Honda ST1100 V-Fours

Service and Repair Manual

by Matthew Coombs

(3384-10X1-264)

UK models covered
ST1100 Pan European. 1085cc. 1990 to 1997
ST1100A (ABS/TCS) Pan European. 1085cc. 1992 to 1995
ST1100A (CBS-ABS/TCS) Pan European. 1085cc. 1996 to 1997

US models covered
ST1100. 1085cc. 1991 to 1997
ST1100A (ABS/TCS). 1085cc. 1992 to 1995
ST1100A (LBS-ABS/TCS). 1085cc. 1996 to 1997

A book in the **Haynes Service and Repair Manual Series**

ISBN **1 85960 384 X**

British Library Cataloguing in Publication Data
A catalogue record for this book is available from the British Library.

Library of Congress Catalog Card Number 97-80417

ABCDE
FGHIJ
KLMNO
PQRS

Printed by **J H Haynes & Co Ltd, Sparkford, Nr Yeovil, Somerset BA22 7JJ, England**

Haynes Publishing
Sparkford, Nr Yeovil, Somerset BA22 7JJ, England

Haynes North America, Inc
861 Lawrence Drive, Newbury Park, California 91320, USA

Editions Haynes S.A.
Tour Aurore - La Défense 2, 18 Place des Reflets,
92975 PARIS LA DEFENSE Cedex, France

Haynes Publishing Nordiska AB
Box 1504, 751 45 UPPSALA, Sweden

Contents

LIVING WITH YOUR HONDA ST

Introduction

The Birth of a Dream	Page **0•4**
Acknowledgements	Page **0•7**
About this manual	Page **0•7**
Identification numbers	Page **0•8**
Buying spare parts	Page **0•8**
Safety first!	Page **0•10**

Daily (pre-ride checks)

Engine/transmission oil level	Page **0•11**
Clutch fluid level	Page **0•11**
Brake fluid levels	Page **0•12**
Coolant level	Page **0•13**
Suspension, steering and final drive checks	Page **0•13**
Tyre checks	Page **0•14**
Legal and safety checks	Page **0•14**

MAINTENANCE

Routine maintenance and servicing

Specifications	Page **1•2**
Recommended lubricants and fluids	Page **1•2**
Maintenance schedule	Page **1•3**
Component locations	Page **1•4**
Maintenance procedures	Page **1•6**

Contents

REPAIRS AND OVERHAUL

Engine, transmission and associated systems

Engine, clutch and transmission Page **2•1**

Cooling system Page **3•1**

Fuel and exhaust systems Page **4•1**

Ignition system Page **5•1**

Chassis components

Frame, suspension and final drive Page **6•1**

Brakes, wheels and tyres Page **7•1**

Bodywork Page **8•1**

Electrical system Page **9•1**

Wiring diagrams Page **9•26**

REFERENCE

Dimensions and Weights Page **REF•1**

Tools and Workshop Tips Page **REF•2**

Conversion factors Page **REF•20**

Motorcycle Chemicals and Lubricants Page **REF•21**

MOT Test Checks Page **REF•22**

Storage Page **REF•26**

Fault Finding Page **REF•28**

Fault Finding Equipment Page **REF•36**

Technical Terms Explained Page **REF•40**

Index Page **REF•44**

The Birth of a Dream

by Julian Ryder

There is no better example of the Japanese post-War industrial miracle than Honda. Like other companies which have become household names, it started with one man's vision. In this case the man was the 40-year old Soichiro Honda who had sold his piston-ring manufacturing business to Toyota in 1945 and was happily spending the proceeds on prolonged parties for his friends. However, the difficulties of getting around in the chaos of post-War Japan irked Honda, so when he came across a job lot of generator engines he realised that here was a way of getting people mobile again at low cost.

A 12 by 18-foot shack in Hamamatsu became his first bike factory, fitting the generator motors into pushbikes. Before long he'd used up all 500 generator motors and started manufacturing his own engine, known as the 'chimney', either because of the elongated cylinder head or the smoky exhaust or perhaps both. The chimney made all of half a horsepower from its 50 cc engine but it was a major success and became the Honda A-type. Less than two years after he'd set up in Hamamatsu, Soichiro Honda founded the Honda Motor Company in September 1948. By then, the A-type had been developed into the 90 cc B-type engine, which Mr Honda decided deserved its own chassis not a bicycle frame. Honda was about to become Japan's first post-War manufacturer of complete motorcycles. In August 1949 the first prototype was ready. With an output of three horsepower, the 98 cc D-type was still a simple two-stroke but it had a two-speed transmission and most importantly a pressed steel frame with telescopic forks and hard tail rear end. The frame was almost triangular in profile with the top rail going in a straight line from the massively braced steering head to the rear axle. Legend has it that after the D-type's first tests the entire workforce went for a drink to celebrate and try and think of a name for the bike. One man broke one of those silences you get when people are thinking, exclaiming 'This is like a dream!' 'That's it!' shouted Honda, and so the Honda Dream was christened.

1970 Honda C90 OHV-engined model

'This is like a dream!' 'That's it' shouted Honda

Mr Honda was a brilliant, intuitive engineer and designer but he did not bother himself with the marketing side of his business. With hindsight, it is possible to see that employing Takeo Fujisawa who would both sort out the home market and plan the eventual expansion into overseas markets was a masterstroke. He arrived in October 1949 and in 1950 was made Sales Director. Another vital new name was Kiyoshi Kawashima, who along with Honda himself, designed the company's first four-stroke after Kawashima had told them that the four-stroke opposition to Honda's two-strokes sounded nicer and therefore sold better. The result of that statement was the overhead-valve 148 cc E-type which first ran in July 1951 just two months after the first drawings were made. Kawashima was made a director of the Honda Company at 34 years old.

The E-type was a massive success, over 32,000 were made in 1953 alone, but Honda's lifelong pursuit of technical innovation sometimes distracted him from commercial reality. Fujisawa pointed out that they were in danger of ignoring their core business, the motorised bicycles that still formed Japan's main means of transport. In May 1952 the F-type Cub appeared, another two-stroke despite the top men's reservations. You could buy a complete machine or just the motor to attach to your own bicycle. The result was certainly distinctive, a white fuel tank with a circular profile went just below and behind the saddle on the left of the bike, and the motor with its horizontal cylinder and bright red cover just below the rear axle on the same side of the bike. This was the machine that turned Honda into the biggest bike maker in Japan

The CB250N Super Dream became a favorite with UK learner riders of the late seventies and early eighties

with 70% of the market for bolt-on bicycle motors, the F-type was also the first Honda to be exported. Next came the machine that would turn Honda into the biggest motorcycle manufacturer in the world.

The C100 Super Cub was a typically audacious piece of Honda engineering and marketing. For the first time, but not the last, Honda invented a completely new type of motorcycle, although the term 'scooterette' was coined to describe the new bike which had many of the characteristics of a scooter but the large wheels, and therefore stability, of a motorcycle. The first one was sold in August 1958, fifteen years later over nine-million of them were on the roads of the world. If ever a machine can be said to have brought mobility to the masses it is the Super Cub. If you add in the electric starter that was added for the C102 model of 1961, the design of the Super Cub has remained substantially unchanged ever since, testament to how right Honda got it first time. The Super Cub made Honda the world's biggest manufacturer after just two years of production.

Honda's export drive started in earnest in 1957 when Britain and Holland got their first bikes, America got just two bikes the next year. By 1962 Honda had half the American market with 65,000 sales. But Soichiro Honda had already travelled abroad to Europe and the USA, making a special point of going to the Isle of Man TT, then the most important race in the GP calendar. He realised that no matter how advanced his products were, only racing success would convince overseas markets for whom 'Made in Japan' still meant cheap and nasty. It took five years from Soichiro Honda's first visit to the Island before his bikes were ready for the TT. In 1959 the factory entered five riders in the 125. They did not have a massive impact on the event being benevolently regarded as a curiosity, but sixth, seventh and eighth were good enough for the team prize. The bikes were off the pace but they were well engineered and very reliable.

The TT was the only time the West saw the Hondas in '59, but they came back for more the following year with the first of a generation of bikes which shaped the future of motorcycling - the double-overhead-cam four-cylinder 250. It was fast and reliable - it revved to 14,000 rpm -

The GL1000 introduced in 1975, was the first in Honda's line of Goldwings

Carl Fogarty in action at Donington on the RC45

but didn't handle anywhere near as well as the opposition. However, Honda had now signed up non-Japanese riders to lead their challenge. The first win didn't come until 1962 (Aussie Tom Phillis in the Spanish 125 GP) and was followed up with a world-shaking performance at the TT. Twenty-one year old Mike Hailwood won both 125 and 250 cc TTs and Hondas filled the top five positions in both races. Soichiro Honda's master plan was starting to come to fruition, Hailwood and Honda won the 1961 250 cc World Championship. Next year Honda won three titles. The other Japanese factories fought back and inspired Honda to produce some of the most fascinating racers ever seen: the awesome six-cylinder 250, the five-cylinder 125, and the 500 four with which the immortal Hailwood battled Agostini and the MV Agusta. When Honda pulled out of racing in '67 they had won sixteen rider's titles, eighteen manufacturer's titles, and 137 GPs, including 18 TTs, and introduced the concept of the modern works team to motorcycle racing. Sales success followed racing victory as Soichiro Honda had predicted, but only because the products advanced as rapidly as the racing machinery. The Hondas that came to Britain in the early '60s were incredibly sophisticated. They had overhead cams where the British bikes had pushrods, they had electric starters when the Brits relied on the kickstart, they had 12V electrics when even the biggest British bike used a 6V system. There seemed no end to the technical wizardry and when in 1968 the first four-cylinder CB750 road bike arrived the world changed for ever. They even had to invent a new word for it: superbike. Honda raced again with the CB750 at Daytona and won the World Endurance title with a prototype DOHC version that became the CB900 roadster. There was the six-cylinder CBX, the first turbocharged production bike, they invented the full-dress tourer with the Goldwing and came back to GPs with the revolutionary oval-pistoned NR500 four-stroke, a much-misunderstood bike that was more rolling experiment than racer. It was true, though, that Mr Honda was not keen on two-strokes - early motocross engines had to be explained away to him as lawnmower motors! However, in 1982 Honda raced the NS500, an agile three-cylinder lightweight against the big four-cylinder opposition in 500 GPs. The bike won in the first year and in '83 took the world title for Freddie Spencer. In four-stroke racing the V4 layout took over from the straight four, dominating TT, F1 and Endurance championships and when Superbike arrived Honda were ready with the RC30. On the roads the VFR V4 became an instant classic while the CBR600 invented another new class of bike on its way to becoming a best-seller.

And then there was the NR750. This limited-edition technological tour-de-force embodied many of Soichiro Honda's ideals. It used the latest techniques and materials in every component, from the oval-piston, 32-valve V4 motor to the titanium coating on the windscreen, it was - as Mr Honda would have wanted - the best it could possibly be. A fitting memorial to the man who has shaped the motorcycle industry and motorcycles as we know them today.

An early CB750 Four

ST1100 - The Gentleman's Express

If you were the company that made the mother of all tourers, the six-cylinder GL1500 Gold Wing and a very competent sports tourer in the shape of the CBR1000, would you think there was room for a model in between them in the range? Honda did and the result was the Pan European. It was a typical Honda trick, creating a market segment where one hadn't existed before. The result was a bike that is almost as comfortable as a Gold Wing over long distances yet can tackle back roads with only fractionally less verve than a CBR1000.

Just reading the spec sheet, you would have thought that was an impossible trick because the Pan European is a big, heavy bike with the obligatory tourer's shaft drive and plenty of room for two behind the chunky fairing. At over 325 kg (kerb weight), you wouldn't have thought the thing could ever be nimble but it is, embodying the roadtester's cliché of shedding weight as soon as the wheels start turning.

Honda ST1100

When it appeared in December 1989, the ST1100 had an all-new 16-valve V4 motor but unlike the rest of Honda's V4s it had the motor arranged longitudinally with the crankshaft running parallel to the bike's axis. It made over 90 hp but it was the way it made it that was so impressive: ultra smoothly with torque everywhere, just the sort of relaxing characteristics you want from a touring bike. The rest of the bike was the usual efficient Honda package with a smattering of original touches like the built in crash bars under sacrificial knock-off sections on the bodywork to keep costs down in the event of something embarrassing like the thing falling off its stand.

The press were impressed but the price scared many potential customers, although a good many were tempted off their BMWs by events like the annual Pan European Rally organised by Honda for riders from all over Europe. Gradually the Pan, as it inevitably came to be known, started to take over other fields previously thought of as BMW's fief. Police forces started using it, rescue services like the AA use them especially in big cities as do paramedic services. This came about not just because of competitive pricing by the importer but because of the enviable reputation for reliability the ST1100 developed.

As the price gradually became less scary so the public started warming to the Pan, and in 1992 it got kitted out with Honda's highest-tech trickery to become the ST1100 ABS/TCS, although you could still buy it in the standard form as well. The initials stood for anti-lock braking and traction control system. The first is without doubt superb and a major safety aid. As you'd expect from Honda, their ABS is generally reckoned to be the smoothest, least obtrusive system yet fitted to a two-wheeler. The traction control seems to be one of those things Honda fitted just because it can, and the same goes for the linked braking system fitted to the ST in 1996.

But these are side issues: the Pan European is a bike that fulfils its design objectives brilliantly. It is a superb long-distance machine that can transport two people and their luggage at high speed and in comfort across three countries in a day and then do the same again the next day. And it does it with a discrete elegance that is very European - unlike the very American brashness of the Gold Wing.

Acknowledgements

Our thanks are due to P.R. Taylor & Sons of Chippenham who supplied the ST1100AS featured in the photographs throughout this manual. We would also like to thank NGK Spark Plugs (UK) Ltd for supplying the colour spark plug condition photos and the Avon Rubber Company for supplying information on tyre fitting.

Thanks are also due to Honda (UK) Ltd for supplying colour transparencies. The introduction, "The Birth of a Dream" was written by Julian Ryder.

About this Manual

The aim of this manual is to help you get the best value from your motorcycle. It can do so in several ways. It can help you decide what work must be done, even if you choose to have it done by a dealer; it provides information and procedures for routine maintenance and servicing; and it offers diagnostic and repair procedures to follow when trouble occurs.

We hope you use the manual to tackle the work yourself. For many simpler jobs, doing it yourself may be quicker than arranging an appointment to get the motorcycle into a dealer and making the trips to leave it and pick it up. More importantly, a lot of money can be saved by avoiding the expense the shop must pass on to you to cover its labour and overhead costs. An added benefit is the sense of satisfaction and accomplishment that you feel after doing the job yourself.

References to the left or right side of the motorcycle assume you are sitting on the seat, facing forward.

We take great pride in the accuracy of information given in this manual, but motorcycle manufacturers make alterations and design changes during the production run of a particular motorcycle of which they do not inform us. No liability can be accepted by the authors or publishers for loss, damage or injury caused by any errors in, or omissions from, the information given.

Frame and engine numbers

The frame serial number is stamped into the right side of the steering head and repeated on an identification plate riveted to the steering head. The engine number is stamped into the bottom of the crankcase behind the oil sump. Both of these numbers should be recorded and kept in a safe place so they can be furnished to law enforcement officials in the event of a theft. There is also a carburettor identification number on the intake side of each carburettor body, and a colour code label on the frame under the seat.

The frame serial number, engine serial number, carburettor identification number and colour code should also be kept in a handy place (such as with your driving licence) so they are always available when purchasing or ordering parts for your machine.

The procedures in this manual identify the bikes by model code for UK models and by production year for US models. The model code or production year is printed on the colour code label, which is located on the frame under the seat; this can be confirmed by reference to the frame number as shown in the accompanying table.

UK model identification details

Model	Year	Code	Engine no.	Frame no.
ST1100	1990	L	SC26E-2000082 to 2006870	SC26-2000063 to 2005860
ST1100	1991	M	SC26E-2101976 to 2105620	SC26-2100456 to 2102874
ST1100	1992	N	SC26E-2200287 to 2203224	SC26-2200255 to 2201703
ST1100A	1992	AN	SC26E-2200016 to 2203648	SC26-4200022 to 4200994
ST1100	1993	P	SC26E-2301169 on	SC26-2300049 on
ST1100A	1993	AP	SC26E-2301594 on	SC26-4300053 on
ST1100	1994	R	Not available	Not available
ST1100A	1994	AR	Not available	Not available
ST1100	1995	S	SC26E-2500543 on	SC26-2500021 on
ST1100A	1995	AS	SC26E-2500518 on	SC26-4500008 on
ST1100	1996	T	SC26E-2600001 on	SC26A-TM000001 on
ST1100A	1996	AT	SC26E-2600001 on	SC26B-TM000001 on
ST1100	1997	V	SC26E-2700001 on	SC26A-VM100001 on
ST1100A	1997	AV	SC26E-2700001 on	SC26B-VM100001 on

US model identification details

Model	Year	Engine no.	Frame no.
ST1100 (49-state)	1991	SC26E-2100014 to 2104220	SC260*MM100004 to MM102131
ST1100 (California)	1991	SC26E-2100009 to 2104702	SC261*MM100005 to MM100390
ST1100 (49-state)	1992	SC26E-2200023 to 2203254	SC260*NM200001 to NM200481
ST1100 (California)	1992	SC26E-2200292 to 2202026	SC261*NM200001 to NM200060
ST1100A (California)	1992	SC26E-2202022 to 2203651	SC264*NM200002 to NM200104
ST1100 (49-state)	1993	SC26E-2300001 on	SC260*PM300001 on
ST1100 (California)	1993	SC26E-2300003 on	SC261*PM300001 on
ST1100A (California)	1993	SC26E-2300061 on	SC264*PM300001 on
ST1100 (49-state)	1994	SC26E-2400001 on	SC260*RM400001 on
ST1100 (California)	1994	SC26E-2400004 on	SC261*RM400001 on
ST1100A (49-state)	1994	SC26E-2400001 on	SC263*RM000001 on
ST1100A (California)	1994	SC26E-2400001 on	SC264*RM400001 on
ST1100 (49-state)	1995	SC26E-2500030 on	SC260*SM500006 on
ST1100 (California)	1995	SC26E-2500203 on	SC261*SM500002 on
ST1100A (49-state)	1995	SC26E-2500001 on	SC263*SM100001 on
ST1100A (California)	1995	SC26E-2500001 on	SC264*SM500007 on
ST1100 (49-state)	1996	SC26E-2600001 on	SC260*TM600001 on
ST1100 (California)	1996	SC26E-2600001 on	SC261*TM600001 on
ST1100A (49-state)	1996	SC26E-2600001 on	SC263*TM200001 on
ST1100A (California)	1996	SC26E-2600001 on	SC264*TM600001 on
ST1100 (49-state)	1997	SC26E-2700001 on	SC260*VM700001 on
ST1100 (California)	1997	SC26E-2700001 on	SC261*VM700001 on
ST1100A (49-state)	1997	SC26E-2700001 on	SC263*VM700001 on
ST1100A (California)	1997	SC26E-2700001 on	SC264*VM700001 on

**The asterisk (*) in frame numbers is a check digit - it can be any number from 0 to 9 or X*

Buying spare parts

Once you have found all the identification numbers, record them for reference when buying parts. Since the manufacturers change specifications, parts and vendors (companies that manufacture various components on the machine), providing the ID numbers is the only way to be reasonably sure that you are buying the correct parts.

Whenever possible, take the worn part to the dealer so direct comparison with the new component can be made. Along the trail from the manufacturer to the parts shelf, there are numerous places that the part can end up with the wrong number or be listed incorrectly.

The two places to purchase new parts for your motorcycle - the accessory store and the franchised dealer - differ in the type of parts they carry. While dealers can obtain virtually every part for your motorcycle, the accessory dealer is usually limited to normal high wear items such as shock absorbers, tune-up parts, various engine gaskets, cables, chains, brake parts, etc. Rarely will an accessory outlet have major suspension components, cylinders, transmission gears, or cases.

Used parts can be obtained for roughly half the price of new ones, but you can't always be sure of what you're getting. Once again, take your worn part to the breaker (wrecking yard) for direct comparison.

Whether buying new, used or rebuilt parts, the best course is to deal directly with someone who specialises in parts for your particular make.

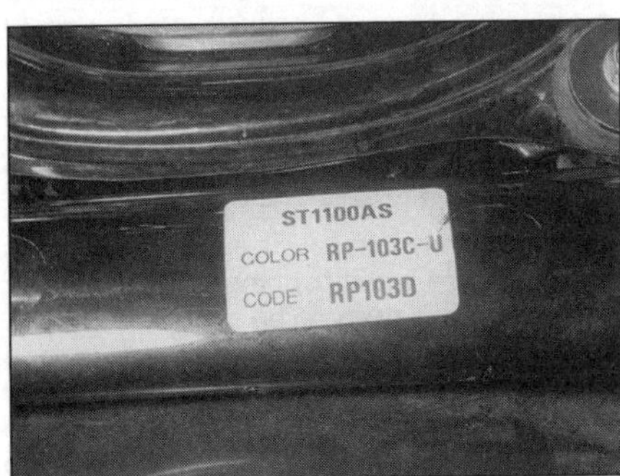

The colour code label is stuck onto the frame cross-member under the seat.

The engine number is stamped into the bottom of the crankcase behind the oil sump.

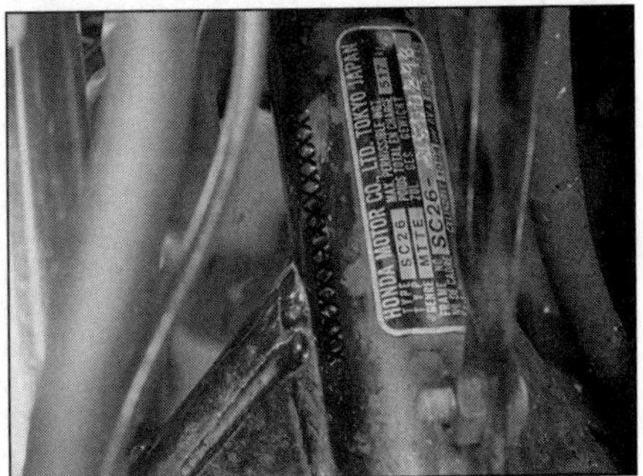

The frame number is stamped into the right-hand side of the steering head

Professional mechanics are trained in safe working procedures. However enthusiastic you may be about getting on with the job at hand, take the time to ensure that your safety is not put at risk. A moment's lack of attention can result in an accident, as can failure to observe simple precautions.

There will always be new ways of having accidents, and the following is not a comprehensive list of all dangers; it is intended rather to make you aware of the risks and to encourage a safe approach to all work you carry out on your bike.

Asbestos

● Certain friction, insulating, sealing and other products - such as brake pads, clutch linings, gaskets, etc. - contain asbestos. Extreme care must be taken to avoid inhalation of dust from such products since it is hazardous to health. If in doubt, assume that they do contain asbestos.

Fire

● Remember at all times that petrol is highly flammable. Never smoke or have any kind of naked flame around, when working on the vehicle. But the risk does not end there - a spark caused by an electrical short-circuit, by two metal surfaces contacting each other, by careless use of tools, or even by static electricity built up in your body under certain conditions, can ignite petrol vapour, which in a confined space is highly explosive. Never use petrol as a cleaning solvent. Use an approved safety solvent.

● Always disconnect the battery earth terminal before working on any part of the fuel or electrical system, and never risk spilling fuel on to a hot engine or exhaust.

● It is recommended that a fire extinguisher of a type suitable for fuel and electrical fires is kept handy in the garage or workplace at all times. Never try to extinguish a fuel or electrical fire with water.

Fumes

● Certain fumes are highly toxic and can quickly cause unconsciousness and even death if inhaled to any extent. Petrol vapour comes into this category, as do the vapours from certain solvents such as trichloroethylene. Any draining or pouring of such volatile fluids should be done in a well ventilated area.

● When using cleaning fluids and solvents, read the instructions carefully. Never use materials from unmarked containers - they may give off poisonous vapours.

● Never run the engine of a motor vehicle in an enclosed space such as a garage. Exhaust fumes contain carbon monoxide which is extremely poisonous; if you need to run the engine, always do so in the open air or at least have the rear of the vehicle outside the workplace.

The battery

● Never cause a spark, or allow a naked light near the vehicle's battery. It will normally be giving off a certain amount of hydrogen gas, which is highly explosive.

● Always disconnect the battery ground (earth) terminal before working on the fuel or electrical systems (except where noted).

● If possible, loosen the filler plugs or cover when charging the battery from an external source. Do not charge at an excessive rate or the battery may burst.

● Take care when topping up, cleaning or carrying the battery. The acid electrolyte, evenwhen diluted, is very corrosive and should not be allowed to contact the eyes or skin. Always wear rubber gloves and goggles or a face shield. If you ever need to prepare electrolyte yourself, always add the acid slowly to the water; never add the water to the acid.

Electricity

● When using an electric power tool, inspection light etc., always ensure that the appliance is correctly connected to its plug and that, where necessary, it is properly grounded (earthed). Do not use such appliances in damp conditions and, again, beware of creating a spark or applying excessive heat in the vicinity of fuel or fuel vapour. Also ensure that the appliances meet national safety standards.

● A severe electric shock can result from touching certain parts of the electrical system, such as the spark plug wires (HT leads), when the engine is running or being cranked, particularly if components are damp or the insulation is defective. Where an electronic ignition system is used, the secondary (HT) voltage is much higher and could prove fatal.

Remember...

✗ **Don't** start the engine without first ascertaining that the transmission is in neutral.

✗ **Don't** suddenly remove the pressure cap from a hot cooling system - cover it with a cloth and release the pressure gradually first, or you may get scalded by escaping coolant.

✗ **Don't** attempt to drain oil until you are sure it has cooled sufficiently to avoid scalding you.

✗ **Don't** grasp any part of the engine or exhaust system without first ascertaining that it is cool enough not to burn you.

✗ **Don't** allow brake fluid or antifreeze to contact the machine's paintwork or plastic components.

✗ **Don't** siphon toxic liquids such as fuel, hydraulic fluid or antifreeze by mouth, or allow them to remain on your skin.

✗ **Don't** inhale dust - it may be injurious to health (see Asbestos heading).

✗ **Don't** allow any spilled oil or grease to remain on the floor - wipe it up right away, before someone slips on it.

✗ **Don't** use ill-fitting spanners or other tools which may slip and cause injury.

✗ **Don't** lift a heavy component which may be beyond your capability - get assistance.

✗ **Don't** rush to finish a job or take unverified short cuts.

✗ **Don't** allow children or animals in or around an unattended vehicle.

✗ **Don't** inflate a tyre above the recommended pressure. Apart from overstressing the carcass, in extreme cases the tyre may blow off forcibly.

✓ **Do** ensure that the machine is supported securely at all times. This is especially important when the machine is blocked up to aid wheel or fork removal.

✓ **Do** take care when attempting to loosen a stubborn nut or bolt. It is generally better to pull on a spanner, rather than push, so that if you slip, you fall away from the machine rather than onto it.

✓ **Do** wear eye protection when using power tools such as drill, sander, bench grinder etc.

✓ **Do** use a barrier cream on your hands prior to undertaking dirty jobs - it will protect your skin from infection as well as making the dirt easier to remove afterwards; but make sure your hands aren't left slippery. Note that long-term contact with used engine oil can be a health hazard.

✓ **Do** keep loose clothing (cuffs, ties etc. and long hair) well out of the way of moving mechanical parts.

✓ **Do** remove rings, wristwatch etc., before working on the vehicle - especially the electrical system.

✓ **Do** keep your work area tidy - it is only too easy to fall over articles left lying around.

✓ **Do** exercise caution when compressing springs for removal or installation. Ensure that the tension is applied and released in a controlled manner, using suitable tools which preclude the possibility of the spring escaping violently.

✓ **Do** ensure that any lifting tackle used has a safe working load rating adequate for the job.

✓ **Do** get someone to check periodically that all is well, when working alone on the vehicle.

✓ **Do** carry out work in a logical sequence and check that everything is correctly assembled and tightened afterwards.

✓ **Do** remember that your vehicle's safety affects that of yourself and others. If in doubt on any point, get professional advice.

● **If** in spite of following these precautions, you are unfortunate enough to injure yourself, seek medical attention as soon as possible.

1 Engine/transmission oil level

Note: *The daily (pre-ride) checks outlined in the owner's manual covers those items which should be inspected on a daily basis.*

Before you start:

✔ Take the motorcycle on a short run to allow it to reach normal operating temperature.
Caution: Do not run the engine in an enclosed space such as a garage or workshop.

✔ Stop the engine and support the motorcycle on its centre stand, making sure it is in an upright position on level ground. Allow it to stand undisturbed for a few minutes to allow the oil level to stabilise.

✔ The oil level is viewed through the window in the right-hand side of the engine via a cutout in the fairing. Wipe the glass clean before inspection to make the check easier.

Bike care:

● If you have to add oil frequently, you should check whether you have any oil leaks. If there is no sign of oil leakage from the joints and gaskets the engine could be burning oil (see *Fault Finding*).

The correct oil

● Modern, high-revving engines place great demands on their oil. It is very important that the correct oil for your bike is used.

● Always top up with a good quality oil of the specified type and viscosity and do not overfill the engine.

Oil type	API grade SF or SG
Oil viscosity	SAE 10W40

1 Check the oil level via the cutout in the fairing. Wipe the oil level window so that it is clean. With the motorcycle vertical, the oil level should lie between the upper and lower level lines.

2 If the level is below the lower line, remove the filler cap from the top of the right-hand valve cover.

3 Top the engine up with the recommended grade and type of oil, to bring the level up to the upper line on the window. For improved access, remove the maintenance cover from the right-hand middle fairing panel (see Chapter 8).

2 Clutch fluid level

Warning: Brake and clutch hydraulic fluid can harm your eyes and damage painted surfaces, so use extreme caution when handling and pouring it and cover surrounding surfaces with rag. Do not use fluid that has been standing open for some time, as it absorbs moisture from the air which can cause a dangerous loss of braking and clutch effectiveness.

Before you start:

✔ Position the motorcycle on its centre stand, and turn the handlebars until the top of the clutch master cylinder is as level as possible. If necessary, place the motorcycle on its sidestand to make it level.

✔ Make sure you have the correct hydraulic fluid - DOT 4 is recommended. Wrap a rag around the reservoir to ensure that any spillage does not come into contact with painted surfaces.

Bike care:

● If the fluid reservoir requires repeated topping-up this is an indication of a hydraulic leak somewhere in the system, which should be investigated immediately.

● Check for signs of fluid leakage from the hydraulic hose and components - if found, rectify immediately.

● Check the operation of the clutch; if there is evidence of air in the system (spongy feel to the lever), bleed the clutch (see Chapter 2).

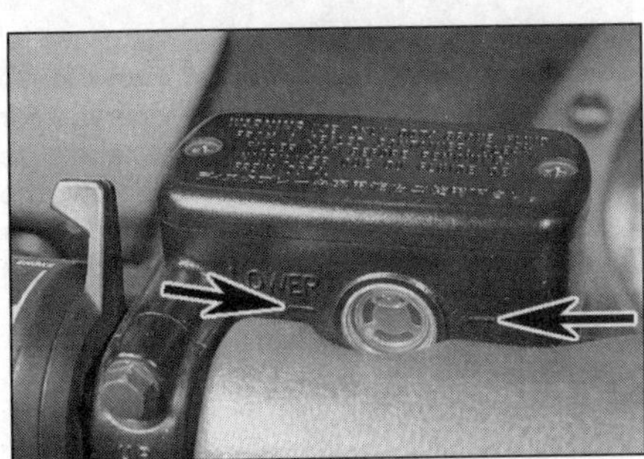

1 The clutch fluid level is checked via the sightglass in the reservoir - it must be above the LOWER level lines (arrowed). To top up, remove the two screws to free the clutch fluid reservoir cover.

2 Top up with new clean DOT 4 hydraulic fluid until the level is up to the upper level line on the inside of the reservoir (arrowed). Take care to avoid spills (see **Warning** above).

3 Ensure that the diaphragm is correctly seated before installing the plate and cover.

3 Brake fluid levels

Warning: Brake and clutch hydraulic fluid can harm your eyes and damage painted surfaces, so use extreme caution when handling and pouring it and cover surrounding surfaces with rag. Do not use fluid that has been standing open for some time, as it absorbs moisture from the air which can cause a dangerous loss of braking and clutch effectiveness.

Before you start:

✔ Position the motorcycle on its centre stand, and turn the handlebars until the top of the front master cylinder is as level as possible. If necessary, place the motorcycle on its sidestand to make it level. Remove the right-hand pannier (see Chapter 8) for access to the rear brake fluid reservoir.

✔ Make sure you have the correct hydraulic fluid - DOT 4 is recommended. Wrap a rag around the reservoir being worked on to ensure that any spillage does not come into contact with painted surfaces.

Bike care:

- The fluid in the front and rear brake master cylinder reservoirs will drop slightly as the brake pads wear down.
- If any fluid reservoir requires repeated topping-up this is an indication of a hydraulic leak somewhere in the system, which should be investigated immediately.
- Check for signs of fluid leakage from the hydraulic hoses and components - if found, rectify immediately.
- Check the operation of both brakes before taking the machine on the road; if there is evidence of air in the system (spongy feel to lever or pedal), it must be bled as described in Chapter 7.

1 The front brake fluid level is checked via the sightglass in the reservoir - it must be above the LOWER level lines (arrowed).

2 If the level is below the LOWER level mark, remove the two screws (arrowed) to free the front brake fluid reservoir cover, and remove the cover, the diaphragm plate and the diaphragm.

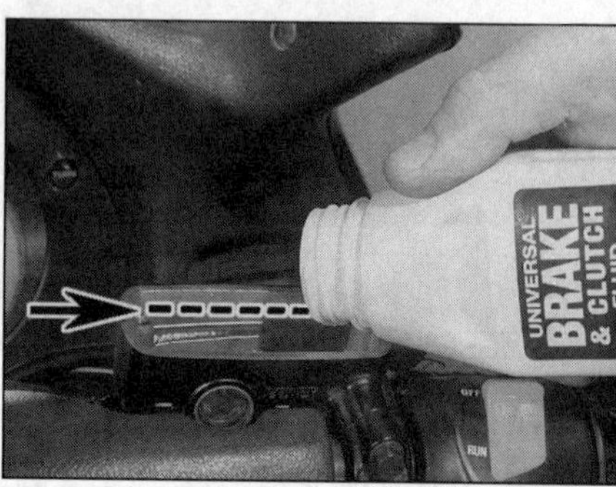

3 Top up with new clean DOT 4 hydraulic fluid until the level is up to the upper level line on the inside of the reservoir (arrowed). Take care to avoid spills (see **Warning** above).

4 Ensure that the diaphragm is correctly seated before installing the plate and cover.

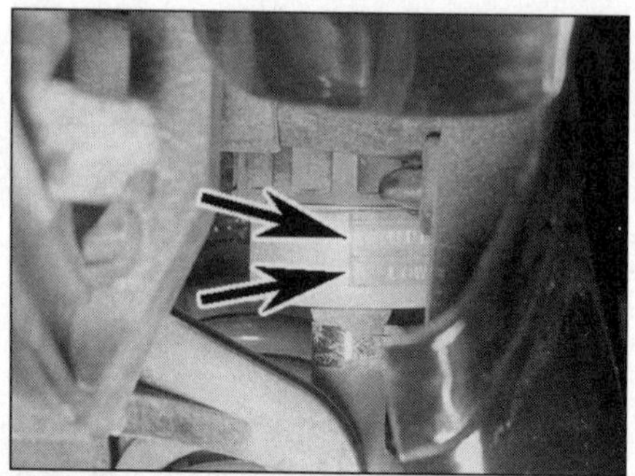

5 The rear brake fluid level can be seen through the translucent body of the reservoir after the right-hand pannier has been removed (see Chapter 8). The fluid must lie between the LOWER and UPPER level lines (arrowed).

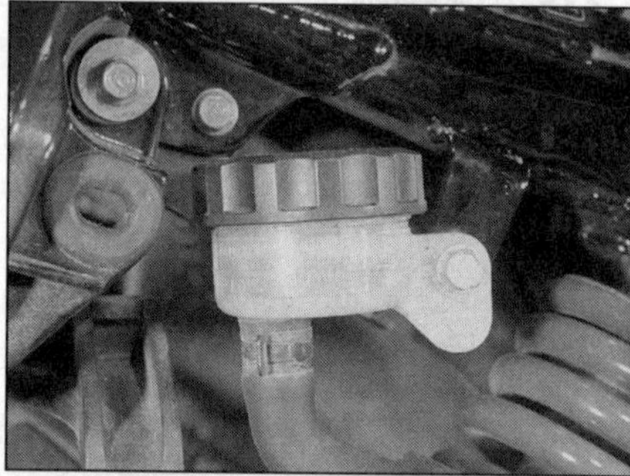

6 To access the rear brake reservoir for topping up, remove the right-hand side panel (see Chapter 8). Unscrew the reservoir cap and top up the fluid to the upper level mark as described for the front brake reservoir.

4 Coolant level

Warning: DO NOT remove the radiator pressure cap to add coolant. Topping up is done via the coolant reservoir tank filler. DO NOT leave open containers of coolant about, as it is poisonous.

Before you start:

✔ Make sure you have a supply of coolant available (a mixture of 50% distilled water and 50% corrosion inhibited ethylene glycol anti-freeze is needed).

✔ Always check the coolant level when the engine is at normal working temperature. Take the motorcycle on a short run to allow it to reach normal temperature.

✔ Support the motorcycle on its centre stand, making sure it is in an upright position on level ground.

Caution: Do not run the engine in an enclosed space such as a garage or workshop.

Bike care:

● Use only the specified coolant mixture. It is important that anti-freeze is used in the system all year round, and not just in the winter. Do not top the system up using only water, as the system will become too diluted.

● Do not overfill the reservoir tank. If the coolant is significantly above the UPPER level line at any time, the surplus should be siphoned or drained off to prevent the possibility of it being expelled out of the overflow hose.

● If the coolant level falls steadily, check the system for leaks (see Chapter 1). If no leaks are found and the level continues to fall, it is recommended that the machine is taken to a Honda dealer for a pressure test.

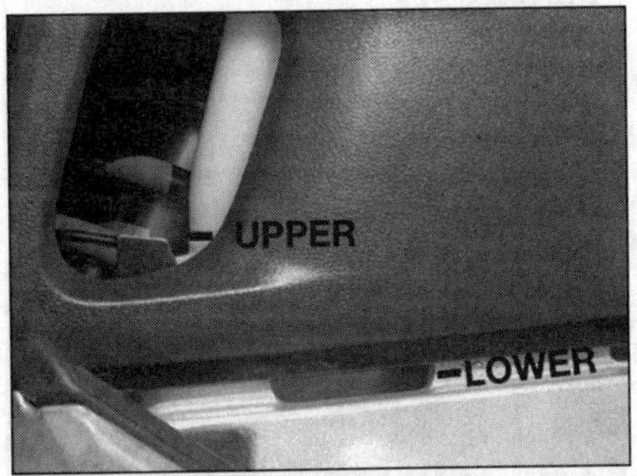

1 On standard models, the coolant reservoir is located behind the right-hand side panel. The coolant UPPER and LOWER level markings are visible through the apertures in the panel.

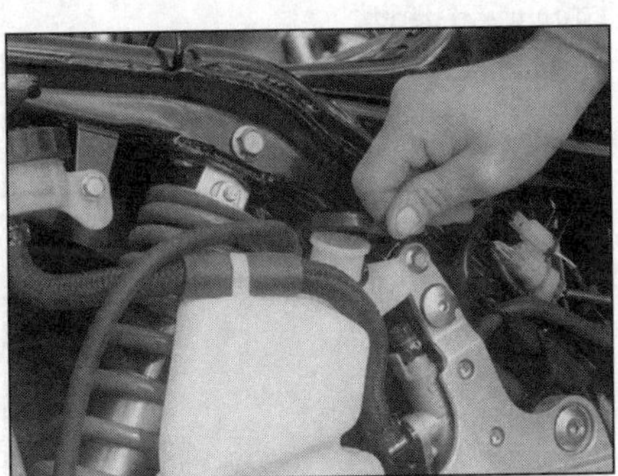

2 If the coolant level is low, remove the side panel and prise off the reservoir filler cap . . .

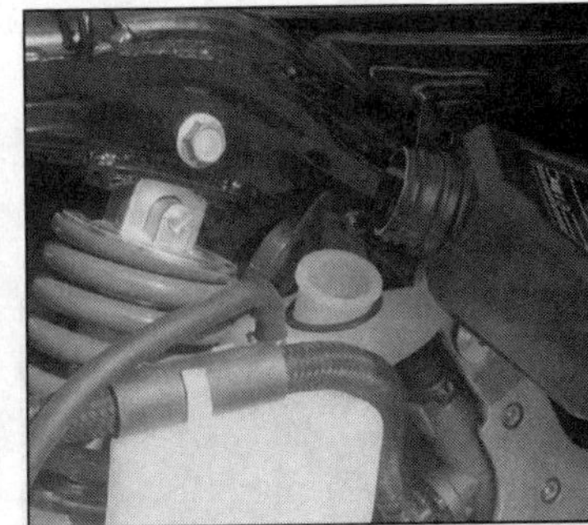

3 . . . top up the reservoir so that the coolant level is between the UPPER and LOWER markings.

4 On ABS/TCS and CBS/LBS-ABS/TCS models, the coolant reservoir is located behind the maintenance cover on the right-hand middle fairing panel. The coolant UPPER and LOWER level markings are visible through the aperture in the panel.

5 If the coolant level is not in between the UPPER and LOWER markings, remove the maintenance cover (see Chapter 8), then remove the reservoir filler cap . . .

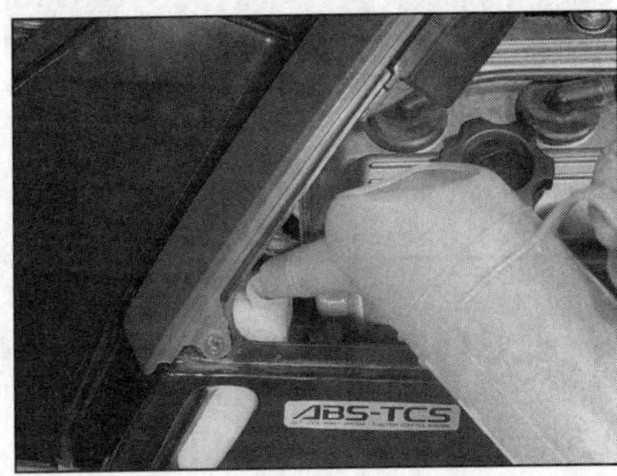

6 . . . and top up with the recommended coolant mixture so that the level is between the UPPER and LOWER markings.

5 Suspension, steering and final drive checks

Suspension and steering:

● Check that the front and rear suspension operates smoothly without binding.

● Check that the suspension is adjusted as required.

● Check that the steering moves smoothly from lock-to-lock.

Final drive:

● Check for signs of oil leakage around the final drive housing. If any is evident, check the final drive oil level (Chapter 1).

6 Tyre checks

Tyre care:

- Check the tyres carefully for cuts, tears, embedded nails or other sharp objects and excessive wear. Operation of the motorcycle with excessively worn tyres is extremely hazardous, as traction and handling are directly affected.
- Check the condition of the tyre valve and ensure the dust cap is in place.
- Pick out any stones or nails which may have become embedded in the tyre tread. If left, they will eventually penetrate through the casing and cause a puncture.
- If tyre damage is apparent, or unexplained loss of pressure is experienced, seek the advice of a tyre fitting specialist without delay.

Tyre tread depth:

- Always take note of the minimun tyre tread depth regulations in your country. At the time of writing UK law requires that tread depth must be at least 1 mm over 3/4 of the tread breadth all the way around the tyre, with no bald patches. Many riders, however, consider 2 mm tread depth minimum to be a safer limit. Honda recommendations are given in the table below.
- Many tyres now incorporate wear indicators in the tread. Identify the triangular pointer or TWI marking on the tyre sidewall to locate the indicator bar and replace the tyre if the tread has worn down to the bar.

Tire tread depth	
Front	1.5 mm (0.06 in)
Rear	2.0 mm (0.08 in)

The correct pressures:

- The tyres must be checked when **cold**, not immediately after riding. Note that low tyre pressures may cause the tyre to slip on the rim or come off. High tyre pressures will cause abnormal tread wear and unsafe handling.
- Use an accurate pressure gauge.
- Proper air pressure will increase tire life and provide maximum stability and ride comfort.

Tire pressures	
Front	36 psi (2.5 Bars)
Rear	42 psi (2.9 Bars)

1 Check the tyre pressures when the tyres are **cold** and keep them properly inflated.

2 Measure tread depth at the centre of the tyre using a tread depth gauge.

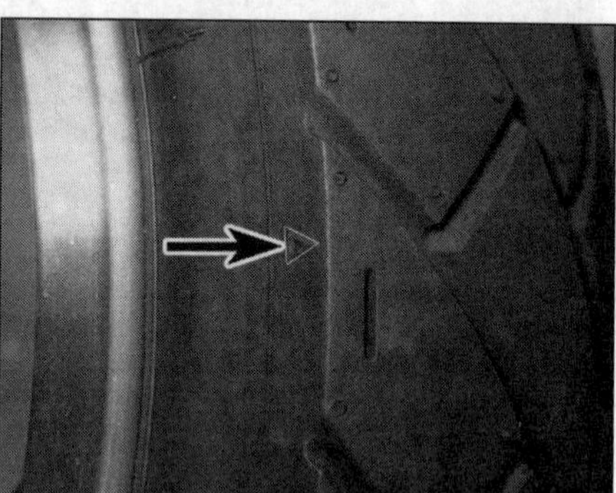

3 Tyre tread wear indicator bar locations can be identified by either an arrow, a triangle or the letters TWI on the sidewall (arrowed).

7 Legal and safety checks

Lighting and signalling:

- Take a minute to check that the headlight, tail light, brake light, instrument lights and turn signals all work correctly.
- Check that the horn sounds when the switch is operated.
- A working speedometer is a statutory requirement in the UK.

Safety:

- Check that the throttle grip rotates smoothly and snaps shut when released, in all steering positions. Also check for the correct amount of freeplay (see Chapter 1).
- Check that the engine shuts off when the kill switch is operated.
- Check that sidestand return spring holds the stand securely up when retracted. The same applies to the centrestand.
- Check the operation of the sidestand switch. Sit astride the motorcycle with the sidestand up. Make sure that the transmission is in neutral and start the engine. Pull in the clutch lever and shift the transmission into gear. With the clutch lever held in, lower the sidestand. If the sidestand switch is working correctly, the engine should cut out. Turn the ignition off when checking is complete. If the switch doesn't operate correctly, check it as described in Chapter 9.

Fuel:

- This may seem obvious, but check that you have enough fuel to complete your journey. If you notice signs of fuel leakage - rectify the cause immediately.
- Ensure you use the correct grade unleaded fuel - see Chapter 4 Specifications. Do not overfill the fuel tank - fill only to the bottom of the filler neck.

Chapter 1
Routine maintenance and servicing

Contents

Air filter - replacement 20
Battery - charging ..... see Chapter 9
Battery - removal, installation, inspection and maintenance ..... see Chapter 9
Brake caliper and master cylinder seals - replacement 32
Brake fluid - change 21
Brake hoses - replacement 33
Brake pads - wear check 3
Brake system - check 12
Carburettors - synchronisation 8
Clutch - check 14
Clutch - fluid change 22
Clutch hose - replacement 34
Cooling system - check 9
Cooling system - draining, flushing and refilling 24
Cylinder compression - check 28
Emission control systems - check (US models only) 10
Engine oil pressure - check 29
Engine oil and oil filter - change 7
Final drive - oil level check 11
Final drive - oil change 25
Front forks - oil change 27
Fuel hoses - replacement 35
Fuel system - check 4
Headlight aim - check and adjustment 13
Idle speed - check and adjustment 2
Nuts and bolts - tightness check 17
Spark plug gaps - check and adjustment 1
Spark plugs - replacement 6
Stands, lever pivots and cables - lubrication 15
Steering head bearings - freeplay check and adjustment 19
Steering head bearings - lubrication 30
Suspension - check 16
Swingarm bearings - lubrication 31
Throttle and choke cables - check 5
Valve clearances - check and adjustment 23
Wheels and tyres - general check 18
Wheel bearings - check 26

1

Degrees of difficulty

Easy, suitable for novice with little experience 

Fairly easy, suitable for beginner with some experience 

Fairly difficult, suitable for competent DIY mechanic 

Difficult, suitable for experienced DIY mechanic

Very difficult, suitable for expert DIY or professional 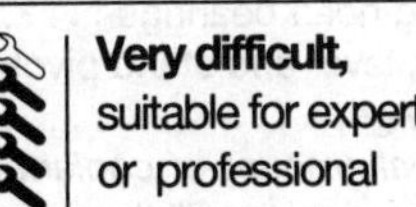

Engine

Spark plugs	
Type	
Standard	NGK CR8EH9 or Nippondenso U24FER9
For extended high speed riding	NGK CR9EH9 or Nippondenso U27FER9
Electrode gap	0.8 to 0.9 mm
Engine idle speed	
UK models	1000 ± 100 rpm
US models	1200 ± 100 rpm
Carburettor synchronisation - max. difference between carburettors	40 mm Hg
Valve clearances (COLD engine)	
Intake valves	0.13 to 0.19 mm
Exhaust valves	0.22 to 0.28 mm
Cylinder compression	171 to 227 psi (12 to 16 Bar)
Oil pressure (with engine warm)	57 to 71 psi (4.0 to 5.0 Bar) at 5000 rpm, oil at 80°C

Miscellaneous

Throttle cable freeplay	2 to 6 mm
Tyre pressures (cold)	
Front	36 psi (2.50 Bar)
Rear	42 psi (2.90 Bar)
Tyre tread depth	
Front	1.5 mm
Rear	2.0 mm

Torque settings

Oil drain plug	38 Nm
Oil filter	10 Nm
Final drive oil filler cap	12 Nm
Final drive oil drain plug	20 Nm
Shock absorber upper mounting bolt	50 Nm
Shock absorber lower mounting bolt	23 Nm
Swingarm right-hand pivot bolt	150 Nm
Swingarm left-hand pivot bolt	
Standard and ABS/TCS models	18 Nm
CBS/LBS-ABS/TCS	22 Nm
Swingarm left-hand pivot bolt locknut	105 Nm
Steering head bearing adjuster nut	28 Nm
Steering stem nut	105 Nm
Top yoke fork clamp bolts	23 Nm

Recommended lubricants and fluids

Engine/transmission oil type	API grade SF or SG motor oil
Engine/transmission oil viscosity	SAE 10W40
Engine/transmission oil capacity	
Oil change	3.6 litres
Oil and filter change	3.7 litres
Following engine overhaul - dry engine, new filter	4.3 litres
Coolant type	50% distilled water, 50% corrosion inhibited ethylene glycol anti-freeze
Coolant capacity	3.0 to 3.5 litres*
Front fork oil	see Chapter 6
Final drive oil type	SAE 80 Hypoid gear oil
Final drive oil capacity	
Oil change	130 cc
Following overhaul	150 cc
Brake and clutch fluid	DOT 4
Miscellaneous	
Wheel bearings	Multi-purpose grease
Rear suspension bearings	Multi-purpose grease
Rear wheel drive hub and driven coupling splines	Moly-based grease containing at least 40% molybdenum disulphide
Steering head bearings	Multi-purpose grease
Cables, lever and stand pivot points	Motor oil
Throttle grip	Multi-purpose grease or dry film lubricant

**The actual amount of coolant required for a refill of the system will vary slightly according to how completely the system was drained. The important point is to fill the system to the correct level in the reservoir.*

Note: *The daily (pre-ride) checks outlined in the owner's manual covers those items which should be inspected on a daily basis. Always perform the pre-ride inspection at every maintenance interval (in addition to the procedures listed). The intervals listed below are the intervals recommended by the manufacturer for each particular operation during the model years covered in this manual. Your owner's manual may have different intervals for your model.*

Daily (pre-ride)

See *'Daily (pre-ride) checks'* at the beginning of this manual.

After the initial 600 miles (1000 km)

Note: *This check is usually performed by a Honda dealer after the first 600 miles (1000 km) from new. Thereafter, maintenance is carried out according to the following intervals of the schedule.*

Every 4000 miles (6400 km) or 6 months

Carry out all the items under the Daily (pre-ride) checks and the 600 mile (1000 km) check, plus the following:

- ☐ Check the spark plug gaps (Section 1).
- ☐ Check and adjust the engine idle speed (Section 2).
- ☐ Check the brake pads for wear (Section 3).

Every 8000 miles (12,800 km) or 12 months

Carry out all the items under the 4000 mile (6400 km) check, plus the following:

- ☐ Check the fuel hoses and system components (Section 4).
- ☐ Check the throttle/choke cable operation and freeplay (Section 5).
- ☐ Replace the spark plugs (Section 6).
- ☐ Change the engine oil and oil filter (Section 7).
- ☐ Check the carburettor synchronisation (Section 8).
- ☐ Check the cooling system (Section 9).
- ☐ Check the emission control systems - US models (Section 10).
- ☐ Check the final drive gear oil level (Section 11).
- ☐ Check the operation of the brakes, and for fluid leakage (Section 12).
- ☐ Check the headlight aim (Section 13).
- ☐ Check the operation of the clutch (Section 14).
- ☐ Check and lubricate the stands, lever pivots and cables (Section 15).
- ☐ Check the front and rear suspension (Section 16).
- ☐ Check the tightness of all nuts and bolts (Section 17).
- ☐ Check the tyre and wheel condition, and the tyre tread depth (Section 18).
- ☐ Check the steering head bearing freeplay (Section 19).

Every 12,000 miles (19,200 km) or 18 months

Carry out all the items under the 4000 mile (6400 km) check, plus the following:

- ☐ Replace the air filter (Section 20).

Every 12,000 miles (19,200 km) or two years

- ☐ Change the brake fluid (Section 21).
- ☐ Change the clutch fluid (Section 22).

Every 16,000 miles (25,600 km) or two years

Carry out all the items under the 8000 mile (12,800 km) check, plus the following:

- ☐ Check the valve clearances (Section 23).

Every 24,000 miles (38,400 km) or two years

- ☐ Change the coolant mixture (Section 24).

Every 24,000 miles (38,400 km) or three years

Carry out all the items under the 8000 mile (12,800 km) check, plus the following:

- ☐ Change the final drive oil (Section 25).

Non-scheduled maintenance

- ☐ Check the wheel bearings (Section 26).
- ☐ Change the front fork oil (Section 27).
- ☐ Check the cylinder compression (Section 28).
- ☐ Check the engine oil pressure (Section 29).
- ☐ Re-grease the steering head bearings (Section 30).
- ☐ Re-grease the swingarm bearings (Section 31).
- ☐ Replace the brake master cylinder and caliper seals (Section 32).
- ☐ Replace the brake hoses (Section 33).
- ☐ Replace the clutch hose (Section 34).
- ☐ Replace the fuel hoses (Section 35).
- ☐ Replace the emission control system hoses (US models only) (Section 36).

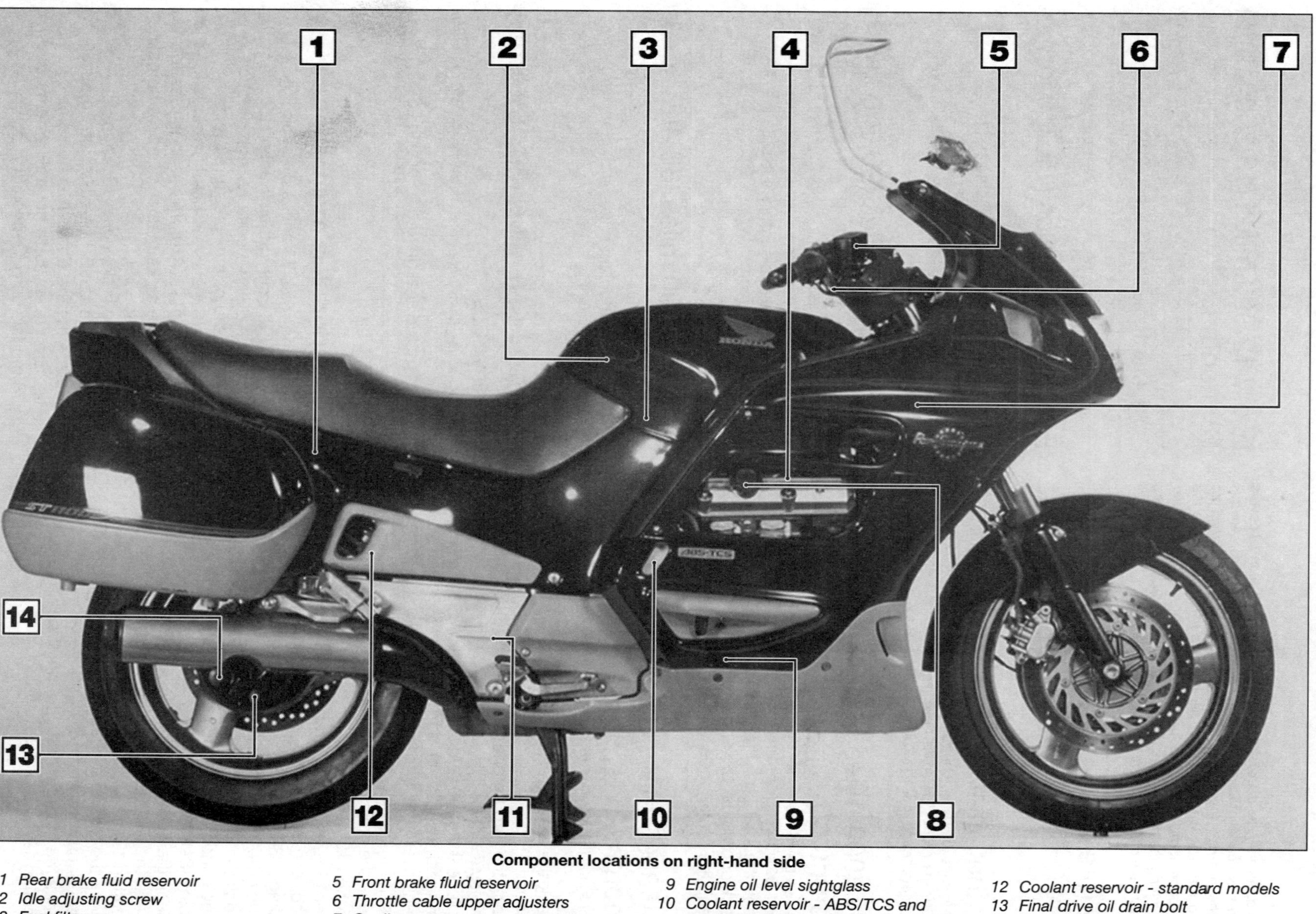

Component locations on right-hand side

1 Rear brake fluid reservoir
2 Idle adjusting screw
3 Fuel filter
4 Spark plugs
5 Front brake fluid reservoir
6 Throttle cable upper adjusters
7 Cooling system pressure cap
8 Engine oil filler
9 Engine oil level sightglass
10 Coolant reservoir - ABS/TCS and CBS/LBS-ABS/TCS models
11 Rear brake light switch
12 Coolant reservoir - standard models
13 Final drive oil drain bolt
14 Final drive oil filler/level cap

Component locations on left-hand side

1 *Fork oil seals*
2 *Steering head bearings*
3 *Clutch fluid reservoir*
4 *Air filter*
5 *Spark plugs*
6 *Battery*
7 *Engine oil filter*
8 *Engine oil drain plug*
9 *Radiator drain plug*

1 This Chapter is designed to help the home mechanic maintain his/her motorcycle for safety, economy, long life and peak performance.

2 Deciding where to start or plug into the routine maintenance schedule depends on several factors. If the warranty period on your motorcycle has just expired, and if it has been maintained according to the warranty standards, you may want to pick up routine maintenance as it coincides with the next mileage or calendar interval. If you have owned the machine for some time but have never performed any maintenance on it, then you may want to start at the nearest interval and include some additional procedures to ensure that nothing important is overlooked. If you have just had a major engine overhaul, then you may want to start the maintenance routine from the beginning. If you have a used machine and have no knowledge of its history or maintenance record, you may desire to combine all the checks into one large service initially and then settle into the maintenance schedule prescribed.

3 Before beginning any maintenance or repair, the machine should be cleaned thoroughly, especially around the oil filter, spark plugs, valve cover, side panels, carburettors, etc. Cleaning will help ensure that dirt does not contaminate the engine and will allow you to detect wear and damage that could otherwise easily go unnoticed.

4 Certain maintenance information is sometimes printed on decals attached to the motorcycle. If the information on the decals differs from that included here, use the information on the decal.

Every 4000 miles (6400 km) or 6 months

1 Spark plug gaps - check and adjustment

1 Make sure your spark plug socket is the correct size before attempting to remove the plugs - a suitable one is supplied in the motorcycle's tool kit which is stored under the seat.

2 Remove the left-hand side panel (see Chapter 8) and disconnect the battery negative (-) lead.

3 Remove the maintenance panel from each middle fairing panel (see Chapter 8).

4 Clean the area around the plug caps to prevent any dirt falling into the spark plug channels.

5 Check that the cylinder location is marked on each plug lead, then pull the spark plug cap off each spark plug. Clean the area around the base of the plugs to prevent any dirt falling into the engine. Using either the plug removing tool supplied in the bike's toolkit or a deep socket type wrench, unscrew the plugs from the cylinder head **(see illustrations)**. Lay each plug out in relation to its cylinder; if any plug shows up a problem it will then be easy to identify the troublesome cylinder.

6 Inspect the electrodes for wear. Both the centre and side electrodes should have square edges and the side electrodes should be of uniform thickness. Look for excessive deposits and evidence of a cracked or chipped insulator around the centre electrode. Compare your spark plugs to the colour spark plug reading chart at the end of this manual. Check the threads, the washer and the ceramic insulator body for cracks and other damage.

7 If the electrodes are not excessively worn, and if the deposits can be easily removed with a wire brush, the plugs can be re-gapped and re-used (if no cracks or chips are visible in the insulator). If in doubt concerning the condition of the plugs, replace them with new ones, as the expense is minimal.

8 Cleaning spark plugs by sandblasting is permitted, provided you clean the plugs with a high flash-point solvent afterwards.

9 Before installing the plugs, make sure they are the correct type and heat range and check the gap between the electrodes. Compare the gap to that specified and adjust as necessary. If the gap must be adjusted, bend the side electrodes only and be very careful not to chip or crack the insulator nose **(see illustrations)**. Make sure the washer is in place before installing each plug.

10 Since the cylinder head is made of aluminium, which is soft and easily damaged, thread the plugs into the heads turning the

1.5a Remove the spark plug cap . . .

1.5b . . . then unscrew the spark plug

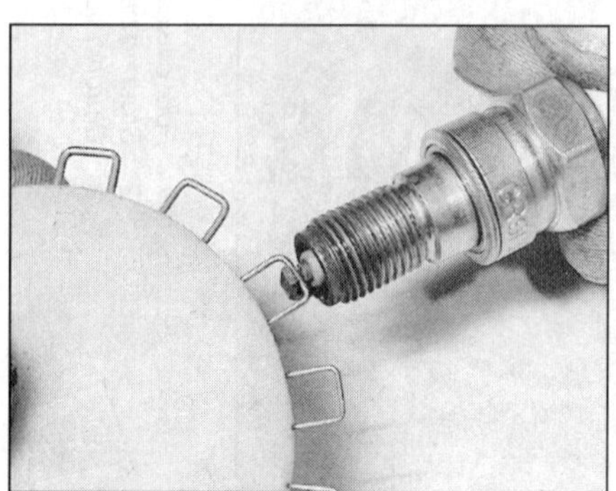

1.9a A wire type gauge is recommended to measure the spark plug electrode gap

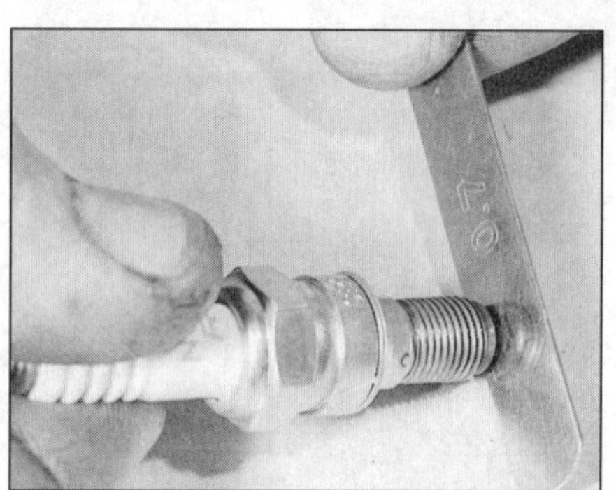

1.9b A blade type feeler gauge can also be used

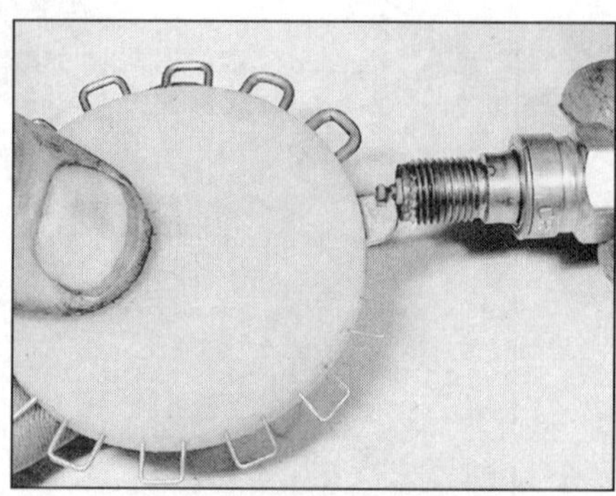

1.9c Adjust the electrode gap by bending the side electrode only

tool by hand **(see illustration)**. Once the plugs are finger-tight, the job can be finished with a spanner on the tool supplied or a socket drive **(see illustration 1.5b)**. Tighten the spark plugs to the specified torque setting - do not over-tighten them.

HAYNES HiNT ***As the plugs are quite recessed, slip a short length of hose over the end of the plug to use as a tool to thread it into place. The hose will grip the plug well enough to turn it, but will start to slip if the plug begins to cross-thread in the hole - this will prevent damaged threads.***

11 Reconnect the spark plug caps, making sure they are securely connected to the correct cylinder. Install all other components previously removed.

HAYNES HiNT ***Stripped plug threads in the cylinder head can be repaired with a Heli-Coil insert - see 'Tools and Workshop Tips' in the Reference section.***

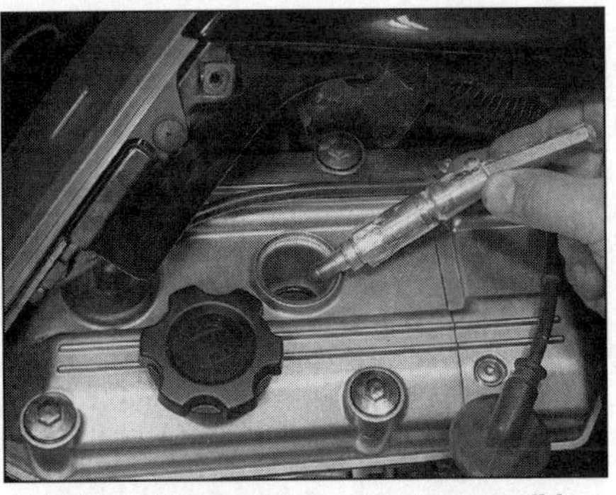

1.10 Thread the plug as far as possible turning the tool by hand

2.3 Open the panel in the tank cover to access the idle speed adjuster (arrowed)

2 Idle speed - check and adjustment

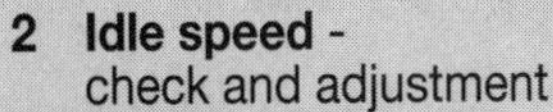

1 The idle speed should be checked and adjusted before and after the carburettors are synchronised (balanced) and when it is obviously too high or too low. Before adjusting the idle speed, make sure the valve clearances and spark plug gaps are correct. Also, turn the handlebars back-and-forth and see if the idle speed changes as this is done. If it does, the throttle cable may not be adjusted or routed correctly, or may be worn out. This is a dangerous condition that can cause loss of control of the bike. Be sure to correct this problem before proceeding.

2 The engine should be at normal operating temperature, which is usually reached after 10 to 15 minutes of stop-and-go riding. Place the motorcycle on its centrestand, and make sure the transmission is in neutral.

3 The idle speed adjuster is located behind the locking panel in the fuel tank cover **(see illustration)**. Use the ignition key to open the panel. With the engine idling, adjust the idle speed by turning the adjuster knob in or out until the idle speed listed in this Chapter's Specifications is obtained.

4 Snap the throttle open and shut a few times, then recheck the idle speed. If necessary, repeat the adjustment procedure.

5 If a smooth, steady idle can't be achieved, the fuel/air mixture may be incorrect (see Chapter 4) or the carburettors may need synchronising (see Section 8).

1

3 Brake pads - wear check

1 Each brake pad has a wear indicator that can be viewed without removing the pads from the caliper. On the front brake caliper, the pad wear indicator cutouts are visible by looking up at the lower edge of the pads. On the rear brake caliper, the pad wear indicators are visible by looking at the rear edge of the pads **(see illustration)**.

2 If the pads are worn to or beyond the cutout, they must be replaced. If the pads are dirty or if you are in doubt as to the amount of friction material remaining, remove them for inspection (see Chapter 7). **Note:** *Some after-market pads may use different indicators to those on the original equipment as shown.*

3 Refer to Chapter 7 for details of pad replacement.

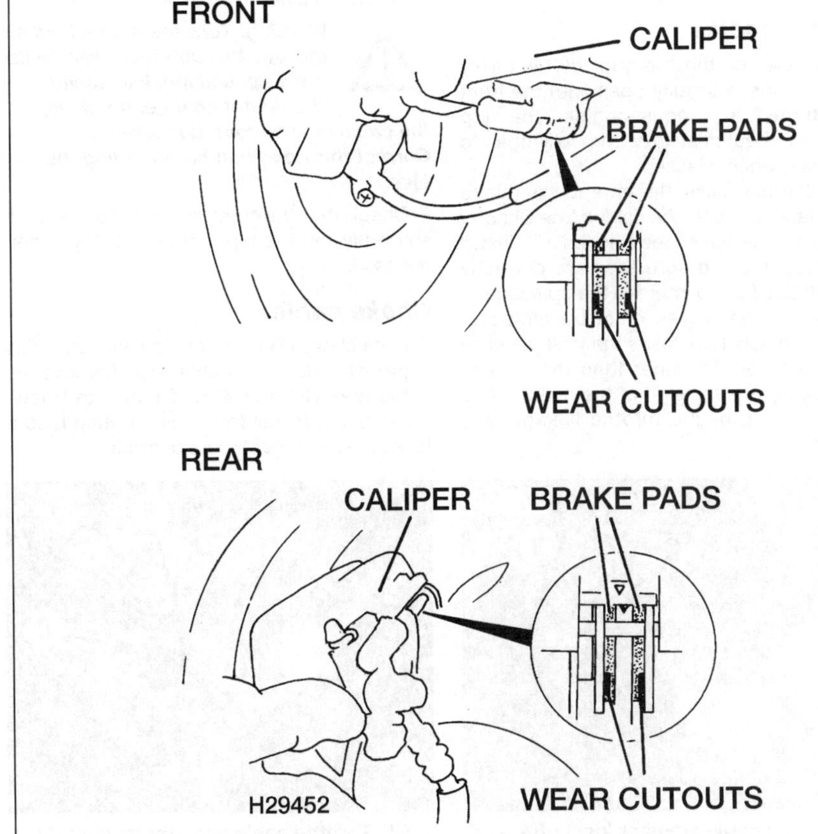

3.1 Brake pad wear indicator locations

Every 8000 miles (12,800 km) or 12 months

Carry out all the items under the 4000 mile (6400 km) check, plus the following:

4 Fuel system - check

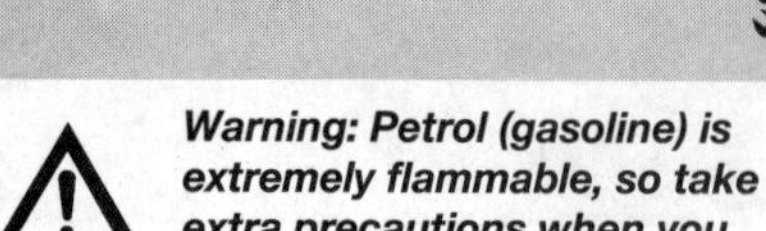

Warning: Petrol (gasoline) is extremely flammable, so take extra precautions when you work on any part of the fuel system. Don't smoke or allow open flames or bare light bulbs near the work area, and don't work in a garage where a natural gas-type appliance is present. If you spill any fuel on your skin, rinse it off immediately with soap and water. When you perform any kind of work on the fuel system, wear safety glasses and have a fire extinguisher suitable for a Class B type fire (flammable liquids) on hand.

Check

1 Remove the fuel tank cover (see Chapter 8) and check the tank, the fuel tap, the filter and the fuel hoses for signs of leakage, deterioration or damage. Replace any hoses which are cracked or deteriorated.

2 If the fuel tap is leaking, remove the tap and tighten the assembly screws (see Chapter 4). If leakage persists remove the screws and disassemble the tap, noting how the components fit. Inspect all components for wear or damage. If any of the components are worn or damaged, a new tap must be fitted.

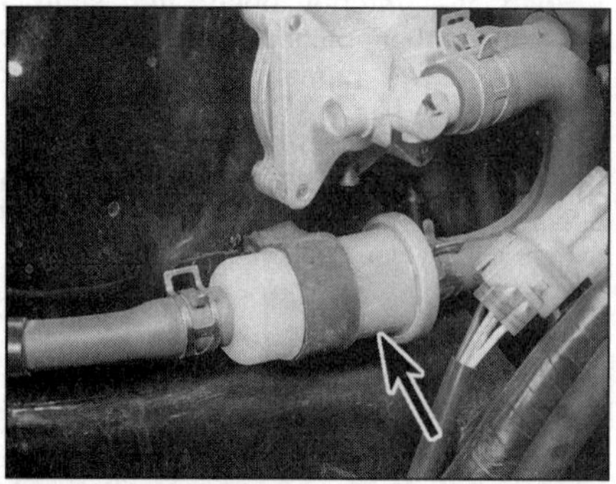

4.5 The fuel filter (arrowed) is below the fuel tap, under the tank cover

3 If the carburettor gaskets are leaking, the carburettors should be disassembled and rebuilt using new gaskets and seals (see Chapter 4).

Filter cleaning

4 Replacement of the fuel filter is advised after a particularly high mileage has been covered. It is also necessary if fuel starvation is suspected.

5 The fuel filter is fitted in the fuel line between the tank and the tap. Remove the fuel tank cover (see Chapter 8). Release the clamps securing the fuel hoses to the filter and detach the filter, being prepared to catch any residue fuel **(see illustration)**. Install the new filter with its narrower end facing back, and secure the hoses with the clamps.

5 Throttle and choke cables - check

Throttle cables

1 Make sure the throttle grip rotates easily from fully closed to fully open with the front wheel turned at various angles. The grip should return automatically from fully open to fully closed when released.

2 If the throttle sticks, this is probably due to a cable fault. Remove the cables (see Chapter 4) and lubricate them (see Section 15). Install the cables, making sure they are correctly routed. If this fails to improve the operation of the throttle, the cables must be replaced. Note that in very rare cases the fault could lie in the carburettors rather than the cables, necessitating the removal of the carburettors and inspection of the throttle linkage (see Chapter 4).

3 With the throttle operating smoothly, check for a small amount of freeplay in the cables, measured in terms of the amount of twistgrip rotation before the throttle opens, and compare the amount to that listed in this Chapter's Specifications **(see illustration)**. If it's incorrect, adjust the cables to correct it.

4 Freeplay adjustments can be made at the throttle end of the cable. Loosen the locknut on the accelerator cable where it leaves the handlebar **(see illustration)**. Turn the adjuster until the specified amount of freeplay is obtained (see this Chapter's Specifications), then retighten the locknut.

5 If the adjuster has reached its limit of adjustment, reset it so that the freeplay is at a maximum, then remove the fuel tank cover (see Chapter 8) and adjust the cable at the carburettor end. Slacken the adjuster locknut, then screw the adjuster out, making sure the lower nut remains captive in the bracket, thereby threading itself down the adjuster as you turn it, until the specified amount of freeplay is obtained, then tighten the locknut **(see illustration)**. Further adjustments can now be made at the throttle end. If the cable cannot be adjusted as specified, replace the cable (see Chapter 4).

Warning: Turn the handlebars all the way through their travel with the engine idling. Idle speed should not change. If it does, the cable may be routed incorrectly. Correct this condition before riding the bike.

6 Check that the throttle twistgrip operates smoothly and snaps shut quickly when released.

Choke cable

7 If the choke does not operate smoothly this is probably due to a cable fault. Remove the cable (see Chapter 4) and lubricate it (see Section 15). Install the cable, routing it so it takes the smoothest route possible.

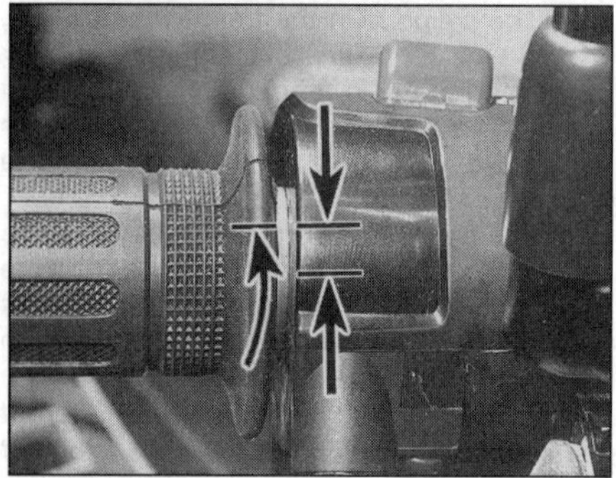

5.3 Throttle cable freeplay is measured in terms of twistgrip rotation

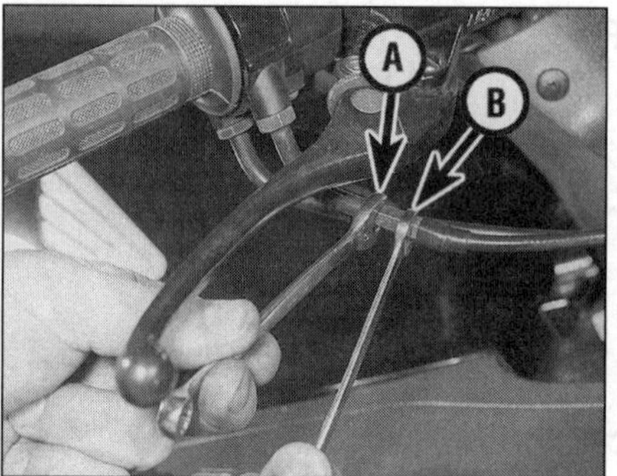

5.4 Throttle cable adjuster locknut(A) and adjuster (B) - throttle end

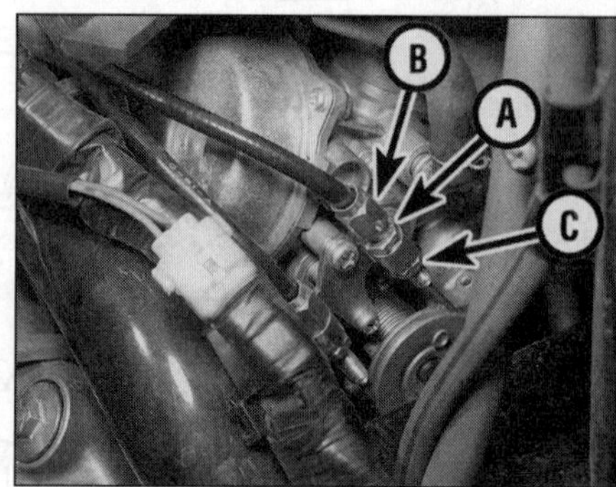

5.5 Throttle cable adjuster locknut (A), adjuster (B) and lower nut (C) - carburettor end

8 If this fails to improve the operation of the choke, the cable must be replaced. Note that in very rare cases the fault could lie in the carburettors rather than the cable, necessitating the removal of the carburettors and inspection of the choke plungers (see Chapter 4). Make sure there is a small amount of freeplay in the cable before the plungers move. If there isn't, check that the cable elbow is threaded fully into the switch housing. If it is, replace the cable.

6 Spark plugs - replacement

1 Remove the old spark plugs as described in Section 1 and install new ones.

7 Engine oil and oil filter - change

Warning: Be careful when draining the oil, as the exhaust pipes, the engine, and the oil itself can cause severe burns.

1 Consistent routine oil and filter changes are the single most important maintenance procedure you can perform on a motorcycle. The oil not only lubricates the internal parts of the engine, transmission and clutch, but it also acts as a coolant, a cleaner, a sealant, and a protectant. Because of these demands, the oil takes a terrific amount of abuse and should be replaced often with new oil of the recommended grade and type. Saving a little money on the difference in cost between a good oil and a cheap oil won't pay off if the engine is damaged. The oil filter should be changed with every oil change.

2 Before changing the oil, warm up the engine so the oil will drain easily.

3 Put the motorcycle on its centre stand, and position a clean drain tray below the engine. Unscrew the oil filler cap on the right-hand valve cover to vent the crankcase and to act as a reminder that there is no oil in the engine **(see illustration)**.

7.3 Remove the oil filler cap (arrowed)

4 Next, unscrew the oil drain plug from the bottom of the engine and allow the oil to flow into the drain tray **(see illustration)**. Check the condition of the sealing washer on the drain plug and discard it if it is any way damaged or worn.

5 When the oil has completely drained, fit the plug to the sump, using a new sealing washer if necessary, and tighten it to the torque setting specified at the beginning of the Chapter. Avoid overtightening, as damage to the sump will result.

6 Now place the drain tray below the oil filter. Unscrew the oil filter using a filter removing strap, chain or wrench and tip any residue oil into the drain tray **(see illustrations)**.

Warning: The starter motor guard just above the oil filter has a sharp edge - take care not to injure yourself when unscrewing or replacing the filter.

7 Smear clean engine oil onto the rubber seal on the new filter, then screw the filter onto the engine and tighten it to the specified torque setting using a filter wrench. If one is not available, tighten the filter as tight as possible by hand **(see illustration)**.

8 Refill the engine to the proper level using the recommended type and amount of oil (see *Daily (pre-ride) checks*). With the motorcycle vertical, the oil level should lie between the upper and lower level lines on the inspection window (see *Daily (pre-ride) checks*). Install the filler cap. Start the engine and let it run for two or three minutes (make sure that the oil

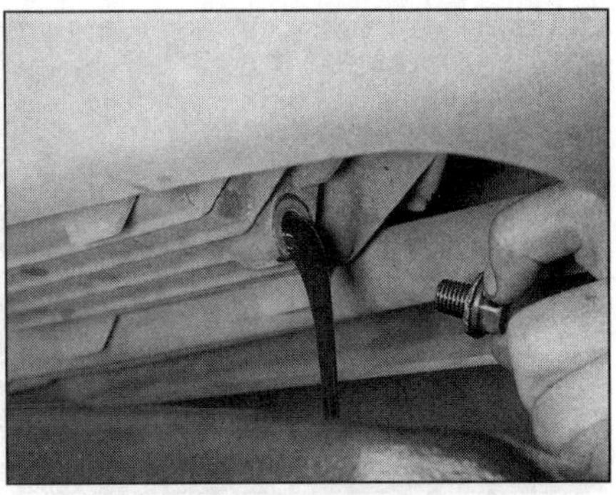

7.4 Remove the drain plug and allow the oil to drain completely

pressure light extinguishes after a few seconds). Shut it off, wait a few minutes, then check the oil level. If necessary, add more oil to bring the level up to the upper level line on the inspection window. Check around the drain plug and the oil filter for leaks.

Saving a little money on the difference between good and cheap oils won't pay off if the engine is damaged as a result.

9 The old oil drained from the engine cannot be re-used and should be disposed of properly. Check with your local refuse disposal company, disposal facility or environmental agency to see whether they will accept the used oil for recycling. Don't pour used oil into drains or onto the ground.

Check the old oil carefully - if it is very metallic coloured, then the engine is experiencing wear from break-in (new engine) or from insufficient lubrication. If there are flakes or chips of metal in the oil, then something is drastically wrong internally and the engine will have to be disassembled for inspection and repair. If there are pieces of fibre-like material in the oil, the clutch is experiencing excessive wear and should be checked.

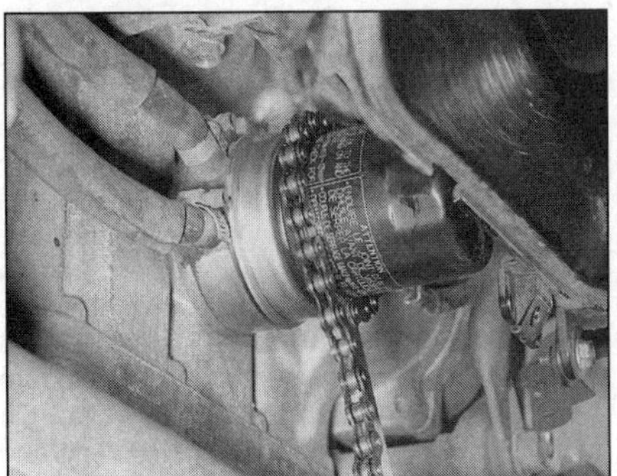

7.6a Unscrew the filter using a filter removing tool (chain type shown) . . .

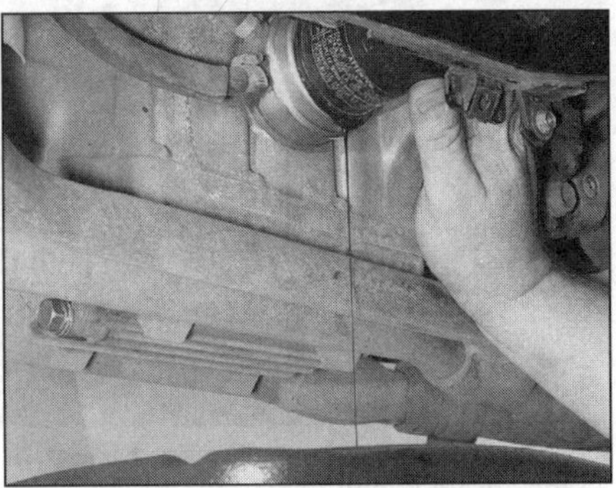

7.6b . . . and allow the oil to drain

7.7 Screw the filter on by hand if a wrench is not available

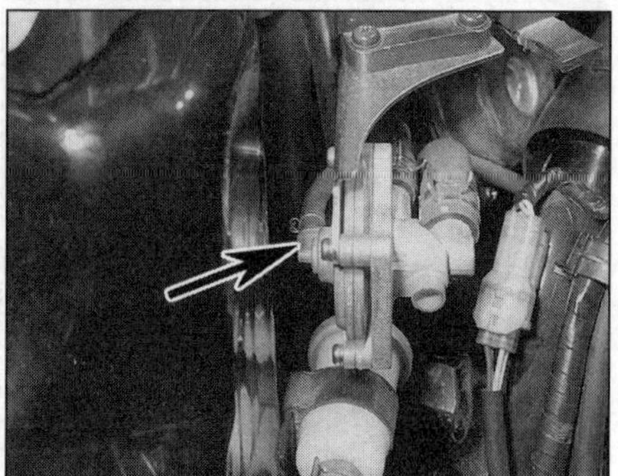
8.5a Detach the vacuum hose (arrowed) from the back of the tap

8.5b Remove the caps (arrowed) from the vacuum hoses of the remaining carburettors

8 Carburettors - synchronisation

Warning: Petrol (gasoline) is extremely flammable, so take extra precautions when you work on any part of the fuel system. Don't smoke or allow open flames or bare light bulbs near the work area, and don't work in a garage where a natural gas-type appliance is present. If you spill any fuel on your skin, rinse it off immediately with soap and water. When you perform any kind of work on the fuel system, wear safety glasses and have a fire extinguisher suitable for a Class B type fire (flammable liquids) on hand.

Warning: Take great care not to burn your hand on the hot engine unit when accessing the gauge take-off points on the intake manifolds. Do not allow exhaust gases to build up in the work area; either perform the check outside or use an exhaust gas extraction system.

1 Carburettor synchronisation is simply the process of adjusting the carburettors so they pass the same amount of fuel/air mixture to each cylinder. This is done by measuring the vacuum produced in each cylinder. Carburettors that are out of synchronisation will result in decreased fuel mileage, increased engine temperature, less than ideal throttle response and higher vibration levels. Before synchronising the carburettors, make sure the valve clearances are properly set.

2 To properly synchronise the carburettors, you will need a set of vacuum gauges or calibrated tubes to indicate engine vacuum. The equipment used should be suitable for a four cylinder engine and come complete with the necessary adapters and hoses to fit the take off points. **Note:** *Because of the nature of the synchronisation procedure and the need for special instruments, most owners leave the task to a Honda dealer.*

3 Start the engine and let it run until it reaches normal operating temperature, then shut it off.

4 Remove the fairing pockets (see Chapter 8).

5 Disconnect the no.3 cylinder vacuum hose from the vacuum take-off stub on the fuel tap. Using an auxiliary length of hose, attach it to the vacuum take-off stub on the fuel tap, then apply a vacuum to the hose and seal it off using a clamp. This ensures the fuel tap is open and can supply fuel to the carburettors. On UK models, remove the blanking caps from the vacuum hoses of the remaining carburettors **(see illustrations)**. On all US models, disconnect the nos. 2 and 4 cylinder vacuum hoses from the three-way joint. On all California models and 1991 to 1993 49 State ABS/TCS models, disconnect the no.1 cylinder vacuum hose from the EVAP system control valve. Using an auxiliary length of hose, attach it to the EVAP system control valve, then apply a vacuum to the hose and seal it off using a clamp. On standard 1991 to 1993 49 State models and all 1994 on 49 State models, remove the blanking cap from the no.1 cylinder vacuum hose.

6 Connect the vacuum gauges to the vacuum hoses. Make sure they are a good fit because any air leaks will result in false readings.

7 Start the engine and adjust the idle speed (see Section 2).

8 If using vacuum gauges fitted with damping adjustment, set this so that the needle flutter is just eliminated but so that they can still respond to small changes in vacuum.

9 The vacuum readings for all of the cylinders should be the same. If the vacuum readings vary, proceed as follows.

10 The carburettors are adjusted by turning the synchronising screws situated in-between the carburettors on each side, in the throttle linkage. **Note:** *Do not press down on the screws whilst adjusting them, otherwise a false reading will be obtained.* First synchronise no. 2 carburettor to no. 4 using the synchronising screw on the left-hand side of the carburettor assembly, until the readings are the same. Then synchronise no. 1 carburettor to no. 3 using the front synchronising screw on the right-hand side of the assembly, and finally synchronise nos. 1 and 3 carburettors to nos. 2 and 4 using the centre synchronising screw on the right-hand side of the assembly **(see illustrations)**. When all the carburettors are synchronised, open and close the throttle quickly to settle the linkage, and recheck the gauge readings, readjusting if necessary.

11 When the adjustment is complete, recheck the vacuum readings, then adjust the idle speed by turning the throttle stop screw (see Section 2) until the idle speed listed in this Chapter's Specifications is obtained. Stop the engine.

12 Remove the vacuum gauges and the auxiliary hoses fitted to the fuel tap (all models) and the EVAP control valve (all California models and 1991 to 1993 49 State ABS/TCS models). Install the no. 3 cylinder vacuum hose onto the fuel tap **(see illustration 8.5a)**. On UK models, fit the blanking caps onto the vacuum hoses of the remaining carburettors. On all US models, connect the nos. 2 and 4 cylinder vacuum hoses to the three-way joint. On all California models and 1991 to 1993 49 State ABS/TCS models, connect the no.1 cylinder vacuum hose to the EVAP system control valve. On standard 1991 to 1993 49 State models and all 1994 on 49 State models, fit the blanking cap to the no.1 cylinder vacuum hose.

13 Install the fairing pockets (see Chapter 8).

8.10a Synchronise no. 2 to no. 4 using the screw (arrowed) on the left-hand side of the carburettors . . .

8.10b . . . then synchronise no. 1 to no. 3 using screw A, and finally synchronise nos. 1 and 3 to nos. 2 and 4 using screw B, both on the right-hand side of the carburettors

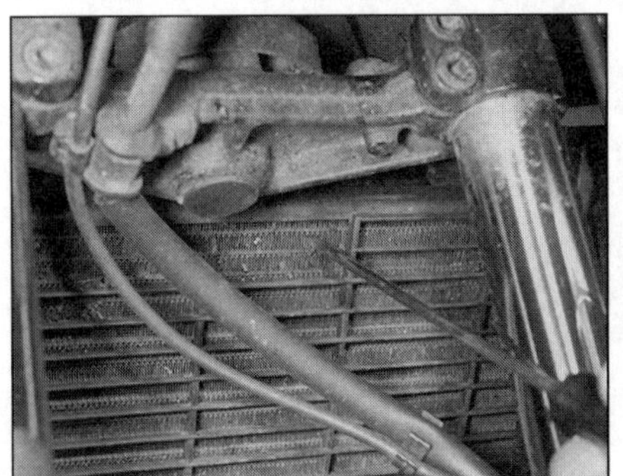

9.5 Carefully straighten any bent fins using a screwdriver

9 Cooling system - check

Warning: The engine must be cool before beginning this procedure.

1 Check the coolant level (see *Daily (pre-ride) checks*).

2 The entire cooling system should be checked for evidence of leakage. Examine each rubber coolant hose along its entire length. Look for cracks, abrasions and other damage. Squeeze each hose at various points. They should feel firm, yet pliable, and return to their original shape when released. If they are dried out or hard, replace them with new ones.

3 Check for evidence of leaks at each cooling system joint. Tighten the hose clips carefully to prevent future leaks.

4 Check the radiator for leaks and other damage. Leaks in the radiator leave tell-tale scale deposits or coolant stains on the outside of the core below the leak. If leaks are noted, remove the radiator (see Chapter 3) and have it repaired at a radiator shop or replace it with a new one.

Caution: Do not use a liquid leak stopping compound to try to repair leaks.

5 Check the radiator fins for mud, dirt and insects, which may impede the flow of air through the radiator. If the fins are dirty, clean them using water or low pressure compressed air directed through the fins from the backside. If the fins are bent or distorted, straighten them carefully with a screwdriver **(see illustration)**. If the air flow is restricted by bent or damaged fins over more than 30% of the radiator's surface area, replace the radiator.

9.6 Cooling system pressure cap

6 Remove the right-hand middle fairing inner pocket (see Chapter 8). Remove the pressure cap from the filler neck by turning it counterclockwise (anti-clockwise) until it reaches a stop **(see illustration)**. If you hear a hissing sound (indicating there is still pressure in the system), wait until it stops. Now press down on the cap and continue turning the cap until it can be removed. Check the condition of the coolant in the system. If it is rust-coloured or if accumulations of scale are visible, drain, flush and refill the system with new coolant (See Section 24). Check the cap seal for cracks and other damage. If in doubt about the pressure cap's condition, have it tested by a Honda dealer or replace it with a new one. Install the cap by turning it clockwise until it reaches the first stop then push down on the cap and continue turning until it can turn no further.

7 Check the antifreeze content of the coolant with an antifreeze hydrometer. Sometimes coolant looks like it's in good condition, but might be too weak to offer adequate protection. If the hydrometer indicates a weak mixture, drain, flush and refill the system (see Section 24).

8 Start the engine and let it reach normal operating temperature, then check for leaks again. As the coolant temperature increases, the fan should come on automatically and the temperature should begin to drop. If it does not, refer to Chapter 3 and check the fan and fan circuit carefully.

9 If the coolant level is consistently low, and no evidence of leaks can be found, have the entire system pressure checked by a Honda dealer.

10 Emission control systems - check (US models only)

1 Visually inspect all the emission control system hoses for kinks and splits and any other damage or deterioration. Make sure that the hoses are securely connected with a clamp on each end. Replace any hoses that are damaged or deteriorated. See Chapter 4 for further information on the systems. **Note:** *The EVAP system hoses can be identified by referring to the vacuum hose routing diagram on the rear mudguard, under the seat.*

11 Final drive - oil level check

1 Place the motorcycle on its centre stand, making sure it is on level ground.

2 The check should be made after the machine has been standing for a few hours. Unscrew the oil filler cap and check that the oil is up to the lower edge of the filler hole **(see illustrations)**. If the level is below this, look for signs of leakage, such as oil staining on the underside of the casing. If leakage is evident, the problem must be rectified to avoid the possibility of damage to the final drive and oil contaminating the rear tyre (see Chapter 6).

3 Replenish the oil if necessary to the correct level using the type and grade specified at the beginning of the Chapter, then install the filler cap, using a new O-ring smeared with clean oil, and tighten it to the torque setting specified at the beginning of the Chapter **(see illustrations)**.

11.2a Remove the cap . . .

11.2b . . . and check the oil is up to the lower edge of the hole

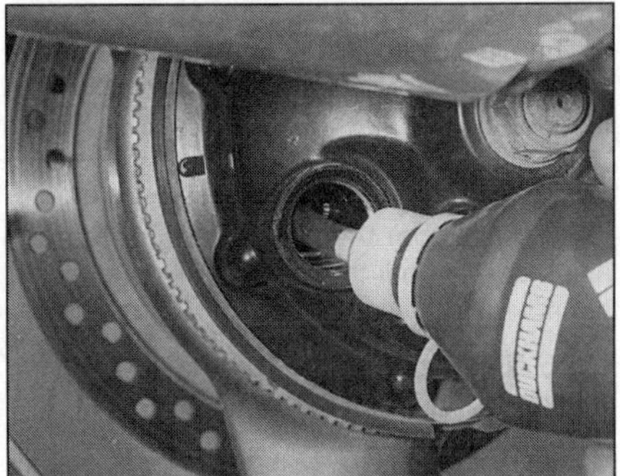

11.3a Top up the oil if necessary . . .

11.3b . . . and replace the cap using a new O-ring

12 Brake system - check

General check - all models

1 A routine general check of the brake system will ensure that any problems are discovered and remedied before the rider's safety is jeopardised.

2 Check the brake lever and pedal for loose connections, improper or rough action, excessive play, bends, and other damage. Replace any damaged parts with new ones (see Chapter 7).

3 Make sure all brake fasteners are tight. Check the brake pads for wear (see Section 3) and make sure the fluid level in the reservoirs is correct (see *Daily (pre-ride) checks*). Look for leaks at the hose connections and check for cracks in the hoses. If the lever or pedal is spongy, bleed the brakes (see Chapter 7).

4 Make sure the brake light operates when the front brake lever is depressed. The front brake light switch is not adjustable. If it fails to operate properly, check it (see Chapter 9).

5 Make sure the brake light is activated just before the rear brake pedal takes effect. If adjustment is necessary, remove the right-hand side panel for access to the switch (see Chapter 8). Hold the switch and turn the adjuster ring on the switch body until the brake light is activated when required **(see illustration)**. If the switch doesn't operate the brake light, check it (see Chapter 9).

6 The front brake lever has a span adjuster which alters the distance of the lever from the handlebar **(see illustration)**. Each setting is identified by a notch in the adjuster which aligns with the arrow on the lever. Pull the lever away from the handlebar and turn the adjuster ring until the setting which best suits the rider is obtained. There are eight settings.

CBS/LBS check - UK AT and AV models, US 1996 and 1997 A models

7 Place the motorcycle on its centrestand and make sure the transmission is in neutral. Check that the rear wheel is off the ground.

12.5 Rear brake light switch adjuster ring (arrowed)

8 Lift the left-hand front brake caliper up so that the secondary master cylinder pushrod is activated. Keeping the caliper raised, check that the rear wheel is locked by the brake. If the wheel can be turned, the CBS/LBS system is faulty and must be checked (see Chapter 7). Also check that the linkage between the left-hand caliper and the secondary master cylinder pushrod moves smoothly and freely.

9 Raise the front wheel off the ground, either by having an assistant press down on the rear or by placing a support under the engine. Press the rear brake pedal down and check that the front wheel is locked by the brake. If the wheel can be turned, the CBS/LBS system is faulty and must be checked (see Chapter 7).

13 Headlight aim - check and adjustment

Note: *An improperly adjusted headlight may cause problems for oncoming traffic or provide poor, unsafe illumination of the road ahead. Before adjusting the headlight aim, be sure to consult with local traffic laws and regulations - for UK models refer to MOT Test Checks in the Reference section.*

1 The headlight beam can adjusted both horizontally and vertically. Before making any adjustment, check that the tyre pressures are correct and the suspension is adjusted as

13.2 Headlight beam vertical adjuster

12.6 Front brake lever span adjuster ring (arrowed)

required. Make any adjustments to the headlight aim with the machine on level ground, with the fuel tank half full and with an assistant sitting on the seat. If the bike is usually ridden with a passenger on the back, have a second assistant to do this.

2 Vertical adjustment is made by turning the adjuster knob mounted in the cockpit **(see illustration)**. Turn it clockwise to move the beam up, and anti-clockwise to move it down, as indicated on the knob.

3 Horizontal adjustment is made by turning the adjuster screw on the left-hand end of the headlight assembly using a screwdriver inserted through the hole in the middle fairing inner panel above the radiator **(see illustration)**. Turn it clockwise to move the beam to the right, and anti-clockwise to move it to the left.

14 Clutch - check

1 All models are fitted with an hydraulic clutch, for which there is no method of adjustment.

2 Check the fluid level in the reservoir (see *Daily (pre-ride) checks*).

3 Inspect the hose and its connections for signs of fluid leakage, cracking, deterioration and wear. The clutch fluid should be changed every two years (see Section 22), and the hoses replaced if they deteriorate, or every

13.3 Headlight beam horizontal adjuster (fairing removed for clarity)

four years irrespective of their condition at that stage (see Section 34).

4 Check the operation of the clutch; if there is evidence of air in the system (spongy feel to the lever), bleed the clutch as described in Chapter 2.

15 Stands, lever pivots and cables - lubrication

1 Since the controls, cables and various other components of a motorcycle are exposed to the elements, they should be lubricated periodically to ensure safe and trouble-free operation.

2 The footrests, clutch and brake levers, brake pedal, gearshift lever linkage and stand pivots should be lubricated frequently. In order for the lubricant to be applied where it will do the most good, the component should be disassembled. However, if chain and cable lubricant is being used, it can be applied to the pivot joint gaps and will usually work its way into the areas where friction occurs. If motor oil or light grease is being used, apply it sparingly as it may attract dirt (which could cause the controls to bind or wear at an accelerated rate). **Note:** *One of the best lubricants for the control lever pivots is a dry-film lubricant (available from many sources by different names).*

3 To lubricate the cables, disconnect the relevant cable at its upper end, then lubricate the cable with a pressure adapter, or if one is not available, using the set-up shown **(see illustrations)**. See Chapter 4 for the choke and throttle cable removal procedures.

4 The speedometer cable should be removed (see Chapter 9) and the inner cable withdrawn from the outer cable and lubricated with motor oil or cable lubricant. Do not lubricate the upper few inches of the cable as the lubricant may travel up into the instrument head.

16 Suspension - check

1 The suspension components must be maintained in top operating condition to ensure rider safety. Loose, worn or damaged suspension parts decrease the motorcycle's stability and control.

Front suspension

2 While standing alongside the motorcycle, apply the front brake and push on the handlebars to compress the forks several times. See if they move up-and-down smoothly without binding. If binding is felt, the forks should be disassembled and inspected (see Chapter 6).

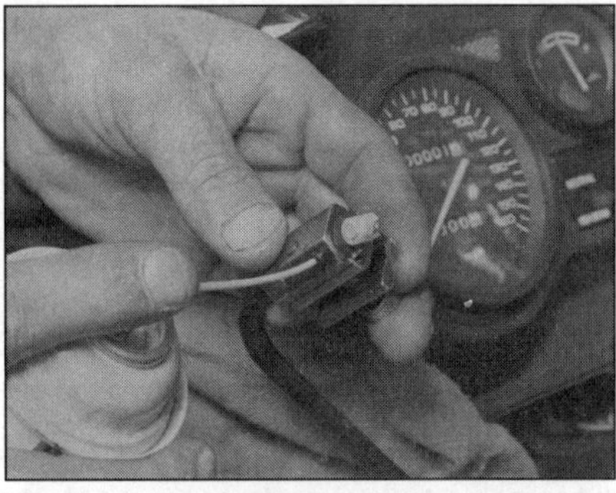

15.3a Lubricating a cable with a pressure lubricator. Make sure the tool seals around the inner cable

3 Inspect the area above the dust seal for signs of oil leakage, then carefully lever off the dust seal using a flat-bladed screwdriver and inspect the area around the fork seal **(see illustration)**. If leakage is evident, the seals must be replaced (see Chapter 6).

4 Check the tightness of all suspension nuts and bolts to be sure none have worked loose.

Rear suspension

5 Inspect the rear shock for fluid leakage and tightness of its mountings **(see illustration)**. If leakage is found, the shock should be replaced (see Chapter 6).

6 With the aid of an assistant to support the bike, compress the rear suspension several times. It should move up and down freely without binding. If any binding is felt, the worn or faulty component must be identified and replaced. The problem could be due to either the shock absorber or the swingarm components.

7 Position the motorcycle on its centrestand so that the rear wheel is off the ground. Grab the swingarm and rock it from side to side - there should be no discernible movement at the rear. If there's a little movement or a slight clicking can be heard, inspect the tightness of all the rear suspension mounting bolts, referring to the torque settings specified at the beginning of the Chapter, and re-check for movement. Next, grasp the top of the rear wheel and pull it upwards - there should be no discernible freeplay before the shock

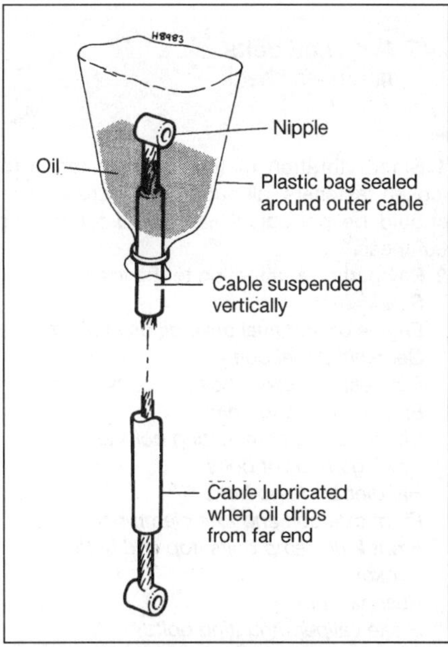

15.3b Lubricating a cable with a makeshift funnel and motor oil

absorber begins to compress. Any freeplay felt in either check indicates worn bearings in the swingarm, or worn shock absorber mountings. The worn components must be replaced (see Chapter 6).

8 To make an accurate assessment of the swingarm bearings, remove the rear wheel (see Chapter 7) and the shock absorber (see Chapter 6). Grasp the rear of the swingarm with one hand and place your other hand at the junction of the swingarm and the frame. Try to move the rear of the swingarm from side-to-side. Any wear (play) in the bearings should be felt as movement between the swingarm and the frame at the front. If there is any play, the swingarm will be felt to move forward and backward at the front (not from side-to-side). Next, move the swingarm up and down through its full travel. It should move freely, without any binding or rough spots. If any play in the swingarm is noted or if the swingarm does not move freely, the bearings must be removed for inspection or replacement (see Chapter 6).

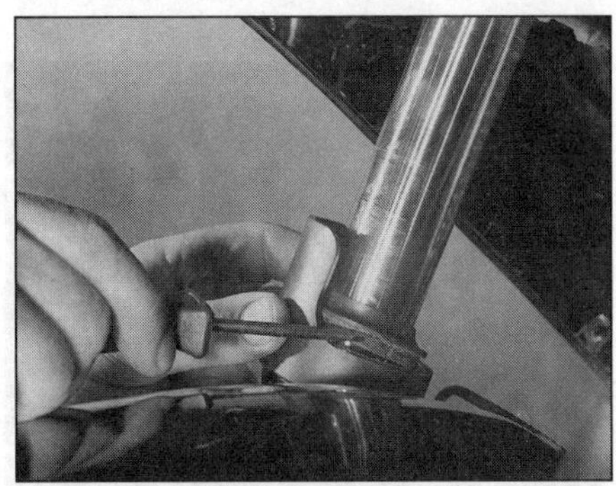

16.3 Lever up the dust seal and check for evidence of leakage from the fork oil seal

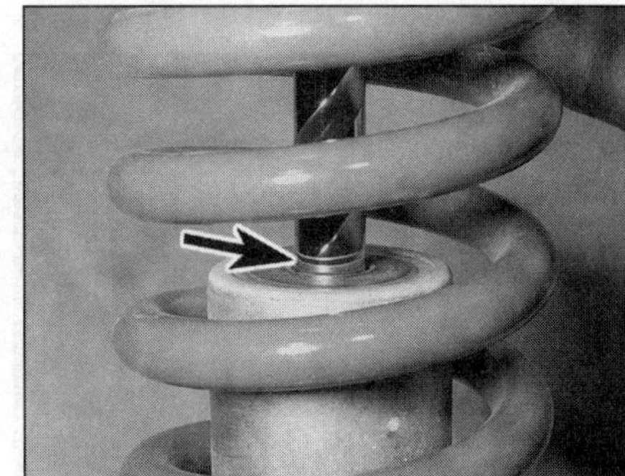

16.5 Check the area around the rod and seal (arrowed) for evidence of leakage from the shock

17 Nuts and bolts - tightness check

1 Since vibration of the machine tends to loosen fasteners, all nuts, bolts, screws, etc. should be periodically checked for proper tightness.

2 Pay particular attention to the following:
Spark plugs
Engine oil and final drive oil drain plugs
Gearshift pedal bolt
Footrest and stand bolts
Engine mounting bolts
Shock absorber mounting bolts and swingarm pivot bolts
Handlebar clamp bolts
Front axle bolt and axle clamp bolts
Front fork clamp bolts (top and bottom yoke)
Rear axle nut
Brake caliper mounting bolts
Brake hose banjo bolts and caliper bleed valves
Brake disc bolts
Exhaust system bolts/nuts

3 If a torque wrench is available, use it along with the torque specifications at the beginning of this and other Chapters.

18 Wheels and tyres - general check

Tyres

1 Check the tyre condition and tread depth thoroughly - see *Daily (pre-ride) checks*.

Wheels

2 Cast wheels are virtually maintenance free, but they should be kept clean and checked periodically for cracks and other damage. Also check the wheel runout and alignment (see Chapter 7). Never attempt to repair damaged cast wheels; they must be replaced with new ones. Check the valve rubber for signs of damage or deterioration and have it replaced if necessary. Also, make sure the valve stem cap is in place and tight.

19 Steering head bearings - freeplay check and adjustment

1 This motorcycle is equipped with caged ball steering head bearings which can become dented, rough or loose during normal use of the machine. In extreme cases, worn or loose steering head bearings can cause steering wobble - a condition that is potentially dangerous.

Check

2 Place the motorcycle on its centrestand. Raise the front wheel off the ground either by having an assistant push down on the rear or by placing a support under the engine.

3 Point the front wheel straight-ahead and slowly move the handlebars from side-to-side. Any dents or roughness in the bearing races will be felt and the bars will not move smoothly and freely.

4 Next, grasp the fork sliders and try to move them forward and backward **(see illustration)**. Any looseness in the steering head bearings will be felt as front-to-rear movement of the forks. If play is felt in the bearings, adjust the steering head as follows.

Freeplay in the fork due to worn fork bushes can be misinterpreted for steering head bearing play - do not confuse the two.

Adjustment

5 Displace the handlebars (see Chapter 6). Although not essential, it is wise to remove the upper fairing and the fuel tank cover (see Chapter 8) to avoid the possibility of damage should a tool slip while adjustment is being made. Unscrew the steering stem nut, then slacken the fork clamp bolts in the top yoke **(see illustration)**.

6 Gently ease the top yoke up off the fork tubes **(see illustration)**.

7 Prise the lockwasher tabs out of the slots in the locknut and adjuster nut. Unscrew the locknut using a C-spanner and discard the lockwasher **(see illustrations)**; a new lockwasher must be used on reassembly.

8 Slacken the adjuster nut slightly until pressure is just released, then tighten it until all freeplay is removed, yet the steering is able to move freely **(see illustration)**. Note that Honda specify a torque setting for the adjuster nut - if this is applied, check afterwards that the steering is still able to move freely from side to side. The object is to set the adjuster nut so that the bearings are

19.4 Checking for play in the steering head bearings

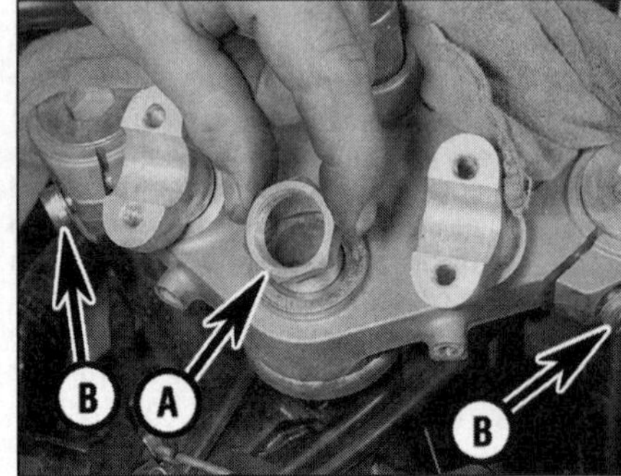

19.5 Remove the steering stem nut (A) and slacken the clamp bolts (B)

19.6 Lift the yoke up off the steering stem and fork tubes

19.7a Bend down the upper lockwasher tabs to free the locknut

19.7b Unscrew the locknut and remove the lockwasher

19.8 Turn the adjuster nut using a C-spanner

19.10 Locate the down-facing tabs in the slots in the adjuster nut

19.11 Tighten the steering stem nut and fork clamp bolts to the specified torque settings

under a very light loading, just enough to remove any freeplay.

Caution: Take great care not to apply excessive pressure because this will cause premature failure of the bearings.

9 If the bearings cannot be set up properly, or if there is any binding, roughness or notchiness, they will have to be removed for inspection or replacement (see Chapter 6).

10 When the bearings are correctly adjusted, install the new lockwasher onto the adjuster nut so that the down-facing tabs fit into the slots in the adjuster nut **(see illustration)**. Install the locknut and tighten it finger-tight, then tighten it further (to a maximum of 90°) until its slots align with the remaining tabs on the lockwasher. Hold the adjuster nut to prevent it from moving if necessary. Bend up the lockwasher tabs to secure the locknut.

11 Fit the top yoke onto the steering stem, then install the washer and nut and tighten it and both the fork clamp bolts to the torque settings specified at the beginning of the Chapter **(see illustration)**.

12 Check the bearing adjustment as described above and re-adjust if necessary. Install the handlebars (see Chapter 6).

Every 12,000 miles (19,200 km) or 18 months

Carry out all the items under the 4000 mile (6400 km) check:

20 Air filter - replacement

Caution: If the machine is continually ridden in continuously wet or dusty conditions, the filter should be replaced more frequently.

1 Remove the fuel tank cover (see Chapter 8).

2 Unscrew the eight screws securing the air filter cover to the filter housing and remove the cover. Remove the filter element from the housing and discard it **(see illustrations)**.

3 Check the condition of the sealing ring in the filter housing and replace it if necessary **(see illustration)**. Install the new filter by reversing the removal procedure. Make sure the filter is properly seated.

4 To clean the filter in between replacement service intervals, tap the filter on a hard surface to dislodge any dirt and use compressed air to clear the element, directing the air from the inside. Also check the condition of the sub-air cleaner element in the box just ahead of the main housing, and clean or replace it as required **(see illustrations)**.

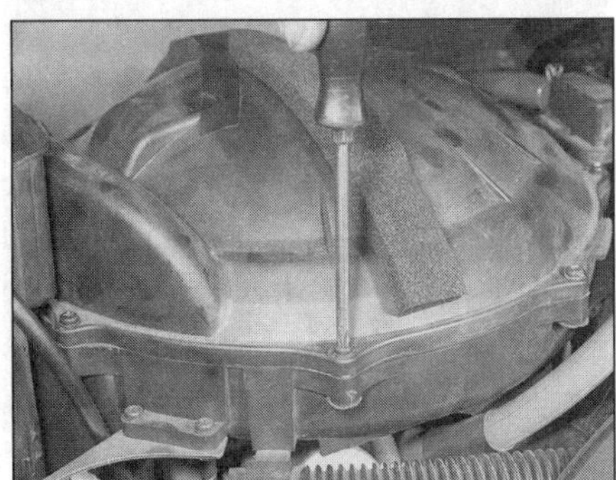
20.2a Unscrew the filter cover screws . . .

20.2b . . . and remove the element

20.3 Check the condition of the sealing ring

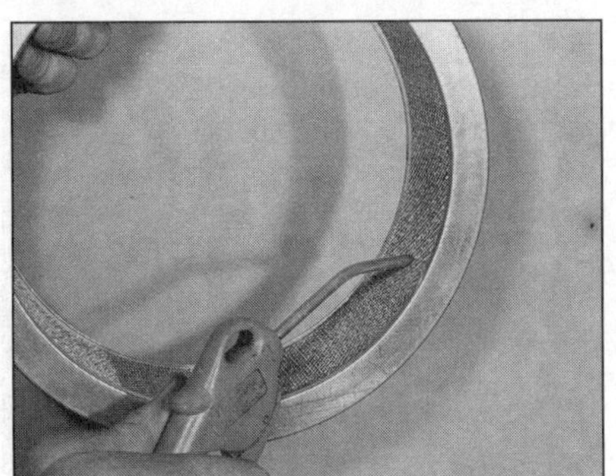
20.4a Use compressed air to clean the element between replacement intervals

20.4b Lift the cover to access the sub-air cleaner element

Every 12,000 miles (19,200 km) or two years

21 Brake fluid - change

1 The brake fluid should be replaced at the prescribed interval or whenever a master cylinder or caliper overhaul is carried out. Refer to the brake bleeding section in Chapter 7, noting that all old fluid must be pumped from the fluid reservoir and hydraulic line before filling with new fluid.

22 Clutch - fluid change

1 The clutch fluid should be replaced at the prescribed interval or whenever a master cylinder or release cylinder overhaul is carried out. Refer to the clutch bleeding section in Chapter 2, noting that all old fluid must be pumped from the fluid reservoir and hydraulic line before filling with new fluid.

HAYNES HiNT

Old brake and clutch fluid is invariably much darker in colour than new fluid, making it easy to see when all old fluid has been expelled from the system.

Every 16,000 miles (25,600 km) or two years

Carry out all the items under the 8000 mile (12,800 km) check, plus the following:

23 Valve clearances - check and adjustment

1 The engine must be completely cool for this maintenance procedure, so let the machine sit overnight before beginning.

2 Remove the spark plugs (see Section 6).

3 Remove the valve covers (see Chapter 2). Each cylinder is referred to by a number. The no.1 cylinder is the front cylinder on the right-hand bank, no.2 cylinder is the front on the left-hand, no.3 the rear on the right and no.4 the rear on the left **(see illustration)**.

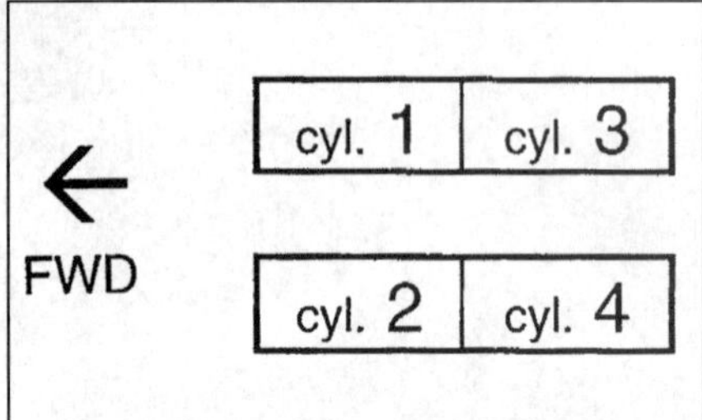

23.3 Cylinder identification

4 Make a chart or sketch of all valve positions so that a note of each clearance can be made against the relevant valve.

5 Remove the lower fairing (see Chapter 8). Unscrew the two bolts securing the timing inspection cover to the timing belt cover on the front of the engine. Discard the cover O-ring as a new one must be used. The engine can be turned using a 17 mm socket on the drive pulley bolt and turning it in a clockwise direction only **(see illustrations)**. Alternatively, place the motorcycle on its centre stand, select a high gear and rotate the rear wheel by hand in its normal direction of rotation.

23.5a The timing inspection cover is secured by two bolts (arrowed)

Caution: DO NOT use the timing rotor bolt to turn the crankshaft - it may snap or strip out. Also be sure to turn the engine in its normal direction of rotation.

6 Turn the engine until the "T1" mark on the drive pulley guide plate aligns with the static timing mark on the timing belt cover, and the index lines on the front end of the camshafts on the right-hand cylinder head are facing out and align with the head mating surface **(see illustration)**. If they are facing in, rotate the engine clockwise one full turn until the "T1" mark again aligns with the static timing mark. The camshaft index lines will now be facing out and the no. 1 cylinder is at TDC on the compression stroke. Do not confuse the index lines with the punchmarks on the camshaft ends.

7 With no. 1 cylinder at TDC on the compression stroke, check the clearances on the no.1 cylinder intake and exhaust valves. Insert a feeler gauge of the same thickness as the correct valve clearance (see Specifications) between the cam base and follower of each valve and check that it is a firm sliding fit - you should feel a slight drag when the you pull the gauge out **(see illustration)**. If not, use the

23.5b Turn the engine in a clockwise direction only

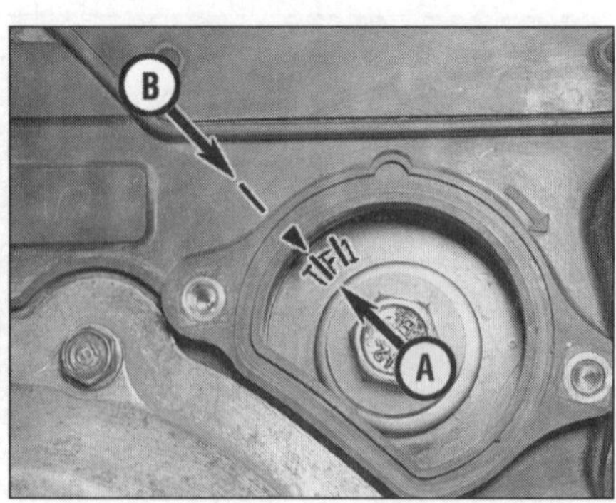

23.6 Align the "T" mark (A) with the static timing mark (B)

23.7 Check the clearance using a feeler gauge

23.13a Lift out the cam follower

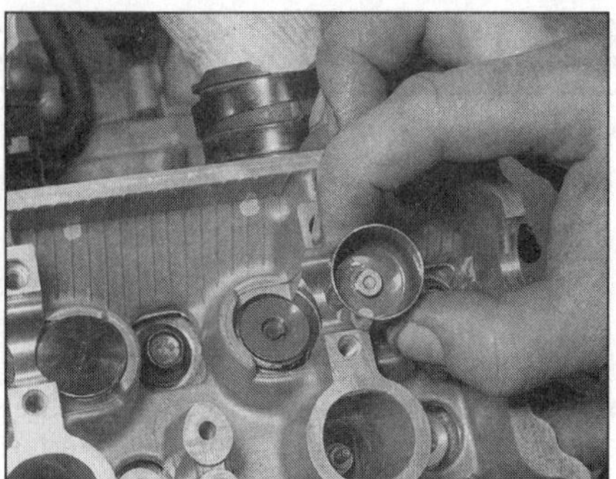
23.13b The shim will either be stuck to the inside of the follower . . .

23.13c . . . or remain in the top of the valve (arrow)

feeler gauges to obtain the exact clearance. Record the measured clearance on the chart.

8 Rotate the engine clockwise so that the timing rotor turns through 90° (1/4 turn) and the "T4" mark aligns with the static timing mark. The index lines on the front of the camshafts on the left-hand cylinder bank should be facing in and align with the top of the cylinder head. Do not confuse the index lines with the punchmarks on the camshaft ends. Measure the valve clearance of the no.4 cylinder valves using the method described in Step 7.

9 Rotate the engine so that the timing rotor turns through 270° (3/4 turn) and the "T1" mark aligns with the static timing mark. The index lines on the front of the camshafts on the right-hand cylinder bank should now be facing in and align with the top of the cylinder head. Measure the valve clearance of the no.3 cylinder valves using the method described in Step 7.

10 Rotate the engine so that the timing rotor turns through 90° (1/4 turn) and the "T4" mark aligns with the static timing mark. The index lines on the front of the camshafts on the left-hand cylinder bank should now be facing out and align with the top of the cylinder head. Measure the valve clearance of the no.2 cylinder valves using the method described in Step 7.

11 When all clearances have been measured and charted, identify whether the clearance on any valve falls outside that specified. If it does, the shim between the follower and the valve must be replaced with one of a thickness which will restore the correct clearance.

12 Shim replacement requires removal of the relevant camshaft (see Chapter 2).

13 With the camshaft removed, remove the cam follower of the valve in question, then remove the shim, which will probably be stuck to the inside of the follower **(see illustrations)**. If the shim remains in the top of the valve, lever it out using a small screwdriver and remove it using a pair of pliers. Do not allow the shim to fall into the engine.

14 The shim size should be stamped on its face. A shim size of 250 denotes a thickness of 2.5 mm, 245 is 2.45 mm. It is recommended that the shim is measured using a micrometer to check that it has not worn. Shims are available in 0.025 mm increments from 1.200 mm to 2.800 mm.

15 Calculate the required replacement shim by using the formula a=b-c+d, where a is the required shim size, b is the measured valve clearance, c is the specified valve clearance, and d is the existing shim thickness. For example:

The measured clearance of a no.1 cylinder inlet valve is 0.21 mm, so b=0.21.

The specified clearance range for an intake valve is 0.13 to 0.19 mm, the mid-point being 0.16 mm, so c=0.16.

The thickness of the existing shim is 1.800 mm.

Therefore, the required replacement shim a=0.21-0.16+1.800 a=1.85

Note: *If the required replacement shim is greater than 2.800 mm (the largest available), the valve is probably not seating correctly due to a build-up of carbon deposits and should be checked and cleaned or resurfaced as required (see Chapter 2).*

16 Obtain and install the replacement shim in the recess in the top of the valve spring retainer **(see illustration)**, noting that its size marking should be installed upwards and that the shim should be lubricated with molybdenum disulphide grease - this will also hold it in position on the valve while the follower and camshaft are installed.

17 Lubricate the follower with molybdenum disulphide grease and install it onto the valve **(see illustration)**. Repeat the process for any other valves until the clearances are correct, then install the camshafts (see Chapter 2).

1

18 Rotate the crankshaft several turns to seat the new shim(s), then check the clearances again.

19 Install all disturbed components in a reverse of the removal sequence. Use a new O-ring on the timing inspection cover **(see illustration)**.

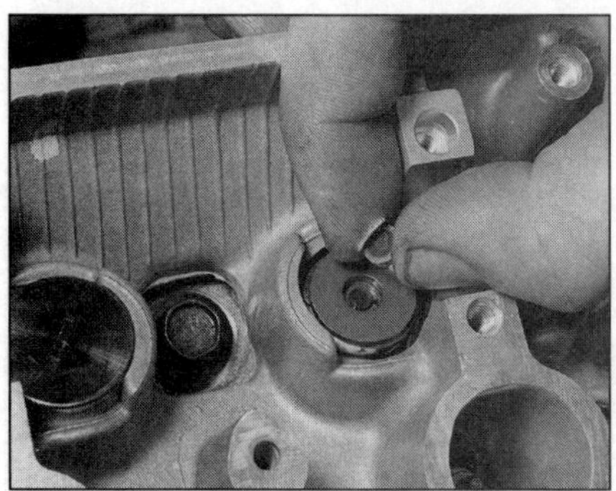
23.16 Fit the shim into the recess in the valve spring retainer . . .

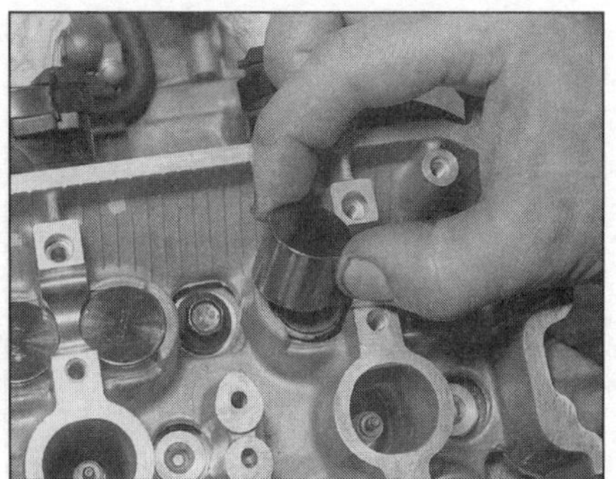
23.17 . . . then install the follower

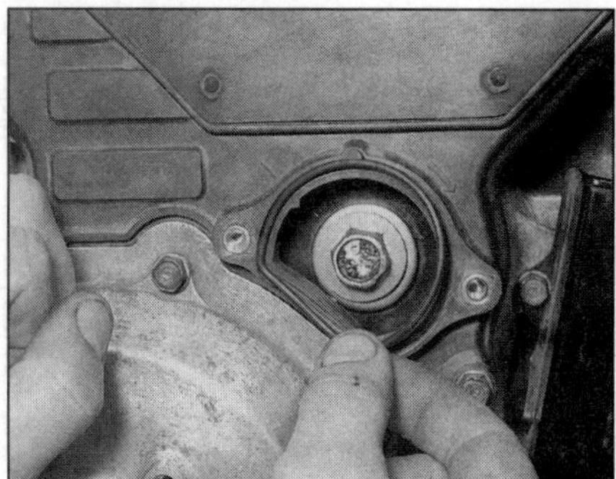
23.19 Use a new O-ring on the timing inspection cover

Every 24,000 miles (38,400 km) or two years

Carry out all the items under the 8000 mile (12,800 km) check, plus the following:

24 Cooling system - draining, flushing and refilling

Warning: Allow the engine to cool completely before performing this maintenance operation. Also, don't allow antifreeze to come into contact with your skin or the painted surfaces of the motorcycle. Rinse off spills immediately with plenty of water. Antifreeze is highly toxic if ingested. Never leave antifreeze lying around in an open container or in puddles on the floor; children and pets are attracted by its sweet smell and may drink it. Check with local authorities (councils) about disposing of antifreeze. Many communities have collection centres which will see that antifreeze is disposed of safely. Antifreeze is also combustible, so don't store it near open flames.

Draining

1 Remove the middle fairing panels (see Chapter 8). Remove the pressure cap by turning it counterclockwise (anti-clockwise) until it reaches a stop **(see illustration 9.6)**. If you hear a hissing sound (indicating there is still pressure in the system), wait until it stops. Now press down on the cap and continue turning the cap until it can be removed.

2 Position a suitable container beneath the left-hand end of the radiator. Remove the radiator drain plug and its sealing washer and allow the coolant to completely drain from the radiator **(see illustration)**. Discard the sealing washer as a new one must be used.

3 Position the container beneath each cylinder head in turn, then remove the drain plug and its sealing washer from the relevant head and allow the coolant to completely drain from the engine. Retain the old sealing washers for use during flushing. The left-hand cylinder head drain plug is difficult to access without a universal drive socket adapter and extension bar. If the tools are not available, remove the left-hand exhaust downpipe assembly (see Chapter 4) **(see illustrations)**.

4 Position the container beneath the coolant reservoir. On standard models, the coolant reservoir is located behind the right-hand side panel. On models equipped with ABS/TCS, the coolant reservoir is located behind the right-hand middle fairing panel (already removed). Detach the radiator overflow hose from the base of the coolant reservoir and drain the reservoir into the container **(see illustration)**. Remove the reservoir for improved access if required (see Chapter 3). Wash out the reservoir with fresh water.

Flushing

5 Flush the system with clean tap water by inserting a garden hose in the radiator filler neck. Allow the water to run through the system until it is clear and flows cleanly out of the drain holes. If the radiator is extremely corroded, remove it (see Chapter 3) and have it cleaned at a radiator shop.

6 Clean the drain holes then install the drain plugs using the old sealing washers.

7 Fill the cooling system with clean water mixed with a flushing compound. Make sure the flushing compound is compatible with aluminium components, and follow the manufacturer's instructions carefully.

8 Start the engine and allow it to reach normal operating temperature. Let it run for about ten minutes.

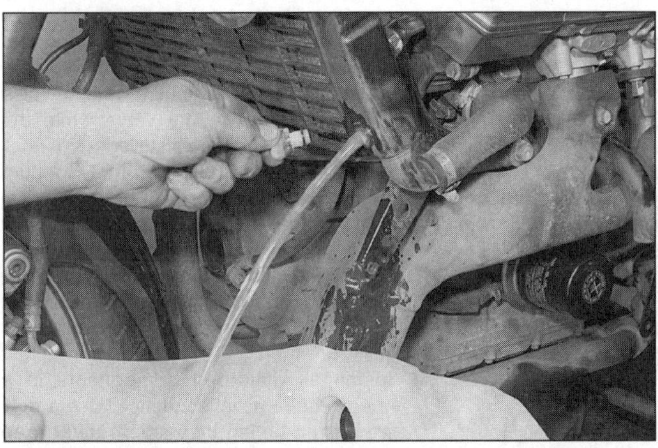

24.2 Remove the drain plug and allow the coolant to drain completely

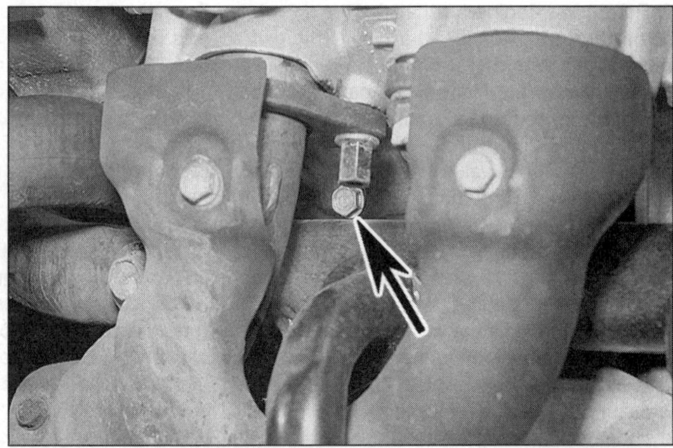

24.3a The left-hand cylinder head drain plug (arrowed) is difficult to access . . .

24.3b . . . without the correct tools. If they are not available . . .

24.3c . . . remove the exhaust downpipe assembly, then drain the head

24.4 Detach the hose and drain the reservoir

9 Stop the engine. Let it cool for a while, then cover the pressure cap with a heavy rag and turn it counterclockwise (anti-clockwise) to the first stop, releasing any pressure that may be present in the system. Once the hissing stops, push down on the cap and remove it completely.
10 Drain the system once again.
11 Fill the system with clean water and repeat the procedure in Steps 8 through 10.

Refilling

12 Fit a new sealing washer to each drain plug and tighten them securely.
13 Fill the system with the proper coolant mixture (see this Chapter's Specifications) **(see illustration)**. **Note:** *Pour the coolant in slowly to minimise the amount of air entering the system.*
14 When the system is full (all the way up to the top of the radiator filler neck), install the pressure cap. Also top up the coolant reservoir to the UPPER level mark (see *Daily (pre-ride) checks)*.
15 Start the engine and allow it to idle for 2 to 3 minutes. Flick the throttle twistgrip part open 3 or 4 times, so that the engine speed rises to approximately 4000 - 5000 rpm, then stop the engine. Any air trapped in the system should have bled back to the radiator filler neck via the small-bore air bleed hoses.
16 Let the engine cool then remove the pressure cap as described in Step 1. Check that the coolant level is still up to the radiator filler neck. If it's low, add the specified mixture until it reaches the top of the filler neck. Reinstall the cap.
17 Check the coolant level in the reservoir and top up if necessary.
18 Check the system for leaks.
19 Do not dispose of the old coolant by pouring it down the drain. Instead pour it into a heavy plastic container, cap it tightly and take it into an authorised disposal site or service station - see **Warning** at the beginning of this Section.

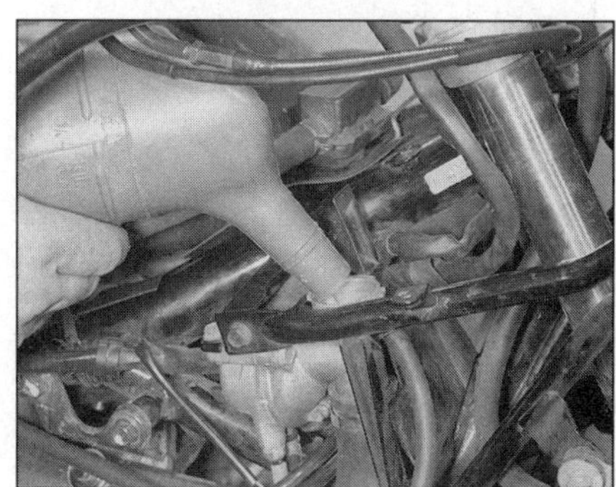
24.13 Refill the system using the specified coolant mixture

Every 24,000 miles (38,400 km) or three years

Carry out all the items under the 8000 mile (12,800 km) check, plus the following:

25 Final drive - oil change

1 Place the motorcycle on its centre stand, making sure it is on level ground.
2 Place an oil drain pan under the drain bolt in the final drive housing. Unscrew the filler cap and the drain plug, and allow the oil to drain into the pan **(see illustrations)**.
3 Check the condition of the drain bolt sealing washer and replace it if necessary (it is advisable to replace it as a matter of course). Install the drain bolt and tighten it to the torque setting specified at the beginning of the Chapter, then fill the housing using the amount and type of oil specified at the beginning of the Chapter **(see illustration)**. The oil should come up to the lower edge of the filler hole **(see illustration 11.2b)**.
4 Install the filler cap, using a new O-ring smeared with clean oil, and tighten it to the specified torque setting **(see illustration)**.

25.2a Remove the filler cap . . .

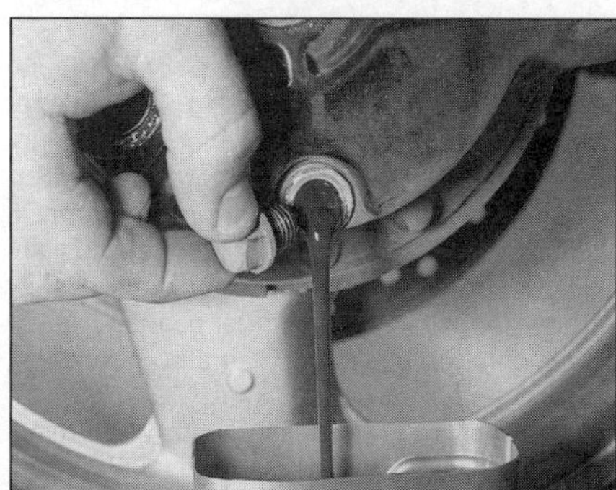
25.2b . . . and the drain plug and allow the oil to drain completely

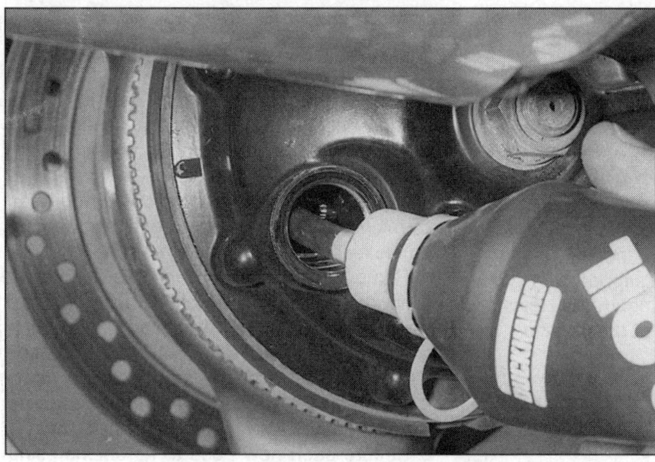

25.3 Fill the housing using the correct oil

25.4 Install the filler cap using a new O-ring

26 Wheel bearings - check

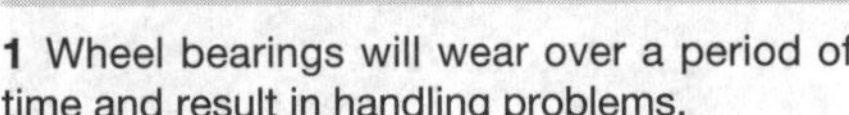

1 Wheel bearings will wear over a period of time and result in handling problems.

2 Place the motorcycle on its centrestand (where fitted) or support it upright using an auxiliary stand. Check for any play in the bearings by pushing and pulling the wheel against the hub. Also rotate the wheel and check that it rotates smoothly.

3 If any play is detected in the hub, or if the wheel does not rotate smoothly (and this is not due to brake or transmission drag), the wheel bearings must be removed and inspected for wear or damage (see Chapter 6).

27 Front forks - oil change

1 Fork oil degrades over a period of time and loses its damping qualities. Refer to Chapter 6 for front fork removal, oil draining and refilling.

28 Cylinder compression - check

1 Among other things, poor engine performance may be caused by leaking valves, incorrect valve clearances, a leaking head gasket, or worn pistons, rings and/or cylinder walls. A cylinder compression check will help pinpoint these conditions and can also indicate the presence of excessive carbon deposits in the cylinder heads.

2 The only tools required are a compression gauge and a spark plug wrench. A compression gauge with a threaded end for the spark plug hole is preferable to the type which requires hand pressure to maintain a tight seal. Depending on the outcome of the initial test, a squirt-type oil can may also be needed.

3 Make sure the valve clearances are correctly set (see Section 23) and that the cylinder head bolts are tightened to the correct torque setting (see Chapter 2 Specifications).

4 Refer to *Fault Finding Equipment* in the Reference section for details of the compression test.

29 Engine oil pressure - check

1 The oil pressure warning light should come on when the ignition (main) switch is turned ON and extinguish a few seconds after the engine is started - this serves as a check that the warning light bulb is sound. If the oil pressure light comes on whilst the engine is running, low oil pressure is indicated - stop the engine immediately and carry out an oil level check (see *Daily (pre-ride) checks*).

2 An oil pressure check must be carried out if the warning light comes on when the engine is running and the oil level is good (Step 1). It can also provide useful information about the condition of the engine's lubrication system.

3 To check the oil pressure, a suitable gauge and adapter piece (which screws into the crankcase) will be needed. Honda provide a kit (part nos. 07501-4220100 and 07506-3000000) for this purpose.

4 Warm the engine up to normal operating temperature then stop it.

5 Remove the oil pressure switch (see Chapter 9) and swiftly screw the adapter into the crankcase threads. Connect the gauge to the adapter.

6 Start the engine and increase the engine speed to 5000 rpm whilst watching the gauge reading. The oil pressure should be similar to that given in the Specifications at the start of this Chapter.

7 If the pressure is significantly lower than the standard, either the pressure regulator is stuck open, the oil pump is faulty, the oil strainer or filter is blocked, or there is other engine damage. Begin diagnosis by checking the oil filter, strainer and regulator, then the oil pump (see Chapter 2). If those items check out okay, chances are the bearing oil clearances are excessive and the engine needs to be overhauled.

8 If the pressure is too high, either an oil passage is clogged, the regulator is stuck closed or the wrong grade of oil is being used.

9 Stop the engine and unscrew the gauge and adapter from the crankcase.

10 Install the oil pressure switch (see Chapter 9). Check the oil level (see *Daily (pre-ride) checks*).

30 Steering head bearings - lubrication

1 Over a period of time the grease will harden or may be washed out of the bearings by incorrect use of jet washes.

2 Disassemble the steering head for re-greasing of the bearings. Refer to Chapter 6 for details.

31 Swingarm bearings - lubrication

1 Over a period of time the grease will harden or dirt will penetrate the bearings.

2 The swingarm is not equipped with grease nipples. Remove the swingarm as described in Chapter 6 for greasing of the bearings.

32 Brake caliper and master cylinder seals - replacement

1 Brake seals will deteriorate over a period of time and lose their effectiveness, leading to sticking operation or fluid loss, or allowing the ingress of air and dirt. Refer to Chapter 7 and dismantle the components for seal replacement.

33 Brake hoses - replacement

1 The hoses will in time deteriorate with age and should be replaced regardless of their apparent condition.

2 Refer to Chapter 7 and disconnect the brake hoses from the master cylinders and calipers. Always replace the banjo union sealing washers with new ones.

34 Clutch hose - replacement

1 The hose will in time deteriorate with age and should be replaced regardless of its apparent condition.

2 Refer to Chapter 2 and disconnect the clutch hose from the master cylinder and release cylinder. Always replace the banjo union sealing washers with new ones.

35 Fuel hoses - replacement

Warning: Petrol (gasoline) is extremely flammable, so take extra precautions when you work on any part of the fuel system. Don't smoke or allow open flames or bare light bulbs near the work area, and don't work in a garage where a natural gas-type appliance is present. If you spill any fuel on your skin, rinse it off immediately with soap and water. When you perform any kind of work on the fuel system, wear safety glasses and have a fire extinguisher suitable for a Class B type fire (flammable liquids) on hand.

1 The fuel delivery and vacuum hoses will deteriorate over a period of time and any cracks which develop may lead to fuel loss (fuel delivery hose) or loss of vacuum (vacuum hose). On US and California models, also renew the emission control system hoses. **Note:** *The emission control system hoses can be identified by referring to the vacuum hose routing diagram on the rear mudguard, under the seat.*

2 Remove the fuel tank cover (see Chapter 4). Disconnect the fuel hoses from the fuel tap and from the carburettors, noting the routing of each hose and where it connects (see Chapter 8 if required). It is advisable to make a sketch of the various hoses before removing them to ensure they are correctly installed.

3 Secure each new hose to its unions using new clamps. Run the engine and check for leaks before taking the machine out on the road.

Chapter 2
Engine, clutch and transmission

Contents

Alternator - removal and installation ....see Chapter 9
Camshafts and followers - removal, inspection and installation 12
Clutch - bleeding 20
Clutch - check ....see Chapter 1
Clutch - removal, inspection and installation 17
Clutch master cylinder - removal, overhaul and installation 18
Clutch release cylinder - removal, overhaul and installation 19
Connecting rods - removal, inspection and installation 32
Crankcase halves and cylinder bores - inspection and servicing ... 30
Crankcase halves - separation and reassembly 29
Crankshaft and main bearings - removal, inspection and installation 35
Cylinder heads - removal and installation 14
Cylinder head and valves - disassembly, inspection and reassembly 16
Engine - compression check ....see Chapter 1
Engine - removal and installation 5
Engine disassembly and reassembly - general information 6
Gearchange mechanism (external components) - removal, inspection and installation 23
General information 1
Idle speed - check and adjustment ....see Chapter 1
Ignition rotor and pulse generator coil assembly - removal and installation ....see Chapter 5
Initial start-up after overhaul 37
Main and connecting rod bearings - general note 31
Major engine repair - general note 4
Neutral switch - check, removal and installation ....see Chapter 9
Oil and filter - change ....see Chapter 1
Oil cooler (early models) - removal and installation 7
Oil level - check ....see Daily (pre-ride) checks
Oil pressure - check ....see Chapter 1
Oil pressure switch - check, removal and installation ...see Chapter 9
Oil pump and pressure relief valve - removal, inspection and installation 22
Oil sump and oil strainer - removal, inspection and installation 21
Operations possible with the engine in the frame 2
Operations requiring engine removal 3
Pistons - removal, inspection and installation 33
Piston rings - inspection and installation 34
Primary drive damper shaft - removal, inspection and installation .. 28
Primary drive gear and starter clutch assembly - removal, inspection and installation 36
Recommended running-in procedure 38
Reduction gear shafts - removal, inspection and installation 13
Selector drum and forks - removal, inspection and installation 27
Spark plug gap - check and adjustment ....see Chapter 1
Starter motor - removal and installation ....see Chapter 9
Timing belt cover - removal and installation 9
Timing belt and tensioner - removal, inspection and installation ... 10
Timing belt pulleys - removal and installation 11
Transmission casing - removal and installation 24
Transmission shafts - disassembly, inspection and reassembly ... 26
Transmission shafts and bearings - removal and installation 25
Valve clearances - check and adjustment ....see Chapter 1
Valve covers - removal and installation 8
Valves/valve seats/valve guides - servicing 15

2

Degrees of difficulty

Easy, suitable for novice with little experience 	**Fairly easy,** suitable for beginner with some experience 	**Fairly difficult,** suitable for competent DIY mechanic	**Difficult,** suitable for experienced DIY mechanic 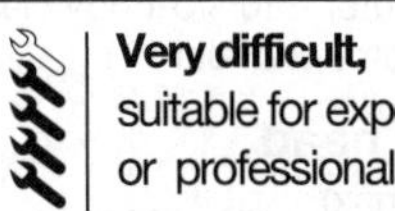	**Very difficult,** suitable for expert DIY or professional

Specifications

General

Type	Four-stroke 90° V-four
Capacity	1085 cc
Bore	73.0 mm
Stroke	64.8 mm
Compression ratio	10.0 to 1
Firing order	1-4-3-2
Cylinder numbering	
Front right	1
Rear right	3
Front left	2
Rear left	4
Clutch	Wet multi-plate
Transmission	Five-speed constant mesh
Final drive	Shaft

← FWD		
	cyl. 1	cyl. 3
	cyl. 2	cyl. 4

Camshafts and followers

Camshaft	
Intake lobe height	
All UK models and standard US 49-state models	
Standard	36.480 to 36.640 mm
Service limit (min)	36.450 mm
All California models and US ABS/TCS and LBS-ABS/TCS models	
Standard	35.680 to 35.840 mm
Service limit (min)	35.650 mm
Exhaust lobe height	
All UK models and standard US 49-state models	
Standard	35.970 to 36.130 mm
Service limit (min)	35.940 mm
All California models and US ABS/TCS and LBS-ABS/TCS models	
Standard	35.770 to 35.930 mm
Service limit (min)	35.740 mm
Journal diameter	
Journal A (centre and rear journal pairs)	
Standard	24.959 to 24.980 mm
Service limit (min)	24.950 mm
Journal B (front journal)	
Standard	24.929 to 24.950 mm
Service limit (min)	24.920 mm
Journal holder diameter	
Journal A (centre and rear journal pairs)	25.000 to 25.021 mm
Journal B (front journal)	25.000 to 25.021 mm
Journal oil clearance	
Journal A (centre and rear journal pairs)	
Standard	0.020 to 0.062 mm
Service limit (min)	0.100 mm
Journal B (front journal)	
Standard	0.050 to 0.092 mm
Service limit (min)	0.130 mm
Runout (max)	0.05 mm
Followers	
Follower diameter	
Standard	25.978 to 25.993 mm
Service limit (min)	25.968 mm
Follower bore diameter	
Standard	26.010 to 26.026 mm
Service limit (max)	26.040 mm

Lubrication system

Oil pressure	see Chapter 1
Oil pump inner rotor tip-to-outer rotor clearance	0.15 mm
Oil pump outer rotor-to-body clearance	0.15 to 0.22 mm
Oil pump rotor endfloat	0.02 to 0.09 mm

Cylinder head

Warpage (max)	0.10 mm

Valves, guides and springs

Valve clearances	see Chapter 1
Intake valve	
Stem diameter	
Standard	4.475 to 4.490 mm
Service limit (min)	4.465 mm
Guide bore diameter	
Standard	4.500 to 4.512 mm
Service limit (max)	4.562 mm
Stem-to-guide clearance	0.010 to 0.037 mm
Seat width	
Standard	1.0 mm
Service limit (max)	1.5 mm
Valve guide height above cylinder head	15.3 to 15.5 mm
Exhaust valve	
Stem diameter	
Standard	4.465 to 4.480 mm
Service limit (min)	4.455 mm
Guide bore diameter	
Standard	4.500 to 4.512 mm
Service limit (max)	4.612 mm
Stem-to-guide clearance	0.020 to 0.047 mm
Seat width	
Standard	1.0 mm
Service limit (max)	1.5 mm
Valve guide height above cylinder head	15.3 to 15.5 mm
Valve spring free length (intake and exhaust)	
Standard	41.72 mm
Service limit (min)	39.6 mm

Clutch

Friction plates	10
Plain plates	9
Friction and plain plate total thickness (all plates together)	
Standard	54.72 to 55.72 mm
Service limit (min)	54.20 mm
Spring free length	
Standard	43.0 mm
Service limit (min)	40.0 mm
Master cylinder bore diameter	
Standard	14.000 to 14.043 mm
Service limit (max)	14.06 mm
Master cylinder piston diameter	
Standard	13.957 to 13.984 mm
Service limit (min)	13.94 mm
Clutch housing guide OD	
Standard	34.975 to 34.991 mm
Service limit (min)	34.965 mm
Clutch housing guide ID	
Standard	27.989 to 28.006 mm
Service limit (max)	28.016 mm
Primary damper shaft OD at clutch housing guide	27.974 to 27.987 mm

Transmission

Gear ratios (no. of teeth)	
Primary reduction	1.8292 to 1 (75/41T)
1st gear	2.2666 to 1 (34/15T)
2nd gear	1.5000 to 1 (27/18T)
3rd gear	1.1428 to 1 (24/21T)
4th gear	0.9166 to 1 (22/24T)
5th gear	0.7586 to 1 (22/29T)
Final reduction	2.8333 to 1 (34/12T)
Input shaft 4th and 5th gears ID	
Standard	31.000 to 31.025 mm
Service limit (max)	31.04 mm
Output shaft 2nd and 3rd gears ID	
Standard	31.000 to 31.025 mm
Service limit (max)	31.04 mm

Transmission (continued)

Input shaft 4th and 5th gears bushing OD	
Standard	30.950 to 30.975 mm
Service limit (min)	30.930 mm
Output shaft 2nd and 3rd gears bushing OD	
Standard	30.950 to 30.975 mm
Service limit (min)	30.930 mm
Gear-to-bushing clearance	
Input shaft 4th and 5th gears	0.025 to 0.075 mm
Output shaft 2nd and 3rd gears	0.025 to 0.075 mm
Input shaft 4th gear bushing ID	
Standard	28.000 to 28.021 mm
Service limit (max)	28.031 mm
Input shaft OD at 4th gear bushing point	
Standard	27.967 to 27.980 mm
Service limit (min)	27.96 mm
Input shaft-to-bushing clearance at 4th gear bushing point	0.020 to 0.054 mm

Selector drum and forks

Selector fork end thickness	
Standard	5.93 to 6.00 mm
Service limit (min)	5.90 mm
Selector fork bore ID	
Standard	14.000 to 14.021 mm
Service limit (max)	14.03 mm
Selector fork shaft OD	
Standard	13.973 to 13.984 mm
Service limit (min)	13.965 mm

Primary drive damper shaft

Damper spring free length	
Standard	95.4 mm
Service limit (min)	93.0 mm

Cylinder block

Bore	
Standard	73.000 to 73.015 mm
Service limit (max)	73.10 mm
Warpage (max)	0.10 mm
Ovality (out-of-round) (max)	0.10 mm
Taper (max)	0.10 mm
Cylinder compression	see Chapter 1

Connecting rods

Small-end internal diameter	
Standard	18.016 to 18.034 mm
Service limit (max)	18.050 mm
Small-end to piston pin clearance	0.016 to 0.040 mm
Big-end side clearance	
Standard	0.1 to 0.3 mm
Service limit (max)	0.4 mm
Big-end oil clearance	
Standard	0.030 to 0.052 mm
Service limit (max)	0.08 mm

Pistons

Piston diameter (measured 19.0 mm up from skirt, at 90° to piston pin axis)	
Standard	72.970 to 72.990 mm
Service limit (min)	72.850 mm
Oversize pistons	+0.25 mm, +0.50 mm
Piston-to-bore clearance	0.010 to 0.045 mm
Piston pin diameter	
Standard	17.994 to 18.000 mm
Service limit (min)	17.98 mm
Piston pin bore diameter in piston	
Standard	18.002 to 18.008 mm
Service limit (max)	18.020 mm
Piston pin-to-bore clearance	0.002 to 0.014 mm

Piston rings

Ring end gap (installed)	
Top ring	
Standard	0.15 to 0.30 mm
Service limit (max)	0.50 mm
2nd ring	
Standard	0.30 to 0.45 mm
Service limit (max)	0.70 mm
Oil ring side-rail	
Standard	0.20 to 0.70 mm
Service limit (max)	1.00 mm
Ring-to-groove clearance	
Top ring	
Standard	0.025 to 0.060 mm
Service limit (max)	0.10 mm
2nd ring	
Standard	0.015 to 0.050 mm
Service limit (max)	0.10 mm
Ring identification	
Top ring	R (facing up)
2nd ring	RN (facing up)
Oversize rings	+0.25 mm, +0.50 mm

Crankshaft and bearings

Main bearing oil clearance	
Standard	0.026 to 0.048 mm
Service limit (max)	0.065 mm
Runout (max)	0.05 mm

Torque settings

Engine mounting bolts (refer to illustration 5.26a for location)	
Sub-frame bolts nos. 1 to 5	40 Nm
10 mm bolts nos. 6 and 7	55 Nm
No. 10 bolt adjusting collar adjusting nut	10 Nm
10 mm bolts nos. 8 and 9	55 Nm
12 mm bolt and nut nos. 10 and 11	65 Nm
Adjusting collar locknut (UK models L to S and AN to AS, and all US 1991 to 1995 models)	21 Nm
Adjusting collar locknuts (UK models T, V, AT and AV, and all US 1996 and 1997 models)	21 Nm
Oil cooler bolt	65 Nm
Valve cover bolts	12 Nm
Timing belt driven pulley bolts	27 Nm
Timing belt tensioner bolt	46 Nm
Timing belt idle pulley bolt	46 Nm
Timing belt drive pulley bolt	65 Nm
Camshaft holder bolts	12 Nm
Cylinder head bolts	58 Nm
Oil pump driven sprocket bolt	15 Nm
Clutch nut	110 Nm
Clutch master cylinder clamp bolts	12 Nm
Clutch hose banjo bolts	35 Nm
Clutch lever pivot bolt	1 Nm
Clutch lever pivot bolt locknut	6 Nm
Clutch release cylinder bleed valve	9 Nm
Oil sump bolts	12 Nm
Selector drum stopper plate assembly bolt	23 Nm
Gearchange linkage arm pinchbolt	12 Nm
Upper crankcase 6 mm bolts	12 Nm
Upper crankcase 8 mm bolt	23 Nm
Lower crankcase 6 mm bolts	12 Nm
Lower crankcase 8 mm bolts	23 Nm
Lower crankcase 10 mm bolts	52 Nm
Connecting rod cap nuts	36 Nm
Starter clutch bolts	16 Nm

1 General information

The engine/transmission unit is a liquid-cooled 90° V-four. The valves are operated by double overhead camshafts which are belt and gear driven. The engine/transmission assembly is constructed from aluminium alloy. The crankcase is divided horizontally.

The crankcase incorporates a wet sump, pressure-fed lubrication system which uses a chain-driven, dual-rotor oil pump, an oil filter and by-pass valve assembly, a relief valve and an oil pressure switch.

Power from the crankshaft is routed to the transmission via the clutch and a damper shaft. The clutch is of the wet, multi-plate type and is gear-driven off the crankshaft. The transmission is a five-speed constant-mesh unit, housed in a separate casing. Final drive to the rear wheel is by shaft.

The alternator is driven by a gear in the starter clutch assembly.

2 Operations possible with the engine in the frame

The components and assemblies listed below can be removed without having to remove the engine/transmission assembly from the frame. If however, a number of areas require attention at the same time, removal of the engine is recommended.

Valve cover
Camshafts
Cylinder heads
Timing belt
Ignition rotor and pulse generator coil assembly
Clutch
Gearchange mechanism (external components)
Alternator
Oil filter and oil cooler (where fitted)
Oil sump, oil pump, oil strainer and oil pressure relief valve
Starter motor
Water pump

3 Operations requiring engine removal

It is necessary to remove the engine/transmission assembly from the frame to gain access to the following components.

Cylinder bores, pistons and piston rings
Starter clutch and idle gear
Transmission shafts
Primary damper shaft
Selector drum and forks
Crankshaft and bearings
Connecting rods and bearings

4 Major engine repair - general note

1 It is not always easy to determine when or if an engine should be completely overhauled, as a number of factors must be considered.

2 High mileage is not necessarily an indication that an overhaul is needed, while low mileage, on the other hand, does not preclude the need for an overhaul. Frequency of servicing is probably the single most important consideration. An engine that has regular and frequent oil and filter changes, as well as other required maintenance, will most likely give many miles of reliable service. Conversely, a neglected engine, or one which has not been run in properly, may require an overhaul very early in its life.

3 Exhaust smoke and excessive oil consumption are both indications that piston rings and/or valve guides are in need of attention, although make sure that the fault is not due to oil leakage.

4 If the engine is making obvious knocking or rumbling noises, the connecting rod and/or main bearings are probably at fault.

5 Loss of power, rough running, excessive valve train noise and high fuel consumption rates may also point to the need for an overhaul, especially if they are all present at the same time. If a complete tune-up does not remedy the situation, major mechanical work is the only solution.

6 An engine overhaul generally involves restoring the internal parts to the specifications of a new engine. The piston rings and main and connecting rod bearings are usually replaced and the cylinder walls honed or, if necessary, re-bored during a major overhaul. Generally the valve seats are re-ground, since they are usually in less than perfect condition at this point. The end result should be a like new engine that will give as many trouble-free miles as the original.

7 Before beginning the engine overhaul, read through the related procedures to familiarise yourself with the scope and requirements of the job. Overhauling an engine is not all that difficult, but it is time consuming. Plan on the motorcycle being tied up for a minimum of two weeks. Check on the availability of parts and make sure that any necessary special tools, equipment and supplies are obtained in advance.

8 Most work can be done with typical workshop hand tools, although a number of precision measuring tools are required for inspecting parts to determine if they must be replaced. Often a dealer will handle the inspection of parts and offer advice concerning reconditioning and replacement. As a general rule, time is the primary cost of an overhaul so it does not pay to install worn or substandard parts.

9 As a final note, to ensure maximum life and minimum trouble from a rebuilt engine, everything must be assembled with care in a spotlessly clean environment.

5 Engine - removal and installation

Warning: The engine is very heavy and difficult to manoeuvre out of the frame. It is highly recommended that a mechanical or hydraulic hoist is used and that you have at least one assistant. If a hoist is not available, a mechanical or hydraulic floor jack is essential and at least two assistants will be needed. Personal injury or damage could occur if the engine falls or is dropped.

Removal

1 Position the bike on its centrestand or support it securely in an upright position using an auxiliary stand. Work can be made easier by raising the machine to a suitable working height on a hydraulic ramp or a suitable platform. Make sure the motorcycle is secure and will not topple over (see *Tools and Workshop Tips* in the Reference section).

2 If the engine is dirty, particularly around its mountings, wash it thoroughly before starting any major dismantling work. This will make work much easier and rule out the possibility of caked on lumps of dirt falling into some vital component.

3 Drain the engine oil and remove the oil filter (see Chapter 1). Also drain the cooling system (see Chapter 1).

4 Remove the seat and the side panels, and remove the fuel tank cover and all the fairing panels (see Chapter 8).

5 Remove the exhaust system and, if required, the engine crash bars (see Chapter 4).

6 Remove the carburettors (see Chapter 4). Plug the engine intake manifolds with clean rag.

7 Remove the radiator (see Chapter 3).

8 If required, remove the swingarm and driveshaft (see Chapter 6). The engine can be removed with them in place, but removing them provides a little extra clearance. It is recommended that they are removed if a hoist is not available to support the engine.

9 Trace the negative (-ve) lead from the battery and remove the bolt securing it to the engine **(see illustration)**.

5.9 Remove the bolt securing the earth cable to the engine (arrowed)

5.10 Disconnect the starter motor lead

5.11a Unscrew the linkage arm pinch bolt (arrowed) . . .

5.11b . . . and the lever pivot bolt (arrowed), and remove the lever and linkage as an assembly

10 Pull back the rubber cover on the starter motor terminal, then unscrew the nut and disconnect the lead **(see illustration)**.

11 On UK L and M models and US 1991 models, make some alignment marks (if none are already visible) between the gearchange linkage arm and the shaft so that they can be correctly aligned on installation. On all other models, a wider spline aligns the arm. Unscrew the linkage arm pinch bolt and remove the arm from the shaft. Unscrew the pivot bolt securing the gearchange lever and remove the lever and linkage as an assembly **(see illustrations)**. Note the breather hose guide secured by the pivot bolt nut.

12 Disconnect all the HT leads from the spark plugs and secure them clear of the engine.

13 Trace the alternator wiring from the left-hand side of the rear of the engine and disconnect it at the connectors **(see illustration)**. Disconnect the red connector first, then press in the clip on the back of the black connector to release it from the bracket. Release the wiring from any clips or ties, noting its routing, and coil it so that it does not impede engine removal.

14 Trace the ignition pulse generator, neutral switch and oil pressure switch wiring from the rear of the engine and disconnect it at the connector **(see illustration)**. Release the wiring from any clips or ties, noting its routing, and coil it on top of the crankcase so that it does not impede engine removal.

15 Free the sidestand wiring connector from the clips on the heat guard plate on the right-hand side of the engine, then unscrew the bolt securing the plate and remove it **(see illustration)**.

16 Unscrew the bolts securing each front valve cover to the main valve cover and remove the covers **(see illustration)**.

17 Remove the rubber heat insulator pad and the side pieces, secured by cable ties, noting how they fit **(see illustration)**.

18 Release the clamp securing the water outlet hose to each cylinder head and detach the hoses. Also detach the water bypass hose from either the water pipe in between the cylinder heads or from the thermostat housing.

19 Disconnect the fuel tap vacuum hose from the take-off stub on no.3 cylinder.

20 Detach the clutch release cylinder from the clutch cover (see Section 19). There is no need to separate the hydraulic hose.

21 At this point, position an hydraulic or mechanical jack under the engine with a block of wood between the jack head and sump. Make sure the jack is centrally positioned so the engine will not topple in any direction when the last mounting bolt is removed. Take the weight of the engine on the jack.

22 The engine is secured to the frame at the

5.13 Alternator wiring connectors (arrowed)

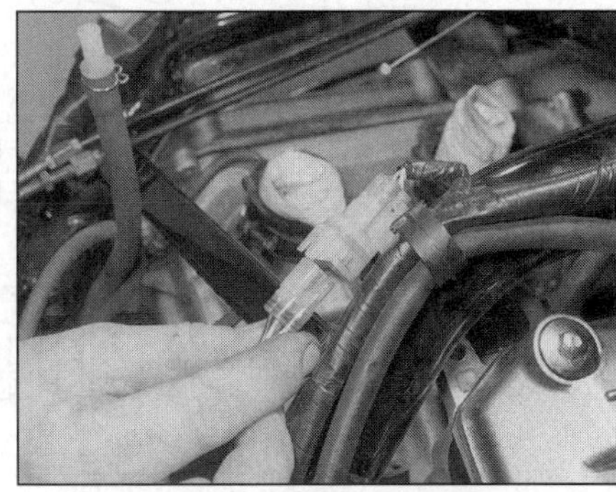
5.14 Disconnect the combined pulse generator, neutral and oil switch wiring connector

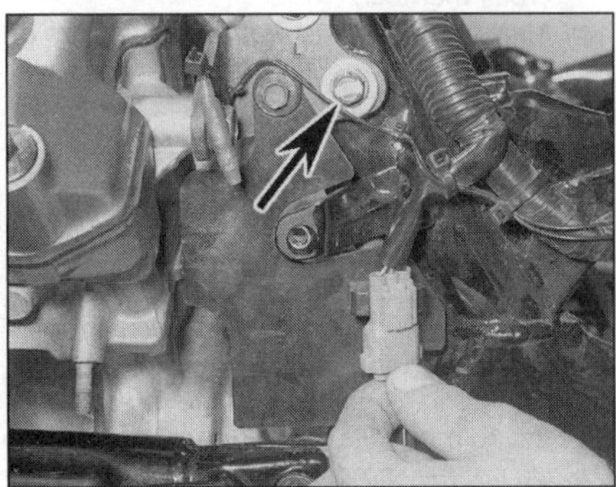
5.15 Release the wiring connector, then unscrew the bolt (arrowed) and remove the plate

5.16 Unscrew the bolts and remove the front valve covers

5.17 Remove the rubber pads, noting how they fit

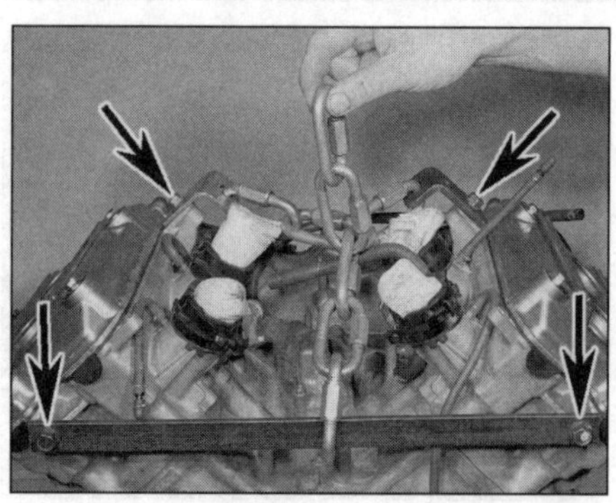
5.22 **If a hoist is being used, bolt the lifting tackle to the upper engine mountings (arrowed)**

5.23 **Removing the sub-frame**

5.25 **Removing the engine using a hoist**

top by four brackets, each secured by three bolts. Unscrew all the bolts and remove the brackets, noting how they fit. If a hoist is being used to remove the engine, the bolt holes where the brackets fit to the engine can be used as mounts for the lifting gear **(see illustration)**.

23 Remove the bolts numbered 1, 3, 4 and 5 **(see illustration 5.26)** which secure the front of the sub-frame to the main-frame downtubes, and the bolts numbered 2 (if not already removed when removing the engine crash bars), 8 and 9 which secure the middle and the rear of the sub-frame to the left-hand side of the engine. Remove the sub-frame, noting how the adjusting collar with bolt 8 fits between it and the engine **(see illustration)**.

24 Make sure the engine is properly supported on the hoist and/or jack, and have an assistant support it as well. Remove the bolts numbered 6 and 7 which secure the right-hand side of the engine to the frame, and the lower rear mounting nut and bolt numbered 10 and 11 (already loosened when removing the engine crash bars), noting how the collars fit between the engine and the frame **(see illustration 5.26)**. On UK T, V, AT and AV models, and all US 1996 and 1997 models, the left-hand collar is an adjustable one.

25 The engine can now be removed from the frame. Check that all wiring, cables and hoses are well clear, then carefully manoeuvre the engine out of the left-hand side of the frame (see ***Warning*** above) **(see illustration)**.

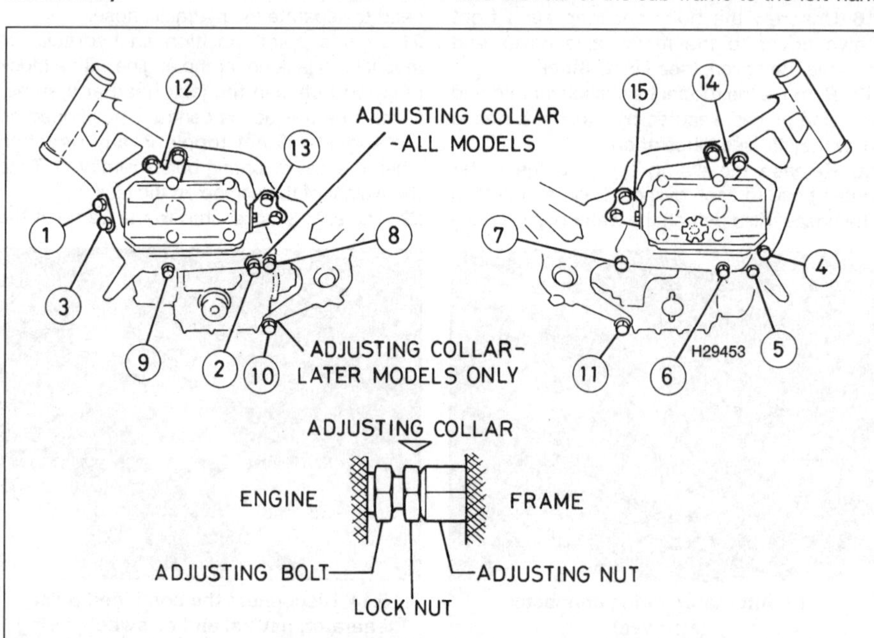

5.26a **Engine mounting bolt locations**

5.26b **No. 8 bolt adjusting collar . . .**

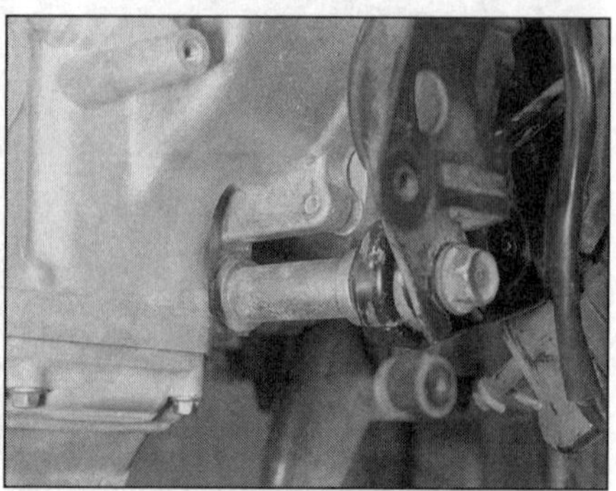
5.26c **. . . and the no. 10 bolt left-hand collar**

Installation

26 Installation is the reverse of removal. Refer to the illustration for bolt number identification **(see illustration)**, and to the following points:

a) Make sure no wires, cables or hoses become trapped between the engine and the frame when installing the engine, and that the clutch hose is routed between the front of the engine and the sub-frame cross-member.

b) Many of the engine mounting bolts are of different size and length. Make sure the correct bolt is installed in its correct location. Do not forget to install the adjusting collar with the bolt numbered 8, and the two collars (the left-hand one of which is adjustable on UK T, V, AT and AV models, and all US 1996 and 1997 models) with the bolt numbered 10 ***(see illustrations)****.*

c) Apply clean engine oil to the threads of the 10 mm bolts ***(see illustration)****.*

d) Do not fully tighten any of the bolts until they have all been installed.

e) First tighten the sub-frame bolts numbered 1 to 5 in sequence to the torque setting specified at the beginning of the Chapter.

f) Tighten the 10 mm bolts numbered 6 and 7 to the specified torque setting.

g) Adjust the length of the adjusting collar on the 10 mm bolt numbered 8 by turning the adjusting nut until the collar ends contact the engine and the frame **(see illustration 5.26a)**. On UK T, V, AT and AV models, and all US 1996 and 1997 models, similarly adjust the length of the adjusting collar on the 12 mm bolt numbered 10. Tighten the adjusting nut on the no. 10 bolt collar to the specified torque setting.

h) Tighten the 10 mm bolts numbered 8 and 9 to the specified torque setting.

i) Tighten the 12 mm bolt and nut numbered 10 and 11 to the specified torque setting.

j) Tighten the adjusting collar locknut(s) to the specified torque setting.

k) Tighten the 8 mm and 10 mm bracket bolts numbered 12 to 15 to the specified torque settings, being sure to distinguish correctly between the two sizes of bolt.

l) Use new gaskets on the exhaust pipe connections.

m) Align the marks made on the gearchange lever linkage arm and shaft when installing the arm onto the shaft, and tighten the pinch bolt securely.

n) Make sure all wires, cables and hoses are correctly routed and connected, and secured by any clips or ties.

o) Refill the engine with oil and coolant (see Chapter 1).

p) Adjust the throttle cable freeplay and idle speed (see Chapter 1).

6 Engine disassembly and reassembly - general information

Disassembly

1 Before disassembling the engine, the external surfaces of the unit should be thoroughly cleaned and degreased. This will prevent contamination of the engine internals, and will also make working a lot easier and cleaner. A high flash-point solvent, such as paraffin (kerosene) can be used, or better still, a proprietary engine degreaser. Use old paintbrushes and toothbrushes to work the solvent into the various recesses of the engine casings. Take care to exclude solvent or water from the electrical components and intake and exhaust ports.

Warning: The use of petrol (gasoline) as a cleaning agent should be avoided because of the risk of fire.

2 When clean and dry, arrange the unit on the workbench, leaving suitable clear area for working. Gather a selection of small containers and plastic bags so that parts can be grouped together in an easily identifiable manner. Some paper and a pen should be on hand to permit notes to be made and labels attached where necessary. A supply of clean rag is also required.

3 Before commencing work, read through the appropriate section so that some idea of the necessary procedure can be gained. When removing components it should be noted that great force is seldom required, unless specified. In many cases, a component's reluctance to be removed is indicative of an incorrect approach or removal method - if in any doubt, re-check with the text.

4 An engine support stand made from short lengths of 2 x 4 inch wood bolted together into a rectangle will help support the engine **(see illustration)**. The perimeter of the mount should be just big enough to accommodate the sump within it so that the engine rests on its crankcase.

5 When disassembling the engine, keep 'mated' parts together (including gears, cylinders, pistons, connecting rods, valves, etc. that have been in contact with each other during engine operation). These 'mated' parts must be reused or replaced as an assembly.

6 A complete engine/transmission disassembly should be done in the following general order with reference to the appropriate Sections.

Remove the valve covers
Remove the camshafts
Timing belt and pulleys
Remove the cylinder heads
Remove the clutch
Remove the alternator (see Chapter 9)
Remove the starter motor (see Chapter 9)
Remove the pulse generator coil assembly (see Chapter 5)
Remove the gearchange mechanism external components
Remove the oil sump
Remove the oil pump
Remove the transmission casing
Remove the primary damper shaft
Separate the crankcase halves
Remove the connecting rods and pistons
Remove the crankshaft
Remove the timing rotor starter clutch and idle gear

Reassembly

7 Reassembly is accomplished by reversing the general disassembly sequence.

7 Oil cooler (early models) - removal and installation

Note: *The oil cooler (fitted to UK L to S models and US 1991 to 1995 models) can be removed with the engine in the frame. If the engine has been removed, ignore the steps which do not apply.*

Removal

1 Remove the left-hand middle fairing panel (see Chapter 8).

2 Drain the engine oil and remove the oil filter (see Chapter 1).

3 Release the clamp securing each hose to the cooler (if the engine is in the frame) or from the water pipe and pump (if the engine has been removed) and detach the hoses **(see illustration)**. If the engine is in the frame have some means of blocking or clamping the hoses to avoid excessive loss of coolant.

4 Unscrew the cooler bolt and remove the cooler, noting how the bracket on the top locates over the lug on the crankcase **(see**

2

5.26d Apply engine oil to the 10 mm bolts

6.4 An engine support made from pieces of 2 x 4 inch wood

7.3 Slacken the hose clamps (arrowed) and detach the hoses . . .

7.4 . . . then unscrew the bolt and remove the cooler, noting how it locates over the lug (arrowed)

7.5 Withdraw the nozzle from the passage and blow it through

7.6a Fit a new O-ring onto the nozzle . . .

7.6b . . . and the cooler

7.6c Tighten the cooler bolt to the specified torque setting

illustration). Discard the cooler O-ring as a new one must be used.

5 If required, withdraw the oil nozzle and its O-ring from the passage, noting which way round it fits **(see illustration)**. Discard the O-ring as a new one must be used.

Installation

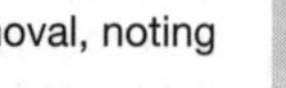

6 Installation is the reverse of removal, noting the following:

a) Make sure that the oil nozzle is clean and blow it through with compressed air, if available.

*b) Always use new O-rings when installing the nozzle and cooler **(see illustrations)**.*

*c) Tighten the cooler bolt to the torque setting specified at the beginning of the Chapter **(see illustration)**.*

d) Make sure the coolant hoses are pressed fully onto their unions and are secured by the clamps.

e) Fit the oil filter using a new O-ring and fill the engine with oil (see Chapter 1).

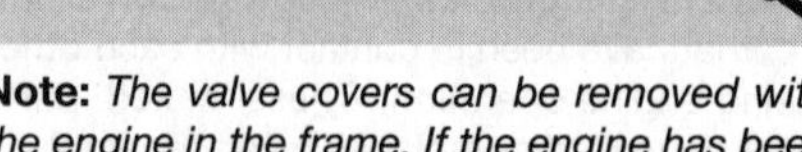

8 Valve covers - removal and installation

Note: *The valve covers can be removed with the engine in the frame. If the engine has been removed, ignore the steps which do not apply.*

Removal

1 Remove the upper fairing, and, if required for easier access or to avoid the possibility of damage, also remove the middle fairing panel for the side being worked on (see Chapter 8).

2 Unscrew the two bolts securing the front valve cover to the main valve cover and remove it **(see illustration)**.

3 Disconnect the spark plug caps from the plugs and secure them clear of the engine.

4 Unscrew the four bolts securing the main valve cover then lift the cover off the cylinder head **(see illustration)**. If it is stuck, do not try to lever it off with a screwdriver. Tap it gently around the sides with a rubber hammer or block of wood to dislodge it. Also remove the gasket. Note the rubber washers fitted in the cover and remove them if they are loose.

Installation

5 Examine the valve cover gasket and the rubber washers for signs of damage or deterioration and replace them if necessary.

6 Clean the mating surfaces of the cylinder head and the valve cover with lacquer thinner, acetone or brake system cleaner. Note that the right-hand cover has the oil filler cap.

7 Apply a smear of a suitable sealant into the grooves in the main valve cover. Install the gasket onto the valve cover, making sure it fits correctly into the groove. Apply the sealant to the cut-outs in the cylinder head where the gasket half-circles fit **(see illustration)**.

8 Position the main cover on the cylinder head, making sure the gasket stays in place and the gasket half-circles locate correctly. Fit the rubber washers into the cover, using new

8.2 The front cover is secured to the main cover by two bolts (arrowed)

8.4 The main cover is secured by four bolts (arrowed)

8.7 Apply a sealant to the cut-outs in the head as shown

8.8a Fit the cover onto the head . . .

8.8b . . . and the washers into the cover . . .

8.8c . . . then install the bolts and tighten them to the specified torque setting

ones if required, and making sure they are installed with the "UP" mark facing up. Install the cover bolts and tighten them to the torque setting specified at the beginning of the Chapter **(see illustrations)**.

9 Install the remaining components in the reverse order of removal.

9 Timing belt cover - removal and installation

Note: *The timing belt cover can be removed with the engine in the frame. If the engine has been removed, ignore the steps which do not apply.*

Removal

1 Drain the engine oil and the cooling system (see Chapter 1).

2 Remove the radiator (see Chapter 3).

3 Unscrew the three bolts securing each camshaft drive pulley cover, then remove the covers **(see illustration)**.

4 Unscrew the nine bolts securing the clutch cover and remove the cover **(see illustration)**. There is no need to detach the clutch slave cylinder. Be prepared to catch any residue oil as the cover is removed. Discard the gasket as a new one must be used.

5 Unscrew the four bolts securing the timing belt cover and remove the cover **(see illustration)**.

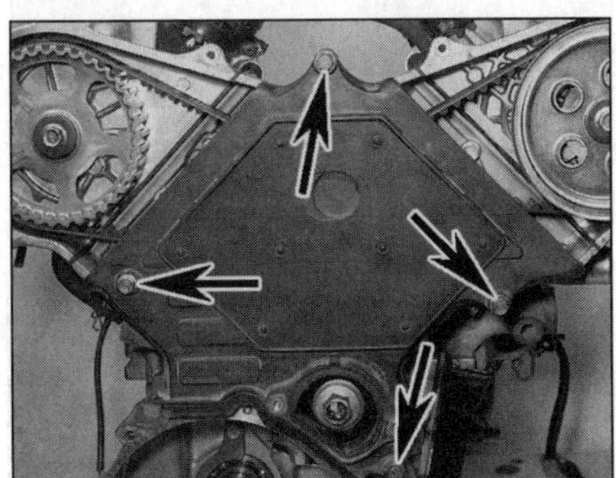

9.5 The timing belt cover is secured by four bolts (arrowed)

Installation

6 Installation is the reverse of removal. Install the clutch cover using a new gasket. Check the condition of the rubber gaskets on the timing belt cover and the camshaft drive pulley covers and replace them if necessary.

10 Timing belt and tensioner - removal, inspection and installation

Note: *The timing belt and tensioner can be removed with the engine in the frame. If the engine has been removed, ignore the steps which do not apply.*

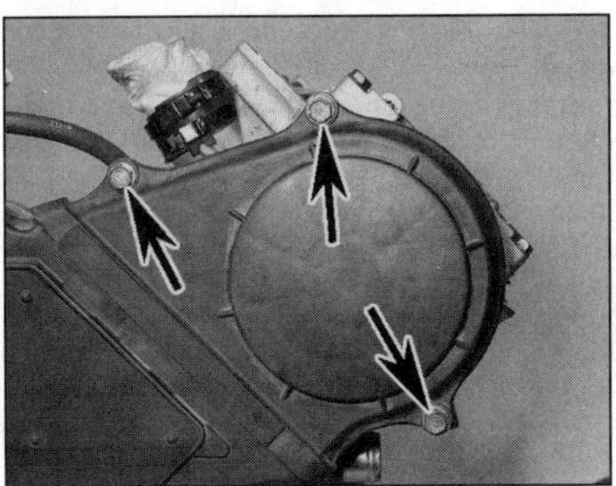

9.3 Each camshaft drive pulley cover is secured by three bolts (arrowed)

10.2 Unscrew the bolt (arrowed) and remove the plate from the pulley

Removal

1 Remove the timing belt cover (see Section 9). Also remove the spark plugs (see Chapter 1).

2 Unscrew the bolt securing the left-hand camshaft drive pulley **(see illustration)**. To prevent the engine from turning, either counter-hold the timing belt drive pulley bolt, or, if the engine is in the frame, select 5th gear and have an assistant push down on the rear brake pedal (on CBS/LBS models either the rear brake pedal or the front brake lever can be applied). Remove the bolt and washer, then remove the belt guide plate from the front of the pulley.

3 Slacken the timing belt tensioner bolt by 1/4 to 1/2 a turn **(see illustration)**. Release the tensioner either by turning the crankshaft

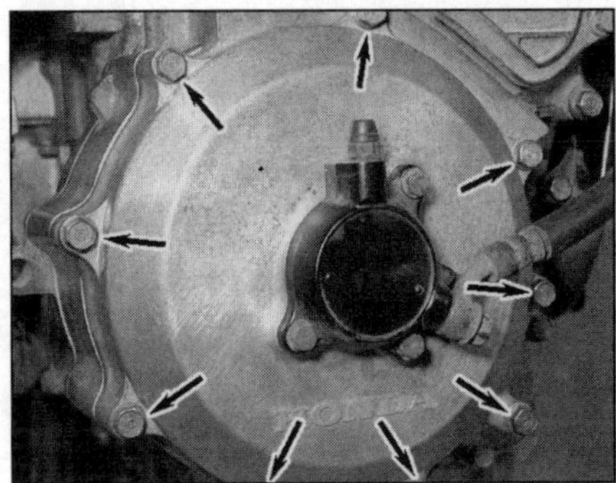

9.4 The clutch cover is secured by nine bolts (arrowed)

10.3 Slacken the tensioner bolt (arrowed), then press down on the tensioner to slacken the belt

10.4a Use a spanner or socket on the drive pulley bolt to turn the engine

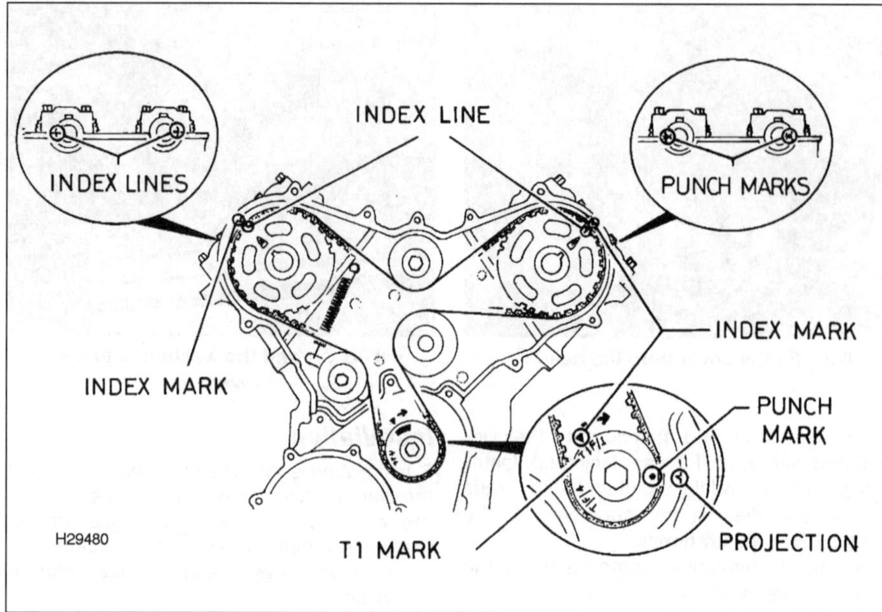

10.4b Align all the marks as shown to set the timing

anti-clockwise using a spanner on the timing belt drive pulley bolt whilst holding the right-hand camshaft drive pulley to prevent it from turning, or by simply pressing down on it against the tension of the spring. When the tensioner moves down, secure it in position by tightening the bolt.

4 Turn the crankshaft clockwise using a 17 mm spanner or socket on the timing belt drive pulley bolt, until the "T1" mark on the drive pulley guide plate aligns with the index mark on the crankcase **(see illustrations)**. Check that the punchmark also on the drive pulley guide plate aligns with the projection on the crankcase. Also make sure that the index line on each camshaft drive pulley aligns with the mark on the reduction shaft casing, and that the index lines on the front end of each camshaft on the right-hand cylinder head and the punchmarks on the front end of each camshaft on the left-hand cylinder are facing away from each other and are level with the head mating surface. If the index marks do not align as stated, rotate the engine clockwise one full turn until the "T1" mark again aligns with the static timing mark. The index marks should now align. Do not confuse the index lines with the punchmarks on the pulleys and camshaft ends.

5 Slide the timing belt off the pulleys and remove it.

6 If required, unscrew the tensioner bolt and remove the tensioner along with the spring and its boot **(see illustration)**.

Caution: Do not turn the camshafts or the crankshaft with the timing belt removed, as the valves will contact the pistons and could be damaged.

Inspection

7 Check the belt along its entire length for splits, cracks, worn or damaged teeth, frays and any other damage or deterioration. Be careful not to bend the belt excessively or to get oil or grease on it. Replace the belt if it is in any way worn, damaged or deteriorated.

8 Check the timing belt and camshaft drive pulleys for signs of wear or damage and replace them if necessary (see Section 11).

9 Check the sliding surface of the tensioner and the pivot point for signs of wear or damage and replace them if necessary. Check the spring for tension and cracks and replace it if it is stretched or damaged.

Installation

10 If removed, install the tensioner, making sure the hole in the bracket fits over the pivot lug on the engine **(see illustration)**. Position the tensioner is in its fully released position and tighten the bolt to secure it there against the tension of the spring. Check that the timing marks align as described in Step 4 **(see illustration 10.4b)**.

11 Fit the timing belt around the drive pulley first, then around the left-hand camshaft drive pulley and finally around the right-hand camshaft drive pulley. Install the left-hand pulley guide plate, washer and bolt, and tighten the bolt to the torque setting specified at the beginning of the Chapter, using the method in Step 2 to stop the engine turning **(see illustrations)**. Check again that all the timing marks align as described in Step 4.

12 Slacken the timing belt tensioner bolt and allow the tensioner to take up the tension. Turn the crankshaft clockwise through 2 to 4

10.6 Unscrew the bolt and remove the tensioner if required

10.10 Tensioner shown in its released position. Note how the bracket locates over the lug on the engine (arrowed)

10.11a Install the timing belt as shown . . .

10.11b . . . then install the guide plate onto the left-hand pulley . . .

10.11c . . . and tighten the bolt to the specified torque setting

10.12 Tighten the tensioner bolt to the specified torque setting

full turns to allow the tensioner to settle, then align the marks and tighten the tensioner bolt to the specified torque setting **(see illustration)**. Check again that all the timing marks align as described in Step 4. If a new belt has been fitted, turn the crankshaft three teeth further on the driven pulley after the marks have aligned, then tighten the tensioner bolt.

13 Install the timing belt cover (see Section 9) and the spark plugs (see Chapter 1).

11 Timing belt pulleys - removal and installation

Note: *The timing belt pulleys can be removed with the engine in the frame.*

Removal

1 Remove the timing belt (see Section 10), noting that when following Step 2 both the left-hand and right-hand camshaft drive pulley bolts should be removed **(see illustration)**. The right-hand pulley does not have a belt guide plate. Also slacken the timing belt drive pulley bolt at this stage, before the belt is removed, to prevent the possibility of the crankshaft turning independently of the camshafts. The clutch removing tool can be used to prevent the engine turning whilst slackening the bolt (see Section 17).

2 Slide the pulleys off the reduction gear shafts. Remove the Woodruff key from each shaft if it is loose **(see illustration)**.

3 Remove the bolt and washer securing the timing belt drive pulley, followed by the front belt guide plate, noting how it fits **(see illustration)**. Slide the pulley off the crankshaft, then slide the rear guide plate off.

4 If required, unscrew the bolt securing the idle pulley and remove the pulley **(see illustration)**.

Caution: Do not turn the camshafts or the crankshaft with the timing belt removed, as the valves will contact the pistons and could be damaged.

Installation

5 If removed, apply a suitable non-permanent thread locking compound to the idle pulley bolt, then install the pulley and tighten the bolt to the torque setting specified at the beginning of the Chapter **(see illustration 11.4)**.

6 Slide the drive pulley rear belt guide plate onto the crankshaft with its flat side facing out. Slide the pulley onto the shaft, aligning the key on the inside of the pulley with the slot in the shaft. Fit the front guide plate with the timing marks facing out, and align the tab on the inside with the slot in the shaft, so that the tab fits in between the pulley key and the shaft **(see illustrations)**. Install the drive pulley bolt but do not yet fully tighten it.

7 Slide each camshaft drive pulley onto its shaft, aligning the key slots, then fit the key

11.1 Right-hand camshaft drive pulley bolt

11.2 Slide each pulley off its shaft and retrieve the Woodruff key

2

11.3 Remove the bolt and timing belt drive pulley assembly

11.4 Idle pulley bolt (arrowed)

11.6a Install the rear guide plate . . .

11.6b . . . and the drive pulley as described . . .

11.6c . . . align the tab on the inside of the front guide plate with the slot in the shaft

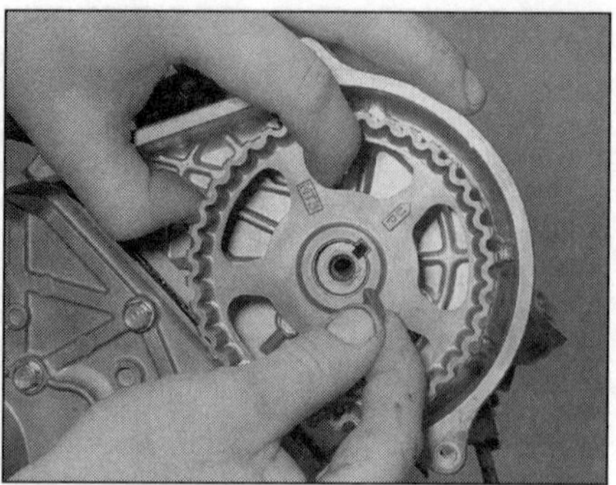
11.7 Align the key slots between the pulley and shaft, then fit the key

into the slots **(see illustration)**. Install the right-hand pulley bolt and washer and tighten it finger-tight at this stage.

8 Install the timing belt (see Section 10), noting that when following Step 11 both the left-hand and right-hand camshaft drive pulley bolts, and the timing belt drive pulley bolt, should be tightened to the specified torque **(see illustration)**. The right-hand pulley does not have a belt guide plate.

12 Camshafts and followers - removal, inspection and installation

Note: *The camshafts can be removed with the engine in the frame.*

Removal

1 Remove the valve covers (see Section 8).

2 Unscrew the three bolts securing each camshaft drive pulley cover, then remove the covers **(see illustration 9.3)**.

3 Unscrew the two bolts securing the timing inspection cover to the timing belt cover. Remove the cover and discard the O-ring as a new one must be used. The engine can be turned using a 17 mm socket on the drive pulley bolt and turning it in a clockwise direction only **(see illustrations)**. Alternatively, place the motorcycle on its centre stand, select a high gear and rotate the rear wheel by hand in its normal direction of rotation.

4 To remove the right-hand cylinder head camshafts, turn the engine clockwise until the "T1" mark on the drive pulley guide plate aligns with the index mark on the timing belt cover **(see illustration and see illustration 10.4b)**. Also make sure that the index line on the camshaft drive pulley aligns with the mark on the reduction shaft casing, and that the index lines on the front end of the camshafts on the right-hand cylinder head are facing away from each other and are level with the head mating surface **(see illustrations)**. If the marks do not align as stated, rotate the engine clockwise one full turn until the "T1" mark again aligns with the static timing mark. The marks should now align. Do not confuse the index lines with the punchmarks on the driven pulley and camshaft ends. Mark the relative positions of the reduction gear and

11.8 Tighten the timing belt drive pulley bolt to the specified torque setting

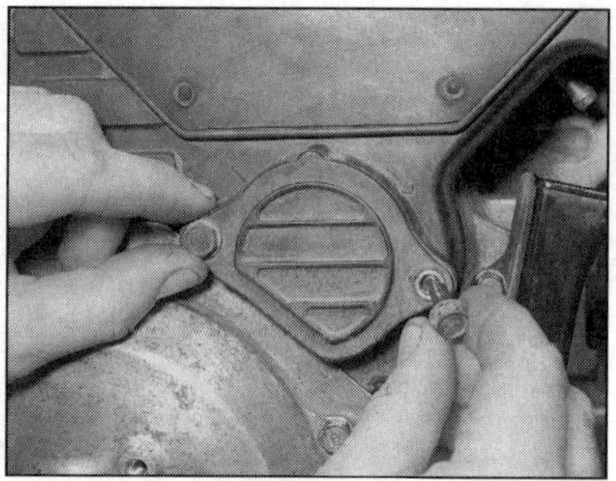
12.3a The inspection cover is secured by two bolts

12.3b Turn the engine using a socket on the drive pulley bolt

12.4a Align the marks as shown

12.4b The index line (A) should align with the mark on the casing (B) . . .

12.4c . . . and the index lines on the camshafts should face away and be level with the head

12.5a The punchmark (A) should align with the mark on the casing (B) . . .

12.5b . . . and the index lines on the camshafts should face away and be level with the head

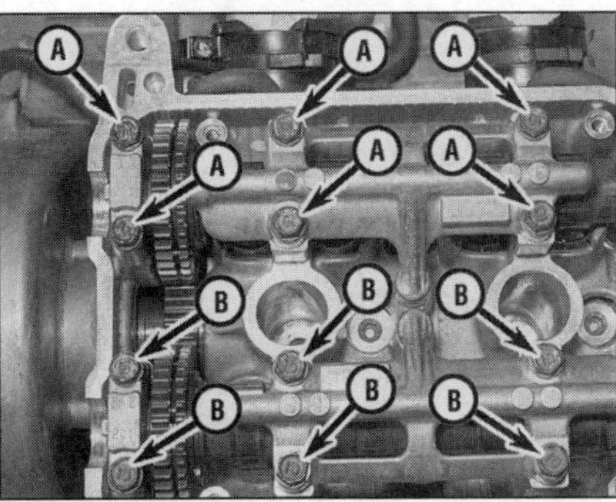

12.7a Intake camshaft holder bolts (A), exhaust camshaft holder bolts (B)

the camshaft driven gears as a further aid for installation.

5 To remove the left-hand cylinder head camshafts, turn the engine clockwise until the "T4" mark on the drive pulley guide plate aligns with the index mark on the crankcase. Also make sure that the punchmark on the camshaft drive pulley aligns with the mark on the reduction shaft casing, and that the index lines on the front end of the camshafts on the left-hand cylinder head are facing away from each other and are level with the head mating surface **(see illustrations)**. If the marks do not align as stated, rotate the engine clockwise one full turn until the "T4" mark again aligns with the static timing mark. The marks should now align. Do not confuse the index lines with the punchmarks on the driven pulley and camshaft ends. Mark the relative positions of the reduction gear and the camshaft driven gears as an aid to installation.

6 Before disturbing the camshaft journal holders, check for identification markings. According to Honda, for the right-hand cylinder head, the intake camshaft holders should be marked RI and the exhaust camshaft holders marked RE. For the left-hand cylinder head the intake camshaft holders should be marked LI and the exhaust camshaft holders marked LE. However, on the model used here, all the holders were identically marked IE. The smaller front holders also have a tab which faces the front. These markings ensure that the holders can be matched up to their original journals on installation. If no markings are visible, or they are all the same, mark your own using a felt pen. If necessary, make a sketch of the layout as a further aid for installation.

7 Unscrew the journal holder bolts for the camshaft being worked on, evenly and a little at a time, until they are all loose **(see illustration)**.

Caution: If the bearing cap bolts aren't loosened evenly, the camshaft may bind.

Remove the bolts and lift off the journal holders, then remove the camshaft **(see illustration)**. Retrieve the dowels from either the holder or the cylinder head if they are loose. The camshafts are marked for identification. For the right-hand cylinder head, the intake camshaft is marked RH IN and the exhaust camshaft is marked RH EX. For the left-hand cylinder head the intake camshaft is marked LH IN and the exhaust camshaft is marked LH EX.

8 Obtain two containers, each divided into eight compartments, and label each compartment with the location of its corresponding valve, whether it belongs with an intake or an exhaust valve, and to the right-hand or left-hand cylinder head. Pick each follower and shim out of the cylinder head and store them in the corresponding compartment in the container. Note that the shim will probably be stuck to the inside of the follower **(see illustrations)**. If the shim remains in the top of the valve, lever it out using a small screwdriver and remove it using a pair of pliers. Do not allow the shim to fall into the engine.

Inspection

9 Inspect the bearing surfaces of the head and the bearing holders and the corresponding journals on the camshaft. Look for score marks, deep scratches and evidence of spalling (a pitted appearance) **(see illustration)**.

10 Check the camshaft lobes for heat discoloration (blue appearance), score marks, chipped areas, flat spots and spalling. Measure the height of each lobe with a micrometer and compare the results to the minimum lobe height listed in this Chapter's

12.7b With the holders removed, lift out the camshaft

2

12.8a Remove the follower . . .

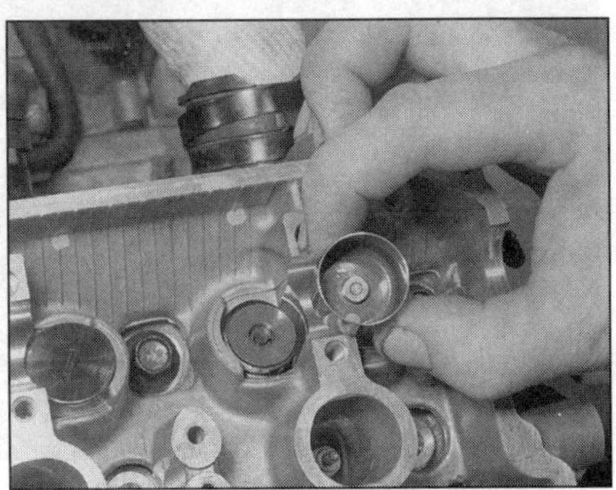
12.8b . . . noting that the shim will probably stick to the inside

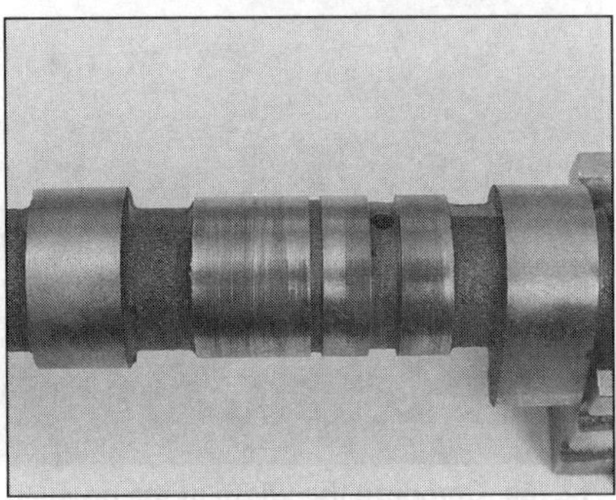
12.9 Check the journal surfaces of the camshaft for scratches or wear

12.10a Check the lobes of the camshaft for wear - here's an example of damage requiring camshaft repair or renewal

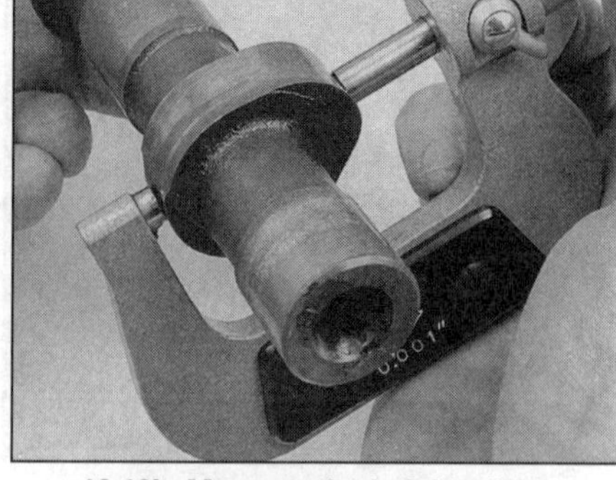
12.10b Measure the height of the camshaft lobes with a micrometer

12.13 Place a strip of Plastigage on each bearing journal

Specifications. If damage is noted or wear is excessive, the camshaft must be replaced. Also, be sure to check the condition of the followers, as described later in this Section **(see illustrations)**.

11 Check the amount of camshaft runout by supporting each end of the camshaft on V-blocks, and measuring any runout using a dial gauge. If the runout exceeds the specified limit the camshaft must be replaced.

> HAYNES HINT
>
> ***Refer to Tools and Workshop Tips in the Reference section for details of how to read a micrometer and dial gauge.***

12 Next, check the camshaft bearing oil clearances. Clean the camshafts, the bearing surfaces in the cylinder head and the bearing caps with a clean, lint-free cloth, then lay the cams in place in the cylinder head.

13 Cut eight strips of Plastigauge (type HPG-1) and lay one piece on each bearing journal, parallel with the camshaft centreline **(see illustration)**.

14 Make sure the journal holder dowels are installed. Install the journal holders in their proper positions (see Step 6) and install the bolts. Tighten the bolts evenly and a little at a time in a criss-cross pattern, to the torque setting specified at the beginning of the Chapter. While doing this, DO NOT let the camshafts rotate!

15 Now unscrew the bolts, a little at a time, and carefully lift off the journal holders.

16 To determine the oil clearance, compare the crushed Plastigauge (at its widest point) on each journal to the scale printed on the Plastigauge container. Compare the results to this Chapter's Specifications. If the oil clearance is greater than specified, either the camshaft journal or journal holder (or both) are worn. Measure the diameter of the camshaft journal with a micrometer **(see illustrations)**. Measure the journal holder diameter by assembling the journals on the cylinder head without the camshaft in place, and measuring the diameter with an internal micrometer or telescoping gauge. If any measurement is outside that specified, the camshaft or journal holder/cylinder head must be replaced.

17 Check the camshaft drive gear on the reduction shaft and the driven gear on each camshaft for wear, cracks and other damage, replacing them if necessary. The driven gears are integral with the camshafts, whilst the drive gear can be removed from the reduction shaft. If wear this severe is apparent, the entire engine should be disassembled for inspection.

18 Inspect the outer surfaces of the cam followers for evidence of scoring or other damage. If a follower is in poor condition, it is probable that the bore in which it works is also damaged. Measure the external diameter of each follower and the diameter of its bore in the cylinder head. If the measurements are outside the service limits specified, or if the bores are seriously out-of-round or tapered, the followers and/or the cylinder head must be replaced.

Installation

19 Lubricate each shim and its follower with mixed (1:1) engine oil and molybdenum grease and install the shim in the recess in the top of the valve spring retainer, with its size marking facing upwards. Install the follower onto the valve **(see illustrations)**. **Note:** *It is*

> HAYNES HINT
>
> ***Before replacing camshafts or the cylinder head and journal holders because of damage, check with local machine shops specialising in motorcycle engine work. In the case of the camshafts, it may be possible for cam lobes to be welded, reground and hardened, at a cost far lower than that of a new camshaft. If the bearing surfaces in the cylinder head are damaged, it may be possible for them to be bored out to accept bearing inserts. Due to the cost of a new cylinder head it is recommended that all options be explored before condemning it as trash!***

12.16a Compare the width of the crushed Plastigage to the scale provided with it to obtain the clearance

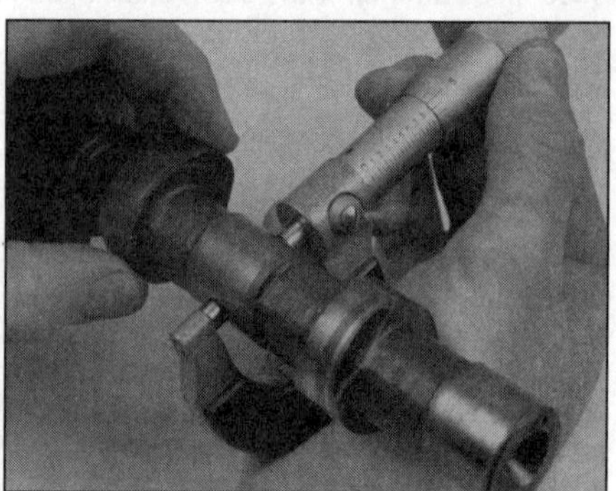
12.16b Measure the cam bearing journals with a micrometer

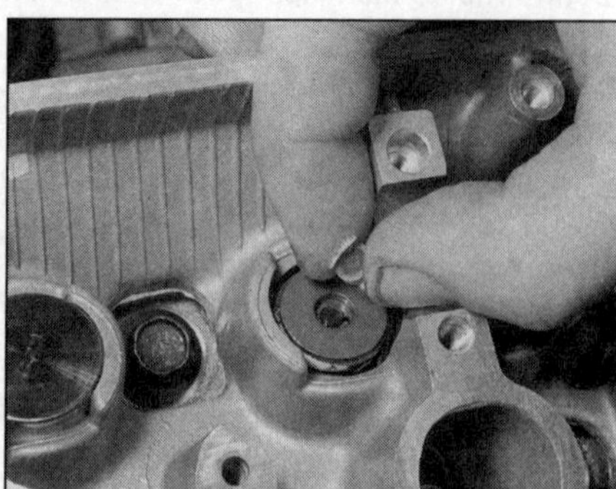
12.19a Fit the shim into its recess . . .

12.19b . . . then install the follower

12.21 Lay the camshaft in the head, making sure it is correctly positioned

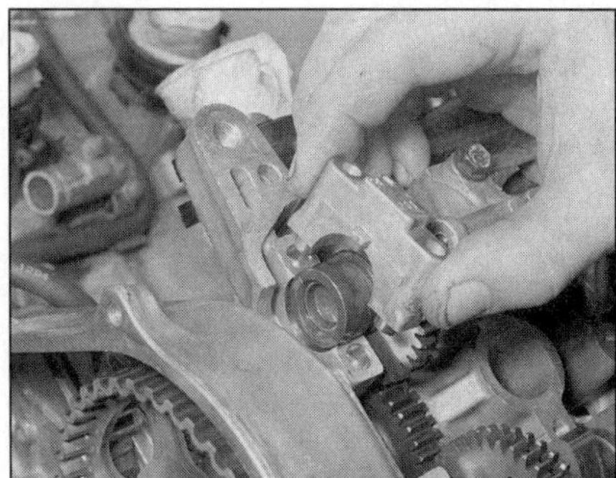
12.22a Make sure the dowels are fitted with the holders . . .

most important that the shims and followers are returned to their original valves otherwise the valve clearances will be inaccurate.

20 Make sure the bearing surfaces in the cylinder head and the journal holders are clean, then apply mixed (1:1) engine oil and molybdenum grease to each of them. Also apply it to the camshaft journals and lobes.

21 Check that the crankshaft is positioned as described in Step 4 when installing the right-hand cylinder head camshafts, and as described in Step 5 for the left-hand head shafts. Work on only one head at a time. The camshafts are marked for identification. For the right-hand cylinder head, the intake camshaft is marked RH IN and the exhaust camshaft is marked RH EX. For the left-hand cylinder head the intake camshaft is marked LH IN and the exhaust camshaft is marked LH EX. Install each camshaft for the head being worked and check that everything aligns as described in Step 4 for the right-hand head or Step 5 for the left-hand head **(see illustration)**, and that the marks made between the reduction gear and the camshaft driven gears align. If not, the valve timing will be inaccurate and the valves could contact the pistons when the engine is turned over. Take extra care at this stage as it is easy to be one tooth out on the timing without it appearing as a drastic misalignment of the timing marks.

22 Make sure the journal holder dowels are in place. Fit the journal holders in their original positions (see Step 6) and install the bolts. Tighten the bolts evenly and a little at a time in a criss-cross pattern, to the torque setting specified at the beginning of the Chapter **(see illustrations)**.

23 With all holders tightened down, check that the valve timing marks still align (see Steps 4 and 5. Also see Step 4, Section 10, and **see illustration 10.4b**). Check that each camshaft is not pinched by turning the crankshaft a few degrees in each direction with a 17 mm socket on the drive pulley bolt.

Caution: If the marks are not aligned exactly as described, the valve timing will be incorrect and the valves may strike the pistons, causing extensive damage to the engine.

12.22b . . . then install the bolts . . .

12.22c . . . and tighten them to the specified torque setting

24 Check the valve clearances and adjust them if necessary (see Chapter 1).

25 Install the timing inspection cover using a new O-ring.

26 Install the camshaft drive pulley covers.

27 Install the valve covers (see Section 8).

13 Reduction gear shafts - removal, inspection and installation

Note: *The reduction gear shafts can be removed with the engine in the frame. It is only necessary to remove the camshafts if the drive gear on the reduction shaft has to be replaced. Otherwise the reduction shaft can be withdrawn leaving the drive gear in situ in the cylinder head.*

Removal

1 Remove the camshaft drive pulleys (see Section 11).

Caution: Do not turn the camshafts or the crankshaft with the timing belt removed, as the valves will contact the pistons and could be damaged.

2 Mark the relative positions of the reduction gear and the camshaft driven gears as an aid to installation. If required, remove the camshafts (see **Note** above) (see Section 12).

3 Unscrew the three bolts securing the reduction shaft holder to the cylinder head **(see illustration)**. Slide the holder forward off the shaft, noting how it locates along the timing belt casing. Discard the gasket between the holder and the cylinder head as a new one must be used. Also check the condition of the rubber gasket and replace it if it is damaged or deteriorated. Remove the dowel from either the holder or the cylinder head if it is loose.

4 Withdraw the shaft from the cylinder head. If it is a tight fit, slide the driven pulley back onto the shaft and secure it with its bolt, then use the pulley to help withdraw the shaft. If the camshafts were removed, remove the reduction gear from the cylinder head **(see**

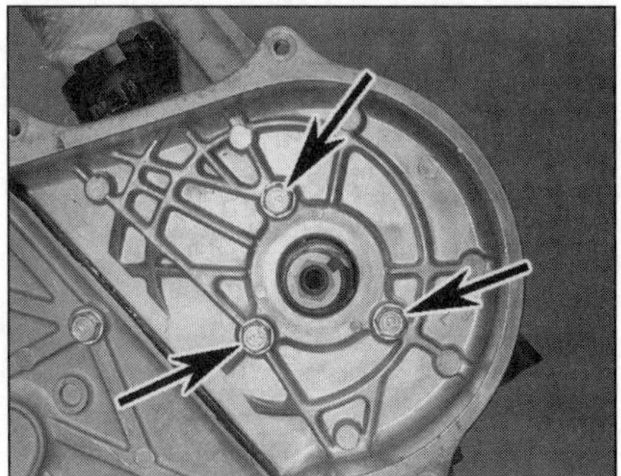
13.3 The reduction shaft holder is secured by three bolts (arrowed)

2

13.4 Withdraw the shaft from the head, noting its alignment with the gear

13.7 Check the oil seal for signs of damage or leakage and replace it if necessary

13.9a Check that the dowel is in place, then install the holder using a new gasket

illustration). Note the wide spline on the shaft which aligns with the wide spline on the gear, indicated by a punchmark.

Inspection

5 The shaft is unlikely to sustain damage unless the engine has seized, or the machine has covered a very high mileage. Check the surface of the shaft, especially the splines, and replace the shaft if there are any cracks or if the splines are worn. Damage of any kind can only be cured by replacement.

6 Check the ball bearings (the right-hand shaft has one, the left-hand two) for play or roughness, and that it is a tight fit on the shaft. Replace the bearing if it is worn, loose or damaged, using a bearing puller to remove it if required. Install the bearing using a press or a length of tubing which bears only on the bearing's inner race.

7 Check the condition of the oil seal in the reduction shaft holder and replace it if worn or damaged, or if there are any signs of oil leakage in the front of the holder **(see illustration)**. Drive or lever the old seal out and make sure the new one is installed squarely.

Installation

8 Lubricate the shaft and the reduction gear with mixed (1:1) engine oil and molybdenum grease. If the camshafts were removed, place the reduction gear in the cylinder head. If the camshafts were left in place, check that the marks between them and the reduction gear align. Slide the shaft into the cylinder head, aligning the wide spline on the shaft with that in the gear, indicated by a punchmark **(see illustration 13.4)**.

9 Make sure the dowel is fitted in either the shaft holder or the cylinder head. Install the holder using a new gasket and apply a non-permanent thread locking compound to the bolt threads **(see illustrations)**.

10 If removed, install the camshafts (see Section 12).

11 Install the timing belt driven pulleys (see Section 11).

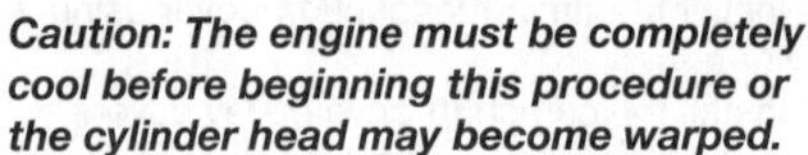

14 Cylinder heads - removal and installation

Caution: The engine must be completely cool before beginning this procedure or the cylinder head may become warped.

Note: *The cylinder head can be removed with the engine in the frame. If the engine has been removed, ignore the steps which don't apply. If required, the heads can be removed with the reduction shafts in place.*

Removal

1 Remove the carburettors (see Chapter 4).

2 Remove the exhaust system (see Chapter 4).

3 Remove the camshafts (see Section 12).

4 If the head is to be removed with the reduction shaft, shaft holder and driven pulley still attached, just remove the timing belt (see Section 10). Otherwise, remove the components as required (see Section 13).

5 On US models, detach the air injection pipes from above each exhaust port.

6 Each cylinder head is secured by six bolts **(see illustration)**. Slacken the bolts evenly and a little at a time until they are all slack. Remove the bolts and their washers.

7 Pull the cylinder head up off the dowels **(see illustration)**. If it is stuck, tap around the joint faces of the cylinder head with a soft-faced mallet to free the head. Do not attempt to free the head by inserting a screwdriver between the head and cylinder block - you'll damage the sealing surfaces. Remove the old cylinder head gasket and discard it as a new one must be used.

8 If they are loose, remove the dowels from the cylinder block. If they appear to be missing they are probably stuck in the underside of the cylinder head.

9 Check the cylinder head gasket and the mating surfaces on the cylinder head and block for signs of leakage, which could indicate warpage. Refer to Section 16 and check the flatness of the cylinder head.

10 Clean all traces of old gasket material from the cylinder head and block. If a scraper is used, take care not to scratch or gouge the soft aluminium. Be careful not to let any of the

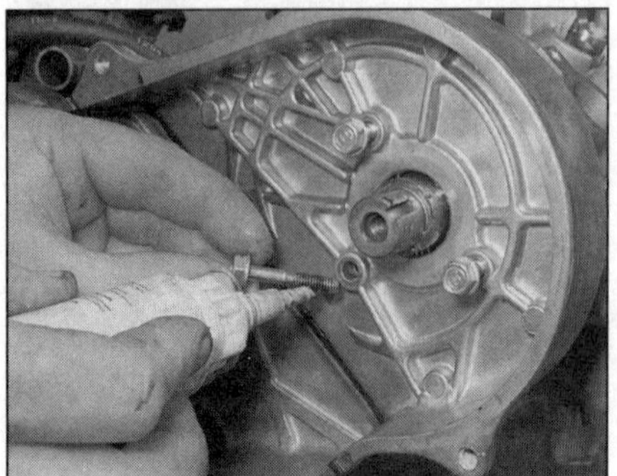
13.9b Apply a thread locking compound to the bolts

14.6 Each head is secured by six bolts (arrowed)

14.7 With all bolts removed, lift the head up off the block

14.12 Make sure the dowels (A) are fitted, then lay a new gasket on the block, making sure the UP mark (B) faces up

14.14a Apply clean engine oil to the bolt threads . . .

14.14b . . . and tighten them to the specified torque setting

gasket material fall into the crankcase, the cylinder bores or the oil passages.

Installation

11 If removed, install the dowels onto the cylinder block. Lubricate the cylinder bores with engine oil.

12 Ensure both cylinder head and block mating surfaces are clean, then lay the new head gasket in place on the cylinder block, making sure all the holes are correctly aligned and the UP mark faces up **(see illustration)**. Never re-use the old gasket.

13 Carefully fit the cylinder head onto the block **(see illustration 14.7)**.

14 Apply clean engine oil to the cylinder head bolts, then install them with their washers and tighten them finger-tight. Now tighten the bolts evenly and a little at a time to the torque setting specified at the beginning of the Chapter **(see illustrations)**.

15 Install the remaining components in a reverse of their removal sequence, referring to the relevant Sections or Chapters (see Steps 1 to 5).

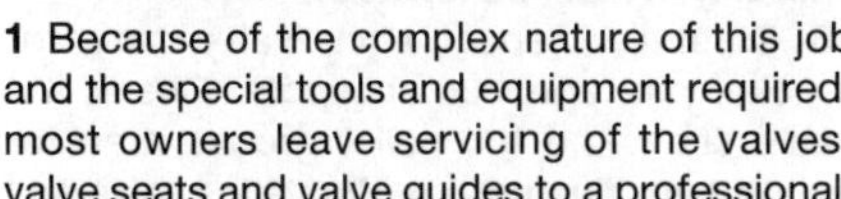

15 Valves/valve seats/valve guides - servicing

1 Because of the complex nature of this job and the special tools and equipment required, most owners leave servicing of the valves, valve seats and valve guides to a professional.

2 The home mechanic can, however, remove the valves from the cylinder head, clean and check the components for wear and assess the extent of the work needed, and, unless a valve service is required, grind in the valves (see Section 16).

3 The dealer service department will remove the valves and springs, replace the valves and guides, recut the valve seats, check and replace the valve springs, spring retainers and collets (as necessary), replace the valve seals with new ones and reassemble the valve components.

4 After the valve service has been performed, the head will be in like-new condition. When the head is returned, be sure to clean it again very thoroughly before installation on the engine to remove any metal particles or abrasive grit that may still be present from the valve service operations. Use compressed air, if available, to blow out all the holes and passages.

16 Cylinder head and valves - disassembly, inspection and reassembly

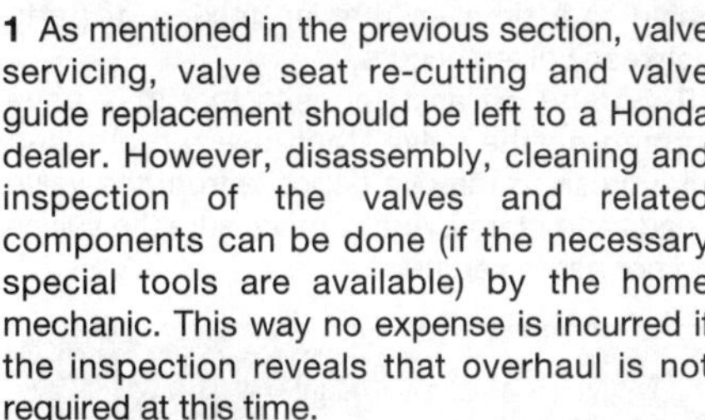

1 As mentioned in the previous section, valve servicing, valve seat re-cutting and valve guide replacement should be left to a Honda dealer. However, disassembly, cleaning and inspection of the valves and related components can be done (if the necessary special tools are available) by the home mechanic. This way no expense is incurred if the inspection reveals that overhaul is not required at this time.

2 To disassemble the valve components without the risk of damaging them, a valve spring compressor is absolutely necessary. This special tool can usually be rented, but if it's not available, have a dealer service department handle the entire process of disassembly, inspection, service or repair (if required) and reassembly of the valves.

Disassembly

3 Before proceeding, arrange to label and store the valves along with their related components in such a way that they can be returned to their original locations without getting mixed up. A good way to do this is to obtain a container which is divided into sixteen compartments, and to label each compartment with the identity of the valve which will be stored in it (i.e. number of cylinder, intake or exhaust valve). Alternatively, labelled plastic bags will do just as well.

4 If not already done, clean all traces of old gasket material from the cylinder head. If a scraper is used, take care not to scratch or gouge the soft aluminium.

Refer to Tools and Workshop Tips for details of gasket removal methods.

5 Compress the valve spring on the first valve with a spring compressor, making sure it is correctly located onto each end of the valve assembly. Do not compress the springs any more than is absolutely necessary. Remove the collets, using either needle-nose pliers, tweezers, a magnet or a screwdriver with a dab of grease on it. Carefully release the valve spring compressor and remove the spring retainer, noting which way up it fits, the springs and the valve from the head. If the valve binds in the guide (won't pull through), push it back into the head and deburr the area around the collet groove with a very fine file or whetstone **(see illustrations)**.

16.5a Compressing the valve springs using a valve spring compressor

16.5b Remove the collets with needle-nose pliers, tweezers, a magnet or a screwdriver with a dab of grease on it

2

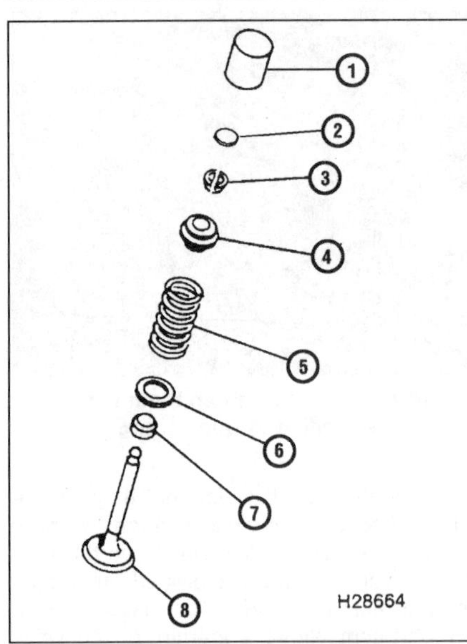

16.5c Valve components

1 *Follower*
2 *Shim*
3 *Collets*
4 *Spring retainer*
5 *Spring*
6 *Spring seat*
7 *Stem seal*
8 *Valve*

6 Repeat the procedure for the remaining valves. Remember to keep the parts for each valve together and in order so they can be reinstalled in the same location.

7 Once the valves have been removed and labelled, pull the valve stem seals off the top of the valve guides with pliers and discard them (the old seals should never be reused), then remove the spring seats, noting which way up they fit.

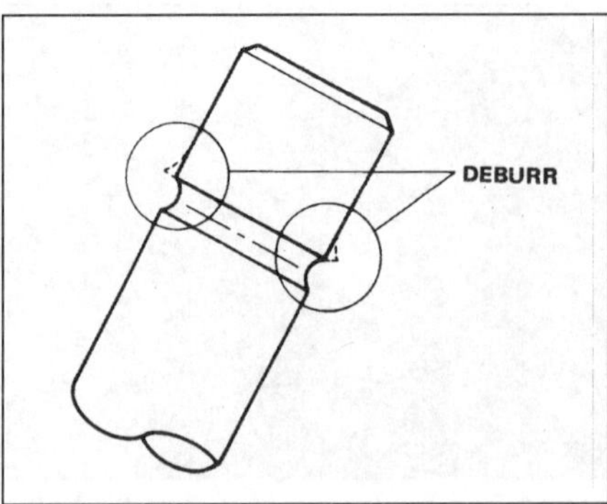

16.5d If the valve stem won't pull through the guide, deburr the area above the collet groove

8 Next, clean the cylinder head with solvent and dry it thoroughly. Compressed air will speed the drying process and ensure that all holes and recessed areas are clean.

9 Clean all of the valve springs, collets, retainers and spring seats with solvent and dry them thoroughly. Do the parts from one valve at a time so that no mixing of parts between valves occurs.

10 Scrape off any deposits that may have formed on the valve, then use a motorised wire brush to remove deposits from the valve heads and stems. Again, make sure the valves do not get mixed up.

16.13 Measure the valve seat width with a ruler (or for greater precision use a vernier caliper)

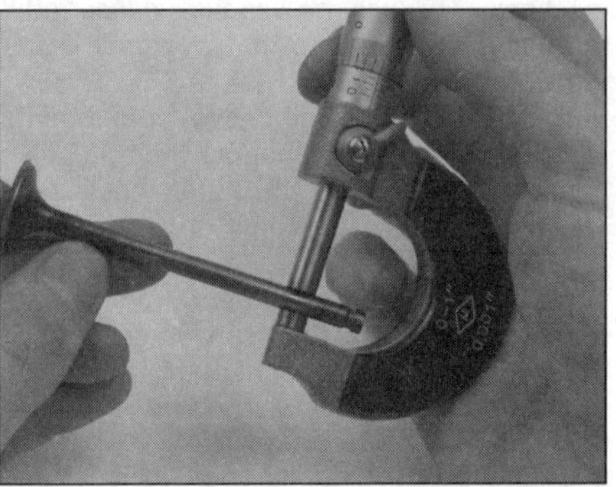

16.14a Measure the valve stem diameter with a micrometer

16.14b Insert a small hole gauge into the valve guide and expand it so there's a slight drag when it's pulled out

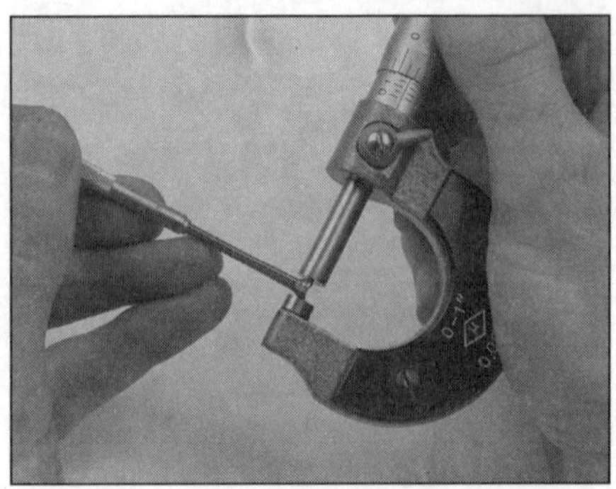

16.14c Measure the small hole gauge with a micrometer

Inspection

11 Inspect the head very carefully for cracks and other damage. If cracks are found, a new head will be required. Check the cam bearing surfaces for wear and evidence of seizure. Check the camshafts for wear as well (see Section 12).

12 Using a precision straight-edge and a feeler gauge set to the warpage limit listed in the specifications at the beginning of the Chapter, check the head gasket mating surface for warpage. Refer to *Tools and Workshop Tips* in the Reference section for details of how to use the straight-edge.

13 Examine the valve seats in the combustion chamber. If they are pitted, cracked or burned, the head will require work beyond the scope of the home mechanic. Measure the valve seat width and compare it to this Chapter's Specifications **(see illustration)**. If it exceeds the service limit, or if it varies around its circumference, valve overhaul is required. If available, use Prussian blue to determine the extent of valve seat wear. Uniformly coat the seat with the Prussian blue, then install the valve and rotate it back and forth using a lapping tool. Remove the valve and check whether the ring of blue on the valve is uniform and continuous around the valve, and of the correct width as specified.

14 Measure the valve stem diameter. Clean the valve guides to remove any carbon build-up, then measure the inside diameters of the guides (at both ends and the centre of the guide) with a small hole gauge and micrometer **(see illustrations)**.The guides are measured at the ends and at the centre to determine if they are worn in a bell-mouth pattern (more wear at the ends). Subtract the stem diameter from the valve guide diameter to obtain the valve stem-to-guide clearance. If the stem-to-guide clearance is greater than listed in this Chapter's Specifications, the guides and valves will have to be replaced with new ones. If the valve stem or guide is worn beyond its limit, or if the guide is worn unevenly, it must be replaced.

15 Carefully inspect each valve face for cracks, pits and burned spots. Check the valve stem and the collet groove area for cracks **(see illustration)**. Rotate the valve and

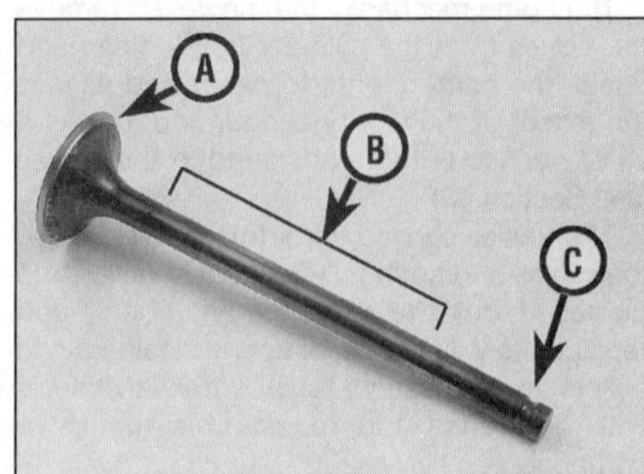

16.15 Check the valve face (A), stem (B) and collet groove (C) for signs of wear and damage

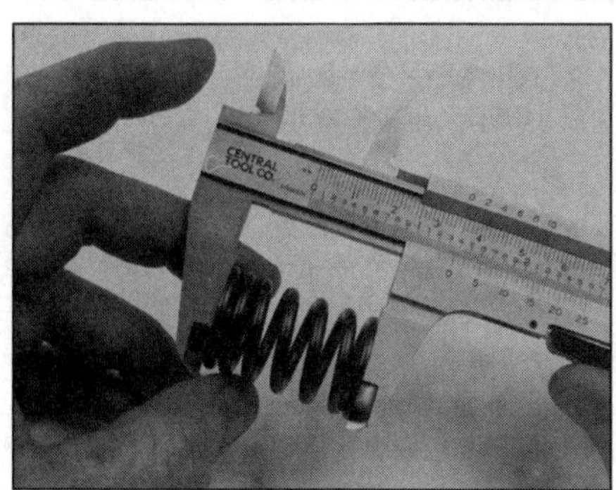
16.16a Measure the free length of the valve springs

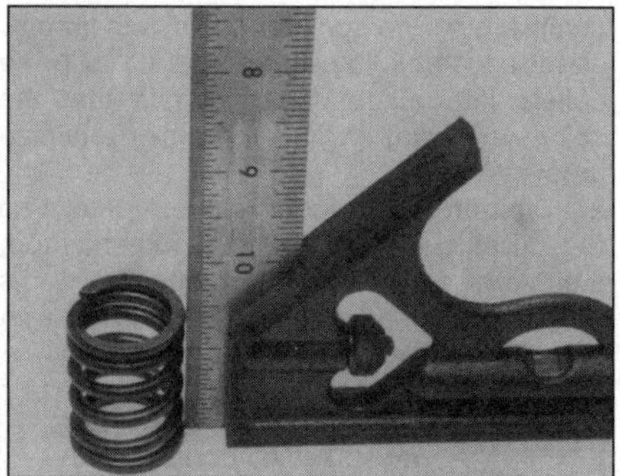
16.16b Check the valve springs for squareness

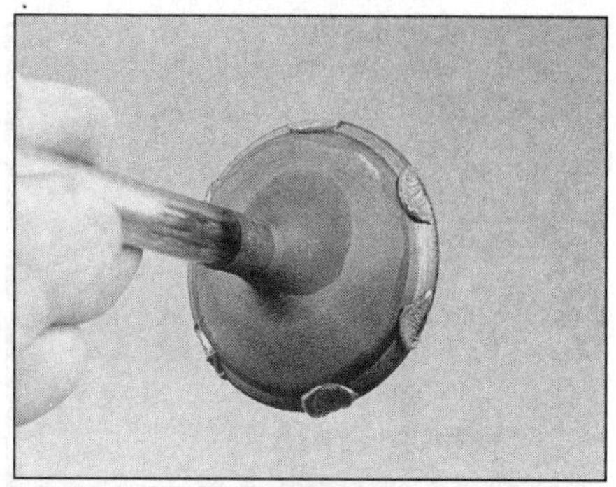
16.20 Apply the lapping compound very sparingly, in small dabs, to the valve face only

check for any obvious indication that it is bent. Check the end of the stem for pitting and excessive wear. The presence of any of the above conditions indicates the need for valve servicing. The stem end can be ground down, provided that the amount of stem above the collet groove after grinding is sufficient.

16 Check the end of each valve spring for wear and pitting. Measure the spring free length and compare it to that listed in the specifications. If any spring is shorter than specified it has sagged and must be replaced. Also place the spring upright on a flat surface and check it for bend by placing a ruler against it **(see illustrations)**. If the bend in any spring is excessive, it must be replaced.

17 Check the spring retainers and collets for obvious wear and cracks. Any questionable parts should not be reused, as extensive damage will occur in the event of failure during engine operation.

18 If the inspection indicates that no overhaul work is required, the valve components can be reinstalled in the head.

Reassembly

19 Unless a valve service has been performed, before installing the valves in the head they should be ground in (lapped) to ensure a positive seal between the valves and seats. This procedure requires coarse and fine valve grinding compound and a valve grinding tool. If a grinding tool is not available, a piece of rubber or plastic hose can be slipped over the valve stem (after the valve has been installed in the guide) and used to turn the valve.

20 Apply a small amount of coarse grinding compound to the valve face, then slip the valve into the guide **(see illustration)**. **Note:** *Make sure each valve is installed in its correct guide and be careful not to get any grinding compound on the valve stem.*

21 Attach the grinding tool (or hose) to the valve and rotate the tool between the palms of your hands. Use a back-and-forth motion (as though rubbing your hands together) rather than a circular motion (i.e. so that the valve rotates alternately clockwise and anti-clockwise rather than in one direction only). Lift the valve off the seat and turn it at regular intervals to distribute the grinding compound properly. Continue the grinding procedure until the valve face and seat contact area is of uniform width and unbroken around the entire circumference of the valve face and seat **(see illustrations)**.

22 Carefully remove the valve from the guide and wipe off all traces of grinding compound. Use solvent to clean the valve and wipe the seat area thoroughly with a solvent soaked cloth.

23 Repeat the procedure with fine valve grinding compound, then repeat the entire procedure for the remaining valves.

24 Lay the spring seats for all the valves in place in the cylinder head with their shouldered side facing up so that they fit into the base of the springs (the spring seat can be identified from the spring retainer by its larger internal diameter - be sure not to mix up the two), then install new valve stem seals on each of the guides. Use an appropriate size deep socket to push the seals over the end of the valve guide until they are felt to clip into place. Don't twist or cock them, or they will not seal properly against the valve stems. Also, don't remove them again or they will be damaged.

25 Coat the valve stems with molybdenum disulphide grease, then install one of them into its guide, rotating it slowly to avoid damaging the seal. Check that the valve moves up and down freely in the guide. Next, install the inner and outer springs, with their closer-wound coils facing down into the cylinder head, followed by the spring retainer, with its shouldered side facing down so that it fits into the top of the springs.

26 Apply a small amount of grease to the collets to help hold them in place as the pressure is released from the springs **(see**

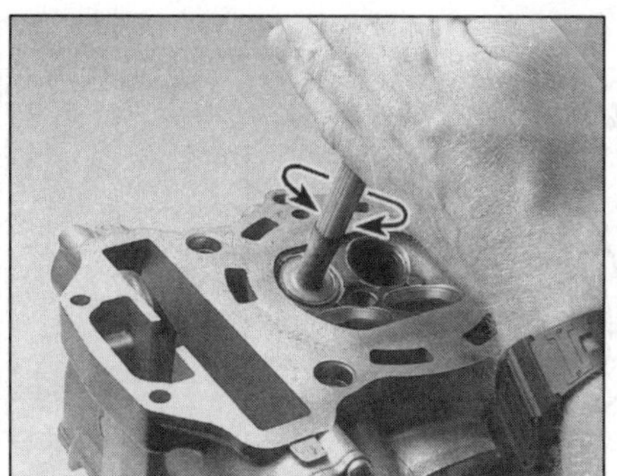
16.21a Rotate the valve grinding tool back and forth between the palms of your hands

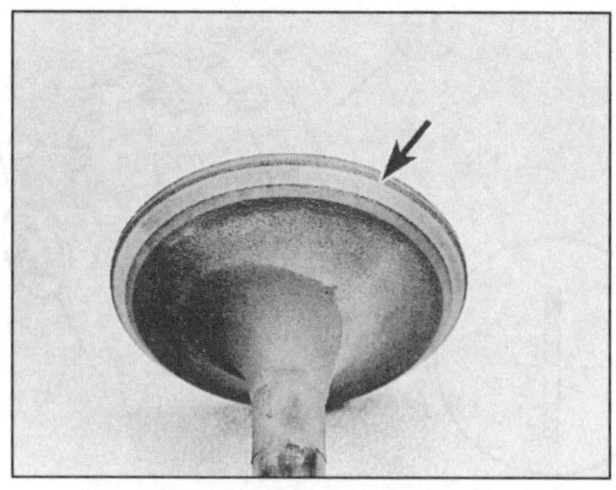
16.21b The valve face and seat should show a uniform unbroken ring . . .

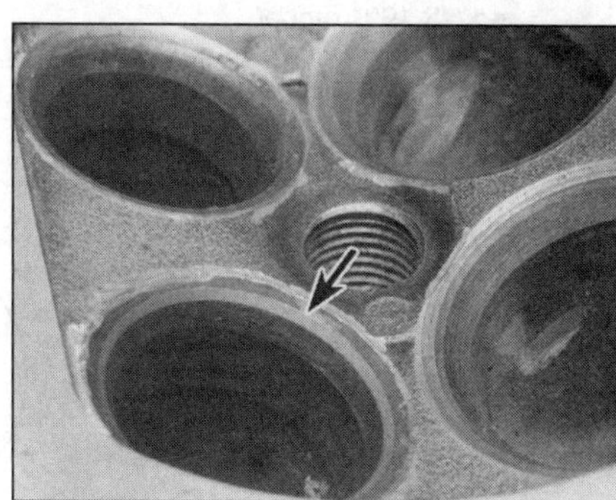
16.21c . . . and the seat (arrowed) should be the specified width all the way round

16.26 A small dab of grease will help to keep the collets in place on the valve while the spring is released

illustration). Compress the springs with the valve spring compressor and install the collets **(see illustrations 16.5a and b)**. When compressing the springs, depress them only as far as is absolutely necessary to slip the collets into place. Make certain that the collets are securely locked in their retaining grooves.

27 Support the cylinder head on blocks so the valves can't contact the workbench top, then very gently tap each of the valve stems with a soft-faced hammer. This will help seat the collets in their grooves.

Check for proper sealing of the valves by pouring a small amount of solvent into each of the valve ports. If the solvent leaks past any valve into the combustion chamber area the valve grinding operation on that valve should be repeated.

17 Clutch - removal, inspection and installation

Note: *The clutch can be removed with the engine in the frame. If the engine has been removed, ignore the steps which don't apply.*

Removal

1 Drain the engine oil (see Chapter 1).

2 Remove the right-hand exhaust downpipe section (see Chapter 4).

3 Remove the clutch release cylinder (see Section 19). There is no need to detach the hydraulic hose from the cylinder.

4 Unscrew the clutch cover bolts and remove the cover, being prepared to catch any residue oil **(see illustrations)**. Discard the gasket as a new one must be used. Remove

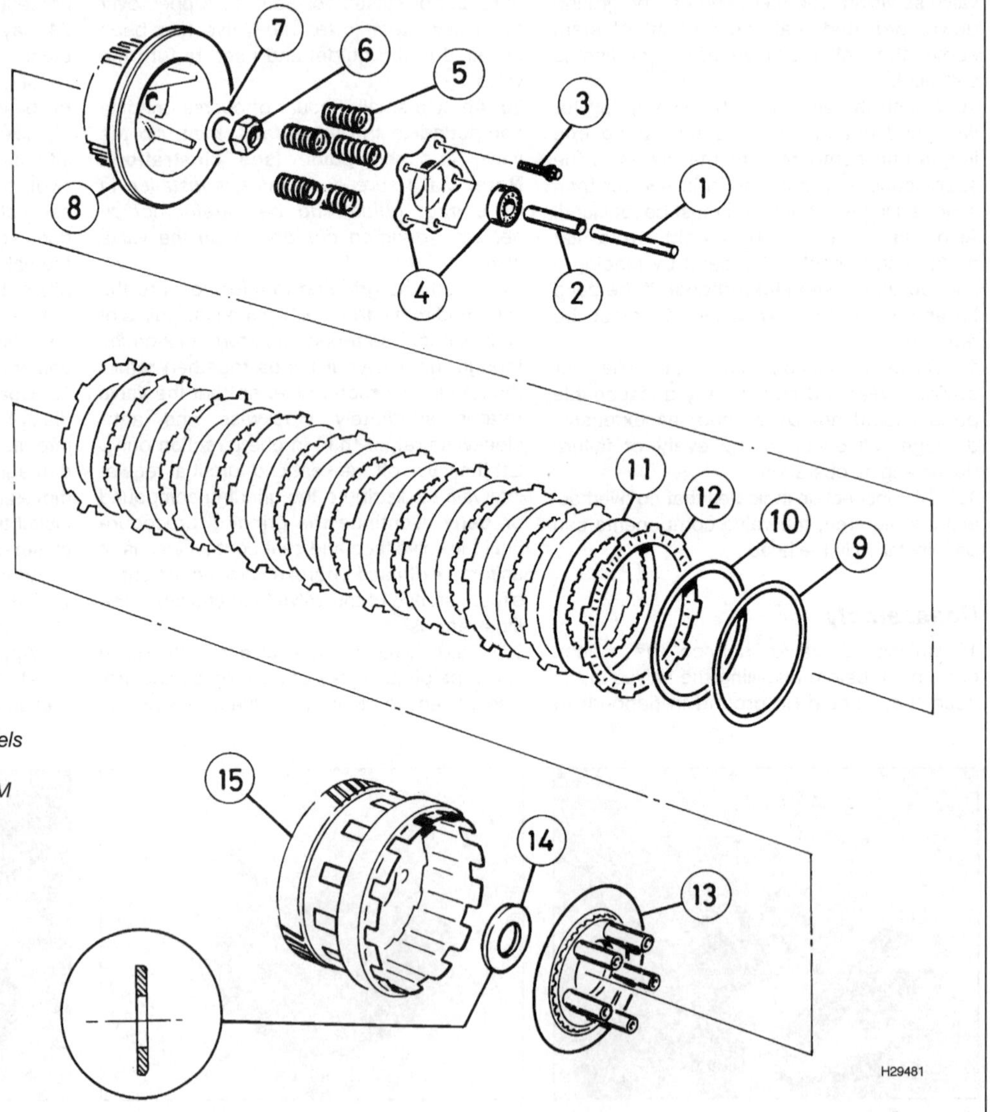

1 Release rod
2 Release rod guide
3 Release plate bolts
4 Release plate and bearing
5 Clutch spring
6 Clutch nut
7 Washer
8 Clutch centre
9 Spring seat - UK L and M models and US 1991 model
10 Anti-judder spring - UK L and M models and US 1991 model
11 Plain plate
12 Friction plate
13 Pressure plate
14 Thrust washer
15 Clutch housing

H29481

17.4a Clutch components

17.4b The clutch cover is secured by nine bolts (arrowed)

17.5 Withdraw the release rod and guide

17.6 Unscrew the release plate bolts (arrowed) evenly and gradually

the dowels from either the cover or the crankcase if they are loose.

5 Withdraw the clutch release rod and its guide from the centre of the release plate **(see illustration)**.

6 Working in a criss-cross pattern, gradually slacken the clutch release plate bolts until spring pressure is released, then remove the bolts, plate and springs **(see illustration)**.

7 The clutch nut is staked against the primary drive damper shaft **(see illustration)**. Unstake the nut using a screwdriver, a punch, or a drill. To remove the clutch nut the damper shaft must be locked. This can be done in several ways:

TOOL TiP

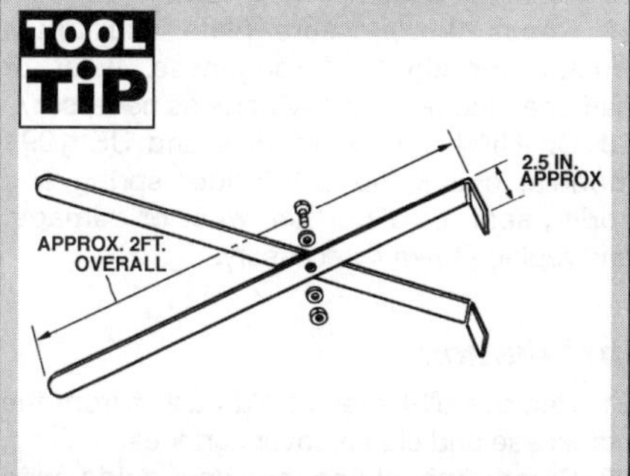

A clutch centre holding tool can easily be made using two strips of steel bent over at the ends and bolted together in the middle

a) If the engine is in the frame, engage 1st gear and have an assistant hold the rear brake on hard with the rear tyre in firm contact with the ground.

b) The Honda service tools (Pt. Nos. 07JMB-MN50300 and 07LMB-MT30100) can be used to stop the clutch centre from turning whilst the nut is slackened.

*c) A home-made tool made from two strips of steel bent at the ends and bolted together in the middle **(see Tool tip)**, can be used to stop the clutch centre from turning whilst the nut is slackened **(see illustration)**.*

8 Unscrew the clutch nut and remove the washer from the shaft, noting which way round it fits. Discard the nut as a new one must be used.

9 Grasp the clutch centre with the complete set of clutch plates and the pressure plate and remove them as a pack **(see illustration)**. Unless the plates are being replaced with new ones, keep them in their original order. Note that of the ten friction plates, there are two types, the two outermost plates (type A) being slightly different to the inner ones (type B). Take care not to mix them up. On UK L and M models and US 1991 models, an anti-judder spring and spring seat fit between the outer friction plate and the clutch centre.

10 Remove the thrust washer from the damper shaft, noting which way round it fits **(see illustration)**.

11 Remove the clutch housing **(see illustration)**.

17.7a The clutch nut (arrowed) is staked against the damper shaft

17.7b Use the holding tool as shown when slackening the clutch nut

17.9 Remove the pressure plate, clutch plates and clutch centre as an assembly

17.10 Remove the thrust washer (arrowed) . . .

17.11 . . . and the clutch housing

17.12a Locate an Allen key as shown to prevent the sprocket turning

17.12b Remove the oil pump chain and sprockets

17.14 Check the plain plates for warpage

12 Note the pins on the oil pump drive sprocket behind the clutch housing which must locate in the holes in the back of the housing on reassembly. Using an Allen key located as shown **(see illustration)** to lock the oil pump driven sprocket, unscrew the sprocket bolt and remove the sprocket from the pump, then disengage the pump drive chain and withdraw the drive sprocket from the damper shaft **(see illustration).** Note the "IN" mark on the back of the oil pump driven sprocket which must face inwards. Remove the washer, thrust bearing and clutch housing guide from the damper shaft.

Inspection

13 After an extended period of service the clutch friction plates will wear and promote clutch slip. Place all the plain and friction plates together and measure their combined thickness using a vernier caliper. If the thickness is less than the service limit given in the Specifications at the beginning of the Chapter, the friction plates must be replaced as a set. Also, if any of the plates smell burnt or are glazed, they must be replaced as a set.

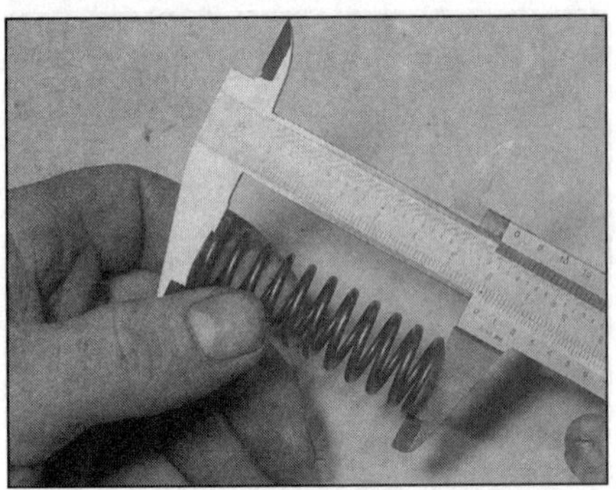
17.15 Measure the free length of the clutch springs

14 The plain plates should not show any signs of excess heating (bluing). Check for warpage using a surface plate and feeler gauges **(see illustration).** If any plate appears warped, or shows signs of bluing, all plain plates must be replaced as a set.

15 Measure the free length of each clutch spring using a vernier caliper **(see illustration).** If any spring is below the service limit specified, replace all the springs as a set.

16 Inspect the clutch assembly for burrs and indentations on the edges of the protruding tangs of the friction plates and/or slots in the edge of the housing with which they engage. Similarly check for wear between the inner tongues of the plain plates and the slots in the clutch centre. Wear of this nature will cause clutch drag and slow disengagement during gear changes, since the plates will snag when the pressure plate is lifted. With care, a small amount of wear can be corrected by dressing with a fine file, but if this is excessive the worn components should be replaced.

17 Check the release plate, release bearing, release rod and guide for signs of roughness, wear or damage, and replace any parts as necessary. Check that the bearing outer race is a tight fit in the centre of the plate, and that the inner race rotates freely without any rough spots. Check that the release rod is straight by rolling it on a flat surface.

18 Measure the clutch housing guide inner and outer diameters, and the diameter of the damper shaft where the guide fits. Compare the measurements to the specifications and replace the guide and/or the shaft if they are worn beyond their service limits. Also check all the above components for signs of damage or scoring, and replace if necessary.

19 Check the pressure plate and thrust washer for signs of roughness, wear or damage, and replace any parts as necessary.

20 On UK L and M models and US 1991 models, check the anti-judder spring and spring seat for distortion, wear or damage, and replace them if necessary.

Installation

21 Remove all traces of old gasket from the crankcase and clutch cover surfaces.

22 Smear the clutch housing guide with clean engine oil, then slide it onto the primary drive damper shaft, followed by the thrust bearing and washer **(see illustrations).**

23 Install the oil pump drive sprocket onto the shaft with its pins facing out, then loop the

17.22a Slide the housing guide . . .

17.22b . . . thrust bearing . . .

17.22c . . . and washer onto the shaft

17.23a Fit the drive sprocket onto the shaft . . .

17.23b . . . then loop the chain around it

17.23c The "IN" mark on the driven sprocket must face in

chain around the sprocket **(see illustrations)**. Fit the driven sprocket into the chain, making sure that the "IN" mark on the driven sprocket faces the engine, and mount it onto the pump **(see illustration)**. Apply a suitable non-permanent thread locking compound to the driven sprocket bolt and tighten it to the torque setting specified at the beginning of the Chapter **(see illustrations and Tool Tip)**.

> **TOOL TiP** *Insert an Allen key through one of the holes in the sprocket and lock it against the crankcase to prevent the sprocket from turning whilst tightening the bolt.*

24 Install the clutch housing onto the housing guide on the mainshaft, making sure that the teeth of the primary driven gear on the clutch housing engage with those of the primary drive gear, and that the pins on the oil pump drive sprocket engage with the holes in the rear of the housing **(see illustration)**. The primary driven gear teeth will be felt to engage with the outer sprung gear on the drive gear and then go no further. At this point twist the housing anti-clockwise using a steel bar to align the sprung gear with the main gear - the housing will be felt to slide further when they engage **(see illustration)**. Use a screwdriver to turn the oil pump driven sprocket to locate the pins in their holes.

25 Install the thrust washer onto the shaft, making sure its chamfered side faces out, followed by the clutch pressure plate **(see illustrations)**.

26 Coat each clutch plate with engine oil, then build up the plates in the housing, making sure the two outermost (type A) friction plates are correctly identified. Start with a type A friction plate, then a plain plate and alternating type B friction and plain plates

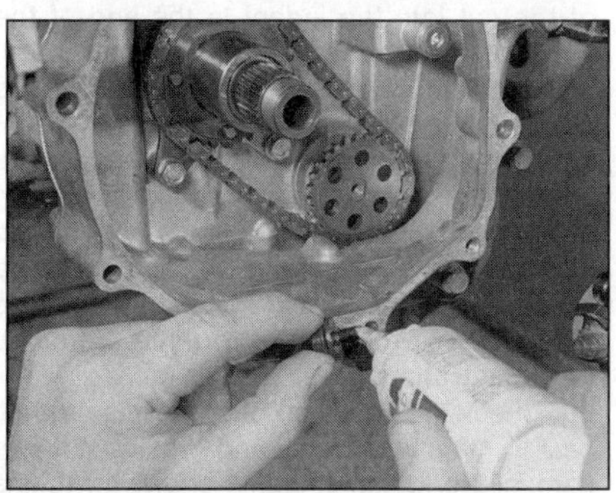
17.23d Apply a thread locking compound to the sprocket bolt . . .

17.23e . . . and tighten it to the specified torque setting

17.24a Align the pins (A) with the holes (B) when installing the housing

17.24b Use a steel bar as shown to help engage the primary drive and driven gear teeth

17.25a Install the thrust washer . . .

17.25b . . . and the pressure plate . . .

17.26a . . . followed by alternating friction . . .

17.26b . . . and plain plates

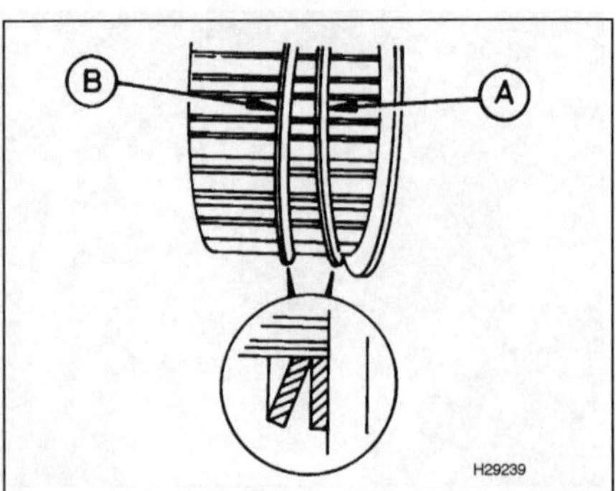

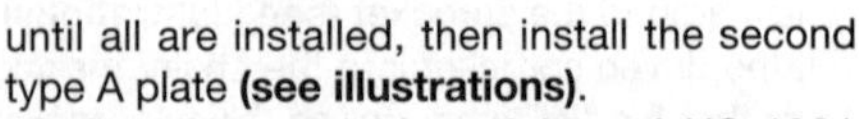
17.27 Correct fitting of spring seat (A) and anti-judder spring (B)

17.28a Install the clutch centre . . .

17.28b . . . aligning the marks as shown . . .

17.28c . . . then fit the washer with its OUT mark facing out

17.28d Fit the clutch nut . . .

until all are installed, then install the second type A plate **(see illustrations)**.

27 On UK L and M models and US 1991 models, install the spring seat onto the clutch centre, followed by the anti-judder spring seat, making sure its raised inner edge faces the front of the engine **(see illustration)**.

28 Install the clutch centre onto the damper shaft splines, aligning the triangle on the centre with that on the pressure plate, then install the washer with its OUT marking facing out **(see illustrations)**. Fit a new clutch nut, and using the method employed on removal to lock the damper shaft, tighten the nut to the torque setting specified at the beginning of the Chapter **(see illustrations)**. Stake the rim of the nut into the indent in the end of the shaft using a suitable punch **(see illustration)**. **Note:** *Check that the clutch centre rotates freely after tightening.*

29 Install the clutch springs, release plate and release plate bolts and tighten them evenly in a criss-cross sequence **(see illustrations)**. Lubricate the release rod guide with clean engine oil and fit it into the release plate, then fit the release rod into the guide **(see illustrations)**.

30 Check the condition of the release rod oil seal in the clutch cover and replace it if it is damaged or deteriorated, or shows any signs of leakage **(see illustrations)**. Apply grease to the lips of the seal. If removed, insert the dowels in the crankcase. Install the clutch

17.28e . . . and tighten it to the specified torque setting

17.28f Stake the nut against the shaft using a punch

17.29a Install the springs . . .

17.29b . . . and the release plate

17.29c Fit the guide into the plate . . .

17.29d . . . and the rod into the guide

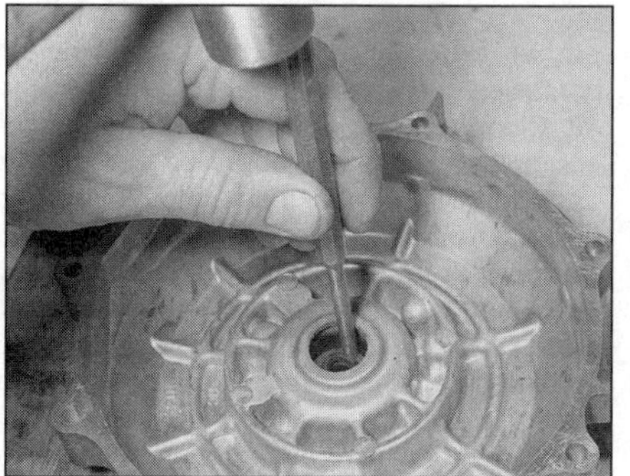
17.30a Drive the old seal out from the inside . . .

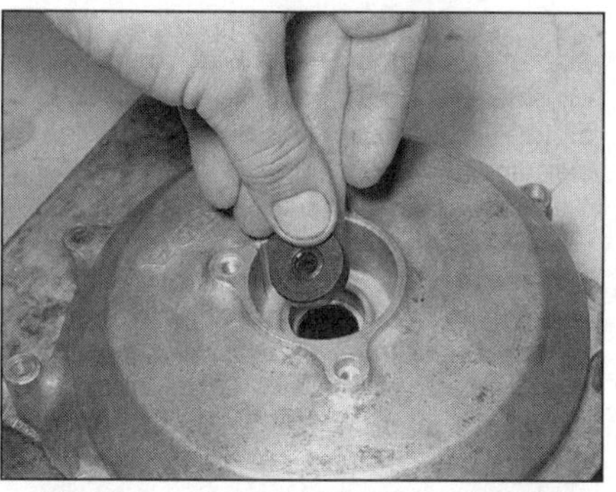
17.30b . . . and press the new seal into place

17.30c Make sure the gasket locates over the dowels . . .

17.30d . . . then fit the cover

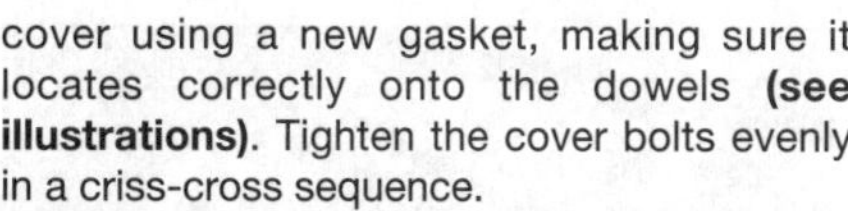
cover using a new gasket, making sure it locates correctly onto the dowels **(see illustrations)**. Tighten the cover bolts evenly in a criss-cross sequence.

31 Install the clutch slave cylinder (see Section 19).

32 Install the right-hand exhaust downpipe section (see Chapter 4).

33 Refill the engine with oil (see Chapter 1).

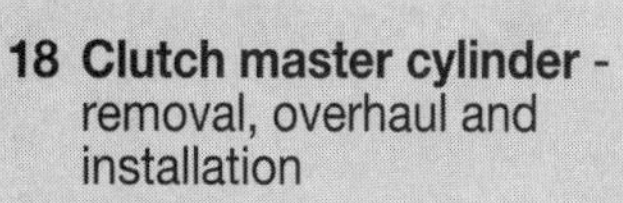
18 Clutch master cylinder - removal, overhaul and installation

1 If the master cylinder is leaking fluid, or if the clutch does not work when the lever is applied, and bleeding the system does not help (see Section 20), and the hydraulic hoses are all in good condition, then master cylinder overhaul is recommended.

2 Before disassembling the master cylinder, read through the entire procedure and make sure that you have the correct rebuild kit **(see illustration)**. Also, you will need some new DOT 4 hydraulic brake and clutch fluid, some clean rags and internal circlip pliers. **Note:** *To*

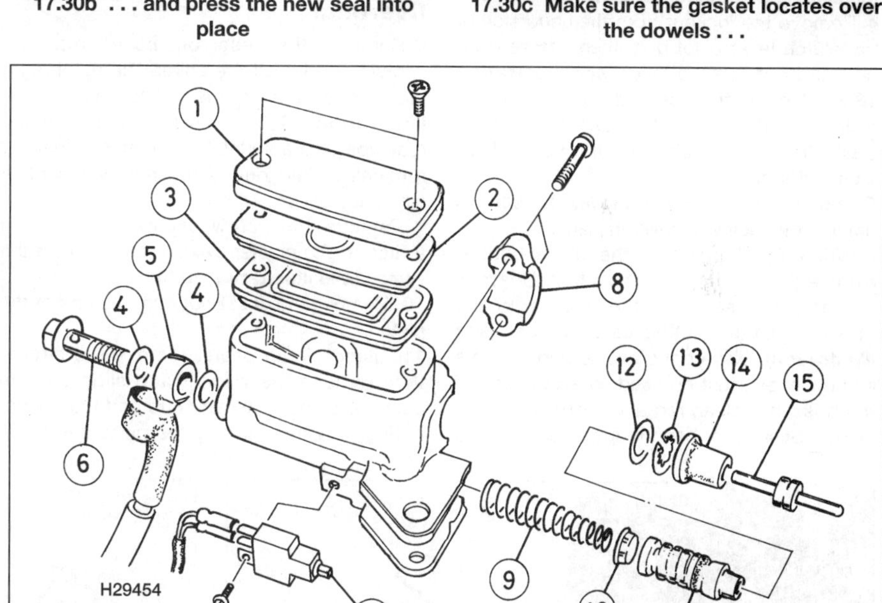

18.2 Clutch master cylinder components

1 Reservoir cover
2 Diaphragm plate
3 Diaphragm
4 Sealing washers
5 Clutch hose
6 Banjo bolt
7 Clutch switch
8 Master cylinder clamp
9 Spring
10 Primary cup
11 Piston
12 Washer
13 Circlip
14 Dust boot
15 Pushrod

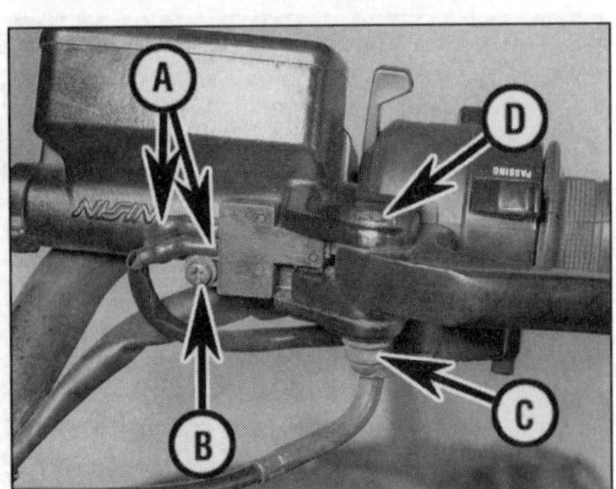

18.3 Clutch switch connectors (A) and mounting screw (B), clutch lever locknut (C) and pivot bolt (D)

18.4a Withdraw the pushrod from the master cylinder . . .

18.4b . . . and remove the bush from the lever

prevent damage to the paint from spilled brake fluid, always cover the fuel tank and fairing (where fitted) when working on the master cylinder.

Caution: Disassembly, overhaul and reassembly of the master cylinder must be done in a spotlessly clean work area to avoid contamination and possible failure of the hydraulic system components.

Removal

3 Disconnect the electrical connectors from the clutch switch **(see illustration)**.

4 Remove the locknut from the underside of the clutch lever pivot bolt, then unscrew the bolt and remove the lever **(see illustration 18.3)**. Remove the pushrod from the master cylinder. Take care not to lose the pushrod bush from its socket in the lever **(see illustrations)**.

5 Loosen, but do not remove, the screws holding the reservoir cover in place.

6 Where fitted, pull back the rubber boot to expose the clutch hose banjo bolt. Unscrew the bolt and separate the hose from the master cylinder, noting its alignment **(see illustration)**. Discard the two sealing washers as new ones must be used. Wrap the end of the hose in a clean rag and suspend it in an upright position or bend it down carefully and place the open end in a clean container. The objective is to prevent excessive loss of clutch fluid, fluid spills and system contamination.

7 Remove the master cylinder clamp mounting bolts, noting how the top mating surfaces of the clamp align with the punch mark on the handlebar **(see illustration)**. Lift the master cylinder and reservoir away from the handlebar.

Caution: Do not tip the master cylinder upside down or fluid will run out.

Overhaul

8 Remove the reservoir cover retaining screws and lift off the cover, the diaphragm plate and the rubber diaphragm **(see illustration 18.2)**. Drain the fluid from the reservoir into a suitable container. Wipe any remaining fluid out of the reservoir with a clean rag.

9 Remove the screw securing the clutch switch to the master cylinder and remove the switch **(see illustration 18.3)**.

10 Remove the dust boot from the end of the piston.

11 Using circlip pliers, remove the circlip, then remove the washer and slide out the piston assembly, primary cup and the spring, noting how they fit. Lay the parts out in the proper order and way round to prevent confusion during reassembly.

12 Clean all parts with clean DOT 4 fluid. If compressed air is available, use it to dry the parts thoroughly (make sure it's filtered and unlubricated).

Caution: Do not, under any circumstances, use a petroleum-based solvent to clean clutch parts.

13 Check the master cylinder bore for corrosion, scratches, nicks and score marks. If the necessary measuring equipment is available, compare the dimensions of the piston and bore to those given in the Specifications Section of this Chapter. If damage or wear is evident, the master cylinder must be replaced with a new one. If the master cylinder is in poor condition, then the release cylinder should be checked as well (see Section 19). Check that the fluid inlet and outlet ports in the master cylinder are clear.

14 The dust boot, circlip, washer, piston assembly, primary cup and spring are included in the rebuild kit. Use all of the new parts, regardless of the apparent condition of the old ones.

15 Install the spring in the master cylinder bore so that its tapered (narrow) end faces out.

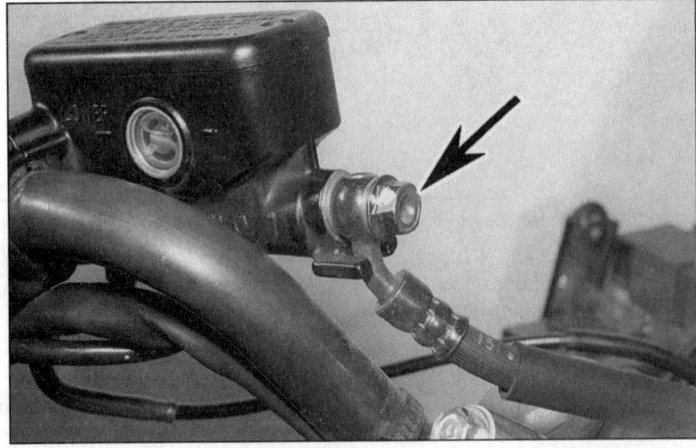

18.6 Note the alignment of the hose before removing the bolt (arrowed)

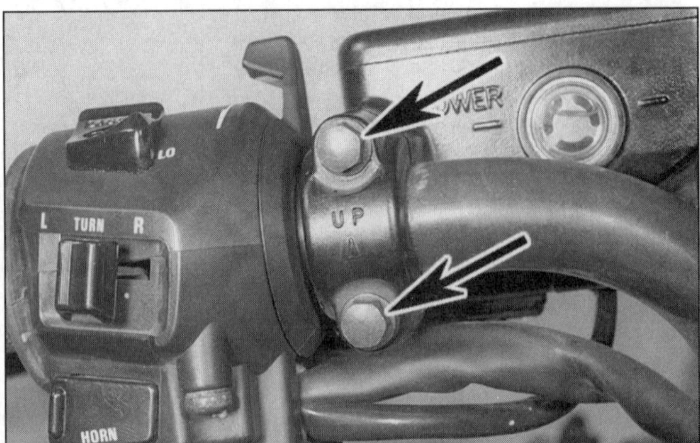

18.7 Clutch master cylinder mounting bolts (arrowed)

18.20 Fit the clamp with the UP mark facing up and align the mating surfaces with the punchmark (arrowed)

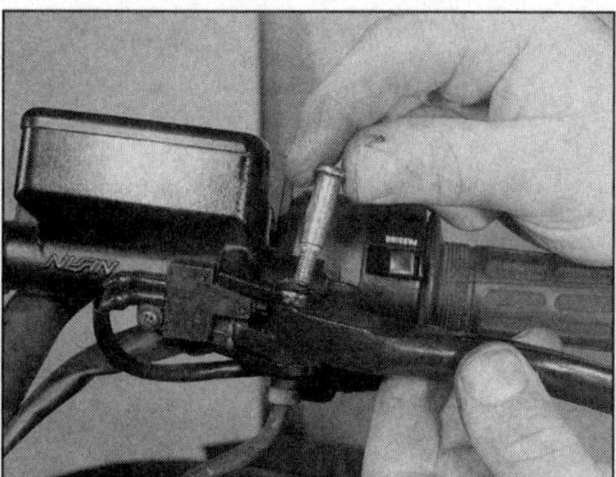
18.22 Install the lever and tighten the pivot bolt

18.25 Make sure the diaphragm is seated before fitting the plate and cover

16 Lubricate the cup and piston with clean brake fluid, and place a dab of silicone grease into the outer end of the piston. Install them into the master cylinder, making sure they are the correct way round. Make sure the lips on the cup do not turn inside out when they are slipped into the bore. Depress the piston and install the washer and circlip, making sure that it locates in the master cylinder groove.
17 Install the rubber dust boot and pushrod **(see illustration 18.4a)**.
18 Install the clutch switch.
19 Inspect the reservoir cover rubber diaphragm and replace if damaged or deteriorated.

Installation

20 Attach the master cylinder to the handlebar and fit the clamp, making sure the UP mark faces up. Align the top mating surfaces of the clamp with the punchmark on the handlebar, then tighten the bolts to the torque setting specified at the beginning of the Chapter **(see illustration)**.
21 Connect the clutch hose to the master cylinder, using new sealing washers on each side of the union, and aligning the hose as noted on removal **(see illustration 18.6)**. Tighten the banjo bolt to the torque setting specified at the beginning of this Chapter.
22 Apply silicone grease to the pushrod bush and to the lever pivot bolt. Fit the pushrod bush into the clutch lever **(see illustration 18.4b)**, then fit the lever into its bracket and tighten the pivot bolt to the specified torque setting **(see illustration)**. Now fit and tighten the pivot bolt locknut to the specified torque.
23 Connect the clutch switch wiring **(see illustration 18.3)**.
24 Fill the fluid reservoir with DOT 4 fluid (see *Daily (pre-ride) checks*). Refer to Section 20 of this Chapter and bleed the air from the system.
25 Fit the rubber diaphragm, making sure it is correctly seated, the diaphragm plate and the cover onto the master cylinder reservoir **(see illustration)**.

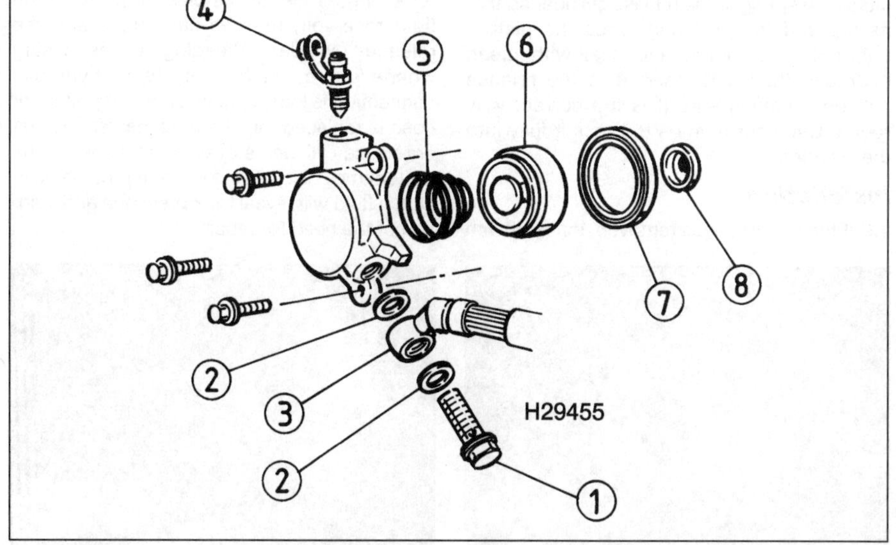

19.2a Clutch release cylinder components

1 *Banjo bolt*
2 *Sealing washer*
3 *Clutch hose*
4 *Bleed valve*
5 *Spring*
6 *Piston*
7 *Piston seal*
8 *Pushrod oil seal*

19 Clutch release cylinder - removal, overhaul and installation

Note: *If the release cylinder is only being removed for access to the clutch, and is not being overhauled, there is no need to disconnect the hydraulic hose (Step 2).*

Removal

1 Remove the lower fairing (see Chapter 8).
2 Remove the clutch hose banjo bolt and separate the hose from the release cylinder, noting its alignment **(see illustrations)**. Plug the hose end or wrap a plastic bag around it to minimise fluid loss and prevent dirt entering the system. Discard the sealing washers as new ones must be used on installation. **Note:** *If you're planning to overhaul the release cylinder and don't have a source of compressed air to blow out the piston, just loosen the banjo bolt at this stage and retighten it lightly. The hydraulic system can then be used to force the piston out of the body once the cylinder has been unbolted. Disconnect the hose once the piston has been sufficiently displaced.*

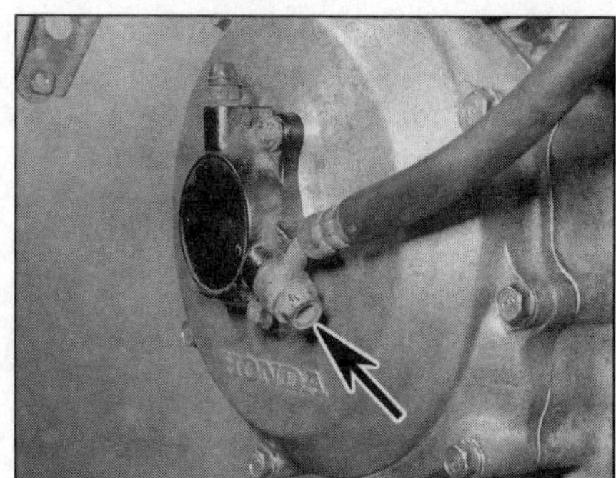
19.2b Note the alignment of the hose before removing the bolt (arrowed)

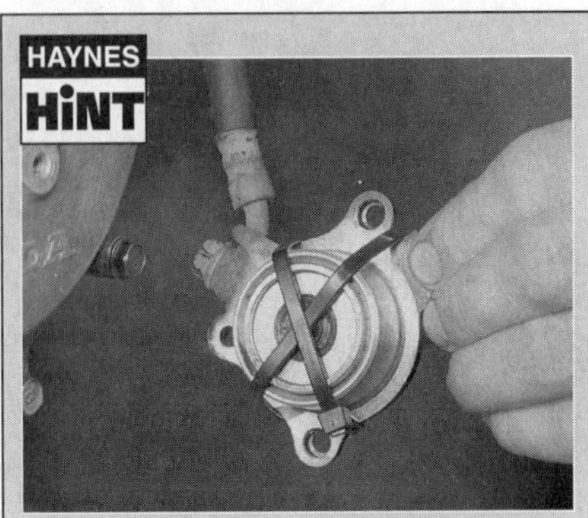

If the release cylinder is not being disassembled, the piston can be prevented from creeping out of the release cylinder by restraining it with a couple of cable ties

3 Unscrew the three bolts securing the release cylinder to the clutch cover and withdraw the cylinder from the cover (see **Haynes Hint**). Retrieve the two dowels if they are loose. Discard the gasket as a new one must be used. If required, withdraw the release rod from the clutch **(see illustrations)**. Do not operate the clutch lever with the release cylinder removed

Overhaul

4 The release cylinder housing in the clutch cover has a slot in its underside which allows the escape of hydraulic fluid in the event of the piston seal failing. Hydraulic fluid might otherwise be forced under pressure past the single-lipped pushrod seal and into the clutch.
5 Have a supply of clean rags on hand, then pump the clutch lever to expel the piston under hydraulic pressure. If the hose has already been detached, use a jet of compressed air directed into the fluid inlet to expel the piston **(see illustration)**.

Warning: Use only low air pressure, otherwise the piston may be forcibly expelled causing injury. Wrap the cylinder in a rag before applying the air.

6 Recover the spring from the piston **(see illustration 19.2a)**.

19.3a Unscrew the three bolts and remove the cylinder

7 Using a plastic or wooden tool, remove the piston seal from the piston groove. Also remove the pushrod oil seal. Discard both seals as new ones must be used.
8 Clean the piston and release cylinder bore with clean hydraulic fluid.
Caution: Do not, under any circumstances, use a petroleum-based solvent to clean hydraulic parts.
9 Inspect the piston and release cylinder bore for signs of corrosion, nicks and burrs and loss of plating. If surface defects are found, the piston and cylinder should be replaced. If the release cylinder is in poor condition the master cylinder should also be overhauled (see Section 18).
10 Check the condition of the release rod oil seal in the clutch cover and replace it if it is damaged or deteriorated, or shows any signs of leakage **(see illustrations 17.30a and b)**. It may be necessary to remove the clutch cover to remove the old seal (see Section 17, Steps 1 to 4). Apply grease to the lips of the seal.
11 Lubricate the new piston seal with clean hydraulic fluid and install it on the piston. Install the spring in the release cylinder so that its tapered (narrow) end faces the piston. Lubricate the piston and seal with clean hydraulic fluid and insert it in the release cylinder, making sure it is the correct way round. Use your thumbs to press it fully into the cylinder.

Installation

12 If the pushrod was removed, smear it with engine oil and slide it back into the clutch cover **(see illustration 19.3b)**.

19.3b Withdraw the release rod if required

13 Fit the dowels into the clutch cover if removed, then install the release cylinder using a new gasket and tighten the bolts securely **(see illustrations)**.
14 If the hydraulic hose was disconnected, use a new sealing washer on each side of the banjo union. Position the union as noted on removal and tighten the banjo bolt to the specified torque setting **(see illustration 19.2b)**.
15 Remove the two master cylinder reservoir cover screws and lift off the cover, diaphragm plate and diaphragm. Fill the reservoir with new hydraulic fluid (see *Daily (pre-ride) checks*) and bleed the system as described in the next Section.

20 Clutch - bleeding

1 Bleeding the clutch is simply the process of removing all the air bubbles from the clutch fluid reservoir, the hydraulic hose and the release cylinder. Bleeding is necessary whenever a clutch system hydraulic connection is loosened, when a component or hose is replaced, or when the master cylinder or release cylinder is overhauled. Leaks in the system may also allow air to enter, but leaking clutch fluid will reveal their presence and warn you of the need for repair.

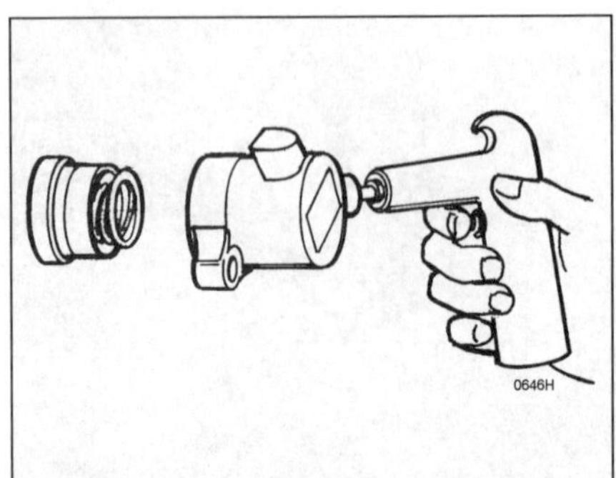

19.5 A jet of compressed air directed into the fluid inlet will expel the piston

19.13a Make sure the gasket locates over the dowels . . .

19.13b . . . then install the release cylinder

2 To bleed the clutch, you will need some new DOT 4 brake and clutch fluid, a length of clear vinyl or plastic tubing, a small container partially filled with clean fluid, a supply of clean rags and a spanner to fit the bleed valve.
3 Cover the fuel tank and other painted components to prevent damage in the event that fluid is spilled.
4 Position the bike on its centrestand so that the master cylinder is level. Remove the two screws securing the master cylinder reservoir cover, then lift off the cover, diaphragm plate and diaphragm. Slowly pump the clutch lever a few times until no air bubbles can be seen floating up from the bottom of the reservoir. Doing this bleeds air from the master cylinder end of the hose.
5 Pull the dust cap off the bleed valve on the release cylinder and attach one end of the clear tubing to the valve. Submerge the other end in the fluid in the container. Check the fluid level in the reservoir. Do not allow it to drop below the lower mark during the bleeding process.
6 Pump the clutch lever three or four times and hold it in against the handlebar whilst opening the bleed valve. When the valve is opened, fluid will flow out of the release cylinder into the clear tubing.
7 Tighten the bleed valve, then release the lever gradually. Repeat the process until no air bubbles are visible in the fluid leaving the release cylinder and the clutch action feels smooth and progressive. On completion, tighten the bleed valve to the torque setting specified at the beginning of the Chapter.
8 Ensure that the reservoir is topped up above the lower level mark on the sightglass, install the diaphragm, diaphragm plate and cover and secure them with the two screws. Wipe up any spilled fluid and check that there are no leaks from the system. Refit the dust cap over the bleed valve.

21 Oil sump and oil strainer - removal, inspection and installation

Note: *The oil sump and strainer can be removed with the engine in the frame. If the engine has been removed, ignore the steps which don't apply.*

Removal

1 Drain the engine oil (see Chapter 1).
2 Remove the exhaust system (see Chapter 4).
3 Unscrew the sump bolts, slackening them evenly in a criss-cross sequence to prevent distortion, and remove the sump **(see illustration)**. Discard the gasket as a new one must be used.
4 Remove the oil strainer from the oil pump. Remove the rubber seal and discard it as a new one must be used **(see illustrations)**.

Inspection

5 Remove all traces of gasket from the sump and crankcase mating surfaces.
6 Clean the sump, making sure all the oil passages are free of any debris.
7 Make sure the oil strainer is clean and remove any debris caught in the mesh. Inspect the strainer for any signs of wear or damage and replace it if necessary.

Installation

8 Fit a new rubber seal into the oil strainer passage in the oil pump **(see illustration)**. Do not fit it onto the strainer as it will distort when the strainer is fitted onto the pump.
9 Install the strainer onto the pump, locating the cutout in the strainer base over the lug on the pump **(see illustration 21.4a)**.
10 Lay a new gasket onto the sump (if the engine is in the frame) or onto the crankcase (if the engine has been removed and is positioned upside down on the work surface) **(see illustration)**. Make sure the holes in the gasket align correctly with the bolt holes.
11 Position the sump onto the crankcase and install the bolts **(see illustration)**. Tighten the bolts evenly in a criss-cross pattern to the torque setting specified at the beginning of the Chapter.
12 Install the exhaust system (see Chapter 3).
13 Fill the engine with the correct type and quantity of oil as described in Chapter 1. Start the engine and check for leaks around the sump.

21.3 The sump is secured by 14 bolts (arrowed)

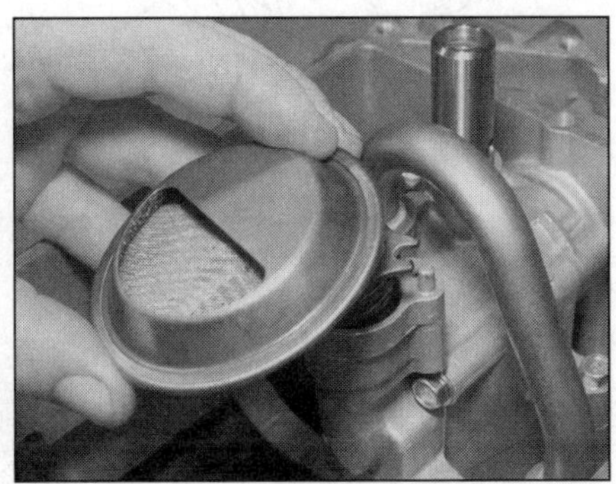

21.4a Remove the oil strainer . . .

21.4b . . . and discard the rubber seal

21.8 Press the new seal into the passage in the pump (arrowed)

21.10 Lay the new gasket on the sump or crankcase as appropriate . . .

21.11 . . . then fit the sump

22.3 Unscrew the three bolts (arrowed) and remove the pipe

22.4 Unscrew the two bolts (arrowed) and remove the pump

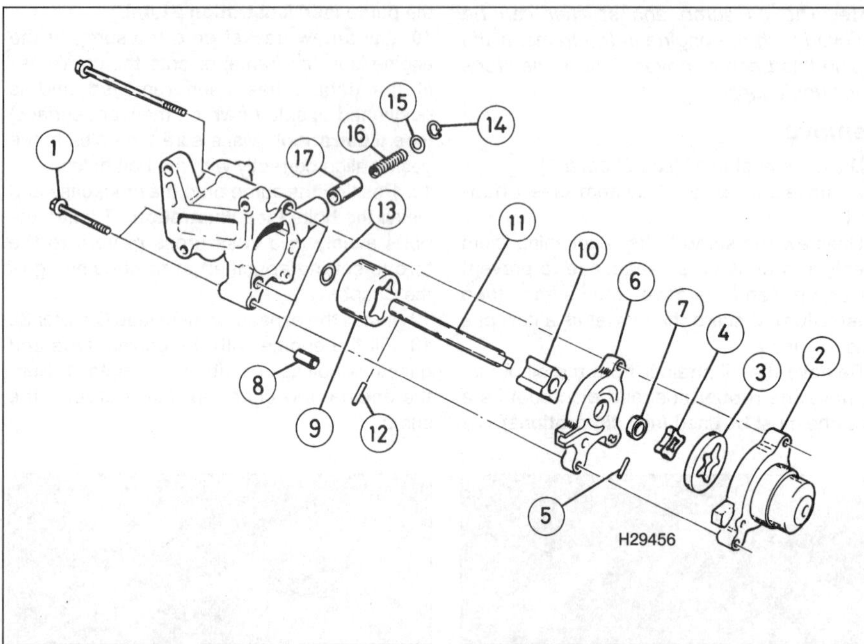

22.5a Oil pump components

1 *Pump bolts*
2 *Cover*
3 *Scavenging pump outer rotor*
4 *Scavenging pump inner rotor*
5 *Scavenging pump drive pin*
6 *Scavenging pump cover*
7 *Oil seal*
8 *Dowels*
9 *Outer rotor*
10 *Inner rotor*
11 *Drive shaft*
12 *Drive pin*
13 *Washer*
14 *Circlip*
15 *Washer*
16 *Spring*
17 *Relief valve plunger*

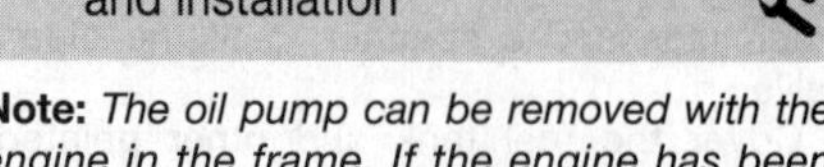

22 Oil pump and pressure relief valve - removal, inspection and installation

Note: *The oil pump can be removed with the engine in the frame. If the engine has been removed, ignore the steps which don't apply.*

Removal

1 Remove the sump and oil strainer (see Section 21).

2 Remove the clutch (see Section 17).

3 Unscrew the bolts securing the oil pipe to the pump and the crankcase **(see illustration)**. Remove the pipe, then remove the O-rings from the oil passages and discard them as new ones must be used.

4 Unscrew the bolts securing the pump to the crankcase, then remove the pump, noting how it fits **(see illustration)**. Remove the O-ring from the pump and discard it as a new one must be used.

Inspection

5 Unscrew the three bolts securing the pump body to the cover, then remove the cover **(see illustrations)**.

6 Remove the outer and inner rotors of the scavenging pump, then slide the drive pin out of the drive shaft. Note how the pin locates through the shaft and in the notches in the inner rotor, and note which way the punchmark on the outer rotor faces. Remove the dowels from either the body or the cover if they are loose.

7 Grasp the end of the shaft and remove the inner cover, shaft and rotors as one **(see illustration)**. The outer rotor may stay in the pump. Note which way the punchmark on the outer rotor faces. Note how the pin locates through the shaft and in the notches in the inner rotor. Remove the washer from inside the pump body or from the end of the drive shaft.

Caution: It is important that the shaft is not withdrawn from the oil seal in the inner cover, as the seal is easily damaged by the sharp edges of the shaft end. The oil seal is not available as a separate component, so if it is damaged the entire pump must

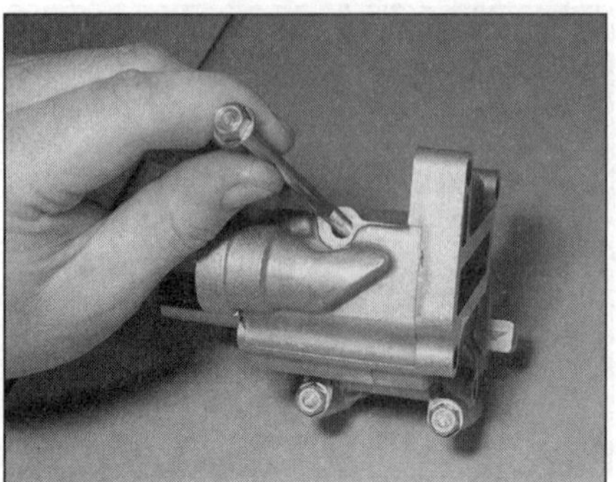
22.5b Unscrew the three bolts . . .

22.5c . . . and remove the cover

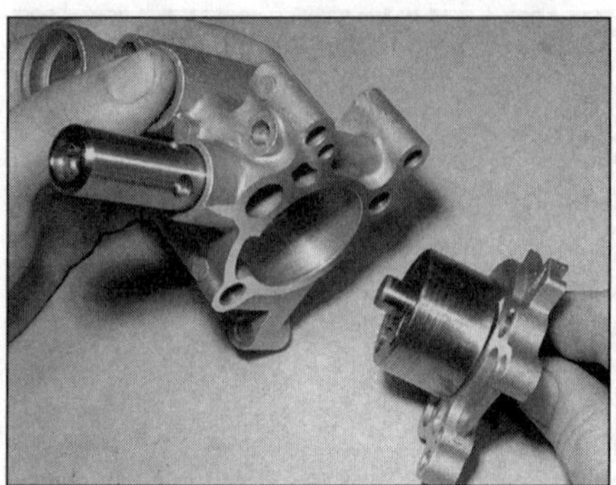
22.7 Withdraw the pump assembly from the body

22.9 Look for scoring and wear, such as on this outer rotor

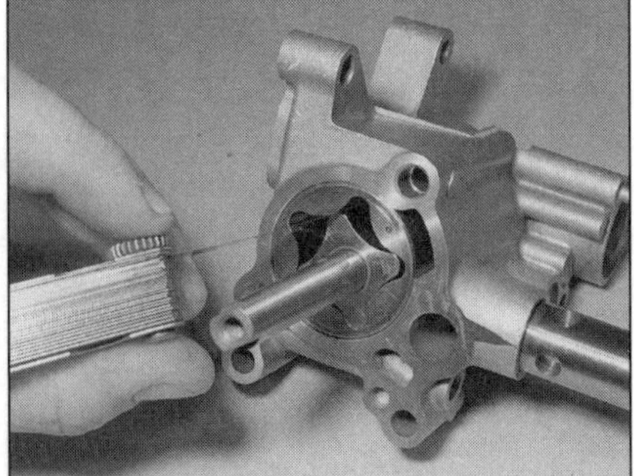
22.10 Measure the inner rotor tip-to-outer rotor clearance as shown (inner cover shown removed for clarity)

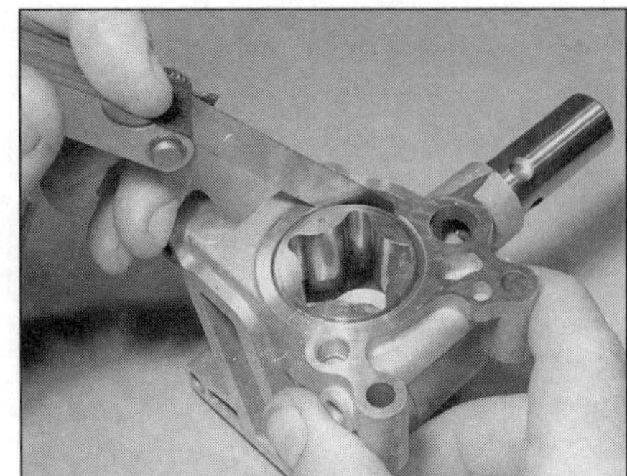
22.11 Measure the outer rotor-to-body clearance as shown

be replaced. The seal has no size markings which makes it difficult to obtain one from a seal supplier.

8 Clean all the components in solvent.

9 Inspect the pump body and rotors for scoring and wear. If any damage, scoring or uneven or excessive wear is evident, replace the pump (individual components are not available) **(see illustration)**.

10 Fit the inner and outer rotors into the pump body. Measure the clearance between the inner rotor tip and the outer rotor with a feeler gauge and compare it to the maximum clearance listed in the specifications at the beginning of the Chapter **(see illustration)**. If the clearance measured is greater than the maximum listed, replace the pump.

11 Measure the clearance between the outer rotor and the pump body with a feeler gauge and compare it to the maximum clearance listed in the specifications at the beginning of the Chapter **(see illustration)**. If the clearance measured is greater than the maximum listed, replace the pump.

12 Lay a straight edge across the rotors and the pump body and, using a feeler gauge, measure the rotor end float (the gap between the rotors and the straight edge) **(see illustration)**. If the clearance measured is greater than the maximum listed, replace the pump.

13 Remove the circlip from the end of the relief valve body and withdraw the washer, spring and valve plunger **(see illustrations)**. Clean all the components in solvent. Check that the plunger moves freely in the body and inspect it for wear or damage. If the valve is good, install the plunger into the body, followed by the spring and the washer, and secure them in place with the circlip.

14 Check the pump drive chain and sprockets for wear or damage, and replace them as a set if necessary.

15 If the pump is good, make sure all the components are clean, then lubricate them with new engine oil. Slide the inner rotor onto the shaft, then fit the drive pin into the hole and locate it in the notches in the back of the rotor. Install the thrust washer onto the end of the shaft, then fit the outer rotor over the inner rotor, with the punchmark facing the inner cover **(see illustrations)**. Install the assembly into the pump body, making sure the washer stays in place on the end of the shaft **(see illustration 22.7)**.

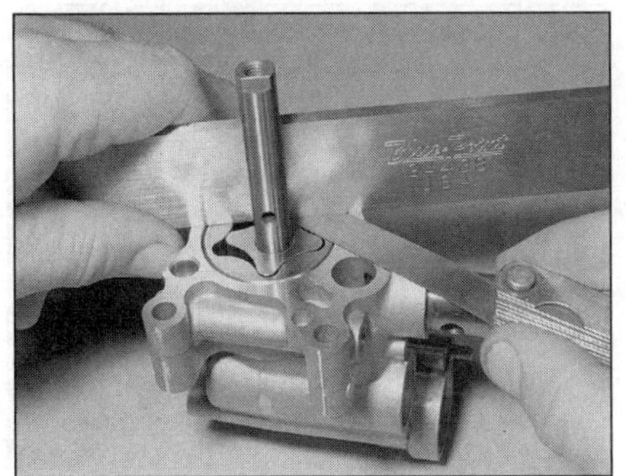
22.12 Measure the rotor end float as shown

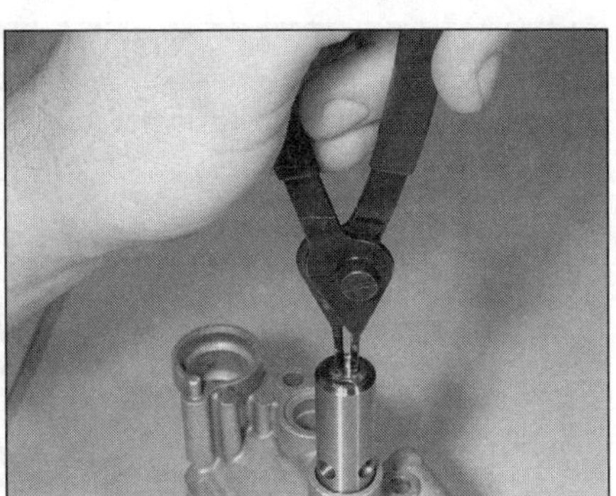
22.13a Remove the circlip . . .

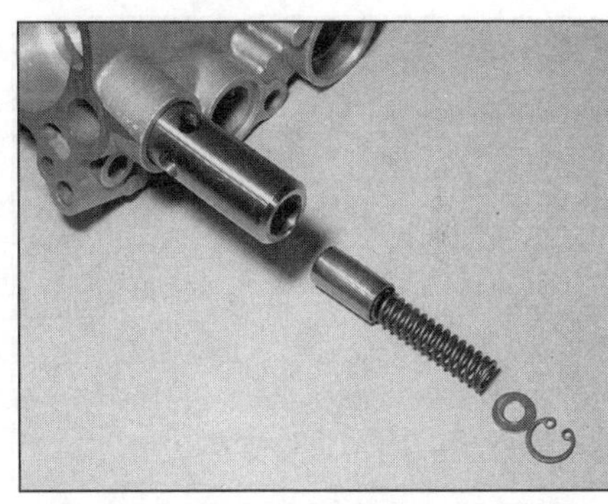
22.13b . . . and relief valve components

2

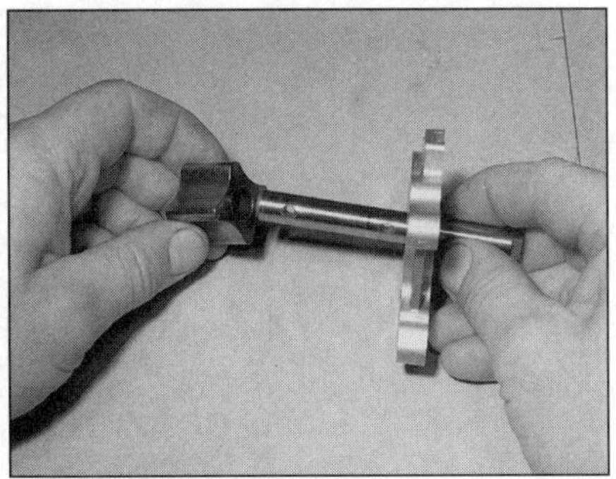
22.15a Slide the inner rotor onto the shaft . . .

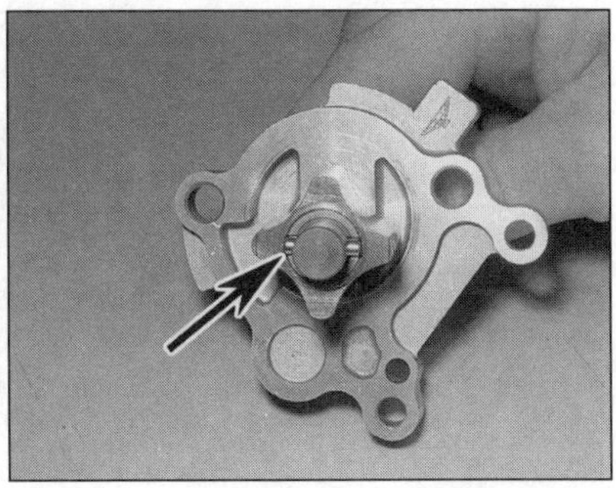
22.15b . . . and secure it with the drive pin (arrowed)

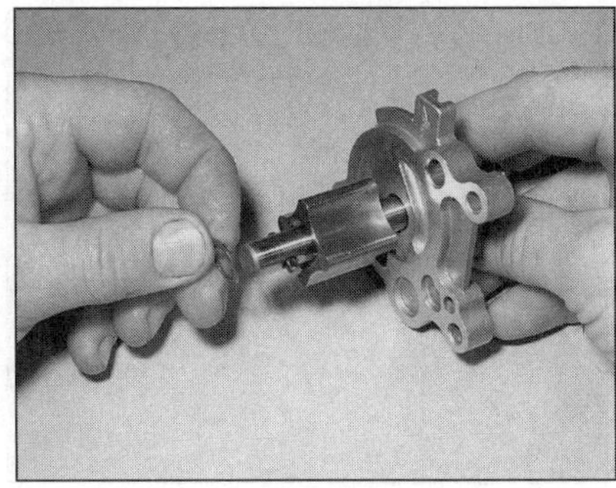
22.15c Fit the thrust washer . . .

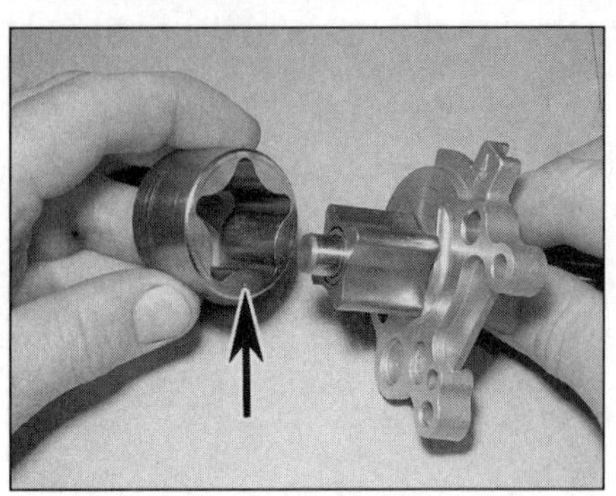

22.15d ... and the outer rotor, with its punchmark (arrowed) facing the inner cover

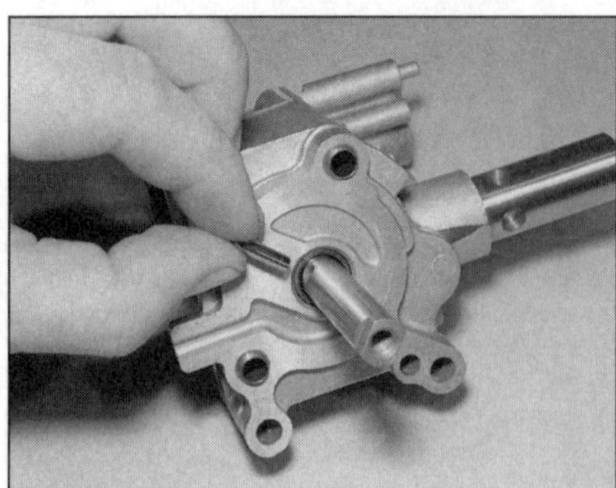

22.16a Fit the drive pin ...

22.16b ... followed by the inner and outer rotors

16 Fit the drive pin into the drive shaft. Install the inner rotor onto the shaft making sure the pin fits into the notches in the rotor. Install the scavenging pump outer rotor with the punchmark facing the way noted on removal (Honda specify that it should face out, but on the model used it faced in) **(see illustrations)**.

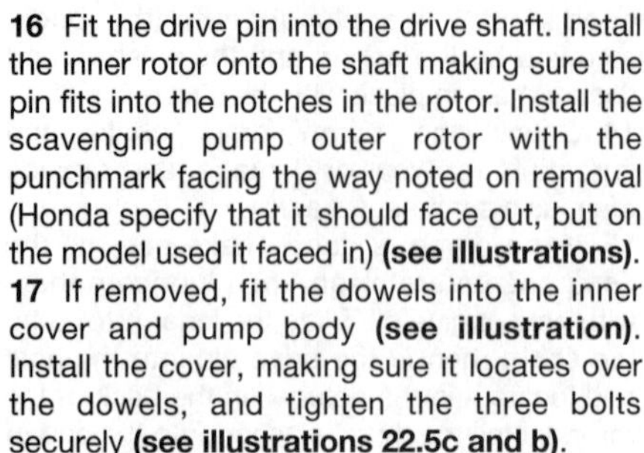

17 If removed, fit the dowels into the inner cover and pump body **(see illustration)**. Install the cover, making sure it locates over the dowels, and tighten the three bolts securely **(see illustrations 22.5c and b)**.

Installation

18 Fit a new O-ring onto the pump, then install the pump into the crankcase **(see illustrations)**.

19 Fit new O-rings into the oil pipe passages in the pump and crankcase, then install the pipe **(see illustrations)**. Install the pump and pipe bolts and tighten them securely **(see illustrations 22.4 and 22.3)**.

20 Install the clutch **(see** Section 17).

21 Install the sump and oil strainer (see Section 21).

23 Gearchange mechanism (external components) - removal, inspection and installation

Note: *The gearchange mechanism (external components) can be removed with the engine in the frame. If the engine has been removed, ignore the steps which don't apply.*

Removal

1 Remove the swingarm (see Chapter 6).

2 Shift the transmission into neutral. On UK L and M models and US 1991 models, make some alignment marks (if none are already visible) between the gearchange linkage arm and the shaft so that they can be correctly aligned on installation. On all other models, a wider spline aligns the arm. Unscrew the linkage arm pinch bolt and remove the arm from the shaft **(see illustration)**.

3 Unscrew the bolts securing the gearchange mechanism cover and remove the cover **(see**

22.17 Fit the dowels through the inner cover and into the pump body

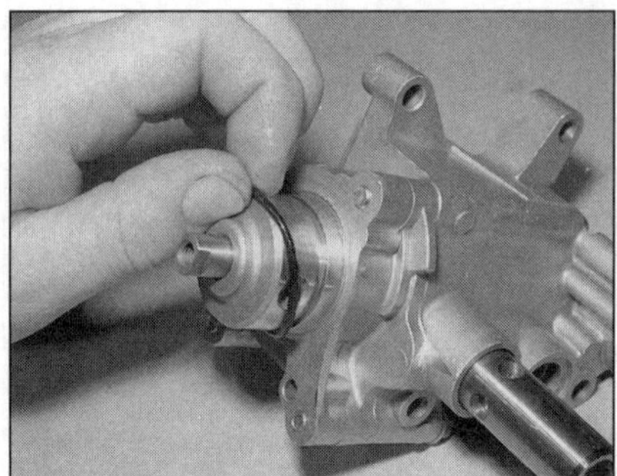

22.18a Fit a new O-ring ...

22.18b ... then install the pump

22.19a Fit new O-rings into the oil pipe passages ...

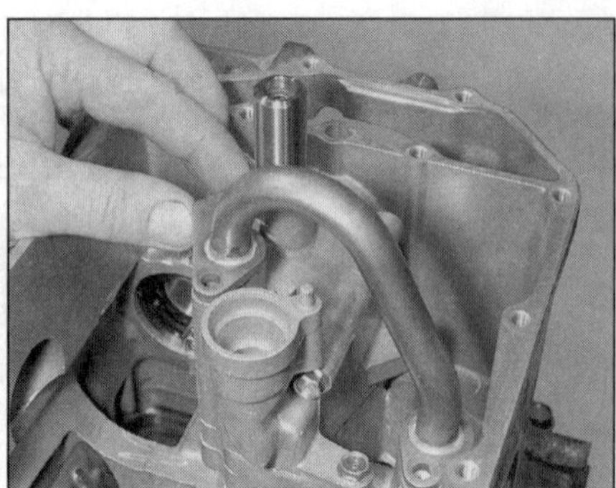

22.19b ... then fit the pipe

23.2 Unscrew the bolt (arrowed) and slide the arm off the shaft

23.3 The cover is secured by seven bolts (arrowed)

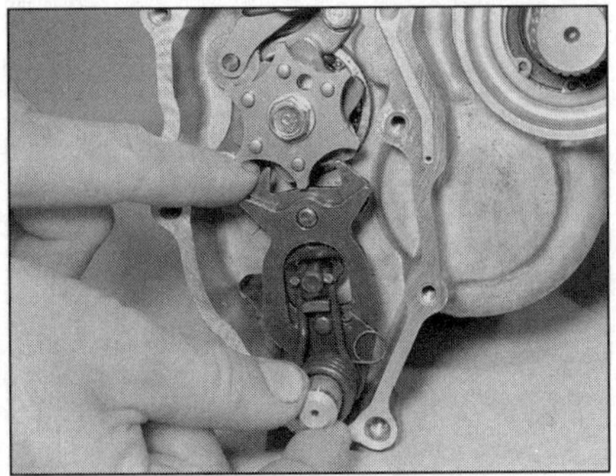
23.4a Press the arm down until it clears the outer stopper plate . . .

23.4b . . . then withdraw the shaft

illustration). Remove the dowels if they are loose. Discard the gasket as a new one must be used.

4 Note how the gearchange shaft centralising spring ends fit on each side of the locating pin in the casing, and how the teeth of the selector arm engage with the dowel pins on the selector drum. Press the selector arm down until it is clear of the stopper plate assembly on the drum and withdraw the gearchange shaft from the casing **(see illustrations)**.

5 Unscrew the bolt securing the selector drum stopper arm, then lift the stopper arm off the stopper plate on the selector drum and remove the arm with its collar, return spring and washer, noting how they fit **(see illustration)**.

6 If the selector drum and forks or transmission shafts are to be removed from the transmission casing, unscrew the bolt securing the stopper plate assembly to the selector drum, then remove the plate assembly, keeping the two plates together, noting how the slot in the back of the inner plate locates over the offset pin in the selector drum. The two plates can be separated if required, but note the relative positions of the plates and the dowel pins and take care not to lose any of the pins. Remove the pin if it is loose **(see illustrations)**.

Inspection

7 Inspect the selector arm and the stopper arm return springs and the shaft centralising spring. If they are fatigued, worn or damaged they must be replaced. Also check that the spring locating pin in the casing is securely tightened.

8 Check the gearchange shaft for straightness and damage to the splines. If the shaft is bent you can attempt to straighten it, but if the splines are damaged the shaft must be replaced. Also check the condition of the shaft oil seal in the casing and replace it if damaged or deteriorated. Lever the old seal out using a screwdriver and drive the new seal in squarely. Also check the condition of the needle bearing, though it is unlikely to wear unless the seal has failed **(see illustrations)**. Refer to *Tools and Workshop Tips (*Sections 5 and 6) in the Reference Section if the bearing requires replacement.

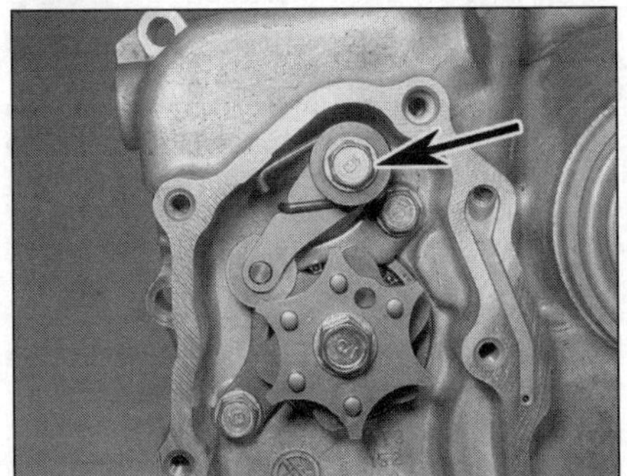
23.5 Unscrew the stopper arm bolt (arrowed) and remove the arm

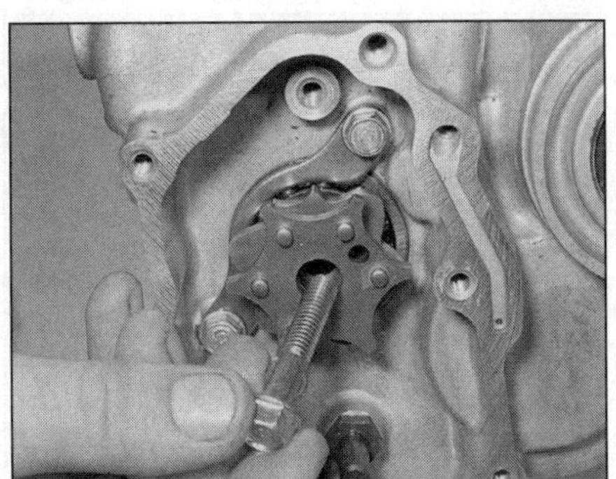
23.6a Unscrew the bolt and remove the plates

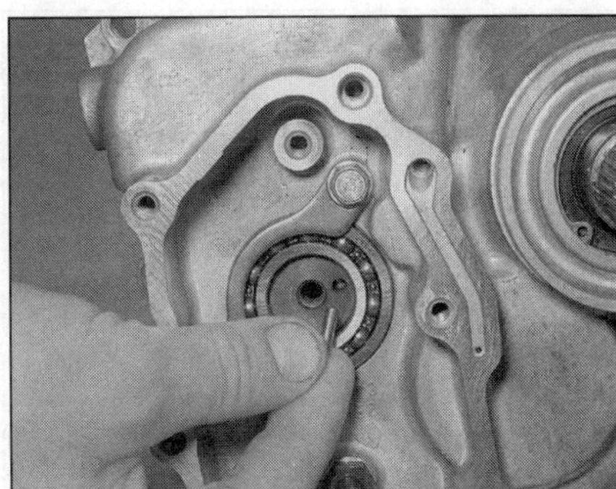
23.6b Remove the pin if it is loose

23.8a Lever out the old seal . . .

23.8b . . . and drive in the new one

23.8c Check the condition of the needle bearing

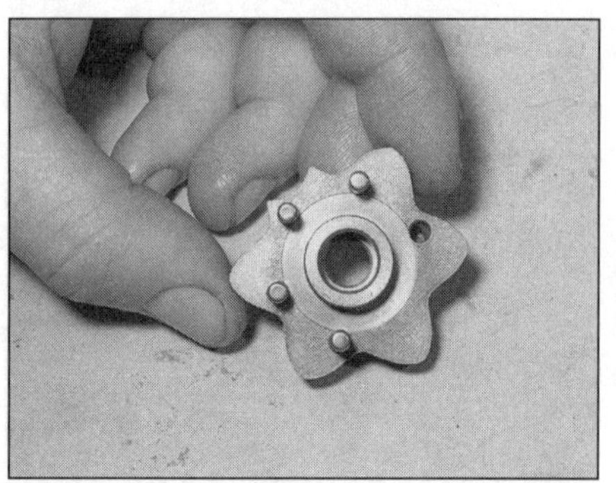

23.10a Locate the pins in the inner plate as shown . . .

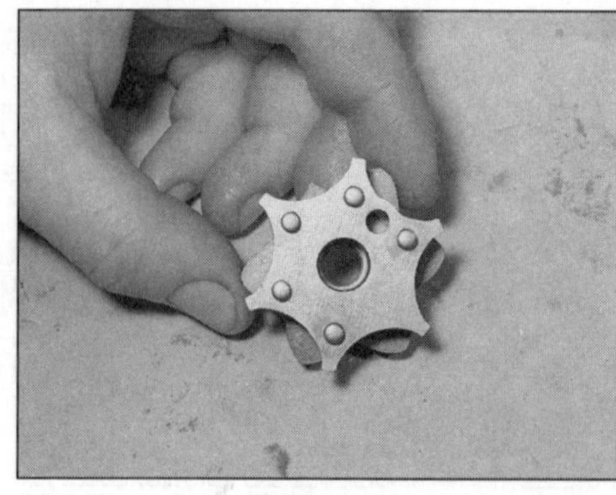

23.10b . . . then fit the outer plate onto the pins

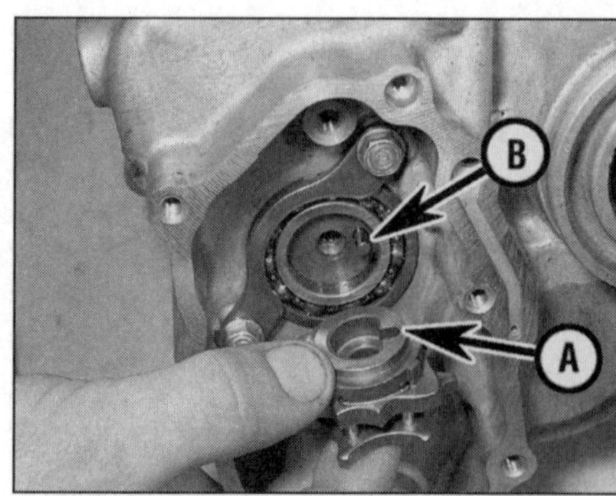

23.10c Locate the slot (A) over the pin (B)

9 Inspect the selector arm claw and the dowel pins, and the stopper arm roller and the stopper plates. If they are worn or damaged they must be replaced.

Installation

10 If removed, install the locating pin in the offset hole in the end of the selector drum **(see illustration 23.6b)**. If the stopper plates were separated and the pins removed, reassemble the plates as shown. Install the plate assembly, locating the slot in the back of the inner plate over the offset pin in the selector drum **(see illustrations)**. Install the bolt and tighten it to the torque setting specified at the beginning of the Chapter **(see illustration 23.6a)**.

11 Install the stopper arm bolt through the collar, the return spring, the stopper arm and the washer **(see illustration)**. Install the assembly onto the casing, positioning the stopper arm onto the stopper plate and making sure the spring ends are located correctly over the stopper arm and against the casing **(see illustration 23.5)**. Tighten the bolt securely. Make sure the stopper arm is free to move and is returned by the pressure of the spring.

12 Check that the shaft assembly components are correctly positioned, the install the shaft into its hole in the casing **(see illustration 23.4b)**. Press the arm down until it clears the stopper plate assembly and slide the shaft fully home, positioning the selector arm on the selector drum dowel pins. Make sure the centralising spring ends are correctly located on each side of the tab on the arm and the pin in the casing **(see illustrations)**.

13 Fit the dowels in the casing if removed, then install the cover using a new gasket and tighten the bolts evenly **(see illustration)**.

14 Install the gearchange linkage arm onto the end of the shaft on the left hand side of the engine, aligning the marks made on removal (UK L and M models and US 1991 models) or the wider splines (all other models), and check that the mechanism works correctly. Tighten the pinch bolt to the specified torque setting.

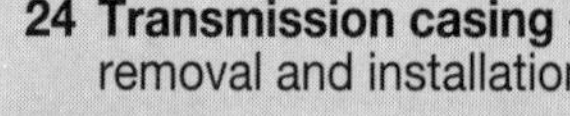

24 Transmission casing - removal and installation

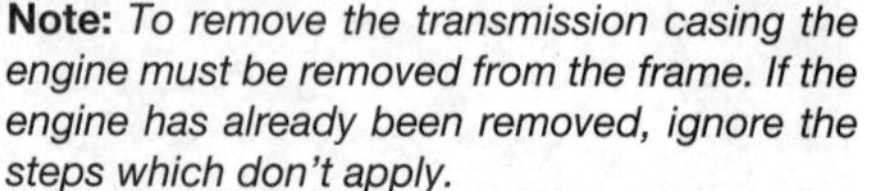

Note: *To remove the transmission casing the engine must be removed from the frame. If the engine has already been removed, ignore the steps which don't apply.*

Removal

1 Remove the engine (see Section 5).

2 Unscrew the eight bolts securing the transmission casing to the engine. Carefully separate the casing from the engine, using a soft-faced hammer to tap around the joint to initially separate the halves if necessary **(see**

23.11 Stopper arm assembly

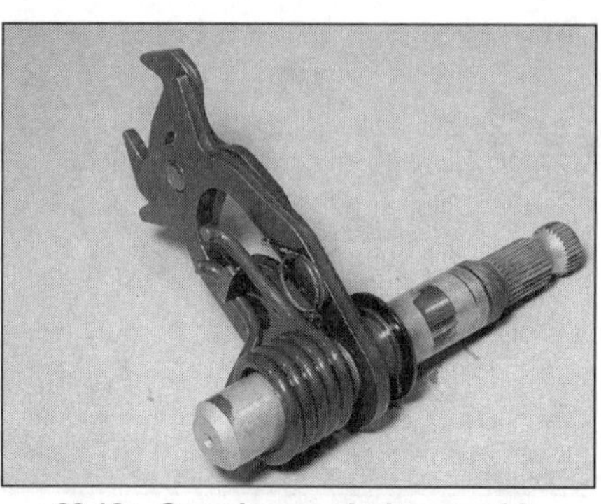

23.12a Gearchange shaft assembly

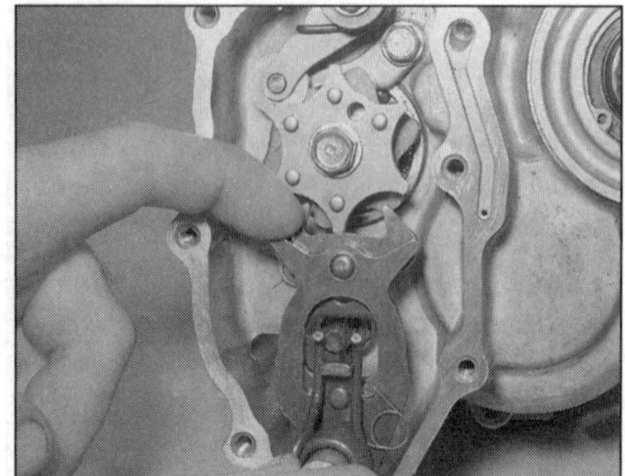

23.12b Press the arm down to clear the plate

23.12c Make sure the spring ends are correctly located

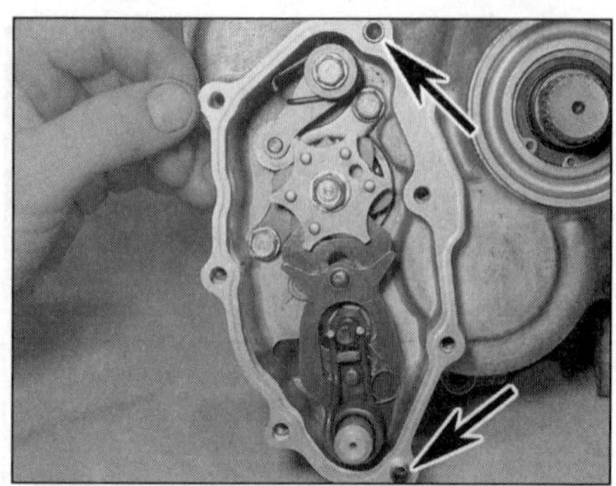

23.13 Use a new gasket, making sure it locates over the dowels (arrowed)

24.2a Unscrew the eight bolts (arrowed) . . .

24.2b . . . and withdraw the casing from the engine

24.3 Make sure the gasket locates over the dowels (arrowed)

illustrations). **Note:** *If the casing does not separate easily, make sure all fasteners have been removed. Do not try and separate the casing by levering against the mating surfaces as they are easily scored and will leak oil. Tap around the joint faces of the casing with a soft-faced mallet.* Remove the dowels if they are loose. Discard the gasket as a new one must be used.

Installation

3 Installation is the reverse of removal. If removed, do not forget to fit the dowels into the engine casing. Install the transmission casing using a new gasket, making sure it locates correctly onto the dowels, and tighten the casing bolts securely **(see illustration)**.

25 Transmission shafts and bearings - removal and installation

Note: *To remove the transmission shafts the engine must be removed from the frame. If the engine has already been removed, ignore the steps which do not apply.*

Removal

1 Remove the engine (see Section 5).
2 Separate the transmission casing from the engine (see Section 24).
3 Remove the gearchange mechanism (external components) (see Section 23).
4 Unscrew the seven bolts securing the inner cover to the transmission casing. Place the inner casing face down, supported on wooden blocks, and carefully lift the rear casing off the inner casing, leaving the shafts in the inner casing **(see illustrations)**. Use a soft-faced hammer to tap around the joint to initially separate the halves if necessary. **Note:** *If the halves do not separate easily, make sure all fasteners have been removed. Do not try and separate the halves by levering against the casing mating surfaces.* Remove the dowels if they are loose.
5 Remove the selector drum and forks (see Section 27).
6 Lift the input shaft and output shaft out of the casing, noting their relative positions and how they fit together **(see illustration)**. If they are stuck, use a soft-faced hammer and gently tap on the ends of the shafts to free them. If necessary, the input shaft and output shaft can be disassembled and inspected for wear or damage (see Section 26).
7 Referring to *Tools and Workshop Tips (*Sections 5 and 6) in the Reference Section, replace the oil seals and check the bearings in the transmission casing. Replace the bearings if necessary. The transmission output shaft oil seal is secured by a circlip, and the selector drum bearing by a retainer plate **(see illustrations)**.

Installation

8 Position the transmission input and output shafts together so that their related pinions are engaged. Install the shafts into the casing **(see illustration 25.6)**. Make sure both shafts

25.4a Unscrew the seven bolts (arrowed) . . .

25.4b . . . then turn the casing over and lift the rear half off the inner half

2

25.6 Lift the transmission shafts out of the casing as a pair

25.7a The output shaft oil seal is secured by a circlip . . .

25.7b . . . and the selector drum bearing by a retainer plate

25.10 The complete assembly should be as shown

are correctly seated in their bearings and their related pinions are still correctly engaged.

HAYNES HiNT ***Standing the shafts upright and fitting the inner casing down onto the shafts, rather than lowering the shafts down into the casing, will prevent the end components on the output shaft from dropping off.***

9 Install the selector drum and forks (see Section 27). Thoroughly lubricate all the transmission components with clean engine oil.

10 Position the gears in the neutral position and check the shafts are free to rotate easily and independently (i.e. the input shaft can turn whilst the output shaft is held stationary) before proceeding further. Rotate the selector drum by hand and select each gear in turn whilst rotating the input shaft. Check that all gears can be selected and that the shafts rotate freely in every gear **(see illustration)**.

11 If removed, fit the dowels into the casing, then install the inner cover and tighten the bolts securely **(see illustrations 25.4b and a)**. Check again that all gears can be selected and that the shafts rotate freely in every gear.

12 The remainder of installation is the reverse of removal, referring to the relevant Sections (see Steps 1 to 3). With the gearchange mechanism (external components) installed, but before fitting the transmission casing to the engine, check again the operation of the transmission in each gear. If there are any signs of undue stiffness, tight or rough spots, or of any other problem, the fault must be rectified before proceeding further.

26 Transmission shafts - disassembly, inspection and reassembly

1 Remove the transmission shafts from the casing (see Section 25). Always disassemble the transmission shafts separately to avoid mixing up the components.

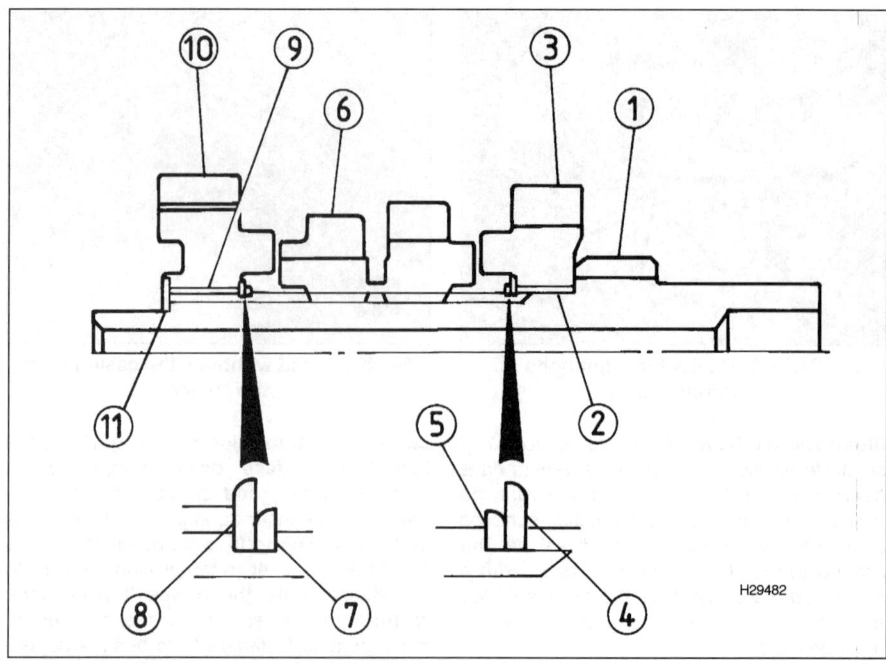

26.2 Transmission input shaft components

1 Input shaft with integral 1st gear pinion
2 4th gear pinion bush
3 4th gear pinion
4 Spline washer
5 Circlip
6 Combined 2nd/3rd gear pinion
7 Circlip
8 Spline washer
9 5th gear pinion bush
10 5th gear pinion
11 Washer

Input shaft disassembly

HAYNES HiNT ***When disassembling the transmission shafts, place the parts on a long rod or thread a wire through them to keep them in order and facing the proper direction.***

2 Slide the washer off the rear end of the shaft, followed by the 5th gear pinion and its bush, and the spline washer **(see illustration)**.

3 Remove the circlip securing the combined 2nd/3rd gear pinion, then slide the pinion off the shaft.

4 Remove the circlip securing the 4th gear pinion, then slide the spline washer, the pinion and its bush off the shaft.

5 The 1st gear pinion is integral with the shaft.

Input shaft inspection

6 Wash all of the components in clean solvent and dry them off.

7 Check the gear teeth for cracking, chipping, pitting and other obvious wear or damage. Any pinion that is damaged as such must be replaced.

8 Inspect the dogs and the dog holes in the gears for cracks, chips, and excessive wear especially in the form of rounded edges. Make sure mating gears engage properly. Replace the paired gears as a set if necessary.

9 Check for signs of scoring or bluing on the pinions, bushes and shaft. This could be caused by overheating due to inadequate lubrication. Check that all the oil holes and passages are clear. Replace any damaged pinions or bushes.

10 Check that each pinion moves freely on the shaft or bush but without undue freeplay. Check that each bush moves freely on the shaft but without undue free play.

11 The shaft is unlikely to sustain damage unless the engine has seized, placing an unusually high loading on the transmission, or the machine has covered a very high mileage. Check the surface of the shaft, especially where a pinion turns on it, and replace the shaft if it has scored or picked up, or if there are any cracks. Damage of any kind can only be cured by replacement.

12 Check the washers and circlips and replace any that are bent or appear weakened or worn. Use new ones if in any doubt.

Input shaft reassembly

13 During reassembly, apply engine oil to the mating surfaces of the shaft, pinions and bushes. When installing the circlips, do not expand the ends any further than is necessary. Install the stamped circlips so that their chamfered side faces the pinion it secures (see *correct fitting of a stamped circlip* illustration in Tools and Workshop Tips of the Reference section).

14 Slide the 4th gear pinion and its bush, with the pinion dog holes facing away from the integral 1st gear, onto the rear end of the shaft. Align the oil hole in the bush with the

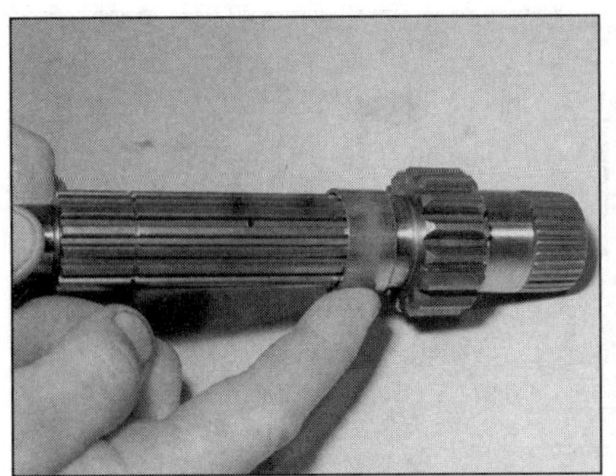
26.14a Slide the bush . . .

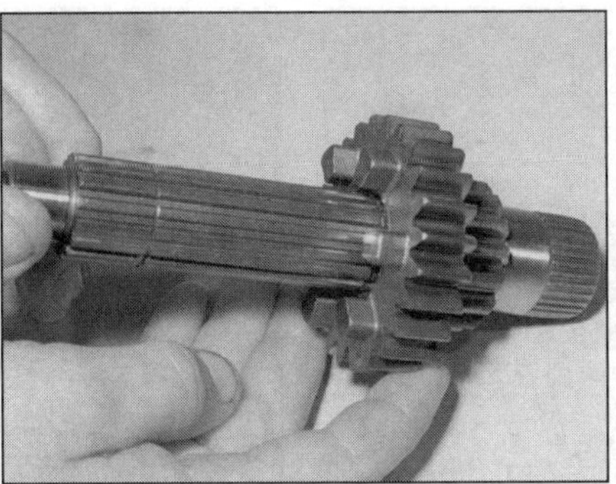
26.14b . . . the 4th gear pinion . . .

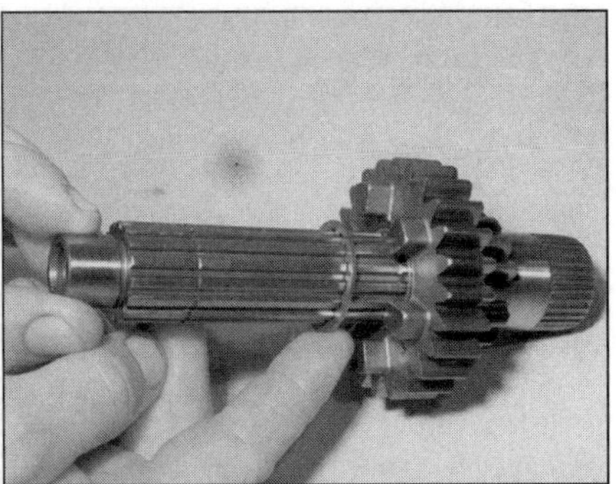
26.14c . . . and the thrust washer onto the shaft . . .

hole in the shaft. Slide the thrust washer onto the shaft, then fit the circlip, making sure that it locates correctly in the groove in the shaft **(see illustrations)**.

15 Slide the combined 2nd/3rd gear pinion onto the shaft with the larger 3rd gear pinion facing the 4th gear pinion. Secure it in place with the circlip, making sure it is properly seated in its groove **(see illustrations)**.

16 Slide the spline washer onto the shaft, followed by the 5th gear pinion and its bush, making sure the dogs in the pinion face the dog holes on the 2nd/3rd gear pinion, and the oil hole in the bush aligns with the hole in the shaft. Slide the washer onto the end of the shaft **(see illustrations)**.

26.14d . . . and secure them with the circlip

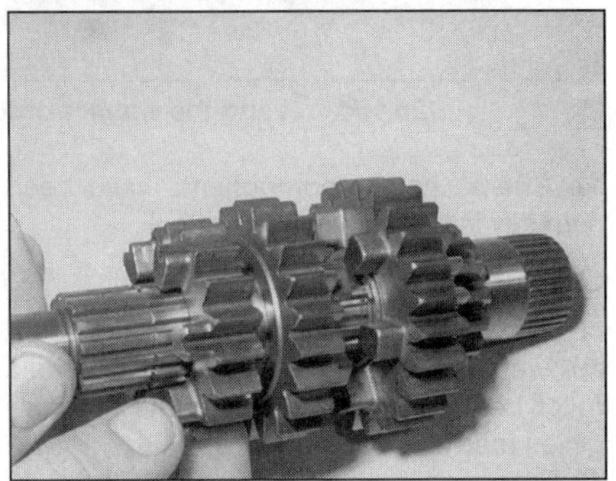
26.15a Slide the combined 2nd/3rd gear pinion onto the shaft . . .

26.15b . . . and secure it with the circlip

26.16a Slide the spline washer . . .

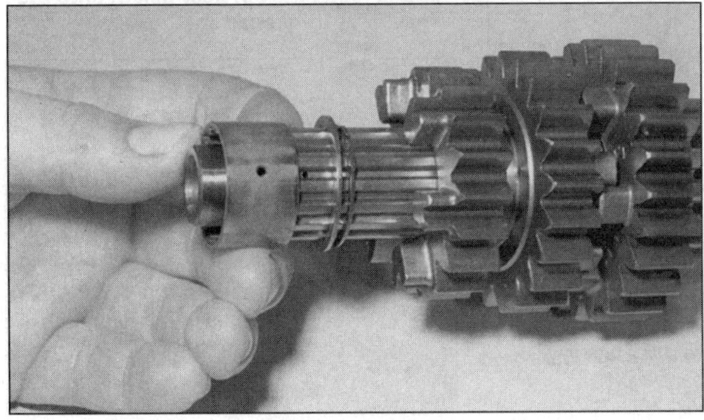
26.16b . . . the bush . . .

26.16c . . . the 5th gear pinion . . .

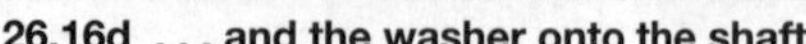

26.16d ... and the washer onto the shaft

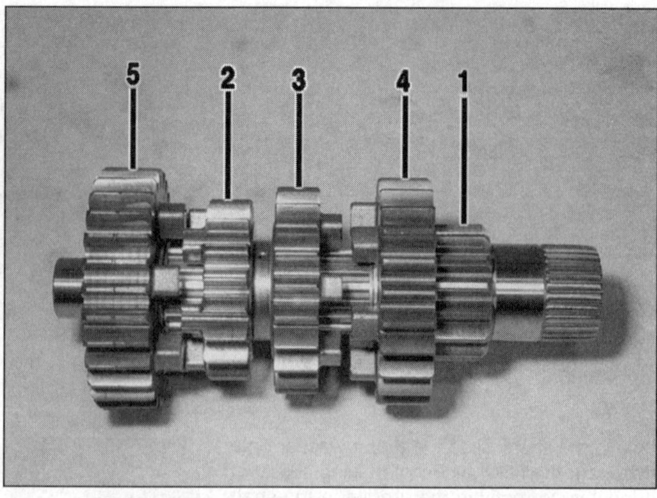

26.17 The assembled shaft should be as shown

17 Check that all components have been correctly installed **(see illustration)**.

Output shaft disassembly

18 Slide the washer off the front of the shaft, followed by the 1st gear pinion and its needle roller bearing, the washer and the 4th gear pinion **(see illustration)**.

19 Remove the circlip securing the 3rd gear pinion, then slide the spline washer, the pinion and its bush off the shaft.

20 Slide the lockwasher and the spline washer off the shaft, noting how they fit together.

21 Slide the 2nd gear pinion and its bush, followed by the spline washer, off the shaft.

22 Remove the circlip securing the 5th gear pinion, then slide the pinion off the shaft.

Output shaft inspection

23 Refer to Steps 6 to 12 above.

24 Install the needle roller bearing onto the shaft, and check it for play or roughness. Replace the bearing if it is worn or damaged.

Output shaft reassembly

25 During reassembly, apply engine oil to the mating surfaces of the shaft, pinions and bushes. When installing the circlips, do not expand the ends any further than is necessary, and install them so that the chamfered side faces the pinion it secures (see *correct fitting of a stamped circlip* illustration in Tools and Workshop Tips of the Reference section).

26 Slide the 5th gear pinion onto the shaft with its selector fork groove facing the front of the shaft and secure it with the circlip, making sure it is properly seated in its groove **(see illustrations)**.

27 Slide the spline washer and the 2nd gear pinion and its bush, onto the shaft, making sure the pinion dog holes face the 5th gear

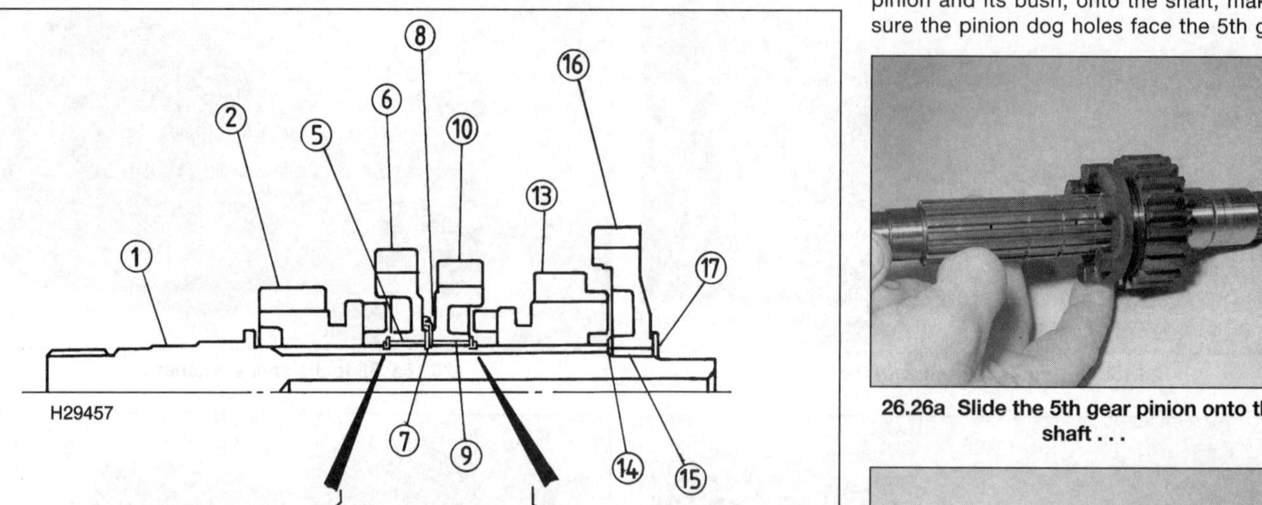

26.18 Transmission output shaft components

1 *Output shaft*
2 *5th gear pinion*
3 *Circlip*
4 *Spline washer*
5 *2nd gear pinion bush*
6 *2nd gear pinion*
7 *Slotted spline washer*
8 *Lockwasher*
9 *3rd gear pinion bush*
10 *3rd gear pinion*
11 *Spline washer*
12 *Circlip*
13 *4th gear pinion*
14 *Washer*
15 *Needle roller bearing*
16 *1st gear pinion*
17 *Washer*

26.26a Slide the 5th gear pinion onto the shaft . . .

26.26b . . . and secure it with the circlip

26.27a Slide the spline washer . . .

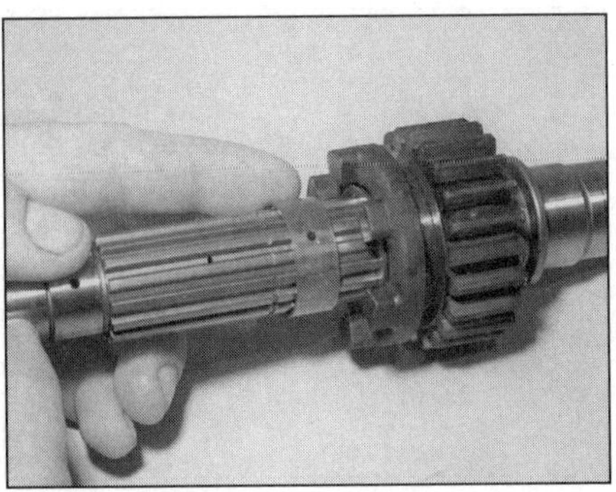
26.27b . . . the bush . . .

26.27c . . . and the 2nd gear pinion onto the shaft

pinion and the oil hole in the bush aligns with the hole in the shaft **(see illustrations)**.

28 Slide the slotted spline washer onto the shaft and locate it in its groove, then turn it in the groove so that the splines on the washer locate between the splines of the shaft and secure the washer in the groove. Slide the lockwasher onto the shaft, so that the tabs on the lockwasher face the rear end of the shaft and locate into the slots in the outer rim of the spline washer **(see illustrations)**.

29 Slide the 3rd gear pinion and its bush onto the shaft, making sure the oil hole in the bush aligns with the hole in the shaft, followed by the spline washer, and secure them in place with the circlip, making sure it is properly seated in its groove **(see illustrations)**.

26.28a Slide the slotted spline washer onto the shaft . .

26.28b . . . and turn it in the groove to secure it between the shaft splines

26.28c Slide the lockwasher onto the shaft . . .

26.28d . . . locating its tabs in the slots on the spline washer

26.29a Slide the bush . . .

26.29b . . . the 3rd gear pinion . . .

26.29c . . . and the spline washer onto the shaft . . .

26.29d . . . and secure them with the circlip

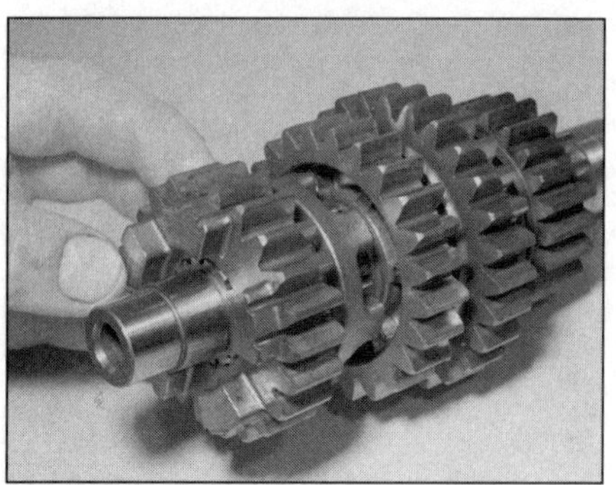
26.30a Slide the 4th gear pinion . . .

26.30b . . . and the washer onto the shaft

26.31a Slide the needle roller bearing onto the shaft . . .

30 Slide the 4th gear pinion onto the shaft with its selector fork groove facing the 3rd gear pinion, followed by the washer **(see illustrations)**.

31 Slide the 1st gear pinion and its needle roller bearing onto the shaft, so that the gear's dog holes face the 4th gear pinion. Slide the washer onto the end of the shaft **(see illustrations)**.

32 Check that all components have been correctly installed **(see illustration)**.

26.31b . . . and fit the 1st gear pinion over it . . .

26.31c . . . then slide the washer onto the shaft

27 Selector drum and forks - removal, inspection and installation

Note: *To remove the selector drum and forks the engine must be removed from the frame.*

Removal

1 Remove the engine (see Section 5).

2 Separate the transmission casing from the engine (see Section 24).

3 Remove the gearchange mechanism (external components) (see Section 23).

4 Unscrew the seven bolts securing the inner cover to the transmission casing **(see illustration 25.4a)**. Place the inner casing face down, supported on wooden blocks, and carefully lift the rear casing off the inner casing, leaving the shafts in the inner casing **(see illustration 25.4b)**. Use a soft-faced hammer to tap around the joint to initially separate the halves if necessary. **Note:** *If the halves do not separate easily, make sure all fasteners have been removed. Do not try and separate the halves by levering against the casing mating surfaces.* Remove the dowels if they are loose.

5 Before removing the selector forks, note that each fork is lettered for identification. The front fork has an "F", the centre fork a "C", and the rear fork an "R" **(see illustration)**. These letters face the rear. If no letters are visible, mark them yourself using a felt pen.

6 Supporting the selector forks, withdraw the fork shaft from the casing, then remove the forks **(see illustration)**. Once removed from the case, slide the forks back onto the shaft in their correct order and way round.

7 Remove the selector drum.

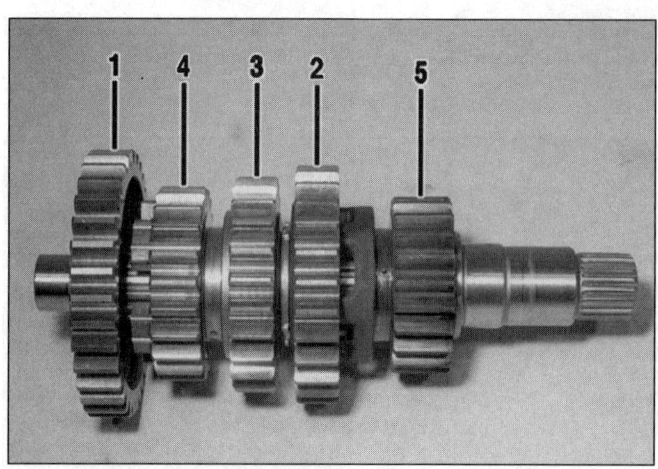

26.32 The assembled shaft should be as shown

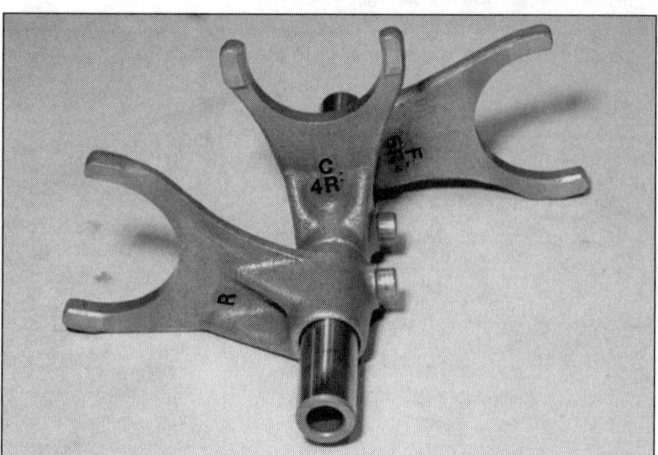

27.5 Each fork is lettered to identify its position on the shaft

27.6 Withdraw the shaft and remove the forks

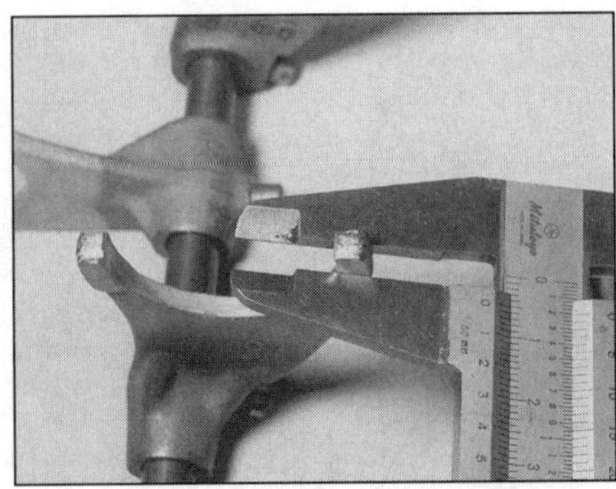
27.9 Measure the fork end thickness as shown

27.14 Fit each fork into its pinion . . .

Inspection

8 Inspect the selector forks for any signs of wear or damage, especially around the fork ends where they engage with the groove in the pinion. Check that each fork fits correctly in its pinion groove. Check closely to see if the forks are bent. If the forks are in any way damaged they must be replaced.

9 Measure the thickness of the fork ends and compare the readings to the specifications **(see illustration)**. Replace the forks if they are worn beyond their specifications.

10 Check that the forks fit correctly on their shaft. They should move freely with a light fit but no appreciable freeplay. Measure the internal diameter of the fork bores and the corresponding diameter of the fork shaft. Replace the forks and/or shaft if they are worn beyond their specifications. Check that the fork shaft holes in the casing and inner cover are not worn or damaged.

11 The selector fork shaft can be checked for trueness by rolling it along a flat surface. A bent rod will cause difficulty in selecting gears and make the gearshift action heavy. Replace the shaft if it is bent.

12 Inspect the selector drum grooves and selector fork guide pins for signs of wear or damage. If either component shows signs of wear or damage the selector(s) and drum must be replaced.

13 Check that the selector drum bearing rotates freely and has no sign of freeplay between it and the casing. Replace the bearing if necessary (see *Tools and Workshop Tips* in the Reference Section). The bearing is secured by a plate with two bolts **(see illustration 25.7b)**.

Installation

14 Fit each selector fork into its groove in the relevant pinion, making sure it is in its correct location and the right way round (see Step 5) **(see illustration)**.

15 Slide the selector drum into position in the crankcase. Locate the guide pin on the end of each fork into its groove in the drum **(see illustrations)**. Lubricate the selector fork shaft with clean engine oil and slide through each fork and into its bore in the crankcase **(see illustration 27.6)**.

16 Rotate the selector drum by hand and select each gear in turn whilst rotating the transmission input shaft. Check that all gears can be selected and that the shafts rotate freely in every gear.

17 If removed, fit the dowels into the casing, then install the inner cover and tighten the bolts securely **(see illustrations 25.4b and a)**. Check again that all gears can be selected and that the shafts rotate freely in every gear.

18 The remainder of installation is the reverse of removal, referring to the relevant Sections (see Steps 1 to 3). With the gearchange mechanism (external components) installed, but before fitting the transmission casing to the engine, check again the operation of the transmission in each gear. If there are any signs of undue stiffness, tight or rough spots, or of any other problem, the fault must be rectified before proceeding further.

28 Primary drive damper shaft - removal, inspection and installation

Note: *To remove the primary damper shaft the engine must be removed from the frame.*

Removal

1 Remove the engine (see Section 5).

2 Remove the clutch (see Section 17).

3 Separate the transmission casing from the engine (see Section 24).

4 Withdraw the damper shaft from the engine **(see illustration)**.

Inspection

5 Using a coil spring compressor located onto the rear end of the shaft, so that the spring is compressed from the middle towards the rear, or a hydraulic press located onto the rear end of the shaft and the washer between the spring and its seat, compress the spring approximately 5 mm until the spring

2

27.15a . . . then install the selector drum . . .

27.15b . . . and locate the fork guide pins into the drum grooves

28.4 Withdraw the shaft from the engine

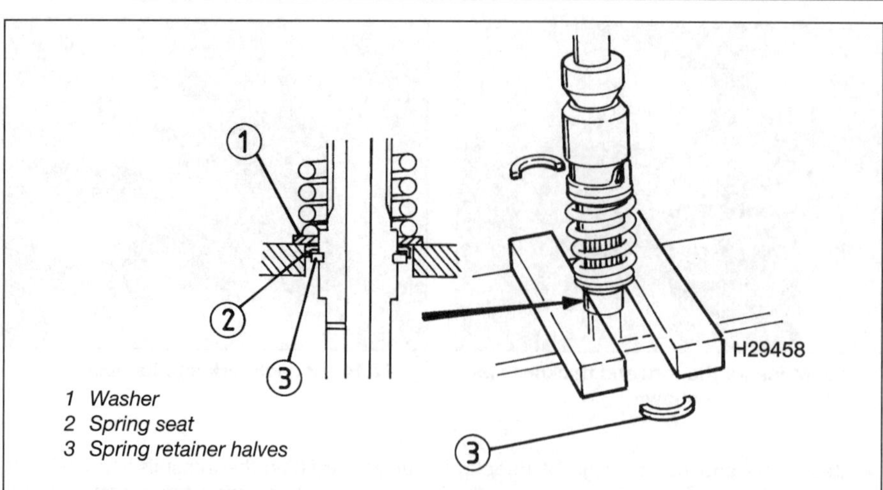

28.5 Compressing the primary damper shaft spring

retainer halves can be removed from their groove in the shaft **(see illustration)**.

Caution: Do not compress the spring by more than 7 mm.

6 Carefully release the compressor until the spring is relaxed, then remove the compressor and slide the spring seat and spring off the front of the shaft **(see illustration)**.

7 Slide the lifter and cam towards the middle of the shaft until the cam retainer halves can be removed from their groove in the shaft. Slide the washer, cam and lifter off the shaft.

8 Measure the free length of the damper spring. If it is shorter than the service limit specified at the beginning of the Chapter, replace the spring.

9 Check the shaft splines and the corresponding splines of the lifter for signs of wear or damage and replace them if necessary.

10 Check the spring retainer and cam retainer halves and their corresponding grooves in the shaft for signs of wear or damage, in particular rounded edges, and replace them if necessary.

11 Reassemble the components onto the shaft in a reverse of their removal order, making sure the retainer halves locate correctly in their grooves **(see illustration 28.5)**. Install the spring with its narrower end facing the front of the shaft, away from the lifter and cam.

Installation

12 Installation is the reverse of removal, referring to the relevant Sections (see Steps 1 to 4).

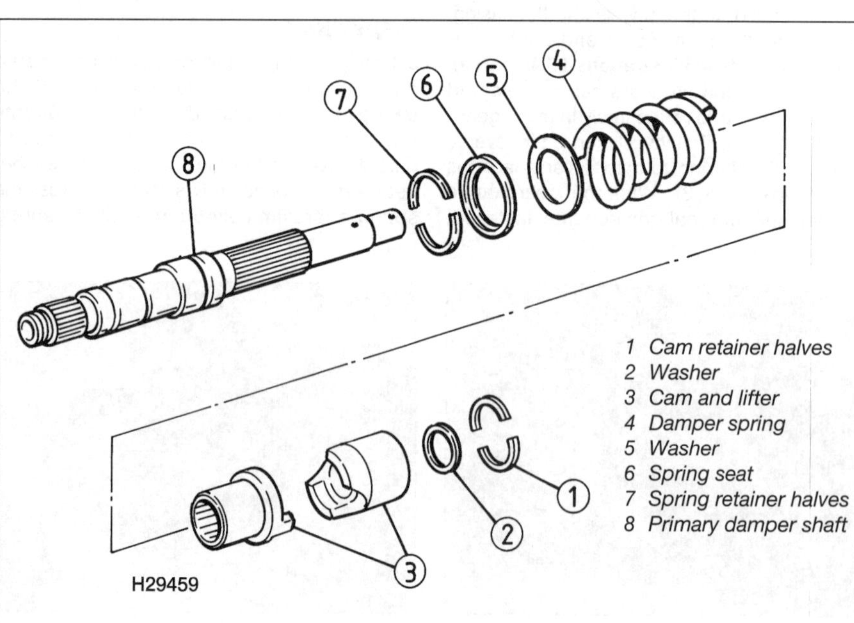

28.6 Primary damper shaft components

29 Crankcase halves - separation and reassembly

Note: *To separate the crankcase halves, the engine must be removed from the frame.*

Separation

1 To access the pistons, connecting rods, crankshaft, bearings and starter clutch, the crankcase must be split into two parts.

2 To enable the crankcases to be separated, the engine must be removed from the frame (see Section 5). Before the crankcases can be separated the following components must be removed:

a) Oil cooler (early models) (Section 7).
b) Timing belt and tensioner (Section 10).
c) Timing belt pulleys (Section 11).
d) Camshafts (Section 12).
e) Cylinder heads (Section 14).
f) Clutch (Section 17).
g) Ignition pulse generator coil assembly (Chapter 5).
h) Gearchange mechanism external components (Section 23).
i) Transmission casing (Section 24).
j) Primary damper shaft (Section 28).
k) Oil sump (Section 21).
l) Alternator (Chapter 9).
m) Starter motor (Chapter 9).
n) Water pump (Chapter 3).

Note: *If the crankcases are being separated to inspect the crankshaft without removing it, or to remove the crankshaft without removing the connecting rods and pistons, the camshafts and cylinder heads can remain in situ. However, if removal of the connecting rod assemblies is intended, full disassembly of the top-end is necessary.*

3 Remove the water pump (see Chapter 3, Step 7, ignoring the other Steps which do not apply).

4 Unscrew the bolts securing the clutch casing to the front of the engine and remove the casing, along with the cooler hose guard (early models) **(see illustration)**. Remove the

29.4 The clutch casing is secured by seven bolts (arrowed)

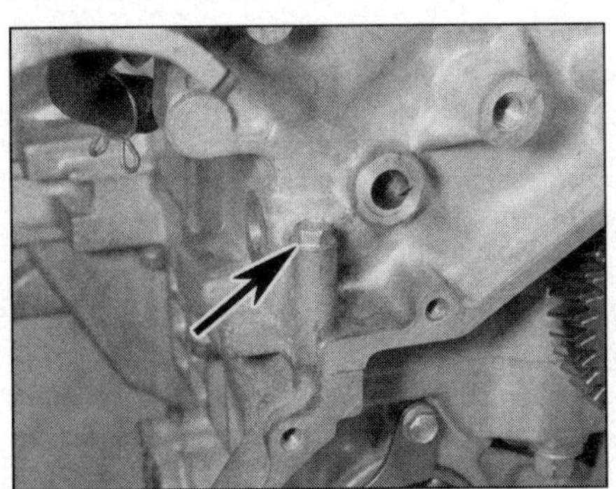
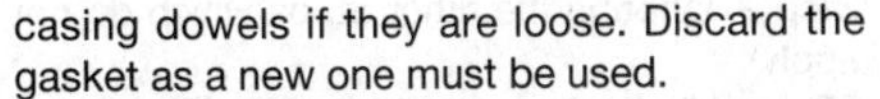

29.5a Remove the 6 mm bolt at the front . . .

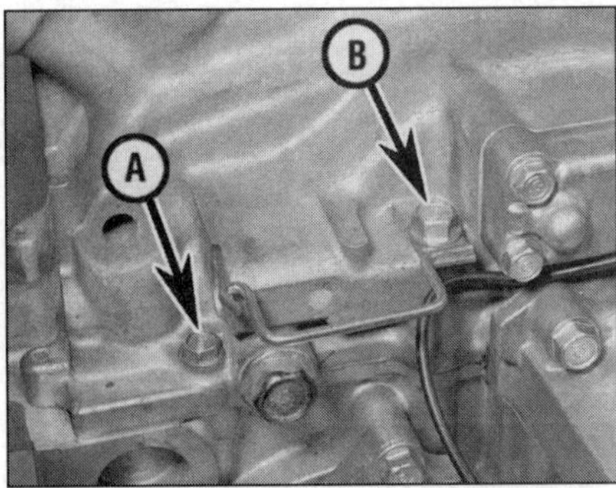

29.5b . . . and the 6 mm bolt (A) and the 8 mm bolt (B) at the back, noting the hose guide with the 8 mm bolt

29.7a Remove the 6 mm bolts (A), noting the hose guide . . .

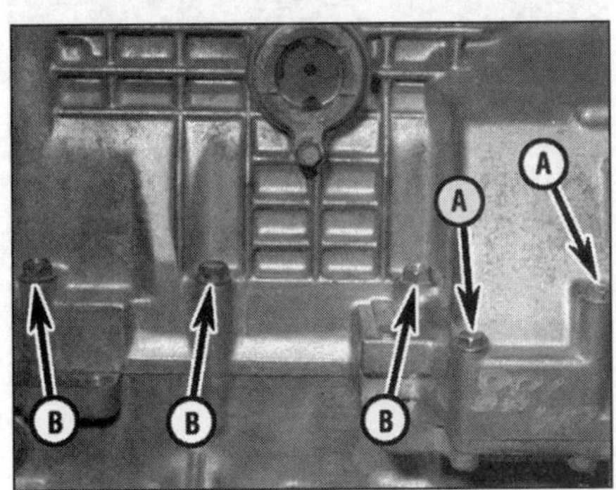

29.7b . . . and the 8 mm bolts (B) . . .

29.7c . . . and finally the 10 mm bolts (arrowed)

casing dowels if they are loose. Discard the gasket as a new one must be used.

5 Unscrew the two 6 mm and one 8 mm upper crankcase bolts **(see illustrations)**. Note the position of the hose guide fitted with the 8 mm bolt.

6 Turn the engine upside down so that it rests on the cylinder block.

7 Unscrew the four 6 mm lower crankcase bolts, followed by the six 8 mm bolts and finally the six 10 mm bolts **(see illustrations)**. Unscrew the bolts evenly, a little at a time and in a criss-cross sequence until they are finger-tight, then remove them. Note the hose guide fitted with one of the 6 mm bolts. Washers are fitted with the 10 mm bolts on all models except UK T, AT, V and AV, and all US 1996 and 1997 models. **Note:** *As each bolt is removed, store it in its relative position in a cardboard template of the crankcase halves. This will ensure all bolts are installed in the correct location on reassembly.*

8 Carefully lift the lower crankcase half off the upper half, using a soft-faced hammer to tap around the joint to initially separate the halves if necessary **(see illustration 29.16)**. **Note:** *If the halves do not separate easily, make sure all fasteners have been removed. Do not try and separate the halves by levering against the crankcase mating surfaces as they are easily scored and will leak oil. Tap around the joint faces with a soft-faced mallet.* The lower crankcase half will come away with the oil pump (if not already removed), leaving the crankshaft in the upper crankcase half.

9 Remove the three locating dowels from the crankcase if they are loose (they could be in either crankcase half), noting their locations.

10 Refer to Sections 30 to 36 for the removal and installation of the components housed within the crankcases.

Reassembly

11 Remove all traces of sealant from the crankcase mating surfaces.

12 Ensure that all components and their bearings are in place in the upper and lower crankcase halves. Check that the crankshaft thrust bearings are correctly located.

13 Generously lubricate the crankshaft, particularly around the bearings, with clean engine oil, then use a rag soaked in high flash-point solvent to wipe over the mating surfaces of both crankcase halves to remove all traces of oil.

14 Install the three locating dowels in the upper crankcase half.

15 Apply a small amount of suitable sealant to the mating surface of the upper crankcase half **(see illustration)**.

Caution: Do not apply an excessive amount of sealant as it will ooze out when the case halves are assembled and may obstruct oil passages. Do not apply the sealant on or too close to any of the bearing inserts or surfaces.

16 Check again that all components are in position, particularly that the bearing shells are still correctly located in the lower crankcase half. Carefully install the lower crankcase half down onto the upper crankcase half, making sure the dowels all locate correctly into the lower crankcase half **(see illustration)**.

17 Check that the lower crankcase half is correctly seated. **Note:** *The crankcase halves should fit together without being forced. If the casings are not correctly seated, remove the lower crankcase half and investigate the problem. Do not attempt to pull them together using the crankcase bolts as the casing will crack and be ruined.*

18 Clean the threads of the six 10 mm lower crankcase bolts and apply clean engine oil to

29.15 Apply a sealant to the mating surface of the upper crankcase half . . .

29.16 . . . then carefully fit the lower half down onto the upper half

29.18 Lubricate the specified bolts with clean engine oil

29.23a Locate the new gasket over the dowels (arrowed) . . .

29.23b . . . then fit the casing

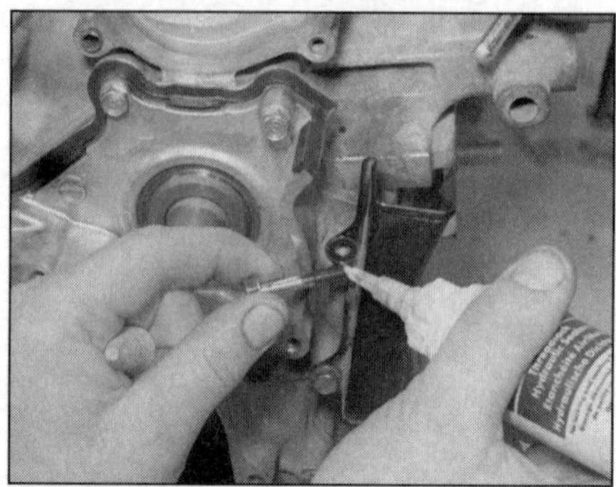
29.23c Apply a thread locking compound to the casing bolts

the threads and under the head **(see illustration)**. Insert them in their original locations, not forgetting the copper washers on all models except UK T, AT, V and AV, and all US 1996 and 1997 models (using new ones if necessary) **(see illustration 29.7c)**. Secure all bolts finger-tight at first, then tighten the bolts evenly a little at a time in a criss-cross sequence to the torque setting specified at the beginning of the Chapter.

19 Clean the threads of the six 8 mm lower crankcase bolts and apply clean engine oil to the threads and under the head. Insert them in their original locations, then tighten the bolts evenly a little at a time in a criss-cross sequence to the torque setting specified at the beginning of the Chapter **(see illustrations 29.7a and b)**.

20 Clean the threads of the four 6 mm lower crankcase bolts and insert them in their original locations, not forgetting the bracket/guide. Tighten the bolts evenly a little at a time in a criss-cross sequence to the specified torque setting **(see illustration 29.7a and b)**.

21 Turn the engine over. Install the single 8 mm upper crankcase bolt with its cable/hose guide, and the two 6 mm bolts **(see illustrations 29.5a and b)**. Tighten the bolts a little at a time to the specified torque setting.

22 With all crankcase fasteners tightened, check that the crankshaft rotates smoothly and easily. If there are any signs of undue stiffness, tight or rough spots, or of any other problem, the fault must be rectified before proceeding further.

23 Check the condition of the oil seal in the clutch casing and replace it if necessary, referring to *Tools and Workshop Tips (*Sections 5 and 6) in the Reference Section. If removed, fit the clutch casing dowels, then install the casing using a new gasket. Apply a suitable non-permanent thread-locking compound to the casing bolts and tighten them securely **(see illustrations)**.

24 Install the water pump (see Chapter 3, Step 9, ignoring the other Steps which do not apply).

25 Install all other removed assemblies in the reverse of the sequence given in Step 2.

30 Crankcase halves and cylinder bores - inspection and servicing

Crankcase halves

1 After the crankcases have been separated, remove the crankshaft, connecting rods and pistons, bearings (referring to *Tools and Workshop Tips (*Sections 5 and 6) in the Reference Section), oil pump and oil pressure switch, and, if required, the cooling system unions, referring to the relevant Sections of this Chapter, to Chapter 9 for the oil pressure switch, and to Chapter 3 for the coolant unions. Unscrew the bolt securing the starter idle/reduction gear shaft, then withdraw the shaft and remove the gear, noting which way round it fits. On all except UK L and M models, and US 1991 model, remove the oil separator plate from the upper crankcase half **(see illustrations)**.

2 The crankcases should be cleaned

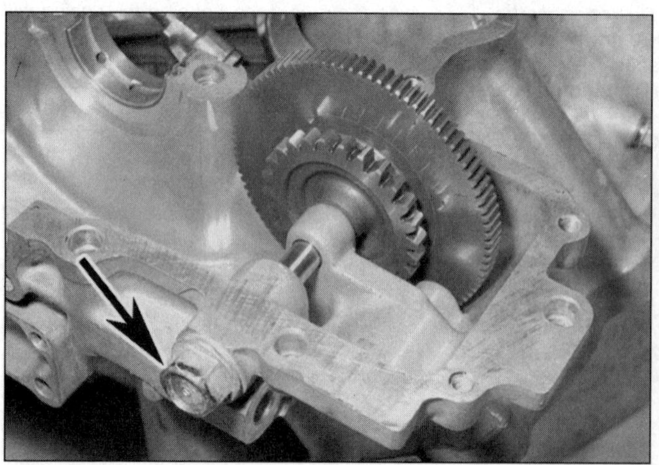
30.1a Unscrew the bolt (arrowed), then withdraw the shaft and remove the gear

30.1b The oil separator plate is a push fit in the casing

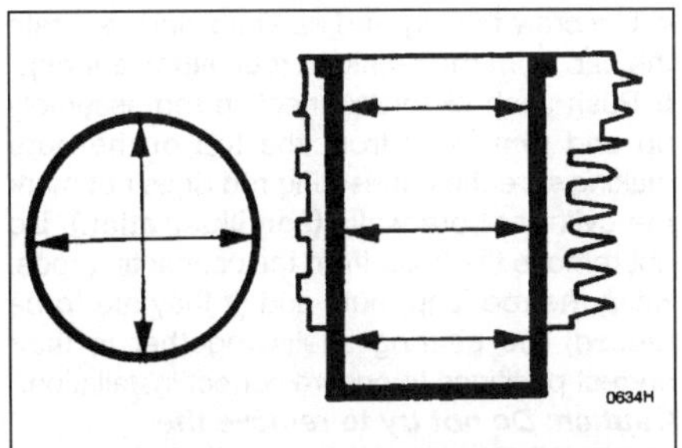

30.11 Measure the cylinder bore in the directions shown with a telescoping gauge, then measure the gauge with a micrometer

thoroughly with new solvent and dried with compressed air. All oil passages should be blown out with compressed air.

3 All traces of old gasket sealant should be removed from the mating surfaces. Minor damage to the surfaces can be cleaned up with a fine sharpening stone or grindstone.

Caution: Be very careful not to nick or gouge the crankcase mating surfaces or oil leaks will result. Check both crankcase halves very carefully for cracks and other damage.

4 Small cracks or holes in aluminium castings may be repaired with an epoxy resin adhesive as a temporary measure. Permanent repairs can only be effected by argon-arc welding, and only a specialist in this process is in a position to advise on the economy or practical aspect of such a repair. If any damage is found that can't be repaired, replace the crankcase halves as a set.

5 Damaged threads can be economically reclaimed by using a diamond section wire insert, of the Heli-Coil type, which is easily fitted after drilling and re-tapping the affected thread.

6 Sheared studs or screws can usually be removed with screw extractors, which consist of a tapered, left thread screw of very hard steel. These are inserted into a pre-drilled hole in the stud, and usually succeed in dislodging the most stubborn stud or screw.

7 Install all components and assemblies,

Refer to Tools and Workshop Tips for details of installing a thread insert and using screw extractors.

referring to the relevant Sections of this Chapter and to Chapter 8, before reassembling the crankcase halves. Install the idle/reduction gear with the smaller pinion facing the rear and lubricate the shaft with clean engine oil.

Cylinder bores

8 Do not attempt to separate the cylinder liners from the cylinder block.

9 Check the cylinder walls carefully for scratches and score marks. A rebore will be necessary to remove any deep scores.

10 Using a precision straight-edge and a feeler gauge set to the warpage limit listed in the specifications at the beginning of the Chapter, check the block gasket mating surface for warpage. Refer to *Tools and Workshop Tips* in the Reference section for details of how to use the straight-edge. If warpage is excessive the block must be replaced with a new one.

11 Using telescoping gauges and a micrometer (see *Tools and Workshop Tips*), check the dimensions of each cylinder to assess the amount of wear, taper and ovality. Measure near the top (but below the level of the top piston ring at TDC), centre and bottom (but above the level of the oil ring at BDC) of the bore, both parallel to and across the crankshaft axis **(see illustration)**. Compare the results to the specifications at the beginning of the Chapter. If the cylinders are worn, oval or tapered beyond the service limit, or badly scratched, scuffed or scored, have them rebored and honed by a Honda dealer or specialist motorcycle repair shop. If the cylinders are rebored, they will require oversize pistons and rings.

12 If the precision measuring tools are not available, take the block to a Honda dealer or specialist motorcycle repair shop for assessment and advice.

13 If the block and cylinders are in good condition and the piston-to-bore clearance is within specifications (see Section 33), the cylinders should be honed (de-glazed). To perform this operation you will need the proper size flexible hone with fine stones, or a bottle-brush type hone, plenty of light oil or honing oil, some clean rags and an electric drill motor.

14 Hold the block sideways (so that the bores are horizontal rather than vertical) in a vice with soft jaws or cushioned with wooden blocks. Mount the hone in the drill motor, compress the stones and insert the hone into the cylinder. Thoroughly lubricate the cylinder, then turn on the drill and move the hone up and down in the cylinder at a pace which produces a fine cross-hatch pattern on the cylinder wall with the lines intersecting at an angle of approximately 60°. Be sure to use plenty of lubricant and do not take off any more material than is necessary to produce the desired effect. Do not withdraw the hone from the cylinder while it is still turning. Switch off the drill and continue to move it up and down in the cylinder until it has stopped turning, then compress the stones and withdraw the hone. Wipe the oil from the cylinder and repeat the procedure on the other cylinder. Remember, do not take too much material from the cylinder wall.

15 Wash the cylinders thoroughly with warm soapy water to remove all traces of the abrasive grit produced during the honing operation. Be sure to run a brush through the stud holes and flush them with running water. After rinsing, dry the cylinders thoroughly and apply a thin coat of light, rust-preventative oil to all machined surfaces.

16 If you do not have the equipment or desire to perform the honing operation, take the block to a Honda dealer or specialist motorcycle repair shop.

31 Main and connecting rod bearings - general note

1 Even though main and connecting rod bearings are generally replaced with new ones during the engine overhaul, the old bearings should be retained for close examination as they may reveal valuable information about the condition of the engine.

2 Bearing failure occurs mainly because of lack of lubrication, the presence of dirt or other foreign particles, overloading the engine and/or corrosion. Regardless of the cause of bearing failure, it must be corrected before the engine is reassembled to prevent it from happening again.

3 When examining the connecting rod bearings, remove them from the connecting rods and caps and lay them out on a clean surface in the same general position as their location on the crankshaft journals. This will enable you to match any noted bearing problems with the corresponding crankshaft journal.

4 Dirt and other foreign particles get into the engine in a variety of ways. It may be left in the engine during assembly or it may pass through filters or breathers. It may get into the oil and from there into the bearings. Metal chips from machining operations and normal engine wear are often present. Abrasives are sometimes left in engine components after reconditioning operations, especially when parts are not thoroughly cleaned using the proper cleaning methods. Whatever the source, these foreign objects often end up imbedded in the soft bearing material and are easily recognised. Large particles will not imbed in the bearing and will score or gouge the bearing and journal. The best prevention for this cause of bearing failure is to clean all parts thoroughly and keep everything spotlessly clean during engine reassembly. Frequent and regular oil and filter changes are also recommended.

5 Lack of lubrication or lubrication breakdown has a number of interrelated causes. Excessive heat (which thins the oil), overloading (which squeezes the oil from the bearing face) and oil leakage or throw off (from excessive bearing clearances, worn oil pump or high engine speeds) all contribute to lubrication breakdown. Blocked oil passages will also starve a bearing and destroy it. When lack of lubrication is the cause of bearing failure, the bearing material is wiped or extruded from the steel backing of the bearing. Temperatures may increase to the point where the steel backing and the journal turn blue from overheating.

6 Riding habits can have a definite effect on

Refer to Tools and Workshop Tips for bearing fault finding.

bearing life. Full throttle low speed operation, or labouring the engine, puts very high loads on bearings, which tend to squeeze out the oil film. These loads cause the bearings to flex, which produces fine cracks in the bearing face (fatigue failure). Eventually the bearing material will loosen in pieces and tear away from the steel backing. Short trip riding leads to corrosion of bearings, as insufficient engine heat is produced to drive off the condensed water and corrosive gases produced. These products collect in the engine oil, forming acid and sludge. As the oil is carried to the engine bearings, the acid attacks and corrodes the bearing material.

7 Incorrect bearing installation during engine assembly will lead to bearing failure as well. Tight fitting bearings which leave insufficient bearing oil clearances result in oil starvation. Dirt or foreign particles trapped behind a bearing insert result in high spots on the bearing which lead to failure.

8 To avoid bearing problems, clean all parts thoroughly before reassembly, double check all bearing clearance measurements and lubricate the new bearings with clean engine oil during installation.

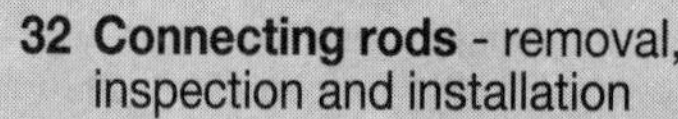

32 Connecting rods - removal, inspection and installation

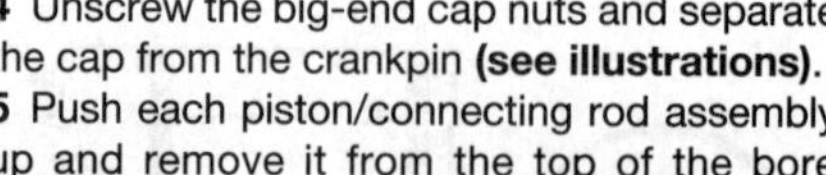

Note: *To remove the connecting rods the engine must be removed from the frame and the crankcases separated.*

Removal

1 Remove the engine from the frame (see Section 5) and separate the crankcase halves (see Section 29).

2 Before removing the rods from the crankshaft, measure the side clearance on each rod with a feeler gauge **(see illustration)**. If the clearance on any rod is greater than the service limit listed in this Chapter's Specifications, replace that rod with a new one.

3 Using paint or a felt marker pen, mark the relevant cylinder identity on each connecting rod and cap. Mark across the cap-to-connecting rod join and note which side of the rod faces the front of the engine to ensure that the cap and rod are fitted the correct way around on reassembly. Note that the number already across the rod and cap indicates bearing size grade, not cylinder number. The oil hole in the big-end of each connecting rod should face in for each left-hand cylinder, and out for each right-hand cylinder.

4 Unscrew the big-end cap nuts and separate the cap from the crankpin **(see illustrations)**.

5 Push each piston/connecting rod assembly up and remove it from the top of the bore making sure the connecting rod does not mark the cylinder bore walls **(see illustration)**. Do not remove the bolts from the connecting rods. Keep the rod, cap, nuts and (if they are to be reused) the bearing shells together in their correct positions to ensure correct installation.

Caution: Do not try to remove the piston/connecting rod from the bottom of the cylinder bore. The piston will not pass the crankcase main bearing webs. If the piston is pulled right to the bottom of the bore the oil control ring will expand and lock the piston in position. If this happens it is likely the ring will be broken.

6 Immediately install the relevant bearing shells (if removed), bearing cap, and nuts on each piston/connecting rod assembly so that they are all kept together as a matched set.

7 Remove the pistons from the connecting rods (see Section 33).

Inspection

8 Check the connecting rods for cracks and other obvious damage.

9 If not already done (see Section 33), apply clean engine oil to the piston pin, insert it into the connecting rod small-end and check for any freeplay between the two **(see illustration)**. Measure the pin external diameter and the small-end bore diameter and compare the measurements to the specifications at the beginning of the Chapter **(see illustrations 33.14b and 33.14d)**. Replace components that are worn beyond the specified limits.

10 Refer to Section 31 and examine the connecting rod bearing shells. If they are scored, badly scuffed or appear to have seized, new shells must be installed. Always replace the shells in the connecting rods as a set. If they are badly damaged, check the corresponding crankpin. Evidence of extreme heat, such as discoloration, indicates that lubrication failure has occurred. Be sure to thoroughly check the oil pump and pressure regulator as well as all oil holes and passages before reassembling the engine.

32.2 Measure the connecting rod side clearance using a feeler gauge

32.4a Unscrew the cap nuts (arrowed) . . .

32.4b . . . and remove the cap

32.5 Withdraw the piston/connecting rod assembly from the top of the bore

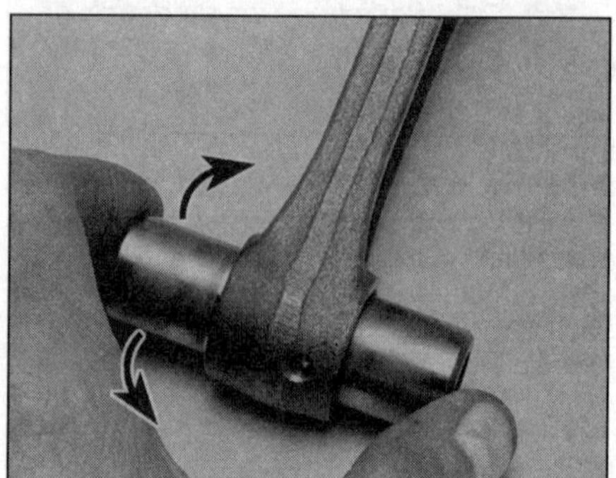

32.9 Slip the piston pin into the rod's small end and rock it back and forth to check for looseness

32.12a Crankpin journal size letters

32.12b Connecting rod size number

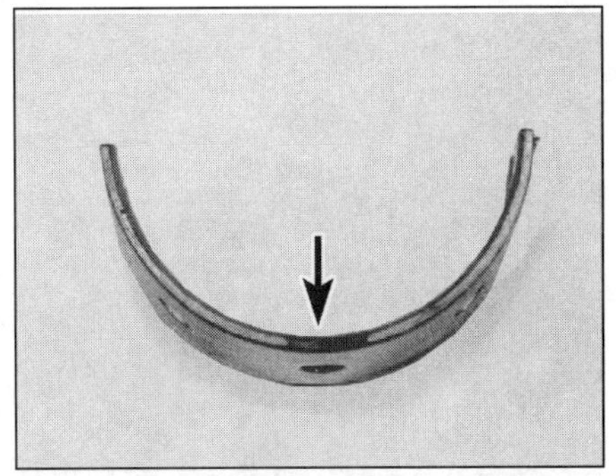
32.13 Bearing shell colour code location

11 Have the rods checked for twist and bend by a Honda dealer if you are in doubt about their straightness.

Bearing shell selection

12 Replacement bearing shells for the big-end bearings are supplied on a selected fit basis. Code letters and numbers stamped on various components are used to identify the correct replacement bearings. The crankpin journal size letters are stamped on the crankshaft webs and will be either an A, a B or a C. Each letter is adjacent to the crankpin journal it represents. The connecting rod size code number is marked on the flat face of the connecting rod and cap and will be either a 1, a 2 or a 3 **(see illustrations)**.

13 A range of bearing shells is available. To select the correct bearing for a particular big-end, using the table below cross-refer the crankpin journal size letter (stamped on the web) with the connecting rod size number (stamped on the rod) to determine the colour code of the bearing required. For example, if the connecting rod size is 2, and the crankpin size is A, then the bearing required is Green. The colour is marked on the side of the shell **(see illustration)**.

Crankpin code	Connecting rod code		
	1	2	3
A	Yellow	Green	Brown
B	Green	Brown	Black
C	Brown	Black	Blue

Oil clearance check

14 Whether new bearing shells are being fitted or the original ones are being re-used, the connecting rod bearing oil clearance should be checked prior to reassembly. If not already done, remove the crankshaft from the crankcase (see Section 35).

15 Clean the backs of the bearing shells and the bearing locations in both the connecting rod and cap.

16 Press the bearing shells into their locations, ensuring that the tab on each shell engages the notch in the connecting rod/cap **(see illustration)**. Make sure the bearings are fitted in the correct locations and take care not to touch any shell's bearing surface with your fingers.

17 Cut a length of the appropriate size Plastigauge (it should be slightly shorter than the width of the crankpin). Place a strand of Plastigauge on the (cleaned) crankpin journal and fit the (clean) connecting rod, shells and cap. Make sure the cap is fitted the correct way around so the previously made markings align, and that the rod is facing the right way, and tighten the bearing cap nuts evenly, in two or three stages, to the torque setting specified at the beginning of the Chapter, whilst ensuring that the connecting rod does not rotate. Slacken the cap nuts and remove the connecting rod, again taking great care not to rotate the crankshaft.

18 Compare the width of the crushed Plastigauge on the crankpin to the scale printed on the Plastigauge envelope to obtain the connecting rod bearing oil clearance **(see illustration 35.19)**. Compare the reading to the specifications at the beginning of the Chapter.

19 On completion carefully scrape away all traces of the Plastigauge material from the crankpin and bearing shells using a fingernail or other object which is unlikely to score the shells.

20 If the clearance is within the range listed in this Chapter's Specifications and the bearings are in perfect condition, they can be reused. If the clearance is beyond the service limit, replace the bearing shells with new ones (see Steps 12 and 13). Check the oil clearance once again (the new shells may be thick enough to bring bearing clearance within the specified range). Always replace all of the inserts at the same time.

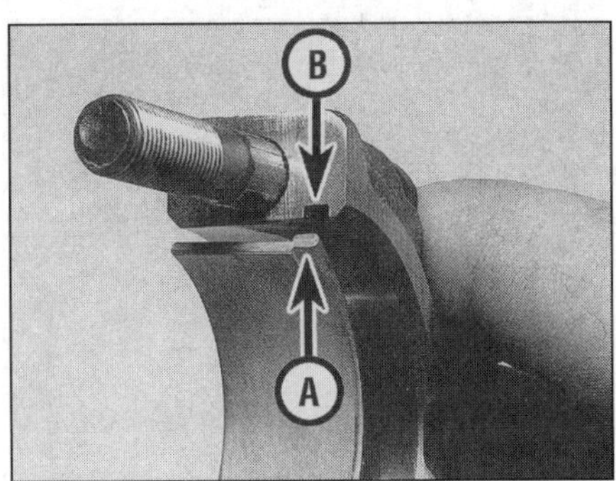

32.16 Make sure the tab (A) locates in the notch (B)

21 If the clearance is still greater than the service limit listed in this Chapter's Specifications, the crankpin is worn and the crankshaft should be replaced

22 Repeat the bearing selection procedure for the remaining connecting rods.

Installation

23 Install the pistons onto the connecting rods (see Section 33).

24 Install the bearing shells in the connecting rods and caps, aligning the notch in the bearing with the groove in the rod or cap **(see illustration 32.16)**. Lubricate the shells with a 50/50 mixture of molybdenum disulphide grease and clean engine oil.

25 Lubricate the pistons, rings and cylinder bore with clean engine oil. Insert the piston/connecting rod assembly into the top of its bore, taking care not to allow the connecting rod to mark the bore **(see illustration 32.5)**. Make sure the "IN" mark on the piston crown is on the intake side of the bore and the connecting rod is the right way round, then carefully compress and feed each piston ring into the bore until the piston crown is flush with the top of the bore **(see illustration)**.

26 Ensure that the connecting rod bearing insert is still correctly installed. Liberally lubricate the crankpin with a 50/50 mixture of molybdenum disulphide grease and clean engine oil. Taking care not to mark the

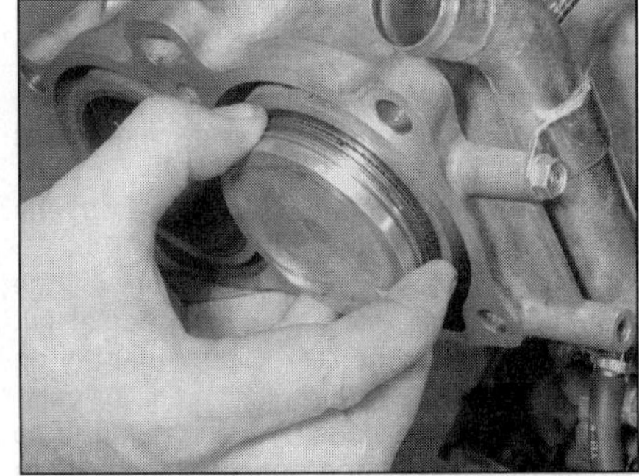
32.25 Compress each ring in turn and feed it into the bore

32.28 Tighten the cap nuts to the specified torque setting

cylinder bores pull the piston/connecting rod assembly down its bore and onto the crankpin.

27 Fit the bearing cap with its shell onto the connecting rod **(see illustration 32.4b)**. Make sure the cap is fitted the correct way around so the connecting rod and bearing cap weight/size markings are correctly aligned.

28 Apply a smear of clean engine oil to the threads and underside of the bearing cap nuts. Fit the nuts to the connecting rod and tighten them evenly, in two or three stages, to the specified torque setting **(see illustration)**.

29 Check that the crankshaft is free to rotate easily, then install the three remaining assemblies in the same way. Check to make sure that all components have been returned to their original locations using the marks made on disassembly.

30 Check that the rods rotate smoothly and freely on the crankpin. If there are any signs of roughness or tightness, remove the rods and re-check the bearing clearance. Sometimes tapping the bottom of the connecting rod cap will relieve tightness, but if in doubt, recheck the clearances.

31 Reassemble the crankcase halves (see Section 29).

33 Pistons - removal, inspection and installation

Note: *To remove the pistons the engine must be removed from the frame and the crankcase halves separated.*

Removal

1 Remove the engine from the frame (see Section 5) and separate the crankcase halves (see Section 29).

2 Separate the connecting rods from the crankshaft (see Section 32).

3 Before removing the piston from the connecting rod, use a sharp scriber or felt marker pen to write the cylinder identity on the crown of each piston (or on the inside of the skirt if the piston is dirty and going to be cleaned). Each piston should also have an "IN" mark on its crown which should face the intake side of the bore **(see illustration)**. If this is not visible, mark the piston accordingly so that it can be installed the correct way round.

4 Carefully prise out the circlip on one side of the piston using needle-nose pliers or a small flat-bladed screwdriver inserted into the notch. Push the piston pin out from the other side to free the piston from the connecting rod **(see illustrations)**. Remove the other circlip and discard them as new ones must be used. When the piston has been removed, install its pin back into its bore so that related parts do not get mixed up.

HAYNES HiNT ***To prevent the circlip from pinging away, pass a rod or screwdriver, whose diameter is greater than the gap between the circlip ends, through the piston pin. This will trap the circlip if it springs out.***

HAYNES HiNT ***If a piston pin is a tight fit in the piston bosses, soak a rag in boiling water then wring it out and wrap it around the piston - this will expand the alloy piston sufficiently to release its grip on the pin. If the piston pin is particularly stubborn, extract it using a drawbolt tool, but be careful to protect the piston's working surfaces.***

Inspection

5 Before the inspection process can be carried out, the pistons must be cleaned and the old piston rings removed. Note that if the cylinders are being rebored, piston inspection can be overlooked as new ones will be fitted.

6 Using your thumbs or a piston ring removal and installation tool, carefully remove the rings from the pistons **(see illustration)**. Do not nick or gouge the pistons in the process. Carefully note which way up each ring fits and in which groove as they must be installed in their original positions if being re-used. The upper surface of each ring is marked with a letter at one end. The top ring is identified by the letter R, and the second (middle) ring by the letters RN.

7 Scrape all traces of carbon from the tops of the pistons. A hand-held wire brush or a piece of fine emery cloth can be used once most of the deposits have been scraped away. Do not, under any circumstances, use a wire brush mounted in a drill motor to remove deposits from the pistons; the piston material is soft and will be eroded away by the wire brush.

8 Use a piston ring groove cleaning tool to remove any carbon deposits from the ring grooves. If a tool is not available, a piece broken off an old ring will do the job. Be very careful to remove only the carbon deposits. Do not remove any metal and do not nick or gouge the sides of the ring grooves.

9 Once the deposits have been removed,

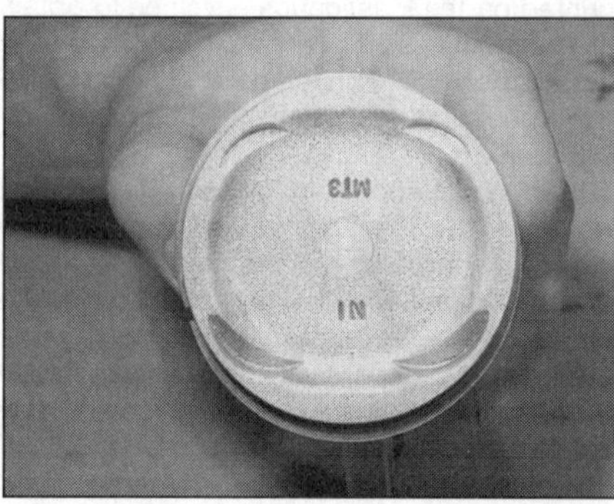

33.3 Note the "IN" mark on the piston which faces the intake side of the bore

33.4a Prise out the circlip . . .

33.4b . . . then push out the pin and remove the piston

33.6 Removing the piston rings using a ring removal and installation tool

33.12 Measure the piston ring-to-groove clearance with a feeler gauge

33.13 Measure the piston diameter with a micrometer at the specified distance from the bottom of the skirt

clean the pistons with solvent and dry them thoroughly. If the identification previously marked on the piston is cleaned off, be sure to re-mark it with the correct identity. Make sure the oil return holes below the oil ring groove are clear.

10 Carefully inspect each piston for cracks around the skirt, at the pin bosses and at the ring lands. Normal piston wear appears as even, vertical wear on the thrust surfaces of the piston and slight looseness of the top ring in its groove. If the skirt is scored or scuffed, the engine may have been suffering from overheating and/or abnormal combustion, which caused excessively high operating temperatures. The oil pump should be checked thoroughly. Also check that the circlip grooves are not damaged.

11 A hole in the piston crown, an extreme to be sure, is an indication that abnormal combustion (pre-ignition) was occurring. Burned areas at the edge of the piston crown are usually evidence of spark knock (detonation). If any of the above problems exist, the causes must be corrected or the damage will occur again.

12 Measure the piston ring-to-groove clearance by laying each piston ring in its groove and slipping a feeler gauge in beside it **(see illustration)**. Make sure you have the correct ring for the groove (see Step 5). Check the clearance at three or four locations around the groove. If the clearance is greater than specified, replace both the piston and rings as a set. If new rings are being used, measure the clearance using the new rings. If the clearance is greater than that specified, the piston is worn and must be replaced.

13 Check the piston-to-bore clearance by measuring the bore (see Section 30) and the piston diameter. Make sure each piston is matched to its correct cylinder. Measure the piston 19.0 mm up from the bottom of the skirt and at 90° to the piston pin axis **(see illustration)**. Subtract the piston diameter from the bore diameter to obtain the clearance. If it is greater than the specified figure, the piston must be replaced (assuming the bore itself is within limits, otherwise a rebore is necessary).

14 Apply clean engine oil to the piston pin, insert it into the piston and check for any freeplay between the two. Measure the pin external diameter and the pin bore in the piston and compare the measurements to the specifications at the beginning of the Chapter. Repeat the measurements between the pin and the connecting rod small-end **(see illustrations)**. Replace components that are worn beyond the specified limits.

15 If the pistons are to be replaced, ensure the correct size of piston is ordered. Honda produce two oversize pistons, as well as the standard piston. The oversize pistons available are: +0.25 mm and +0.50 mm. **Note:** *Oversize pistons usually have their relevant size stamped on top of the piston crown, e.g. a 0.50 mm oversize piston will be marked 0.50. Be sure to obtain the correct oversize rings for the pistons.*

Installation

16 Inspect and install the piston rings (see Section 34).

17 Lubricate the piston pin, the piston pin bore and the connecting rod small-end bore with a 50/50 mixture of molybdenum disulphide grease and clean engine oil.

18 When installing the pistons onto the connecting rods, make sure that the "IN" mark is on the same side as the oil hole in the connecting rod on the left-hand cylinder pistons, but is on the opposite side to the hole on the right-hand cylinder pistons. Install a new circlip in one side of the piston (do not re-use old circlips) **(see illustration)**. Line up the

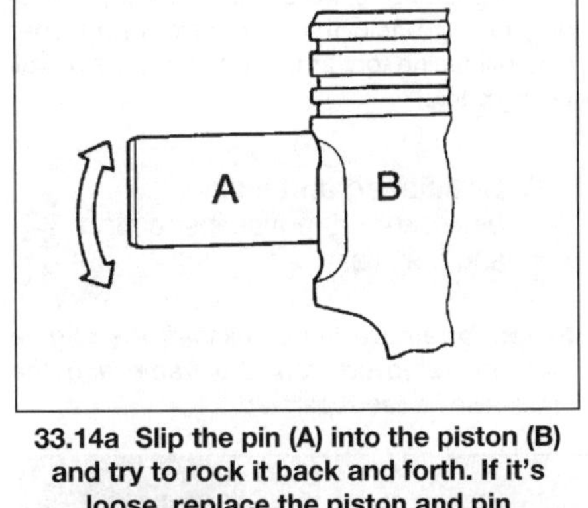

33.14a Slip the pin (A) into the piston (B) and try to rock it back and forth. If it's loose, replace the piston and pin

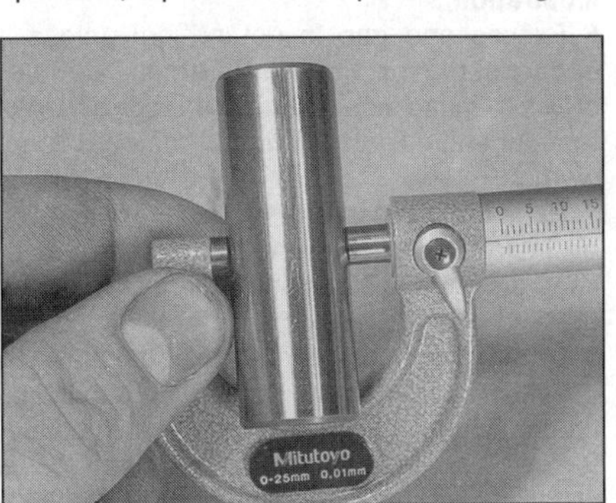

33.14b Measure the external diameter of the pin . . .

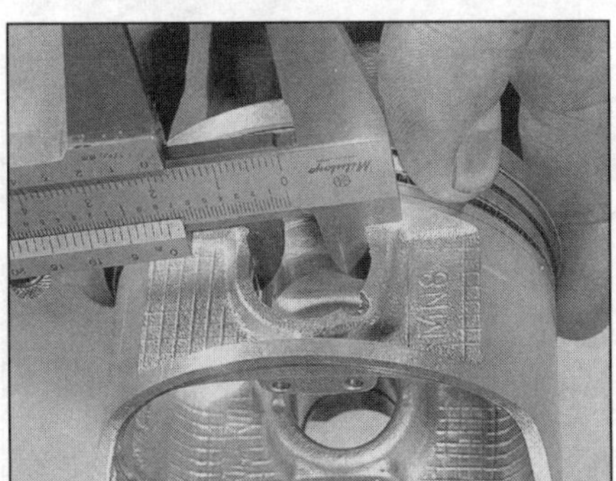

33.14c . . . the internal diameter of the bore in the piston . . .

33.14d . . . and the internal diameter of the connecting rod small-end

33.18 Do not over-compress the circlip when fitting it into the piston

34.3 Measuring piston ring installed end gap

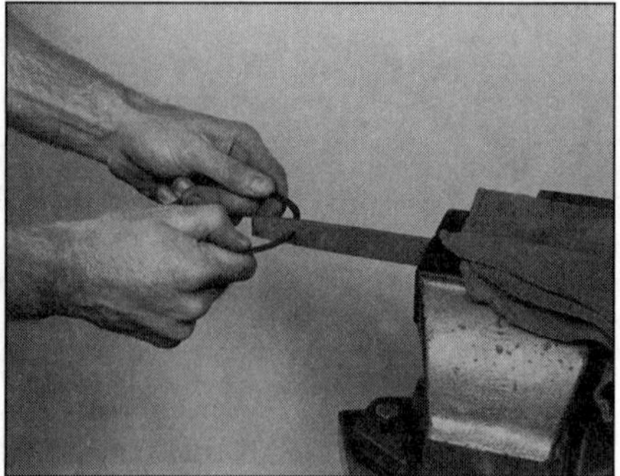
34.5 Ring end gap can be enlarged by clamping a file in a vice and filing the ring ends

piston on its correct connecting rod, and insert the piston pin from the other side **(see illustration 33.4b)**. Secure the pin with the other new circlip. When installing the circlips, compress them only just enough to fit them in the piston, and make sure they are properly seated in their grooves with the open end away from the removal notch.

19 Install the connecting rods onto the crankshaft (see Section 32) and reassemble the crankcase halves (see Section 29).

34 Piston rings - inspection and installation

1 It is good practice to replace the piston rings when an engine is being overhauled. Before installing the new piston rings, the ring end gaps must be checked with the rings installed in the cylinder.

2 Lay out the pistons and the new ring sets so the rings will be matched with the same piston and cylinder during the end gap measurement procedure and engine assembly.

3 To measure the installed ring end gap, insert the top ring into the top of the first cylinder and square it up with the cylinder walls by pushing it in with the top of the piston. The ring should be about 20 mm below the top edge of the cylinder. To measure the end gap, slip a feeler gauge between the ends of the ring and compare the measurement to the specifications at the beginning of the Chapter **(see illustration)**.

4 If the gap is larger or smaller than specified, double check to make sure that you have the correct rings before proceeding.

5 If the gap is too small, it must be enlarged or the ring ends may come in contact with each other during engine operation, which can cause serious damage. The end gap can be increased by filing the ring ends very carefully with a fine file. When performing this operation, file only from the outside in **(see illustration)**.

6 Excess end gap is not critical unless it exceeds the service limit. Again, double-check to make sure you have the correct rings for your engine and check that the bore is not worn.

7 Repeat the procedure for each ring that will be installed in the cylinders. Remember to keep the rings, pistons and cylinders matched up.

8 Once the ring end gaps have been checked/corrected, the rings can be installed on the pistons.

9 The oil control ring (lowest on the piston) is installed first. It is composed of three separate components, namely the expander and the upper and lower side rails. Slip the expander into the groove, then install the upper side rail. Do not use a piston ring installation tool on the oil ring side rails as they may be damaged. Instead, place one end of the side rail into the groove between the expander and the ring land. Hold it firmly in place and slide a finger around the piston while pushing the rail into the groove. Next, install the lower side rail in the same manner **(see illustrations)**. Make sure the ends of the expander do not overlap.

10 After the three oil ring components have been installed, check to make sure that both the upper and lower side rails can be turned smoothly in the ring groove.

11 The upper surface of each compression ring is marked with a letter at one end. The top ring is identified by the letter R, and the second (middle) ring by the letters RN. Install the second (middle) ring next. Make sure that the identification letter near the end gap is facing up. Fit the ring into the middle groove in the piston. Do not expand the ring any more than is necessary to slide it into place. To avoid breaking the ring, use a piston ring installation tool.

12 Finally, install the top ring in the same manner into the top groove in the piston. Make sure the identification letter near the end gap is facing up.

13 Once the rings are correctly installed, check they move freely without snagging and stagger their end gaps 180° apart, with the top ring facing forward, the second (middle) ring facing back, the oil control ring upper side rail facing forward, and the lower side rail facing back.

35 Crankshaft and main bearings - removal, inspection and installation

Note: *To remove the crankshaft the engine must be removed from the frame and the crankcase halves separated.*

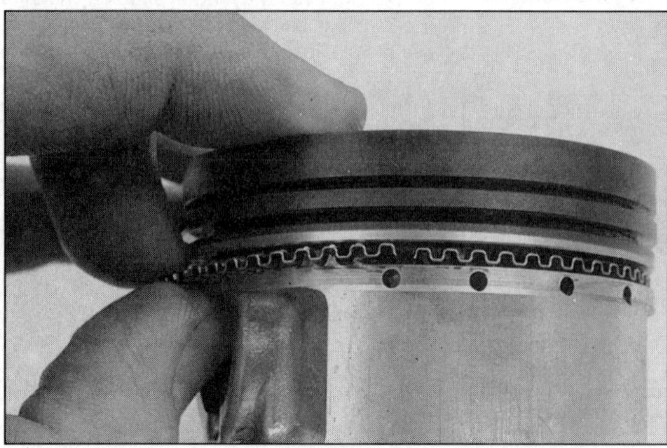
34.9a Install the oil ring expander in its groove . . .

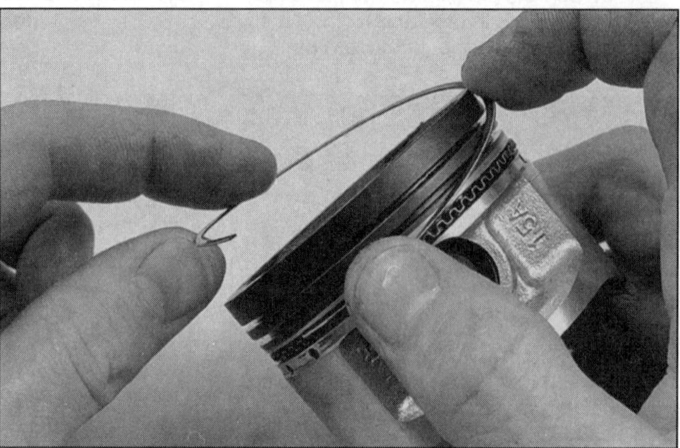
34.9b . . . and fit the side rails each side of it. The oil ring must be installed by hand

35.3 Remove the two thrust bearings (arrowed), noting how they fit

Removal

1 Remove the engine from the frame (see Section 5) and separate the crankcase halves (see Section 29).

2 Separate the connecting rods from the crankshaft (see Section 32).

Note: *If no work is to be carried out on the piston/connecting rod assemblies there is no need to remove them from the bores. The cylinder heads can be left in position although the connecting rod bearing caps must be removed (see Section 32, Steps 2 to 4) and the pistons pushed up to the top of the bores so that the connecting rod ends are positioned clear of the crankshaft.*

3 Lift the crankshaft out of the upper crankcase half, taking care not to dislodge the main bearing shells. Remove the two thrust bearings, noting which way round they fit **(see illustration)**.

4 If required, remove the primary drive gear and starter clutch assembly from the crankshaft (see Section 36).

5 The main bearing shells can be removed from the crankcase halves by pushing their centres to the side, then lifting them out. Keep the shells in order.

Inspection

6 Clean the crankshaft with solvent, using a rifle-cleaning brush to scrub out the oil passages. If available, blow the crank dry with compressed air, and also blow through the oil passages. Check the primary drive gear for wear or damage. If any of the gear teeth are excessively worn, chipped or broken, the crankshaft must be replaced.

7 Refer to Section 31 and examine the main bearing shells. If they are scored, badly scuffed or appear to have been seized, new bearings must be installed. Always replace the main bearings as a set. If they are badly damaged, check the corresponding crankshaft journals. Evidence of extreme heat, such as discoloration, indicates that lubrication failure has occurred. Be sure to thoroughly check the oil pump and pressure regulator as well as all oil holes and passages before reassembling the engine.

8 The crankshaft journals should be given a close visual examination, paying particular attention where damaged bearings have been discovered. If the journals are scored or pitted in any way a new crankshaft will be required. Note that undersizes are not available, precluding the option of re-grinding the crankshaft.

9 Place the crankshaft on V-blocks and check the runout at the main bearing journals using a dial gauge. Compare the reading to the maximum specified at the beginning of the Chapter. If the runout exceeds the limit, the crankshaft must be replaced.

Main bearing shell selection

10 Replacement bearing shells for the main bearings are supplied on a selected fit basis. Code letters and numbers stamped on various components are used to identify the correct replacement bearings. The crankshaft main bearing journal size numbers are stamped on the crankshaft webs and will be either a 1, a 2 or a 3 **(see illustration 32.12a)**. Each number is adjacent to the journal it represents. The corresponding main bearing housing size letters are stamped into the front of the upper crankcase half and will be either an A, a B or a C, with a number above each letter denoting the corresponding journal **(see illustration)**. No.1 is the front journal, no.2 the middle and no.3 the rear.

11 A range of bearing shells is available. To select the correct bearing for a particular journal, using the table below cross-refer the main bearing journal size number (stamped on the crank web) with the main bearing housing size letter (stamped on the crankcase) to determine the colour code of the bearing required. For example, if the journal code is 1, and the housing code is A, then the bearing required is Yellow. The colour is marked on the side of the shell **(see illustration 32.13)**.

Crankshaft journal code	Crankcase housing code		
	A	B	C
1	Yellow	Green	Brown
2	Green	Brown	Black
3	Brown	Black	Blue

Oil clearance check

12 Whether new bearing shells are being fitted or the original ones are being re-used, the main bearing oil clearance should be checked before the engine is reassembled. Main bearing oil clearance is measured with a product known as Plastigauge.

13 Clean the backs of the bearing shells and the bearing housings in both crankcase halves.

14 Press the bearing shells into their cut-outs, ensuring that the tab on each shell engages in the notch in the crankcase **(see illustration)**. Make sure the bearings are fitted in the correct locations and take care not to touch any shell's bearing surface with your fingers.

15 Ensure the shells and crankshaft are clean and dry. Lay the crankshaft in position in the upper crankcase.

16 Cut several lengths of the appropriate size

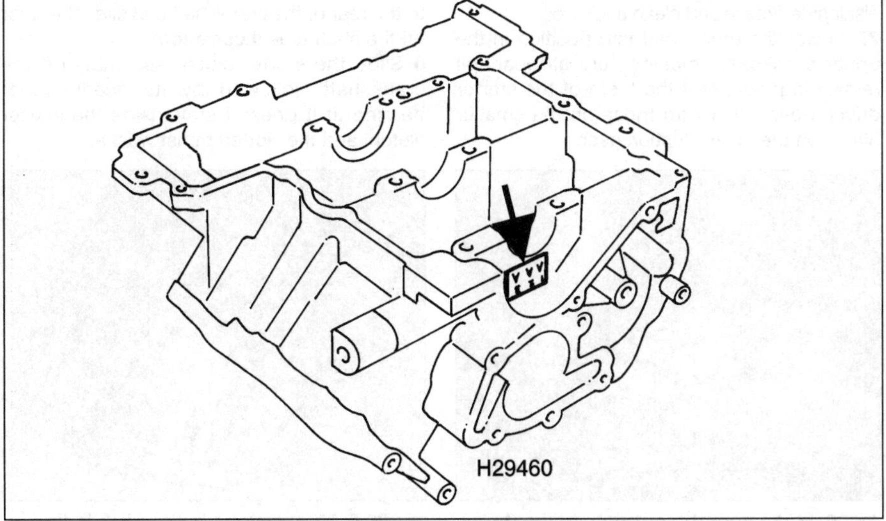

35.10 Main bearing housing size letters

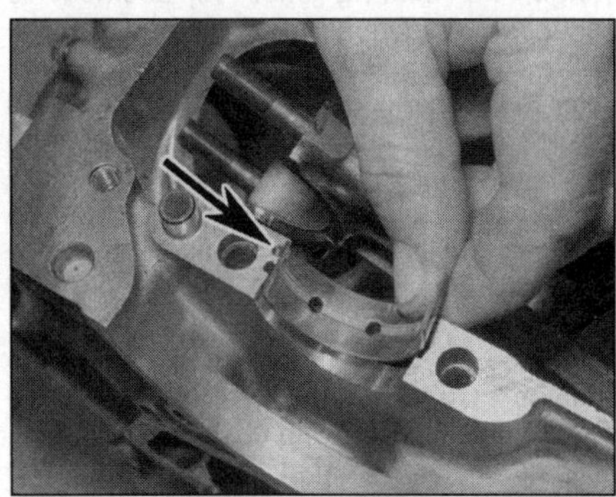
35.14 Make sure the tab on the shell locates in the notch in the housing (arrowed)

2

35.16 Lay a strand of Plastigage (arrowed) on each journal parallel to the crankshaft centreline

35.19 Measure the width of the crushed Plastigage (be sure to use the correct scale - metric and imperial are included)

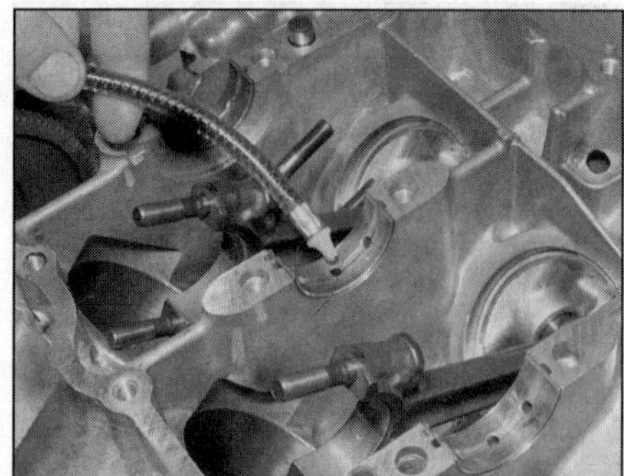
35.25 Generously lubricate all the bearing shells

Plastigauge (they should be slightly shorter than the width of the crankshaft journals). Place a strand of Plastigauge on each (cleaned) journal **(see illustration)**. Make sure the crankshaft is not rotated.

17 Carefully install the lower crankcase half on to the upper half. Check that the lower crankcase half is correctly seated. **Note:** *Do not tighten the crankcase bolts if the casing is not correctly seated.* Install the lower crankcase 10 mm bolts in their original locations and tighten them evenly a little at a time in a criss-cross sequence to the torque setting specified at the beginning of the Chapter. Make sure that the crankshaft is not rotated as the bolts are tightened.

18 Slacken each bolt evenly a little at a time in a criss-cross sequence until they are all finger-tight, then remove the bolts. Carefully lift off the lower crankcase half, making sure the Plastigauge is not disturbed.

19 Compare the width of the crushed Plastigauge on each crankshaft journal to the scale printed on the Plastigauge envelope to obtain the main bearing oil clearance **(see illustration)**. Compare the reading to the specifications at the beginning of the Chapter.

20 On completion carefully scrape away all traces of the Plastigauge material from the crankshaft journal and bearing shells; use a fingernail or other object which is unlikely to score them.

21 If the oil clearance falls into the specified range, no bearing shell replacement is required (provided they are in good condition). If the clearance is beyond the service limit, refer to the marks on the case and the marks on the crankshaft and select new bearing shells (see Steps 10 and 11). Install the new shells and check the oil clearance once again (the new shells may bring bearing clearance within the specified range). Always replace all of the shells at the same time.

22 If the clearance is still greater than the service limit listed in this Chapter's Specifications (even with replacement shells), the crankshaft journal is worn and the crankshaft should be replaced.

Installation

23 If removed, install the primary drive gear and starter clutch assembly onto the crankshaft (see Section 36).

24 Clean the backs of the bearing shells and the bearing cut-outs in both crankcase halves. If new shells are being fitted, ensure that all traces of the protective grease are cleaned off using paraffin (kerosene). Wipe dry the shells and crankcase halves with a lint-free cloth. Make sure all the oil passages and holes are clear, and blow them through with compressed air if it is available.

25 Press the bearing shells into their locations. Make sure the tab on each shell engages in the notch in the casing **(see illustration 35.14)**. Make sure the bearings are fitted in the correct locations and take care not to touch any shell's bearing surface with your fingers. Lubricate each shell with a 50/50 mixture of molybdenum disulphide grease and clean engine oil **(see illustration)**.

26 Lubricate each thrust bearing with a 50/50 mixture of molybdenum disulphide grease and clean engine oil. Install them into the upper crankcase half, aligning the tab on each bearing with the groove in the crankcase so that the cut-outs in the bearing face out **(see illustration)**. Also lubricate the primary drive gear on the crankshaft with the mixture of molybdenum disulphide grease and clean engine oil.

27 Lower the crankshaft into position in the upper crankcase, making sure all bearings remain in place, and the teeth of the starter driven gear mesh with those on the smaller pinion on the idle/reduction gear.

35.26 Make sure the cut-outs in the thrust bearings face out

28 Fit the connecting rods onto the crankshaft (see Section 32).

29 Reassemble the crankcase halves (see Section 29).

36 Primary drive gear and starter clutch assembly - removal, inspection and installation

Note: *To remove the starter clutch and idle/reduction gear the engine must be removed from the frame and the crankcase halves separated.*

Removal

1 Remove the engine from the frame (see Section 5) and separate the crankcase halves (see Section 29).

2 Remove the crankshaft (see Section 35).

3 Remove the collar and O-ring from the front of the crankshaft. Check the condition of the O-ring and replace it if necessary.

4 Remove the stopper circlip and slide the primary drive gear off the front of the crankshaft, noting which way round they fit.

5 Unscrew the bolt securing the ignition rotor to the rear of the crankshaft and slide the rotor off the shaft **(see illustration)**.

6 Slide the starter clutch assembly off the crankshaft, followed by its needle roller bearing (if it doesn't stay inside the starter clutch) and the slotted thrust washer.

36.5 Unscrew the bolt and slide the ignition rotor and starter clutch assembly off the end of the crankshaft

Inspection

7 Install the starter driven gear into the starter clutch (if removed) and, with the clutch face down on a workbench, check that the gear rotates freely in an anti-clockwise direction and locks against the rotor in a clockwise direction. If it doesn't, replace the starter clutch.

8 Withdraw the starter driven gear from the starter clutch. If it appears stuck, rotate it anti-clockwise as you withdraw it to free it from the starter clutch.

9 Check the bearing surface of the starter driven gear hub and the condition of the rollers inside the clutch body. If the bearing surface shows signs of excessive wear or the rollers are damaged, marked or flattened at any point, they should be replaced. The rollers are secured in the clutch body by a circlip.

10 Check the teeth of the starter idle/reduction gear in the crankcase and the corresponding teeth of the starter driven gear and starter motor drive shaft. Replace the gears and/or starter motor if worn or chipped teeth are discovered on related gears. Also check the idle/reduction gear shaft for damage, and check that the gear is not a loose fit on the shaft. Replace the shaft if necessary. Unscrew the bolt securing the shaft, then withdraw the shaft and remove the idle/reduction gear **(see illustration 30.1a)**. Install the idle/reduction gear with the smaller pinion facing the rear and lubricate the shaft with clean engine oil.

11 Check the teeth of the alternator drive gear and the corresponding teeth of the alternator driven gear. Replace the gear and/or alternator if worn or chipped teeth are discovered on related gears. The drive gear is secured to the starter clutch body by eight bolts.

12 Check that all the starter clutch bolts are tight. If any are loose, remove them and apply a suitable non-permanent thread locking compound to their threads, then tighten them to the torque setting specified at the beginning of the Chapter.

Installation

13 Lubricate the hub of the starter driven gear with clean engine oil, then install the starter driven gear into the clutch, rotating it anti-clockwise as you do so to spread the rollers and allow the hub of the gear to enter.

14 Slide the slotted thrust washer onto the rear end of the crankshaft. Lubricate the needle roller bearing with clean engine oil and slide it onto the shaft.

15 Slide the starter clutch assembly onto the rear end of the crankshaft, with the starter driven gear facing in and aligning the wide spline in the clutch body with that on the crankshaft. Make sure the starter driven gear fits correctly over the needle roller bearing.

16 Slide the ignition rotor onto the end of the crankshaft, aligning the wide spline in the rotor with that on the crankshaft. Install the rotor bolt with its washer and tighten it securely.

17 Slide the primary drive gear onto the front of the crankshaft, making sure the OUT mark is facing out **(see illustration)**. Secure the gear with the stopper circlip, making sure its dished side faces in.

18 Slide the O-ring onto the front of the shaft, using a new one if necessary, and lubricate it with clean engine oil. Slide the collar onto the shaft.

19 Install the crankshaft (see Section 35).

37 Initial start-up after overhaul

1 Make sure the engine oil level is correct (see *Daily (pre-ride) checks*).

2 Pull the plug caps off the spark plugs and insert a spare spark plug into each cap. Position the spare plugs so that their bodies are earthed (grounded) against the engine. Turn on the ignition switch and crank the engine over with the starter until the oil pressure indicator light goes off (which indicates that oil pressure exists). Turn off the ignition. Remove the spare spark plugs and reconnect the plug caps.

3 Make sure there is fuel in the tank and set the choke as required.

4 Start the engine and allow it to run at a moderately fast idle until it reaches operating temperature.

Warning: If the oil pressure indicator light doesn't go off, or it comes on while the engine is running, stop the engine immediately.

5 Check carefully for oil leaks and make sure the transmission and controls, especially the brakes, function properly before road testing the machine. Refer to Section 38 for the recommended running-in procedure.

6 Upon completion of the road test, and after the engine has cooled down completely, recheck the valve clearances (see Chapter 1) and check the engine oil level (see *Daily (pre-ride) checks*).

36.17 The OUT mark (arrowed) on the primary drive bear must face out

38 Recommended running-in procedure

1 Treat the machine gently for the first few miles to make sure oil has circulated throughout the engine and any new parts installed have started to seat.

2 Even greater care is necessary if the engine has been rebored or a new crankshaft has been installed. In the case of a rebore, the bike will have to be run in as when new. This means greater use of the transmission and a restraining hand on the throttle until at least 600 miles (1000 km) have been covered. There's no point in keeping to any set speed limit - the main idea is to keep from labouring the engine and to gradually increase performance up to the 600 mile (1000 km) mark. These recommendations can be lessened to an extent when only a new crankshaft is installed. Experience is the best guide, since it's easy to tell when an engine is running freely. The following maximum engine speed limitations, which Honda provide for new motorcycles, can be used as a guide.

Up to 600 miles (1000 km)
4000 rpm max
Vary throttle position/speed
600 to 1000 miles (1000 to 1600 km)
6000 rpm max
Vary throttle position/speed.
Use full throttle for short bursts
Over 1000 miles (1600 km)
8000 rpm max
Do not exceed tachometer red line

3 If a lubrication failure is suspected, stop the engine immediately and try to find the cause. If an engine is run without oil, even for a short period of time, severe damage will occur.

Notes

Chapter 3
Cooling system

Contents

Coolant hoses - removal and installation 9
Coolant level check . . . . . see Daily (pre-ride) checks
Coolant reservoir - removal and installation 3
Coolant temperature gauge and sensor - check and replacement . 5
Cooling fan and cooling fan switch - check and replacement 4
Cooling system checks . . . . . see Chapter 1
Cooling system draining, flushing and refilling . . . . . see Chapter 1
General information 1
Radiator - removal and installation 7
Radiator pressure cap - check 2
Thermostat - removal, check and installation 6
Water pump - check, removal and installation 8

Degrees of difficulty

Easy, suitable for novice with little experience 	**Fairly easy,** suitable for beginner with some experience 	**Fairly difficult,** suitable for competent DIY mechanic	**Difficult,** suitable for experienced DIY mechanic	**Very difficult,** suitable for expert DIY or professional

Specifications

Coolant

Mixture type and capacity	see Chapter 1

Radiator

Cap valve opening pressure	16 to 20 psi (1.1 to 1.4 Bar)

Fan switch

Cooling fan cut-in temperature	98 to 102°C
Cooling fan cut-out temperature	93 to 97°C

Temperature gauge sensor

Resistance	
@ 50°C	130 to 180 ohms
@ 80°C	45 to 60 ohms
@ 120°C	10 to 20 ohms

Thermostat

Opening temperature	80 to 84°C
Valve lift	8 mm (min) @ 95°C

Torque settings

Fan switch	12 Nm
Thermostat housing bolts	10 Nm
Timing belt idle pulley bolt	46 Nm

1 General information

The cooling system uses a water/antifreeze coolant to carry away excess energy in the form of heat. The cylinders are surrounded by a water jacket from which the heated coolant is circulated by thermo-syphonic action in conjunction with a water pump, driven by the timing belt. The hot coolant passes upwards to the thermostat and through to the radiator. The coolant then flows across the radiator core, where it is cooled by the passing air, to the water pump and back to the engine where the cycle is repeated.

A thermostat is fitted in the system to prevent the coolant flowing through the radiator when the engine is cold, therefore accelerating the speed at which the engine reaches normal operating temperature. A thermostatically-controlled cooling fan is also fitted to aid cooling in extreme conditions.

The complete cooling system is partially sealed and pressurised, the pressure being controlled by a valve contained in the spring-loaded radiator cap. By pressurising the coolant the boiling point is raised, preventing premature boiling in adverse conditions. The overflow pipe from the system is connected to a reservoir into which excess coolant is expelled under pressure. The discharged coolant automatically returns to the radiator when the engine cools.

Warning: Do not remove the pressure cap from the radiator when the engine is hot. Scalding hot coolant and steam may be blown out under pressure, which could cause serious injury. When the engine has cooled, place a thick rag, like a towel over the pressure cap; slowly rotate the cap anti-clockwise to the first stop. This procedure allows any residual pressure to escape. When the steam has stopped escaping, press down on the cap while turning it anti-clockwise and remove it.

Warning: Do not allow antifreeze to come in contact with your skin or painted surfaces of the motorcycle. Rinse off any spills immediately with plenty of water. Antifreeze is highly toxic if ingested. Never leave antifreeze lying around in an open container or in puddles on the floor; children and pets are attracted by its sweet smell and may drink it. Check with the local authorities about disposing of used antifreeze. Many communities will have collection centres which will see that antifreeze is disposed of safely.

Caution: At all times use the specified type of antifreeze, and always mix it with distilled water in the correct proportion. The antifreeze contains corrosion inhibitors which are essential to avoid damage to the cooling system. A lack of these inhibitors could lead to a build-up of corrosion which would block the coolant passages, resulting in overheating and severe engine damage. Distilled water must be used as opposed to tap water to avoid a build-up of scale which would also block the passages.

2 Radiator pressure cap - check

If problems such as overheating or loss of coolant occur, check the entire system as described in Chapter 1. The radiator cap opening pressure should be checked by a Honda dealer with the special tester required to do the job. If the cap is defective, replace it with a new one.

3 Coolant reservoir - removal and installation

Removal

1 On all standard models, remove the right-hand side panel (see Chapter 8). Free the rear brake master cylinder reservoir hose from its guide pegs on the top of the coolant reservoir. If necessary, unscrew the master cylinder reservoir bolt and lift the reservoir up to free the hose. Support the reservoir in an upright position so that no strain is placed on the hose.

2 On all ABS/TCS and CBS/LBS-ABS/TCS models, remove the right-hand middle fairing panel (see Chapter 8). Release the coolant reservoir breather/overflow hose (coming out of the top of the reservoir) from its clamp **(see illustration)**.

3 Place a suitable container underneath the reservoir, then release the clamp securing the radiator overflow hose to the base of the reservoir. Detach the hose and allow the coolant to drain into the container **(see illustration 3.2)**.

4 Unscrew the two reservoir mounting bolts and remove the reservoir from the bike **(see illustration)**. On standard models, note the breather/overflow hose clamp secured by the rear bolt.

Installation

5 Installation is the reverse of removal. Make sure the hoses are correctly installed and secured with their clamps. On completion refill the reservoir as described in Chapter 1.

4 Cooling fan and cooling fan switch - check and replacement

Cooling fan

Check

1 If the engine is overheating and the cooling fan isn't coming on, first check the cooling fan circuit fuse (see Chapter 9) and then the fan switch as described in Steps 8 to 12 below.

2 If the fan does not come on, (and the fan switch is good), the fault lies in either the cooling fan motor or the relevant wiring. Test all the wiring and connections as described in Chapter 9.

3 To test the cooling fan motor, disconnect the fan wiring connector behind the radiator **(see illustration)**. Using a 12 volt battery and two jumper wires, connect battery positive (+ve) lead to the black/blue fan wire and the battery negative (-ve) lead to earth. Once connected the fan should operate. If it does

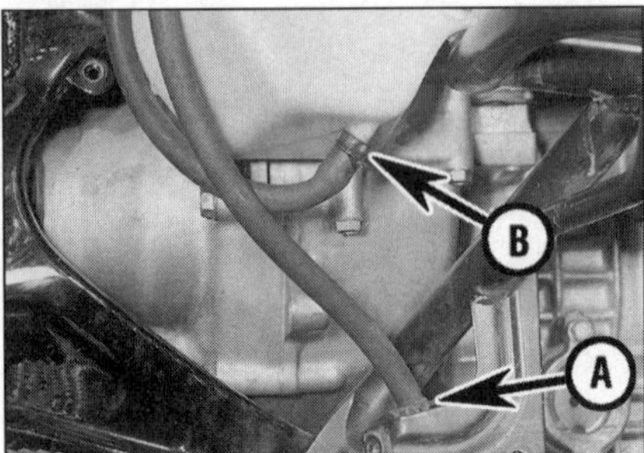

3.2 Free the overflow hose from its clamp (A), then detach the radiator hose (B) and drain the coolant

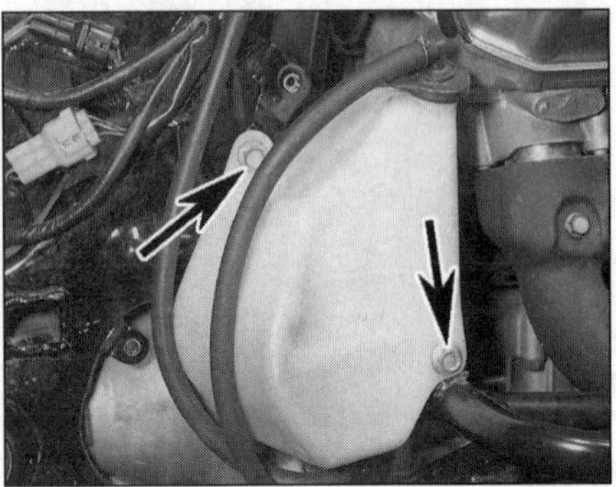

3.4 The reservoir is secured by two bolts (arrowed)

4.3 The fan wiring connector fits in a bracket on the frame behind the radiator

4.5a Disconnect the fan switch wiring connector . . .

4.5b . . . then unscrew the two bolts at the back (arrowed) . . .

4.5c . . . and the bolt at the front (arrowed) and remove the fan assembly

not, and the wiring is all good, then the fan is faulty. As no individual components are available for the fan assembly, it must be replaced as a unit.

Replacement

Warning: The engine must be completely cool before carrying out this procedure.

4 Remove the radiator (see Section 7).

5 Disconnect the wiring connector from the fan switch in the radiator. Unscrew the three bolts, two on the back at the bottom and one on the front at the top, securing the fan shroud and fan assembly to the radiator, noting that the lower left-hand bolt also secures the earth (ground) cable **(see illustrations)**. Unscrew the three nuts on the front of the fan securing the fan assembly to the shroud and remove the shroud.

6 Installation is the reverse of removal. Apply a suitable non-permanent thread locking compound to the threads of the fan mounting nuts and tighten them securely. Do not forget to attach the earth (ground) cable to the shroud.

7 Install the radiator (see Section 7).

Cooling fan switch

Check

8 If the engine is overheating and the cooling fan isn't coming on, first check the cooling fan circuit fuse (see Chapter 9). If the fuse is blown, check the fan circuit for a short to earth (see the wiring diagrams at the end of this manual).

9 If the fuse is good, disconnect the wire from the fan switch fitted to the left side of the radiator **(see illustration 4.5a)**. Using a jumper wire if necessary, connect the wire to earth (ground). The fan should come on. If it does, the fan switch is defective and must be replaced. If it does not come on, the fan should be tested (see Step 3).

10 If the fan works but is suspected of cutting in at the wrong temperature, a more comprehensive test of the switch can be made as follows.

11 Remove the switch (see Steps 13 to 16). Fill a small heatproof container with coolant and place it on a stove. Connect the positive (+ve) probe of an ohmmeter to the terminal of the switch and the negative (-ve) probe to the switch body, and using some wire or other support suspend the switch in the coolant so that just the sensing portion and the threads are submerged. Also place a thermometer capable of reading temperatures up to 110°C in the coolant so that its bulb is close to the switch. The testing set-up is similar to that used for the temperature gauge sensor **(see illustration 5.7)**. **Note:** *None of the components should be allowed to directly touch the container.*

12 Initially the ohmmeter reading should be very high indicating that the switch is open (OFF). Heat the coolant, stirring it gently.

Warning: This must be done very carefully to avoid the risk of personal injury.

When the temperature reaches around 98 to 102°C the meter reading should drop to around zero ohms, indicating that the switch has closed (ON). Now turn the heat off. As the temperature falls below 93 to 97°C the meter reading should show infinite (very high) resistance, indicating that the switch has opened (OFF). If the meter readings obtained are different, or they are obtained at different temperatures, then the switch is faulty and must be replaced.

Replacement

Warning: The engine must be completely cool before carrying out this procedure.

13 Drain the cooling system (see Chapter 1).

14 The fan switch is located in the left-hand side of the radiator **(see illustration)**. Disconnect the wiring connector, then unscrew the switch and withdraw it from the radiator. Discard the O-ring as a new one must be used.

15 Install the switch using a new O-ring and tighten it to the torque setting specified at the beginning of the Chapter.

16 Reconnect the switch wiring and refill the cooling system (see Chapter 1).

4.14 The fan switch (arrowed) is screwed into the left-hand side of the radiator

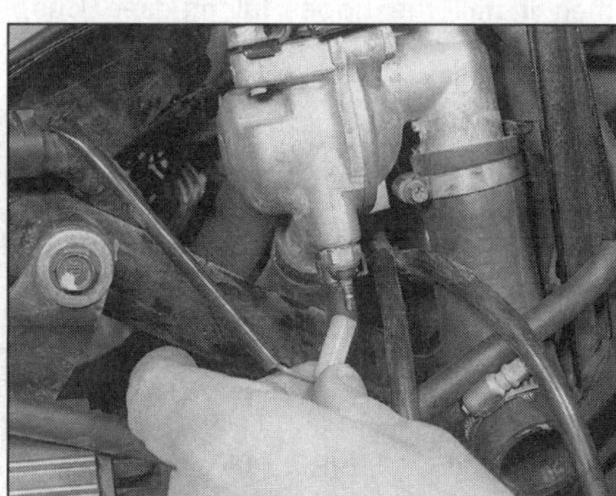
5.2 Disconnect the sensor wiring connector from the base of the thermostat housing

5 Coolant temperature gauge and sensor - check and replacement

Coolant temperature gauge

Check

1 The circuit consists of the sensor mounted in the bottom of the thermostat housing and the gauge assembly mounted in the instrument panel. If the system malfunctions check first that the battery is fully charged and that the fuses are all good.

2 If the gauge is not working, disconnect the wire from the sensor and turn the ignition switch ON **(see illustration)**. The temperature gauge needle should be on the "C" on the

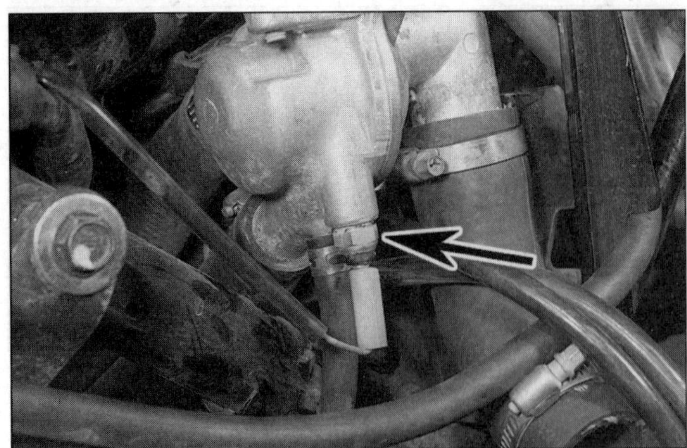

5.5 The temperature sensor screws into the base of the thermostat housing

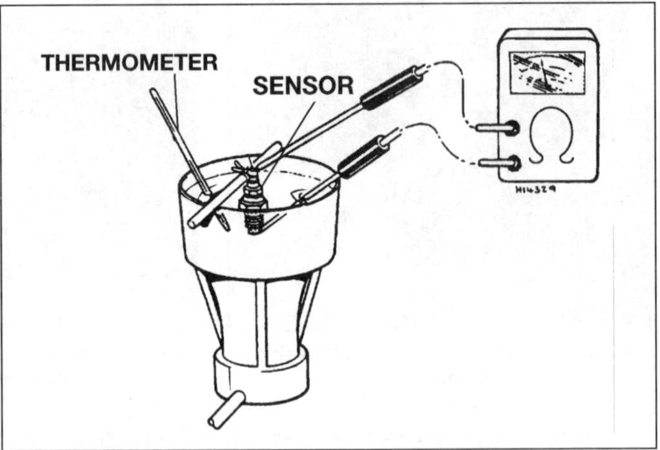

5.7 Temperature gauge sensor testing set-up

gauge. Now earth the sensor wire on the engine. The needle should swing immediately over to the "H" on the gauge. If the needle moves as described above, the sensor is proven defective and must be replaced.

Caution: Do not earth the wire for any longer than is necessary to take the reading, or the gauge may be damaged.

3 If the needle movement is still faulty, or if it does not move at all, the fault lies in the wiring or the gauge itself. Check all the relevant wiring and wiring connectors (see Chapter 9). If all appears to be well, the gauge is defective and must be replaced.

Replacement

4 See Chapter 9.

Temperature gauge sensor

Check

5 Remove the upper fairing (see Chapter 8). The sensor is fitted to the bottom of the thermostat housing **(see illustration)**.

6 Disconnect the sensor wiring connector **(see illustration 5.2)**. Using a continuity tester, check for continuity between the sensor body and earth (ground). There should be continuity. If there is no continuity, check that the thermostat mounting is secure.

7 Remove the sensor (see Steps 9 to 11 below). Fill a small heatproof container with coolant and place it on a stove. Using an ohmmeter, connect the positive (+ve) probe of the meter to the terminal on the sensor, and the negative (-ve) probe to the body of the sensor. Using some wire or other support, suspend the sensor in the coolant so that just the sensing portion and the threads are submerged. Also place a thermometer capable of reading temperatures up to 110°C in the water so that its bulb is close to the sensor **(see illustration)**. **Note:** *None of the components should be allowed to directly touch the container.*

8 Heat the coolant, stirring it gently. When the temperature reaches around 50°C the meter should read between 130 and 180 ohms. When the temperature reaches around 80°C the meter should read between 45 and 60 ohms. When the temperature reaches around 120°C the meter should read between 10 and 20 ohms. If the meter readings obtained are different, or they are obtained at different temperatures, then the sensor is faulty and must be replaced.

Warning: This must be done very carefully to avoid the risk of personal injury.

Replacement

Warning: The engine must be completely cool before carrying out this procedure.

9 Drain the cooling system (see Chapter 1).

10 If not already done, remove the upper fairing (see Chapter 8). The sensor is fitted to the bottom of the thermostat housing **(see illustration 5.5)**.

11 Disconnect the sensor wiring connector **(see illustration 5.2)**. Unscrew the sensor and remove it from the thermostat housing.

12 Apply a smear of sealant to the threads of the new sensor, then install it into the thermostat housing and tighten it securely. Connect the sensor wiring.

13 Refill the cooling system (see Chapter 1), then install the upper fairing (see Chapter 8).

6 Thermostat - removal, check and installation

Removal

Warning: The engine must be completely cool before carrying out this procedure.

1 The thermostat is automatic in operation and should give many years service without requiring attention. In the event of a failure, the valve will probably jam open, in which case the engine will take much longer than normal to warm up. Conversely, if the valve jams shut, the coolant will be unable to circulate and the engine will overheat. Neither condition is acceptable, and the fault must be investigated promptly.

2 Remove the upper fairing (see Chapter 8) and drain the cooling system (see Chapter 1).

3 The thermostat is located in the thermostat housing adjacent to the filler neck pressure cap. Unscrew the single bolt securing the thermostat housing to the frame, then move the housing to access the two bolts securing the thermostat housing to the filler neck. Unscrew these bolts and separate the housing from the filler neck, then withdraw the thermostat, noting how it fits **(see illustrations)**. Discard the O-ring as a new one must be fitted.

6.3a Remove the top bolt . . .

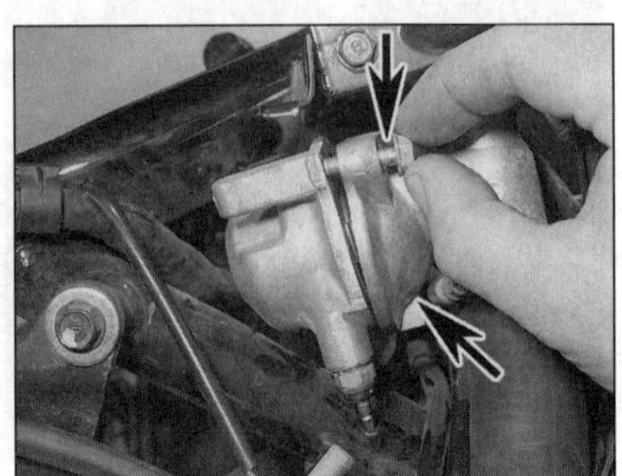

6.3b . . . and the front bolts (arrowed) . . .

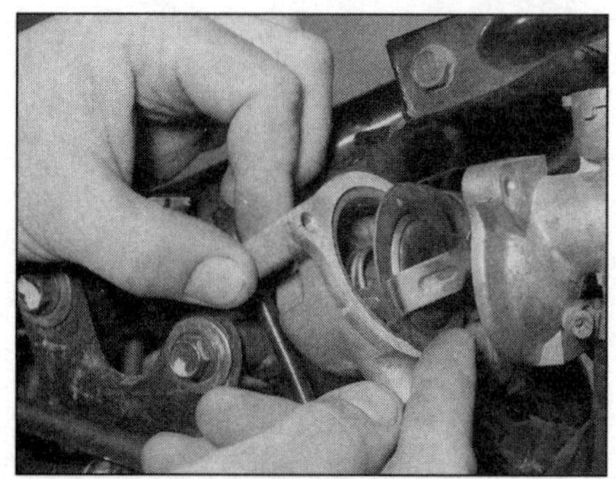

6.3c . . . then separate the housing from the filler and remove the thermostat

Check

4 Examine the thermostat visually before carrying out the test. If it remains in the open position at room temperature, it should be replaced.

5 Suspend the thermostat by a piece of wire in a container of cold water. Place a thermometer in the water so that the bulb is close to the thermostat **(see illustration)**. Heat the water, noting the temperature when the thermostat opens, and compare the result with the specifications given at the beginning of the Chapter. Also check the amount the valve opens after it has been heated at 95°C for a few minutes and compare the measurement to the specifications. If the readings obtained differ from those given, the thermostat is faulty and must be replaced.

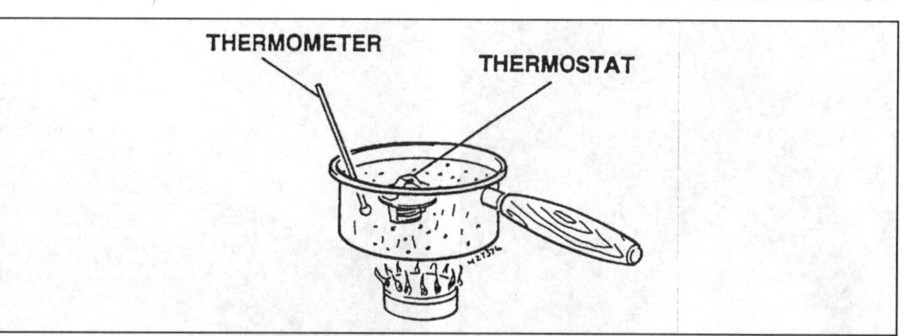

6.5 Thermostat opening check

6 In the event of thermostat failure, as an emergency measure only, it can be removed and the machine used without it. **Note:** *Take care when starting the engine from cold as it will take much longer than usual to warm up.* Ensure that a new unit is installed as soon as possible.

Installation

7 Fit the thermostat into the housing, making sure that it seats correctly and that the hole is at the top **(see illustration)**.

8 Fit a new O-ring into the groove in the filler neck, using a dab of grease to keep it in place if required **(see illustration)**. Join the thermostat housing to the filler neck, then install the two bolts and tighten them to the torque setting specified at the beginning of the Chapter **(see illustration 6.3b)**. Install the bolt securing the housing to the frame **(see illustration 6.3a)**.

9 Refill the cooling system (see Chapter 1).

10 Install the upper fairing (see Chapter 8).

7 Radiator - removal and installation

Removal

Warning: The engine must be completely cool before carrying out this procedure.

1 Remove the middle fairing panels and the upper fairing (see Chapter 8) and drain the cooling system (see Chapter 1).

2 Trace the cooling fan wiring back from the fan and disconnect it at its connector **(see illustration)**. Release the connector from its clip on the frame.

3 Slacken the clamps securing the top and bottom radiator hoses and detach them from the radiator **(see illustrations)**.

4 Remove the horn (see Chapter 9).

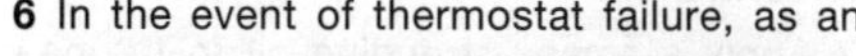

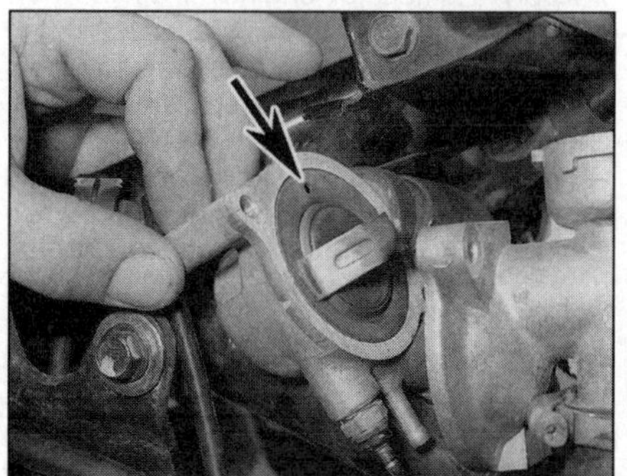

6.7 Install the thermostat with the hole at the top (arrow)

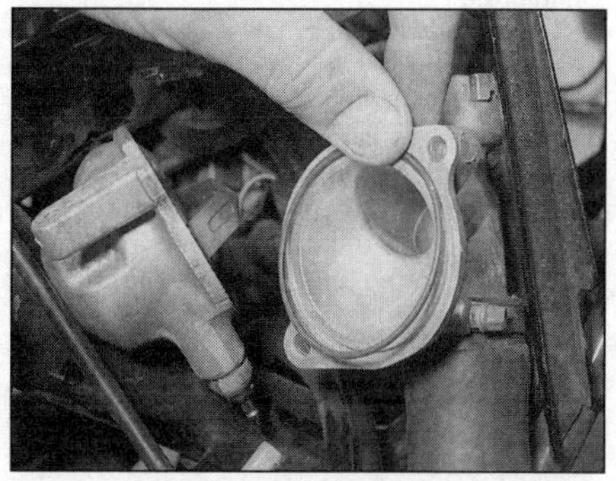

6.8 Always use a new O-ring, making sure it fits into the groove

7.2 Disconnect the wiring connector and release the wiring from the clip (arrowed)

3

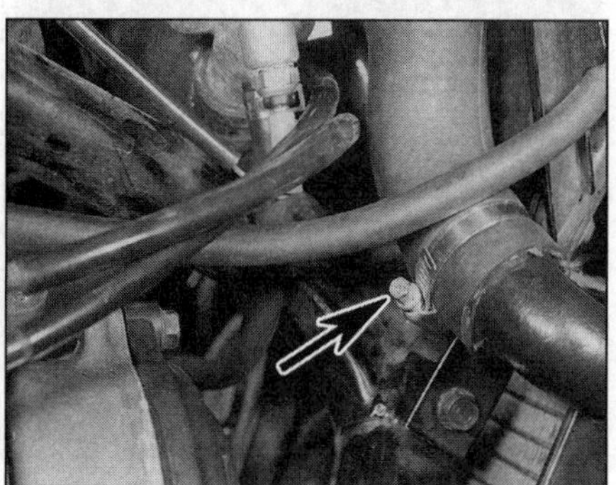

7.3a Slacken the top hose clamp (arrowed) . . .

7.3b . . . and the bottom hose clamp . . .

7.3c . . . and detach the hoses

7.5 The radiator is secured by two bolts at the top . . .

7.6 . . . and by a lug fitting into a grommet at the bottom (arrow)

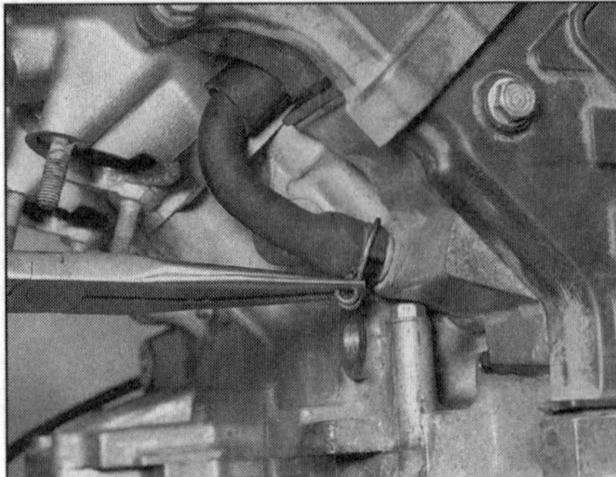

8.4 Release the clamp and detach the hose

5 Unscrew the two bolts securing the top of the radiator to the frame **(see illustration)**. Note the arrangement of the collars and rubber grommets.

6 Carefully lift the radiator until the bottom locating lug is clear of its rubber grommet, then remove the radiator assembly **(see illustration)**.

7 If necessary, remove the cooling fan (see Section 4) from the radiator.

8 Remove the stone guard from the radiator. Check the stone guard and the radiator for signs of damage and clear any dirt or debris that might obstruct air flow and inhibit cooling. If the radiator fins are badly damaged or broken the radiator must be replaced. Also check the rubber mounting grommets, and replace them if necessary.

Installation

9 Installation is the reverse of removal, noting the following.

a) Make sure the bottom locating lug fits correctly into the rubber grommet.

b) Make sure that the fan wiring is correctly connected.

c) Ensure the coolant hoses are securely retained by their clamps, using new ones if necessary.

d) On completion refill the cooling system as described in Chapter 1.

8 Water pump - check, removal and installation

Check

1 The water pump is located inside the housing behind the timing belt cover on the front of the engine. Remove the timing belt cover (see Chapter 2) and visually check the area around the pump housing for signs of leakage.

Removal

2 Drain the coolant (see Chapter 1).

3 Remove the timing belt and tensioner (see Chapter 2).

4 On all models except UK L and M, and US 1991 models, release the clamp securing the breather hose to the right-hand side of the water pump housing and detach the hose **(see illustration)**. On all models except UK T, AT, V and AV, and all US 1996 and 1997 models, release the clamp securing the oil cooler hose to the left-hand side of the water pump housing and detach the hose.

5 Unscrew the bolts securing the pump housing to the engine and remove the housing, taking care not to damage the reduction shaft holder gaskets as you do **(see illustration)**. Discard the pump sealing ring as a new one must be used. Remove the two dowels from the pump or the cover if they are loose, noting their locations. On all models except UK L and M, and US 1991 models, remove the breather hose O-ring from the housing and discard it as a new one must be used.

6 Wiggle the water pump impeller back-and-forth and in-and-out. If there is excessive movement the pump must be replaced. Also check for corrosion or a build-up of scale in the pump body and clean or replace the pump as necessary. Individual components are not available. The pump and its housing come as an assembly.

Installation

7 Apply a smear of engine oil to the new pump sealing ring and install it onto the housing, making sure it seats correctly in its groove. On all models except UK L and M, and US 1991 models, fit a new breather hose O-ring onto the housing. A dab of grease can be used to keep the rings in place when installing the housing if required. Fit the dowels if removed, then install the pump housing onto the engine, taking care not to damage the reduction shaft holder gaskets as you do. Apply a suitable non-permanent thread locking compound to the housing bolts and tighten them securely **(see illustrations)**.

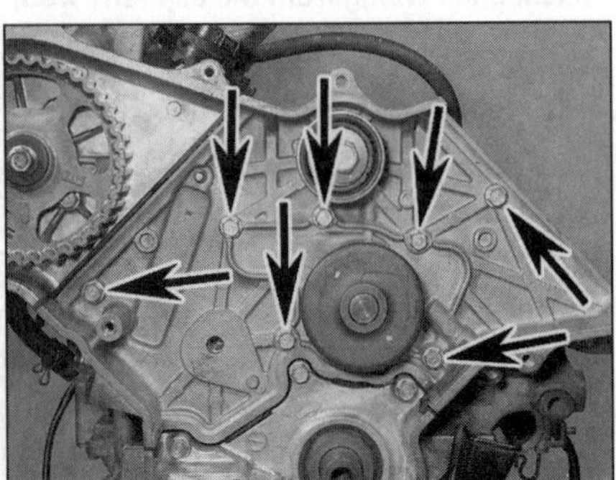

8.5 The pump housing is secured by seven bolts (arrowed)

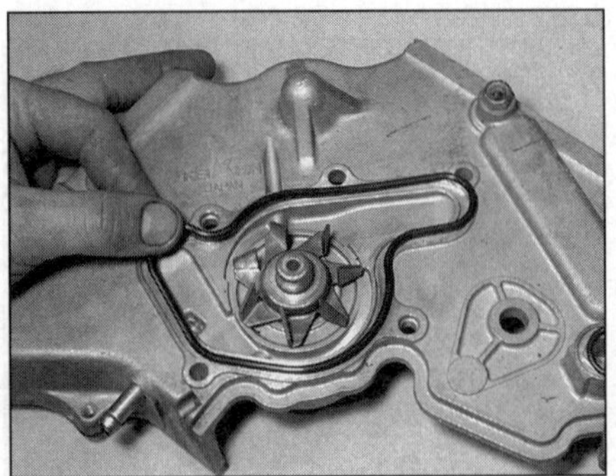

8.7a Use a new pump sealing ring and, where fitted, breather hose O-ring. Make sure they fit into the grooves

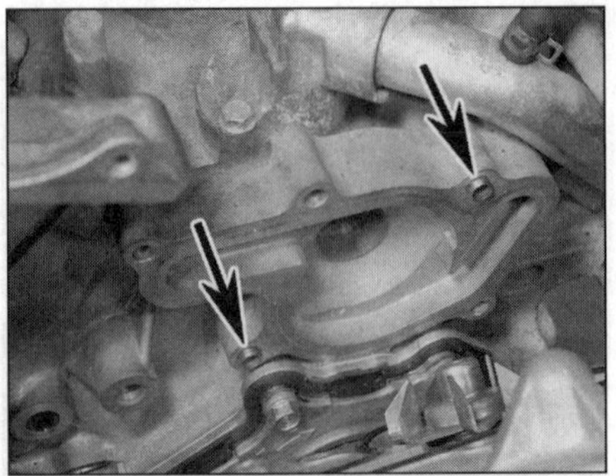

8.7b Make sure the dowels (arrowed) are installed . . .

8.7c . . . then fit the housing . . .

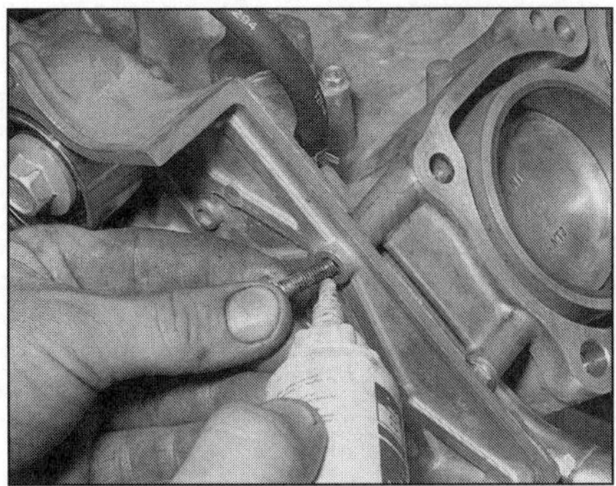
8.7d . . . and apply a thread locking compound to its bolts

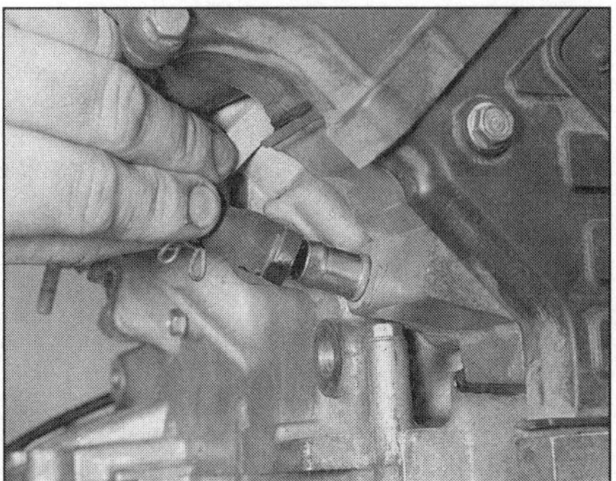
8.8 Fit the breather hose onto its union

8 On all models except UK L and M, and US 1991 models, attach the breather hose onto its union on the right-hand side of the pump housing **(see illustration)**. On all models except UK T, AT, V and AV, and all US 1996 and 1997 models, attach the oil cooler hose to the left-hand side of the pump housing.

9 Install the timing belt and tensioner (see Chapter 2).

10 Refill the cooling system (see Chapter 1).

9 Coolant hoses - removal and installation

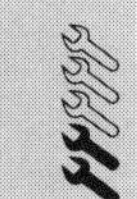

Removal

1 Before removing a hose, drain the coolant (see Chapter 1).

2 Use a screwdriver to slacken the larger-bore hose clamps, then slide them back along the hose and clear of the union spigot **(see illustrations 7.3b and 7.3c)**. The smaller-bore hoses are secured by spring clamps which can be expanded by squeezing their ears together with pliers **(see illustration 8.4)**.

Caution: The radiator unions are fragile. Do not use excessive force when attempting to remove the hoses.

3 If a hose proves stubborn, release it by rotating it on its union before working it off. If all else fails, cut the hose with a sharp knife then slit it at each union so that it can be peeled off in two pieces. Whilst this means replacing the hose, it is preferable to buying a new radiator.

4 The water pipe inlet union to the cylinder block can be removed by unscrewing the two retaining bolts. If it is removed, the O-ring must be replaced. The outlet pipes from the cylinder heads are also secured by two bolts **(see illustrations)**. If they are removed, their O-rings must be replaced.

Installation

5 Slide the clips onto the hose and then work it onto its respective union.

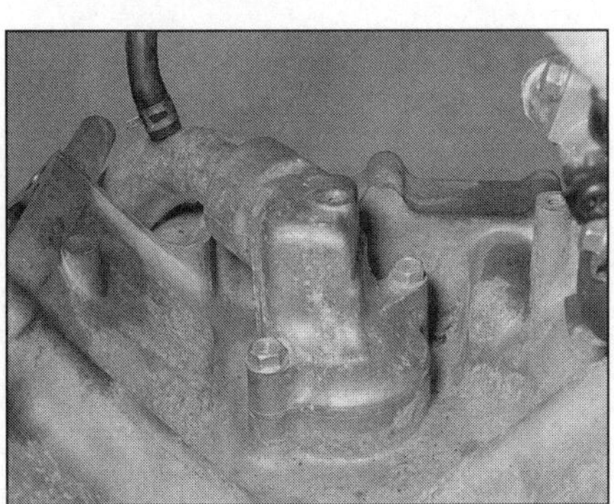
9.4a Water pipe inlet union . . .

If the hose is difficult to push on its union, it can be softened by soaking it in very hot water, or alternatively a little soapy water can be used as a lubricant.

6 Rotate the hose on its unions to settle it in position before sliding the clamps into place and tightening them securely.

7 If either the inlet union to the cylinder block or the outlet unions from the cylinder heads have been removed, fit a new O-ring, then install the union and tighten the mounting bolts securely.

9.4b . . . and outlet union (there is one for each head)

Notes

Chapter 4
Fuel and exhaust systems

Contents

Air filter replacement .... see Chapter 1
Air filter housing - removal and installation 12
Carburettor overhaul - general information 5
Carburettor synchronisation .... see Chapter 1
Carburettors - disassembly, cleaning and inspection 7
Carburettors - reassembly and float height check 9
Carburettors - removal and installation 6
Carburettors - separation and joining 8
Choke cable - removal and installation 11
Crankcase breather - general 15
EVAP and PAIR systems - (California and US ABS/TCS and LBS-ABS/TCS models) 14
Exhaust system - removal and installation 13
Fuel cut-off relay - check and replacement .... see Chapter 9
Fuel hoses - check and replacement .... see Chapter 1
Fuel gauge and level sender - check and replacement .... see Chapter 9
Fuel pump - check, removal and installation .... see Chapter 9
Fuel system - check .... see Chapter 1
Fuel tank - cleaning and repair 3
Fuel tank and fuel tap - removal and installation 2
Fuel indicator light circuit - check and replacement .... see Chapter 9
General information and precautions 1
Idle fuel/air mixture adjustment - general information 4
Idle speed - check and adjustment .... see Chapter 1
Throttle and choke cables - check .... see Chapter 1
Throttle cables - removal and installation 10

Degrees of difficulty

Easy, suitable for novice with little experience 	**Fairly easy,** suitable for beginner with some experience 	**Fairly difficult,** suitable for competent DIY mechanic	**Difficult,** suitable for experienced DIY mechanic	**Very difficult,** suitable for expert DIY or professional 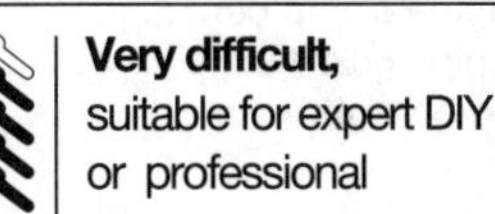

Specifications

Fuel

Grade	Unleaded, minimum 91 RON (Research Octane Number)
Fuel tank capacity	28 litres

Carburettors

Type	CV
Bore	34.5 mm
I.D. no.	
UK	
L, M, N, AN, P, AP, R and AR models	VD B1A
S, AS, T, AT, V and AV models	VD B1B
US	
All standard 49 state models	VD BDA
All standard California and all 1991 to 1993 US ABS/TCS models	VD BEA
1993-on 49-state ABS/TCS and LBS-ABS/TCS models	VD BJA
Pilot screw setting (turns out)	
UK	
L and M models	
Initial setting	1 7/8 turns out
Final setting	1/4 turn out (see text)
N, AN, P, AP, R and AR models	
Initial setting	1 7/8 turns out
Final setting	7/8 turn out (see text)
S, AS, T, AT, V and AV models	
Initial setting	1 5/8 turns out
Final setting	7/8 turn out (see text)
US	
All standard 49-state models	
Initial setting	2 1/4 turns out
Final setting	7/8 turn out (see text)
All California and all 49-state ABS/TCS and LBS-ABS/TCS models	
Initial setting	2 5/8 turns out
Final setting	7/8 turn out (see text)
Float height	7.0 mm
Idle speed	see Chapter 1

4

Carburettor jet sizes

Pilot jet	
All UK models	40
All US models	38
Main jet	
UK	
L, M, N, AN, P, AP, R and AR models	128
S, AS, T, AT, V and AV models	125
US	
All 1991 to 1993 49-state models	128
1993-on standard 49-state models	128
All California models	125
1993-on ABS/TCS and LBS-ABS/TCS models	125

Torque settings

Fuel tank mounting bolts	12 Nm
Carburettor joining screws	8 Nm
Silencer clamp bolts	22 Nm
Silencer mounting bolt	27 Nm
Footpeg bracket bolts	
8 mm bolt	27 Nm
10 mm bolts	35 Nm
Exhaust downpipe flange nuts	
Initial setting (see text)	10 Nm
Final setting	17 Nm
Downpipe clamp bolt	22 Nm
Downpipe guard bolts	12 Nm
Fairing bracket bolts	40 Nm

1 General information and precautions

General information

The fuel system consists of the fuel tank, automatic fuel tap, fuel filter, the carburettors, fuel pump, fuel hoses and control cables. There is also a fuel gauge, fuel level sender, low fuel level warning light and a fuel cut-off relay.

The fuel tap is automatic and opens by vacuum when the engine is turned. The fuel filter is fitted externally in the fuel line between the tank and the tap.

The carburettors used on all models are CV types. On all models there is a carburettor for each cylinder. For cold starting, a choke lever mounted on the left-handlebar and connected by a cable controls an enrichment circuit in the carburettor.

Air is drawn into the carburettors via an air filter which is housed under the fuel tank cover.

The exhaust system is a four piece four-into-two design.

Many of the fuel system service procedures are considered routine maintenance items and for that reason are included in Chapter 1.

Precautions

Warning: Petrol (gasoline) is extremely flammable, so take extra precautions when you work on any part of the fuel system. Don't smoke or allow open flames or bare light bulbs near the work area, and don't work in a garage where a natural gas-type appliance is present. If you spill any fuel on your skin, rinse it off immediately with soap and water. When you perform any kind of work on the fuel system, wear safety glasses and have a fire extinguisher suitable for a class B type fire (flammable liquids) on hand.

Always perform service procedures in a well-ventilated area to prevent a build-up of fumes.

Never work in a building containing a gas appliance with a pilot light, or any other form of naked flame. Ensure that there are no naked light bulbs or any sources of flame or sparks nearby.

Do not smoke (or allow anyone else to smoke) while in the vicinity of petrol (gasoline) or of components containing it. Remember the possible presence of vapour from these sources and move well clear before smoking.

Check all electrical equipment belonging to the house, garage or workshop where work is being undertaken (see the Safety first! section of this manual). Remember that certain electrical appliances such as drills, cutters etc. create sparks in the normal course of operation and must not be used near petrol (gasoline) or any component containing it. Again, remember the possible presence of fumes before using electrical equipment.

Always mop up any spilt fuel and safely dispose of the rag used.

Any stored fuel that is drained off during servicing work must be kept in sealed containers that are suitable for holding petrol (gasoline), and clearly marked as such; the containers themselves should be kept in a safe place. Note that this last point applies equally to the fuel tank if it is removed from the machine; also remember to keep its filler cap closed at all times.

Read the Safety first! section of this manual carefully before starting work.

Owners of machines used in the US, particularly California, should note that their machines must comply at all times with Federal or State legislation governing the permissible levels of noise and of pollutants such as unburnt hydrocarbons, carbon monoxide etc. that can be emitted by those machines. All vehicles offered for sale must comply with legislation in force at the date of manufacture and must not subsequently be altered in any way which will affect their emission of noise or of pollutants.

In practice, this means that adjustments may not be made to any part of the fuel, ignition or exhaust systems by anyone who is not authorised or mechanically qualified to do so, or who does not have the tools, equipment and data necessary to properly carry out the task. Also if any part of these systems is to be replaced it must be replaced with only genuine Honda components or by components which are approved under the relevant legislation. The machine must never be used with any part of these systems removed, modified or damaged.

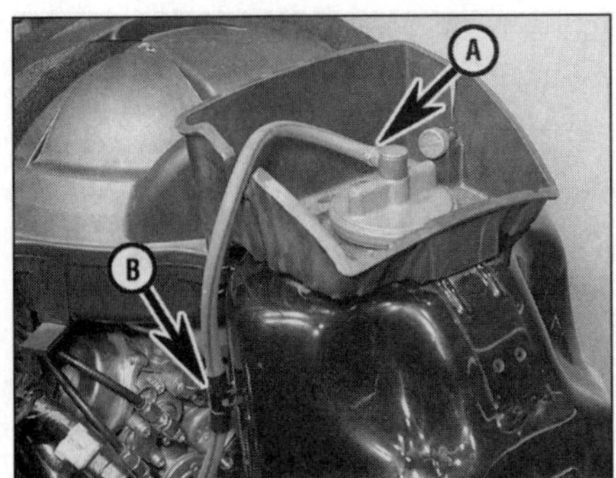

2.3 Detach the hose (A) and free it from the guide (B)

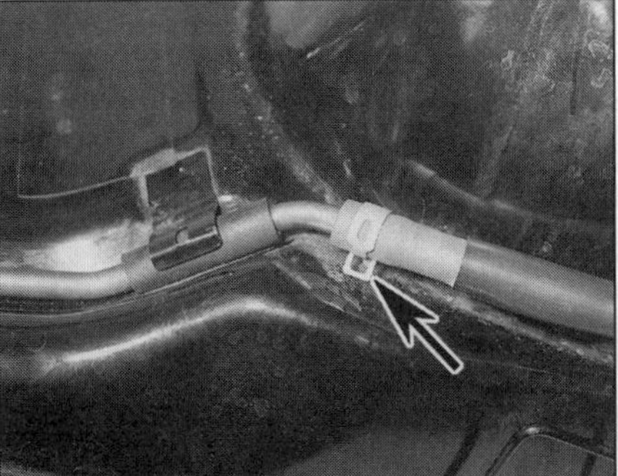

2.4 Release the clamp (arrowed) and pull the hose off the pipe

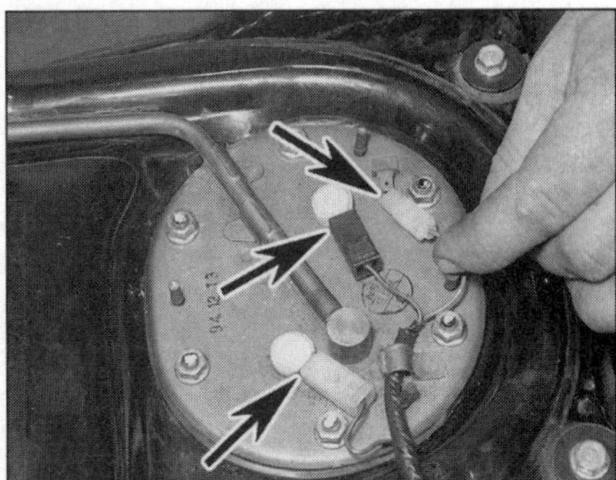

2.5a Disconnect the pump wiring connectors (arrowed) . . .

2.5b . . . and the fuel level sender connector (arrowed)

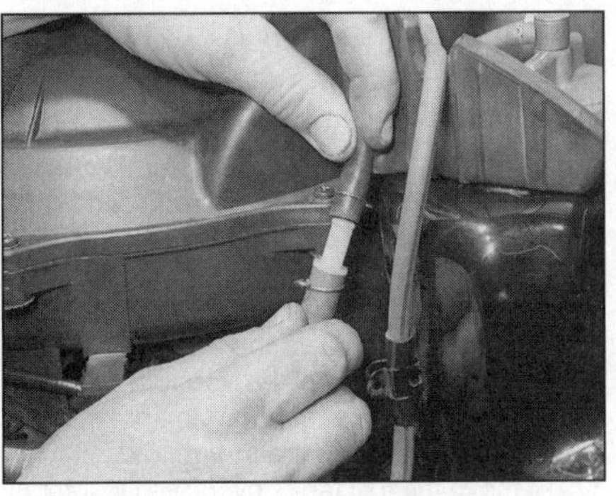

2.6a Detach the drain hose . . .

2.6b . . . and displace the idle speed cable

2 Fuel tank and fuel tap - removal and installation

Warning: Refer to the precautions given in Section 1 before starting work.

Fuel tank

Removal

1 Remove the fuel tank cover (see Chapter 8). Make sure the fuel cap is secure.

2 Remove the air filter housing (see Section 12).

3 Release the clamp securing the tank breather hose and detach the hose **(see illustration)**. Free the hose from its guide.

4 Release the clamp securing the fuel hose to the fuel pipe on the tank and detach the hose, being prepared to catch any residue fuel **(see illustration)**.

5 Disconnect the fuel pump and fuel level sender wiring connectors **(see illustrations)**.

6 Detach the filler drain tray hose and lift the idle speed adjuster cable out if its slot in the tray **(see illustrations)**. Remove the fuel filler cap and lift the drain tray off the tank if required **(see illustration 2.10)**. Fit the cap back onto the tank.

7 Unscrew the four bolts securing the tank to the frame. Check that all hoses and wiring have been disconnected, then carefully lift the tank away from the machine **(see illustrations)**. If required, remove the heat protector, secured by two clips, from the base of the tank.

8 Inspect the tank mounting rubbers for signs of damage or deterioration and replace them if necessary.

Installation

9 If removed, fit the heat protector to the base of the fuel tank and secure it with the clips. Check that the tank mounting rubbers are fitted, then carefully lower the fuel tank into position. Tighten the bolts to the torque setting specified at the beginning of the Chapter.

10 Remove the fuel filler cap and fit the filler drain tray onto the tank. Fit the cap back onto the tank, aligning the triangle on the cap with that on the tray **(see illustrations)**. Attach the

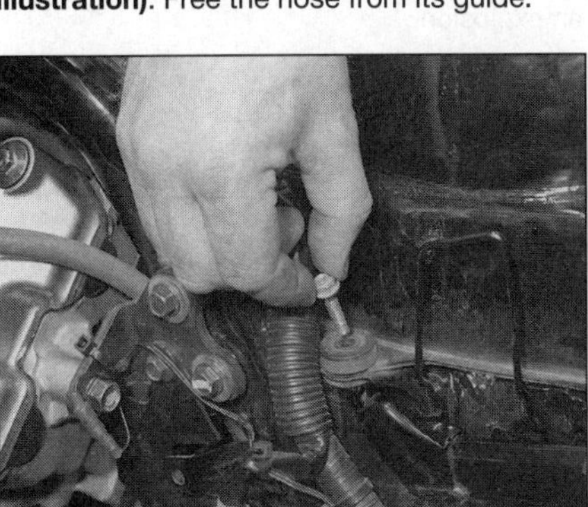

2.7a Remove the four bolts securing the tank . . .

2.7b . . . and carefully lift it out of the frame

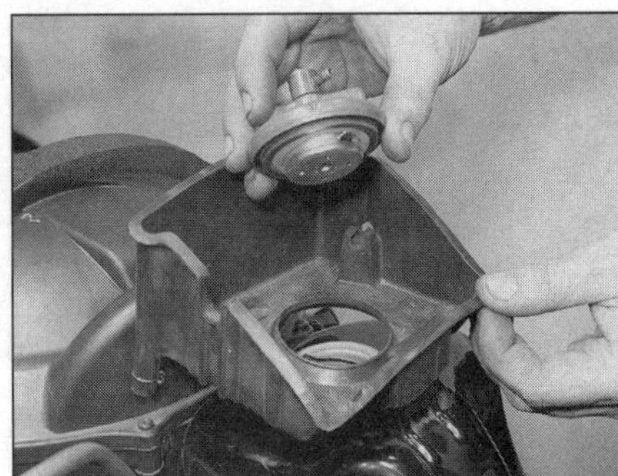

2.10a Position the drain tray onto the tank . . .

2.10b ... then fit the cap, aligning the marks

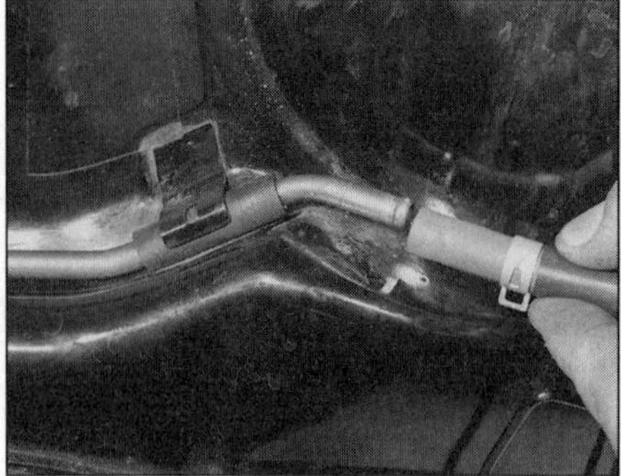

2.12a Attach the fuel hose to the pipe ...

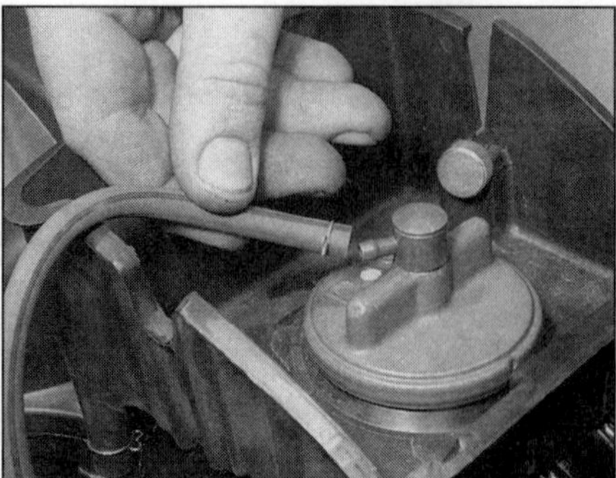

2.12b ... and the breather hose to the filler cap

drain hose and position the throttle stop screw in its slot **(see illustrations 2.6a and 2.6b)**.

11 Connect the fuel pump and fuel level sender wiring connectors, making sure they are secure and correctly routed and cannot be trapped between the seat and the frame **(see illustrations 2.5a and 2.5b)**.

12 Attach the fuel hose and the breather hose, making sure they are secured by their clamps **(see illustrations)**.

13 Install the air filter housing (see Section 12).

14 Start the engine and check that there is no sign of fuel leakage, then shut if off.

15 Install the fuel tank cover (see (Chapter 8).

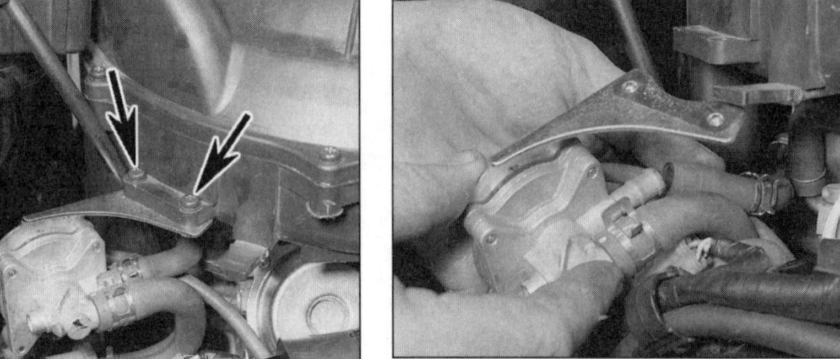

2.18 The tap is secured to the air filter housing by two screws (arrowed)

2.19a Detach the fuel hoses ...

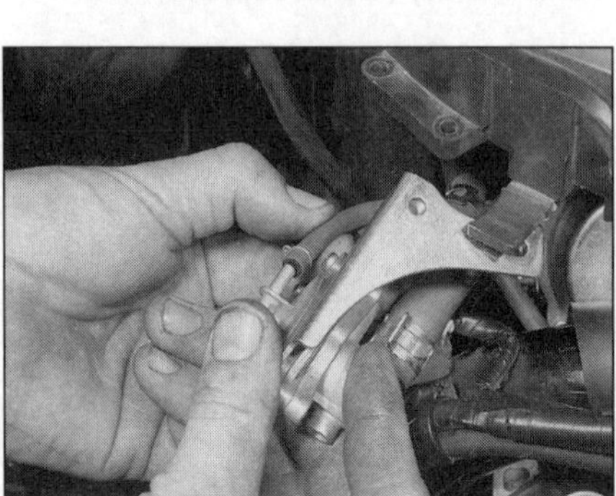

2.19b ... and the vacuum hose

Fuel tap

Removal

16 The fuel tap is automatic, operated by a vacuum created when the engine is turned over. If it is faulty, it must be replaced as no internal parts are available. Before discarding the tap, check that the vacuum hose is securely attached at both ends, and that there are no splits or cracks in the hose. If in doubt, attach a spare hose to the vacuum union on the tap and apply a vacuum to the hose. If fuel does not flow through the tap, replace it.

17 Remove the fuel tank cover (see Chapter 8).

18 Unscrew the two screws securing the tap and displace it to provide better access for detaching the hoses **(see illustration)**.

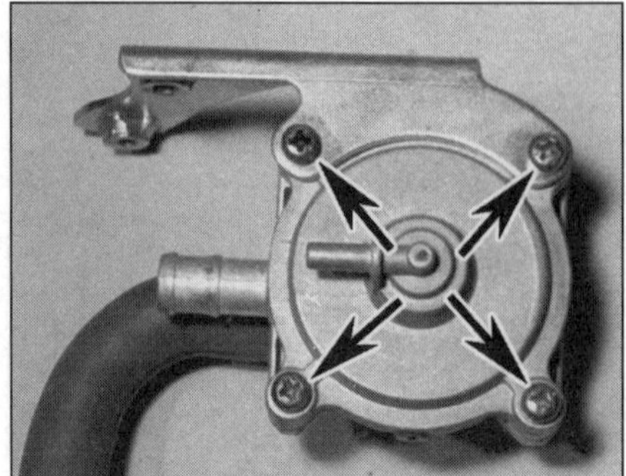

2.20 If the tap leaks, tighten the screws (arrowed)

19 Release the clamps securing the fuel inlet and outlet hoses and detach the hoses, being prepared to catch any residue fuel. Also detach the vacuum hose from the back of the tap **(see illustrations)**.

20 If the fuel tap is leaking, tighten the assembly screws on the back of the tap **(see illustration)**. If leakage persists unscrew the screws and disassemble the tap, noting how the components fit. Inspect all components for wear or damage. If any of the components are worn or damaged, a new tap must be fitted.

Installation

21 Installation is the reverse of removal. Make sure the fuel hose and vacuum hose are secured by their clamps.

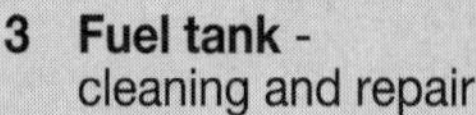

3 Fuel tank - cleaning and repair

1 All repairs to the fuel tank should be carried out by a professional who has experience in this critical and potentially dangerous work. Even after cleaning and flushing of the fuel system, explosive fumes can remain and ignite during repair of the tank.

2 If the fuel tank is removed from the bike, it should not be placed in an area where sparks or open flames could ignite the fumes coming out of the tank. Be especially careful inside garages where a natural gas-type appliance is located, because the pilot light could cause an explosion.

4 Idle fuel/air mixture adjustment - general information

1 Due to the increased emphasis on controlling motorcycle exhaust emissions, certain governmental regulations have been formulated which directly affect the carburation of this machine. In order to comply with the regulations, the carburettors on US models are fitted with special screws requiring a special tool so they can't be tampered with. The pilot screws on other models are adjustable using normal tools, but the use of an exhaust gas analyser and an auxiliary tachometer capable of accurately displaying changes of 50 rpm is the only certain way to adjust the idle fuel/air mixture and be sure the machine doesn't exceed the emissions regulations.

2 The pilot screws are set to their correct position by the manufacturer and should not be adjusted or removed unless it is necessary to do so during a carburettor overhaul. If the screws are to be removed, record the pilot screw's current setting by turning the screw it in until it seats lightly, counting the number of turns necessary to achieve this, then fully unscrew it. On installation, the screw is simply backed out the number of turns you've recorded.

3 If the engine runs extremely rough at idle or continually stalls, and if a carburettor overhaul does not cure the problem, take the motorcycle to a Honda dealer equipped with an exhaust gas analyser. They will be able to properly adjust the idle fuel/air mixture to achieve a smooth idle and restore low speed performance.

5 Carburettor overhaul - general information

1 Poor engine performance, hesitation, hard starting, stalling, flooding and backfiring are all signs that major carburettor maintenance may be required.

2 Keep in mind that many so-called carburettor problems are really not carburettor problems at all, but mechanical problems within the engine or ignition system malfunctions. Try to establish for certain that the carburettors are in need of maintenance before beginning a major overhaul.

3 Check the fuel filter, the fuel hoses, the fuel pump, the fuel cut-off relay, the intake manifold joint clamps, the air filter, the ignition system, the spark plugs and carburettor synchronisation before assuming that a carburettor overhaul is required.

4 Most carburettor problems are caused by dirt particles, varnish and other deposits which build up in and block the fuel and air passages. Also, in time, gaskets and O-rings shrink or deteriorate and cause fuel and air leaks which lead to poor performance.

5 When overhauling the carburettors, disassemble them completely and clean the parts thoroughly with a carburettor cleaning solvent and dry them with filtered, unlubricated compressed air. Blow through the fuel and air passages with compressed air to force out any dirt that may have been loosened but not removed by the solvent. Once the cleaning process is complete, reassemble the carburettor using new gaskets and O-rings.

6 Before disassembling the carburettors, make sure you have all necessary O-rings and other parts, some carburettor cleaner, a supply of clean rags, some means of blowing out the carburettor passages and a clean place to work. It is recommended that only one carburettor be overhauled at a time to avoid mixing up parts.

6 Carburettors - removal and installation

Warning: Refer to the precautions given in Section 1 before starting work.

Removal

1 Remove the fuel tank cover and the fairing pockets (see Chapter 8).

2 Remove the air filter housing (see Section 12).

3 Detach the choke cable from the carburettors (see Section 11).

4 Detach the throttle cables from the carburettors (see Section 10).

5 Release the clamp securing the fuel supply hose to the fuel tap and detach the hose, being prepared to catch any residue fuel **(see illustration 2.19a)**.

6 Lift the idle speed cable out of the holder in the fuel filler drain tray **(see illustration 2.6b)**.

7 On all California models and all US ABS/TCS models, disconnect the no.6 EVAP system purge hose from the T-piece union on the carburettors, the no.15 EVAP system purge hoses from the carburettors, and the no.4 hose from the purge control valve. **Note:** *The EVAP system hoses can be identified by referring to the vacuum hose routing diagram on the rear mudguard, under the seat.*

8 Slacken the clamps securing the carburettors to the cylinder head adapters **(see illustration)**.

9 Ease the carburettors off the adapters, noting how they fit. As it becomes accessible, detach the main drain hose from the union of the individual hoses **(see illustration)**. Lift the carburettors out of the top of the frame, noting the routing of the various hoses. **Note:** *Keep the carburettors upright to prevent fuel spillage from the float chambers and the possibility of the piston diaphragms being damaged.*

Caution: On the model stripped down, a lot of dirt and dust had collected on the rubber heat insulator pad around the intake adapters. On removing the carburettors, there is a danger of some dirt falling into the intakes, which would mean removing the cylinder heads for cleaning. Try to blow away as much dirt as possible before removing the carburettors, and take great care when lifting them off the adapters. Stuff clean rag into each intake after removal.

10 Place a suitable container below the drain tube hose union, then slacken the drain screws and drain all the fuel from the carburettors. Once all the fuel has been drained, tighten the drain screws securely.

11 If necessary, slacken the clamps securing the intake adapters to the cylinder head and remove the adapters, noting how they fit **(see illustration)**. If the rubber heat insulator pad has collected dirt and dust, remove it for cleaning, noting how it fits.

Installation

12 Installation is the reverse of removal, noting the following.

a) *Check for cracks or splits in the cylinder head intake adapters, and replace them if necessary.*
b) *If removed, make sure the intake adapters are installed with the CARB marking facing out (towards the carburettor), and so that the slots align with the lugs on the cylinder head* ***(see illustration 6.11)****.*

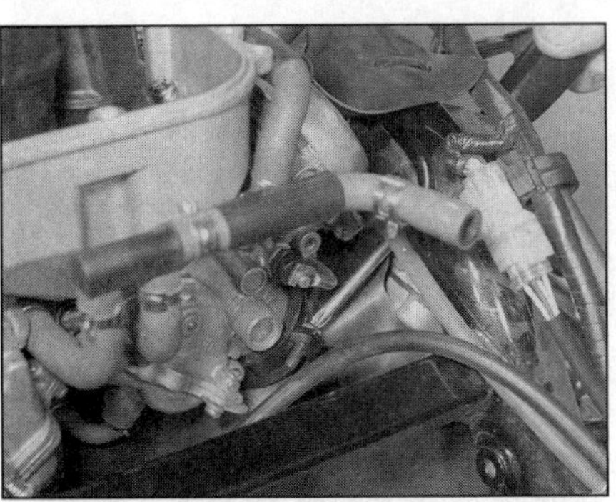

6.8 Slacken the clamps . . .

6.9 . . . and lift the carburettors off the adapters, detaching the drain hose (arrowed) when accessible

6.11 The adapters are secured by clamps, locate on lugs, and have a CARB marking which faces out

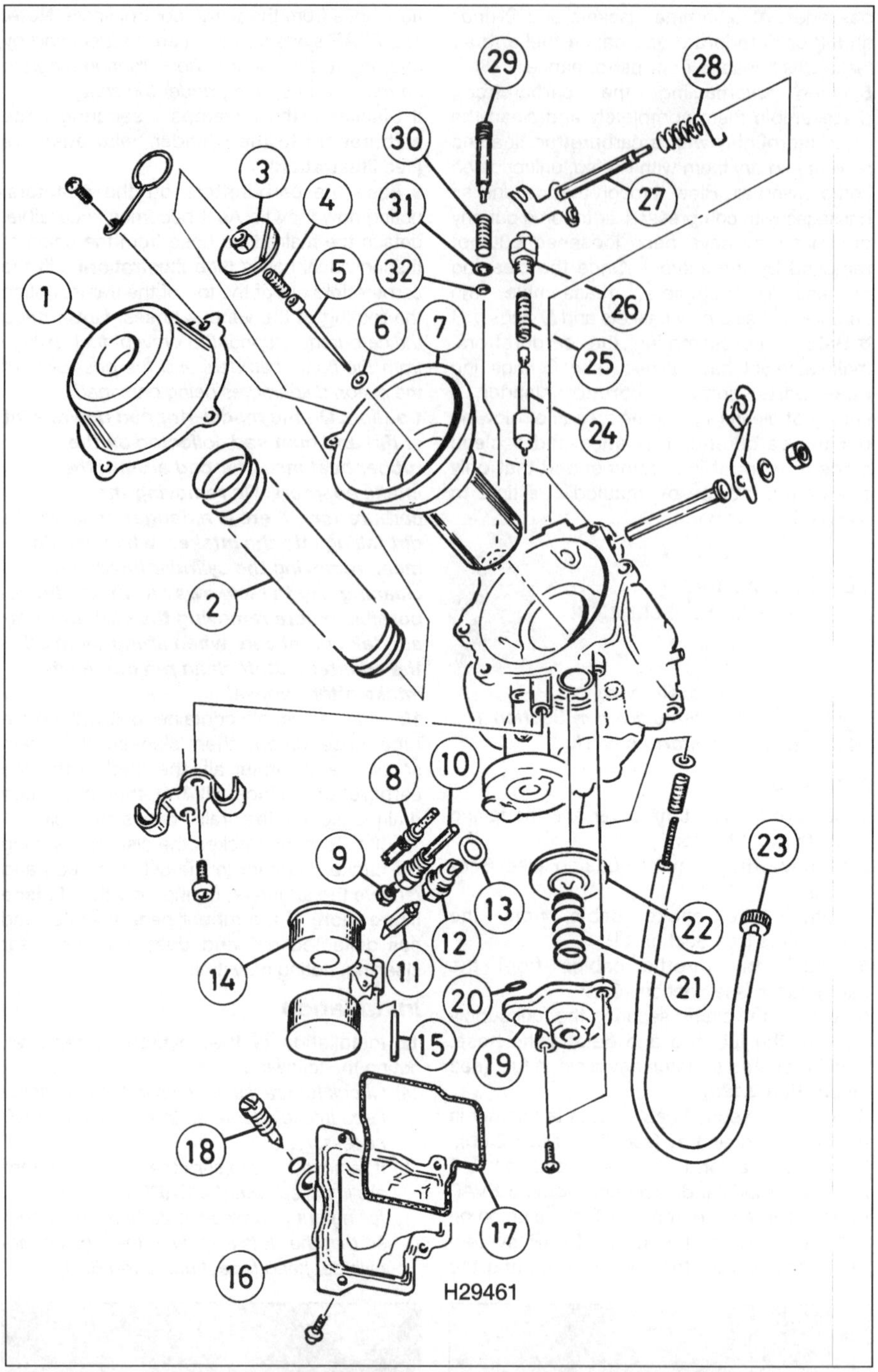

7.1 Carburettor components

1 Top cover
2 Spring
3 Jet needle retainer
4 Spring
5 Jet needle
6 Washer
7 Diaphragm/piston assembly
8 Pilot jet
9 Main jet
10 Needle jet holder
11 Float needle valve
12 Float needle valve seat
13 Sealing washer
14 Float
15 Float pin
16 Float chamber
17 Rubber gasket
18 Drain screw and washer
19 Air cut-off valve cover
20 O-ring
21 Spring
22 Air cut-off valve diaphragm
23 Idle speed adjuster screw
24 Choke plunger
25 Spring
26 Choke plunger nut
27 Choke arm
28 Spring
29 Pilot screw
30 Spring
31 Washer
32 O-ring

c) Make sure the cylinder head intake adapters are fully engaged with the carburettors and their retaining clamps are securely tightened.

d) Make sure all hoses are correctly routed and secured and not trapped or kinked.

e) Check the operation of the choke and throttle cables and adjust them as necessary (see Chapter 1).

f) Check idle speed and carburettor synchronisation and adjust as necessary (see Chapter 1).

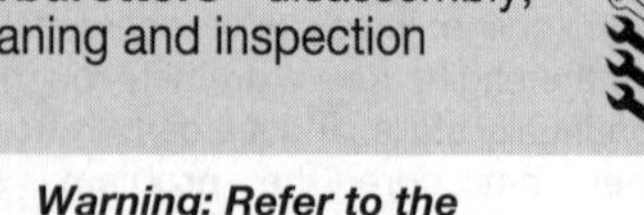

7 Carburettors - disassembly, cleaning and inspection

Warning: Refer to the precautions given in Section 1 before starting work.

Disassembly

1 Remove the carburettors from the machine as described in the previous Section. **Note:** *Do not separate the carburettors unless absolutely necessary; each carburettor can be dismantled sufficiently for all normal cleaning and adjustments while in place on the mounting brackets. Dismantle the carburettors separately to avoid interchanging parts* ***(see illustration)***.

2 If required, remove the air duct assembly and housing from the carburettors as follows, but note that this is not necessary for carburettor disassembly and cleaning, unless they are being separated (see Section 8). Bend back the tabs on the four screws securing the air duct assembly to the duct housing, then unscrew the screws and remove the duct assembly. Bend back the tabs on the screws securing the duct housing to the carburettors, then unscrew the screws and remove the housing. Remove the dowels from each carburettor intake if they are loose.

3 Unscrew and remove the top cover retaining screws. Lift off the cover and remove the spring from inside the piston **(see illustrations)**.

7.3a Remove the screws (arrowed) and the cover . . .

7.3b . . . then withdraw the spring

7.4 Withdraw the diaphragm and piston assembly from the carburettor

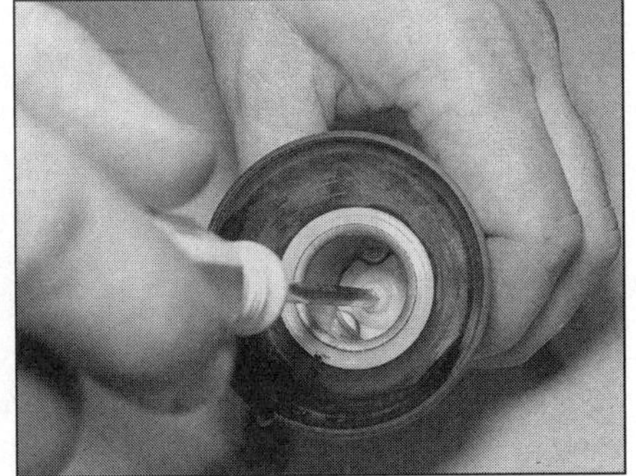

7.5a Push down on the retainer and turn it to release it . . .

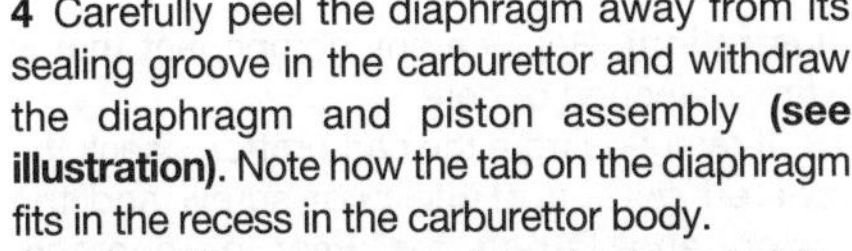

4 Carefully peel the diaphragm away from its sealing groove in the carburettor and withdraw the diaphragm and piston assembly **(see illustration)**. Note how the tab on the diaphragm fits in the recess in the carburettor body.

Caution: Do not use a sharp instrument to displace the diaphragm as it is easily damaged.

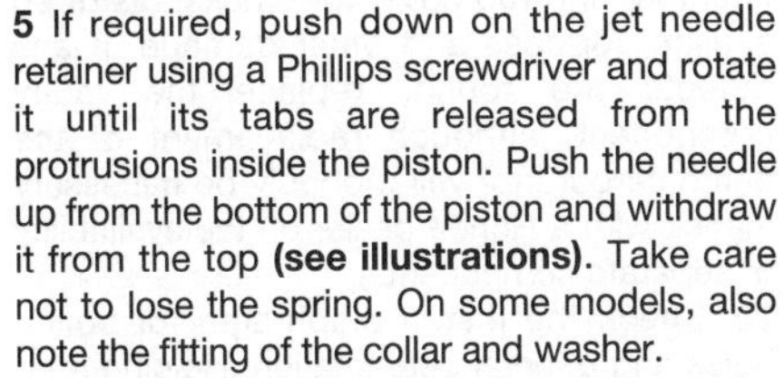

5 If required, push down on the jet needle retainer using a Phillips screwdriver and rotate it until its tabs are released from the protrusions inside the piston. Push the needle up from the bottom of the piston and withdraw it from the top **(see illustrations)**. Take care not to lose the spring. On some models, also note the fitting of the collar and washer.

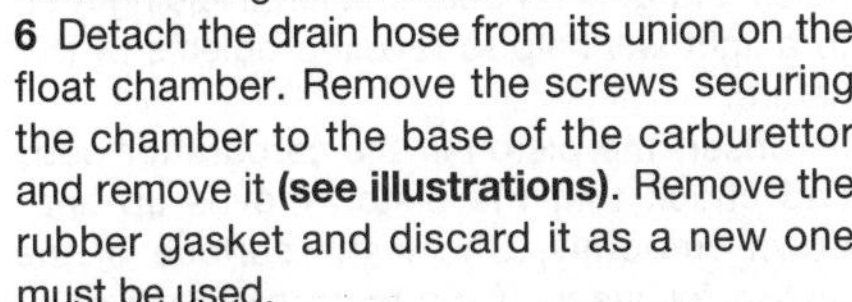

6 Detach the drain hose from its union on the float chamber. Remove the screws securing the chamber to the base of the carburettor and remove it **(see illustrations)**. Remove the rubber gasket and discard it as a new one must be used.

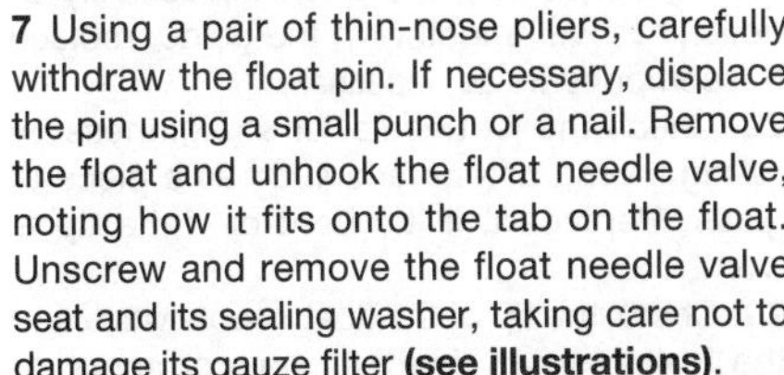

7 Using a pair of thin-nose pliers, carefully withdraw the float pin. If necessary, displace the pin using a small punch or a nail. Remove the float and unhook the float needle valve, noting how it fits onto the tab on the float. Unscrew and remove the float needle valve seat and its sealing washer, taking care not to damage its gauze filter **(see illustrations)**.

8 Unscrew and remove the main jet from the base of the needle jet holder **(see illustration)**.

9 Unscrew and remove the needle jet holder **(see illustration)**.

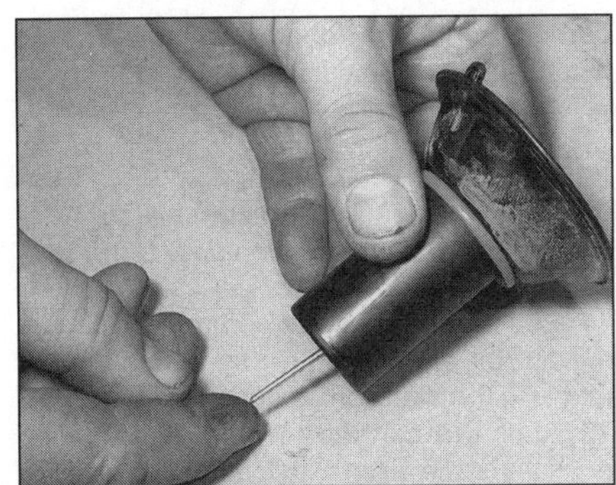

7.5b . . . then push the needle up from the bottom

7.6a Detach the drain hose . . .

7.6b . . . then remove the four screws (arrowed) and lift off the chamber

7.7a Withdraw the float pin and remove the float assembly

7.7b Unscrew the float needle valve seat (arrowed)

7.8 Remove the main jet (arrowed) . . .

7.9 . . . the needle jet holder (arrowed) . . .

7.10 . . . and the pilot jet (arrowed)

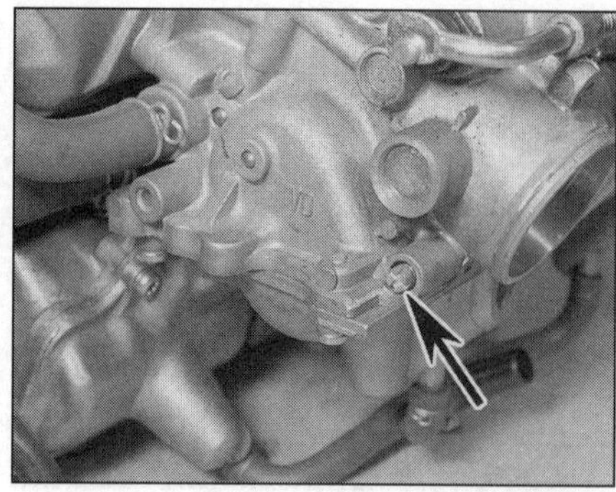
7.11 If required, remove the pilot screw (arrowed)

7.12 The air cut-off valve cover is secured by two screws (arrowed)

10 Unscrew and remove the pilot jet **(see illustration)**.

11 The pilot screw can be removed if required, but note that its setting will be disturbed (see **Haynes Hint**). Unscrew and remove the pilot screw along with its spring, washer and O-ring **(see illustration)**. Discard the O-ring as a new one must be used.

> **HAYNES HiNT** ***To record the pilot screw's current setting, turn the screw in until it seats lightly, counting the number of turns necessary to achieve this, then fully unscrew it. On installation, the screw is simply backed out the number of turns you've recorded.***

12 Unscrew the two screws securing the air cut-off valve cover, noting that it is under spring pressure **(see illustration)**. Carefully release the cover and remove the spring and cut-off valve diaphragm, noting how they fit. Do not remove the O-ring unless it is obviously damaged or deteriorated as Honda do not supply it as an individual component (see Step 26).

13 Slacken the screw securing the choke linkage bar, then lift the bar arm off the choke plunger. Unscrew the choke plunger nut and withdraw the plunger and spring from the carburettor body, noting how they fit **(see illustrations)**. Take care not to lose the spring when removing the nut.

Cleaning

Caution: Use only a petroleum based solvent for carburettor cleaning. Don't use caustic cleaners.

14 Submerge the metal components in the solvent for approximately thirty minutes (or longer, if the directions recommend it).

15 After the carburettor has soaked long enough for the cleaner to loosen and dissolve most of the varnish and other deposits, use a nylon-bristled brush to remove the stubborn deposits. Rinse it again, then dry it with compressed air.

16 Use a jet of compressed air to blow out all of the fuel and air passages in the main and upper body, not forgetting the air jets in the carburettor inlet.

Caution: Never clean the jets or passages with a piece of wire or a drill bit, as they will be enlarged, causing the fuel and air metering rates to be upset.

Inspection

17 Check the operation of the choke plunger. If it doesn't move smoothly, inspect the needle on the end of the choke plunger, the spring and the plunger linkage bar or arm **(see illustration)**. Replace any component that is worn, damaged or bent.

18 If removed from the carburettor, check the tapered portion of the pilot screw and the spring and O-ring for wear or damage. Replace them if necessary.

19 Check the carburettor body, float chamber and top cover for cracks, distorted sealing surfaces and other damage. If any defects are found, replace the faulty component, although replacement of the entire carburettor will probably be necessary (check with a Honda dealer on the availability of separate components).

20 Check the piston diaphragm for splits, holes and general deterioration. Holding it up to a light will help to reveal problems of this nature.

21 Insert the piston in the carburettor body and check that the piston moves up-and-down smoothly. Check the surface of the piston for wear. If it's worn excessively or doesn't move smoothly in the guide, replace the components as necessary.

22 Check the jet needle for straightness by rolling it on a flat surface such as a piece of glass. Replace it if it's bent or if the tip is worn.

23 Check the tip of the float needle valve and the valve seat. If either has grooves or scratches in it, or is in any way worn, they must be replaced as a set. Also check the

7.13a Slacken the screw (A), then lift the bar arms off the plungers (B) and withdraw the bar

7.13b The choke plunger is retained by a nut (arrowed)

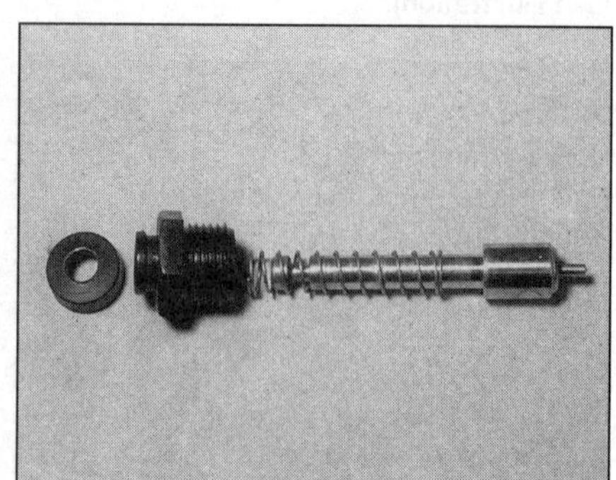
7.17 Choke plunger components

7.23 Check the gauze for holes and splits

condition of the valve seat filter and of the sealing washer **(see illustration)**.

24 Operate the throttle shaft to make sure the throttle butterfly valve opens and closes smoothly. If it doesn't, cleaning the throttle linkage may help. Otherwise, replace the carburettor.

25 Check the floats for damage. This will usually be apparent by the presence of fuel inside one of the floats. If the floats are damaged, they must be replaced.

26 Check the air cut-off valve assembly components and O-ring for wear or damage and replace the assembly if necessary (individual components are not available). Note that it may be possible to obtain an O-ring from a specialist supplier, if required.

8 Carburettors - separation and joining

Warning: Refer to the precautions given in Section 1 before proceeding

Separation

1 The carburettors do not need to be separated for normal overhaul. If you need to separate them (to replace a carburettor body, for example), refer to the following procedure.

2 Remove the carburettors from the machine (see Section 6). Mark the body of each carburettor with its cylinder location to ensure that it is positioned correctly on reassembly **(see illustration)**.

1 Drain tube joint piece
2 Air duct lock plates
3 Air duct holder
4 Air duct holder retainer plates
5 No. 3 carburettor
6 No. 1 carburettor
7 No. 4 carburettor
8 No. 2 carburettor
9 Carburettor joining bracket
10 Carburettor joining screws
11 Fuel joint pipe and O-rings
12 Air joint pipe and O-rings
13 Throttle linkage thrust spring
14 Synchronisation screw spring
15 Throttle linkage joining bar
16 Choke linkage joining bar
17 Fuel hose joint piece
18 Drain tube joint
19 Choke linkage bar and spring
20 Choke linkage arm
21 Sub air cleaner hose
22 Air vent hose
23 Sub air cleaner hose
24 Air vent hose

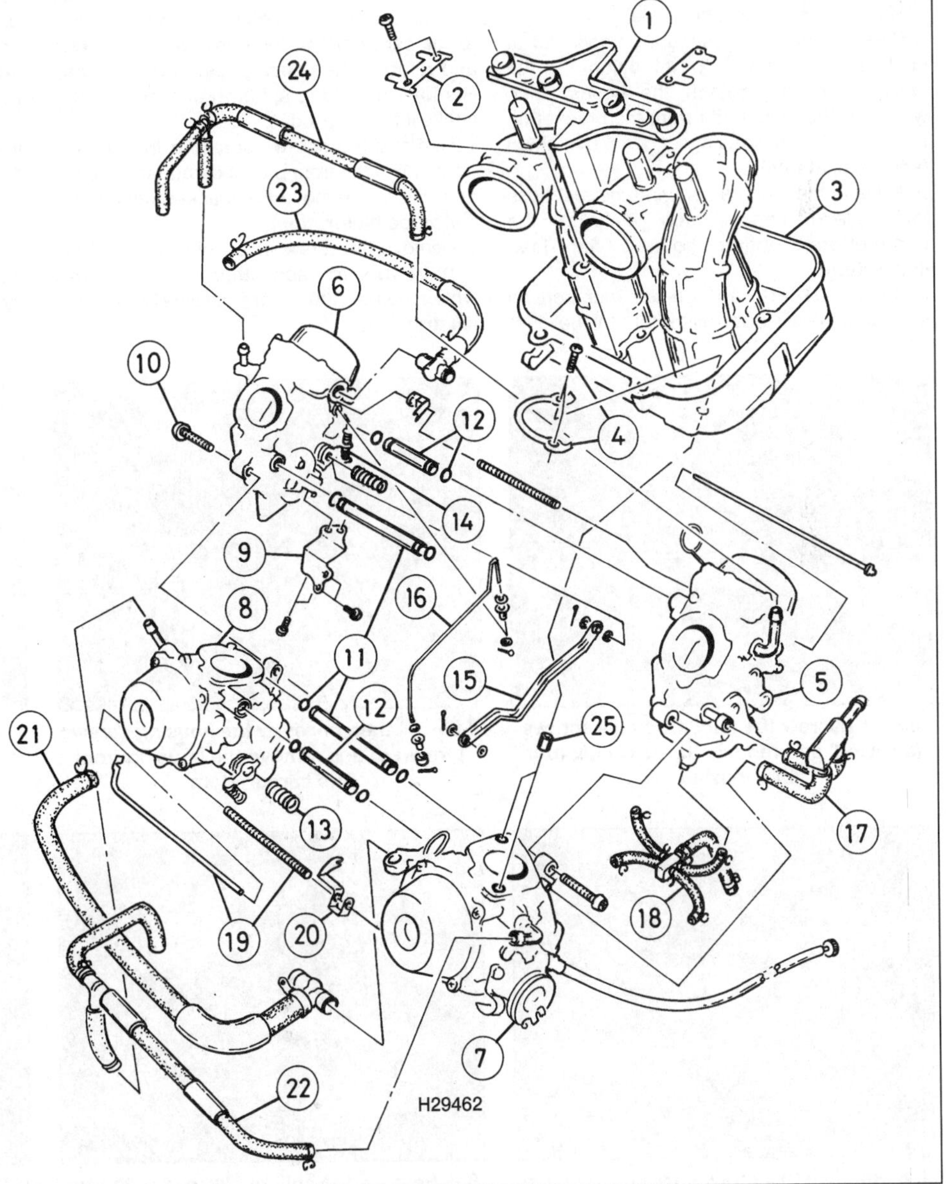

H29462

8.2 Carburettor assembly components

8.4a Release the clamps (arrowed) and detach the hoses . . .

8.4b . . . then withdraw the hose ends from the bracket (arrowed) and remove the hoses

8.5 Release the clamps (arrowed) and detach the fuel hose joint

3 Detach the drain tube from the bottom of each carburettor and remove the drain tube joint piece **(see illustration 7.6a)**.

4 Release the clamp securing each end of each air vent hose to its union on the carburettor and detach the hoses, then withdraw the hose ends from the bracket on the front of the housing and remove them **(see illustrations)**.

5 Release the clamps securing the fuel hose joint piece and detach it from the carburettors, noting how it fits **(see illustration)**.

6 Bend back the tabs on the four screws securing the air duct assembly to the duct housing, then unscrew the screws and remove the duct assembly. Bend back the tabs on the screws securing the duct housing to the carburettors, then unscrew the screws and remove the housing **(see illustrations)**. Remove the dowels from each carburettor intake if they are loose.

7 Remove the screws securing the bracket which joins the front pair of carburettors to the rear pair and remove the bracket, noting how it fits **(see illustration)**.

8 Remove the screw which joins the two front carburettors to each other, and the screw which joins the rear carburettors **(see illustration)**.

9 Remove the split pin securing each end of the choke linkage joining bar, then remove the bar, noting the arrangement of the washers and collars **(see illustration)**.

10 Remove the split pin securing each end of the throttle linkage joining bar, then remove the bar, noting the arrangement of the washers **(see illustration)**.

11 Slacken the screw securing the choke linkage bar, then lift the bar arms off the choke plungers and withdraw it, recovering the spring as you do **(see illustration 7.13)**.

12 Make a note of how the carburettor synchronisation springs and thrust springs are arranged to ensure that they are fitted

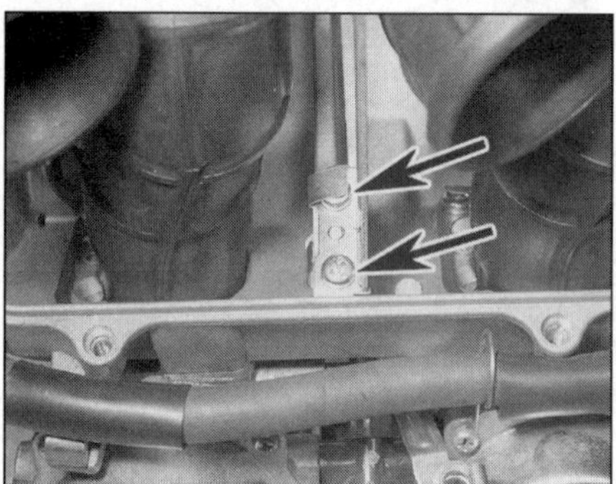
8.6a Unscrew the duct assembly screws (arrowed) and remove the assembly from the housing . . .

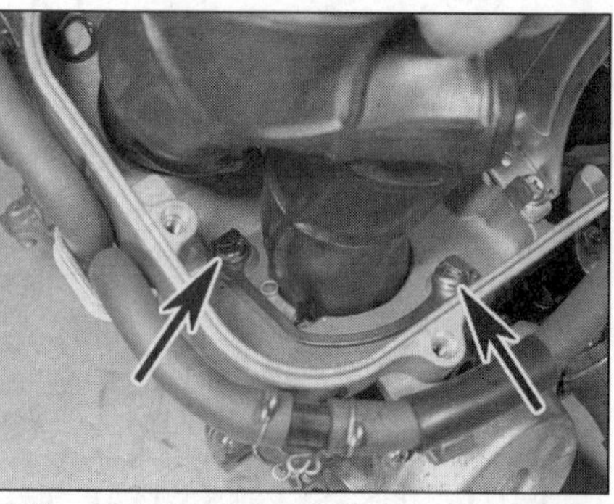
8.6b . . . then unscrew the housing screws (arrowed) and remove the housing from the carburettors

8.7 Unscrew the screws (arrowed) and remove the bracket

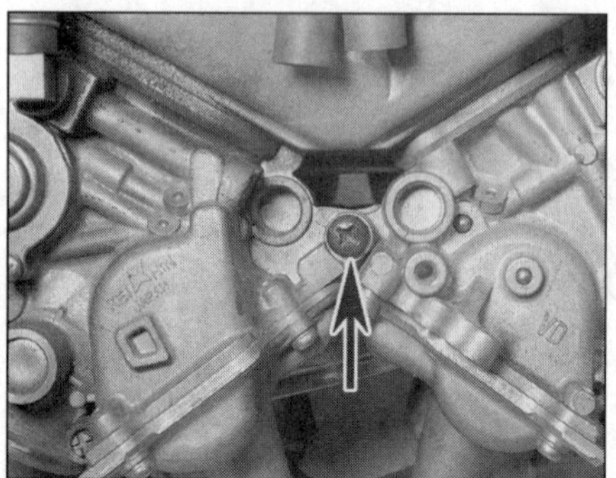
8.8 Remove the screw (arrowed) on each end of the assembly

8.9 Remove the split pin (arrowed) to free the choke linkage joining bar

8.10 Remove the split pin (arrowed) to free the throttle linkage joining bar

8.12 Make a careful note of the arrangement of the various springs before separating the carburettors

8.17a Slide the bar through the carburettor and fit the spring . . .

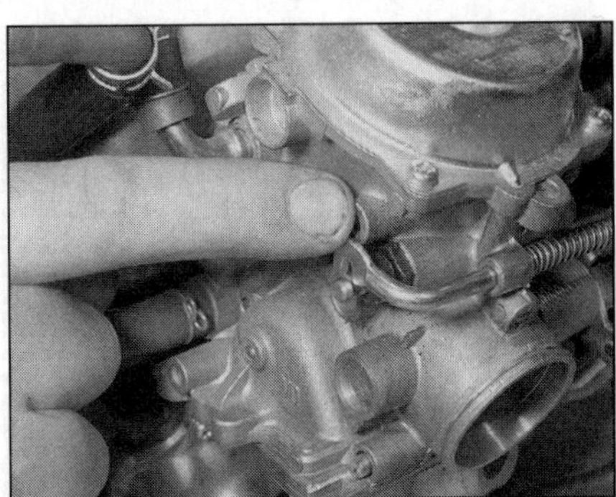

8.17b . . . then locate the arm on the plunger . . .

correctly on reassembly **(see illustration)**. Also note the arrangement of the various hoses and their unions.

13 Carefully separate the carburettors. Retrieve the synchronisation springs and note the fitting of the two fuel joint pipes and their O-rings, the two air joint pipes and their O-rings, and the two sub air cleaner hoses, as they are separated. Discard the O-rings as new ones must be used.

Joining

14 Fit a new O-ring onto each end of the fuel joint pipes and air joint pipes. Apply clean engine oil to each O-ring. Fit the two fuel joint pipes, the two air joint pipes, and the two sub air cleaner hoses into either the front or the rear carburettors **(see illustration 8.2)**.

15 Install the screw which joins the two front carburettors to each other, and the screw which joins the rear carburettors, but do not yet fully tighten them **(see illustration 8.8)**.

16 Join the front carburettors to the rear, making sure the fuel joint pipes, air vent joint pipes and sub air cleaner hose unions all locate correctly into their bores. Install the carburettor joining bracket, but do not fully tighten the screws **(see illustration 8.7)**.

17 Slide each choke linkage bar through its carburettor and then slide the spring onto the bar. Fit each choke linkage arm onto its plunger **(see illustrations)**. Do not yet tighten the bar clamp screw.

18 Install the throttle linkage joining bar with its washers and secure it using new split pins **(see illustration 8.10)**.

19 Install the choke linkage joining bar with its collars and washers and secure it using new split pins **(see illustration 8.9)**.

20 If removed, fit the dowels into each carburettor intake. Fit the air duct housing onto the carburettors, aligning the duct flanges with the grooves in the carburettors, and making sure the assembly locates correctly onto the dowels. Do not yet fit the assembly retainer plates.

21 Tighten the carburettor joining screws **(see illustration 8.8)** to the torque setting specified at the beginning of the Chapter. Also tighten the joining bracket screws **(see illustration 8.7)** and the choke linkage bar clamp screws **(see illustration)**.

22 Install the air duct housing retainer plates and tighten their screws **(see illustration 8.6b)**. Install the air duct assembly **(see illustration 8.6a)**.

23 Install the three carburettor synchronisation springs, making sure they locate correctly and squarely between their plates **(see illustration 8.12)**. Also install the two thrust springs.

24 Install the fuel hose joint piece and secure it with its clamps **(see illustration 8.5)**.

25 Install both air vent hoses and secure them with their clamps **(see illustration 8.4a and b)**.

26 Install the drain tube joint piece, making sure each tube is secure on its carburettor **(see illustration 7.6a)**.

27 Install the carburettors (see Section 6).

8.21 Tighten the choke bar clamp screw

9 Carburettors - reassembly and float height check

Warning: Refer to the precautions given in Section 1 before proceeding.

Note: *When reassembling the carburettors, be sure to use new O-rings and seals. Do not overtighten the carburettor jets and screws as they are easily damaged* ***(see illustration 7.1)****.*

1 If removed, install the air cut-off valve O-ring into its recess, followed by the air cut-off valve diaphragm, making sure it is properly seated. Fit the spring against the diaphragm, then install the cover and tighten its screws securely **(see illustrations)**.

2 Install the choke plunger and spring into the

9.1a Fit the O-ring if removed . . .

9.1b . . . then fit the diaphragm . . .

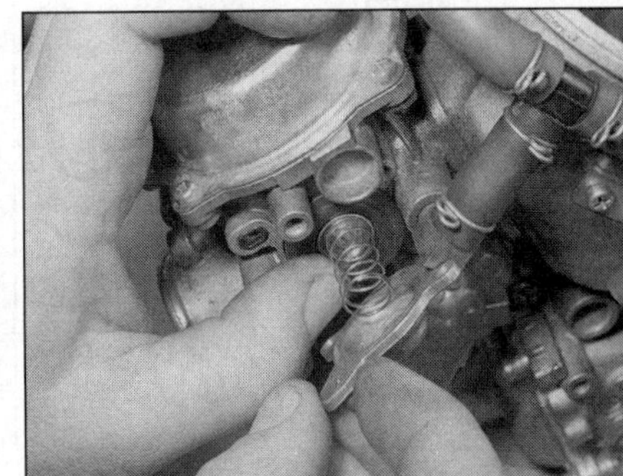

9.1c . . . the spring and the cover

9.4 Install the pilot jet . . .

9.5a . . . the needle jet holder . . .

9.5b . . . and the main jet

carburettor body and tighten the nut to secure it **(see illustration)**. Locate the choke arm or bar onto the plunger nipple and tighten the clamp screw **(see illustration 8.17b and 8.21)**.

3 Install the pilot screw (if removed) along with its spring, washer and O-ring, turning it in until it seats lightly **(see illustration 7.11)**. Now, turn the screw out the number of turns previously recorded on disassembly. If the carburettors have been idling roughly, or if the pilot screw settings are believed to be out, check and adjust the settings according to the procedure described in Section 10.

4 Install the pilot jet into the carburettor **(see illustration)**.

5 Install the needle jet holder into the carburettor. Screw the main jet into the end of the needle jet holder **(see illustrations)**.

6 If removed, install the float needle valve seat and its sealing washer, making sure its filter is attached **(see illustration)**.

7 Hook the float needle valve onto the float tab, then position the float assembly in the carburettor and install the pin, making sure it is secure **(see illustrations)**.

8 To check the float height, hold the carburettor so the float hangs down, then tilt it back until the needle valve is just seated, but not so far that the needle's spring-loaded tip is compressed. Measure the distance between the gasket face (with the gasket removed) and the bottom of the float with an accurate ruler. The correct setting should be as given in the Specifications at the beginning of the Chapter. If it is incorrect, adjust the float height by carefully bending the float tab a little at a time until the correct height is obtained. Repeat the procedure for all carburettors **(see illustration)**.

9 With the float height checked, fit a new rubber gasket onto the float chamber, making sure it is seated properly in its groove, and install the chamber onto the carburettor. Attach the drain hose to its union **(see illustrations)**.

10 If removed, carefully install the jet needle, spring and retainer into the piston, and where fitted the collar and washer, making sure all the components are correctly fitted, then push down on the needle retainer using a Phillips

9.6 Install the float needle valve seat

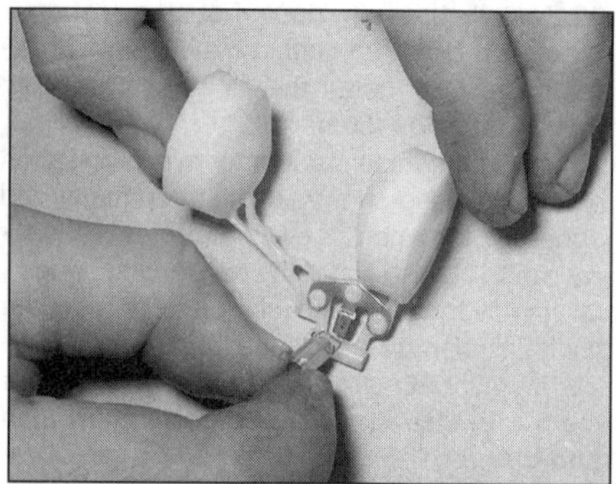
9.7a Fit the needle valve onto the float . . .

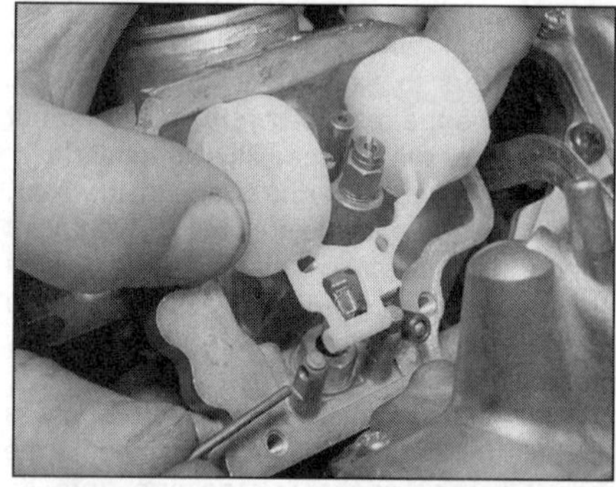
9.7b . . . then install the float

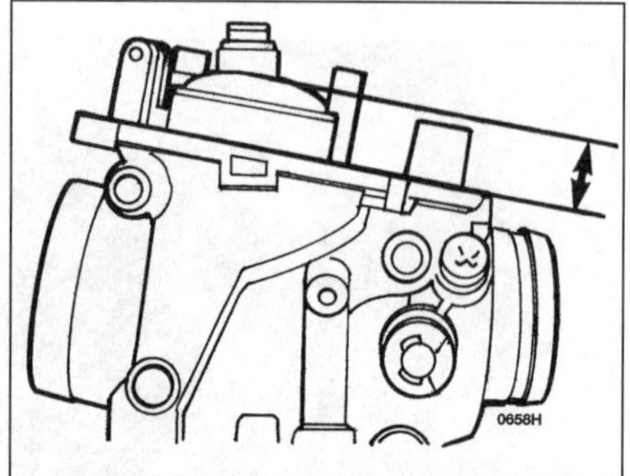

9.8 Measure the height of the top of the float above the gasket surface

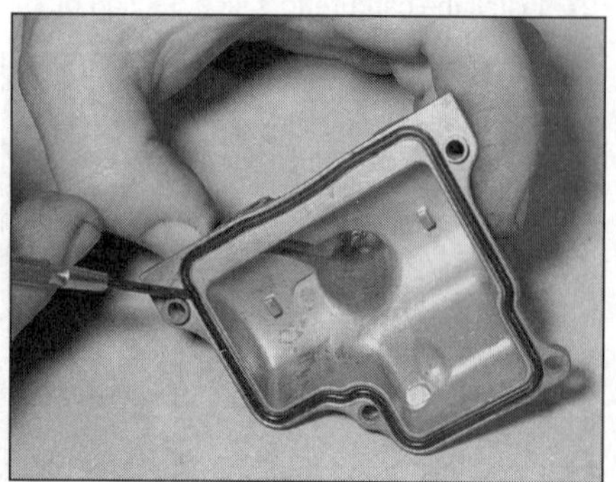
9.9a Fit a new gasket into the groove in the chamber . . .

9.9b . . . then install the chamber . . .

9.9c . . . and attach the drain hose

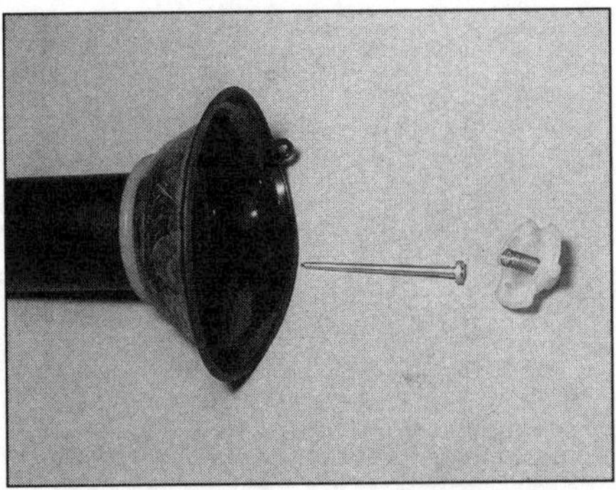
9.10 Install the needle and its retainer components into the piston

9.11 Make sure the tab is located in the recess around the air passage (arrowed)

9.12a Install the spring . . .

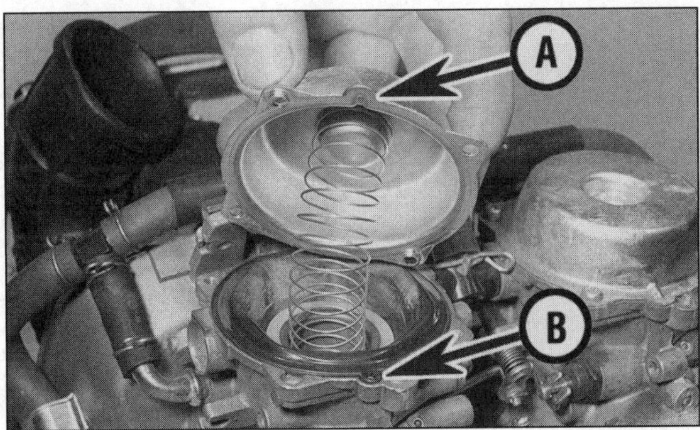

9.12b . . . then fit the cover, aligning the protrusion (A) with the tab (B). Check that the spring is located correctly in the cover

screwdriver and rotate it until its tabs lock under the protrusions in the piston **(see illustration and see illustration 7.5a)**.

11 Insert the piston assembly into the body and lightly push it down, ensuring the needle is correctly aligned with the needle jet **(see illustration 7.4)**. Align the tab on the diaphragm with the recess in the carburettor body, then press the diaphragm outer edge into its groove, making sure it is correctly seated and that the tab locates in the recess **(see illustration)**. Check the diaphragm is not creased, and that the piston moves smoothly up and down in its guide.

12 Install the spring into the piston. Fit the top cover to the carburettor, aligning the protrusion on the cover with the tab on the diaphragm and making sure the top of the spring locates onto the protrusion in the cover, and tighten its screws securely **(see illustrations)**.

13 Install the carburettors (see Section 6).

10 Throttle cables - removal and installation

Warning: Refer to the precautions given in Section 1 before proceeding.

Removal

1 Remove the fuel tank cover and the fairing pockets (see Chapter 8).

2 Remove the air filter housing (see Section 12).

3 Slacken the accelerator cable adjuster locknut, then unscrew the adjuster so that it threads out of the lower nut, which is captive against a small lug on the bracket. Thread the lower nut off the adjuster, then lift the adjuster out of the bracket **(see illustrations)**.

4 Unscrew the decelerator cable adjuster until the lower nut is free, then slip the cable out of the bracket **(see illustration)**. Mark each cable according to its location. Withdraw

4

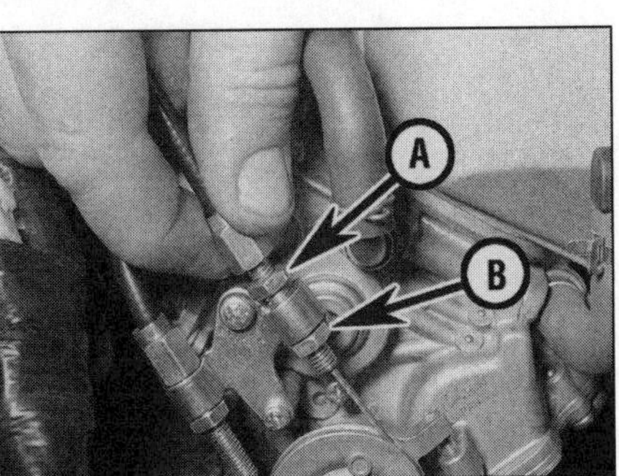

10.3a Slacken the accelerator cable adjuster locknut (A), then unscrew the adjuster until the lower nut (B) threads off . . .

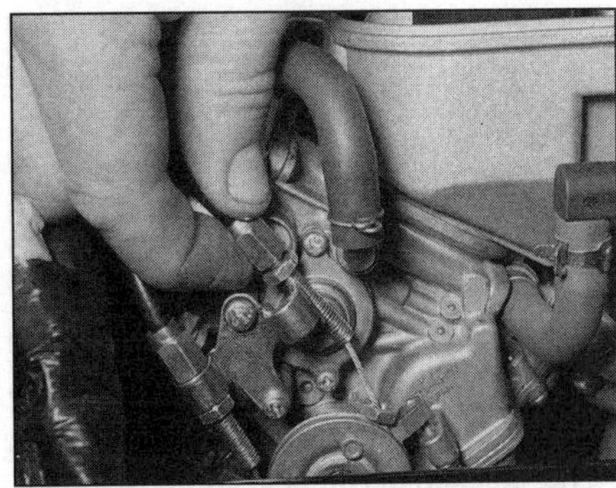
10.3b . . . then slip the cable out of the bracket

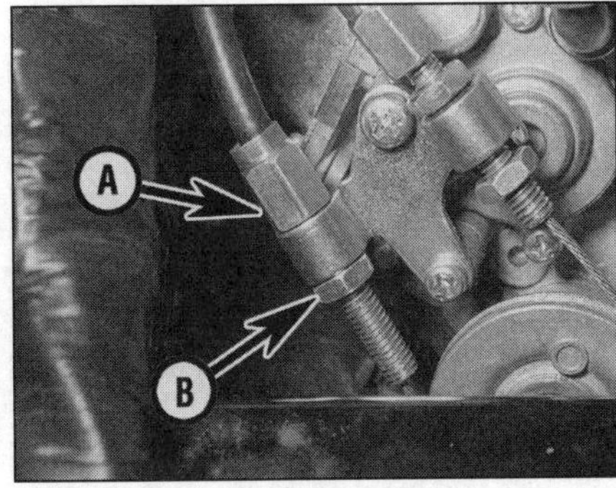

10.4 Decelerator cable adjuster (A) and lower nut (B)

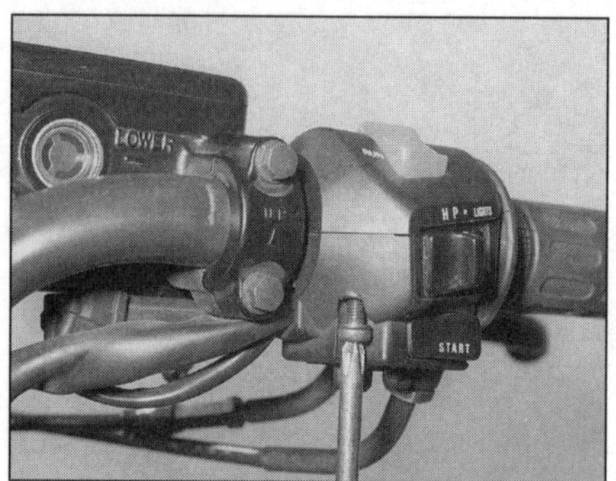

10.5a Remove the housing screws and separate the halves . . .

10.5b . . . then detach the cables

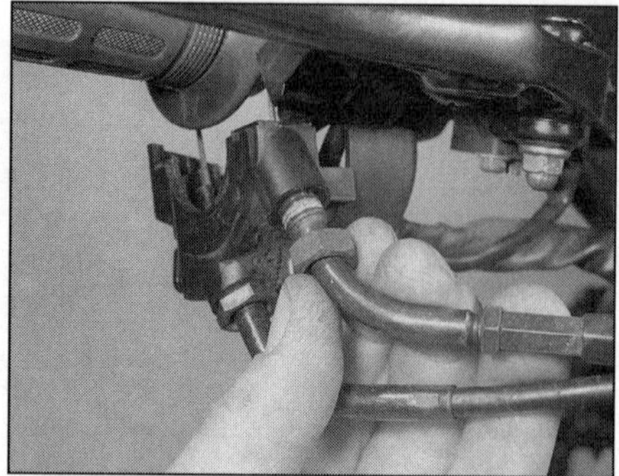

10.5c Unscrew the accelerator cable locknut and the cable elbow . . .

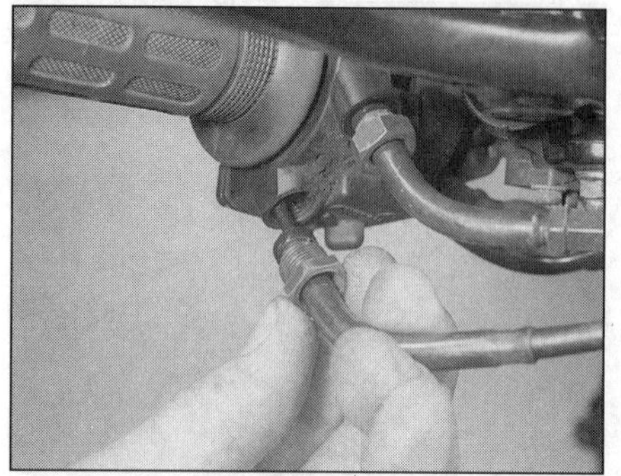

10.5d . . . then unscrew the decelerator cable nut and withdraw the elbow

the cables from the machine noting the correct routing of each cable.

5 Unscrew the two right side handlebar switch/throttle pulley housing screws, and separate the two halves. Detach the cable nipples from the pulley. Unscrew the accelerator cable elbow locknut, then unscrew the elbow and remove the cable from the housing. Unscrew the decelerator cable elbow nut and withdraw the cable **(see illustrations)**. Mark each cable to ensure it is connected correctly on installation.

Installation

6 Thread the accelerator cable elbow into the forward socket of the lower half of the switch/throttle pulley housing, then tighten the locknut **(see illustration 10.5c)**. Feed the decelerator cable into the rear socket and tighten the nut **(see illustration 10.5d)**. Lubricate the cable nipples with multi-purpose grease and install them into the throttle pulley **(see illustration 10.5b)**.

7 Fit the two halves of the housing onto the handlebar, making sure the pin in the lower half of the housing locates in the hole in the underside of the handlebar, and install the screws, tightening them securely **(see illustration)**.

8 Feed the cables through to the carburettors, making sure they are correctly routed. The cables must not interfere with any other component and should not be kinked or bent sharply.

9 Lubricate the lower cable nipples with multi-purpose grease and attach them to the carburettor throttle cam.

10 Fit the decelerator cable adjuster into the outer bracket, locating the nut against the lug so that it is captive, then thread the adjuster into the nut until it is tight **(see illustration 10.4)**.

11 Fit the accelerator cable adjuster into the inner bracket, then thread the lower nut onto the end of the adjuster **(see illustration 10.3b)**. Locate the nut against the lug so that it is captive, then thread the adjuster into the nut until the specified amount of cable freeplay is obtained (see Chapter 1) **(see illustration 10.3a)**. Tighten the locknut against the bracket.

12 Operate the throttle to check that it opens and closes freely.

13 Check and adjust the throttle cable freeplay if required (see Chapter 1). Turn the handlebars back and forth to make sure the cable doesn't cause the steering to bind.

14 Install the air filter housing (see Section 12).

15 Install the fairing pockets and the fuel tank cover (see Chapter 8).

16 Start the engine and check that the idle speed does not rise as the handlebars are turned. If it does, the throttle cable is routed incorrectly. Correct the problem before riding the motorcycle.

11 Choke cable - removal and installation

Removal

1 Remove the fuel tank cover and the fairing pockets (see Chapter 8).

2 Remove the air filter housing (see Section 12).

3 Slacken the bracket screw and free the choke outer cable from its bracket on the carburettor, then detach the inner cable end from the choke linkage lever **(see illustration)**. Withdraw the cable from the machine noting the correct routing.

4 Unscrew the two left side handlebar switch/choke lever housing screws and separate the two halves. Detach the cable nipple from the choke lever. Slacken the cable elbow locknut, then unscrew the elbow and remove the cable from the housing **(see illustrations)**.

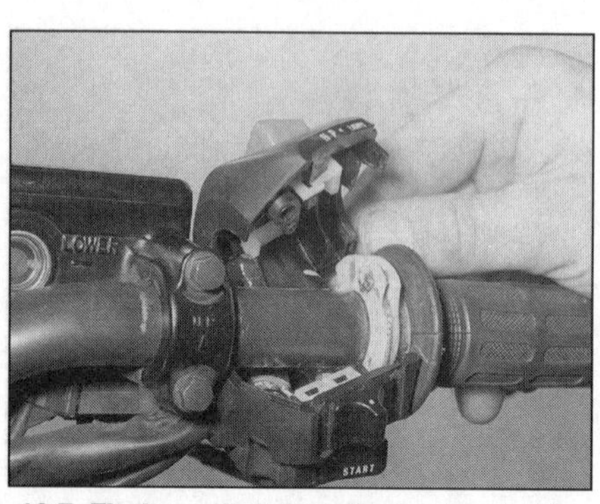

10.7 Fit the switch housing back onto the handlebars

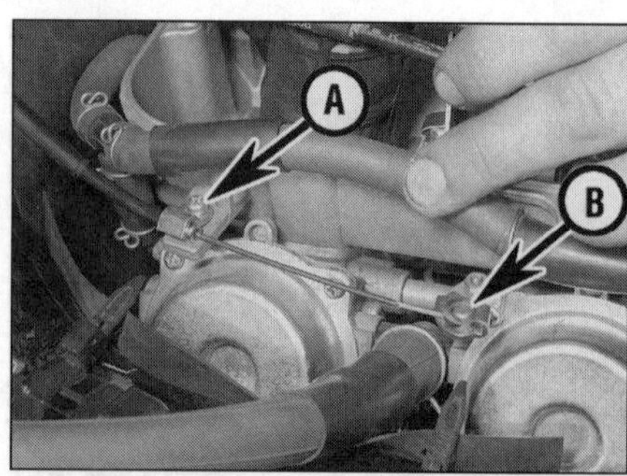

11.3 Slacken the bracket screw (A), then free the outer cable and remove the inner cable end from the linkage (B)

11.4a Remove the housing screws . . .

11.4b ... and separate the halves

11.4c Detach the inner cable end ...

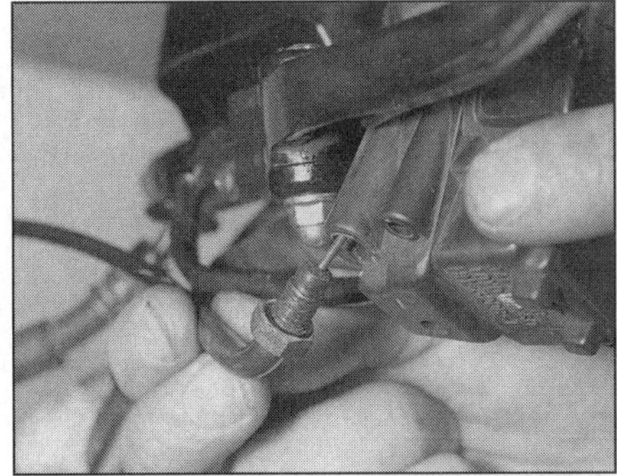
11.4d ... then unscrew the locknut and the elbow

Installation

5 Lubricate the upper cable nipple with multi-purpose grease. Thread the cable elbow into the switch/choke lever housing lower half and attach the nipple to the choke lever **(see illustrations 11.4c and d)**. Tighten the cable elbow locknut securely. Fit the two halves of the housing onto the handlebar, making sure the pin in the lower half of the housing locates in the hole in the underside of the handlebar **(see illustration 11.4b)**, and install the screws, tightening them securely **(see illustration 11.4a)**.

6 Feed the cable through to the carburettors, making sure it is correctly routed. The cable must not interfere with any other component and should not be kinked or bent sharply.

7 Lubricate the lower cable nipple with multi-purpose grease and attach it to the choke linkage lever on the carburettor. Fit the outer cable into its bracket and tighten the screw **(see illustrations)**.

8 Check the operation of the choke cable (see Chapter 1).

9 Install the air filter housing (see Section 12).

10 Install the fairing pockets and the fuel tank cover (see Chapter 8).

12 Air filter housing - removal and installation

Removal

1 Remove the fuel tank cover (see Chapter 8).

2 Unscrew the eight screws securing the air filter cover to the filter housing and remove the cover, then remove the filter element **(see illustrations)**. Do not remove the O-rings from the cover and the filter element sealing ring unless they are damaged or deteriorated and are to be replaced.

3 Release the clamp securing each sub-air cleaner hose to the union on the front of the housing and detach the hoses **(see illustration)**.

4 Release the clamp securing the breather hose to the bottom of the housing and detach the hose **(see illustration)**.

5 Unscrew the two screws securing the fuel tap to the housing and detach the air hose from its lug. Unscrew the six screws securing

11.7a Grease the nipple and slot it into the arm ...

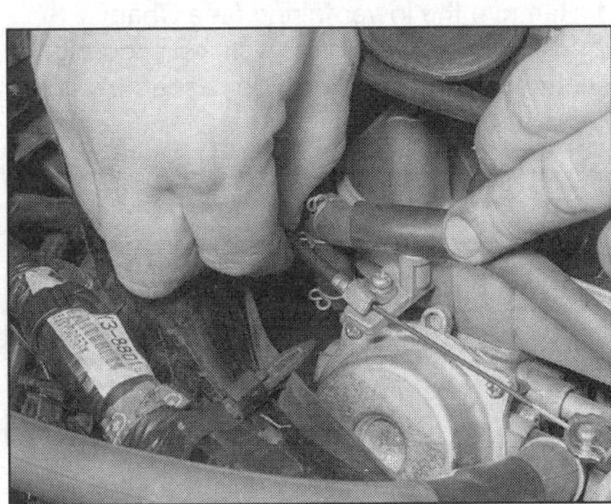
11.7b ... then secure the outer cable end in the bracket and tighten the screw

12.2a The housing cover is secured by eight screws (arrowed)

4

12.2b Remove the cover and lift out the element

12.3 Detach the sub-air cleaner hoses (arrowed) ...

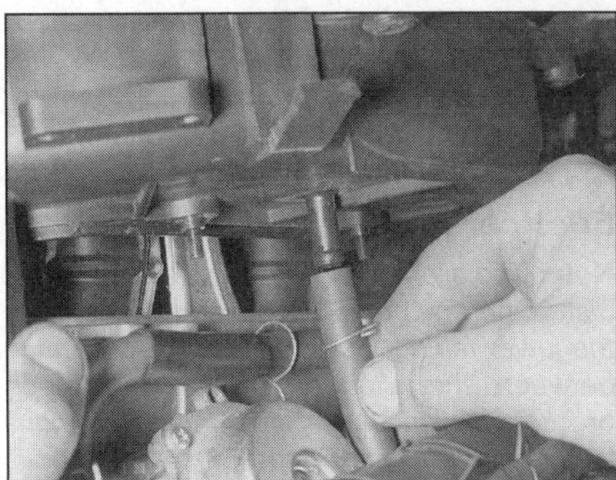
12.4 ... and the breather hose

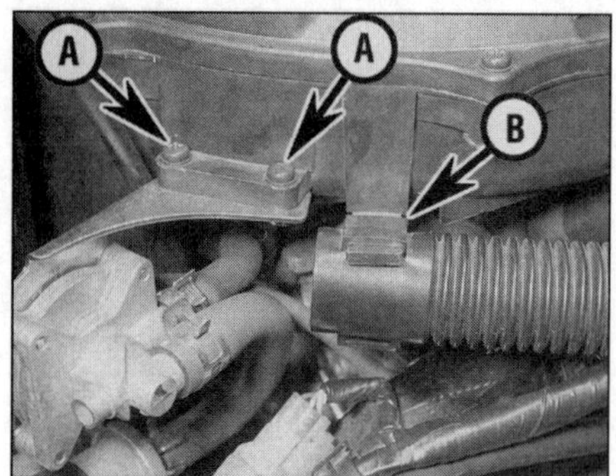

12.5a Remove the two screws (A) securing the fuel tap and detach the air hose from its lug (B) . . .

12.5b . . . then remove the six screws securing the housing . . .

12.6 . . . then lift off the housing

12.7 Check the sealing ring and O-rings and replace them if necessary

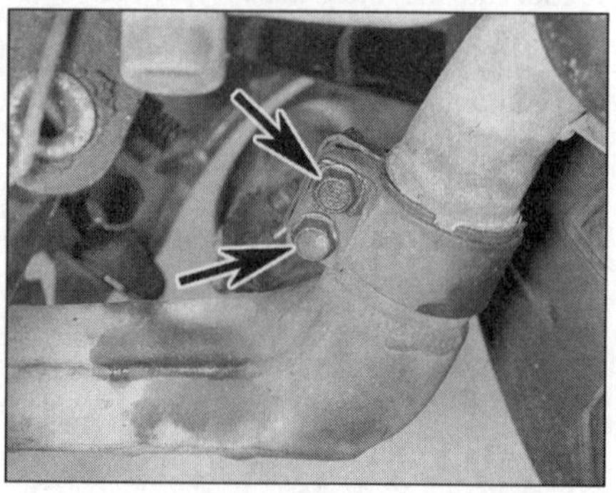
13.2 Slacken the silencer clamp bolts (arrowed) . . .

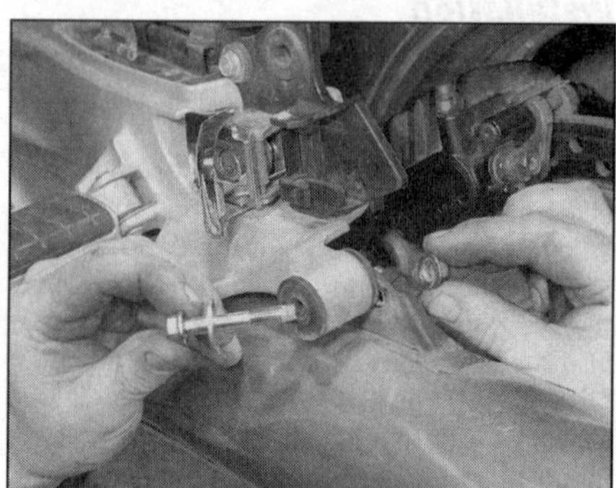
13.3 . . . and remove the mounting bolt . . .

the housing to the air duct holder **(see illustrations)**.

6 Lift the housing up off the air duct holder and remove it **(see illustration)**. Remove the O-ring from the base of the housing and discard it as a new one must be used.

Installation

7 Installation is the reverse of removal. Use a new O-ring for the base of the housing. Check the condition of the element sealing ring and the cover O-rings and replace them if necessary **(see illustration)**.

13 Exhaust system - removal and installation

Warning: If the engine has been running the exhaust system will be very hot. Allow the system to cool before carrying out any work.

Silencers

Note: *The silencers can be removed without disturbing any other components apart from the lower fairing, but there is little clearance between the silencers and the footpeg brackets. If difficulty is encountered, remove the side panels (see Chapter 8), and the bolts securing the footpeg bracket, then displace the bracket to provide more clearance. There is no need to disconnect any wiring or hoses.*

Removal

1 Remove the lower fairing (see Chapter 8).

2 Slacken the bolts on the clamp securing the silencer to the downpipe assembly **(see illustration)**.

The silencer clamp bolts tend to become corroded and seized. It is advisable to spray them with WD40 or a similar product before attempting to Slacken them.

3 Unscrew the bolt securing the silencer to the footpeg bracket, noting the arrangement of the collar and washer **(see illustration)**.

4 Release the silencer from the exhaust downpipe assembly using a twisting motion **(see illustration)**.

5 Inspect the bushes for signs of damage and replace them if necessary. Remove the sealing ring from either the end of the silencer or inside the downpipe assembly and discard it as a new one should be used.

Installation

6 Installation is the reverse of removal. Use a new sealing ring Tighten the silencer mounting bolt and clamp bolts to the torque settings specified at the beginning of the Chapter. Run the engine and check the system for leaks **(see illustrations)**.

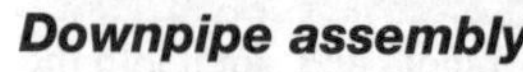

Downpipe assembly

Note: *Whilst it is possible to remove each side of the downpipe assembly separately, the join*

13.4 . . . then remove the silencer

13.6a Fit a new sealing ring . . .

13.6b . . . and tighten the bolts to the specified torque settings

13.9 Slacken the fairing bracket bolts (A), then unscrew the downpipe guard bolts (B) and remove the guard

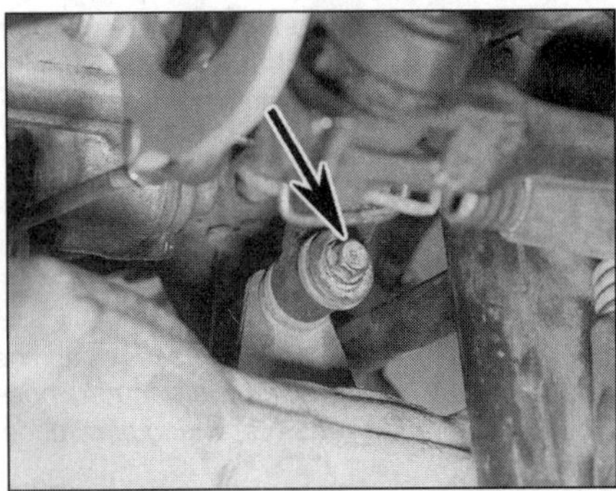

13.10 Unscrew the rear mounting bolt (arrowed)

between the two is likely to be seized, making it very difficult. It is advisable therefore to remove the downpipes as a complete assembly, thus avoiding the possibility of damaging anything.

Removal

7 Remove the middle fairing panels (see Chapter 8) and the silencers (see above). Place the machine on its sidestand for easier removal of the downpipe assembly.

8 On all ABS/TCS and CBS/LBS-ABS/TCS models, remove the coolant reservoir (see Chapter 3).

9 Slacken the two frame bolts securing the fairing bracket on the right hand side of the engine **(see illustration)**. There is no need to fully remove the bolts, but slacken them enough to provide the clearance required to remove the downpipe guard. Unscrew the four bolts securing the guard and manoeuvre it away. Also remove the left-hand guard, though there is no need to slacken the fairing bracket bolts on that side.

HAYNES HiNT ***The downpipe guard bolts tend to become corroded and seized. It is advisable to spray them with WD40 or a similar product before attempting to Slacken them. Apply copper grease to the bolt threads on installation.***

10 Unscrew the bolt securing the downpipe collector section to the frame, noting the collar fitted between it and the frame **(see illustration)**.

11 Unscrew the four nuts securing each side of the downpipe assembly to the cylinder heads. Carefully manoeuvre the assembly off the heads and lower it to the floor **(see illustrations)**.

12 Remove the gasket from each port in the cylinder heads and discard them as new ones must be fitted **(see illustration)**.

Installation

13 Fit a new gasket into each of the cylinder head ports. Apply a smear of grease to the gaskets to keep them in place whilst fitting the downpipe if necessary **(see illustration)**.

14 Manoeuvre the assembly into position so that the head of each downpipe is located in its port in the cylinder head **(see illustration 13.11b)**. Install the flange nuts and tighten one of each pair to the initial torque setting specified at the beginning of the Chapter **(see illustration)**. Now tighten the other nut of each pair to the final torque setting specified, then tighten the first nut to the final torque setting.

15 The remainder of installation is the reverse of removal. Apply copper grease to the downpipe guard bolts and tighten them and

13.11a Each side is secured to its head by four nuts (arrowed)

13.11b Carefully manoeuvre the assembly down to the floor

13.12 Remove the old gaskets . . .

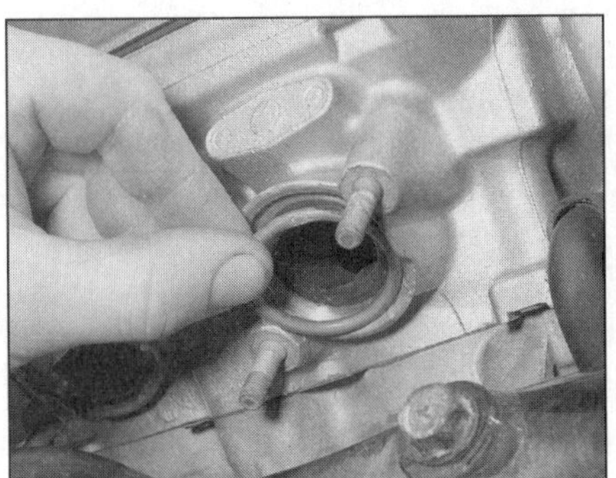

13.13 . . . and fit new ones

13.14 Fit the flange nuts and tighten them as described

the fairing bracket bolts to the specified torque settings **(see illustration)**. Run the engine and check the system for leaks.

14 EVAP and PAIR systems - (California and US ABS/TCS and LBS-ABS/TCS models)

Note: *The EVAP system hoses can be identified by referring to the vacuum hose routing diagram on the rear mudguard, under the seat.*

13.15 Apply copper grease to the threads of the guard bolts

Evaporative emission control system (EVAP)

1 This system prevents the escape of fuel vapour into the atmosphere by storing it in a charcoal-filled canister.

2 When the engine is stopped, fuel vapour from the tank is directed into the canister where it is absorbed and stored whilst the motorcycle is standing. When the engine is started, intake manifold depression opens the purge control valves, thus drawing vapours which are stored in the canister into the carburettors to be burned during the normal combustion process.

3 The system is not adjustable and can be tested only by a Honda dealer. Checks which can be performed by the owner are given in Chapter 1.

Pulse secondary air injection system (PAIR)

4 When the engine is running, the depression present in the intake manifold of a particular carburettor acts on a diaphragm in the purge control valve, opening the valve. With the purge control valve open, whenever there is a negative pulse in the exhaust system, filtered fresh air is drawn from the PAIR air cleaner, through the reed valves and into the exhaust ports in the front of the cylinder head.

5 This fresh air promotes the burning of any excess fuel present in the exhaust gases, so reducing the amount of harmful hydrocarbons emitted into the atmosphere via the exhaust gases. Exhaust gases are prevented from passing back into the PAIR system by the reed valves.

6 The system is not adjustable and can be tested only by a Honda dealer. Checks which can be performed by the owner are given in Chapter 1.

15 Crankcase breather - general

UK L and M and US 1991 models are fitted with a crankcase breather. Hoses from the crankcase and gearchange cover route vapour up to a storage tank on the frame. Another hose carries this vapour from the storage tank to the air filter housing for reburning.

Chapter 5
Ignition system

Contents

General information 1
Ignition control unit - check, removal and installation 5
Ignition (main) switch - check, removal and installation .see Chapter 9
Ignition HT coils - check, removal and installation 3
Ignition system - check 2
Ignition timing - general information and check 6
Neutral switch - check and replacement ....see Chapter 9
Pulse generator coil assembly - check, removal and installation ... 4
Sidestand switch - check and replacement ....see Chapter 9
Spark plug gaps - check and replacement ....see Chapter 1

Degrees of difficulty

Easy, suitable for novice with little experience 

Fairly easy, suitable for beginner with some experience 

Fairly difficult, suitable for competent DIY mechanic 

Difficult, suitable for experienced DIY mechanic

Very difficult, suitable for expert DIY or professional 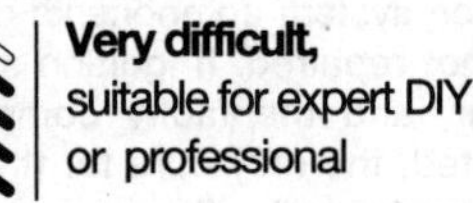

Specifications

General information

Firing order	1-4-3-2
Cylinder numbering	
Front right	1
Rear right	3
Front left	2
Rear left	4
Spark plugs	See Chapter 1

← FWD

cyl. 1	cyl. 3
cyl. 2	cyl. 4

Ignition timing

At idle	12° BTDC
Full advance	27° BTDC @ 5000 rpm

Pulse generator coils

Resistance	405 to 495 ohms

Ignition HT coils

Primary winding resistance	2.16 to 3.19 ohms
Secondary winding resistance	
With plug cap	22.5 to 27.5 K ohms
Without plug cap	13.5 to 16.5 K ohms

1 General information

All models are fitted with a fully transistorised electronic ignition system, which due to its lack of mechanical parts is totally maintenance free. The system comprises a rotor, pulse generator coil, ignition control unit and ignition HT coils (refer to the wiring diagrams at the end of Chapter 9 for details).

The trigger on the rotor, which is fitted to the rear end of the crankshaft, magnetically operates the pulse generator coil as the crankshaft rotates. The pulse generator coil sends a signal to the ignition control unit which then supplies the ignition HT coils with the power necessary to produce a spark at the plugs.

The system uses two coils mounted across the frame behind the steering head. The upper coil supplies nos. 2 and 4 cylinder spark plugs and the lower coil supplies nos. 1 and 3 cylinder plugs.

The system incorporates an electronic advance system controlled by signals generated by the rotor and the pick-up coil.

The system incorporates a safety interlock circuit which will cut the ignition if the sidestand is put down whilst the engine is running and in gear, or if a gear is selected whilst the engine is running and the sidestand is down. There is also a lean angle sensor which cuts the ignition in the event of the bike falling over.

Because of their nature, the individual ignition system components can be checked but not repaired. If ignition system troubles occur, and the faulty component can be isolated, the only cure for the problem is to replace the part with a new one. Keep in mind that most electrical parts, once purchased, cannot be returned. To avoid unnecessary expense, make very sure the faulty component has been positively identified before buying a replacement part.

Note that there is no provision adjusting the ignition timing on these models.

2 Ignition system - check

Warning: The energy levels in electronic systems can be very high. On no account should the ignition be switched on whilst the plugs or plug caps are being held. Shocks from the HT circuit can be most unpleasant. Secondly, it is vital that the engine is not turned over or run with any of the plug caps removed, and that the plugs are soundly earthed (grounded) when the system is checked for sparking. The ignition system components can be seriously damaged if the HT circuit becomes isolated.

1 As no means of adjustment is available, any failure of the system can be traced to failure of a system component or a simple wiring fault. Of the two possibilities, the latter is by far the most likely. In the event of failure, check the system in a logical fashion, as described below.

2 Disconnect the HT leads from the spark plugs. Connect each lead to a spare spark plug and lay each plug on the engine with the threads contacting the engine. If necessary, hold each spark plug with an insulated tool.

Warning: Do not remove any of the spark plugs from the engine to perform this check - atomised fuel being pumped out of the open spark plug hole could ignite, causing severe injury!

3 Having observed the above precautions, check that the kill switch is in the RUN position, turn the ignition switch ON and turn the engine over on the starter motor. If the system is in good condition a regular, fat blue spark should be evident at each plug electrode. If the spark appears thin or yellowish, or is non-existent, further investigation will be necessary. Before proceeding further, turn the ignition off and remove the key as a safety measure.

4 The ignition system must be able to produce a spark which is capable of jumping a particular size gap. Honda do not provide a specification, but a healthy system should produce a spark capable of jumping at least 6 mm. A simple testing tool can be made to test the minimum gap across which the spark will jump (see **Tool Tip**).

5 Connect one of the spark plug HT leads from one coil to the protruding electrode on the test tool, and clip the tool to a good earth (ground) on the engine or frame. Check that the kill switch is in the RUN position, turn the ignition switch ON and turn the engine over on the starter motor. If the system is in good condition a regular, fat blue spark should be seen to jump the gap between the nail ends. Repeat the test for the other coil. If the test results are good the entire ignition system can be considered good. If the spark appears thin or yellowish, or is non-existent, further investigation will be necessary.

TOOL TiP

A simple spark gap testing tool can be made from a block of wood, a large alligator clip and two nails, one of which is fashioned so that a spark plug cap or bare HT lead end can be connected to its end. Make sure the gap between the two nail ends is the same as specified

6 Ignition faults can be divided into two categories, namely those where the ignition system has failed completely, and those which are due to a partial failure. The likely faults are listed below, starting with the most probable source of failure. Work through the list systematically, referring to the subsequent sections for full details of the necessary checks and tests. **Note:** *Before checking the following items ensure that the battery is fully charged and that all fuses are in good condition.*

- *a) Loose, corroded or damaged wiring connections, broken or shorted wiring between any of the component parts of the ignition system (see Chapter 9).*
- *b) Faulty HT lead or spark plug cap, faulty spark plug, dirty, worn or corroded plug electrodes, or incorrect gap between electrodes.*
- *c) Faulty ignition (main) switch or engine kill switch (see Chapter 9).*
- *d) Faulty neutral or sidestand switch or lean angle sensor (see Chapter 9).*
- *e) Faulty pulse generator coil or damaged rotor.*
- *f) Faulty ignition HT coil(s).*
- *g) Faulty ignition control unit.*

7 If the above checks don't reveal the cause of the problem, have the ignition system tested by a Honda dealer. Honda produce a tester which can perform a complete diagnostic analysis of the ignition system.

3 Ignition HT coils - check, removal and installation

Check

1 In order to determine conclusively that the ignition coils are defective, they should be tested by a Honda dealer equipped with the special diagnostic tester.

2 However, the coils can be checked visually (for cracks and other damage) and the primary and secondary coil resistance can be measured with a multimeter. If the coils are undamaged, and if the resistance readings are as specified at the beginning of the Chapter, they are probably capable of proper operation.

3 Remove the left-hand side panel (see Chapter 8) and disconnect the battery negative (-ve) lead.

4 Remove the upper fairing (see Chapter 8). The coils are mounted across the frame behind the steering head.

5 Disconnect the primary circuit electrical

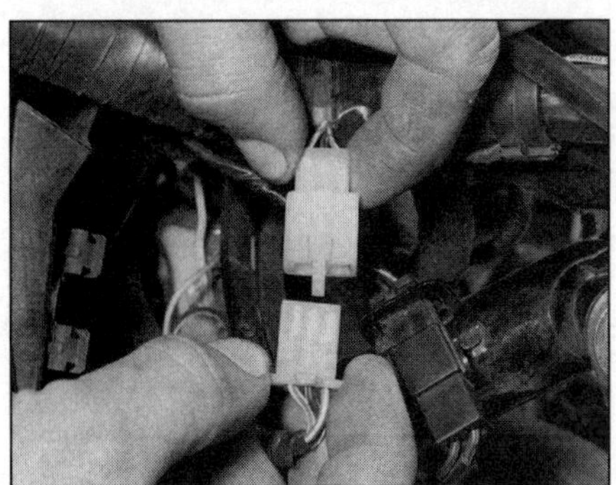

3.5 Disconnect the coils' primary circuit wiring connector

connector and the HT leads from the spark plugs **(see illustration)**. Mark the locations of all wires and leads before disconnecting them.

6 The primary winding test is made on the ignition coil side of the three-pin connector described in Step 5. Set the meter to the ohms x 1 scale and insert the positive probe into the blue/yellow wire terminal, and the negative probe into the black/white wire terminal. This will give a resistance reading of the primary windings of the coil for cylinders 2 and 4 and should be consistent with the value given in the Specifications at the beginning of the Chapter. Now insert the positive probe into the yellow/blue wire terminal, leaving the negative probe in place on the black/white wire terminal. This will give a resistance reading of the primary windings of the coil for cylinders 1 and 3 and should be consistent with the value given in the Specifications at the beginning of the Chapter.

7 To check the condition of the secondary windings, set the meter to the K ohm scale and work on one coil at a time. Connect one meter probe to one spark plug cap and the other probe to the other spark plug cap **(see illustration)**. If the reading obtained is not within the range shown in the Specifications, unscrew the caps from the ends of the HT leads and repeat the measurement. If the reading is now as specified, the spark plug caps are confirmed faulty and should be replaced with new ones. If the reading is still outside the specified range, it is likely that the coil or either HT lead is defective; note that the HT leads can be detached from the coil by unscrewing the knurled retainer and renewed separately if there is any doubt about their condition.

8 Should any of the above checks not produce the expected result, have your findings confirmed on the diagnostic tester (see Step 1). If the coil is confirmed to be faulty, it must be replaced; the coil is a sealed unit and cannot therefore be repaired.

Removal

9 Remove the left-hand side panel (see Chapter 8) and disconnect the battery negative (-ve) lead.

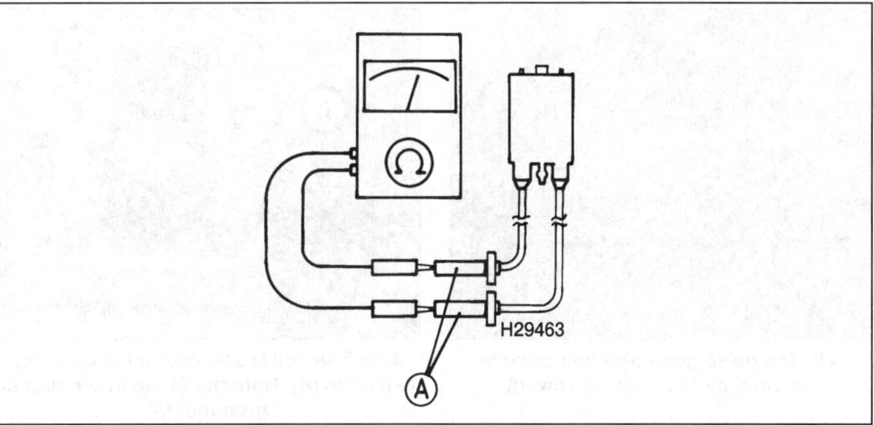

3.7 To test the coil secondary resistance, connect the multimeter leads between the spark plug caps. Perform a second test by unscrewing the plug caps (A) from the leads and connecting the multimeter between the plug leads

10 Remove the upper fairing (see Chapter 8).

11 The coils are mounted across the frame behind the steering stem. Disconnect the primary circuit electrical connector **(see illustration 3.5)** and disconnect the HT leads from the spark plugs. Mark the locations of all wires and leads before disconnecting them.

12 Unscrew the two bolts securing each coil, noting the position of the spacers, and remove the coils **(see illustration)**. Note the routing of the HT leads.

Installation

13 Installation is the reverse of removal. Make sure the wiring connectors and HT leads are securely connected.

4 Pulse generator coil assembly - check, removal and installation

Check

1 Remove the left-hand side panel (see Chapter 8) and disconnect the battery negative (-ve) lead.

2 On standard models, remove the right-hand side panel and on ABS/TCS or CBS/LBS-ABS/TCS models remove the fuel tank cover (see Chapter 8).

3 Trace the pulse generator coil/neutral switch/oil pressure switch wiring back from the rear of the engine and disconnect it at the 4-pin connector **(see illustration)**. Using a multimeter set to the ohms x 100 scale, measure the resistance between the white/yellow and yellow terminals on the pulse generator coil side of the connector.

4 Compare the reading obtained with that given in the Specifications at the beginning of this Chapter. The pulse generator coil must be replaced if the reading obtained differs greatly from that given, particularly if the meter indicates a short circuit (no measurable resistance) or an open circuit (infinite, or very high resistance).

5 If the pulse generator coil is thought to be faulty, first check that this is not due to a damaged or broken wire from the coil to the connector; pinched or broken wires can usually be repaired. Note that the coil is not available individually but comes as an assembly with the mounting plate and wiring.

Removal

6 Remove the left-hand side panel (see Chapter 8) and disconnect the battery negative (-ve) lead.

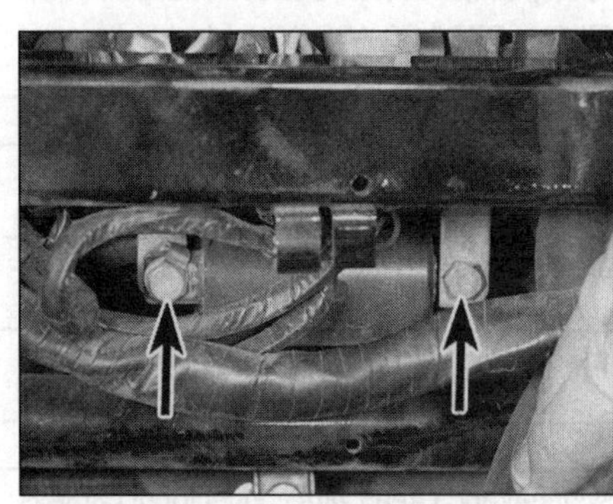

3.12 The coils are mounted behind the steering head. Each is secured by two bolts (arrowed)

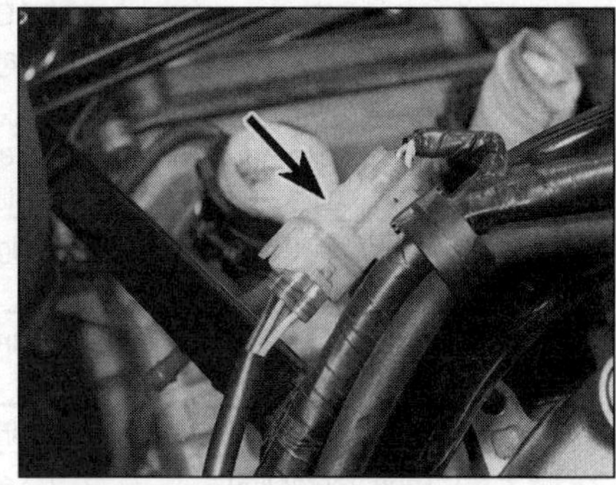

4.3 Disconnect the pulse generator wiring connector (arrowed)

4.9 The pulse generator coil cover is secured by four bolts (arrowed)

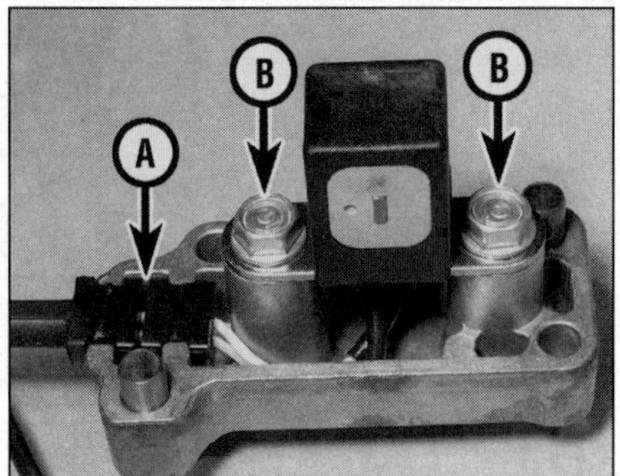

4.10 The coil is secured to the cover by two bolts (B). Note the fitting of the rubber grommet (A)

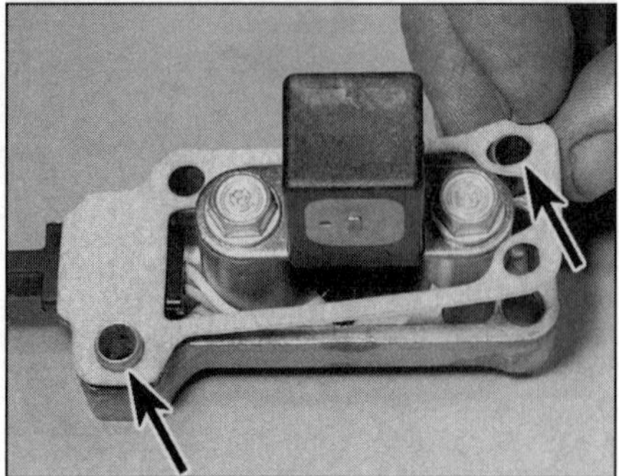
4.13a Locate the new gasket over the dowels (arrowed) . . .

4.13b . . . then install the coil and tighten the cover bolts

7 On standard models, remove the right-hand side panel and on ABS/TCS or CBS/LBS-ABS/TCS models remove the fuel tank cover (see Chapter 8).

8 Trace the pulse generator coil/neutral switch/oil pressure switch wiring back from the rear of the engine and disconnect it at the 4-pin connector **(see illustration 4.3)**. Free the wiring from any clips or ties and feed it through to the rear of the engine. Disconnect the neutral switch wiring connector from its terminal on the switch and release it from its guide, then remove the screw securing the oil pressure switch wiring connector and disconnect it (see Chapter 9 if required).

9 Unscrew the four bolts securing the pulse generator coil cover to the rear of the engine **(see illustration)**. Remove the cover. Discard the gasket as a new one must be used. Remove the dowels from the engine or cover if they are loose.

10 Unscrew the two bolts securing the pulse generator coil to the cover **(see illustration)**. Remove the rubber wiring grommet from its recess in the cover, then remove the coil, noting how it fits.

11 Examine the rotor for signs of damage and replace it if necessary. It is mounted onto the end of the crankshaft, which must be removed to access the rotor (see Chapter 2).

Installation

12 Install the pulse generator coil assembly onto the cover and tighten the bolts securely **(see illustration 4.10)**. Position the wiring grommet in its recess.

13 Fit the cover dowels if removed, then install the assembly using a new gasket and tighten the bolts securely **(see illustrations)**.

14 Connect the oil pressure switch wire to its terminal on the switch and tighten the screw securely, then connect the neutral switch wiring connector to the switch terminal and place the wiring in its guide (see Chapter 9 if required). Connect the pulse generator coil/neutral switch/oil pressure switch wiring at the 4-pin connector **(see illustration 4.3)**. Secure the wiring in its clips or ties.

15 On standard models, install the right-hand side panel and on ABS/TCS or CBS/LBS-ABS/TCS models install the fuel tank cover (see Chapter 8).

16 Reconnect the battery negative (-ve) lead and install the left-hand side panel (see Chapter 8).

5 Ignition control unit - check, removal and installation

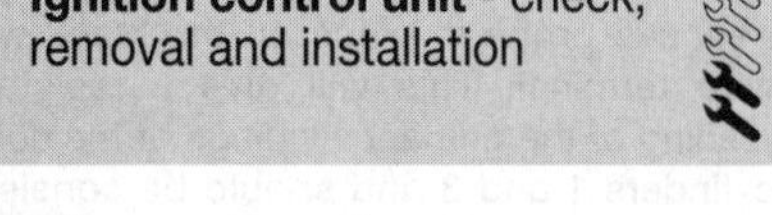

Check

1 If the tests shown in the preceding Sections have failed to isolate the cause of an ignition fault, it is likely that the ignition control unit itself is faulty. Remove the ignition control unit as described below.

2 Using the table shown **(see illustration)**, make the supply line tests on the wiring harness side of the connector. Note that there

Component	Wire connections	Value
Battery voltage input line	Standard models: Black/white and earth (ground) with engine stop switch in RUN position and ignition ON ABS/TCS or CBS/LBS-ABS/TCS: Black/yellow and earth (ground) with ignition ON	Battery voltage should be shown
Pulse generator line	Yellow and White/yellow	405 to 495 ohms
Ignition primary coil line	Yellow/blue and Black/white (cyls. 1 and 3) Blue/yellow and Black/white (cyls. 2 and 4)	2.16 to 3.19 ohms
Neutral switch line	Light green and earth (ground)	Continuity in neutral No continuity in any gear
Sidestand switch line	Green/white and earth (ground)	Continuity with stand up No continuity with stand down
Earth (ground) line	Green and earth (ground)	Continuity
Tachometer line	Yellow/green and Green wire connector of harness side at the instruments	Continuity

5.2 Ignition control unit supply line test table

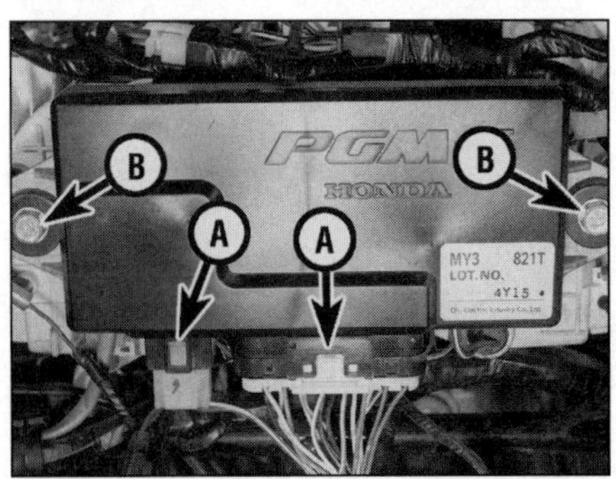

5.5 Ignition control unit wiring connectors (A) and mounting bolts (B)

is no test data available for the ignition control unit; if the supply line tests in the table indicate a problem, take the machine to a Honda dealer for further testing on the diagnostic tester.

Removal

3 Remove the left-hand side panel (see Chapter 8) and disconnect the battery negative (-ve) lead.

4 On standard models remove the left fairing pocket, and on ABS/TCS or CBS/LBS-ABS/TCS models remove the middle fairing inner panel for access to the ignition control unit (see Chapter 8).

5 Disconnect the wiring connector(s) from the ignition control unit **(see illustration)**.

6 On standard models remove the ignition control unit from its rubber sleeve, or lift the sleeve and unit together off the sleeve's mounting lugs, and remove the unit. On ABS/TCS or CBS/LBS-ABS/TCS models, the unit is secured by two bolts with collars **(see illustration 5.5)**.

Installation

7 Installation is the reverse of removal. Make sure the wiring connectors are correctly and securely connected.

6 Ignition timing - general information and check

General information

1 Since no provision exists for adjusting the ignition timing and since no component is subject to mechanical wear, there is no need for regular checks; only if investigating a fault such as a loss of power or a misfire, should the ignition timing be checked.

2 The ignition timing is checked dynamically (engine running) using a stroboscopic lamp. The inexpensive neon lamps should be adequate in theory, but in practice may produce a pulse of such low intensity that the timing mark remains indistinct. If possible, one of the more precise xenon tube lamps should be used, powered by an external source of the appropriate voltage. **Note:** *Do not use the machine's own battery as an incorrect reading may result from stray impulses within the machine's electrical system.*

Check

3 Warm the engine up to normal operating temperature then stop it.

4 Unscrew the two bolts securing the timing inspection cover to the timing belt cover on the front of the engine **(see illustration)**. Discard the O-ring as a new one should be used.

5 The timing mark on the rotor for the no. 1 cylinder is a line with the mark F1 which indicates the firing point at idle speed for that cylinder **(see illustration)**. The timing mark on the rotor for the no. 4 cylinder is a line with the mark F4. The static timing mark with which these should align is the index mark on the timing belt cover.

> **HAYNES HiNT** ***The rotor timing mark can be highlighted with white paint to make it more visible under the stroboscope light.***

6 Connect the timing light to the no.1 cylinder HT lead as described in the manufacturer's instructions.

7 Start the engine and aim the light at the static timing mark.

8 With the machine idling at the specified speed, the timing mark F1 should align with the static timing mark.

9 Slowly increase the engine speed whilst observing the timing mark. The timing mark should move anti-clockwise, increasing in relation to the engine speed until it reaches full advance (no identification mark).

10 Repeat Steps 6 to 9 for the no. 4 cylinder, using the F4 mark.

11 As already stated, there is no means of adjustment of the ignition timing on these machines. If the ignition timing is incorrect, or suspected of being incorrect, one of the ignition system components is at fault, and the system must be tested as described in the preceding Sections of this Chapter.

12 When the check is complete, install the timing inspection cover using a new O-ring and tighten its bolts.

6.4 Unscrew the bolts and remove the cover

6.5 No. 1 cylinder timing marks. The static mark is the sharp protrusion, indicated by a line (arrowed)

Notes

Chapter 6
Frame, suspension and final drive

Contents

Driveshaft joint and final drive - removal, inspection and installation .. 14
Final drive oil change .... see Chapter 1
Final drive oil level check .... see Chapter 1
Footrests, brake pedal and gearchange lever - removal and installation 3
Forks - disassembly, inspection and reassembly 7
Forks - oil change .... see Chapter 1
Forks - removal and installation 6
Frame - inspection and repair 2
General information 1
Handlebars and levers - removal and installation 5
Handlebar switches - check .... see Chapter 9
Handlebar switches - removal and installation .... see Chapter 9
Rear shock absorber - removal, inspection and installation 10
Rear suspension bearings - lubrication .... see Chapter 1
Stands - lubrication .... see Chapter 1
Stands - removal and installation 4
Steering head bearings - freeplay check and adjustment .see Chapter 1
Steering head bearings - inspection and replacement 9
Steering head bearings - lubrication .... see Chapter 1
Steering stem - removal and installation 8
Suspension - adjustments 11
Suspension - check .... see Chapter 1
Swingarm and driveshaft - inspection and bearing replacement ... 13
Swingarm and driveshaft - removal and installation 12

Degrees of difficulty

Easy, suitable for novice with little experience 	**Fairly easy,** suitable for beginner with some experience 	**Fairly difficult,** suitable for competent DIY mechanic 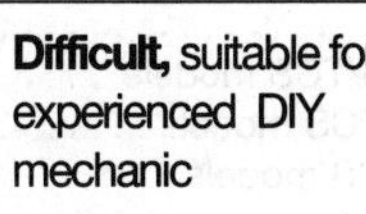	**Difficult,** suitable for experienced DIY mechanic	**Very difficult,** suitable for expert DIY or professional

Specifications

Front forks

Fork oil type	Pro Honda suspension fluid SS-7
Fork oil capacity	
Right fork	
Standard models	382.5 to 387.5 cc
ABS/TCS models	369.5 to 374.5 cc
CBS/LBS-ABS/TCS models	530.5 to 535.5 cc
Left fork	
Standard models	432.5 to 437.5 cc
ABS/TCS models	415.5 to 420.5 cc
CBS/LBS-ABS/TCS models	483.5 to 488.5 cc
Fork oil level*	
Right fork	
Standard models	190 mm
ABS/TCS models	177 mm
CBS/LBS-ABS/TCS models	140 mm
Left fork	
Standard models	187 mm
ABS/TCS models	174 mm
CBS/LBS-ABS/TCS models	136 mm
Fork spring free length (min)	
Standard models	
Standard	415.6 mm
Service limit	407.3 mm
ABS/TCS models	
Standard	474.2 mm
Service limit	464.7 mm
CBS/LBS-ABS/TCS models	
Standard	483.1 mm
Service limit	473.4 mm
Fork tube runout limit	0.2 mm

**Oil level is measured from the top of the tube with the fork spring removed and the leg fully compressed.*

6

Rear suspension

Shock absorber spring free length	
Standard models	
Standard	256.5 mm
Service limit	251.4 mm
ABS/TCS and CBS/LBS-ABS/TCS models	
Standard	258.9 mm
Service limit	253.7 mm

Final drive

Final drive oil type	SAE 80 Hypoid gear oil
Final drive oil capacity	
Oil change	130 cc
Following overhaul	150 cc
Final drive gear backlash	
Standard	0.05 to 0.15 mm
Service limit	0.30 mm

Torque settings

Handlebar clamp bolts	27 Nm
Front brake master cylinder clamp bolts	12 Nm
Top yoke fork clamp bolts	23 Nm
Bottom yoke fork clamp bolts	50 Nm
Damper rod Allen bolt	20 Nm
Fork top bolt	
Right-hand fork - standard and ABS/TCS models	
Against damper rod locknut	20 Nm
In fork tube	23 Nm
Left-hand fork - standard and ABS/TCS models	20 Nm
Right-hand fork - CBS/LBS-ABS/TCS models	23 Nm
Left-hand fork - CBS/LBS-ABS/TCS models	
Against damper rod locknut	20 Nm
In fork tube	23 Nm
Anti-dive assembly cover bolts	4 Nm
Steering head bearing adjuster nut	28 Nm
Steering stem nut	105 Nm
Rear shock absorber	
Upper mounting bolt	50 Nm
Lower mounting bolt	23 Nm
Swingarm right-hand pivot bolt	105 Nm
Swingarm left-hand pivot bolt	
Standard models	18 Nm
ABS/TCS and CBS/LBS-ABS/TCS models	22 Nm
Swingarm left-hand pivot bolt locknut	105 Nm
Final drive housing nuts	65 Nm

1 General information

All models use a full cradle twin spar steel frame. The left-hand side frame downtube is detachable to ease engine removal.

Front suspension is by a pair of oil-damped telescopic forks.

At the rear, a steel swingarm acts on a single shock absorber.,The shock absorber is adjustable for spring pre-load and rebound damping.

The drive to the rear wheel is by shaft, housed inside the right-hand longitudinal section of the swingarm. The final drive housing turns the drive through 90¡ to the rear wheel.

2 Frame - inspection and repair

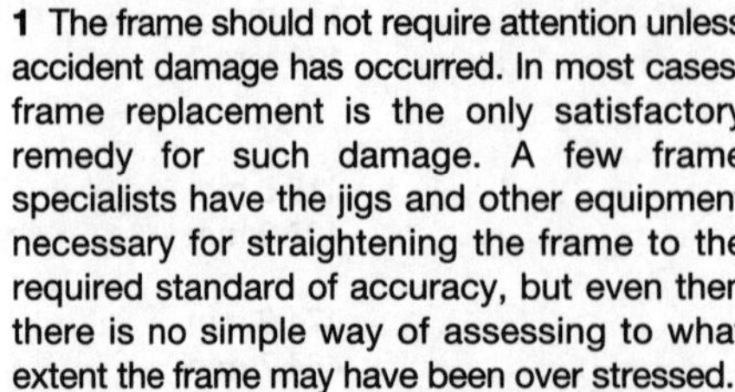

1 The frame should not require attention unless accident damage has occurred. In most cases, frame replacement is the only satisfactory remedy for such damage. A few frame specialists have the jigs and other equipment necessary for straightening the frame to the required standard of accuracy, but even then there is no simple way of assessing to what extent the frame may have been over stressed.

2 After the machine has accumulated a lot of miles, the frame should be examined closely for signs of cracking or splitting at the welded joints. Loose engine mount bolts can cause ovaling or fracturing of the mounting tabs. Minor damage can often be repaired by welding, depending on the extent and nature of the damage.

3 Remember that a frame which is out of alignment will cause handling problems. If misalignment is suspected as the result of an accident, it will be necessary to strip the machine completely so the frame can be thoroughly checked.

3 Footrests, brake pedal and gearchange lever - removal and installation

Footrests

Removal

1 Remove the split pin and washer from the bottom of the footrest pivot pin, then

3.4 The footrest bracket is secured by five bolts (arrowed)

3.5 Unhook the brake pedal return spring (A) and the brake light switch spring (B)

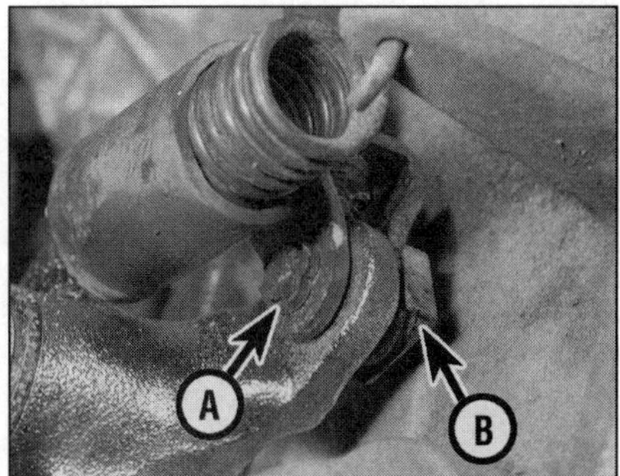

3.6 Remove the split pin (A) and the clevis pin (B)

withdraw the pivot pin and remove the footrest. On the front footrests, note the fitting of the return spring. On the rear footrests, note the fitting of the detent ball and spring, and take care that they do not spring out when removing the footrest.

2 If necessary, the footrest rubber can be separated from the footrest by removing the two screws or bolts on the underside of the footrest.

Installation

3 Installation is the reverse of removal.

Brake pedal

Removal

4 Unscrew the five bolts securing the right-hand footrest bracket, noting that the rear bolt is also the silencer mounting bolt **(see illustration)**. Carefully draw the bracket away from the bike until there is enough room to access the brake pedal. There is no need to disconnect any hoses or remove any components, though the modulator hose bracket bolt can be removed for improved clearance if required. There should be no need to disconnect any wiring, though if a wiring clip or cable tie restricts movement of the bracket, release it.

5 Unhook the brake pedal return spring bracket and the brake light switch spring from the brake pedal **(see illustration)**.

6 Remove the split pin from the clevis pin securing the brake pedal to the master cylinder pushrod **(see illustration)**. Remove the clevis pin and separate the pedal from the pushrod.

7 Remove the circlip securing the pedal on its pivot on the inside of the footpeg bracket **(see illustration)**. Remove the washer and slide the pedal off the pivot.

Installation

8 Installation is the reverse of removal. Check the operation of the rear brake light switch (see Chapter 9).

Gearchange lever

Removal

9 Slacken the gearchange lever linkage rod locknuts, then unscrew the rod and separate it from the lever and the arm (the rod is reverse-threaded on one end and so will simultaneously unscrew from both lever and arm when turned in the one direction) **(see illustration)**. Note the how far the rod is threaded into the lever and arm as this determines the height of the lever relative to the footrest.

10 Unscrew the pivot bolt and remove the lever, noting the breather hose guide secured by the pivot bolt nut **(see illustration)**.

Installation

11 Installation is the reverse of removal.

3.7 Remove the circlip (arrowed) and slide the pedal off the pivot

Remove the bush from the lever, clean it and re-grease it **(see illustration)**. Adjust the gear lever height as required by screwing the rod in or out of the lever and arm. Tighten the locknuts securely.

4 Stands - removal and installation

Centrestand

1 The centrestand is secured in the frame by a pivot shaft. Support the bike on its sidestand and unhook the centre stand springs, then remove the split pin from the

3.9 Slacken the linkage rod locknuts (arrowed) and unscrew the rod

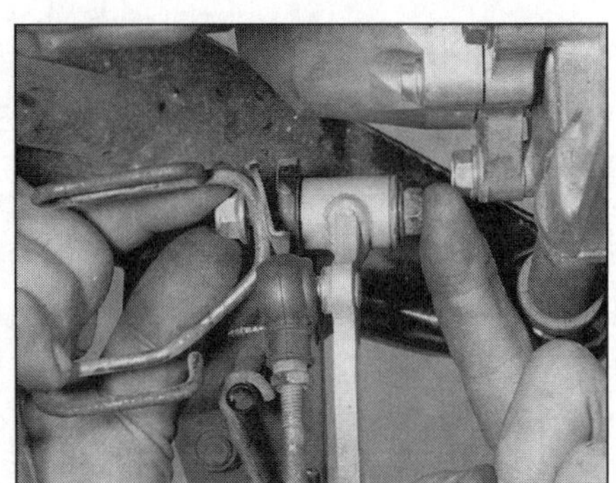
3.10 Remove the pivot bolt and the lever, noting how the hose guide fits

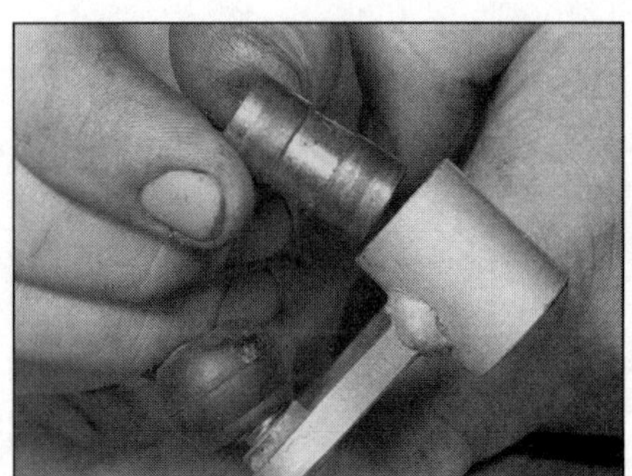
3.11 Grease the pivot bush before refitting

6

4.1a Unhook the spring . . .

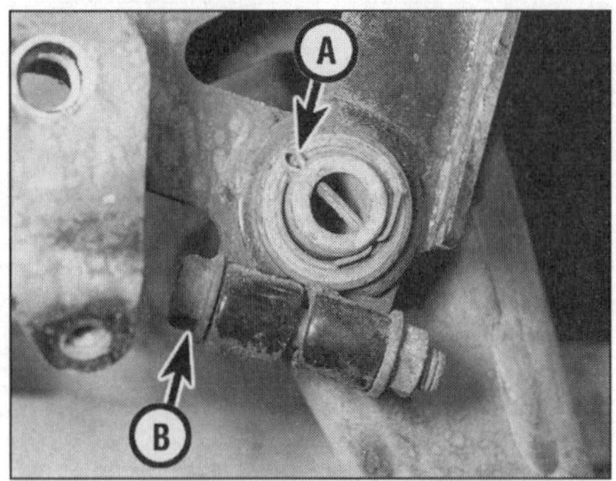

4.1b . . . then remove the split pin (A) and slacken the pinchbolt (B)

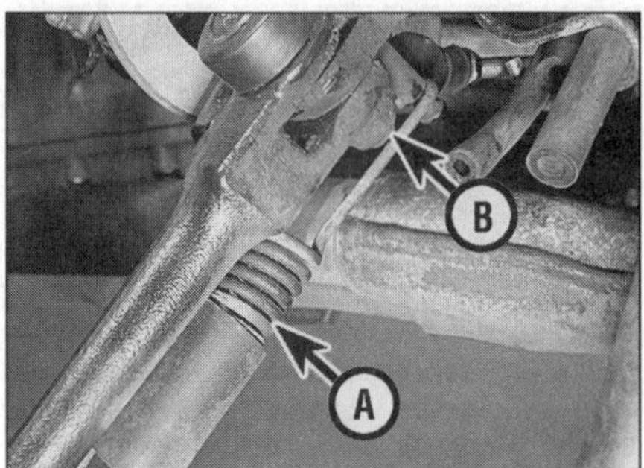

4.6 Unhook the spring (A), then unscrew the nut (B) and remove the pivot bolt and stand

right-hand end of the pivot shaft and slacken the pinchbolt **(see illustrations)**. Withdraw the shaft from the left and remove the stand.

2 Inspect the stand and pivot shaft for signs of wear and replace them if necessary. Apply a smear of grease to the outside of the shaft and fit the stand back on the bike. Use a new split pin on the end of the shaft and tighten the pinchbolt. Reconnect the return springs.

3 Make sure the springs are in good condition and capable of holding the stand up when not in use. A broken or weak spring is an obvious safety hazard.

Sidestand

4 The sidestand is attached to a bracket on the frame. Springs anchored to the bracket ensure that the stand is held in the retracted or extended position.

5 Support the bike on its centrestand. Remove the sidestand switch (see Chapter 9).

6 Unhook the stand springs and unscrew the nut from the pivot bolt **(see illustration)**. Remove the pivot bolt to free the stand from its bracket. On installation apply grease to the pivot bolt shank and tighten the bolt securely. Reconnect the sidestand springs and check that the return spring holds the stand securely up when not in use - an accident is almost certain to occur if the stand extends while the machine is in motion.

5 Handlebars and levers - removal and installation

Handlebars

Removal

Note: *If required, the handlebars can be displaced for access to the fork top bolts or the steering stem nut without removing the switch housings and the front brake master cylinder assembly and the clutch lever/master cylinder assembly.*

1 On UK L, M, N, AN, P, AP, R and AR models, and all US 1991 to 1994 models, unscrew the two screws securing the upper handlebar cover and separate it from the lower covers, noting how it fits. Unscrew the two bolts securing each lower cover half and remove them, noting how they fit.

2 On UK S, AS, T, AT ,V and AV models, and all US 1995-on models, remove the four trim clips and four screws securing the handlebar front and rear covers together, then remove the screw securing the front cover to the bracket **(see illustrations)**. Remove the covers, noting how they fit.

3 Disconnect the brake light switch wiring connectors from the underside of the brake master cylinder and the clutch switch connectors from the front of the clutch master cylinder **(see illustrations)**.

4 Remove the screws securing both the left- and right-hand switch housings to the handlebar, then separate the switch halves and displace them from the handlebar, noting how they fit **(see illustration)**. There is no

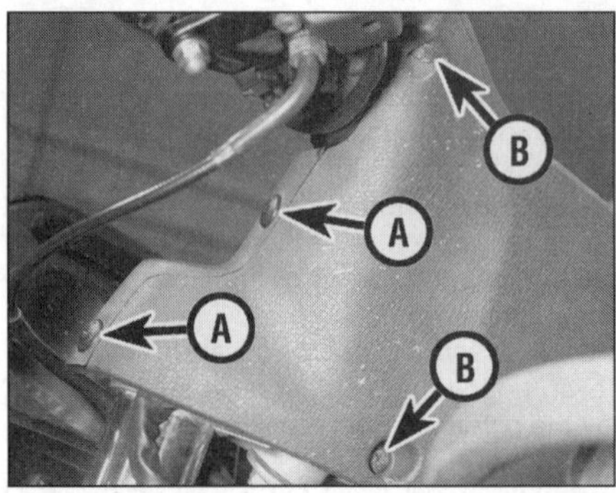

5.2a The covers are secured on each side by two trim clips (A) and two screws (B) . . .

5.2b . . . and in the middle by a screw (arrowed)

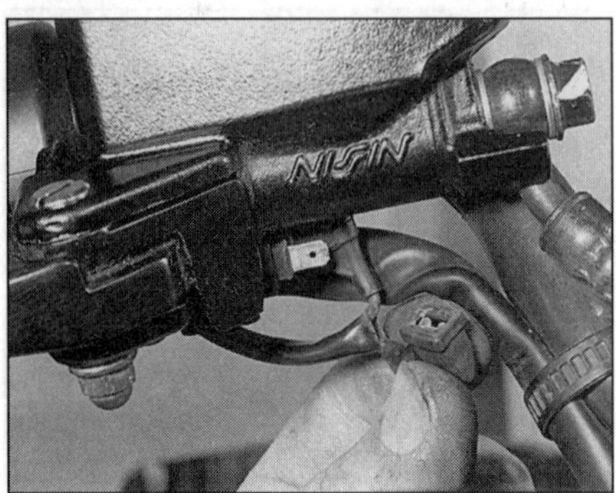

5.3a Disconnect the front brake switch wiring connectors . . .

5.3b . . . and the clutch switch wiring connectors

5.4 The switch housings are secured by two screws on the underside

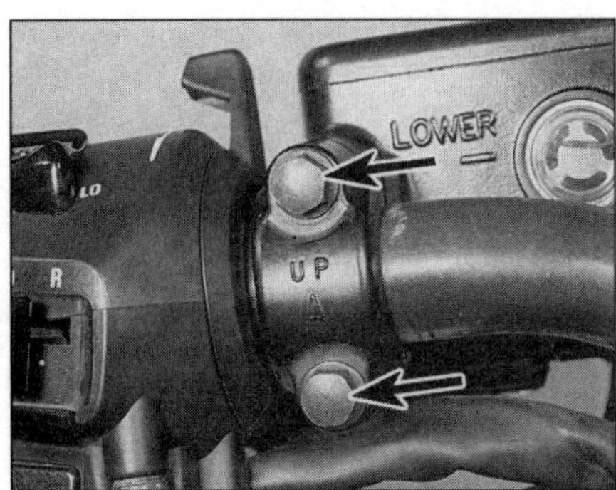

5.5 Each master cylinder clamp is secured by two bolts (arrowed)

5.6 Handlebar clamp bolts (arrowed)

need to disconnect the switch housing wiring at its connector blocks, but release it from the ties on the handlebar. Also there is no need to withdraw the throttle or choke cables from the housings, unless required (see Chapter 4).

5 Unscrew the two clamp bolts securing the front brake master cylinder assembly and the clutch master cylinder assembly to the handlebar, noting how the top mating surfaces of each clamp align with the punch mark on the top of the handlebar, and lift the assembly away **(see illustration)**. There is no need to disconnect the hose from the master cylinder. Support the assemblies in an upright position and so that no strain is placed on the hoses.

6 Unscrew the bolts securing the handlebar clamp tops and remove the clamp tops and the handlebars **(see illustration)**. Note the punch mark on the front of the handlebar which aligns with the mating surfaces of the left-hand clamp, and the punchmark on each clamp top which must be at the front.

7 If necessary, unscrew the handlebar end-weight retaining screws, then remove the weights from the end of the handlebars. If replacing the grips, it may be necessary to slit them using a sharp knife as they are adhered to the throttle twist (right-hand) and the handlebar (left-hand).

Installation

8 Installation is the reverse of removal, noting the following.

a) Fit each clamp top with the punchmark at the front. Align the handlebars so that the punchmark on the front of the handlebar aligns with the front mating surfaces of the left-hand clamp ***(see illustration)****.*

b) Make sure the handlebars are central in the clamps. Tighten the handlebar mounting bolts to the torque setting specified at the beginning of the Chapter, making sure that the gap between the mating surfaces of the clamps are equal front and rear ***(see illustration)****.*

c) Make sure the front brake and clutch master cylinder assembly clamps are installed with the UP mark facing up, and the top clamp mating surfaces aligned with the punchmark on the top of the handlebar ***(see illustration)****. Tighten the brake master cylinder clamp bolts to the torque setting specified at the beginning of the Chapter.*

d) Make sure the pin in the lower half of each switch housing locates in the hole in the underside of the handlebar ***(see illustration)****.*

e) If removed, apply a suitable non-permanent locking compound to the handlebar end-weight retaining screws. If new grips are being fitted, secure them using a suitable adhesive.

Levers

Removal

9 To remove either lever, unscrew the pivot bolt locknut, then withdraw the pivot bolt and remove the lever **(see illustrations)**. Take care not to lose the pushrod bush from its socket in the clutch lever.

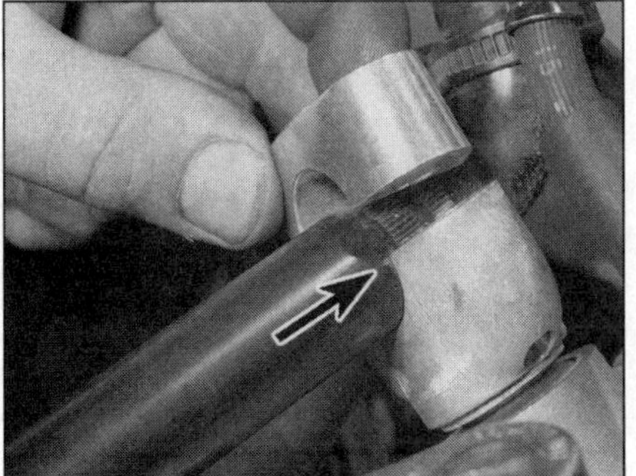
5.8a Align the punchmark (arrowed) with the clamp mating surfaces

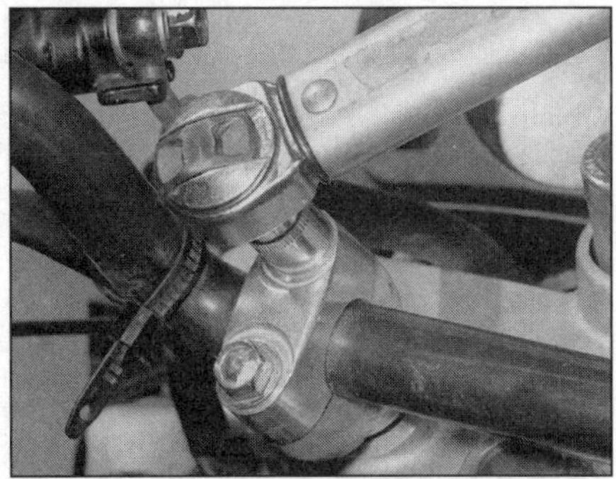
5.8b Tighten the clamp bolts to the specified torque setting

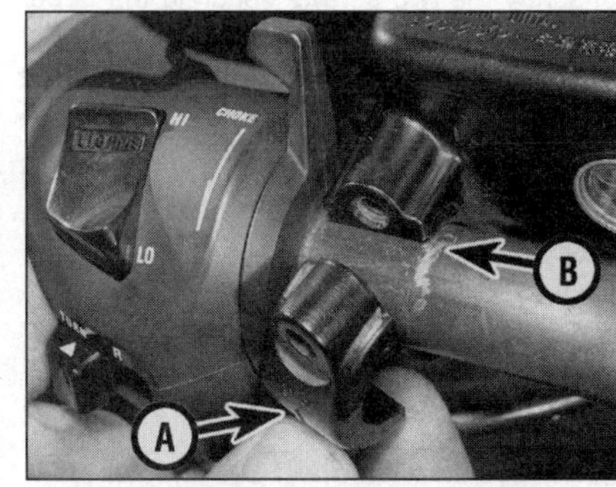

5.8c The UP mark (A) must face up, and align the mating surfaces with the punchmark (B)

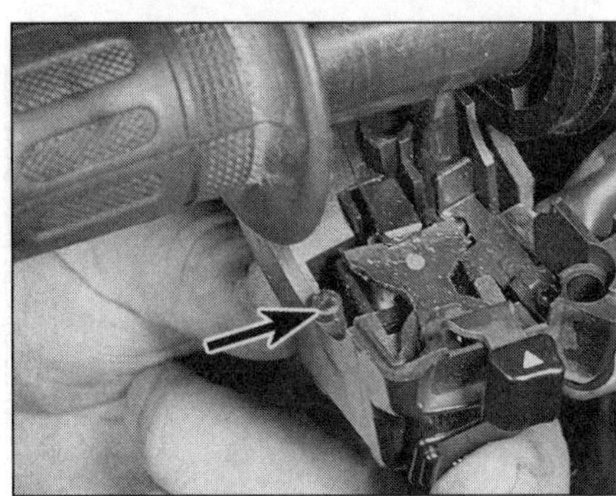
5.8d Locate the pin (arrowed) in the hole in the handlebar

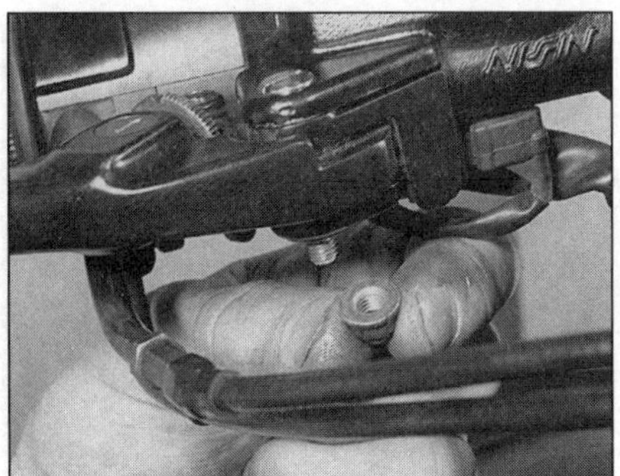
5.9a Unscrew the locknut . . .

5.9b . . . then unscrew the pivot bolt and remove the lever

5.10 Apply some grease to the pushrod bush in the clutch lever

6.7 Slacken each top yoke fork clamp bolt (arrowed) . . .

6.8 . . . and the bottom yoke fork clamp bolts (arrowed)

Installation

10 Installation is the reverse of removal. Apply grease to the pivot bolt shafts and the contact areas between the lever and its bracket, and to the clutch lever pushrod bush **(see illustration)**.

6 Forks - removal and installation

Removal

1 On UK L, M, N, AN, P, AP, R and AR models, and all US 1991 to 1994 models, unscrew the two screws securing the upper handlebar cover and separate it from the lower covers, noting how it fits. Unscrew the two bolts securing each lower cover half and remove them, noting how they fit.

2 On UK S, AS, T, AT ,V and AV models, and all US 1995-on models, remove the four trim clips and four screws securing the handlebar front and rear covers together, then remove the screw securing the front cover to the bracket **(see illustrations 5.2a and b)**. Remove the covers, noting how they fit.

3 Remove the front wheel (see Chapter 7).

4 Remove the front mudguard and brace (see Chapter 8).

5 On standard models, unscrew the bolt securing the brake hose clamp to the right-hand fork and displace the clamp.

6 Remove the left-hand brake caliper (see Chapter 7). There is no need to disconnect the hydraulic hose. Support the caliper so that no strain is placed on the hose.

7 Slacken, but do not remove, the fork clamp bolts in the top yoke **(see illustration)**. If the forks are to be disassembled, or if the fork oil is being changed, it is advisable to slacken the fork top bolts at this stage.

Slackening the fork clamp bolts in the top yoke before slackening the fork top bolts releases pressure on the top bolt. This makes it much easier to remove and helps to preserve the threads.

8 Note the position of the top of the fork tubes relative to the top yoke so that they can be installed in the same position. Slacken but do not remove the fork clamp bolts in the bottom yoke, and remove the forks by twisting them and pulling them downwards **(see illustration)**.

If the fork legs are seized in the yokes, spray the area with penetrating oil and allow time for it to soak in before trying again.

Installation

9 Remove all traces of corrosion from the fork tubes and the yokes and slide the forks up through the yokes **(see illustration)**. Align the forks with the top yoke as noted on removal.

10 Tighten the fork clamp bolts in the bottom yoke to the torque setting specified at the beginning of the Chapter. If the fork legs have been dismantled or if the fork oil has been changed, the fork top bolts should now be tightened to the specified torque setting. Now tighten the fork clamp bolts in the top yoke to the specified torque setting **(see illustrations)**.

11 Install the front wheel and front brake calipers (see Chapter 7), and the front brace and mudguard (see Chapter 8). Install the brake hose clamp onto the right-hand fork.

12 Install the handlebar covers in a reverse of the removal procedure (see Step 1 or 2, according to model). On UK L, M, N, AN, P, AP, R and AR models, and all US 1991 to 1994 models, align the pins in the front of the upper cover with the holes in the lower covers, and engage the tab on the inside of the upper cover with the latch in the plate under the handlebars.

13 Check the operation of the front forks and brakes before taking the machine out on the road.

6.9 Slide the fork up through the yokes . . .

6.10a . . . then tighten the bottom yoke clamp bolts . . .

6.10b . . . and the top yoke clamp bolts to the specified torque settings

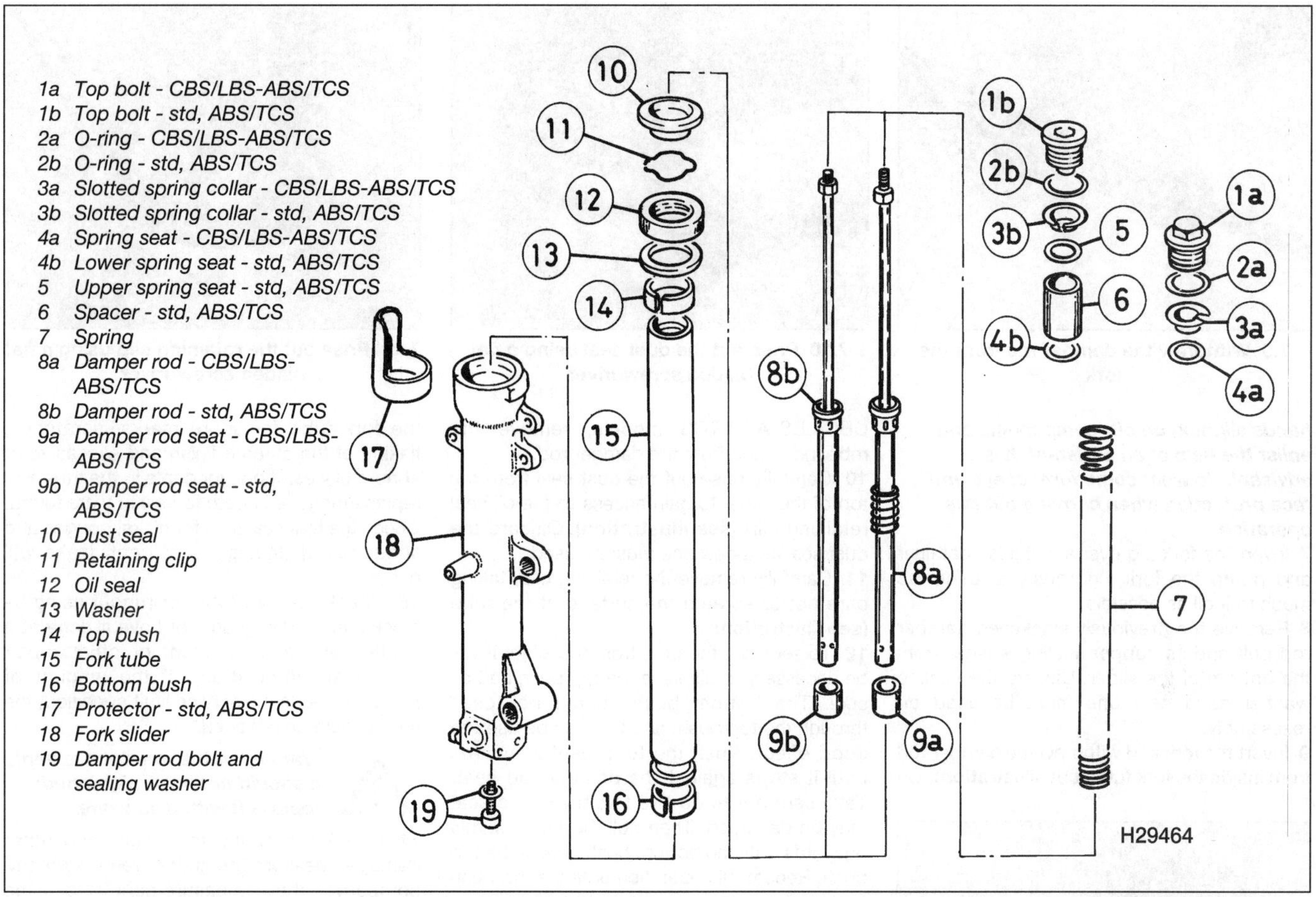

1a *Top bolt - CBS/LBS-ABS/TCS*
1b *Top bolt - std, ABS/TCS*
2a *O-ring - CBS/LBS-ABS/TCS*
2b *O-ring - std, ABS/TCS*
3a *Slotted spring collar - CBS/LBS-ABS/TCS*
3b *Slotted spring collar - std, ABS/TCS*
4a *Spring seat - CBS/LBS-ABS/TCS*
4b *Lower spring seat - std, ABS/TCS*
5 *Upper spring seat - std, ABS/TCS*
6 *Spacer - std, ABS/TCS*
7 *Spring*
8a *Damper rod - CBS/LBS-ABS/TCS*
8b *Damper rod - std, ABS/TCS*
9a *Damper rod seat - CBS/LBS-ABS/TCS*
9b *Damper rod seat - std, ABS/TCS*
10 *Dust seal*
11 *Retaining clip*
12 *Oil seal*
13 *Washer*
14 *Top bush*
15 *Fork tube*
16 *Bottom bush*
17 *Protector - std, ABS/TCS*
18 *Fork slider*
19 *Damper rod bolt and sealing washer*

H29464

7.1 Right-hand fork components (standard and ABS/TCS models), left-hand fork components (CBS/LBS-ABS/TCS models)

7 Forks - disassembly, inspection and reassembly

Right-hand fork (standard and ABS/TCS models), left-hand fork (CBS/LBS-ABS/TCS models)

Disassembly

1 Always dismantle the fork legs separately to avoid interchanging parts and thus causing an accelerated rate of wear. Store all components in separate, clearly marked containers **(see illustration)**.

2 Before dismantling the fork, it is advised that the damper rod bolt be slackened at this stage. Compress the fork tube in the slider so that the spring exerts maximum pressure on the damper rod head, then have an assistant slacken the damper rod bolt in the base of the fork slider. Where fitted, remove the protector from the top of the fork slider.

3 If the fork top bolt was not slackened with the fork in situ, carefully clamp the fork tube in a vice equipped with soft jaws, taking care not to overtighten or score its surface, and slacken the top bolt.

4 Unscrew the fork top bolt from the top of the fork tube. The bolt will remain threaded on the damper rod.

5 Carefully clamp the fork slider in a vise and slide the fork tube down into the slider a little way (wrap a rag around the spring and the top of the tube to minimise oil spillage) while, with the aid of an assistant if necessary, keeping the damper rod and top cap fully extended. Counter-hold the locknut immediately below the top cap and unscrew the fork top bolt from the damper rod **(see illustration)**.

6 Remove the slotted spring collar by holding down the fork spring (keeping the damper rod fully extended) and slipping the collar out to the side **(see illustration)**. Slowly release the spring until all pressure has been relieved, then remove the spring seat, and on standard and ABS/TCS models, the spacer and the lower spring seat. Withdraw the spring from the tube, noting which way up it fits.

Warning: The fork spring may be exerting considerable pressure, making this a potentially dangerous operation. Wipe off as much oil as possible to minimise the risk of your

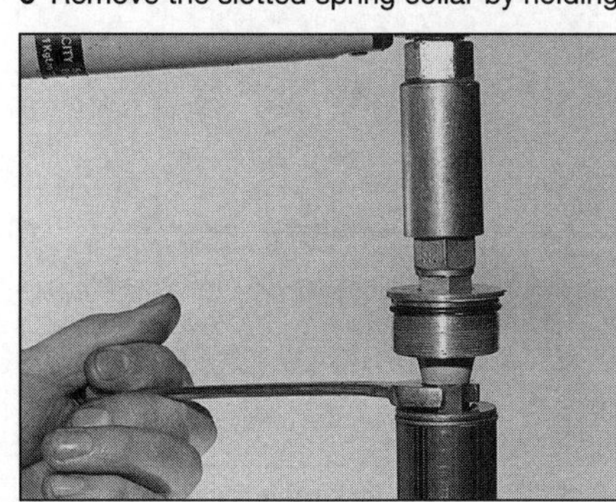

7.5 Counter-hold the locknut and unscrew the top bolt

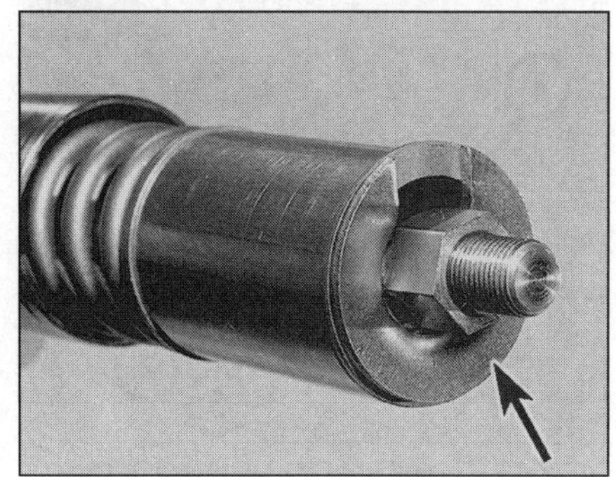

7.6 Compress the spring and slip the collar (arrowed) out

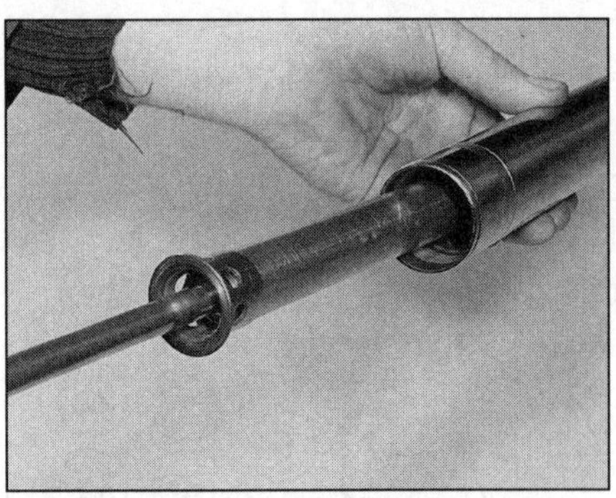
7.9 Withdraw the damper rod from the fork

7.10 Prise out the dust seal using a flat bladed screwdriver

7.11 Prise out the retaining clip using a flat bladed screwdriver

hands slipping on oily components and enlist the help of an assistant. It is advisable to wear some form of eye and face protection when carrying out this operation.

7 Invert the fork leg over a suitable container and pump the fork vigorously to expel as much fork oil as possible.

8 Remove the previously slackened damper rod bolt and its copper sealing washer from the bottom of the slider. Discard the sealing washer as a new one must be used on reassembly.

9 Invert the fork and withdraw the damper rod from inside the fork tube **(see illustration)**. On CBS/LBS-ABS/TCS models, remove the rebound spring from the damper rod.

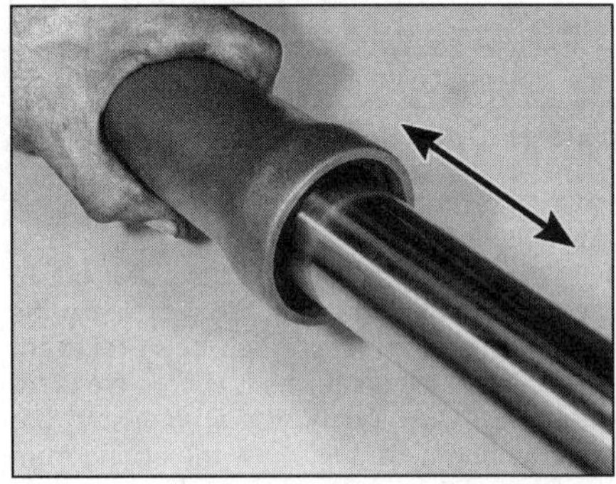
7.12 To separate the inner and outer fork tubes, pull them apart firmly several times - the slide hammer effect will pull the tubes apart

10 Carefully prise out the dust seal from the top of the slider to gain access to the oil seal retaining clip **(see illustration)**. Discard the dust seal as a new one must be used.

11 Carefully remove the retaining clip, taking care not to scratch the surface of the tube **(see illustration)**.

12 To separate the tube from the slider it will be necessary to displace the top bush and oil seal. The bottom bush should not pass through the top bush, and this can be used to good effect. Push the tube gently inwards until it stops against the damper rod seat. Take care not to do this forcibly or the seat may be damaged. Then pull the tube sharply outwards until the bottom bush strikes the top bush. Repeat this operation until the top bush and seal are tapped out of the slider **(see illustration)**.

13 With the tube removed, slide off the oil seal, washer and top bush, noting which way up they fit **(see illustration)**. Discard the oil seal as a new one must be used.

Caution: Do not remove the bottom bush from the tube unless it is to be replaced.

14 Tip the damper rod seat out of the slider, noting which way up it fits.

Inspection

15 Clean all parts in solvent and blow them dry with compressed air, if available. Check the fork tube for score marks, scratches, flaking of the chrome finish and excessive or abnormal wear. Look for dents in the tube and replace the tube in both forks if any are found. Check the fork seal seat for nicks, gouges and scratches. If damage is evident, leaks will occur.

16 Check the fork tube for runout using V-blocks and a dial gauge, or have it done at a dealer service department or other repair shop **(see illustration)**. If the amount of runout exceeds the service limit specified, the tube should be replaced.

Warning: If the fork tube is bent, it should not be straightened; replace it with a new one.

17 Check the spring for cracks and other damage. Measure the spring free length and compare the measurement to the specifications at the beginning of the Chapter. If it is defective or sagged below the service limit, replace the springs in both forks with new ones. Never replace only one spring. On CBS/LBS-ABS/TCS models, also check the rebound spring.

18 Examine the working surfaces of the two bushes; if worn or scuffed they must be replaced. To remove the bottom bush from the fork tube, prise it apart at the slit using a flat-bladed screwdriver and slide it off **(see illustration)**. Make sure the new one seats properly.

19 Check the damper rod assembly for

7.13 The oil seal (1), washer (2), top bush (3) and bottom bush (4) will come out with the fork tube

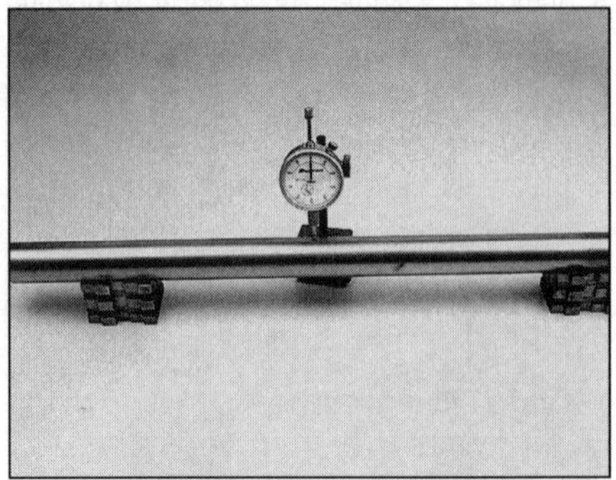
7.16 Check the fork tube for runout using V-blocks and a dial gauge

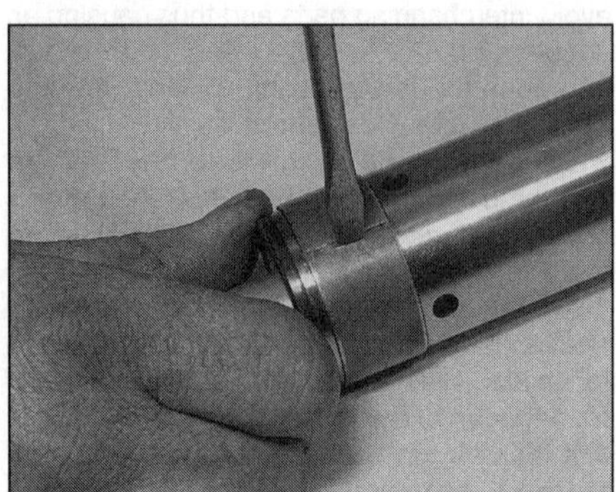
7.18 Prise off the bottom bush using a flat bladed screwdriver

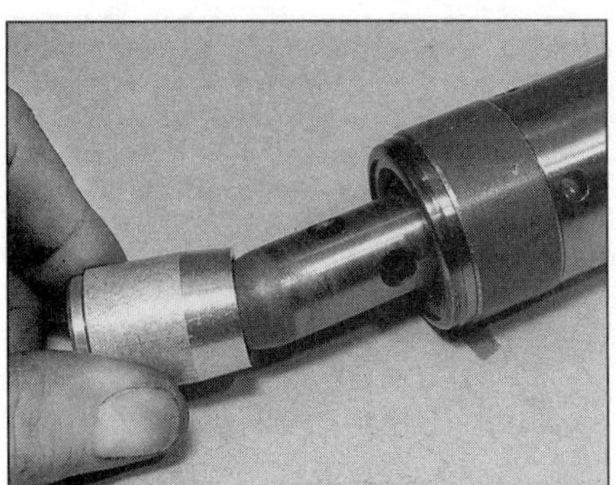
7.20 Fit the seat to the bottom of the rod

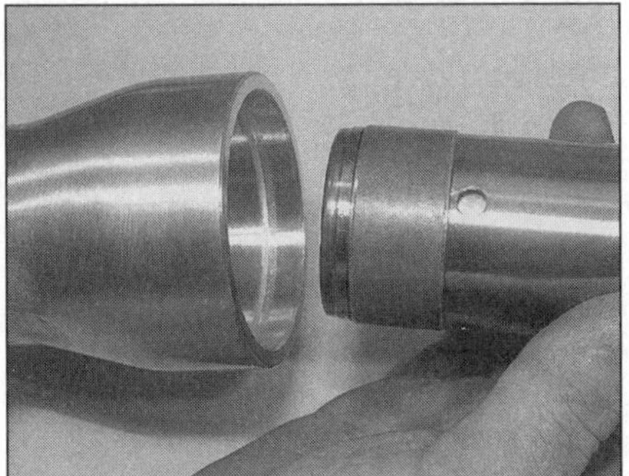
7.21a Slide the tube into the slider

7.21b Apply a thread locking compound to the damper rod bolt and use a new sealing washer

damage and wear, and replace it if necessary. Holding the outside of the damper, pump the rod in and out of the damper. If the rod does not move smoothly in the damper it must be replaced.

Reassembly

20 On CBS/LBS-ABS/TCS models, if removed, slide the rebound spring onto the rod. Insert the damper rod into the fork tube and slide it into place so that it projects fully from the bottom of the tube, then install the seat on the bottom of the damper rod **(see illustration)**.

21 Oil the fork tube and bottom bush with the specified fork oil and insert the assembly into the slider. Fit a new copper sealing washer to the damper rod bolt and apply a few drops of a suitable non-permanent thread locking compound, then install the bolt into the bottom of the slider **(see illustrations)**. Tighten the bolt to the specified torque setting. If the damper rod rotates inside the tube, wait until the fork is fully reassembled before tightening the bolt.

22 Push the fork tube fully into the slider, then oil the top bush and slide it down over the tube. Press the bush squarely into its recess in the slider as far as possible, then install the oil seal washer **(see illustrations)**. Either use the service tool (Pt. Nos. 07947-KA50100 and 07947-KF00100) or a suitable piece of tubing to tap the bush fully into place; the tubing must be slightly larger in diameter than the fork tube and slightly smaller in diameter than the bush recess in the slider. Take care not to scratch the fork tube during this operation; it is best to make sure that the fork tube is pushed fully into the slider so that any accidental scratching is confined to the area above the oil seal.

23 When the bush is seated fully and squarely in its recess in the slider, (remove the washer to check, wipe the recess clean, then reinstall the washer), install the new oil seal. Smear the seal's lips with fork oil and slide it over the tube so that its markings face upwards and drive the seal into place as described in Step 22 until the retaining clip groove is visible above the seal.**(see illustration)**.

24 Once the seal is correctly seated, fit the retaining clip, making sure it is correctly located in its groove **(see illustration)**.

25 Lubricate the lips of the new dust seal then slide it down the fork tube and press it into position **(see illustration)**.

26 Slowly pour in the specified quantity of the specified grade of fork oil and pump the fork to distribute it evenly; the oil level should also be measured and adjustment made by adding or subtracting oil. Fully compress the fork tube into the slider and measure the fork oil level from the top of the tube **(see**

7.22a Install the top bush . . .

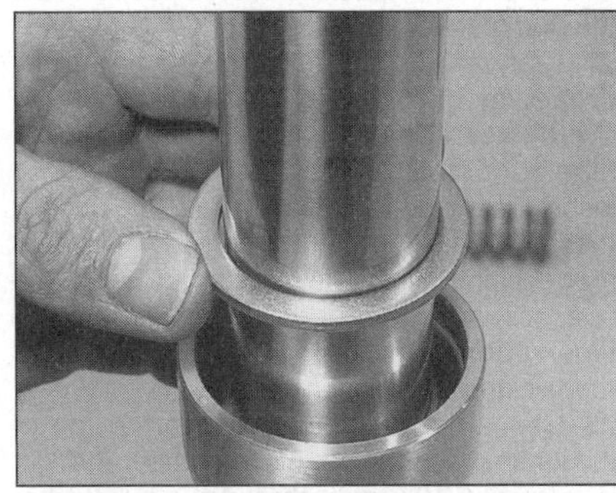
7.22b . . . followed by the washer

7.23 Make sure the oil seal is the correct way up

7.24 Install the retaining clip . . .

7.25 . . . followed by the dust seal

7.26a Pour the oil into the top of the tube

7.26b Measure the oil level with the fork held vertical

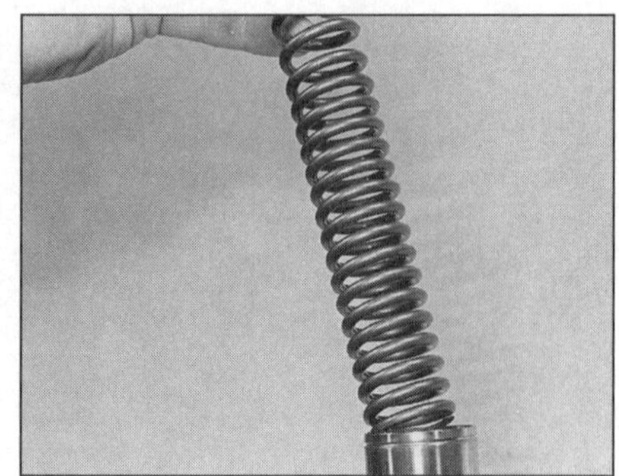
7.27a Install the spring . . .

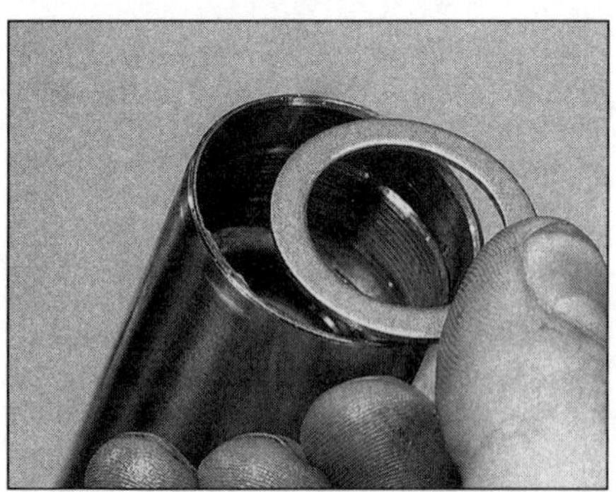
7.27b . . . followed by the spring seat . . .

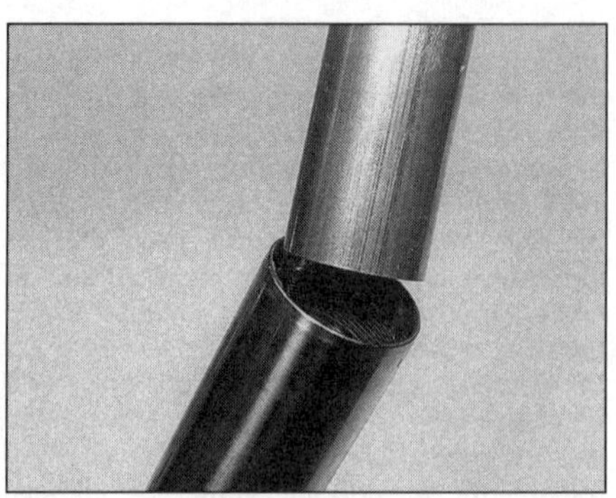
7.27c . . . the spacer and the upper spring seat

illustrations). Add or subtract fork oil until the oil is at the level specified in the Specifications Section of this Chapter.

27 Clamp the slider in a vice via the brake caliper mounting lugs, taking care not to overtighten and damage them. Pull the fork tube out of the slider as far as possible then install the spring with its closer-wound coils at the bottom. On standard and ABS/TCS models, install the lower spring seat, the spacer and the upper spring seat **(see illustrations)**. On CBS/LBS-ABS/TCS models, install the spring seat.

28 Check the distance between the top of the locknut and the top of the damper rod. If it is less than 10.5 mm, thread the nut further onto the rod until the distance is 10.5 mm or more. If the nut was removed from the rod, fit it so that its threaded end faces up **(see illustration)**. Fit a new O-ring to the fork top bolt.

29 With the aid of an assistant, push down on the spring seat, compressing the fork spring, and slide the slotted spring collar into position **(see illustration 7.6)**.

Warning: This is a potentially dangerous operation and should be performed with care, using an assistant if necessary. Wipe off any excess oil before starting to prevent the possibility of slipping.

Screw the top bolt onto the damper rod **(see illustration)**,and, counter-holding the locknut, tighten it to the specified torque setting **(see illustration 7.5)**. Slowly release the fork spring, making sure the slotted collar is correctly seated against the base of the locknut.

30 Withdraw the tube fully from the slider and carefully screw the top bolt into the fork tube making sure it is not cross-threaded. **Note:** *The top bolt can be tightened to the specified torque setting at this stage if the tube is held between the padded jaws of a vise, but do not risk distorting the tube by doing so. A better method is to tighten the top bolt when the fork leg has been installed and is securely held in the triple clamps.* If the damper rod Allen bolt requires tightening (see Step 21), clamp the fork slider between the padded jaws of a vise and have an assistant compress the tube into the slider so that maximum spring pressure is placed on the damper rod head - tighten the damper Allen bolt to the specified torque setting.

31 Where fitted, fit the protector onto the top of the fork slider, making sure its tab fits into the slot in the top of the slider **(see illustration)**.

32 Install the forks (see Section 6).

Left-hand fork (standard and ABS/TCS models), right-hand fork (CBS/LBS-ABS/TCS models)

Disassembly

33 Always dismantle the fork legs separately to avoid interchanging parts and thus causing

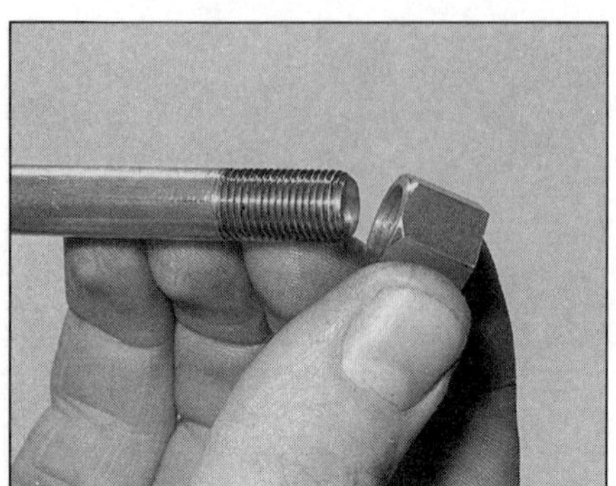
7.28 Thread the locknut onto the damper rod as described

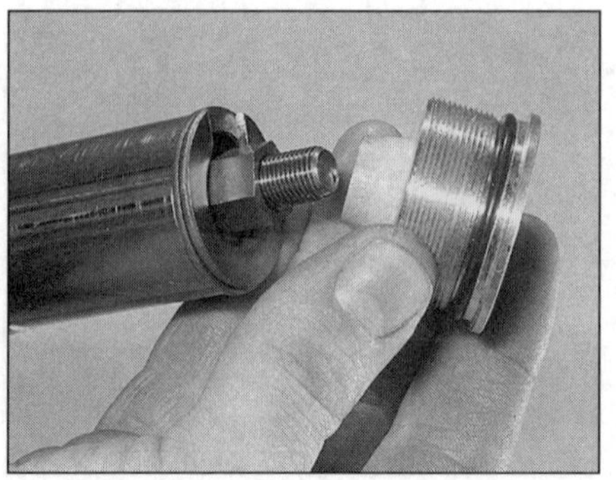
7.29 Thread the top bolt onto the damper rod

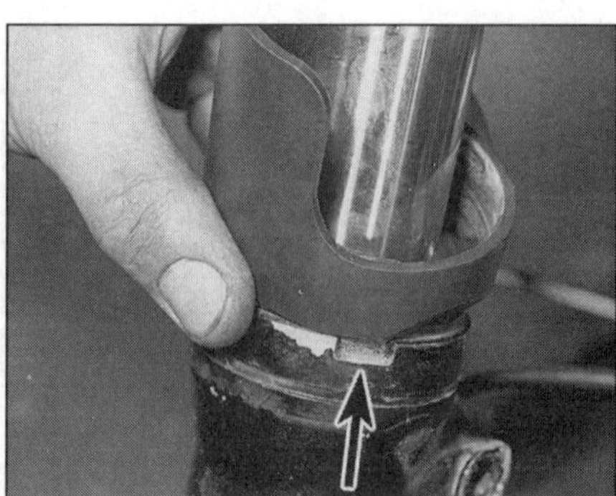
7.31 Locate the tab in the slot (arrowed)

1a Top bolt - CBS/LBS-ABS/TCS
1b Top bolt - std, ABS/TCS
2 O-ring
3 Spacer
4 Spring seat
5 Spring
6 Damper rod assembly
7 Piston rings
8 Damper rod
9 Rebound spring
10 Circlip
11 Spring seat
12 Spring
13 Damper rod seat
14 Circlip
15 Dust seal
16 Retaining clip
17 Oil seal
18 Upper washer
19 Spacer - CBS/LBS-ABS/TCS
20 Lower washer - CBS/LBS-ABS/TCS
21 Top bush
22 Fork tube
23 Bottom bush
24 Fork slider
25 Damper rod bolt and sealing washer

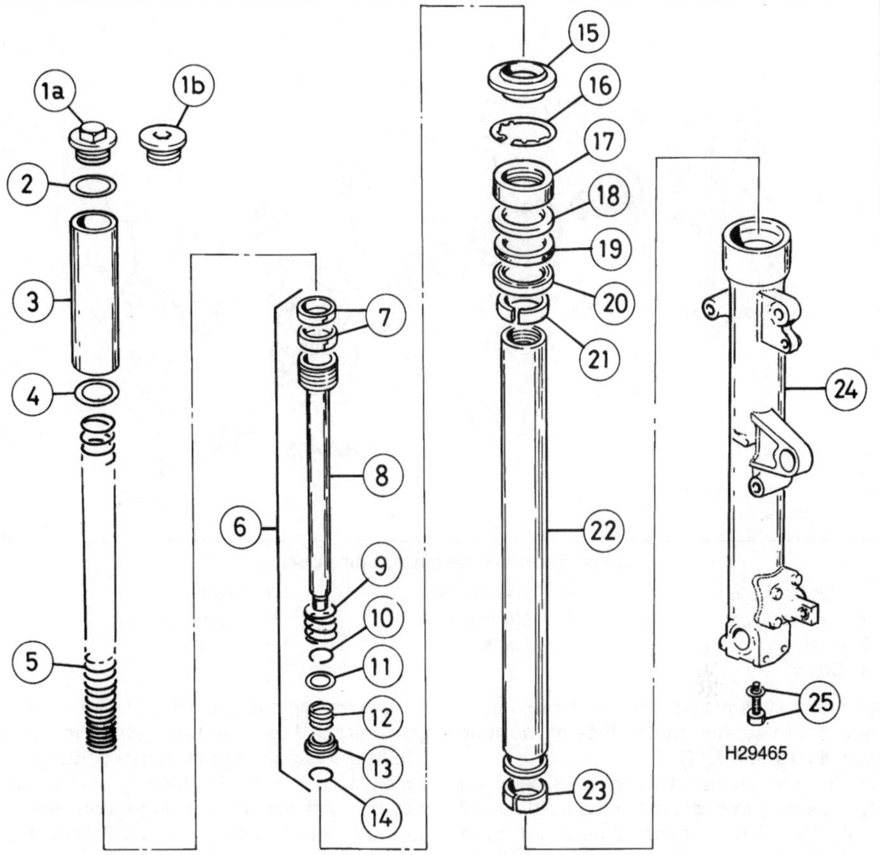

H29465

7.33 Left-hand fork components (standard and ABS/TCS models), right-hand fork components (CBS/LBS-ABS/TCS models)

an accelerated rate of wear. Store all components in separate, clearly marked containers **(see illustration)**.

34 Before dismantling the fork, it is advised that the damper rod bolt be slackened at this stage. Compress the fork tube in the slider so that the spring exerts maximum pressure on the damper rod head, then have an assistant slacken the damper rod bolt in the base of the fork slider. Where fitted, remove the protector from the top of the fork slider.

35 If the fork top bolt was not slackened with the fork in situ, carefully clamp the fork tube in a vice equipped with soft jaws, taking care not to overtighten or score its surface, and slacken the top bolt.

36 Unscrew the fork top bolt from the top of the fork tube.

Warning: The fork spring is pressing on the fork top bolt with considerable pressure. Unscrew the bolt very carefully, keeping a downward pressure on it and release it slowly as it is likely to spring clear. It is advisable to wear some form of eye and face protection when carrying out this operation.

37 Slide the fork tube down into the slider and withdraw the spacer, spring seat and the spring from the tube. Note which way up the spring is fitted.

38 Invert the fork leg over a suitable container and pump the fork vigorously to expel as much fork oil as possible.

39 Remove the previously slackened damper rod bolt and its copper sealing washer from the bottom of the slider. Discard the sealing washer as a new one must be used on reassembly. If the damper rod bolt was not slackened before dismantling the fork, it may be necessary to re-install the spring, spring seat, spacer and top bolt to prevent the damper rod from turning. Alternatively, a long metal bar or length of wood doweling passed down through the fork tube and pressed hard into the damper rod head quite often suffices.

40 Invert the fork and withdraw the damper rod from inside the fork tube. Remove the snap-ring securing the damper rod seat assembly on the bottom of the rod, then remove the seat, spring, spring seat and upper snap-ring **(see illustrations)**. Slide the rebound spring off the rod.

41 Carefully prise out the dust seal from the top of the slider to gain access to the oil seal retaining clip **(see illustration 7.10)**. Discard the dust seal as a new one must be used.

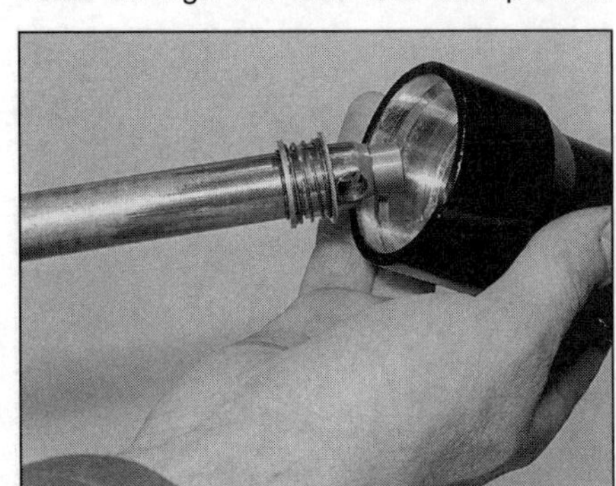

7.40a Withdraw the damper rod from the tube . . .

7.40b . . . then remove the snap-ring and the damper rod seat assembly components

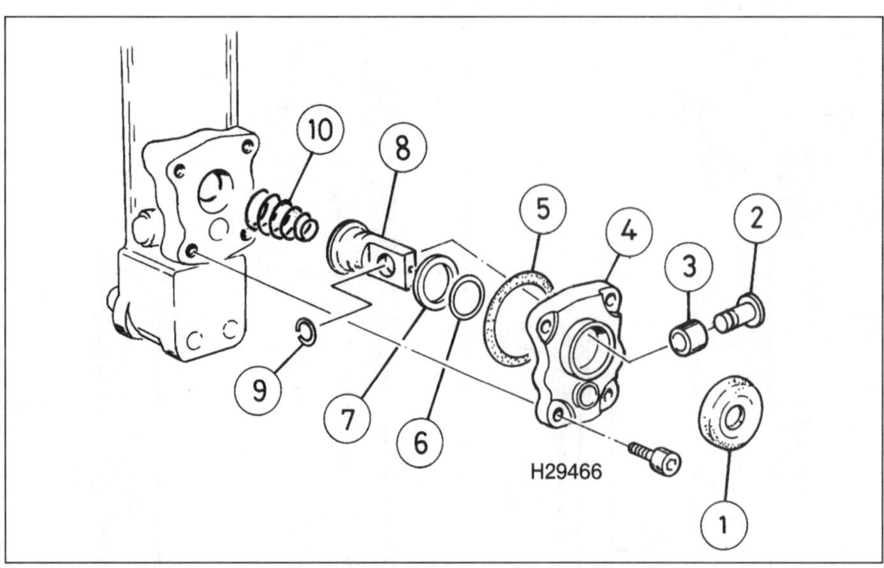

7.45a Anti-dive assembly components

1 *Rubber boot*
2 *Pivot collar*
3 *Bush*
4 *Cover*
5 *Cover O-ring*
6 *Piston seal*
7 *Oil seal*
8 *Piston*
9 *Snap-ring*
10 *Spring*

42 Carefully remove the retaining clip, taking care not to scratch the surface of the tube **(see illustration 7.11)**.

43 To separate the tube from the slider it will be necessary to displace the top bush and oil seal. The bottom bush should not pass through the top bush, and this can be used to good effect. Push the tube gently inwards until it stops against the damper rod seat. Take care not to do this forcibly or the seat may be damaged. Then pull the tube sharply outwards until the bottom bush strikes the top bush. Repeat this operation until the top bush and seal are tapped out of the slider **(see illustration 7.12)**.

44 With the tube removed, slide off the oil seal, followed on standard and ABS/TCS models by the washer and top bush **(see illustration 7.13)**, and on CBS/LBS-ABS/TCS models by the upper washer, spacer and lower washer, noting how they fit together, and the top bush. Discard the oil seal as a new one must be used.

45 If required, remove the snap-ring securing the pivot collar in the anti-dive assembly piston and remove the collar **(see illustration)**. Remove the rubber boot from the cover. Unscrew the four bolts securing the anti-dive assembly cover, noting that it is under spring pressure. Carefully remove the cover, being prepared to recover the internal components in case they are sprung out. Examine the components for wear or damage and replace them as necessary. Remove and discard the cover O-ring, piston seal and oil seal as new ones must be used. Fit the rubber boot onto the cover, using a new one if necessary. Lubricate the new oil seal and piston seal with clean fork oil, then install them on the piston. Install the piston in the cover, then fit the collar into the hole in the piston and secure them with the snap-ring **(see illustrations)**. Lubricate the cover O-ring with clean fork oil and fit it into its groove in the cover. Fit the spring into the slider with its tapered end facing out, then fit the cover, making sure the O-ring stays in place **(see illustration)**. Apply a suitable non-permanent thread locking compound to the cover bolts and tighten them to the torque setting specified at the beginning of the Chapter **(see illustration)**. Check that the piston moves smoothly and freely and that it returns quickly under spring pressure.

Caution: Do not remove the bottom bush from the tube unless it is to be replaced.

Inspection

46 Clean all parts in solvent and blow them dry with compressed air, if available. Check the fork tube for score marks, scratches, flaking of the chrome finish and excessive or

7.45b Fit the piston into the cover . . .

7.45c . . . then install the collar . . .

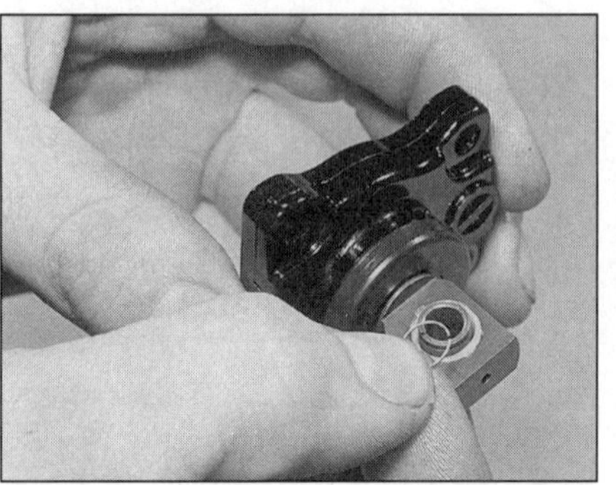

7.45d . . . and secure it with the snap-ring

7.45e Fit the spring with its narrower end out

7.45f Apply thread-locking compound to the cover bolts and tighten them to the specified torque setting

7.50 Replace the damper rod piston rings if they are worn or damaged

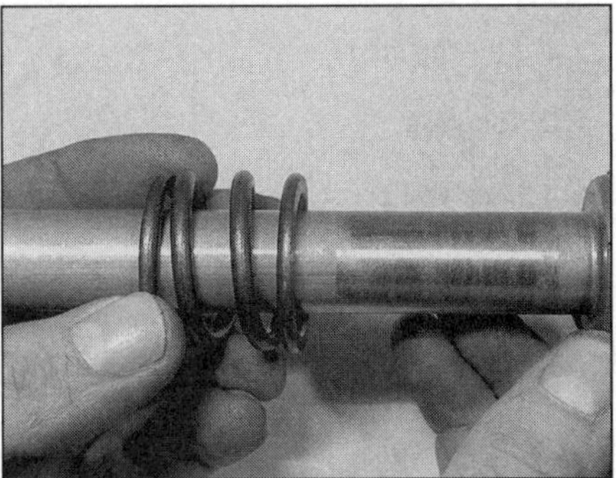

7.51a Slide the rebound spring onto the damper rod

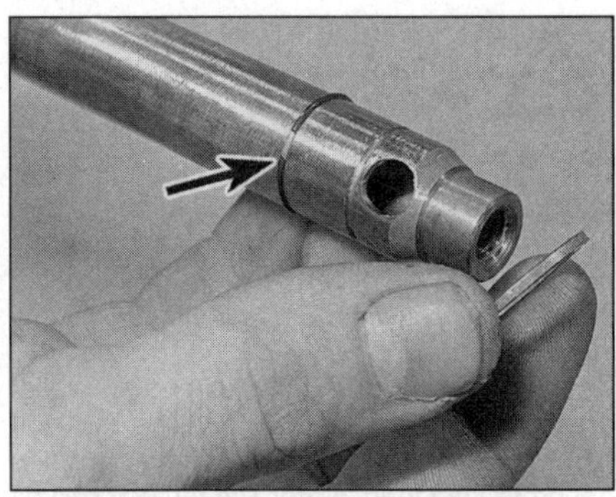

7.51b Fit the upper snap-ring into its groove (arrowed), then fit the spring seat . . .

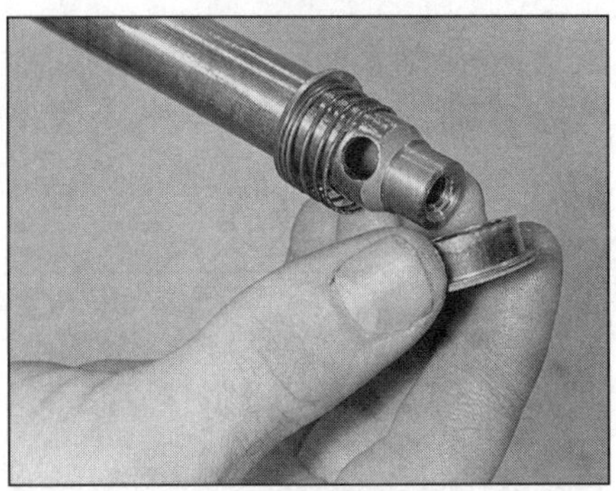

7.51c . . . the spring and the damper rod seat

7.60 Fit a new O-ring onto the top bolt and thread the bolt into the fork tube

abnormal wear. Look for dents in the tube and replace the tube in both forks if any are found. Check the fork seal seat for nicks, gouges and scratches. If damage is evident, leaks will occur.

47 Check the fork tube for runout using V-blocks and a dial gauge, or have it done at a dealer service department or other repair shop **(see illustration 7.16)**.

Warning: If it is bent, it should not be straightened; replace it with a new one.

48 Check the spring for cracks and other damage. Measure the spring free length and compare the measurement to the specifications at the beginning of the Chapter. If it is defective or sagged below the service limit, replace the springs in both forks with new ones. Never replace only one spring. Also check the rebound spring.

49 Examine the working surfaces of the two bushes; if worn or scuffed they must be replaced. To remove the bottom bush from the fork tube, prise it apart at the slit using a flat-bladed screwdriver and slide it off **(see illustration 7.18)**. Make sure the new one seats properly.

50 Check the damper rod and its piston rings for damage and wear, and replace them if necessary **(see illustration)**. Do not remove the rings from the piston unless they are being replaced

Reassembly

51 If removed, install the piston rings into the groove in the damper rod head **(see illustration 7.50)**, then slide the rebound spring onto the rod **(see illustration)**. Fit the upper snap-ring into its groove in the rod, then slide the spring seat, spring and damper rod seat onto the rod **(see illustrations)**. Secure the assembly with the snap-ring **(see illustration 7.40b)**. Insert the damper rod into the fork tube and slide it into place so that it projects fully from the bottom of the tube **(see illustration 7.40a)**.

52 Oil the fork tube and bottom bush with the specified fork oil and insert the assembly into the slider **(see illustration 7.21a)**. Fit a new copper sealing washer to the damper rod bolt and apply a few drops of a suitable non-permanent thread locking compound, then install the bolt into the bottom of the slider **(see illustration 7.21b)**. Tighten the bolt to the specified torque setting. If the damper rod rotates inside the tube, temporarily install the fork spring and top bolt (see Steps 57 and 58) and compress the fork to hold the damper rod. Alternatively, pass a metal bar or length of wood dowel down the fork tube and press it into the damper rod head. Otherwise, wait until the fork is fully reassembled before tightening the bolt.

53 Push the fork tube fully into the slider, then oil the top bush and slide it down over the tube **(see illustration 7.22a)**. Press the bush squarely into its recess in the slider as far as possible, then install the oil seal washer (upper washer on CBS/LBS-ABS/TCS models) **(see illustration 7.22b)**. Either use the service tool (Pt. Nos. 07947-KA50100 and 07947-KF40200) or a suitable piece of tubing to tap the bush fully into place; the tubing must be slightly larger in diameter than the fork tube and slightly smaller in diameter than the bush recess in the slider. Take care not to scratch the fork tube during this operation; it is best to make sure that the fork tube is pushed fully into the slider so that any accidental scratching is confined to the area above the oil seal. Remove the washer and check that the bush is properly seated. On standard and ABS/TCS models, reinstall the washer.

54 On CBS/LBS-ABS/TCS models, remove the upper washer and check that the bush is seated fully and squarely in its recess in the slider. Install the lower washer onto the bush with its flat side facing down, then install the spacer with its grooved side facing down so that it fits into the raised section of the lower washer. Now install the upper washer with its chamfered side facing down.

55 Install the new oil seal. Smear the seal's lips with fork oil and slide it over the tube so that its markings face upwards and drive the seal into place as described in Step 52 until the retaining clip groove is visible above the seal.**(see illustration 7.23)**.

56 Once the seal is correctly seated, fit the retaining clip, making sure it is correctly located in its groove **(see illustration 7.24)**.

57 Lubricate the lips of the new dust seal then slide it down the fork tube and press it into position **(see illustration 7.25)**.

58 Slowly pour in the specified quantity of the specified grade of fork oil and pump the fork to distribute it evenly **(see illustration 7.26a)**; the oil level should also be measured and adjustment made by adding or subtracting oil. Fully compress the fork tube into the slider and measure the fork oil level from the top of the tube **(see illustration 7.26b)**. Add or subtract fork oil until the oil is at the level specified in the Specifications Section of this Chapter.

59 Clamp the slider in a vice via the brake caliper mounting lugs, taking care not to overtighten and damage them. Pull the fork tube out of the slider as far as possible then install the spring with its closer-wound coils at the bottom, followed by the spring seat and the spacer **(see illustrations 7.27a, b and c)**.

60 Fit a new O-ring to the fork top bolt and thread the bolt into the top of the fork tube **(see illustration)**.

Warning: It will be necessary to compress the spring by pressing it down using the top bolt to engage the threads of the top bolt with the fork tube. This is a potentially dangerous operation and should be performed with care, using an assistant if necessary. Wipe off any excess oil before starting to prevent the possibility of slipping.

Keep the fork tube fully extended whilst pressing on the spring. Screw the top bolt carefully into the fork tube making sure it is not cross-threaded. **Note:** *The top bolt can be tightened to the specified torque setting at this stage if the tube is held between the padded jaws of a vice, but do not risk distorting the tube by doing so. A better method is to tighten the top bolt when the fork has been installed in the bike and is securely held in the bottom yoke.*

TOOL TiP

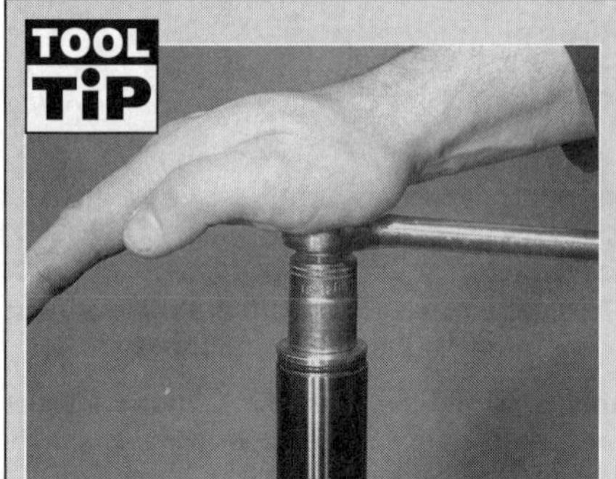

Use a ratchet-type tool when installing the fork top bolt. This makes it unnecessary to remove the tool from the bolt whilst threading it in, thus making it easier to maintain a downward pressure on the spring.

61 Where fitted, fit the protector onto the top of the fork slider, making sure its tab fits into the slot in the top of the slider **(see illustration 7.31)**.

62 Install the forks (see Section 6).

8 Steering stem - removal and installation

Caution: Although not strictly necessary, before removing the steering stem it is recommended that the upper fairing and fuel tank cover are removed. This will prevent accidental damage to the paintwork.

Removal

1 Remove the upper fairing and the fuel tank cover (see Chapter 8).

2 Remove the handlebars (see Section 5).

3 Remove the front forks (see Section 6).

4 Trace the ignition switch wiring and disconnect it at the white connector behind the steering head. Remove the air filter housing for better access to the connector (see Chapter 4).

5 Remove the steering stem nut and washer. Lift the top yoke off the steering stem **(see illustrations)**.

6 Bend back the tabs of the steering stem lockwasher to release it from the locknut, then unscrew and remove the locknut using a suitable C-spanner **(see illustration)**. Remove the lockwasher and discard it as a new one must be used.

7 Supporting the bottom yoke, unscrew the adjuster nut and remove the bearing cover from the steering stem **(see illustration)**.

8 Gently lower the bottom yoke and steering stem out of the frame. The lower bearing can be slid off the steering stem. Remove the

1 Steering stem nut
2 Top yoke
3 Locknut
4 Lockwasher
5 Adjuster nut
6 Bearing cover
7 Upper bearing inner race
8 Upper bearing
9 Upper bearing outer race
10 Lower bearing outer race
11 Lower bearing
12 Lower bearing inner race
13 Dust seal
14 Bottom yoke and steering stem

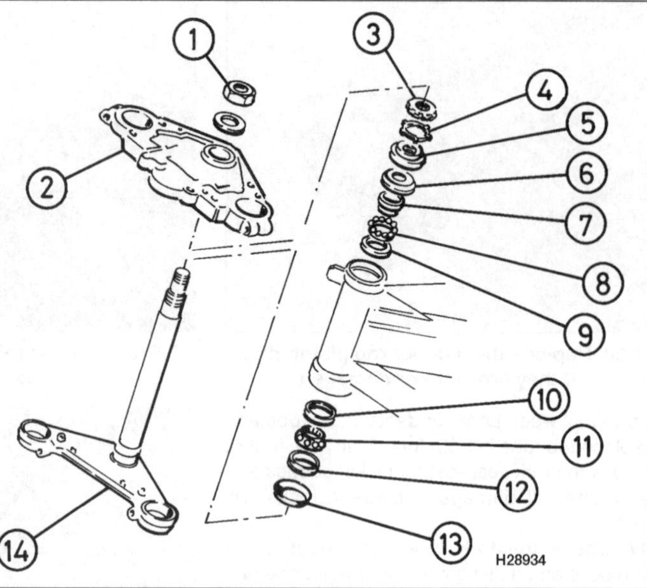

8.5a Steering stem components

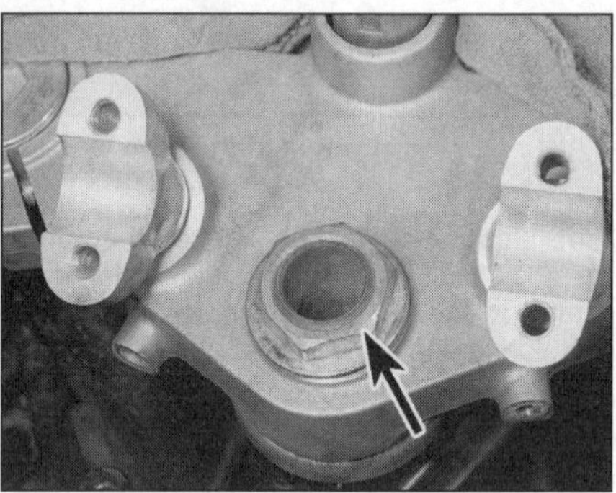

8.5b Remove the nut and washer (arrowed) . . .

8.5c . . . then lift the yoke off the stem

8.6 Bend down the lockwasher tabs using a screwdriver

8.7 Unscrew the locknut and adjuster nut using a C-spanner

8.12a Fit the bent lockwasher tabs down into the adjuster nut slots . . .

8.12b . . . then fit the locknut as described . . .

8.12c . . . and bend up the flat tabs to secure it

inner race and upper bearing from the top of the steering head.

9 Remove all traces of old grease from the bearings and races and check them for wear or damage as described in Section 9. **Note:** *Do not attempt to remove the outer races from the frame or the lower bearing inner race from the steering stem unless they are to be replaced.*

Installation

10 Smear a liberal quantity of grease on the bearing outer races in the frame. Work the grease well into both the upper and lower bearings.

11 Slip the lower bearing over the steering stem and seat it on the inner race. Carefully lift the steering stem/bottom yoke up through the frame. Install the upper bearing and its inner race in the top of the steering head. Install the bearing cover and thread the adjuster nut on the steering stem. Tighten the adjuster nut to the torque setting specified at the beginning of the Chapter, then turn the steering stem through its full lock four or five times and tighten the adjuster nut again to the specified setting. If it is not possible to apply a torque wrench to the adjuster nut, tighten the nut and adjust the bearings as described in Chapter 1 after the installation procedure is complete. **Caution:** *Take great care not to apply excessive pressure because this will cause premature failure of the bearings.*

Caution: Take great care not to apply excessive pressure because this will cause premature failure of the bearings.

12 When the bearings are correctly adjusted, install the new lockwasher onto the adjuster nut so that the down-facing tabs fit into the slots in the adjuster nut **(see illustration)**. Install the locknut and tighten it finger-tight, then tighten it further (to a maximum of 90°) until its slots align with the remaining tabs on the lockwasher **(see illustration)**. Hold the adjuster nut to prevent it from moving if necessary. Bend up the lockwasher tabs to secure the locknut **(see illustration)**.

13 Install the top yoke onto the steering stem. Install the steering stem nut and its washer and tighten it finger-tight at this stage. Temporarily install one of the forks to align the top and bottom yokes, and secure it by tightening the bottom yoke clamp bolt only.

14 Tighten the steering stem nut to the specified torque setting **(see illustration)**.

15 Reconnect the ignition switch wiring connector.

16 Install the front forks (see Section 6).

17 Install the handlebars (see Section 5).

18 Install the upper fairing and the fuel tank cover (see Chapter 8).

19 Carry out a check of the steering head bearing freeplay as described in Chapter 1, and if necessary re-adjust.

9 Steering head bearings - inspection and replacement

Inspection

1 Remove the steering stem (see Section 8).

2 Remove all traces of old grease from the bearings and races and check them for wear or damage.

3 The outer races should be polished and free from indentations. Inspect the bearing balls for signs of wear, damage or discoloration, and examine the ball retainer cage for signs of cracks or splits. Spin the bearings by hand. They should spin freely and smoothly. If there are any signs of wear on any of the above components both upper and lower bearing assemblies must be replaced as a set. Only remove the races if they need to be replaced - do not re-use them once they have been removed.

Replacement

4 The outer races are an interference fit in the steering head and can be tapped from position with a suitable drift **(see illustration)**. Tap firmly and evenly around each race to ensure that it is driven out squarely. It may prove advantageous to curve the end of the drift slightly to improve access.

5 Alternatively, the races can be removed

8.14 Tighten the steering stem nut to the specified torque setting

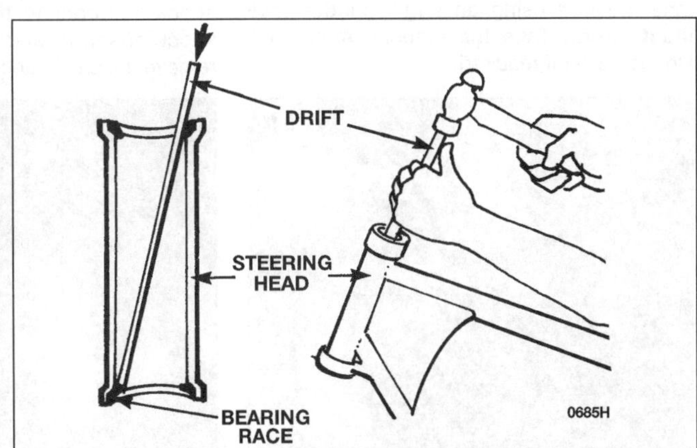

9.4 Drive the bearing races out with a brass drift as shown

6

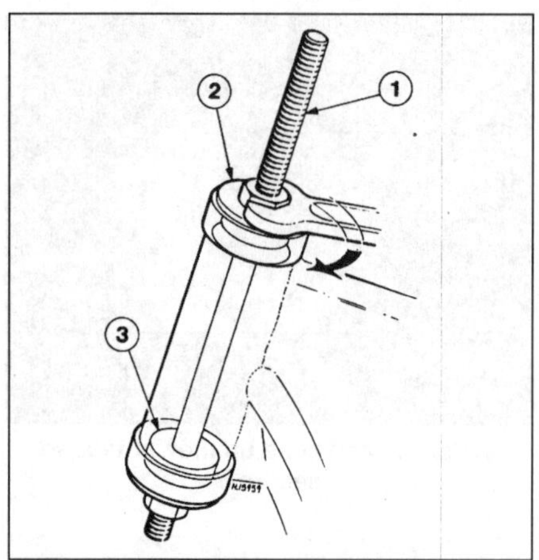

9.6 Drawbolt arrangement for fitting steering stem bearing races

1 *Long bolt or threaded bar*
2 *Thick washer*
3 *Guide for lower race*

using a slide-hammer type bearing extractor; these can often be hired from tool shops.

6 The new outer races can be pressed into the head using a drawbolt arrangement **(see illustration)**, or by using a large diameter tubular drift which bears only on the outer edge of the race. Ensure that the drawbolt washer or drift (as applicable) bears only on the outer edge of the race and does not contact the working surface. Alternatively, have the races installed by a Honda dealer equipped with the bearing race installing tools.

Installation of new bearing outer races is made much easier if the races are left overnight in the freezer. This causes them to contract slightly making them a looser fit.

7 To remove the lower bearing inner race from the steering stem, use two screwdrivers placed on opposite sides of the race to work it free. If the bearing is firmly in place it will be necessary to use a bearing puller, or in extreme circumstances to split the bearing's inner section using an angle grinder **(see illustration)**. Take the steering stem to a Honda dealer if required.

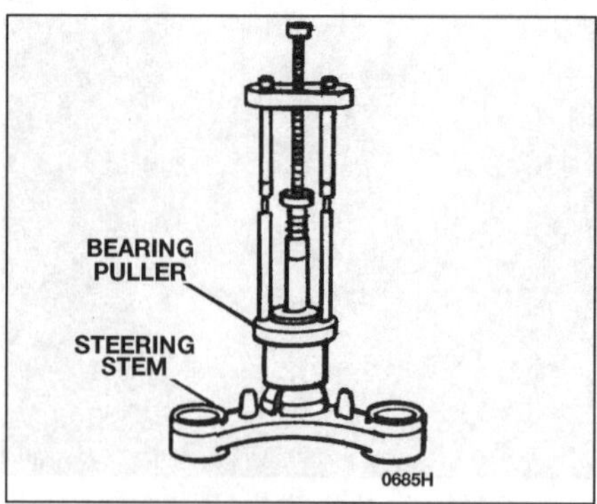

9.7 It is best to remove the lower bearing inner race using a puller

8 Fit the dust seal and new lower bearing inner race onto the steering stem. A length of tubing with an internal diameter slightly larger than the steering stem will be needed to tap the inner race into position **(see illustration)**. Ensure that the drift bears only on the inner edge of the race and does not contact the working face.

9 Install the steering stem (see Section 8).

10 Rear shock absorber - removal, inspection and installation

Removal

1 Place the machine on its centrestand. Position a support under the rear wheel so that it does not drop when the shock absorber is removed, but also making sure that the weight of the machine is off the rear suspension so that the shock is not compressed.

2 Note the shock absorber spring pre-load current setting, then adjust it to its softest setting (see Section 11).

3 Remove the right-hand side panel (see Chapter 8).

4 Unscrew and remove the bolt securing the bottom of the shock absorber to the swingarm **(see illustration)**.

5 Unscrew the bolt securing the top of the shock absorber to the frame. Support the shock absorber and remove the bolt, then remove the shock absorber **(see illustration)**.

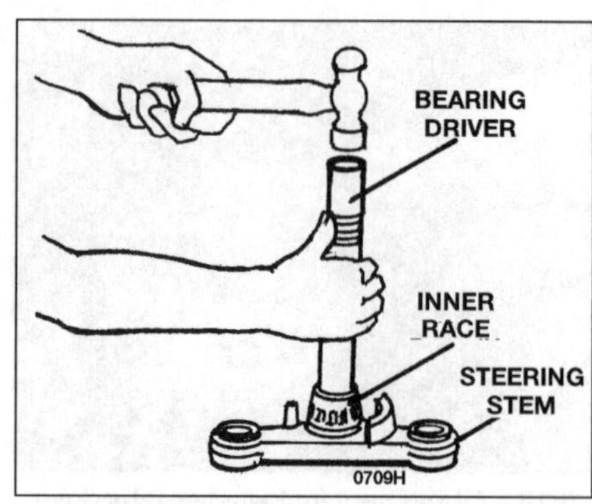

9.8 Drive the new inner race on using a suitable bearing driver or a length of pipe

Inspection

6 Inspect the shock absorber for obvious physical damage and the coil spring for looseness, cracks or signs of fatigue.

7 Inspect the damper rod for signs of bending, pitting and oil leakage.

8 Inspect the pivot hardware at the top and bottom of the shock for wear or damage.

9 To measure the shock absorber spring free length, compress the spring using a coil spring compressor by just enough to access the spring stopper ring. Remove the ring and the upper spring seat, then carefully release the compressor until the spring is relaxed. Remove the spring, noting which way up it fits. Measure the free length of the spring and compare it to the specifications. If the spring has relaxed below its service limit, it must be replaced.

10 Individual components for the rear shock absorber are available for some models. Check with your Honda dealer for availability. Otherwise the entire unit must be replaced if it is worn or damaged.

Installation

11 Installation is the reverse of removal, noting the following.

a) Apply molybdenum disulphide paste to the pivot points.
*b) Tighten the bolts to the torque settings specified at the beginning of the Chapter **(see illustration)**.*
c) Adjust the suspension as required (see Section 11).

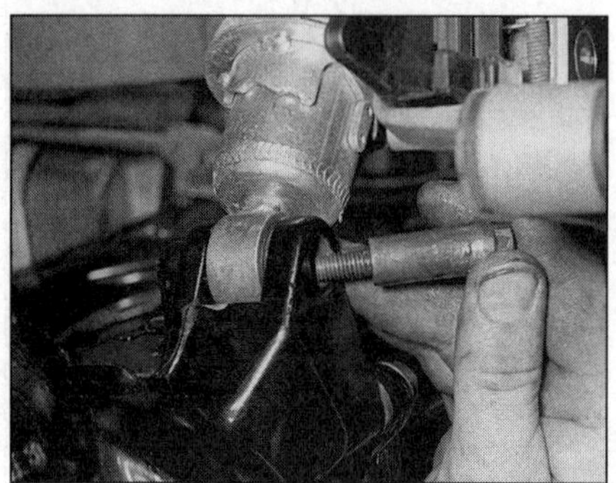

10.4 Remove the lower mounting bolt . . .

10.5 . . . then the upper mounting bolt

10.11 Tighten the mounting bolts to the specified torque settings

11.3 Adjust the pre-load using the tool in the toolkit, or a suitable C-spanner

11 Suspension - adjustments

Front forks

1 The front forks are not adjustable.

Rear shock absorber

2 On all models the rear shock absorber is adjustable for spring pre-load and rebound damping. Remove the right-hand side panel and pannier for access to the pre-load adjuster (see Chapter 8). The damping adjuster is accessed on some models via the hole in the right-hand side panel, or on other models by removing the side panel.

11.5 Adjust the damping using a screwdriver

3 Pre-load adjustment is made using a suitable C-spanner (one is provided in the toolkit) to turn the spring seat on the base of the shock absorber **(see illustration)**. There are five positions. Position 1 is the softest setting, position 5 is the hardest. Align the setting required with the adjustment stopper. Position 2 is the standard setting.

4 To increase the pre-load, turn the spring seat clockwise. To decrease the pre-load, turn the spring seat anti-clockwise.

5 Rebound damping adjustment is made by turning the adjuster on the top of the shock absorber using a flat-bladed screwdriver **(see illustration)**. To set the standard position, turn the adjuster clockwise until it stops, then turn it anti clockwise 1 turn (standard and ABS/TCS models) or 1/2 turn (CBS/LBS-ABS/TCS models) until the punchmark on the adjuster aligns with the index mark on the shock absorber.

6 To increase the damping from the standard position (position 1), turn the adjuster clockwise. On standard and ABS/TCS models, turn the adjuster 1/2 turn for position 2, 3/4 turn for position 3 and 1 full turn for position 4. On CBS/LBS-ABS/TCS models, turn the adjuster 1/4 turn for position 2 and 1/2 turn for position 3. To decrease the damping, turn the adjuster anti-clockwise.

12 Swingarm and driveshaft - removal and installation

Removal

1 Remove the side panels (see Chapter 8). Unscrew the three bolts securing each swingarm pivot cover and remove the covers **(see illustration)**.

2 Remove the final drive housing (see Section 14). Pull the driveshaft out from the rear of swingarm as far as possible so that the universal joint disengages from the transmission output shaft.

3 On ABS/TCS and CBS/LBS-ABS/TCS models, release the wheel speed sensor wiring from the clips on the swingarm **(see illustration)**.

4 Unscrew the brake hose clamp bolts and displace the clamps from the swingarm **(see illustrations)**. Support the brake caliper so that no strain is placed on the hose.

5 Counter-hold the pivot bolt on the left-hand side and slacken the locknut. This requires the use of a Honda service tool, Pt. No. 07908-4690003, which is a special wrench that fits the locknut **(see illustrations)**. There is no alternative to the use of this tool, particularly for the tightening procedure (see Step 10); if you do not have access to it, the swingarm pivot locknut must be unscrewed and later tightened by a Honda dealer service department.

6 With the aid of an assistant to support the swingarm if necessary, unscrew the pivot bolts on both sides and then carefully withdraw the swingarm from the frame.

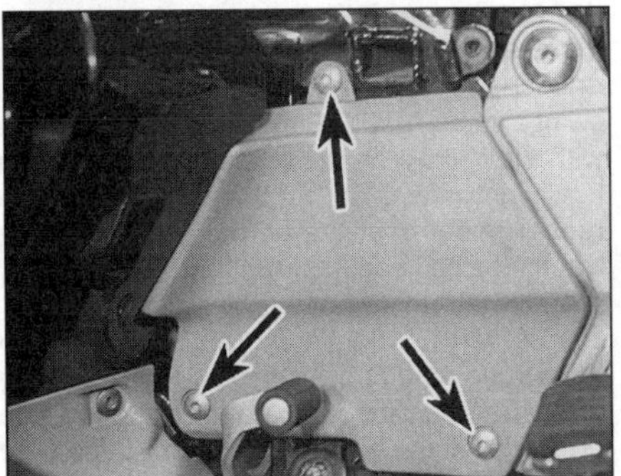

12.1 Each swingarm pivot cover is secured by three screws (arrowed)

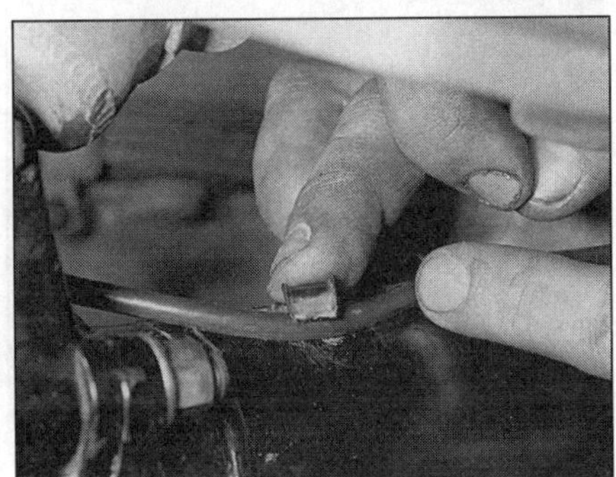

12.3 Release the wheel speed sensor wiring from its clips

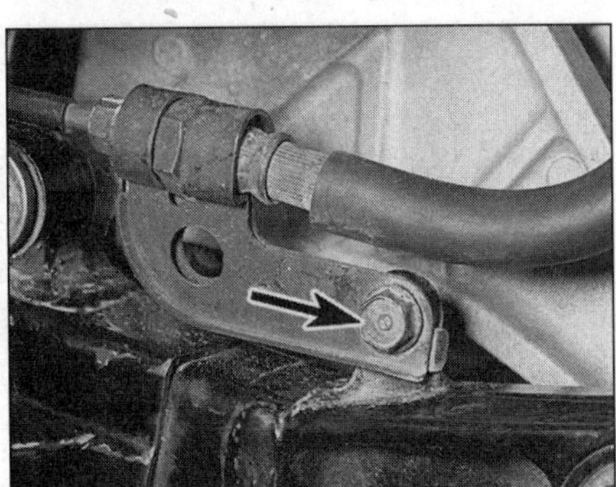

12.4a Unscrew the rear . . .

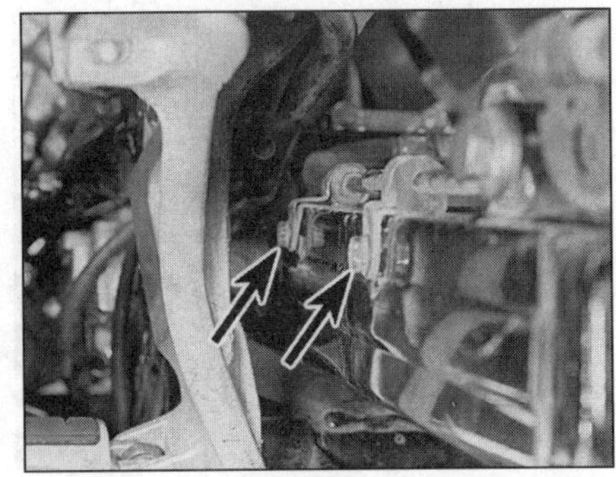

12.4b . . . middle and front brake hose clamps (arrowed)

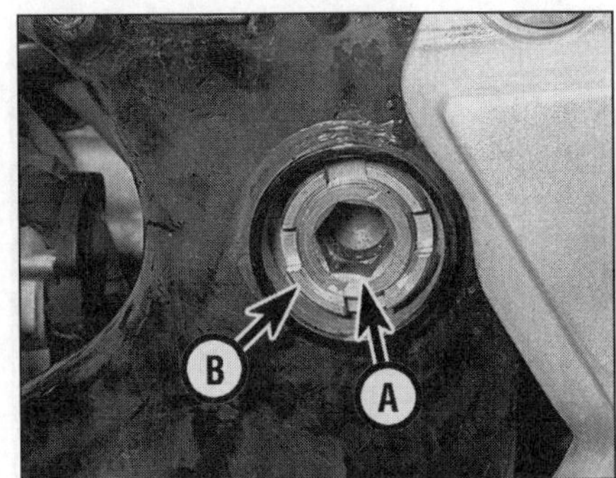

12.5a Pivot bolt (A), locknut (B)

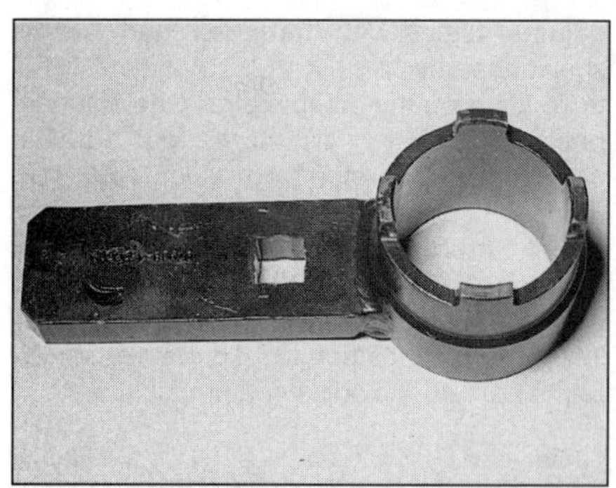

12.5b This tool MUST be used for the swingarm tightening procedure

12.6a Unscrew the left-hand . . .

12.6b . . . and right-hand pivot bolts . . .

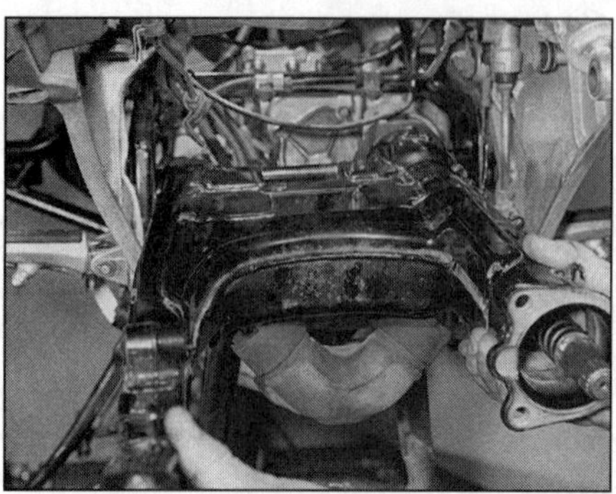

12.6c . . . and remove the swingarm

12.6d Withdraw the driveshaft from the swingarm

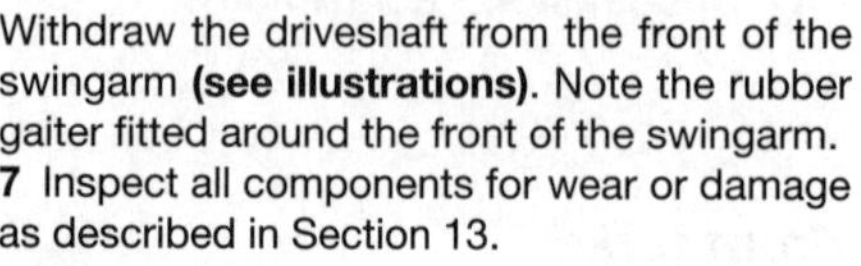

Withdraw the driveshaft from the front of the swingarm **(see illustrations)**. Note the rubber gaiter fitted around the front of the swingarm.

7 Inspect all components for wear or damage as described in Section 13.

Installation

8 Lubricate the driveshaft splines with molybdenum disulphide grease **(see illustration)**. Slide the driveshaft as far as possible into the front of the swingarm **(see illustration 12.6d)**. Fit the rubber gaiter around the front of the swingarm, making sure the "ENG SIDE" mark faces the engine and the "UP" mark faces up **(see illustrations)**. Check that the bearings are in place in the swingarm.

9 Manoeuvre the swingarm into position in the frame, and install the pivot bolts **(see illustrations 12.6c, b and a)**. Slide the driveshaft forward from the rear of the swingarm so that the universal joint engages with the splines on the output shaft, and slide it fully onto the shaft. Fit the front edge of the rubber gaiter over the output section on the transmission casing, making sure it fits properly into the groove.

10 Tighten the right-hand side pivot bolt to the torque setting specified at the beginning of the Chapter, then tighten the left hand side pivot bolt to the torque setting specified **(see illustrations)**. Move the swingarm up and down several times to settle the bearings,

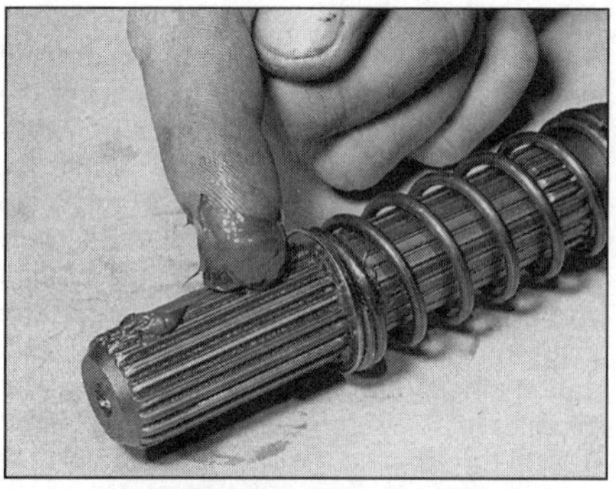

12.8a Lubricate the splines with molybdenum disulphide grease

12.8b Fit the rubber gaiter . . .

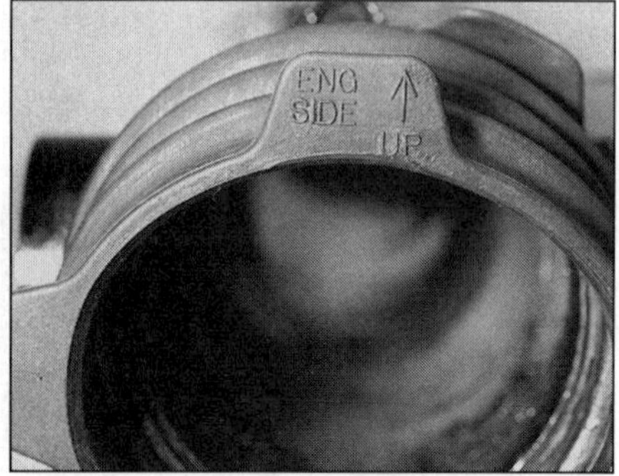

12.8c . . . making sure it is the right way round and up

12.10a Tighten the right-hand pivot bolt . . .

12.10b . . . then the left-hand pivot bolt to the specified torque settings

12.10c Fit the locknut . . .

12.10d . . . and tighten it to the specified torque setting using ONLY the special tool whilst counter-holding the pivot bolt

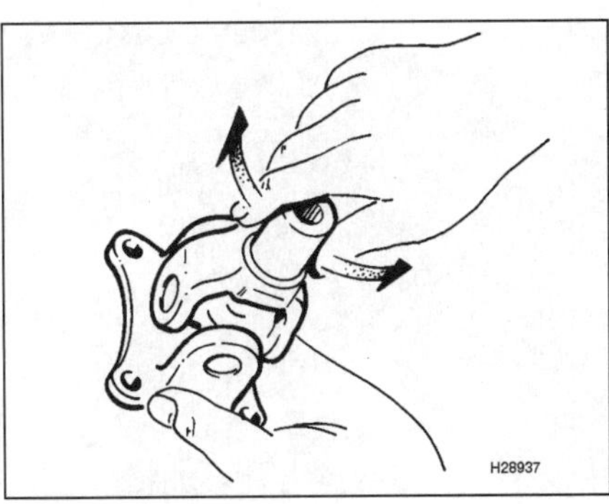

13.4 Check for any signs of freeplay or roughness in the universal joint

then check that the left hand side pivot bolt is still tightened to the torque setting specified and adjust if necessary. Install the locknut onto the left side pivot bolt and tighten it to the specified torque setting using a torque wrench applied to the socket in the arm of the special tool (see Step 4) **(see illustrations)**. **Note:** *The specified torque setting takes into account the extra leverage provided by the service tool and cannot be duplicated without it.* Counter-hold the pivot bolt to prevent it from turning whilst tightening the locknut.

11 Install the brake hose clamps onto the swingarm **(see illustrations 12.4a and b)**.

12 On ABS/TCS and CBS/LBS-ABS/TCS models, secure the wheel speed sensor wiring in the clips on the swingarm **(see illustration 12.3)**.

13.5a Remove the bearings and clean them

13 Install the final drive housing onto the swingarm (see Section 14).

14 Check again that the rubber gaiter is correctly fitted over the swingarm and the transmission casing.

15 Install the pivot covers **(see illustration 12.1)**, and the side panels (see Chapter 8).

16 Check the operation of the rear suspension and driveshaft before taking the machine on the road.

13 Swingarm and driveshaft - inspection and bearing replacement

Inspection

1 Thoroughly clean all components, removing all traces of dirt, corrosion and grease.

2 Inspect all components closely, looking for obvious signs of wear such as heavy scoring, and cracks or distortion due to accident damage. Any damaged or worn component must be replaced.

3 Inspect the driveshaft splines for wear or damage. If wear is evident and there is excessive clearance between the driveshaft and the final drive housing, the shaft must be replaced.

4 Inspect the universal joint for signs of wear or damage. There should be no noticeable play in the bearings, and the joint should move smoothly and freely with no signs of roughness or notchiness **(see illustration)**. If any wear or damage is evident, the universal joint must be replaced.

Bearing replacement

5 Remove the bearings, then clean them and inspect them for wear or damage. If the bearings do not run smoothly and freely or if there is excessive freeplay, they must be replaced. Inspect the bearing races in the swingarm for signs of pitting or other damage **(see illustrations)**.

6 Lubricate the races and the bearings using a multi-purpose lithium based grease and fit the bearings into the swingarm **(see illustration)**.

14 Driveshaft joint and final drive - removal, inspection and installation

Removal

1 Drain the final drive gear oil (see Chapter 1).

2 On ABS/TCS and CBS/LBS-ABS/TCS models, free the wheel speed sensor wiring from its clip on the top of the final drive housing, then unscrew the mounting bolts and withdraw the sensor from is socket **(see illustrations)**. Note the shim fitted between the sensor and the housing.

3 Remove the rear wheel (see Chapter 7).

4 Unscrew the shock absorber lower

13.5b Inspect the races for wear and damage

13.6 Lubricate the races and bearings with grease

14.2a Free the speed sensor wiring from the clip . . .

14.2b . . . then remove the bolts and withdraw the sensor

14.5a The final drive housing is secured to the swingarm by four nuts (arrowed)

14.5b Unscrew the nuts and remove the housing

14.5c Remove the driveshaft joint from either the housing or the swingarm

14.7a Replace the driveshaft joint oil seal (arrowed)

14.7b Lubricate the splines on each end of the joint

mounting bolt and swing the shock backwards so that it is clear of its mounting **(see illustration 10.4)**.

5 Support the final drive housing and unscrew the four nuts securing it to the swingarm. Remove the housing from the swingarm **(see illustrations)**. Remove the driveshaft joint from the front of the final drive housing or from the end of the driveshaft in the swingarm **(see illustration)**. Withdraw the collar from the middle of the housing **(see illustration 14.9)**.

Inspection

6 Install the driveshaft joint into the final drive housing and rotate the shaft. Check that the shaft is able to rotate smoothly and freely and that the power is transmitted correctly through the bevel gear assembly to the output boss. If there are any signs of roughness or notchiness or any evidence of wear on the input and output boss splines, the unit must be disassembled and examined further.

7 Check the housing for any evidence of oil leakage from the seals. Withdraw the driveshaft joint from the housing. Remove the oil seal and discard it as a new one must be used. Fit the new seal, then smear the seal lips and the driveshaft joint inner and outer splines with molybdenum disulphide grease **(see illustrations)**. Wipe the grease off one of the spline grooves to allow air to pass between the components. Install the joint into the housing, taking care not to damage the oil seal lip.

8 If attention to the final drive housing is required, the complete unit should be taken to a Honda dealer or service agent who will have the necessary special tools and expertise to carry out the rather complicated inspection and overhaul procedure.

Installation

9 Install the collar into the drive housing **(see illustration)**.

10 Install the final drive housing, making sure the driveshaft joint engages correctly with the driveshaft **(see illustration 14.5b)**. Fit and tighten the housing nuts finger-tight only at this stage.

11 Install the rear wheel (see Chapter 7). Now tighten the final drive housing nuts evenly and in a criss-cross pattern to the torque setting specified at the beginning of the Chapter.

12 Install the shock absorber lower mounting bolt and tighten it to the specified torque setting **(see illustration 10.4)**.

13 On ABS/TCS and CBS/LBS-ABS/TCS models, install the wheel speed sensor with its shim and tighten the bolts **(see illustration)**. Secure the wiring in its clip on the housing **(see illustration 14.2a)**.

14 Fill the final drive housing with the correct grade and quantity of oil (see Chapter 1).

14.9 Fit the collar into the housing

14.13 Do not omit the shim when fitting the wheel speed sensor

Chapter 7
Brakes, wheels and tyres

Contents

ABS and TCS systems - general information and operation 17
Brake discs (front and rear) - inspection, removal and installation .. 4
Brake fluid level check ....see Daily (pre-ride) checks
Brake hoses, pipes and unions - inspection and replacement 9
Brake light switches - check and replacement ....see Chapter 9
Brake pad wear check ....see Chapter 1
Brake pads (front and rear) - replacement 2
Brake system bleeding 10
Brake system check ....see Chapter 1
Front brake calipers - removal, overhaul and installation 3
Front brake master cylinder - removal, overhaul and installation ... 5
Front wheel - removal and installation 13
General information 1
Rear brake caliper - removal, overhaul and installation 7
Rear brake master cylinder - removal, overhaul and installation ... 8
Rear wheel - removal and installation 14
Secondary master cylinder, delay valve and proportional control valve - overhaul 6
Tyres - general information and fitting 16
Tyres - pressure, tread depth and condition ....see Daily (pre-ride) checks
Wheel bearings - check ....see Chapter 1
Wheel bearings - removal, inspection and installation 15
Wheels - alignment check 12
Wheels - general check ....see Chapter 1
Wheels - inspection and repair 11

Degrees of difficulty

Easy, suitable for novice with little experience 	**Fairly easy,** suitable for beginner with some experience 	**Fairly difficult,** suitable for competent DIY mechanic 	**Difficult,** suitable for experienced DIY mechanic 	**Very difficult,** suitable for expert DIY or professional

Specifications

Front brakes

Brake fluid type	DOT 4
Caliper bore ID	
Standard and ABS/TCS models	
Standard	27.000 to 27.050 mm
Service limit	27.06 mm
CBS/LBS-ABS/TCS models	
Right-hand caliper - upper bore	
Standard	27.000 to 27.050 mm
Service limit	27.06 mm
Right-hand caliper - middle bore	
Standard	22.650 to 22.700 mm
Service limit	22.71 mm
Right-hand caliper - lower bore	
Standard	25.400 to 25.450 mm
Service limit	25.46 mm
Left-hand caliper - upper and middle bores	
Standard	25.400 to 25.450 mm
Service limit	25.46 mm
Left-hand caliper - lower bore	
Standard	22.650 to 22.700 mm
Service limit	22.71 mm

Front brakes (continued)

Caliper piston OD
- Standard and ABS/TCS models
  - Standard: 26.918 to 26.968 mm
  - Service limit: 26.91 mm
- CBS/LBS-ABS/TCS models
  - Right-hand caliper - upper bore
    - Standard: 26.935 to 26.968 mm
    - Service limit: 26.91 mm
  - Right-hand caliper - middle bore
    - Standard: 22.585 to 22.618 mm
    - Service limit: 22.56 mm
  - Right-hand caliper - lower bore
    - Standard: 25.335 to 25.368 mm
    - Service limit: 25.31 mm
  - Left-hand caliper - upper and middle bores
    - Standard: 25.335 to 25.368 mm
    - Service limit: 25.31 mm
  - Left-hand caliper - lower bore
    - Standard: 22.585 to 22.618 mm
    - Service limit: 22.56 mm

Disc minimum thickness
- Standard: 4.8 to 5.2 mm
- Service limit: 4.0 mm

Disc maximum runout: 0.3 mm

Master cylinder bore ID
- Standard and ABS/TCS models
  - Standard: 14.000 to 14.043 mm
  - Service limit: 14.06 mm
- CBS/LBS-ABS/TCS models
  - Standard: 12.700 to 12.743 mm
  - Service limit: 12.76 mm

Master cylinder piston OD
- Standard and ABS/TCS models
  - Standard: 13.957 to 13.984 mm
  - Service limit: 13.95 mm
- CBS/LBS-ABS/TCS models
  - Standard: 12.657 to 12.684 mm
  - Service limit: 12.65 mm

Secondary master cylinder bore ID - CBS/LBS-ABS/TCS models
- Standard: 14.000 to 14.043 mm
- Service limit: 14.06 mm

Secondary master piston OD - CBS/LBS-ABS/TCS models
- Standard: 13.957 to 13.984 mm
- Service limit: 13.95 mm

Rear brake

Brake fluid type: DOT 4

Caliper bore ID
- Standard and ABS/TCS models
  - Standard: 27.000 to 27.050 mm
  - Service limit: 27.06 mm
- CBS/LBS-ABS/TCS models
  - Front and rear bores
    - Standard: 22.650 to 22.700 mm
    - Service limit: 22.71 mm
  - Middle bore
    - Standard: 27.000 to 27.050 mm
    - Service limit: 27.06 mm

Caliper piston OD
- Standard and ABS/TCS models
  - Standard: 26.918 to 26.968 mm
  - Service limit: 26.91 mm
- CBS/LBS-ABS/TCS models
  - Front and rear bores
    - Standard: 22.585 to 22.618 mm
    - Service limit: 22.56 mm
  - Middle bore
    - Standard: 26.935 to 26.968 mm
    - Service limit: 26.91 mm

Rear brake (continued)

Disc minimum thickness	
Standard and ABS/TCS models	
Standard	7.3 to 7.7 mm
Service limit	6.0 mm
CBS/LBS-ABS/TCS models	
Standard	7.3 to 7.7 mm
Service limit	6.5 mm
Disc maximum runout	0.3 mm
Master cylinder bore ID	
Standard and ABS/TCS models	
Standard	12.700 to 12.743 mm
Service limit	12.76 mm
CBS/LBS-ABS/TCS models	
Standard	17.460 to 17.503 mm
Service limit	17.515 mm
Master cylinder piston OD	
Standard and ABS/TCS models	
Standard	12.657 to 12.684 mm
Service limit	12.65 mm
CBS/LBS-ABS/TCS models	
Standard	17.417 to 17.444 mm
Service limit	17.405 mm

Wheels

Maximum wheel runout (front and rear)	
Axial (side-to-side)	2.0 mm
Radial (out-of-round)	2.0 mm
Maximum axle runout (front and rear)	0.20 mm
Front wheel sensor air gap	
ABS/TCS models	0.4 to 1.2 mm
CBS/LBS-ABS/TCS models	0.4 to 0.5 mm
Rear wheel sensor air gap	0.7 to 1.2 mm

Tyres

Tyre pressures	see Chapter 1
Tyre sizes*	
Standard and ABS/TCS models	
Front	110/80-V18
Rear	160/70-V17
CBS/LBS-ABS/TCS models	
Front	120/70-ZR18
Rear	160/70-ZR17

**Refer to the owner's handbook or the tyre information label on the swingarm for approved tyre brands.*

Torque settings

Brake pad retaining pin plug	2.5 Nm
Brake pad retaining pin	18 Nm
Front brake caliper mounting bolts	
Standard and ABS/TCS models	
Right hand caliper	27 Nm
Left-hand caliper	
Upper mounting bolt	27 Nm
Lower mounting bolt	12 Nm
CBS/LBS-ABS/TCS models	
Right hand caliper	
Upper mounting bolt	30 Nm
Lower mounting bolt	12 Nm
Left-hand caliper	30 Nm
Caliper body joining bolts	33 Nm
Brake hose banjo bolts	35 Nm
Brake pipe joint nuts	17 Nm
Brake disc bolts	43 Nm
Front master cylinder clamp bolts	12 Nm
Secondary master cylinder bolts	12 Nm
Linkage arm to caliper bracket pivot bolt	30 Nm
Linkage plate bolts	30 Nm
Delay valve mounting bolts	12 Nm

Torque settings (continued)

Rear caliper body joining bolts (CBS/LBS-ABS/TCS models)	33 Nm
Rear axle nut	90 Nm
Rear axle pinch bolt	27 Nm
Rear caliper bracket stopper bolt	70 Nm
Silencer mounting bolt	27 Nm
Footrest bracket bolts	
8 mm bolt	27 Nm
10 mm bolts	35 Nm
Brake caliper bleed valves	5.5 Nm
Front axle bolt	90 Nm
Front axle clamp bolts	22 Nm
Front wheel speed sensor bracket bolt	12 Nm

1 General information

All models covered in this manual are fitted with cast alloy wheels designed for tubeless tyres only. Both front and rear brakes are hydraulically operated disc brakes.

On Standard and ABS/TCS models, both front and rear brakes have twin piston sliding calipers. On CBS/LBS-ABS/TCS models, both front and rear brakes have triple piston sliding calipers.

The anti-lock braking system (ABS) fitted on some models prevents the wheels from locking up under hard braking. The traction control system (TCS) prevents the rear wheel from losing traction under hard acceleration or on slippery surfaces. These systems are managed by a highly complex system of electronics and hydraulics. Such is the nature of these systems that no attempt is being made to cover them fully in this manual. Faultfinding and troubleshooting is very complicated and requires specific and specialised equipment exclusive to Honda. A functional and operational description of the systems is given later in this Chapter.

The combined or linked braking system (CBS (UK models) or LBS (US models)) applies both front and rear brakes even if only either the front brake lever or rear brake pedal is applied. Operating the front brake lever activates two pistons on each front brake caliper and a proportion of the rear caliper, the amount depending upon how hard the front brake lever is applied. The left front caliper is hinged and linked to the rear caliper via a secondary master cylinder and a proportional control valve. When the braking force is sufficient, the left caliper operates the secondary master cylinder and the rear brake is applied. Operating the rear brake pedal activates one piston on the rear brake caliper and one piston on each front caliper equally.

Caution: Disc brake components rarely require disassembly. Do not disassemble components unless absolutely necessary. If a hydraulic brake line is loosened, the entire system must be disassembled, drained, cleaned and then properly filled and bled upon reassembly. Do not use solvents on internal brake components. Solvents will cause the seals to swell and distort. Use only clean brake fluid or denatured alcohol for cleaning. Use care when working with brake fluid as it can injure your eyes and it will damage painted surfaces and plastic parts.

2 Brake pads (front and rear) - replacement

Warning: The dust created by the brake system may contain asbestos, which is harmful to your health. Never blow it out with compressed air and don't inhale any of it. An approved filtering mask should be worn when working on the brakes.

1 Unscrew the pad retaining pin plug followed by the pad retaining pin, then remove the pads **(see illustrations)**. Note how the pad spring is fitted and remove it if required.

2 Inspect the surface of each pad for contamination and check that the friction material has not worn down level with or beyond the wear grooves in the pad face **(see illustration)**; additionally, check that the pads have not worn down to expose the cutouts in the side of the pads **(see illustration 3.1 in Chapter 1)**. If either pad is worn, fouled with oil or grease, or heavily scored or damaged by dirt and debris, both pads must be replaced as a set. Note that it is not possible to degrease the friction material; if the pads are contaminated in any way they must be replaced.

2.1a Remove the pad pin plug . . .

2.1b . . . then unscrew the pad pin . . .

2.1c . . . and withdraw the pads from the back of the caliper

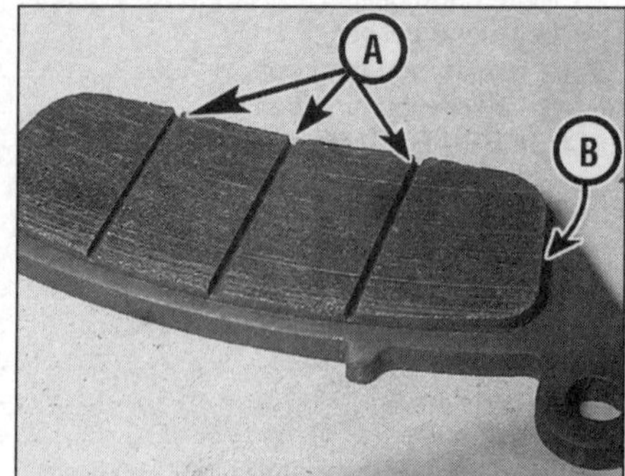

2.2 Brake pads must be replaced when the wear grooves (A) are no longer visible, or when the cutout (B) in the pad's edge is exposed

H29467

Standard and ABS/TCS models (front)

CBS/LBS-ABS/TCS models (front and rear)

2.8a Correct fitting of pad spring

2.8b Install the outer pad and slide the pad pin part-way in to locate it . . .

2.8c . . . then install the inner pad

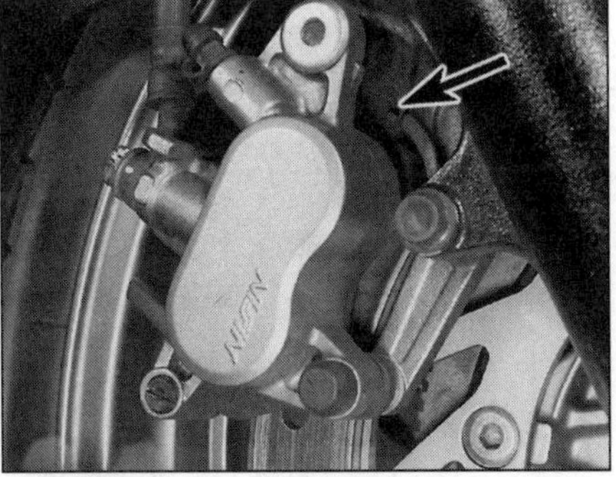
2.8d Check the pads locate correctly against the guide plate (arrowed) . . .

2.8e . . . then tighten the pad pin to the specified torque setting

3 If the pads are in good condition clean them carefully, using a fine wire brush which is completely free of oil and grease to remove all traces of road dirt and corrosion. Using a pointed instrument, clean out the grooves in the friction material and dig out any embedded particles of foreign matter. Any areas of glazing may be removed using emery cloth.

4 Check the condition of the brake disc (see Section 4).

5 Remove all traces of corrosion from the pad pin. Inspect the pin for signs of damage and replace if necessary.

6 Push the pistons as far back into the caliper as possible using hand pressure only. Due to the increased friction material thickness of new pads, it may be necessary to remove the master cylinder reservoir cover and diaphragm and siphon out some fluid.

7 On all models, smear the backs of the pads and the shank of the pad pin with copper-based grease, making sure that none gets on the front or sides of the pads. On CBS/LBS-ABS/TCS models, apply silicone grease to the inner end of the pad pin.

8 Installation of the pads is the reverse of removal. Make sure the pad spring is correctly positioned in the caliper. Insert the outer pad into the caliper so that the friction material faces the disc, then slide the pad retaining pin part-way through to keep the pad in place whilst installing the inner pad **(see illustrations)**. Make sure the pin passes through the hole in each pad, and the pads locate correctly against the guide plate **(see illustration)**. Tighten the pad retaining pin to the torque setting specified at the beginning of the Chapter **(see illustration)**. Install the pad pin plug and tighten it to the specified torque.

9 Top up the master cylinder reservoir if necessary (see *Daily (pre-ride) checks*), and replace the reservoir cover and diaphragm.

10 Operate the brake lever or pedal several times to bring the pads into contact with the disc. Check the operation of the brake before riding the motorcycle.

3 Front brake calipers - removal, overhaul and installation

Warning: If a caliper indicates the need for an overhaul (usually due to leaking fluid or sticky operation), all old brake fluid should be flushed from the system. Also, the dust created by the brake system may contain asbestos, which is harmful to your health. Never blow it out with compressed air and don't inhale any of it. An approved filtering mask should be worn when working on the brakes. Do not, under any circumstances, use petroleum-based solvents to clean brake parts. Use clean brake fluid, brake cleaner or denatured alcohol only.

Removal

1 Remove the brake hose banjo bolt(s), noting their alignment on the caliper and separate the hose(s) from the caliper **(see illustration)**. Plug the hose end or wrap a plastic bag tightly around it to minimise fluid loss and prevent dirt entering the system. Discard the sealing washers as new ones must be used on installation. **Note:** *If you are planning to overhaul the caliper and don't have a source of compressed air to blow out the pistons, just loosen the banjo bolt at this stage and*

3.1 Note the alignment of the hose before removing the banjo bolt (arrowed)

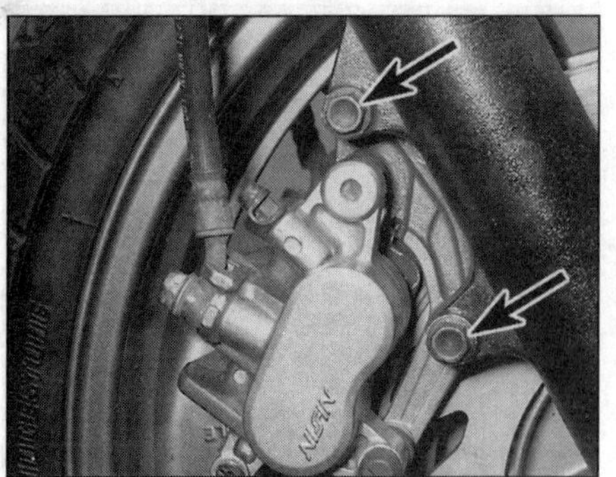

3.3a Right-hand caliper mounting bolts . . .

3.3b . . . and left-hand caliper mounting bolts - standard and ABS/TCS models

retighten it lightly. The bike's hydraulic system can then be used to force the pistons out of the body once the pads have been removed. Disconnect the hose once the pistons have been sufficiently displaced.

2 Remove the brake pads (see Section 2).

3 Unscrew the caliper mounting bolts, and slide the caliper off the disc **(see illustrations)**. Remove the pad spring from the caliper and the pad guide from the bracket, noting how they fit.

Overhaul

4 Clean the exterior of the caliper with denatured alcohol or brake system cleaner **(see illustrations)**.

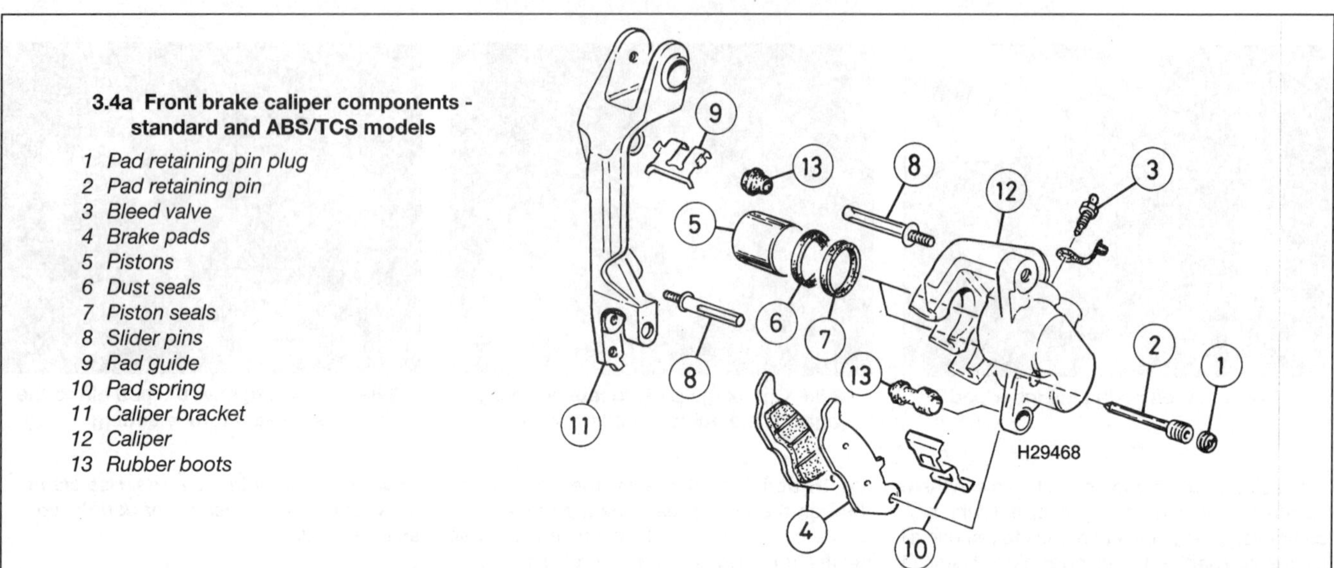

3.4a Front brake caliper components - standard and ABS/TCS models

1 *Pad retaining pin plug*
2 *Pad retaining pin*
3 *Bleed valve*
4 *Brake pads*
5 *Pistons*
6 *Dust seals*
7 *Piston seals*
8 *Slider pins*
9 *Pad guide*
10 *Pad spring*
11 *Caliper bracket*
12 *Caliper*
13 *Rubber boots*

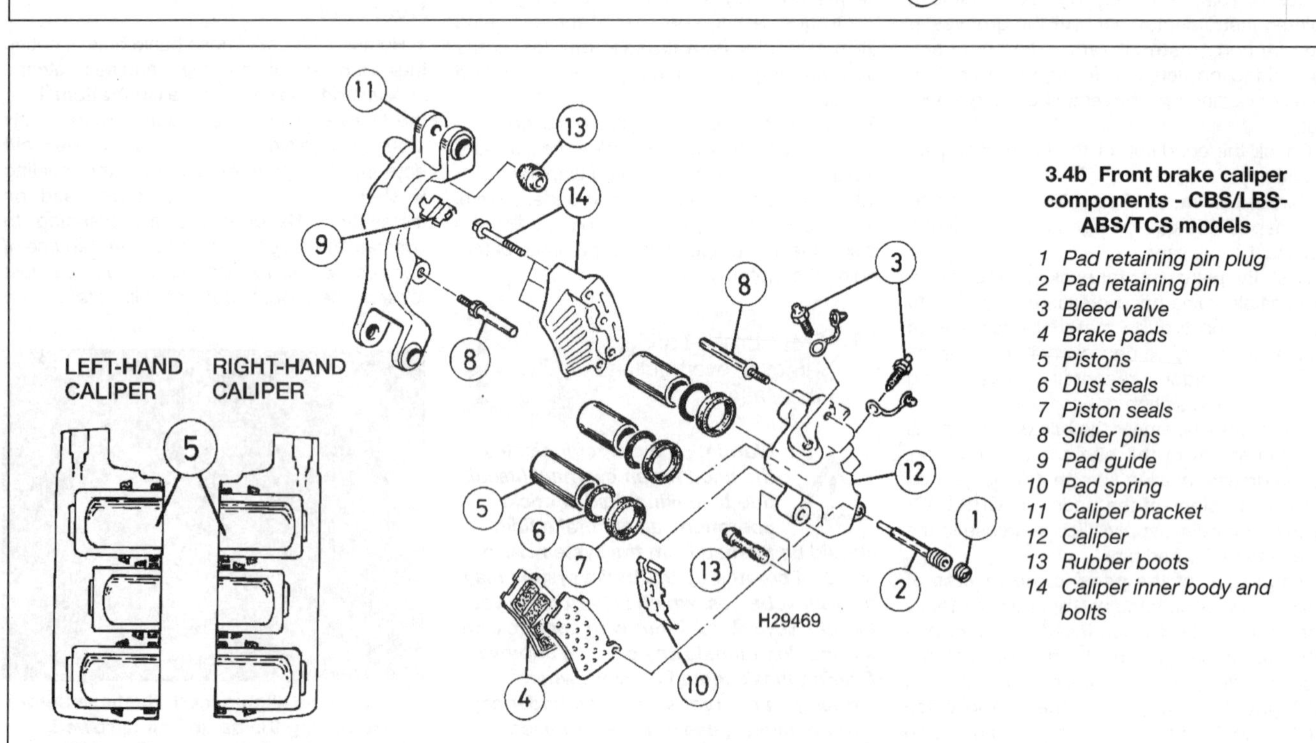

3.4b Front brake caliper components - CBS/LBS-ABS/TCS models

1 *Pad retaining pin plug*
2 *Pad retaining pin*
3 *Bleed valve*
4 *Brake pads*
5 *Pistons*
6 *Dust seals*
7 *Piston seals*
8 *Slider pins*
9 *Pad guide*
10 *Pad spring*
11 *Caliper bracket*
12 *Caliper*
13 *Rubber boots*
14 *Caliper inner body and bolts*

3.7 Remove the dust seal with a plastic or wooden tool (a pencil works well) to avoid damage to the bore and seal groove

3.17 Slide the caliper onto the disc . . .

3.18 . . . and tighten the mounting bolts to the specified torque setting

5 On CBS/LBS-ABS/TCS models, separate the caliper and caliper bracket, then unscrew the bolts securing the caliper inner body to the main body and separate them.
6 Remove the pistons from the caliper body, either by pumping them out by operating the front brake lever until the pistons are displaced, or by forcing them out using compressed air. Mark each piston head and caliper body with a felt marker to ensure that the pistons can be matched to their original bores on reassembly. If the compressed air method is used, place a wad of rag between the pistons and the caliper to act as a cushion, then use compressed air directed into the fluid inlet to force the pistons out of the body. Use only low pressure to ease the pistons out and make sure both pistons are displaced at the same time. If the air pressure is too high and the pistons are forced out, the caliper and/or pistons may be damaged.

Warning: Never place your fingers in front of the pistons in an attempt to catch or protect them when applying compressed air, as serious injury could result.

7 Using a wooden or plastic tool, remove the dust seals from the caliper bores. Discard them as new ones must be used on installation. If a metal tool is being used, take great care not to damage the caliper bores **(see illustration)**.
8 Remove and discard the piston seals in the same way. **Note:** *The piston seals on certain models may have chamfered edges - note their direction of fitting as they are removed from the caliper bores.*
9 Clean the pistons and bores with denatured alcohol, clean brake fluid or brake system cleaner. If compressed air is available, use it to dry the parts thoroughly (make sure it's filtered and unlubricated).
Caution: Do not, under any circumstances, use a petroleum-based solvent to clean brake parts.
10 Inspect the caliper bores and pistons for signs of corrosion, nicks and burrs and loss of plating. If surface defects are present, the caliper assembly must be replaced. If the necessary measuring equipment is available, compare the dimensions of the pistons and bores to those given in the Specifications Section of this Chapter, replacing any component that is worn beyond the service limit. If the caliper is in bad shape the master cylinder should also be checked.
11 Check that the caliper body is able to slide freely on the slider pins. If seized due to corrosion, separate the caliper and bracket and clean off all traces of corrosion and hardened grease. Apply a smear of copper or silicone based grease to the slider pins and reassemble the two components. Replace the rubber boots if they are damaged or deteriorated.
12 Lubricate the new piston seals with clean brake fluid and install them in their grooves in the caliper bores. Where the piston seals have chamfered edges, ensure that they are installed in the correct direction **(see illustration 3.4b)**. Note that on CBS/LBS-ABS/TCS models, different sizes of bore and piston are used (see Specifications), and care must therefore be taken to ensure that the correct size seals are fitted to the correct bores. The same applies when fitting the new dust seals and pistons.
13 Lubricate the new dust seals with clean brake fluid and install them in their grooves in the caliper bores.
14 Lubricate the pistons with clean brake fluid and install them closed-end first into the caliper bores. Using your thumbs, push the pistons all the way in, making sure they enter the bore squarely.
15 On CBS/LBS-ABS/TCS models, install the caliper inner body and tighten the bolts to the torque setting specified at the beginning of the Chapter.

Installation

16 Make sure that the pad spring and pad guide are correctly fitted, then install the brake pads (see Section 2).
17 On CBS/LBS-ABS/TCS models, apply grease to the caliper bracket pivot points. Install the caliper on the brake disc making sure the pads sit squarely either side of the disc **(see illustration)**.
18 Install the caliper mounting bolts, and tighten them to the torque setting specified at the beginning of this Chapter **(see illustration)**. On Standard and ABS/TCS models, install the bolt with the longer threads in the upper mounting. On CBS/LBS-ABS/TCS models, on the left-hand caliper, install the bolt with the longer threads in the lower mounting.
19 Connect the brake hose(s) to the caliper, using new sealing washers on each side of the fitting. Align the hose(s) as noted on removal. Tighten the banjo bolt(s) to the torque setting specified at the beginning of the Chapter.
20 Fill the master cylinder reservoir with DOT 4 brake fluid (see *Daily (pre-ride) checks*) and bleed the hydraulic system as described in Section 10.
21 Check for leaks and thoroughly test the operation of the brake before riding the motorcycle.

4 Brake discs (front and rear) - inspection, removal and installation

Inspection

1 Visually inspect the surface of the disc for score marks and other damage. Light scratches are normal after use and won't affect brake operation, but deep grooves and heavy score marks will reduce braking efficiency and accelerate pad wear. If a disc is badly grooved it must be machined or replaced.
2 To check disc runout, position the bike on its centrestand and support it so that the wheel is raised off the ground. Mount a dial gauge to a fork leg or on the swingarm, according to wheel, with the plunger on the gauge touching the surface of the disc about 10 mm (1/2 in) from the outer edge **(see illustration overleaf)**. Rotate the wheel and watch the indicator needle, comparing the reading with the limit listed in the Specifications at the beginning of the Chapter. If the runout is greater than the

4.2 Set up a dial gauge with the probe contacting the brake disc, then rotate the wheel to check for runout

4.3a The minimum disc thickness is marked on each disc

4.3b Using a micrometer to measure disc thickness

service limit, check the wheel bearings for play (see Chapter 1). If the bearings are worn, replace them (see Section 15) and repeat this check. If the disc runout is still excessive, it will have to be replaced, although machining by an engineer may be possible.

3 The disc must not be machined or allowed to wear down to a thickness less than the service limit as listed in this Chapter's Specifications and as marked on the disc itself. The thickness of the disc can be checked with a micrometer **(see illustrations)**. If the thickness of the disc is less than the service limit, it must be replaced.

Removal

4 Remove the wheel (see Section 13 or 14). ***Caution: Do not lay the wheel down and allow it to rest on the disc - the disc could become warped. Set the wheel on wood blocks so the disc doesn't support the weight of the wheel.***

5 Mark the relationship of the disc to the wheel, so it can be installed in the same position. Unscrew the disc retaining bolts, loosening them a little at a time in a criss-cross pattern to avoid distorting the disc, then remove the disc from the wheel **(see illustration)**. On the front wheel, each disc is marked with either an "R" for the right-hand disc, or an "L" for the left-hand disc. Honda recommend that the disc bolts are discarded on removal and new ones used on installation.

Installation

6 Install the disc on the wheel, on the front wheel making sure the disc marked "R" is on the right-hand side and the disc marked "L" is on the left, and on the rear wheel making sure the "OUTSIDE" mark is on the outside **(see illustration)**. Align the previously applied matchmarks (if you're reinstalling the original disc).

7 Install the bolts and tighten them in a criss-cross pattern evenly and progressively to the torque setting specified at the beginning of the Chapter. Clean off all grease from the brake disc(s) using acetone or brake system cleaner. If a new brake disc has been installed, remove any protective coating from its working surfaces.

8 Install the wheel (see Section 13 or 14).

9 Operate the brake lever or pedal several times to bring the pads into contact with the disc. Check the operation of the brakes carefully before riding the bike.

5 Front brake master cylinder - removal, overhaul and installation

1 If the master cylinder is leaking fluid, or if the lever does not produce a firm feel when the brake is applied, and bleeding the brakes does not help (see Section 11), and the hydraulic hoses are all in good condition, then master cylinder overhaul is recommended **(see illustration)**.

2 Before disassembling the master cylinder, read through the entire procedure and make sure that you have the correct rebuild kit. Also, you will need some new DOT 4 brake fluid, some clean rags and internal circlip pliers. **Note:** *To prevent damage to the paint from spilled brake fluid, always cover the fuel tank when working on the master cylinder.*

Caution: Disassembly, overhaul and reassembly of the brake master cylinder must be done in a spotlessly clean work area to avoid contamination and possible failure of the brake hydraulic system components.

4.5 Each disc is secured by six bolts (arrowed)

4.6 Make sure the disc is correctly installed according to its markings

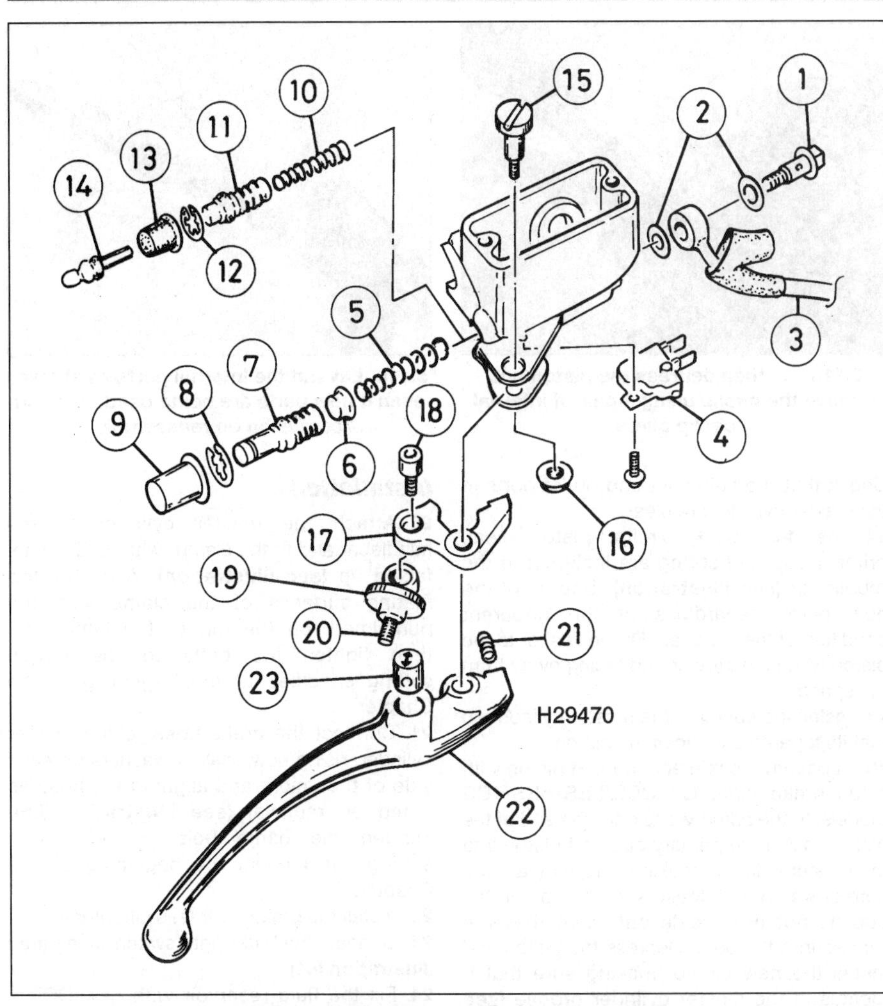

5.1 Front brake master cylinder components

1 Brake hose banjo bolt
2 Sealing washers
3 Brake hose
4 Brake light switch
5 Spring - std, ABS/TCS
6 Primary cup - std, ABS/TCS
7 Piston - std, ABS/TCS
8 Circlip - std, ABS/TCS
9 Rubber boot - std, ABS/TCS
10 Spring - CBS/LBS-ABS/TCS
11 Piston assembly - CBS/LBS-ABS/TCS
12 Circlip - CBS/LBS-ABS/TCS
13 Rubber boot - CBS/LBS-ABS/TCS
14 Pushrod - CBS/LBS-ABS/TCS
15 Brake lever pivot bolt
16 Brake lever pivot bolt locknut
17 Adjuster arm
18 Span adjuster bolt
19 Adjuster
20 Adjuster rod
21 Spring
22 Brake lever
23 Adjuster joint

5.3 Slacken the two reservoir cover screws

Removal

3 Loosen, but do not remove, the screws holding the reservoir cover in place **(see illustration)**.

4 Disconnect the electrical connectors from the brake light switch **(see illustration)**.

5 Remove the front brake lever (see Chapter 6).

6 Unscrew the brake hose banjo bolt and separate the hose from the master cylinder, noting its alignment **(see illustration)**. Discard the two sealing washers as they must be replaced with new ones. Wrap the end of the hose in a clean rag and suspend it in an upright position or bend it down carefully and place the open end in a clean container. The objective is to prevent excessive loss of brake fluid, fluid spills and system contamination.

7 Unscrew the master cylinder clamp bolts, then lift the master cylinder and reservoir away from the handlebar, noting how the top mating surfaces of the clamp align with the punch mark on the top of the handlebar **(see illustration)**.

Caution: Do not tip the master cylinder upside down or brake fluid will run out.

Overhaul

8 Remove the reservoir cover retaining screws and lift off the cover, the diaphragm plate and the rubber diaphragm. Drain the brake fluid from the reservoir into a suitable container. Wipe any remaining fluid out of the reservoir with a clean rag.

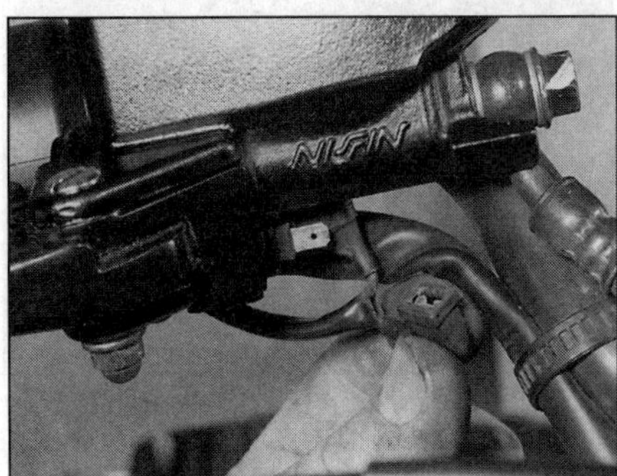

5.4 Disconnect the brake light switch wiring connectors

5.6 Note the alignment of the hose before removing the banjo bolt (arrowed)

5.7 Unscrew the clamp bolts and remove the master cylinder assembly

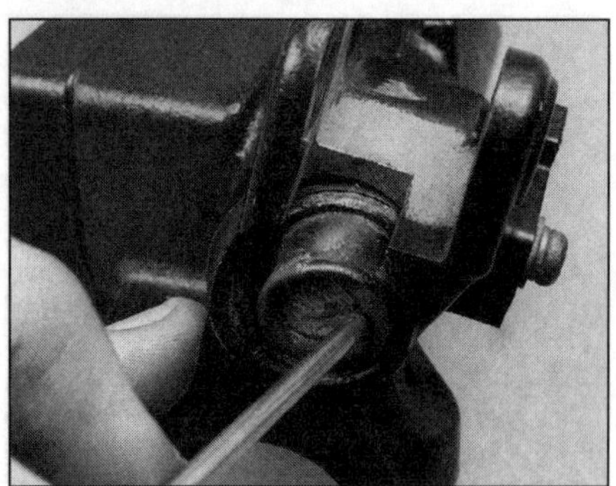

5.10 Remove the dust boot from the end of the master cylinder piston . . .

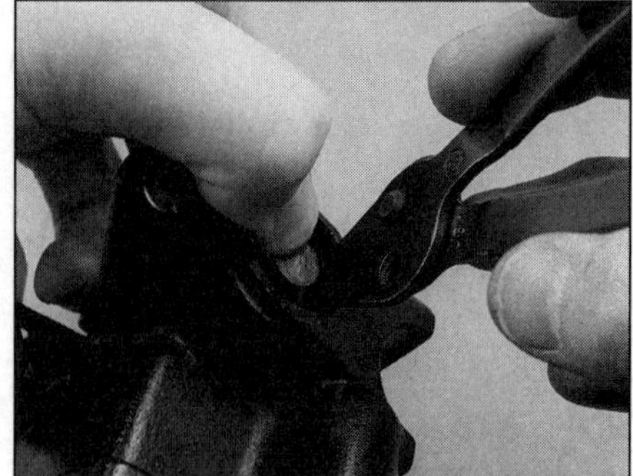

5.11a . . . then depress the piston and remove the circlip using a pair of internal circlip pliers

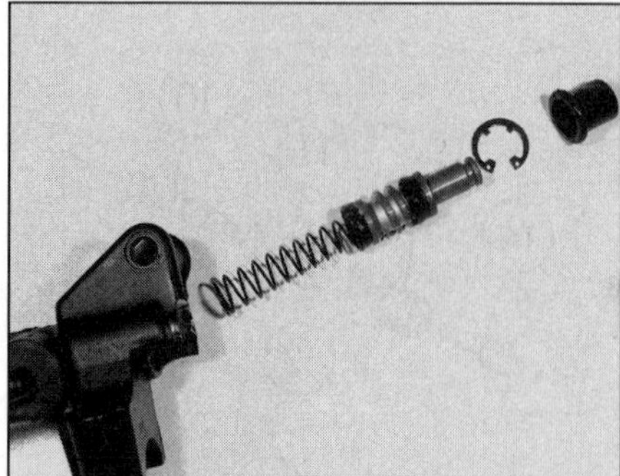

5.11b Lay out the internal parts as shown, even if new parts are being used, to avoid confusion on reassembly

9 Remove the screw securing the brake light switch to the bottom of the master cylinder and remove the switch.

10 Carefully remove the dust boot from the end of the piston **(see illustration)**. On CBS/LBS-ABS/TCS models, withdraw the pushrod.

11 Using circlip pliers, remove the circlip and slide out the piston assembly and the spring, noting how they fit. Lay the parts out in the proper order to prevent confusion during reassembly **(see illustrations)**.

12 Clean all parts with clean brake fluid or denatured alcohol. If compressed air is available, use it to dry the parts thoroughly (make sure it's filtered and unlubricated).

Caution: Do not, under any circumstances, use a petroleum-based solvent to clean brake parts.

13 Check the master cylinder bore for corrosion, scratches, nicks and score marks. If the necessary measuring equipment is available, compare the dimensions of the piston and bore to those given in the Specifications Section of this Chapter. If damage or wear is evident, the master cylinder must be replaced with a new one. If the master cylinder is in poor condition, then the caliper(s) should be checked as well. Check that the fluid inlet and outlet ports in the master cylinder are clear.

14 The dust boot, circlip, piston, seal, primary cup and spring are included in the rebuild kit **(see illustration)**. Use all of the new parts, regardless of the apparent condition of the old ones. Fit the seal onto the piston with its narrower end facing away from the spring.

15 Install the spring in the master cylinder so that its tapered end faces the piston.

16 Lubricate the primary cup and piston with clean brake fluid. On CBS/LBS-ABS/TCS models, fit the primary cup onto the end of the piston. Install the primary cup and piston into the master cylinder, making sure they are the correct way round. Make sure the lips on the cup do not turn inside out when they are slipped into the bore. Depress the piston and install the new circlip, making sure that it locates in the master cylinder groove **(see illustration 5.11a)**.

17 Install the rubber dust boot, making sure the lip is seated correctly in the piston groove **(see illustration 5.10)**. On CBS/LBS-ABS/TCS models, install the pushrod.

18 Install the brake light switch.

19 Inspect the reservoir cover rubber diaphragm and replace if damaged or deteriorated.

Installation

20 Attach the master cylinder to the handlebar and fit the clamp, with its UP mark facing up **(see illustration)**. Align the top mating surfaces of the clamp with the punchmark on the top of the handlebar, then tighten the bolts to the torque setting specified at the beginning of the Chapter.

21 Connect the brake hose to the master cylinder, using new sealing washers on each side of the union, and aligning the hose as noted on removal **(see illustration 5.6)**. Tighten the banjo bolt to the torque setting specified at the beginning of this Chapter.

22 Install the brake lever (see Chapter 6).

23 Connect the brake light switch wiring **(see illustration 5.4)**.

24 Fill the fluid reservoir with new DOT 4 brake fluid as described in *Daily (pre-ride) checks*. Refer to Section 10 of this Chapter and bleed the air from the system.

25 Fit the rubber diaphragm, making sure it is correctly seated, the diaphragm plate and the cover onto the master cylinder reservoir **(see illustration)**.

26 Check the operation of the front brake before riding the motorcycle.

5.14 Front brake master cylinder rebuild kit components

1 *Dust boot*
2 *Circlip*
3 *Piston*
4 *Seal*
5 *Primary cup*
6 *Spring*

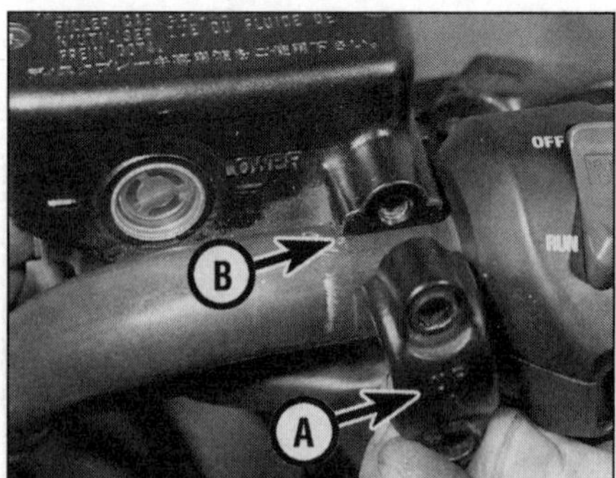

5.20 Make sure the UP mark (A) faces up, and align the top mating surfaces of the clamp with the punchmark on the handlebar (B)

5.25 Make sure the diaphragm is correctly seated, then fit the plate and cover

6 Secondary master cylinder, delay valve and proportional control valve - overhaul

Secondary master cylinder

Removal

1 Before disassembling the master cylinder, read through the entire procedure and make sure that you have the correct rebuild kit. Also, you will need some new DOT 4 brake fluid, some clean rags and internal circlip pliers. **Note:** *To prevent damage to the paint from spilled brake fluid, always cover the fuel tank when working on the master cylinder.*

Caution: Disassembly, overhaul and reassembly of the brake master cylinder must be done in a spotlessly clean work area to avoid contamination and possible failure of the brake hydraulic system components.

2 Remove the front mudguard (see Chapter 8).

3 Unscrew the brake hose banjo bolts, noting their alignment on the caliper, and separate the hoses from the caliper **(see illustration)**. Plug the hose ends or wrap a plastic bag tightly around them to minimise fluid loss and prevent dirt entering the system. Discard the sealing washers as new ones must be used on installation.

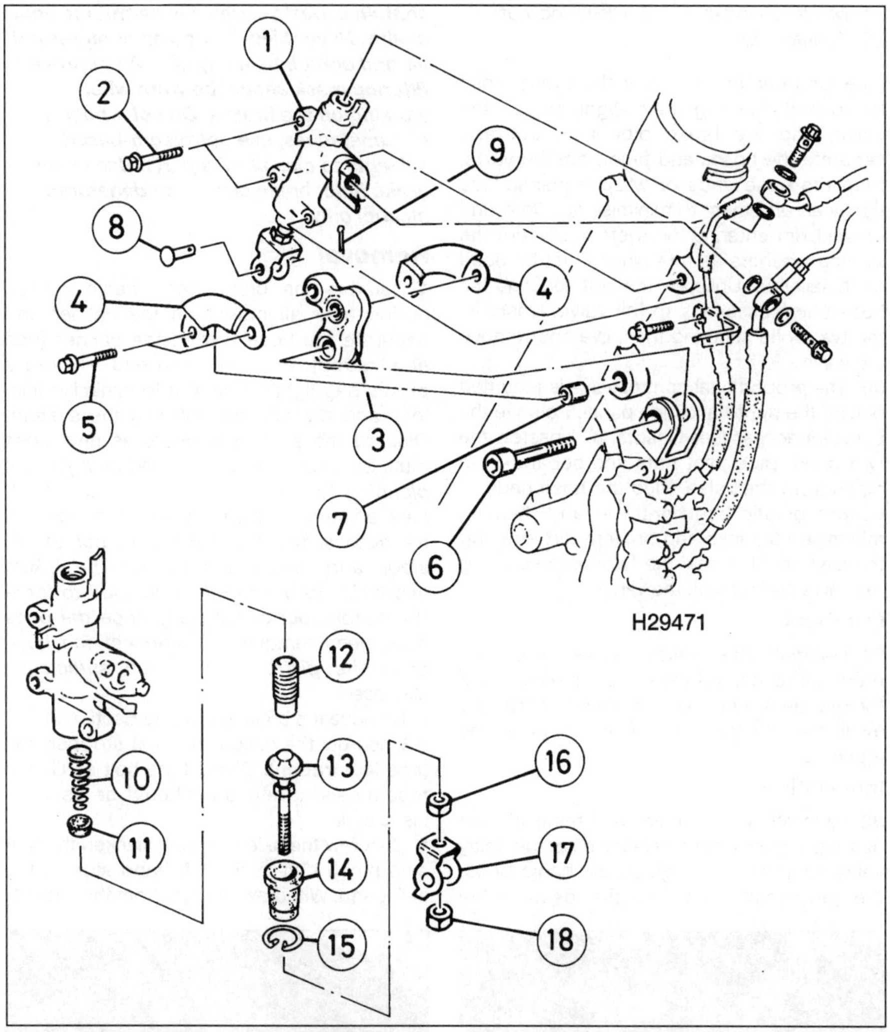

4 Unscrew the bolt securing the front caliper hose bracket to the secondary master cylinder, and pull the hose out of its guide.

5 Unscrew the bolts securing the linkage plates to the linkage arm and the fork slider and remove the plates, noting how they fit.

6 Unscrew the pivot bolt securing the top of the caliper bracket to the linkage arm.

7 Unscrew the bolts securing the secondary master cylinder, then remove the master cylinder and linkage arm. Remove the split pin from the clevis pin securing the linkage arm to the master cylinder pushrod. Withdraw the clevis pin and separate the arm from the pushrod. Discard the split pin as a new one must be used.

1
2
9
8
4
4
5
3
7
6
H29471
12
10
13
16
11
14
17
15
18

6.3 Secondary master cylinder components - CBS/LBS-ABS/TCS models

1 Secondary master cylinder
2 Secondary master cylinder bolts
3 Linkage arm
4 Linkage plates
5 Linkage plate bolts
6 Linkage arm to caliper bracket bolt
7 Inner sleeve
8 Clevis pin
9 Split pin
10 Spring
11 Primary cup
12 Piston
13 Pushrod
14 Rubber boot
15 Circlip
16 Clevis locknut
17 Clevis
18 Clevis nut

Overhaul

8 If necessary, slacken the clevis locknut, then unscrew the clevis with its nut and locknut and remove them from the pushrod.

9 Dislodge the rubber dust boot from the base of the master cylinder to reveal the pushrod retaining circlip.

10 Depress the pushrod and, using circlip pliers, remove the circlip. Slide out the piston assembly and spring. If they are difficult to remove, apply low pressure compressed air to the fluid outlet. Lay the parts out in the proper order to prevent confusion during reassembly.

11 Clean all of the parts with clean brake fluid or denatured alcohol.

Caution: Do not, under any circumstances, use a petroleum-based solvent to clean brake parts. If compressed air is available, use it to dry the parts thoroughly (make sure it's filtered and unlubricated).

12 Check the master cylinder bore for corrosion, scratches, nicks and score marks. If the necessary measuring equipment is available, compare the dimensions of the piston and bore to those given in the Specifications Section of this Chapter. If damage is evident, the master cylinder must be replaced with a new one. If the master cylinder is in poor condition, then the caliper should be checked as well.

13 The dust boot, circlip, piston assembly and spring are included in the rebuild kit. Use all of the new parts, regardless of the apparent condition of the old ones.

14 Install the spring in the master cylinder so that its tapered end faces the piston.

15 Lubricate the primary cup and piston with clean hydraulic fluid and install them into the master cylinder, making sure they are the correct way round. Make sure the lips on the cup seals do not turn inside out when they are slipped into the bore.

16 Install and depress the pushrod, then install a new circlip, making sure it is properly seated in the groove.

17 Install the rubber dust boot, making sure the lip is seated properly in the groove.

6.18 Withdraw the inner sleeve to examine the needle roller bearing

18 Withdraw the spacers from the linkage arm and lever out the dust seals. Thoroughly clean all components, removing all traces of dirt, corrosion and grease. Check the condition of the needle roller bearings in the linkage arm **(see illustration)**. Lubricate the bearings and the pivot bolts with grease and install the spacers

Installation

19 If removed, install the clevis locknut, the clevis and its nut onto the master cylinder pushrod end, but do not yet tighten the locknut. The distance between the centre of the clevis hole and the centre of the lower mounting hole on the master cylinder should be 57 mm **(see illustration)**. Turn the pushrod as required until the distance is as specified, then tighten the clevis locknut securely.

20 Fit the linkage arm into the clevis and insert the clevis pin. Secure the clevis pin using a new split pin.

21 Install the secondary master cylinder, noting that the bolt with the longer threads fits in the upper mounting. Tighten the bolts to the torque setting specified at the beginning of the Chapter.

22 Position the linkage arm in the top of the front caliper bracket. Install the pivot bolt and tighten it to the specified torque setting.

23 Install the linkage plates and tighten their bolts to the specified torque setting.

24 Connect the brake hose banjo bolts to the master cylinder, using new sealing washers on each side of the banjo unions. Ensure that the hoses are positioned so that they butt against the lugs. Tighten the banjo bolts to the specified torque setting.

25 Position the front caliper hose into its guide on the secondary master cylinder and secure the triangular bracket with its bolt.

26 Install the front mudguard (see Chapter 8).

27 Bleed the system following the procedure in Section 10.

28 Check the operation of the brake carefully before riding the motorcycle.

Delay valve and proportional control valve

Removal

29 The delay valve is mounted on the front fork. Remove the front mudguard for access

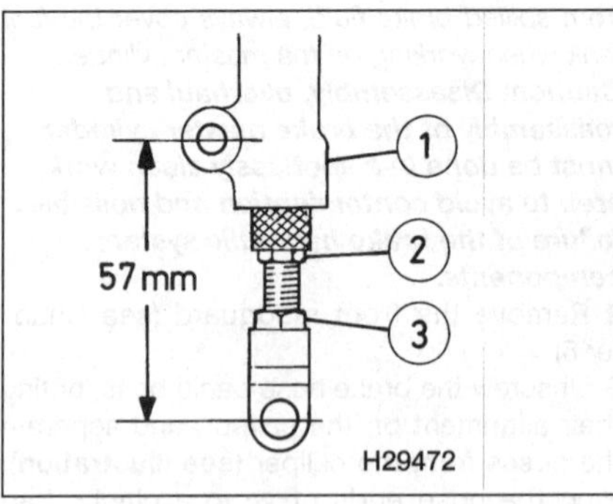

6.19 Secondary master cylinder pushrod length

1 *Master cylinder*
2 *Pushrod nut*
3 *Clevis locknut*

(see Chapter 8). Unscrew the brake hose banjo bolts, noting their alignment on the valve, and the brake pipe joint nut and separate the hoses and pipe from the valve. Plug the hose ends or wrap a plastic bag tightly around them to minimise fluid loss and prevent dirt entering the system. Discard the sealing washers as new ones must be used on installation. Unscrew the bolt securing the hose union assembly to the valve. Unscrew the two bolts securing the valve and remove the valve.

30 The proportional control valve is mounted behind the right-hand side panel. Remove the panel for access (see Chapter 8). Unscrew the two brake pipe joint nuts and separate the pipes from the valve. Plug the hose ends or wrap a plastic bag tightly around them to minimise fluid loss and prevent dirt entering the system. Unscrew the two bolts securing the valve and remove the valve.

Overhaul

31 Neither the delay valve nor the proportional control valve can be dismantled for overhaul, and no component parts are available. If the valve fails, it must be replaced.

Installation

32 Installation is the reverse of removal. Use new sealing washers on each side of the delay valve banjo unions. Tighten the banjo bolts, the pipe joint nuts and the delay valve mounting bolts to the torque settings specified at the beginning of the Chapter. Bleed the hydraulic system as described in Section 10.

7 Rear brake caliper - removal, overhaul and installation

Warning: *If a caliper indicates the need for an overhaul (usually due to leaking fluid or sticky operation), all old brake fluid should be flushed from the system. Also, the dust created by the brake system may contain asbestos, which is harmful to your health. Never blow it out with compressed air and don't inhale any of it. An approved filtering mask should be worn when working on the brakes. Do not, under any circumstances, use petroleum-based solvents to clean brake parts. Use clean brake fluid, brake cleaner or denatured alcohol only.*

Removal

1 Remove the brake hose banjo bolt(s), noting their alignment on the caliper and separate the hose(s) from the caliper **(see illustration)**. Plug the hose end or wrap a plastic bag tightly around it to minimise fluid loss and prevent dirt entering the system. Discard the sealing washers as new ones must be used on installation. **Note:** *If you are planning to overhaul the caliper and don't have a source of compressed air to blow out the pistons, just loosen the banjo bolt at this stage and retighten it lightly. The bike's hydraulic system can then be used to force the pistons out of the body once the pads have been removed. Disconnect the hose once the pistons have been sufficiently displaced.*

2 Remove the brake pads (see Section 2).

3 Unscrew the caliper bracket stopper bolt **(see illustration)**. Discard the bolt as Honda recommend a new one should be used on installation.

4 Unscrew the axle nut, then slacken the rear axle pinch bolt in the left-hand side of the swingarm. Withdraw the axle from the left until

7.1 Note the alignment of the hose before removing the banjo bolt (arrowed)

7.3 Remove the caliper bracket stopper bolt (arrowed)

7.4a Unscrew the axle nut (arrowed) . . .

7.4b . . . and slacken the axle pinch bolt (arrowed)

7.4c Withdraw the axle far enough for the caliper bracket to be removed

it clears the caliper bracket, then slide the caliper with its bracket off the disc **(see illustrations)**. Install the axle back into the wheel as a safety measure, but there is no need to tighten the nut or the pinch bolt. Remove the pad spring from the caliper and the pad guide from the bracket, noting how they fit.

Overhaul

5 Clean the exterior of the caliper with denatured alcohol or brake system cleaner **(see illustrations)**.

6 On CBS/LBS-ABS/TCS models, separate the caliper and caliper bracket, then unscrew the bolts securing the caliper inner body to the main body and separate them.

7 Remove the pistons from the caliper body, either by pumping them out by operating the front brake lever until the pistons are displaced, or by forcing them out using compressed air. Mark each piston head and caliper body with a felt marker to ensure that the pistons can be matched to their original

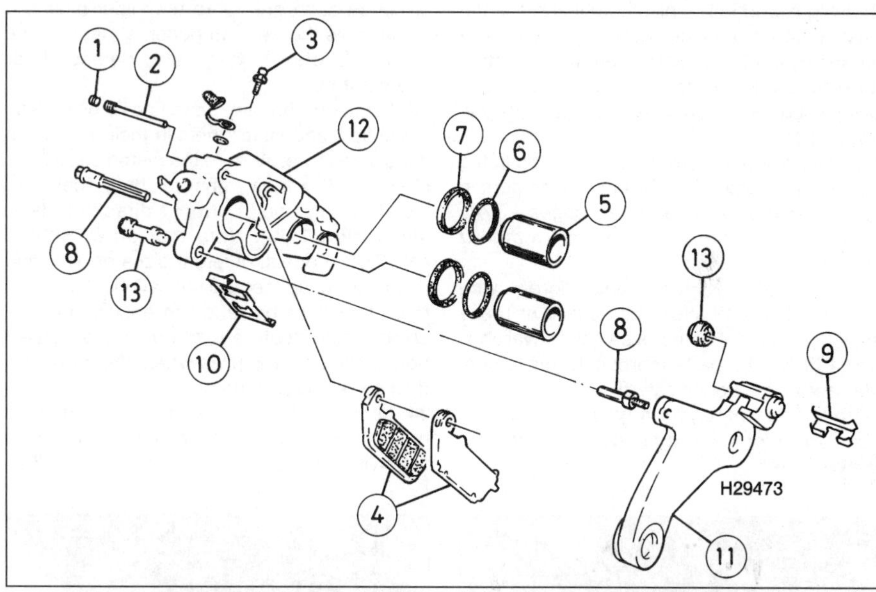

7.5a Rear brake caliper components - standard and ABS/TCS models

1 *Pad retaining pin plug*
2 *Pad retaining pin*
3 *Bleed valve*
4 *Brake pads*
5 *Pistons*
6 *Dust seals*
7 *Piston seals*
8 *Slider pins*
9 *Pad guide*
10 *Pad spring*
11 *Caliper bracket*
12 *Caliper*
13 *Rubber boots*

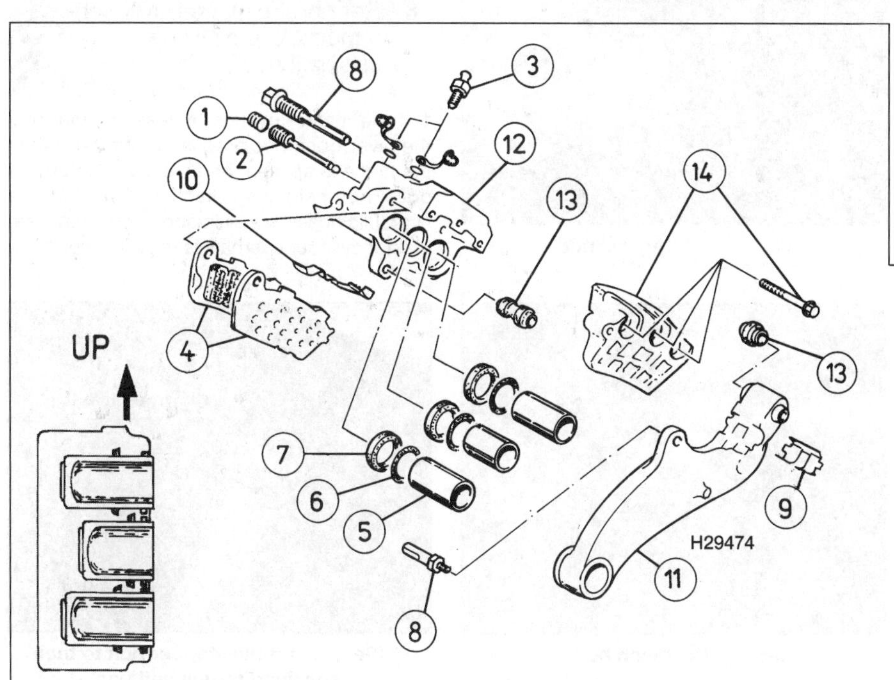

7.5b Rear brake caliper components - CBS/LBS-ABS/TCS models

1 *Pad retaining pin plug*
2 *Pad retaining pin*
3 *Bleed valves*
4 *Brake pads*
5 *Pistons*
6 *Dust seals*
7 *Piston seals*
8 *Slider pins*
9 *Pad guide*
10 *Pad spring*
11 *Caliper bracket*
12 *Caliper*
13 *Rubber boots*
14 *Caliper inner body*

bores on reassembly. If the compressed air method is used, place a wad of rag between the pistons and the caliper to act as a cushion, then use compressed air directed into the fluid inlet to force the pistons out of the body. Use only low pressure to ease the pistons out and make sure both pistons are displaced at the same time. If the air pressure is too high and the pistons are forced out, the caliper and/or pistons may be damaged.

Warning: Never place your fingers in front of the pistons in an attempt to catch or protect them when applying compressed air, as serious injury could result.

8 Using a wooden or plastic tool, remove the dust seals from the caliper bores **(see illustration 3.7)**. Discard them as new ones must be used on installation. If a metal tool is being used, take great care not to damage the caliper bores.

9 Remove and discard the piston seals in the same way. **Note:** *The piston seals on certain models may have chamfered edges - note their direction of fitting as they are removed from the caliper bores.*

10 Clean the pistons and bores with denatured alcohol, clean brake fluid or brake system cleaner. If compressed air is available, use it to dry the parts thoroughly (make sure it's filtered and unlubricated).

Caution: Do not, under any circumstances, use a petroleum-based solvent to clean brake parts.

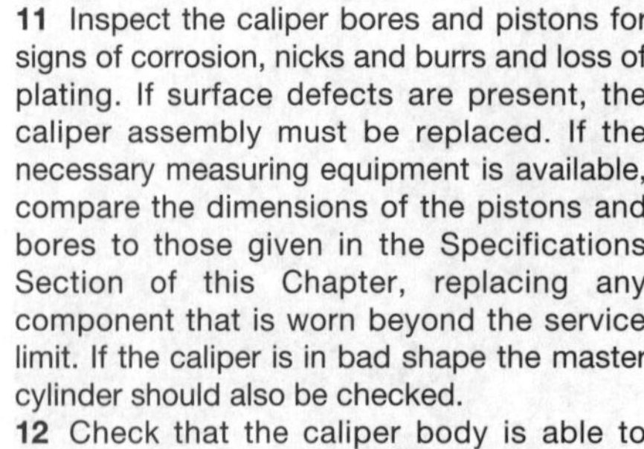

11 Inspect the caliper bores and pistons for signs of corrosion, nicks and burrs and loss of plating. If surface defects are present, the caliper assembly must be replaced. If the necessary measuring equipment is available, compare the dimensions of the pistons and bores to those given in the Specifications Section of this Chapter, replacing any component that is worn beyond the service limit. If the caliper is in bad shape the master cylinder should also be checked.

12 Check that the caliper body is able to slide freely on the slider pins. If seized due to corrosion, separate the caliper and bracket and clean off all traces of corrosion and hardened grease. Apply a smear of copper or silicone based grease to the slider pins and reassemble the two components. Replace the rubber boots if they are damaged or deteriorated.

13 Lubricate the new piston seals with clean brake fluid and install them in their grooves in the caliper bores. Where the piston seals have chamfered edges, ensure that they are installed in the correct direction **(see illustration 7.5b)**. Note that on CBS/LBS-ABS/TCS models, different sizes of bore and piston are used (see Specifications), and care must therefore be taken to ensure that the correct size seals are fitted to the correct bores. The same applies when fitting the new dust seals and pistons.

14 Lubricate the new dust seals with clean brake fluid and install them in their grooves in the caliper bores.

15 Lubricate the pistons with clean brake fluid and install them closed-end first into the caliper bores. Using your thumbs, push the pistons all the way in, making sure they enter the bore squarely.

16 On CBS/LBS-ABS/TCS models, install the caliper inner body and tighten the bolts to the torque setting specified at the beginning of the Chapter.

Installation

17 Make sure that the pad spring and pad guide are correctly fitted, then install the brake pads (see Section 2).

18 Withdraw the axle from the rear wheel. Install the caliper on the brake disc making sure the pads sit squarely either side of the disc, then slide the axle back into the wheel, making sure it passes through the caliper bracket **(see illustration 7.4c)**.

19 Install the caliper stopper bolt, then fit the axle nut and tighten it to the torque setting specified at the beginning of this Chapter. Also tighten the axle pinch bolt and the caliper stopper bolt to the specified torque settings **(see illustrations)**.

20 Connect the brake hose(s) to the caliper, using new sealing washers on each side of the fitting. Align the hose(s) as noted on removal **(see illustration 7.1)**. Tighten the banjo bolt(s) to the torque setting specified at the beginning of the Chapter.

21 Fill the master cylinder reservoir with DOT 4 brake fluid (see *Daily (pre-ride) checks*) and bleed the hydraulic system as described in Section 10.

22 Check for leaks and thoroughly test the operation of the brake before riding the motorcycle.

8 Rear brake master cylinder - removal, overhaul and installation

1 If the master cylinder is leaking fluid, or if the lever does not produce a firm feel when the brake is applied, and bleeding the brakes does not help (see Section 10), and the hydraulic hoses are all in good condition, then master cylinder overhaul is recommended.

7.19a Fit the stopper bolt . . .

7.19b . . . and the axle nut . . .

7.19c . . . then tighten the nut . . .

7.19d . . . the pinch bolt . . .

7.19e . . . and the stopper bolt to their specified torque settings

8.4 Disconnect the brake light switch wiring connector

8.5 Remove the bolt (arrowed) to free the bracket

8.6a The reservoir is secured by a single bolt (arrowed)

2 Before disassembling the master cylinder, read through the entire procedure and make sure that you have the correct rebuild kit. Also, you will need some new DOT 4 brake fluid, some clean rags and internal circlip pliers. **Note:** *To prevent damage to the paint from spilled brake fluid, always cover the surrounding components when working on the master cylinder.*

Caution: Disassembly, overhaul and reassembly of the brake master cylinder must be done in a spotlessly clean work area to avoid contamination and possible failure of the brake hydraulic system components.

Removal

3 Remove the right-hand side panel (see Chapter 8).

4 Unscrew the three screws securing the swingarm right-hand pivot cover and remove the cover. Disconnect the brake light switch wiring connector **(see illustration)**.

5 On ABS/TCS models, loosen the wiring harness and remove the modulator hose bracket bolt **(see illustration)**.

6 Unscrew the bolt securing the reservoir to the frame, then remove the reservoir cover and pour the fluid into a container. Separate the fluid reservoir hose from the elbow on the master cylinder by releasing the hose clamp **(see illustrations)**.

8.6b Release the clamp (arrowed) and detach the hose

8.8 The bracket is secured by five bolts (arrowed)

7 On CBS/LBS-ABS/TCS models, unscrew the three bolts securing the modulator.

8 Unscrew the five bolts securing the footrest bracket **(see illustration)**. Draw the bracket away from the bike, noting that the rear brake master cylinder and brake light switch are still connected.

9 Unscrew the brake hose banjo bolt and separate the brake hose from the master cylinder, noting its alignment **(see illustration)**. Discard the two sealing washers as they must be replaced with new ones. Wrap the end of the hose in a clean rag and suspend the hose in an upright position or bend it down carefully and place the open end in a clean container. The objective is to prevent excessive loss of brake fluid, fluid spills and system contamination.

10 Remove the split pin from the clevis pin securing the brake pedal to the master cylinder pushrod **(see illustration)**. Withdraw the clevis pin and separate the pedal from the pushrod. Discard the split pin as a new one must be used.

11 Unscrew the two bolts securing the master cylinder to the bracket **(see illustration)**.

Overhaul

12 If necessary, slacken the clevis locknut, then drive out the spring pin securing the pushrod in the clevis and remove the

8.9 Note the alignment of the hose before removing the banjo bolt (arrowed)

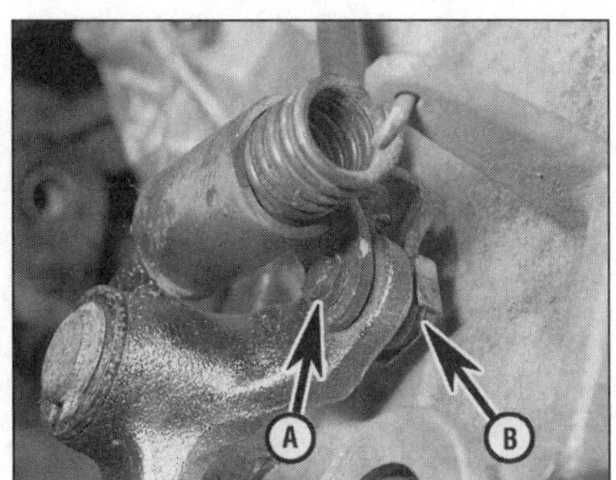

8.10 Remove the split pin (A) and withdraw the clevis pin (B)

8.11 The master cylinder is secured to the bracket by two bolts (arrowed)

7

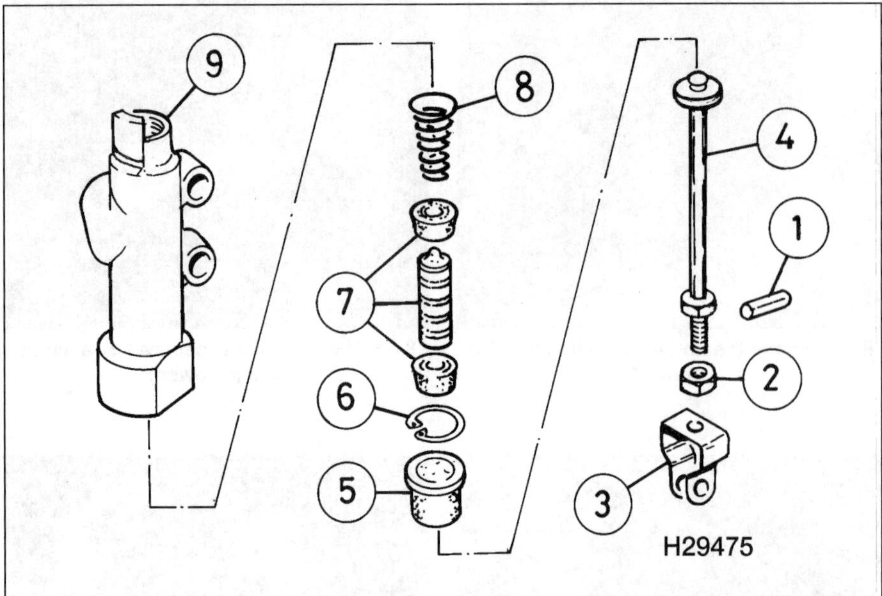

8.12 Rear master cylinder components

1 *Spring pin*
2 *Locknut*
3 *Clevis*
4 *Pushrod*
5 *Rubber boot*
6 *Circlip*
7 *Piston and cup assembly*
8 *Spring*
9 *Master cylinder*

clevis from the pushrod **(see illustration)**. Discard the spring pin as a new one must be used.

13 Dislodge the rubber dust boot from the base of the master cylinder to reveal the pushrod retaining circlip.

14 Depress the pushrod and, using circlip pliers, remove the circlip. Slide out the piston and cup assembly and spring. If they are difficult to remove, apply low pressure compressed air to the fluid outlet. Lay the parts out in the proper order to prevent confusion during reassembly.

15 Clean all of the parts with clean brake fluid or denatured alcohol.

Caution: Do not, under any circumstances, use a petroleum-based solvent to clean brake parts. If compressed air is available, use it to dry the parts thoroughly (make sure it's filtered and unlubricated).

16 Check the master cylinder bore for corrosion, scratches, nicks and score marks. If the necessary measuring equipment is available, compare the dimensions of the piston and bore to those given in the Specifications Section of this Chapter. If damage is evident, the master cylinder must be replaced with a new one. If the master cylinder is in poor condition, then the caliper should be checked as well.

17 If required, unscrew the fluid reservoir hose union screw and detach the elbow from the master cylinder. Discard the O-ring as a new one must be used. Inspect the reservoir hose for cracks or splits and replace if necessary.

18 The dust boot, circlip, piston and cup assembly and spring are included in the rebuild kit. Use all of the new parts, regardless of the apparent condition of the old ones.

19 Install the spring in the master cylinder so that its tapered end faces the piston.

20 Lubricate the piston and cups with clean hydraulic fluid and install the assembly into the master cylinder, making sure all the components are the correct way round. Make sure the lips on the cup seals do not turn inside out when they are slipped into the bore.

21 Install and depress the pushrod, then install a new circlip, making sure it is properly seated in the groove.

22 Install the rubber dust boot, making sure the lip is seated properly in the groove.

23 If removed, fit a new O-ring to the fluid reservoir hose union, then install the union onto the master cylinder and secure it with its screw.

Installation

24 If removed, install the clevis locknut and the clevis onto the master cylinder pushrod end and secure them using a new spring pin. Tighten the clevis locknut securely.

25 Install the master cylinder onto the footrest bracket and tighten its mounting bolts securely **(see illustration 8.11)**.

26 Align the brake pedal with the master cylinder pushrod clevis, then slide in the clevis pin and secure it using a new split pin **(see illustration 8.10)**.

27 Connect the brake hose banjo bolt to the master cylinder, using a new sealing washer on each side of the banjo union. Ensure that the hose is positioned so that it butts against the lug and tighten the banjo bolt to the specified torque setting **(see illustration 8.9)**.

28 Install the footrest bracket and tighten its bolts to the torque settings specified at the beginning of the Chapter **(see illustration 8.8)**.

29 Secure the fluid reservoir to the frame with its retaining bolt **(see illustration 8.6a)**. Ensure that the hose is correctly routed behind the frame tube, then connect it to the union on the master cylinder and secure it with the clamp **(see illustration 8.6b)**. Check that the hose is secure and clamped at the reservoir end as well. If the clamps have weakened, use new ones.

30 On CBS/LBS-ABS/TCS models, install the three bolts securing the modulator.

31 Install all other disturbed components in the reverse order of removal.

32 Fill the fluid reservoir with new DOT 4 brake fluid (see *Daily (pre-ride) checks*) and bleed the system following the procedure in Section 10.

33 Check the operation of the brake carefully before riding the motorcycle.

9 **Brake hoses, pipes and unions** - inspection and replacement

Inspection

1 Brake hose and pipe condition should be checked regularly and the hoses replaced at the specified interval (see Chapter 1).

2 Twist and flex the rubber hoses while looking for cracks, bulges and leaking fluid **(see illustration)**. Check extra carefully around the areas where the hoses connect with the banjo fittings, as these are common areas for hose failure.

3 Inspect the metal brake pipes and the banjo union fittings connected to the brake hoses. If the fittings are rusted, scratched or cracked, replace them.

Replacement

4 The brake hoses have banjo union fittings on each end and the brake pipes have joint nuts. Cover the surrounding area with plenty of rags and unscrew the banjo bolt or joint nut at each end of the hose or pipe, noting its alignment. Free the hose or pipe from any

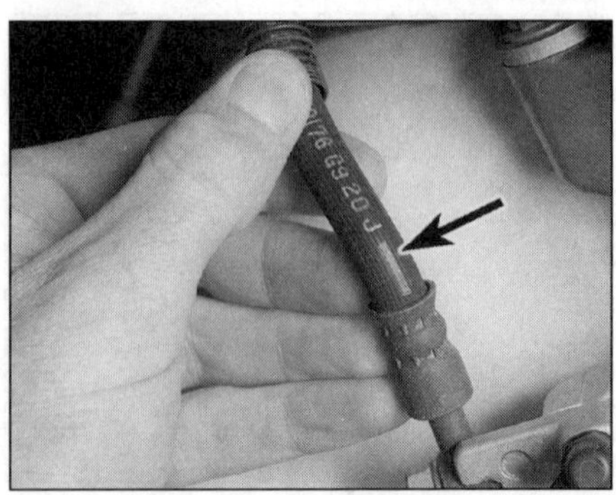

9.2 Flex the brake hoses and check for cracks, bulges and leaking fluid

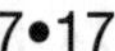

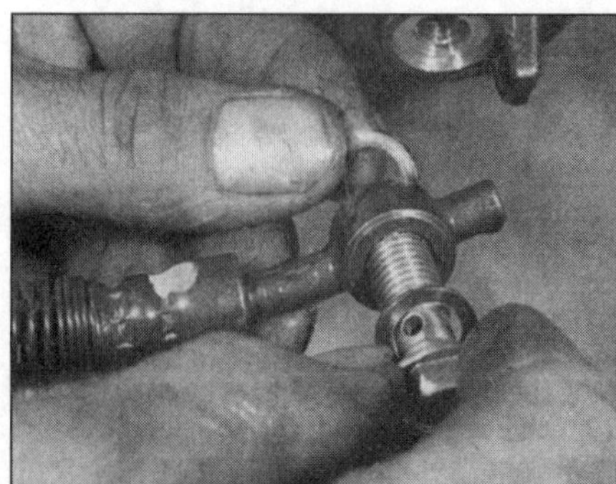

9.4 Remove the banjo bolt and separate the hose from the caliper; there is a sealing washer on each side of the fitting

10.6a Brake caliper bleed valve

10.6b To bleed the brakes, you need a spanner, a short section of clear tubing, and a clear container half-filled with brake fluid

clips or guides and remove it. Discard the sealing washers on the hose banjo unions **(see illustration)**.

5 Position the new hose or pipe, making sure it isn't twisted or otherwise strained, and abut the tab on the hose union with the lug on the component casting, where present. Otherwise align the hose or pipe as noted on removal. Install the hose banjo bolts using new sealing washers on both sides of the unions. Tighten the banjo bolts and joint nuts to the torque settings specified at the beginning of this Chapter. Make sure the hoses and pipes are correctly aligned and routed clear of all moving components.

6 Flush the old brake fluid from the system, refill with new DOT 4 brake fluid (see *Daily (pre-ride) checks*) and bleed the air from the system (see Section 10). Check the operation of the brakes carefully before riding the motorcycle.

10 Brake system - bleeding

1 Bleeding the brakes is simply the process of removing all the air bubbles from the brake fluid reservoirs, the hoses and the brake calipers. Bleeding is necessary whenever a brake system hydraulic connection is loosened, when a component or hose is replaced, or when the master cylinder or caliper is overhauled. Leaks in the system may also allow air to enter, but leaking brake fluid will reveal their presence and warn you of the need for repair.

Standard and ABS/TCS models

2 To bleed the brakes, you will need some new DOT 4 brake fluid, a length of clear vinyl or plastic tubing, a small container partially filled with clean brake fluid, some rags and a spanner to fit the brake caliper bleed valves.

3 Cover the fuel tank and other painted components to prevent damage in the event that brake fluid is spilled.

4 If bleeding the rear brake, remove the right-hand pannier (see Chapter 8) for access to the fluid reservoir.

5 Remove the reservoir cover, diaphragm plate (where fitted) and diaphragm and slowly pump the brake lever or pedal a few times, until no air bubbles can be seen floating up from the holes in the bottom of the reservoir. Doing this bleeds the air from the master cylinder end of the line. Loosely refit the reservoir cover.

6 Pull the dust cap off the bleed valve. Attach one end of the clear vinyl or plastic tubing to the bleed valve and submerge the other end in the brake fluid in the container **(see illustrations)**.

7 Remove the reservoir cover and check the fluid level. Do not allow the fluid level to drop below the lower mark during the bleeding process.

8 Carefully pump the brake lever or pedal three or four times and hold it in (front) or down (rear) while opening the caliper bleed valve. When the valve is opened, brake fluid will flow out of the caliper into the clear tubing and the lever will move toward the handlebar or the pedal will move down.

9 Retighten the bleed valve, then release the brake lever or pedal gradually. Repeat the process until no air bubbles are visible in the brake fluid leaving the caliper and the lever or pedal is firm when applied. On completion, disconnect the bleeding equipment, then tighten the bleed valve to the torque setting specified at the beginning of the Chapter and install the dust cap.

10 Install the diaphragm and cover assembly, wipe up any spilled brake fluid and check the entire system for leaks.

HAYNES HiNT ***If it's not possible to produce a firm feel to the lever or pedal the fluid my be aerated. Let the brake fluid in the system stabilise for a few hours and then repeat the procedure when the tiny bubbles in the system have settled out.***

CBS/LBS-ABS/TCS models

Note: *Honda recommend using a commercially available brake bleeding tool. If bleeding the system using the conventional method does not work sufficiently well, it is advisable to obtain a bleeder and repeat the procedure detailed below, following the manufacturers instructions for using the tool. If the tool is not available, take the machine to a Honda dealer.*

11 The principle involved in bleeding the brakes on these models is the same as on standard models, and the appropriate steps detailed above for the standard models should be followed. The difference is that the order in which the components are bled is important.

12 The brake system should be bled in the following order, using the front brake lever or rear brake pedal as instructed:

1. *Left front caliper - upper bleed valve - front brake lever*
2. *Right front caliper - upper bleed valve - front brake lever*
3. *Left front caliper - lower bleed valve - rear brake pedal*
4. *Right front caliper - lower bleed valve - rear brake pedal*
5. *Rear caliper - front bleed valve - rear brake pedal*
6. *Rear caliper - rear bleed valve - rear brake pedal*

11 Wheels - inspection and repair

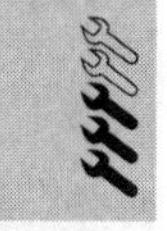

1 In order to carry out a proper inspection of the wheels, it is necessary to support the bike upright so that the wheel being inspected is raised off the ground. Position the motorcycle on its centrestand or an auxiliary stand. Clean the wheels thoroughly to remove mud and dirt that may interfere with the inspection procedure or mask defects. Make a general check of the wheels (see Chapter 1) and tyres (see *Daily (pre-ride) checks*).

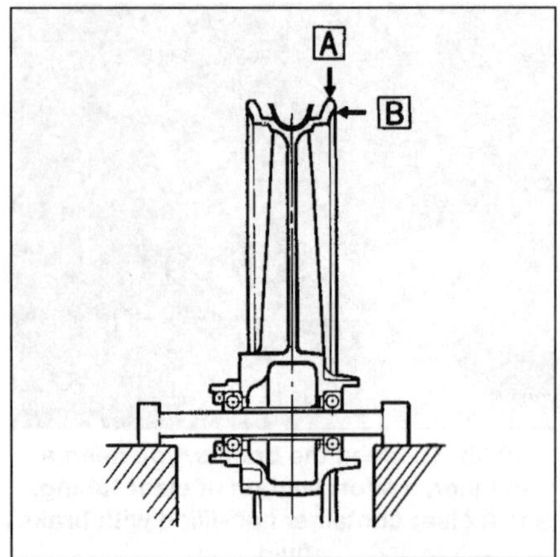

11.2 Check the wheel for radial (out-of-round) runout (A) and axial (side-to-side) runout (B)

2 Attach a dial gauge to the fork slider or the swingarm and position its stem against the side of the rim. Spin the wheel slowly and check the axial (side-to-side) runout of the rim. In order to accurately check radial (out-of-round) runout with the dial gauge, the wheel would have to be removed from the machine, and the tyre from the wheel. With the axle clamped in a vice and the dial gauge positioned on the top of the rim, the wheel can be rotated to check the runout **(see illustration)**.

3 An easier, though slightly less accurate, method is to attach a stiff wire pointer to the fork slider or the swingarm and position the end a fraction of an inch from the wheel (where the wheel and tyre join). If the wheel is true, the distance from the pointer to the rim will be constant as the wheel is rotated. **Note:** *If wheel runout is excessive, check the wheel bearings very carefully before replacing the wheel.*

4 The wheels should also be visually inspected for cracks, flat spots on the rim and other damage. Look very closely for dents in the area where the tyre bead contacts the rim. Dents in this area may prevent complete sealing of the tyre against the rim, which leads to deflation of the tyre over a period of time. If damage is evident, or if runout in either direction is excessive, the wheel will have to be replaced with a new one. Never attempt to repair a damaged cast alloy wheel.

12 Wheels - alignment check

1 Misalignment of the wheels, which may be due to a cocked rear wheel or a bent frame or fork yokes, can cause strange and possibly serious handling problems. If the frame or yokes are at fault, repair by a frame specialist or replacement with new parts are the only alternatives.

2 To check the alignment you will need an assistant, a length of string or a perfectly straight piece of wood and a ruler. A plumb bob or other suitable weight will also be required.

3 In order to make a proper check of the wheels it is necessary to support the bike in an upright position, either on its centrestand or on an auxiliary stand. Measure the width of both tyres at their widest points. Subtract the smaller measurement from the larger measurement, then divide the difference by two. The result is the amount of offset that should exist between the front and rear tyres on both sides.

4 If a string is used, have your assistant hold one end of it about halfway between the floor and the rear axle, touching the rear sidewall of the tyre.

5 Run the other end of the string forward and pull it tight so that it is roughly parallel to the floor. Slowly bring the string into contact with the front sidewall of the rear tyre, then turn the front wheel until it is parallel with the string. Measure the distance from the front tyre sidewall to the string.

6 Repeat the procedure on the other side of the motorcycle. The distance from the front tyre sidewall to the string should be equal on both sides.

7 As was previously pointed out, a perfectly straight length of wood may be substituted for the string. The procedure is the same.

8 If the front-to-back alignment is correct, the wheels still may be out of alignment vertically.

9 Using the plumb bob, or other suitable weight, and a length of string, check the rear wheel to make sure it is vertical. To do this, hold the string against the tyre upper sidewall and allow the weight to settle just off the floor. When the string touches both the upper and lower tyre sidewalls and is perfectly straight, the wheel is vertical. If it is not, place thin spacers under one leg of the stand.

10 Once the rear wheel is vertical, check the front wheel in the same manner. If both wheels are not perfectly vertical, the frame and/or major suspension components are bent.

13 Front wheel - removal and installation

Removal

1 Position the motorcycle on its centre stand and support it under the crankcase so that the front wheel is off the ground. Always make sure the motorcycle is properly supported.

2 On ABS/TCS models, release the wheel speed sensor wiring from its bracket by pulling out the grommet **(see illustration)**.

3 On CBS/LBS-ABS/TCS models, unscrew the wheel speed sensor bracket bolt and displace the sensor. It is advisable to tie a rag around the sensor to avoid the possibility of damage, and to suspend it out of the way.

4 Remove the right-hand front brake caliper mounting bolts and slide the caliper off the disc **(see illustration 3.3a)**. Support the caliper with a piece of wire or a bungee cord so that no strain is placed on its hydraulic hose. There is no need to disconnect the hose from the caliper.

5 Remove the screw securing the speedometer cable to its drive housing on the left-hand side of the wheel hub, and detach the cable **(see illustration)**.

6 Unscrew the axle bolt on the right-hand end of the axle, then slacken the axle clamp bolts on the bottom of each fork **(see illustration)**.

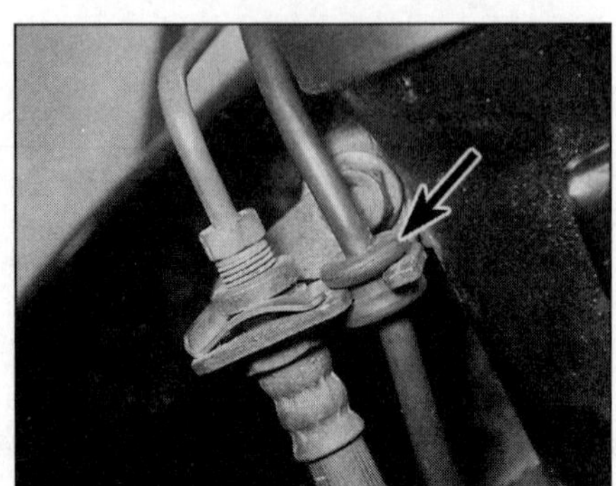

13.2 Free the wiring from its bracket (arrowed)

13.5 Remove the screw (arrowed) and withdraw the cable from the housing

13.6 Remove the axle bolt (A), then slacken the clamp bolts (B) on each fork

13.7 Withdraw the axle from the left

13.8a Remove the spacer . . .

13.8b . . . and the speedometer drive from the wheel

7 Support the wheel, then withdraw the axle from the left-hand side and carefully lower the wheel **(see illustration)**.

8 Remove the wheel spacer from the right-hand side of the wheel and the speedometer drive housing from the left-hand side **(see illustrations)**. **Note:** *Do not operate the front brake lever with the wheel removed.*

Caution: Don't lay the wheel down and allow it to rest on the disc - the disc could become warped. Set the wheel on wood blocks so the disc doesn't support the weight of the wheel.

9 Check the axle for straightness by rolling it on a flat surface such as a piece of plate glass (first wipe off all old grease and remove any corrosion using fine emery cloth). If the equipment is available, place the axle in V-blocks and measure the runout using a dial gauge. If the axle is bent or the runout exceeds the limit specified, replace it.

10 Check the condition of the wheel bearings (see Section 15).

Installation

11 Apply a smear of grease to the speedometer drive components. Fit the speedometer drive to the wheel's left-hand side, aligning its driven gear slots with the drive plate tabs **(see illustration 13.8b)**.

12 Apply a smear of grease to the inside of the wheel spacer, and also to the outside where it fits into the wheel. Fit the spacer into the right-hand side of the wheel **(see illustration 13.8a)**.

13 Manoeuvre the wheel into position. Apply a thin coat of grease to the axle.

14 Lift the wheel into place between the fork sliders, making sure the spacer and speedometer drive remain in position. Slide the axle in from the left-hand side **(see illustration 13.7)**. Align the speedometer drive housing so that the protrusion on the top of the housing locates against the lug on the fork slider.

15 Install the axle bolt and tighten it to the torque setting specified at the beginning of the Chapter **(see illustrations)**.

16 Tighten the axle clamp bolts to the specified torque setting **(see illustration)**.

17 Install the brake caliper, making sure the pads sit squarely on either side of the disc **(see illustration 3.17)**. Tighten the caliper mounting bolts to the torque setting specified at the beginning of the Chapter **(see illustration 3.18)**.

18 Connect the speedometer cable to the drive housing, aligning the slot in the cable end with the drive tab, and securely tighten its screw **(see illustration)**.

19 On ABS/TCS models, fit the wheel speed sensor wiring in its bracket **(see illustration 13.2)**.

20 On CBS/LBS-ABS/TCS models, fit the wheel speed sensor bracket and tighten the bolt. Check the air gap between the sensor and one of the poles on the ABS pulse ring using feeler gauges. If the gap is not as specified at the beginning of the Chapter, slacken the mounting bolt and adjust the air gap with a 0.5 mm feeler gauge positioned between the pole and the sensor. When the gap is correct, there should be a slight drag on the gauge as you withdraw it. Check the gap in different places by rotating the wheel. On completion tighten the bracket bolt to the specified torque setting. If the gap cannot be set up properly, the shim between the sensor and the bracket must be changed to bring the air gap within specifications.

21 Apply the front brake a few times to bring the pads back into contact with the discs. Move the motorcycle off its stand, apply the front brake and pump the front forks a few times to settle all components in position.

22 Check for correct operation of the front brake before riding the motorcycle.

13.15a Install the axle bolt . . .

13.15b . . . and tighten it to the specified torque setting . . .

13.16 . . . then tighten the clamp bolts to the specified torque

13.18 Install the speedometer cable and secure it with the screw

14.2 Remove the caliper bracket stopper bolt (arrowed)

14.3a Unscrew the axle nut (arrowed) . . .

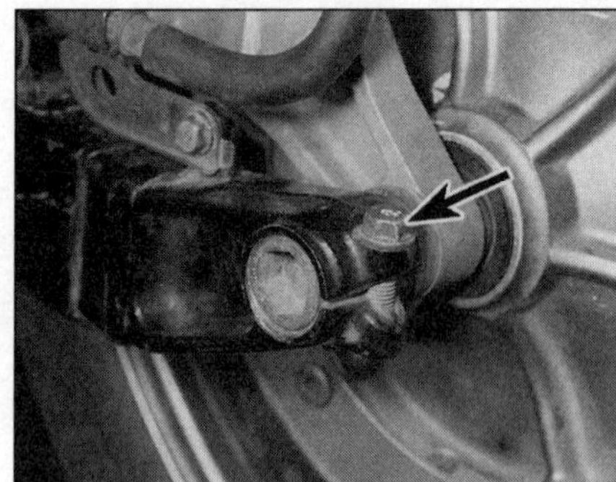

14.3b . . . and slacken the axle pinch bolt (arrowed)

14 Rear wheel - removal and installation

Removal

1 Position the motorcycle on its centrestand. To make it easier to remove the wheel, unscrew the four bolts securing the mudguard/number plate assembly and remove it.

2 Unscrew the caliper bracket stopper bolt **(see illustration)**. Discard the bolt as Honda recommend a new one should be used on installation.

3 Unscrew the axle nut, then slacken the rear axle pinch bolt in the left-hand side of the swingarm. Withdraw the axle from the left **(see illustrations)**. Slide the brake caliper off the disc and support it out of the way, making sure no strain is placed on the hose.

4 Grasp the wheel and draw it off the final drive housing. If necessary, use a screwdriver or the handle of the pliers in the tool kit inserted through the hole in the bottom of the dust guard plate on the drive housing to prise off the wheel.

5 Remove the spacer from the left-hand side of the wheel **(see illustration)**.

Caution: Do not lay the wheel down and allow it to rest on the disc or the final drive coupling - they could become warped. Set the wheel on wood blocks so the disc or the sprocket doesn't support the weight of the wheel. Do not operate the brake pedal with the wheel removed.

6 Check the axle for straightness by rolling it on a flat surface such as a piece of plate glass (if the axle is corroded, first remove the corrosion with fine emery cloth). If the equipment is available, place the axle in V-blocks and measure the runout using a dial gauge. If the axle is bent or the runout exceeds the limit specified at the beginning of the Chapter, replace it.

7 Check the condition of the wheel bearings (see Section 15).

Installation

8 Apply a thin coat of grease to the lips of each bearing seal, and also to the inside and the inner faces of the spacer where they contact the seals.

9 Manoeuvre the wheel into position and apply a thin coat of grease to the axle. Also apply molybdenum disulphide grease to the splines on the drive hub and the driven coupling. **Note:** *Honda specify using a grease which has more than 40% molybdenum disulphide, otherwise the components may tend to stick - refer to your Honda dealer for approved types of grease.* Install the spacer into the left-hand side of the wheel **(see illustrations)**.

14.3c Withdraw the axle and remove the wheel

10 Lift the wheel into position. Make sure the spacer remains correctly in place and the splines engage correctly.

11 Install the caliper on the brake disc making sure the pads sit squarely either side of the disc.

12 Slide the axle back into the wheel, making sure it passes through the caliper bracket **(see illustration 14.3c)**. Install the caliper stopper bolt, then fit the axle nut and tighten it to the torque setting specified at the beginning of this Chapter. Also tighten the axle pinch bolt and the caliper stopper bolt to

14.5 Remove the spacer (arrowed) from the wheel

14.9a Apply moly grease to the drive and driven hub splines

14.9b Fit the spacer into the wheel

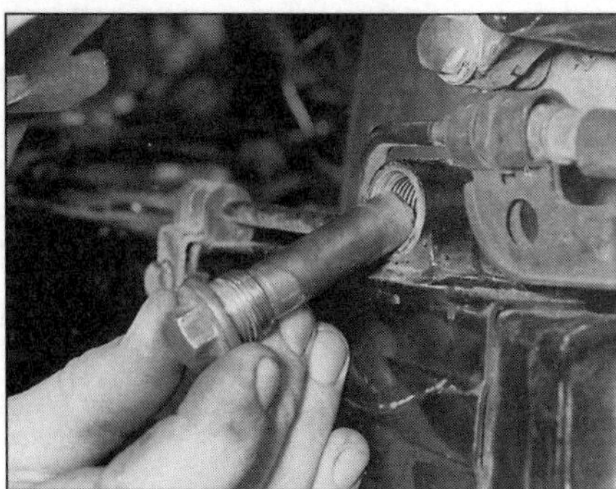
14.12a Fit the stopper bolt . . .

14.12b . . . and the axle nut . . .

14.12c . . . then tighten the nut . . .

14.12d . . . the pinch bolt . . .

14.12e . . . and the stopper bolt to their specified torque settings

the specified torque settings **(see illustrations)**.

13 Operate the brake pedal several times to bring the pads into contact with the disc. Check the operation of the rear brake carefully before riding the bike. Do not forget to install the mudguard/number plate assembly, if removed.

15 Wheel bearings - removal, inspection and installation

Front wheel bearings

Note: *Always replace the wheel bearings in pairs. Never replace the bearings individually. Avoid using a high pressure cleaner on the wheel bearing area.*

1 Remove the wheel (see Section 13) **(see illustration)**.

2 Set the wheel on blocks so as not to allow the weight of the wheel to rest on the brake disc.

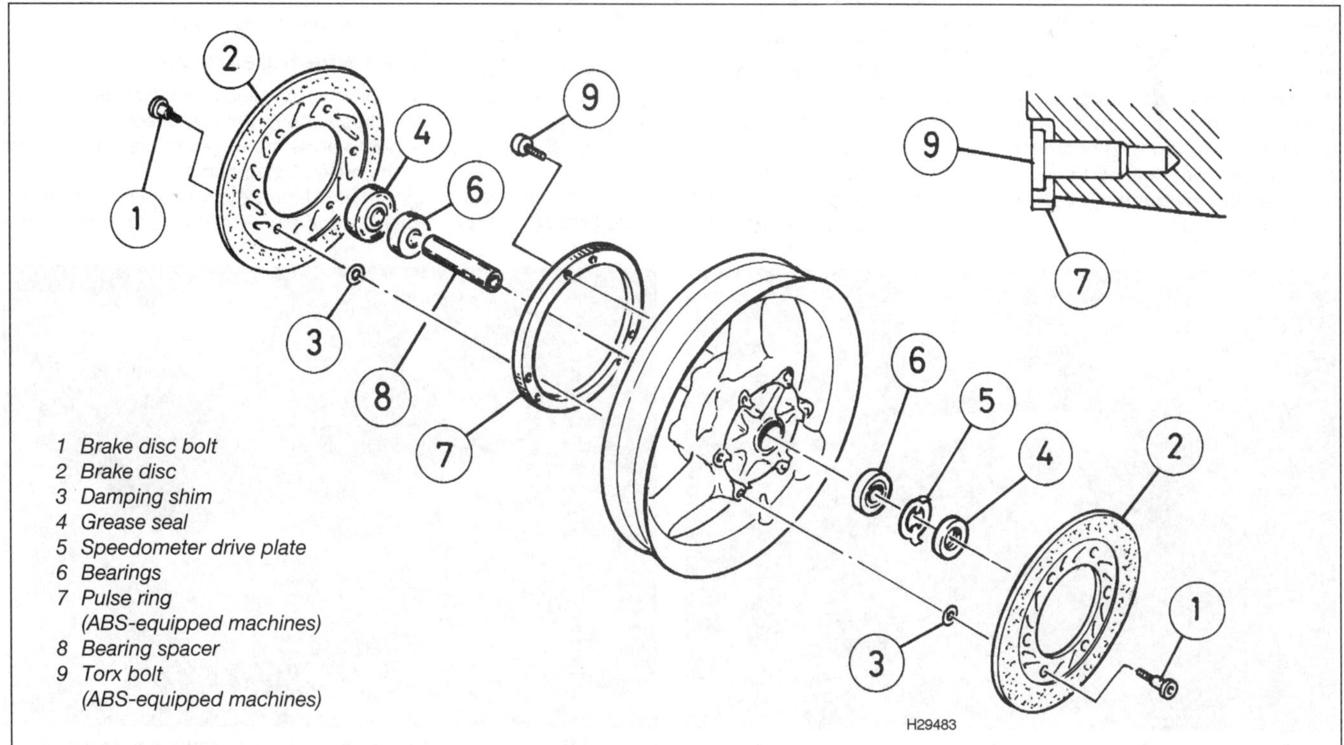

15.1 Front wheel components

15.3 Lever out the grease seals and discard them

15.4a Use a drift to knock out the bearings

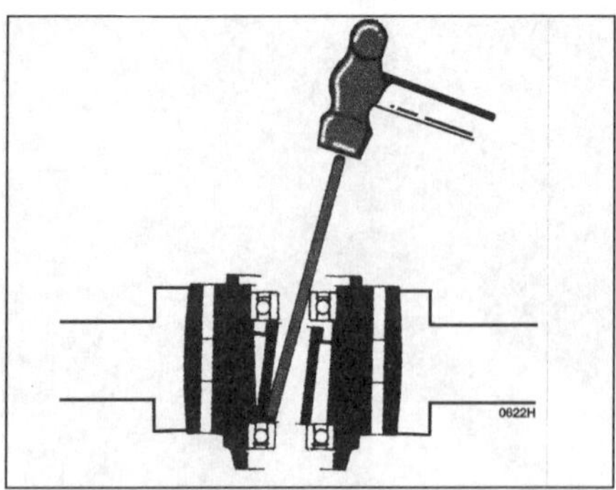
15.4b Locate the drift as shown when driving out the bearing

15.9 The bearing can be driven in using a suitable socket

3 Prise out the grease seal on each side of the wheel using a flat-bladed screwdriver, taking care not to damage the rim of the hub **(see illustration)**. Discard the seals as new ones must be used. Remove the speedometer drive plate after removing the left-hand seal, noting how it fits.

4 Using a metal rod (preferably a brass drift punch) inserted through the centre of the upper bearing, tap evenly around the inner race of the lower bearing to drive it from the hub **(see illustrations)**. The bearing spacer will also come out.

5 Lay the wheel on its other side so that the remaining bearing faces down. Drive the bearing out of the wheel using the same technique as above.

6 If the bearings are of the unsealed type or are only sealed on one side, clean them with a high flash-point solvent (one which won't leave any residue) and blow them dry with compressed air (don't let the bearings spin as you dry them). Apply a few drops of oil to the bearing. **Note:** *If the bearing is sealed on both sides don't attempt to clean it.*

7 Hold the outer race of the bearing and rotate the inner race - if the bearing doesn't turn smoothly, has rough spots or is noisy, replace it with a new one.

Refer to Tools and Workshop Tips for more information about bearings.

8 If the bearing is good and can be re-used, wash it in solvent once again and dry it, then pack the bearing with grease. Honda recommend that the bearings should be renewed if they are removed.

9 Thoroughly clean the hub area of the wheel. First install the left-hand side bearing into its recess in the hub, with the marked or sealed side facing outwards. Using the old bearing (if new ones are being fitted), a bearing driver or a socket large enough to contact the outer race of the bearing, drive it in until it's completely seated **(see illustration)**.

10 Turn the wheel over and install the bearing spacer. Drive the right-hand side bearing into place as described above.

11 Fit the speedometer drive plate into the left-hand side of the wheel, locating its outer tabs in the slots in the hub **(see illustration)**. Apply a smear of grease to the lips of the new grease seals, then install them in the wheel **(see illustration 15.3)**. Drive them into place using a seal or bearing driver, a suitable socket or a flat piece of wood **(see illustration)**.

12 Clean off all grease from the brake discs using acetone or brake system cleaner then install the wheel (see Section 13).

Rear wheel bearings

13 Remove the rear wheel (see Section 14) **(see illustration)**. Set the wheel on blocks so as not to allow the weight of the wheel to rest on the brake disc or hub.

14 Lift the final driven coupling out of the wheel, noting how it fits, and remove the

15.11a Locate the outer drive plate tabs into the slots in the wheel (arrowed)

15.11b The seal can be driven in using a flat piece of wood

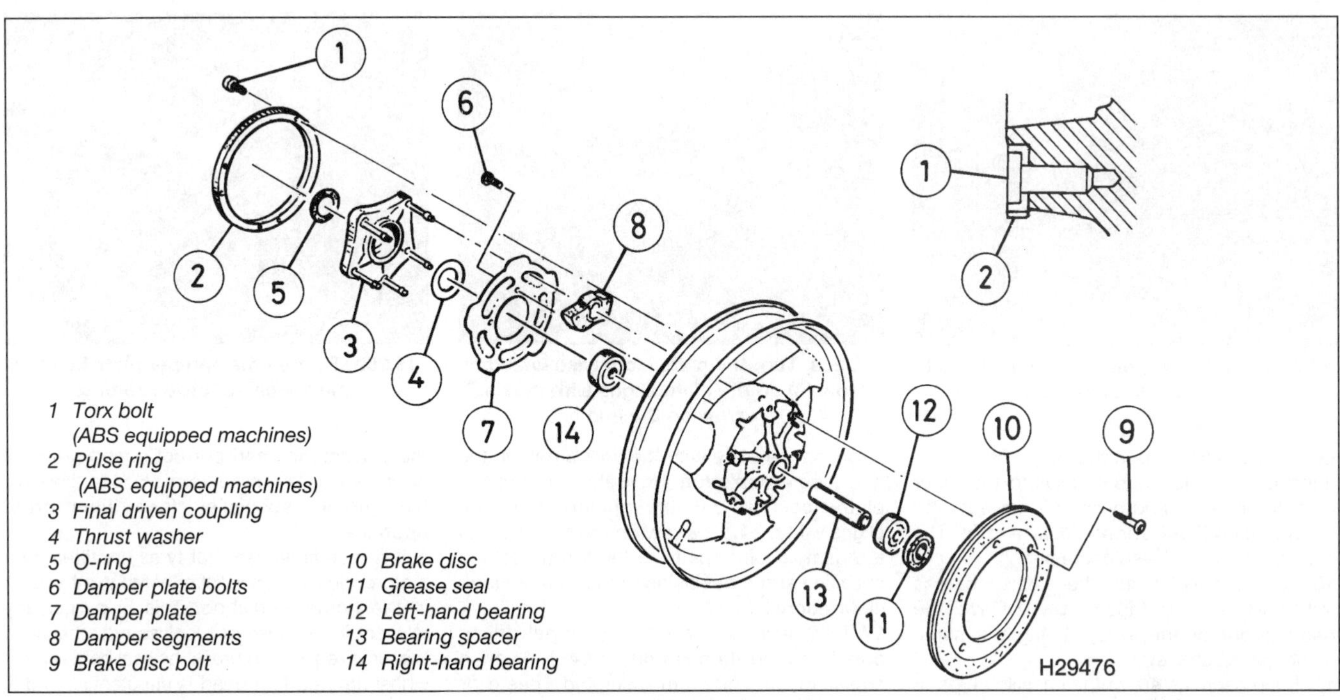

15.13 Rear wheel components

thrust washer. Remove the coupling O-ring and discard it as a new one must be used **(see illustrations)**.

15 Unscrew the bolts securing the damper plate to the hub **(see illustration 15.26)**. Turn the plate anti-clockwise from arrow no.2 until the arrow on the plate aligns with the arrow no.1 on the hub. Remove the plate and lift out the damper segments, noting how they fit **(see illustrations)**.

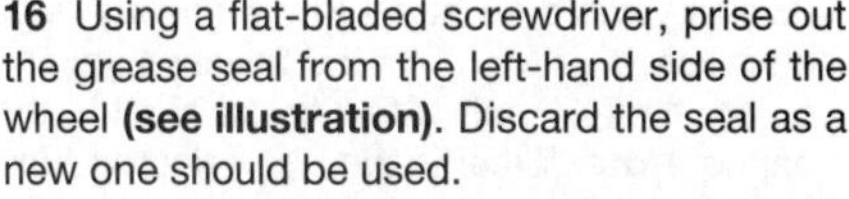

16 Using a flat-bladed screwdriver, prise out the grease seal from the left-hand side of the wheel **(see illustration)**. Discard the seal as a new one should be used.

17 Using a metal rod (preferably a brass drift

15.14a Lift out the coupling . . .

15.14b . . . and remove the thrust washer . . .

15.14c . . . and the O-ring (arrowed)

15.15a Turn the plate anti-clockwise until the arrow (A) on the plate aligns with the no.1 arrow on the hub

15.15b Lift out the damper segments

15.16 Lever out the grease seal and discard it

15.24 Fit the new grease seal into the left-hand side of the hub

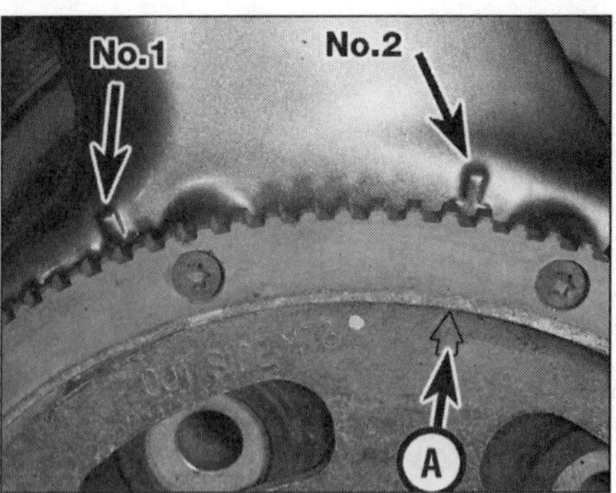

15.26a Turn the plate clockwise until the arrow (A) on the plate aligns with the no.2 arrow on the hub

15.26b Tighten the damper plate bolts to the specified torque setting

punch) inserted through the centre of the left-hand bearing, tap evenly around the inner race of the right-hand bearing to drive it from the hub **(see illustrations 15.4a and b)**. The bearing spacer will also come out.

18 Lay the wheel on its other side so that the left-hand bearing faces down. Drive the bearing out of the wheel using the same technique as above.

19 If the bearings are of the unsealed type or are only sealed on one side, clean them with a high flash-point solvent (one which won't leave any residue) and blow them dry with compressed air (don't let the bearings spin as you dry them). Apply a few drops of oil to the bearing. **Note:** *If the bearing is sealed on both sides don't attempt to clean it.*

20 Hold the outer race of the bearing and rotate the inner race - if the bearing doesn't turn smoothly, has rough spots or is noisy, replace it with a new one (see **Haynes Hint**).

21 If the bearing is good and can be re-used, wash it in solvent once again and dry it, then pack the bearing with grease. Honda recommend that the bearings should be renewed if they are removed.

22 Thoroughly clean the hub area of the wheel. First install the left-hand side bearing into its recess in the hub, with the marked or sealed side facing outwards. Using the old bearing (if new ones are being fitted), a bearing driver or a socket large enough to contact the outer race of the bearing, drive it in squarely until it's completely seated **(see illustration 15.9)**.

23 Turn the wheel over and install the bearing spacer. Drive the right-hand side bearing into place as described above.

24 Apply a smear of grease to the lips of the new grease seal, and install it into the left-hand side of the hub **(see illustration)**. Use a seal or bearing driver, a suitable socket or a flat piece of wood to drive it into place **(see illustration 15.11b)**.

25 Check the condition of the damper segments and replace them if they are worn, damaged or deteriorated. Fit the segments into the wheel with the "OUTSIDE" mark facing out **(see illustration 15.15b)**.

26 Install the damper plate with the "OUTSIDE" mark facing out, aligning the arrow on the plate with the no.1 arrow on the hub **(see illustration 15.15a)**, then turn the plate clockwise until the arrow on the plate aligns with the no.2 arrow on the hub. Tighten the damper plate bolts to the torque setting specified at the beginning of the Chapter **(see illustrations)**.

27 Fit a new O-ring on to the final driven coupling **(see illustration 15.14c)**. Apply a smear of molybdenum disulphide paste or grease to the thrust washer, the inside of the coupling and its mating surface on the outside of the hub. **Note:** *Honda specify using a grease which has more than 40% molybdenum disulphide, otherwise the components may tend to stick - refer to your Honda dealer for approved types of grease.* Install the thrust washer and the coupling **(see illustrations 15.14b and a)**.

28 Clean off all grease from the brake disc using acetone or brake system cleaner. Install the wheel (see Section 14).

16 Tyres - general information and fitting

General information

1 The wheels fitted to all models are designed to take tubeless tyres only. Tyre sizes are given in the Specifications at the beginning of this Chapter.

Warning: The ABS and TCS control units work by comparing the relative wheel speed of the front and rear wheels, and is programmed using the tyre and wheel sizes specified by Honda. If non-specified tyres or wheels are fitted, the computer may become confused and the system may function incorrectly

2 Refer to the Daily (pre-ride) checks listed at the beginning of this manual for tyre maintenance.

Fitting new tyres

3 When selecting new tyres, refer to the tyre information label on the swingarm and the tyre options listed in the owners handbook. Ensure that front and rear tyre types are compatible, the correct size and correct speed rating; if necessary seek advice from a Honda dealer or tyre fitting specialist **(see illustration opposite)**.

4 It is recommended that tyres are fitted by a motorcycle tyre specialist rather than attempted in the home workshop. This is particularly relevant in the case of tubeless tyres because the force required to break the seal between the wheel rim and tyre bead is substantial, and is usually beyond the capabilities of an individual working with normal tyre levers. Additionally, the specialist will be able to balance the wheels after tyre fitting.

5 Note that punctured tubeless tyres can in some cases be repaired. Honda recommend that such repairs are carried out only by an authorised dealer.

17 ABS and TCS systems - general information and operation

Warning: The ABS and TCS control units work by comparing the relative wheel speed of the front and rear wheels, and are programmed using the tyre and wheel sizes specified by Honda. If non-specified tyres or wheels are fitted, the computer may become confused and the system may function incorrectly.

ABS (Anti-lock Braking System)

1 The ABS prevents the wheels from locking up under hard braking or on uneven road surfaces. A sensor on each wheel transmits information about the speed of wheel rotation, and if the control unit senses that a wheel is about to lock, it releases brake pressure momentarily to that wheel, preventing a skid.

2 The ABS system is self-checking, and is always switched on, although it will not function at speeds of less than 5 mph (8 kph) or if the battery is flat.

3 When the ignition (main) switch is turned on, the ABS indicator light on the instrument panel comes on, then extinguishes when setting off. If the indicator light remains on, or starts flashing, then there is probably a fault in

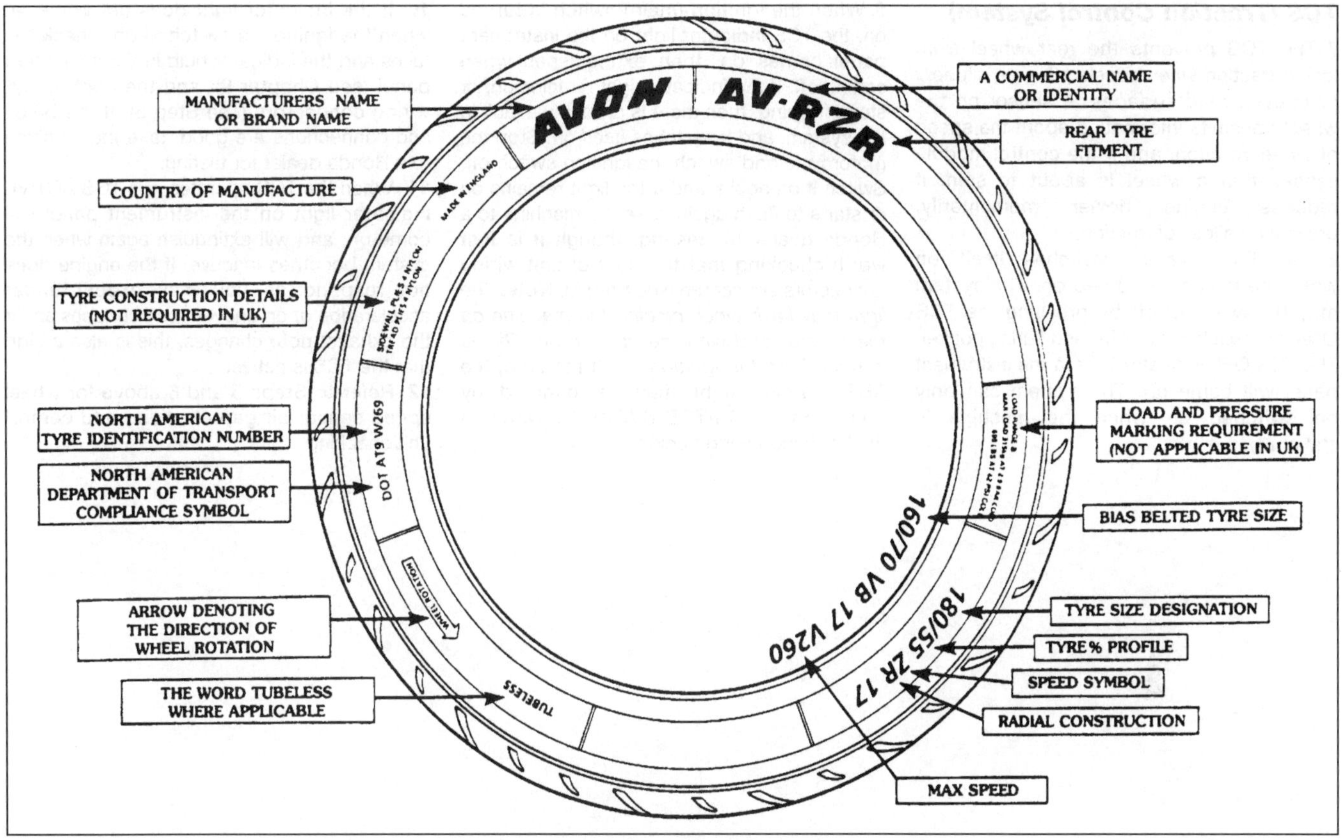

AVON AV·RZR
MADE IN ENGLAND
DOT AT9 W269
160/70 VB 17 V260
180/55 ZR 17
TUBELESS

MANUFACTURERS NAME OR BRAND NAME
COUNTRY OF MANUFACTURE
TYRE CONSTRUCTION DETAILS (NOT REQUIRED IN UK)
NORTH AMERICAN TYRE IDENTIFICATION NUMBER
NORTH AMERICAN DEPARTMENT OF TRANSPORT COMPLIANCE SYMBOL
ARROW DENOTING THE DIRECTION OF WHEEL ROTATION
THE WORD TUBELESS WHERE APPLICABLE
A COMMERCIAL NAME OR IDENTITY
REAR TYRE FITMENT
LOAD AND PRESSURE MARKING REQUIREMENT (NOT APPLICABLE IN UK)
BIAS BELTED TYRE SIZE
TYRE SIZE DESIGNATION
TYRE % PROFILE
SPEED SYMBOL
RADIAL CONSTRUCTION
MAX SPEED

16.3 Common tyre sidewall markings

the system, and it switches itself off. Stop the motorcycle and switch the ignition switch off. Switch it on again, and if the light remains on or starts to flash again, take the machine to a Honda dealer for testing, though it is first worth checking that the control unit wiring connectors are secure (see Step 6). **Note:** *The light may flash when placing the machine on the centrestand with the ignition on. This is normal. Turn the ignition off.* If required, the ABS warning light may be dimmed by pressing the ABS/TCS WARNING switch in the left-hand fairing pocket.

4 If the indicator light does not come on when the ignition is switched on, check the fuses and the indicator bulbs in the instrument panel (see Chapter 9), and the control unit wiring connectors (see Step 6). If the bulbs and connections are good, take the machine to a Honda dealer for testing.

5 The only maintenance required is to check the air gap between the wheel speed sensor and one of the poles on the ABS/TCS pulse ring, though once set, this is unlikely to change. It is only specified when removing and installing the front wheel on CBS/LBS-ABS/TCS models, which have a more critical tolerance. Check the gap by inserting a feeler gauge between the sensor and the tip of one of the poles **(see illustration)**. If the gap is not as specified at the beginning of the Chapter, remove the mounting bolts and adjust the air gap by inserting a replacement shim of the required thickness to bring the gap within specifications **(see illustration)**. Check the gap in different places by rotating the wheel. On completion tighten the bracket bolts to the specified torque setting.

6 The ABS control unit is mounted inside the upper fairing on the left-hand side, and is secured by two bolts **(see illustration)**. If the indicator light stays on or flashes, check that the wiring connectors on the bottom of the unit are secure. Remove the upper fairing for access (see Chapter 8).

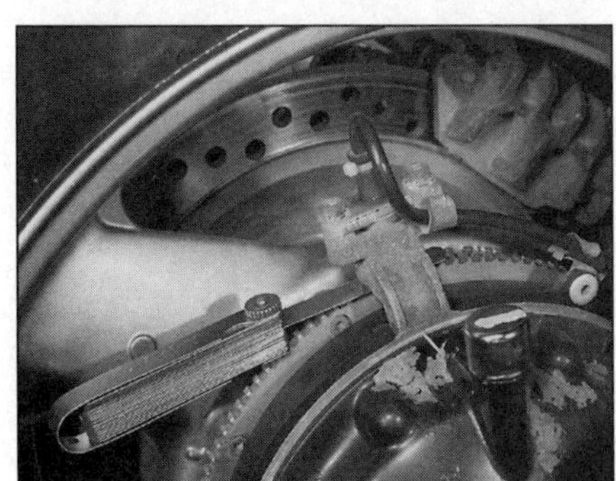

17.5a Check the wheel speed sensor air gap using feeler gauges

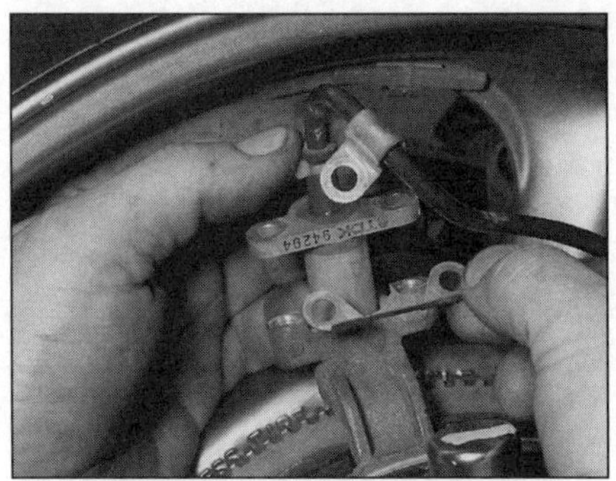

17.5b Unscrew the two bolts, then withdraw the sensor and remove the shim

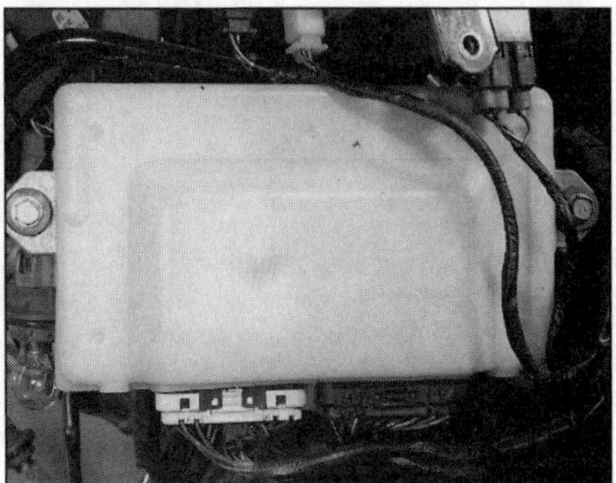

17.6 ABS/TCS control unit

TCS (Traction Control System)

7 The TCS prevents the rear wheel from losing traction when accelerating on slippery or uneven road surfaces. A sensor on the wheel transmits information about the speed of wheel rotation, and if the control module senses that a wheel is about to spin, it reduces engine power momentarily, preventing a loss of traction.

8 The TCS system switches itself on when the ignition is turned on. The system may be switched off by pressing the TCS ON/OFF switch in the left-hand fairing pocket. The TCS OFF indicator light in the instrument panel will come on. The system can only be switched off when the machine is stationary.

9 When the ignition (main) switch is turned on, the TCS indicator light on the instrument panel comes on, then extinguishes when setting off. If the indicator light remains on, or starts flashing, then there is probably a fault in the system, and it switches itself off. Stop the motorcycle and switch the ignition switch off. Switch it on again, and if the light remains on or starts to flash again, take the machine to a Honda dealer for testing, though it is first worth checking that the control unit wiring connectors are secure (see Step 6). **Note:** *The light may flash when placing the machine on the centrestand with the ignition on. This is normal. Turn the ignition off.* If required, the ABS warning light may be dimmed by pressing the ABS/TCS WARNING switch in the left-hand fairing pocket.

10 If the indicator light does not come on when the ignition is switched on, check the fuses and the indicator bulb in the instrument panel (see Chapter 9), and the control unit wiring connectors (see Step 6). If the bulbs and connections are good, take the machine to a Honda dealer for testing.

11 When the TCS operates, the TCS ACTIVE indicator light on the instrument panel will come on, and will extinguish again when the system becomes inactive. If the engine does not respond as you may expect under acceleration or on uneven road surfaces and if the exhaust note changes, this is also a sign that the TCS is active.

12 Refer to Steps 5 and 6 above for wheel speed sensor air gap checking and control unit checking.

Chapter 8
Bodywork

Contents

Fairing panels - removal and installation 6
Front mudguard - removal and installation 9
Fuel tank cover - removal and installation 4
General information 1
Panniers - removal and installation 5
Rear panel - removal and installation 10
Rear view mirrors - removal and installation 7
Seat - removal and installation 2
Side panels - removal and installation 3
Windshield - removal and installation 8

Degrees of difficulty

Easy, suitable for novice with little experience 	**Fairly easy,** suitable for beginner with some experience 	**Fairly difficult,** suitable for competent DIY mechanic 	**Difficult,** suitable for experienced DIY mechanic 	**Very difficult,** suitable for expert DIY or professional

1 General information

This Chapter covers the procedures necessary to remove and install the body parts. Since many service and repair operations on these motorcycles require the removal of the body parts, the procedures are grouped here and referred to from other Chapters.

In the case of damage to the body parts, it is usually necessary to remove the broken component and replace it with a new (or used) one. The material that the body panels are composed of doesn't lend itself to conventional repair techniques. There are however some shops that specialise in 'plastic welding', so it may be worthwhile seeking the advice of one of these specialists before consigning an expensive component to the bin.

When attempting to remove any body panel, first study it closely, noting any fasteners and associated fittings, to be sure of returning everything to its correct place on installation. In some cases the aid of an assistant will be required when removing panels, to help avoid the risk of damage to paintwork. Once the evident fasteners have been removed, try to withdraw the panel as described but DO NOT FORCE IT - if it will not release, check that all fasteners have been removed and try again. Where a panel engages another by means of tabs, be careful not to break the tab or its mating slot or to damage the paintwork. Remember that a few moments of patience at this stage will save you a lot of money in replacing broken fairing panels!

When installing a body panel, first study it closely, noting any fasteners and associated fittings removed with it, to be sure of returning everything to its correct place. Check that all fasteners are in good condition, including all trim nuts or clips and damping/rubber mounts; any of these must be replaced if faulty before the panel is reassembled. Check also that all mounting brackets are straight and repair or replace them if necessary before attempting to install the panel. Where assistance was required to remove a panel, make sure your assistant is on hand to install it.

Tighten the fasteners securely, but be careful not to overtighten any of them or the panel may break (not always immediately) due to the uneven stress.

HAYNES HiNT ***Note that a small amount of lubricant (liquid soap or similar) applied to the mounting rubbers of the side panels will assist the panel retaining pegs to engage without the need for undue pressure.***

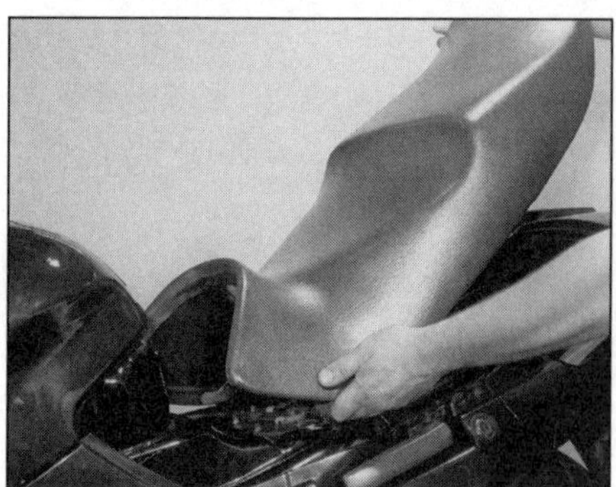

2.3 Align the tabs as described when fitting the seat

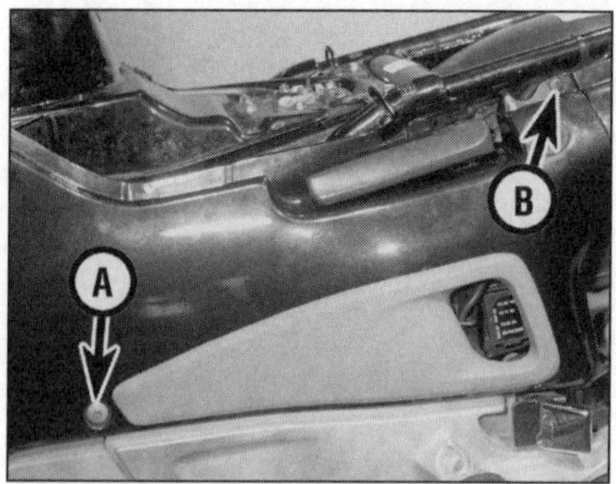

3.2a Remove the screw (A) and the trim clip (B) . . .

3.2b . . . then pull the panel away to release the pegs (arrowed) from their grommets

2 Seat - removal and installation

Removal

1 Insert the ignition key into the seat lock located at the front of the left-hand pannier, and turn it clockwise to unlock the seat.

2 Push down on the front of the seat and lift the rear and draw it back and away from the bike.

Installation

3 Locate the tabs at the front and in the middle of the seat under their holders, and align the hole in the front of the seat with the knob on the back of the fuel tank **(see illustration)**. Align the seat at the rear and push down on it to engage the latches.

3 Side panels - removal and installation

Removal

1 Remove the seat (see Section 2).

2 Each side panel is secured by one screw, one clip-type fastener, three pegs which fit into rubber grommets, and by a tab which locates in the rear panel. The pegs are located one at the front and two at the rear of each panel. Remove the screw and the clip fastener, then gently pull each panel away from the frame to release the pegs and the tab **(see illustrations)**. When removing the left-hand panel, pull out the centre stand lifting lever. Do not force or bend the panel while removing it.

Installation

3 Installation is the reverse of removal.

4 Fuel tank cover - removal and installation

Removal

1 Remove the side panels (see Section 3).

2 Unscrew the two screws at the front and the bolt on each side of the cover and remove the cover **(see illustration)**.

Installation

3 Installation is the reverse of removal.

5 Panniers - removal and installation

Removal

1 Insert the ignition key into the pannier lock located at the front of each pannier, and turn it clockwise to unlock the pannier. Pull the release lever and slide the pannier to the rear and slightly up to release it **(see illustrations)**.

Installation

2 Installation is the reverse of removal.

6 Fairing panels - removal and installation

Upper fairing

Removal

1 Remove the rear view mirrors (see Section 7).

2 Remove the windshield, trim and inner screen (see Section 8).

3 Remove the fairing pockets (see Steps 23 to 25).

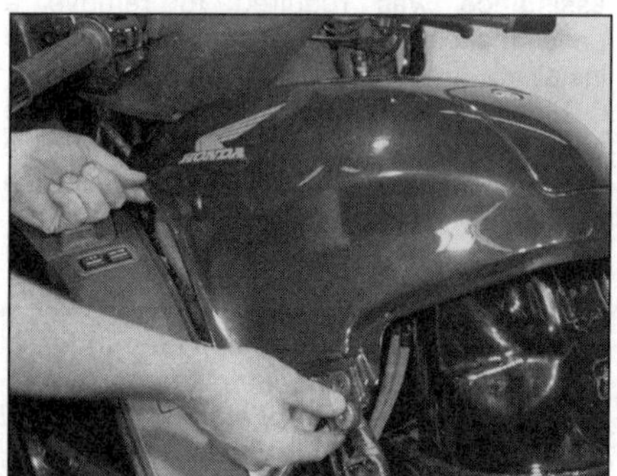

4.2 The tank cover is secured by two screws at the front and a bolt on each side at the back

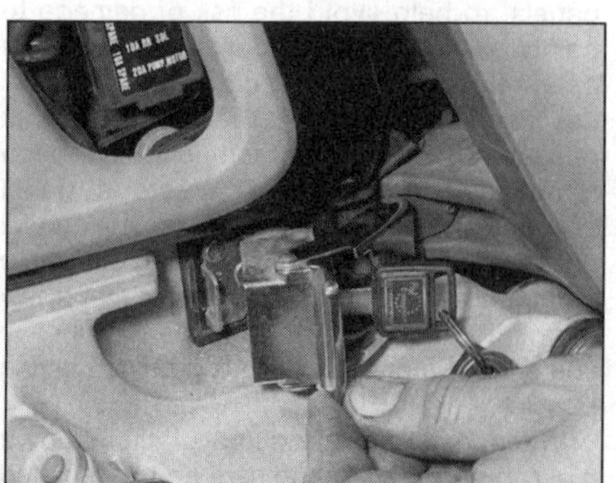

5.1a Turn the key and release the lever . . .

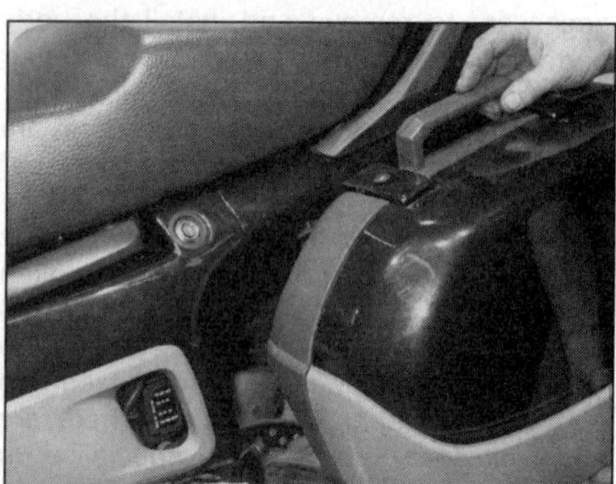

5.1b . . . then unhook the pannier and remove it

6.5a Remove the screw . . .

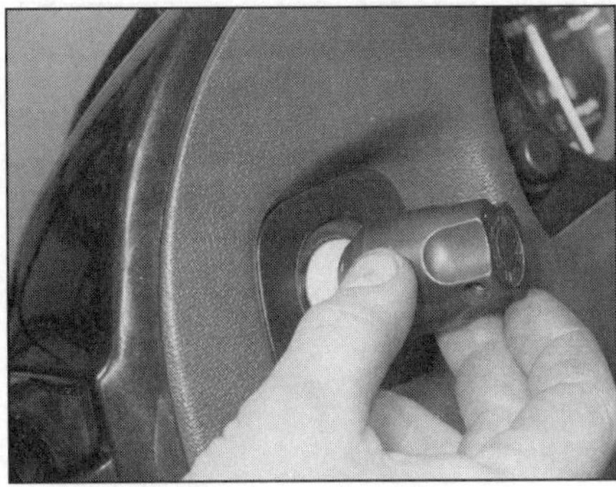
6.5b . . . the knob . . .

6.5c . . . and its set plate . . .

4 Disconnect the clock wiring connectors from under the instrument cluster.

5 Remove the screw from the headlight adjuster knob in the instrument surround, then remove the knob and its set plate. Unscrew the plastic nut and remove the washers, then draw the headlight adjuster cable out of the back of the surround **(see illustrations)**. Remove the two screws securing the surround to the fairing, then release the four tabs and remove the surround.

6 Remove the middle fairing inner cover (see Steps 12 and 13).

7 Remove the fuel tank cover (see Section 4). Detach the air duct hose from its lug on the right-hand side of the air filter housing **(see illustration)**.

8 Disconnect the headlight and sidelight wiring connectors **(see illustration)**.

9 Remove the trim clips, screws, Allen bolts and normal bolts securing the upper fairing to the middle fairing and to the brackets on the frame. Double check that all fasteners have been removed, then carefully draw the fairing away from the machine **(see illustrations)**.

10 If required, remove the headlight from the fairing (see Chapter 9) and separate the fairing into its halves.

Installation

11 Installation is the reverse of removal. Make sure the fairing stay ends locate into the

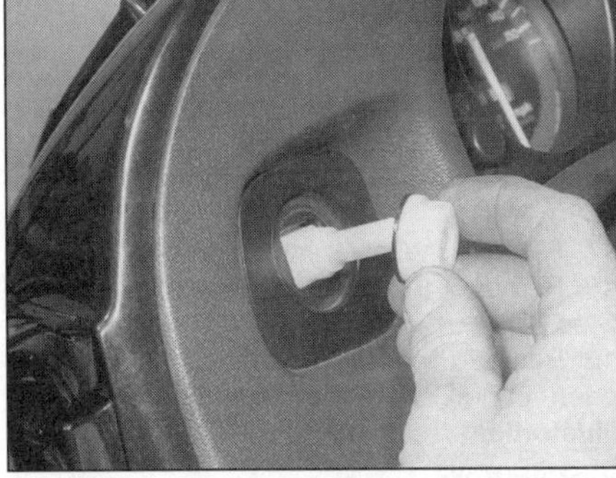
6.5d . . . then unscrew the plastic nut

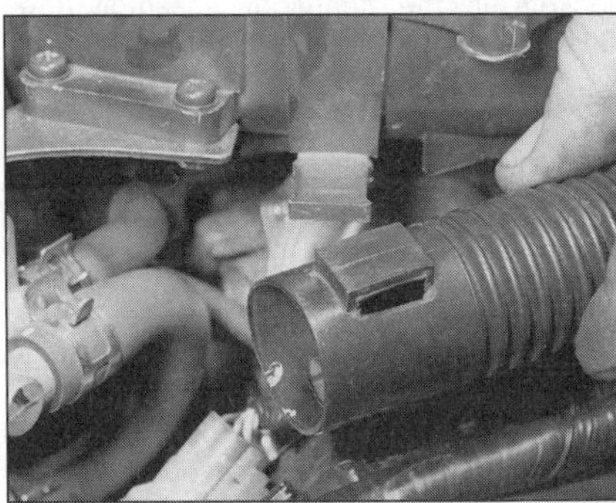
6.7 Detach the hose from its lug

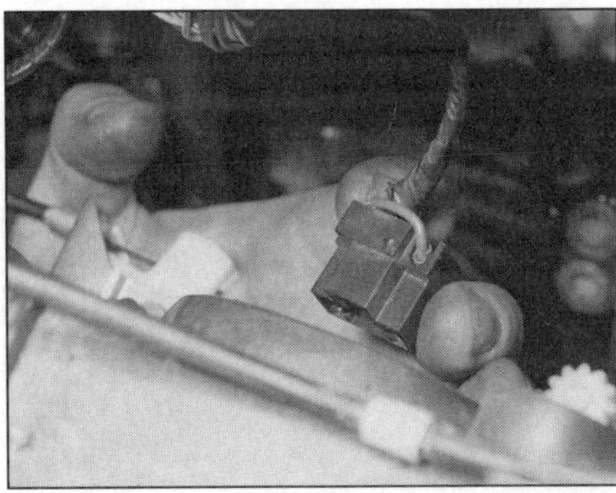
6.8 Disconnect the headlight and sidelight wiring connectors

6.9a Remove the front . . .

6.9b . . . and rear screws securing the upper fairing to the middle fairing . . .

6.9c . . . and the bolts securing the upper fairing to the frame . . .

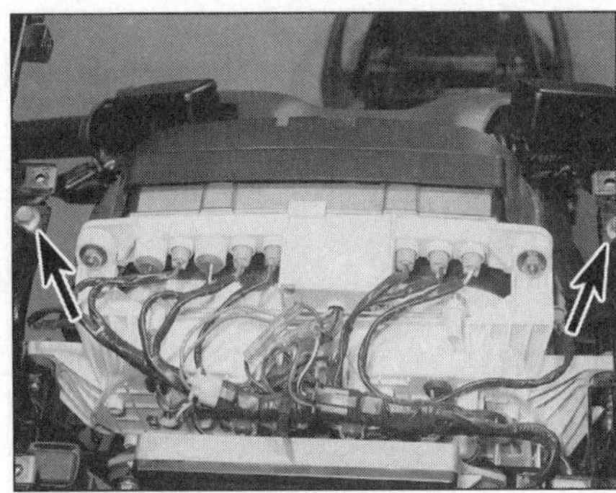
6.9d . . . and the fairing stay

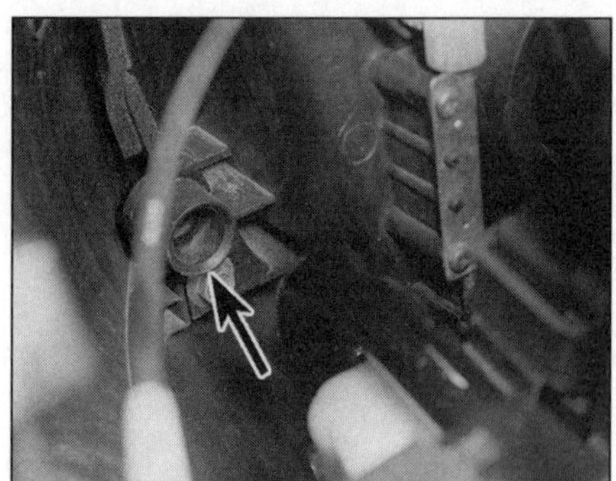

6.11 Fairing stay location sockets

sockets in the headlight assembly **(see illustration)**.

Middle fairing inner cover

Removal

12 Remove the screw securing the speedometer cable to the drive housing on the front wheel **(see illustration)**.

13 Remove the two trim clips and the six screws securing the inner cover to the middle fairing panels, then carefully remove the cover, drawing the cable up through the hole in the inner cover as you do **(see illustrations)**.

Installation

14 Installation is the reverse of removal.

6.12 Remove the screw (arrowed) and detach the cable, then draw it through the hole in the inner cover

Middle fairing panels

Removal

15 Remove the middle fairing inner cover (see Steps 12 and 13).

16 Remove the fairing pockets (see Steps 23 to 25).

17 Remove the lower fairing (see Step 21).

18 Remove the maintenance covers (see Step 27).

19 Remove the screws and bolts securing each panel, then remove the panel **(see illustration)**.

Installation

20 Installation is the reverse of removal. Make sure the peg at the front of each panel

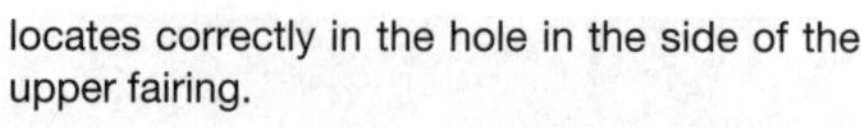

locates correctly in the hole in the side of the upper fairing.

Lower fairing

Removal

21 Remove the nine Allen bolts securing the lower fairing to the middle fairing panels and the brackets on the frame, then carefully lower the panel, noting how the tabs locate **(see illustrations)**.

Installation

22 Installation is the reverse of removal. Make sure the tabs fit correctly in their slots before installing any bolts.

Fairing pockets

Removal

23 Remove the maintenance covers (see Step 26). If only one fairing pocket is being removed, only remove the maintenance cover for that side.

24 Remove the fuel tank cover (see Section 4).

25 Remove the screws securing each pocket, three of which are located within the pocket under the flap or lid, then lift the pocket away. On ABS/TCS models, when removing the left-hand pocket, disconnect the ABS/TCS switch wiring

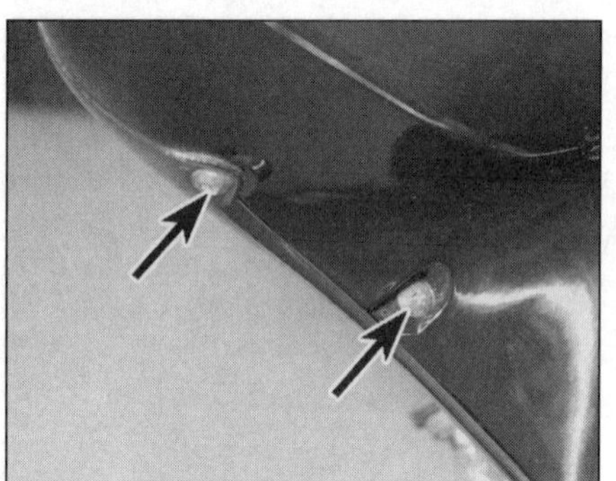

6.13a Remove the two upper screws (arrowed) . . .

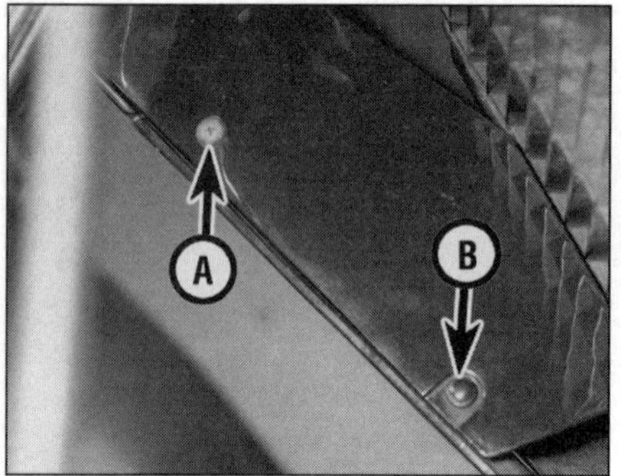

6.13b . . . the lower screw (A) and the trim clip (B) securing each side of the cover . . .

6.13c . . . and manoeuvre it away

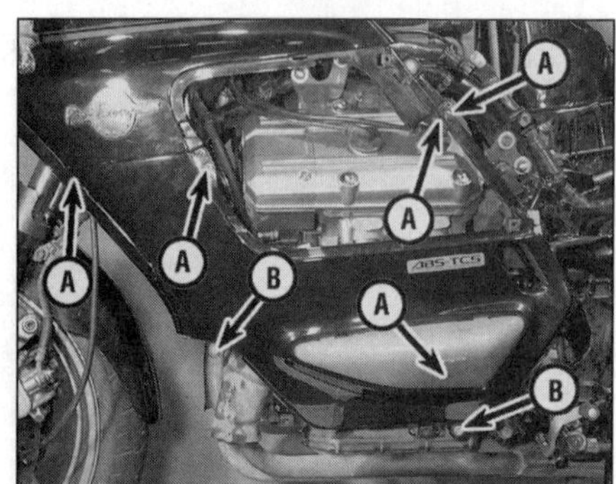

6.19 Each middle panel is secured by five screws (A) and two bolts (B)

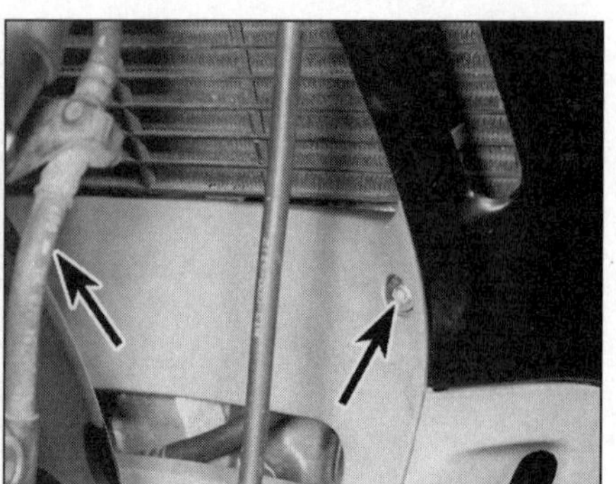

6.21a The lower fairing is secured by two bolts at the front (arrowed) . . .

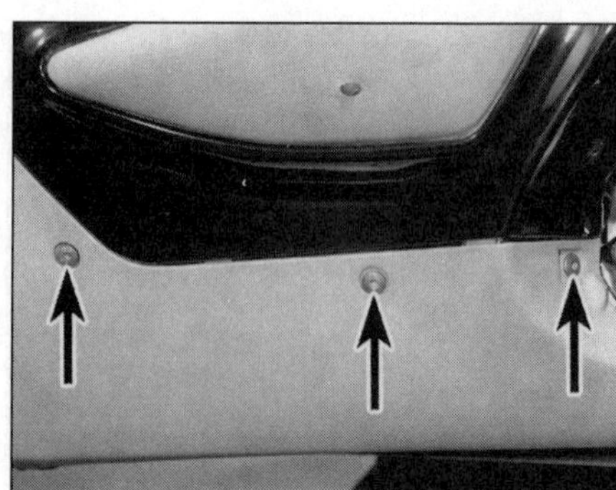

6.21b . . . three on the left-hand side (arrowed), and four on the right

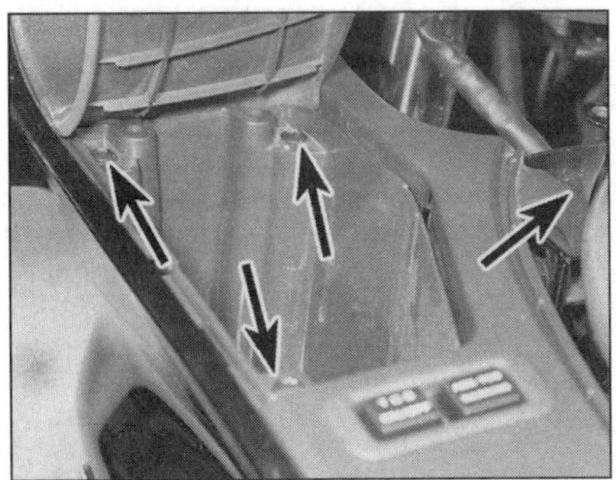
6.25a Remove the fairing pocket upper screws (arrowed) . . .

6.25b . . . and the lower screws

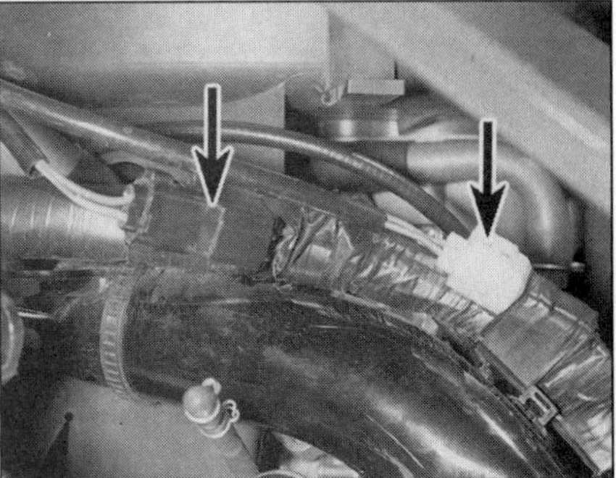
6.25c Disconnect the wiring connectors (arrowed) when they become accessible

6.27a Remove the screws (arrowed) . . .

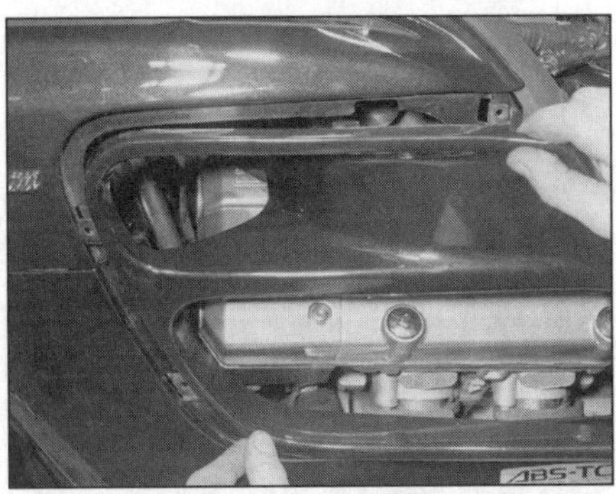

6.27b . . . then release the tabs and draw the cover away

6.30 Each pivot cover is secured by three bolts (arrowed)

connectors as they become accessible **(see illustrations)**.

Installation

26 Installation is the reverse of removal. On models equipped with TCS, reset the system as required after installation of the left-hand pocket (see Chapter 7).

Maintenance covers

Removal

27 Remove the two screws securing each cover, then carefully slide the cover back to release the tabs and remove the cover **(see illustrations)**.

Installation

28 Installation is the reverse of removal. Fit the tabs on the cover into the slots in the middle fairing panel, then slide it forwards to engage them.

Swingarm pivot covers

Removal

29 Remove the side panels (see Section 3). If only one cover is being removed, only remove the side panel for that side.

30 Remove the three Allen bolts and remove the cover **(see illustration)**.

Installation

31 Installation is the reverse of removal.

7 Rear view mirrors - removal and installation

Removal

1 The mirror housing is a press fit onto the fairing. Carefully remove the housing by drawing it away from the fairing until it releases from its clips **(see illustration)**. Disconnect the front turn signal wiring connector as it becomes accessible. Allow the mirror to dangle on its safety strap.

2 Unscrew the two mirror mounting bolts and remove the mirror **(see illustration)**.

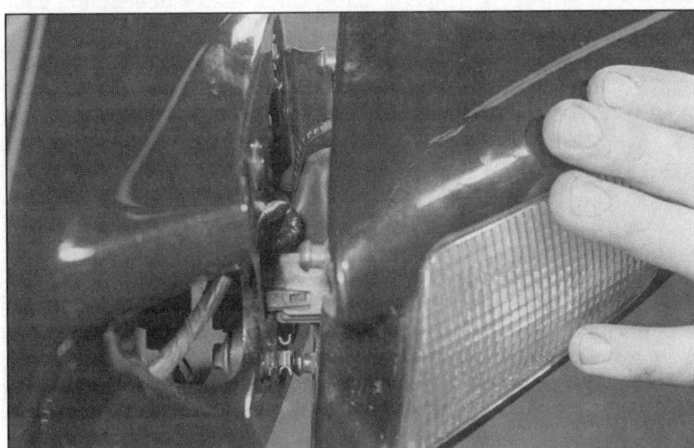
7.1 Release the mirror housing from its clips in the fairing

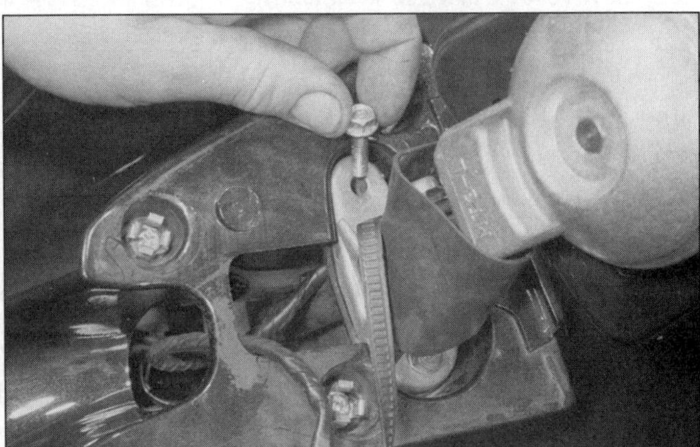
7.2 Each mirror is secured by two bolts

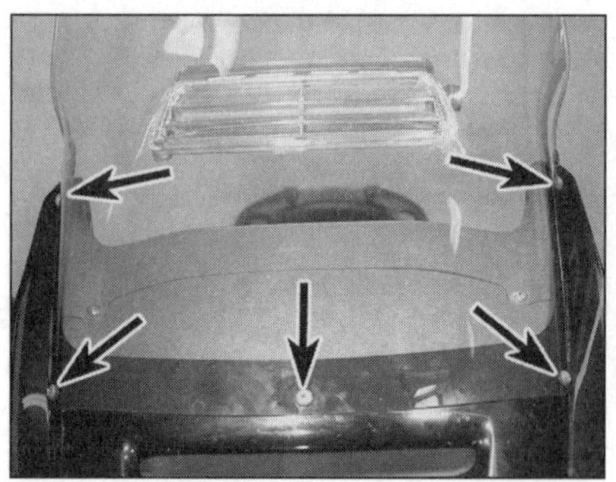
8.1 The windshield is secured by five screws (arrowed)

8.2a Remove the screws on each side . . .

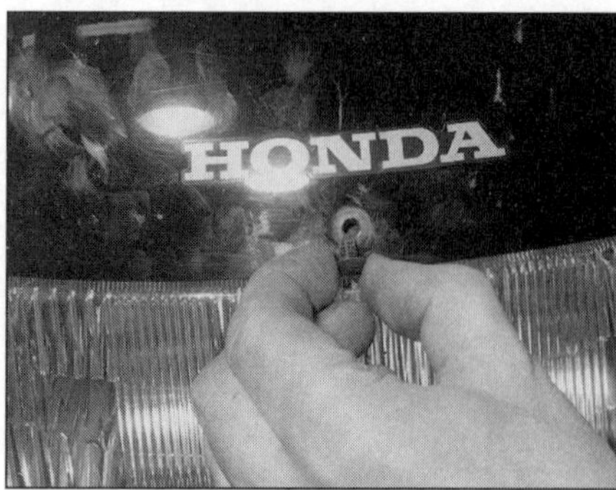

8.2b . . . and the trim clip in the middle . . .

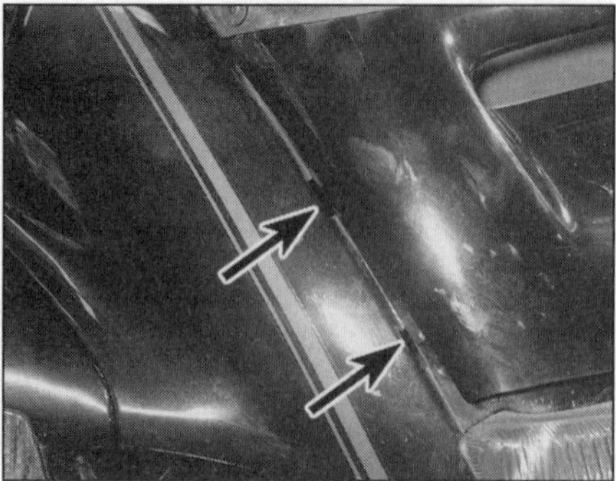
8.2c . . . then release the trim tabs (arrowed) and remove the trim

Installation

3 Installation is the reverse of removal. Make sure the housing is securely held in its clips.

8 Windshield - removal and installation

Removal

1 Unscrew the five screws and remove the windshield **(see illustration)**.

2 Unscrew the two screws and release the trim clip securing the windshield trim to the fairing, then slide the trim up to release the tabs, and remove the trim **(see illustrations)**.

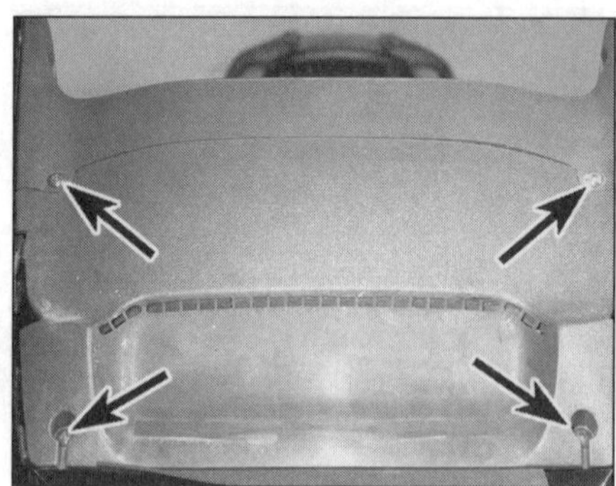
8.3 The inner screen is secured by four screws (arrowed)

3 Unscrew the four screws and remove the inner screen **(see illustration)**.

Installation

4 Installation is the reverse of removal.

9 Front mudguard - removal and installation

Removal

Standard and ABS/TCS models

1 Unscrew the four bolts securing the mudguard, two of which also secure the brake hose brackets **(see illustration)**.

2 Remove the mudguard and its mounting plate, noting how they fit **(see illustration)**.

CBS/LBS-ABS/TCS models

3 Unscrew the bolt securing each side of the rear section to the front section.

4 Unscrew the two bolts securing the top of the front section to the rear section.

5 Remove the front section, noting how the cutout on each side locates onto the tabs on the rear section.

6 Remove the rear section, noting how the holes locate over the raised sections on the mudguard plate.

7 If required, unscrew the bolts securing the mudguard plate and remove the plate.

Installation

8 Installation is the reverse of removal.

10 Rear panel - removal and installation

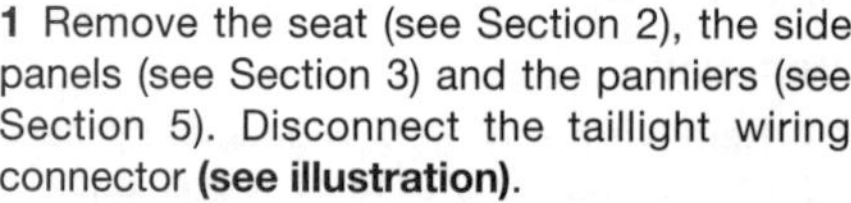

Removal

1 Remove the seat (see Section 2), the side panels (see Section 3) and the panniers (see Section 5). Disconnect the taillight wiring connector **(see illustration)**.

2 Where fitted, remove the caps from the top bolts securing the passenger grab-handles, then unscrew the three bolts securing each

9.1 Remove the two bolts (arrowed) on each side, the rear of which secure the brake hose brackets . . .

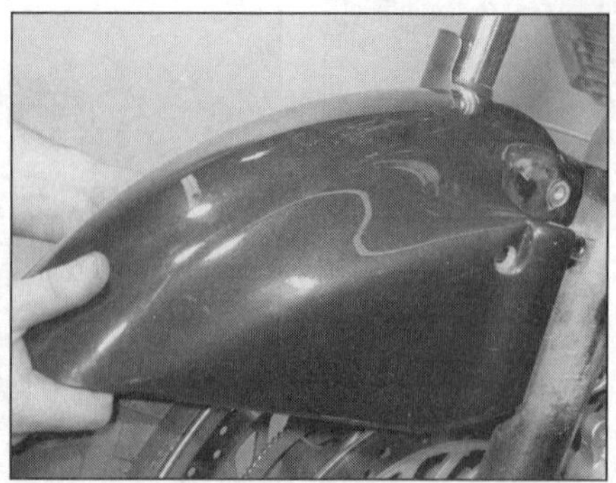
9.2 . . . and draw the mudguard forward to remove it

10.1 Disconnect the taillight wiring connector

handle and remove the handle **(see illustration)**.

3 Remove the two bolts securing the front of the panel, noting that the left-hand bolt also secures an earth terminal on later models **(see illustration)**, then carefully remove the rear panel.

Installation

4 Installation is the reverse of removal. Tighten the grab-handle bolts to 27 Nm. Do not forget to connect the taillight wiring connector, and the earth (ground) terminal with the left-hand bolt on later models.

10.2 Remove the three bolts securing each grab-handle . . .

10.3 . . . and the bolt securing each side of the front of the panel

Notes

Chapter 9
Electrical system

Contents

Alternator/regulator/rectifier - check, removal and installation 36
Battery - charging 4
Battery - removal, installation, inspection and maintenance 3
Brake light switches - check and replacement 14
Brake/tail light bulb - replacement 9
Charging system - leakage and output test 35
Charging system testing - general information and precautions 34
Clutch switch - check and replacement 24
Diode - check and replacement 25
Electrical system - fault finding 2
Fuel indicator light circuit - check 29
Fuel level sender - check and replacement 27
Fuel pump and cut-off relay - check, removal and installation 28
Fuses - check and replacement 5
General information 1
Handlebar switches - check 20
Handlebar switches - removal and installation 21
Headlight aim - check and adjustment .....see Chapter 1
Headlight bulb and sidelight bulb - replacement 7
Headlight assembly - removal and installation 8
Horn(s) - check and replacement 30
Ignition (main) switch - check, removal and installation 19
Ignition system components .....see Chapter 5
Instrument and warning light bulbs - replacement 17
Instrument cluster and speedometer cable - removal and installation 15
Instruments - check and replacement 16
Lean angle sensor and relay - check and replacement 26
Lighting system - check 6
Neutral switch - check, removal and installation 22
Oil pressure switch - check, removal and installation 18
Sidestand switch - check and replacement 23
Starter motor - disassembly, inspection and reassembly 33
Starter motor - removal and installation 32
Starter relay - check and replacement 31
Tail light assembly - removal and installation 10
Turn signal bulbs - replacement 12
Turn signal assemblies - removal and installation 13
Turn signal circuit - check 11

Degrees of difficulty

Easy, suitable for novice with little experience 	**Fairly easy,** suitable for beginner with some experience 	**Fairly difficult,** suitable for competent DIY mechanic	**Difficult,** suitable for experienced DIY mechanic	**Very difficult,** suitable for expert DIY or professional

Specifications

Battery

Capacity	12 V, 12 Ah
Voltage	
Fully charged	13.1 V
Uncharged	below 12.3 V
Charging rate	
Normal	1.4 A for 5 hrs
Quick	6.0 A for 1hr
Current leakage	
UK T, AT, V, AV models, US 1996 and 1997 models	2 mA (max)
All other models	3 mA (max)

Alternator

Slip ring diameter - UK T, AT, V, AV models, US 1996 and 1997 models	
Standard	14.4 mm
Service limit	12.0 mm
Brush length UK T, AT, V, AV models, US 1996 and 1997 models	
Standard	13.7 mm
Service limit	4.7 mm
Rotor coil resistance	
UK T, AT, V, AV models, US 1996 and 1997 models	2.6 to 3.2 ohms
All other models	0 to 4.0 ohms
Stator coil resistance	
UK T, AT, V, AV models, US 1996 and 1997 models	0.22 to 0.26 ohms
All other models	0 to 1.0 ohms

Regulator/rectifier

Regulated voltage	
UK T, AT, V, AV models, US 1996 and 1997 models	14.2 to 14.8 V at 5000 rpm
All other models	12.6 to 15.0 V at 5000 rpm

Starter motor

Brush length	12.0 to 13.0 mm

Fuel level sender

Resistance	
Fuel tank full	10 ohms
Fuel tank empty	90 ohms

Fuses

UK T, AT, V, AV models, US 1996 and 1997 models	
Main	30 A
Alternator	55 A
Accessories	5 A
Others	
Standard models	10 A x 6, 20 A x 1
CBS/LBS-ABS/TCS	10 A x 5, 15 a x 2
All other models	
Main	30 A
Accessories	5 A
Others	10 A x 6, 20 A x 1
ABS fuses	
ABS/TCS models	10 A x 3, 20 A x 1
CBS/LBS-ABS/TCS models	10 A x 1, 30 A x 2

Bulbs

Headlight	
UK models	60/55 W
US models	
Standard and ABS/TCS models	45/45 W
LBS-ABS/TCS models	60/55 W
Sidelight (UK only)	5 W
Brake/tail light	
UK models	21/5 W
US models	32/3 cp
Turn signal lights	
UK models	21 W
US models	
Running light/front	3/32 cp
Rear	32 cp
Instrument lights	1.7 W
Turn signal indicator light	
Standard models	3.4 W
ABS/TCS and CBS/LBS-ABS/TCS models	3 W
Neutral indicator light	
Standard models	3.4 W
ABS/TCS and CBS/LBS-ABS/TCS models	1.7 W
Oil pressure indicator light	
Standard models	3.4 W
ABS/TCS and CBS/LBS-ABS/TCS models	3 W
High beam indicator light	
Standard models	3.4 W
ABS/TCS and CBS/LBS-ABS/TCS models	3 W
Sidestand indicator light	
Standard models	3.4 W
ABS/TCS and CBS/LBS-ABS/TCS models	1.7 W
Low fuel indicator light	
Standard models	3.4 W
ABS/TCS and CBS/LBS-ABS/TCS models	3 W
TCS activation light	3 W
TCS "OFF" indicator light	3 W
TCS indicator light	LED
ABS indicator lights	LED

Torque settings

Instrument cluster bolts	9 Nm
Oil pressure switch	12 Nm
Neutral switch	12 Nm
Sidestand switch bolt	10 Nm
Fuel pump cover nuts	10 Nm
Alternator mounting bolts	
UK T, AT, V, AV models, US 1996 and 1997 models	Not available
All other models	58 Nm
Alternator shaft nut	58 Nm

1 General information

All models have a 12-volt electrical system charged by a three-phase alternator. On UK T, AT, V, AV models, and US 1996 and 1997 models, the alternator has an integral regulator/rectifier unit. On all other models the regulator/rectifier is separate.

The regulator maintains the charging system output within the specified range to prevent overcharging, and the rectifier converts the ac (alternating current) output of the alternator to dc (direct current) to power the lights and other components and to charge the battery. The alternator rotor is driven by a gear incorporated in the starter clutch unit, which is mounted on the end of the crankshaft.

The starter motor is mounted on the left-hand side of the engine. The starting system includes the motor, the battery, the relay and the various wires and switches. If the engine kill switch in the RUN position and the ignition (main) switch is ON, the starter relay allows the starter motor to operate only if the transmission is in neutral (neutral switch on) or, if the transmission is in gear, if the clutch lever is pulled into the handlebar and the sidestand is up.

The anti-lock braking (ABS) and traction control (TCS) systems fitted on some models are managed by a highly complex system of electronics and hydraulics. Such is the nature of these systems that no attempt is being made to cover them fully in this manual. Fault finding is very complicated and requires specific and specialised equipment exclusive to Honda. A functional and operational description of the systems is given in Chapter 7.

Note: *Keep in mind that electrical parts, once purchased, cannot be returned. To avoid unnecessary expense, make very sure the faulty component has been positively identified before buying a replacement part.*

2 Electrical system - fault finding

Warning: To prevent the risk of short circuits, the ignition (main) switch must always be OFF and the battery negative (-ve) terminal should be disconnected before any of the bike's other electrical components are disturbed. Don't forget to reconnect the terminal securely once work is finished or if battery power is needed for circuit testing.

1 A typical electrical circuit consists of an electrical component, the switches, relays, etc. related to that component and the wiring and connectors that hook the component to both the battery and the frame. To aid in locating a problem in any electrical circuit, refer to the wiring diagrams at the end of this Chapter.

2 Before tackling any troublesome electrical circuit, first study the wiring diagram (see end of Chapter) thoroughly to get a complete picture of what makes up that individual circuit. Trouble spots, for instance, can often be narrowed down by noting if other components related to that circuit are operating properly or not. If several components or circuits fail at one time, chances are the fault lies in the fuse or earth (ground) connection, as several circuits often are routed through the same fuse and earth (ground) connections.

3 Electrical problems often stem from simple causes, such as loose or corroded connections or a blown fuse. Prior to any electrical fault finding, always visually check the condition of the fuse, wires and connections in the problem circuit. Intermittent failures can be especially frustrating, since you can't always duplicate the failure when it's convenient to test. In such situations, a good practice is to clean all connections in the affected circuit, whether or not they appear to be good. All of the connections and wires should also be wiggled to check for looseness which can cause intermittent failure.

3.1a Disconnect the negative lead . . .

4 If testing instruments are going to be utilised, use the wiring diagram to plan where you will make the necessary connections in order to accurately pinpoint the trouble spot.

5 The basic tools needed for electrical fault finding include a battery and bulb test circuit, a continuity tester, a test light, and a jumper wire. A multimeter capable of reading volts, ohms and amps is also very useful as an alternative to the above, and is necessary for performing more extensive tests and checks.

Refer to Fault Finding Equipment in the Reference section for details of how to use electrical test equipment.

3 Battery - removal, installation, inspection and maintenance

Caution: Be extremely careful when handling or working around the battery. The electrolyte is very caustic and an explosive gas (hydrogen) is given off when the battery is charging.

Removal and installation

1 Remove the left-hand side panel (see Chapter 8). Unscrew the negative (-ve) terminal screw and disconnect the lead from the battery. Unscrew the nut securing the battery holder, then lower the holder (it is hinged at the bottom) to access the positive (+ve) terminal. Unscrew the screw and disconnect the lead. Remove the battery from its box **(see illustrations)**.

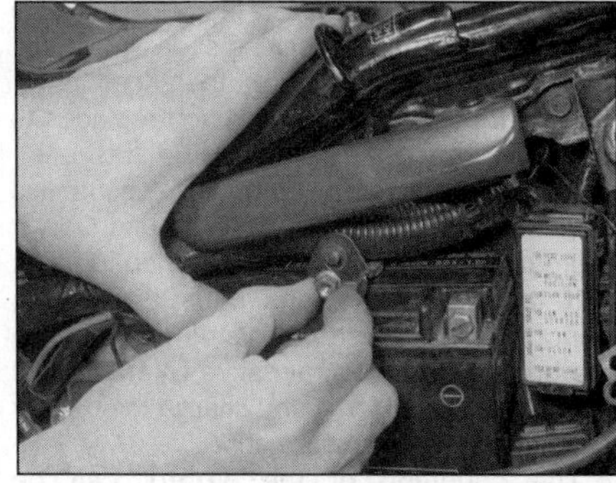

3.1b . . . then remove the holder nut and lower the holder . . .

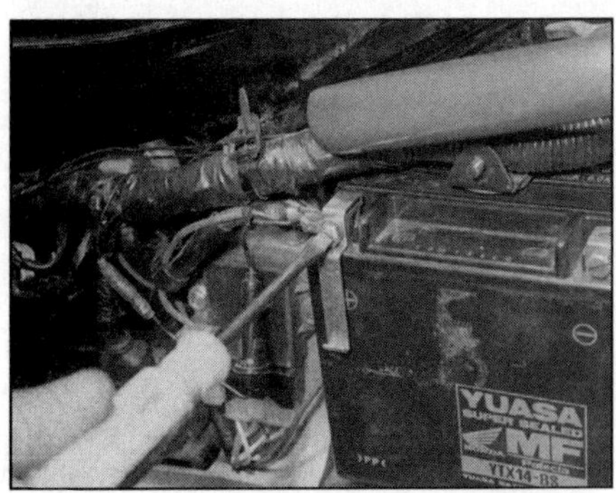
3.1c ... and disconnect the positive lead ...

3.1d ... then remove the battery

3.8a Release the booster cable cover (arrowed) ...

2 On installation, clean the battery terminals and lead ends with a wire brush or knife and emery paper. Reconnect the leads, connecting the positive (+ve) terminal first, then raise the holder and secure it with the nut. Install the side panel (see Chapter 8).

Battery corrosion can be kept to a minimum by applying a layer of petroleum jelly to the terminals after the cables have been connected.

Inspection and maintenance

3 The battery fitted to the models covered in this manual is of the maintenance free (sealed) type, therefore requiring no regular maintenance. However, the following checks should still be regularly performed.

4 Check the battery terminals and leads for tightness and corrosion. If corrosion is evident, unscrew the terminal screws and disconnect the leads from the battery, disconnecting the negative (-ve) terminal first, and clean the terminals and lead ends with a wire brush or knife and emery paper. Reconnect the leads, connecting the negative (-ve) terminal last, and apply a thin coat of petroleum jelly to the connections to slow further corrosion.

5 The battery case should be kept clean to prevent current leakage, which can discharge the battery over a period of time (especially when it sits unused). Wash the outside of the case with a solution of baking soda and water. Rinse the battery thoroughly, then dry it.

6 Look for cracks in the case and replace the battery if any are found. If acid has been spilled on the frame or battery box, neutralise it with a baking soda and water solution, dry it thoroughly, then touch up any damaged paint.

7 If the motorcycle sits unused for long periods of time, disconnect the cables from the battery terminals, negative (-ve) terminal first. Refer to Section 4 and charge the battery once every month to six weeks.

8 The condition of the battery can be assessed by measuring the voltage present at the battery terminals. Connect the voltmeter positive (+ve) probe to the battery positive (+ve) booster cable terminal behind the flip-cover, and the negative (-ve) probe to the battery negative (-ve) terminal **(see illustrations)**. When fully charged there should be more than 12.5 volts present. If the voltage falls below 12.0 volts the battery must be removed, disconnecting the negative (-ve) terminal first, and recharged as described below in Section 4.

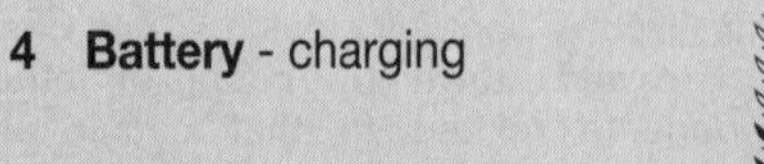
4 Battery - charging

Caution: Be extremely careful when handling or working around the battery. The electrolyte is very caustic and an explosive gas (hydrogen) is given off when the battery is charging.

1 Remove the battery (see Section 3). Connect the charger to the battery, making sure that the positive (+ve) lead on the charger is connected to the positive (+ve) terminal on the battery, and the negative (-ve) lead is connected to the negative (-ve) terminal.

2 Honda recommend that the battery is charged at a maximum rate of 1.4 amps for 5 hours. Exceeding this figure can cause the battery to overheat, buckling the plates and rendering it useless. Few owners will have access to an expensive current controlled charger, so if a normal domestic charger is used check that after a possible initial peak, the charge rate falls to a safe level **(see illustration)**. If the battery becomes hot during charging **stop**. Further charging will cause damage. **Note:** *In emergencies the battery can be charged at a higher rate of around 6.0 amps for a period of 1 hour. However, this is not recommended and the low amp charge is by far the safer method of charging the battery.*

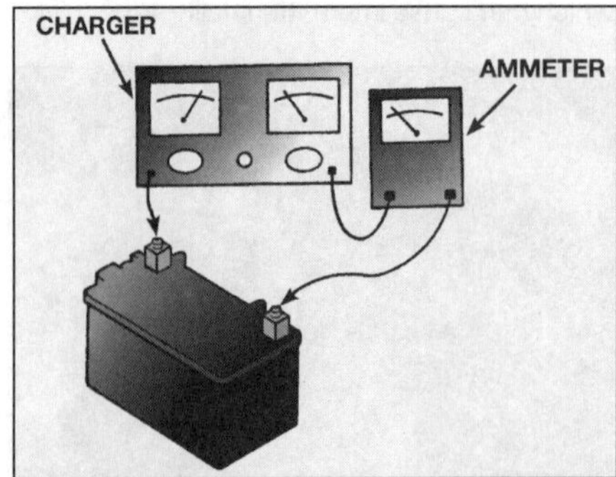

4.2 If the charger doesn't have ammeter built in, connect one in series as shown. DO NOT connect the ammeter between the battery terminals or it will be ruined

3.8b ... to access the terminal, which can be used for connecting a multimeter or, if required, jump leads

3 If the recharged battery discharges rapidly if left disconnected it is likely that an internal short caused by physical damage or sulphation has occurred. A new battery will be required. A sound item will tend to lose its charge at about 1% per day.

4 Install the battery (see Section 3).

5 If the motorcycle sits unused for long periods of time, charge the battery once every month to six weeks and leave it disconnected.

5 Fuses - check and replacement

1 The electrical system is protected by fuses of different ratings. All except the main fuse and the ABS/TCS fuses (and on some models the accessory fuse) are housed in the main fusebox, which is located behind the left-hand side panel. The main fuse is integral with the

5.1a Main fusebox

5.1b The main fuse (arrowed) is housed in the starter relay

5.1c ABS/TCS fusebox

starter relay, which is also behind the left-hand side panel. On ABS/TCS models, the system fuses are housed in their own box below the main fusebox **(see illustrations)**. The accessory fuse is located adjacent to the main fusebox. On later models, the charging circuit has a fuse located in its own box, also behind the left-hand side panel.

2 To access the fuses, remove the left-hand side panel (see Chapter 8) and unclip the fusebox lid **(see illustration)**.

3 The fuses can be removed and checked visually. If you can't pull the fuse out with your fingertips, use a pair of needle-nose pliers. A blown fuse is easily identified by a break in the element **(see illustration)**. Each fuse is clearly marked with its rating and must only be replaced by a fuse of the correct rating. A spare fuse of each rating is housed in the relevant fusebox, and a spare main fuse is housed in the bottom of the starter relay. If a spare fuse is used, always replace it so that a spare of each rating is carried on the bike at all times.

Warning: Never put in a fuse of a higher rating or bridge the terminals with any other substitute, however temporary it may be. Serious damage may be done to the circuit, or a fire may start.

4 If a fuse blows, be sure to check the wiring circuit very carefully for evidence of a short-circuit. Look for bare wires and chafed, melted or burned insulation. If the fuse is replaced before the cause is located, the new fuse will blow immediately.

5 Occasionally a fuse will blow or cause an open-circuit for no obvious reason. Corrosion of the fuse ends and fusebox terminals may occur and cause poor fuse contact. If this happens, remove the corrosion with a wire brush or emery paper, then spray the fuse end and terminals with electrical contact cleaner.

6 Lighting system - check

1 The battery provides power for operation of the headlight, tail light, brake light and instrument cluster lights. If none of the lights operate, always check battery voltage before proceeding. Low battery voltage indicates either a faulty battery or a defective charging system. Refer to Section 3 for battery checks and Sections 34 and 35 for charging system tests. Also, check the condition of the fuses.

Headlight

2 If the headlight fails to work, first check the fuse with the key ON (see Section 5), and then the bulb (see Section 7). If they are both good, use jumper wires to connect the bulb directly to the battery terminals. If the light comes on, the problem lies in the wiring, the relay(s), or one of the switches in the circuit. Refer to Section 20 for the switch testing procedures, and also the wiring diagrams at the end of this Chapter. If either the high beam or low beam relay is suspected of being faulty, substitute it with the other relay. If the beam in question then works, the faulty relay must be replaced. If not, check for voltage at the white terminal of the low beam relay and the blue terminal of the high beam relay. If no voltage is present, check the wiring between the relays and the switches (see *Wiring diagrams* at the end of the Chapter).

Tail light

3 If the tail light fails to work, check the bulb and the bulb terminals first, then the fuse, then check for battery voltage on the supply side of the tail light wiring connector. If voltage is present, check the earth (ground) circuit for an open or poor connection.

4 If no voltage is indicated, check the wiring between the tail light and the ignition switch, then check the switch. Also check the lighting switch.

Brake light

5 See Section 14 for brake switch check and Section 9 for tail light bulb replacement.

Instrument and warning lights

6 See Section 17 for instrument light bulb replacement.

Turn signal lights

7 See Section 11 for turn signal circuit check.

7 Headlight bulb and sidelight bulb - replacement

Note: *The headlight bulb is of the quartz-halogen type. Do not touch the bulb glass as skin acids will shorten the bulb's service life. If the bulb is accidentally touched, it should be wiped carefully when cold with a rag soaked in methylated spirit and dried before fitting.*

Warning: Allow the bulb time to cool before removing it if the headlight has just been on.

Headlight

1 Remove the access panel from middle fairing inner cover, on the underside of the upper fairing.

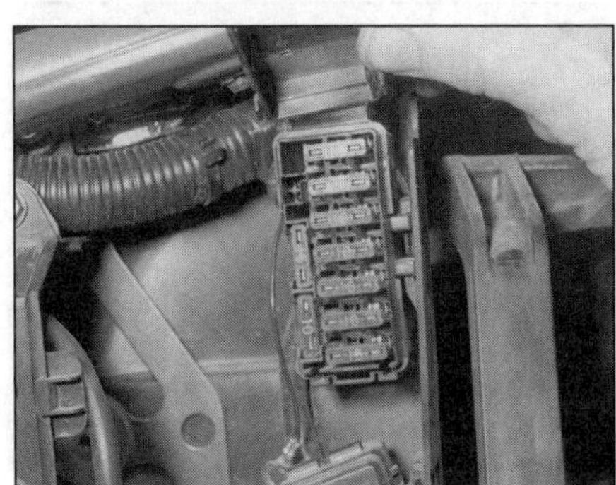

5.2 Unclip the lid to access the fuses

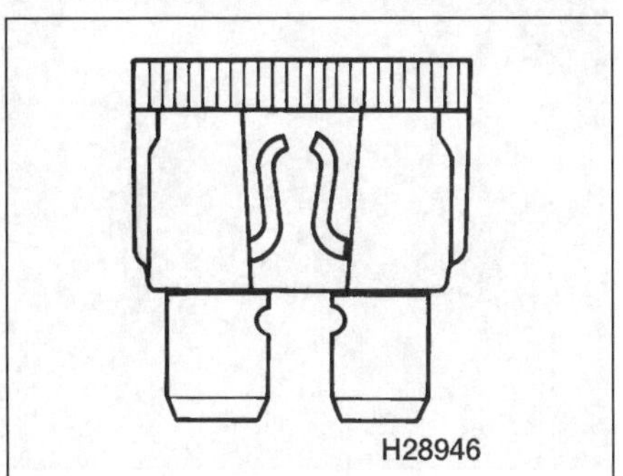

5.3 A blown fuse can be identified by a break in its element

7.2a Disconnect the wiring connector . . .

7.2b . . . and remove the dust cover

7.3a Release the clip . . .

7.3b . . . and remove the bulb

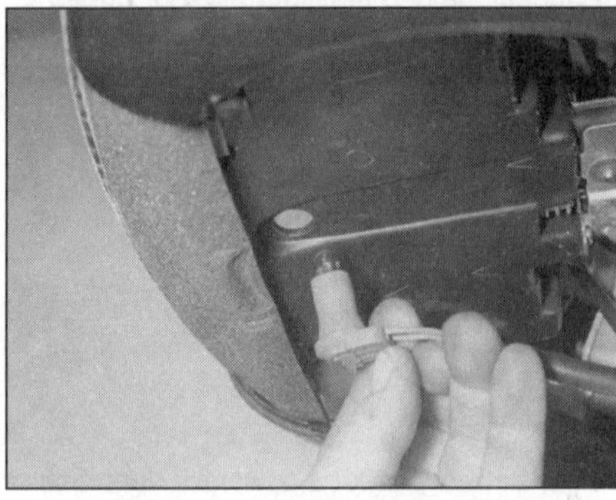

7.8a Remove the bulbholder . . .

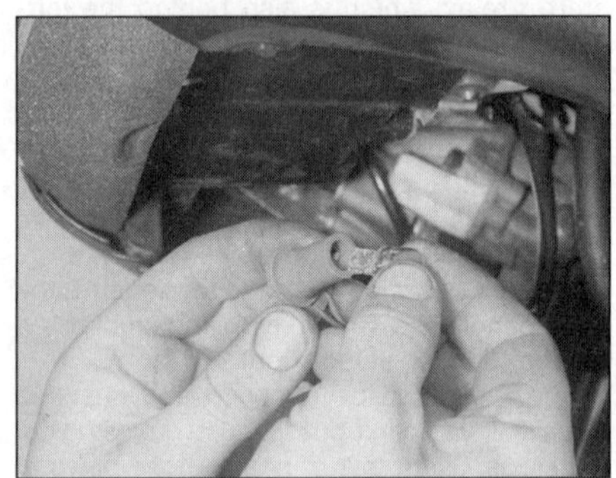

7.8b . . . and pull out the bulb

2 Disconnect the relevant wiring connector from the back of the headlight assembly and remove the rubber dust cover, noting how it fits **(see illustrations)**.

3 Release the bulb retaining clip, noting how it fits, then remove the bulb **(see illustrations)**.

4 Fit the new bulb, bearing in mind the information in the **Note** above. Make sure the tabs on the bulb fit correctly in the slots in the bulb housing, and secure it in position with the retaining clip.

5 Install the dust cover, making sure it is correctly seated and with the "TOP" mark at the top, and connect the wiring connector.

6 Check the operation of the headlight, then fit the access panel.

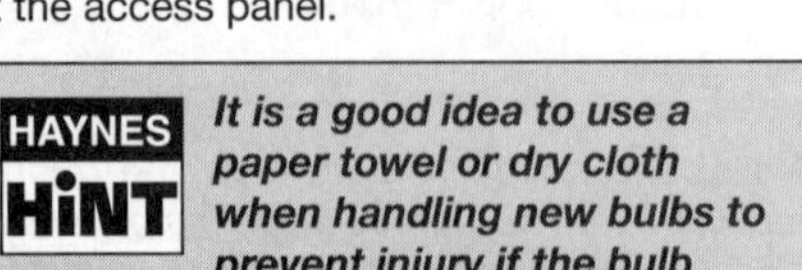

It is a good idea to use a paper towel or dry cloth when handling new bulbs to prevent injury if the bulb should break and to increase bulb life.

Sidelight (UK models only)

7 Remove the access panel from middle fairing inner cover, on the underside of the upper fairing.

8 Pull the bulbholder out of its socket in the base of the headlight, then carefully pull the bulb out of the holder **(see illustrations)**.

9 Install the new bulb in the bulbholder, then install the bulbholder by pressing it in. Make sure the rubber cover is correctly seated.

10 Check the operation of the sidelight, then fit the access panel.

8 Headlight assembly - removal and installation

Removal

1 Remove the upper fairing (see Chapter 8).

2 Unscrew the four bolts securing the headlight unit to the fairing and remove the headlight, noting how it fits **(see illustrations)**.

8.2a The headlight assembly is secured to the fairing by two bolts at the front (arrowed) . . .

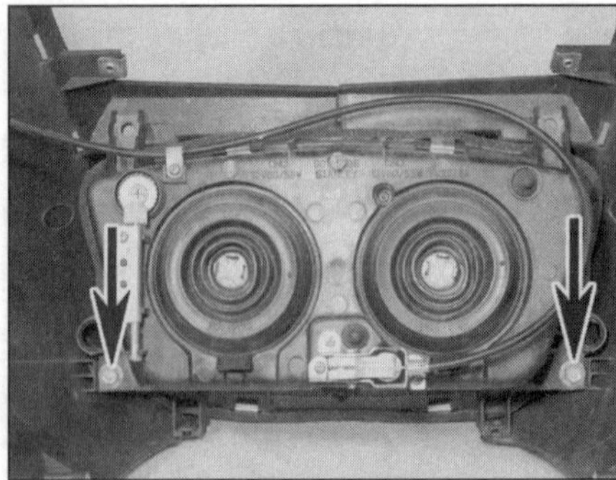

8.2b . . . and two bolts at the back (arrowed)

Installation

3 Installation is the reverse of removal. Make sure all the wiring is correctly connected and secured. Check the operation of the headlight and sidelight. Check the headlight aim (see Chapter 1).

9 Brake/tail light bulb - replacement

1 Remove the seat (see Chapter 8).

2 Fold the tail light cover side pieces in to the middle, then fold the middle piece down to access the bulbholders **(see**

9.2a Fold the side pieces in . . .

9.2b . . . and the middle piece down . . .

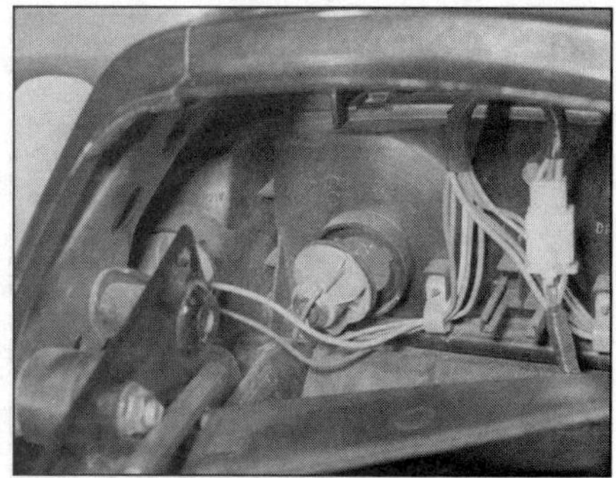

9.3 . . . then remove the bulbholder . . .

9.4 . . . and the bulb

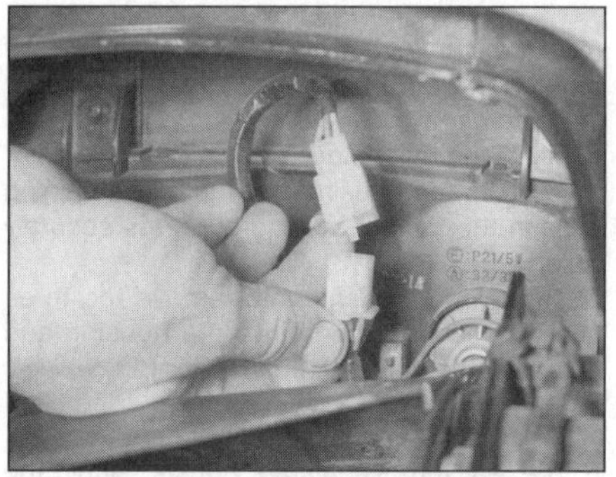

10.3 Disconnect the wiring connector . . .

illustrations). The tail light bulbholders are the middle two of the four.

3 Turn the bulbholder anti-clockwise and withdraw it from the tail light **(see illustration)**.

4 Push the bulb into the holder and twist it anti-clockwise to remove it **(see illustration)**. Check the socket terminals for corrosion and clean them if necessary. Line up the pins of the new bulb with the slots in the socket, then push the bulb in and turn it clockwise until it locks into place. **Note:** *The pins on the bulb are offset so it can only be installed one way. It is a good idea to use a paper towel or dry cloth when handling the new bulb to prevent injury if the bulb should break and to increase bulb life.*

5 Install the bulbholder into the tail light and turn it clockwise to secure it.

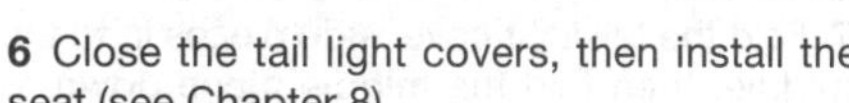

6 Close the tail light covers, then install the seat (see Chapter 8).

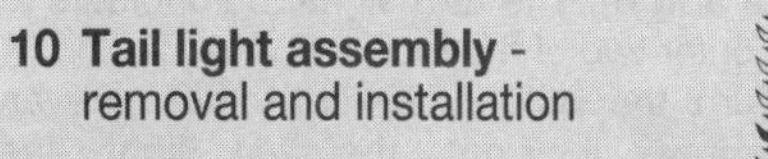

10 Tail light assembly - removal and installation

Removal

1 Remove the seat (see Chapter 8).

2 Fold the tail light cover side pieces in to the middle, then fold the middle piece down to access the bulbholders **(see illustrations 9.1a and b)**.

3 Disconnect the tail light assembly wiring connector **(see illustration)**.

4 Remove the four screws securing the tail light assembly and carefully withdraw it from the bike **(see illustrations)**. If required, turn the bulbholders anti-clockwise and withdraw them from the tail light.

Installation

5 Installation is the reverse of removal. Check the operation of the tail light, the brake light and the rear turn signals.

11 Turn signal circuit - check

1 The battery provides power for operation of the turn signal lights, so if they do not operate, always check the battery voltage first. Low battery voltage indicates either a faulty battery or a defective charging system. Refer to Section 3 for battery checks and Sections 34 and 35 for charging system tests. Also, check the fuse (see Section 5) and the switch (see Section 20).

2 Most turn signal problems are the result of a burned out bulb or corroded socket. This is especially true when the turn signals function properly in one direction, but fail to flash in the other direction. Check the bulbs and the sockets (see Section 12).

3 If the bulbs and sockets are good, check for power at the turn signal relay white/green wire with the ignition ON. The relay is mounted behind the right-hand side panel **(see illustration)**. Remove the side panel for

10.4a . . . then remove the two inner screws (arrowed) . . .

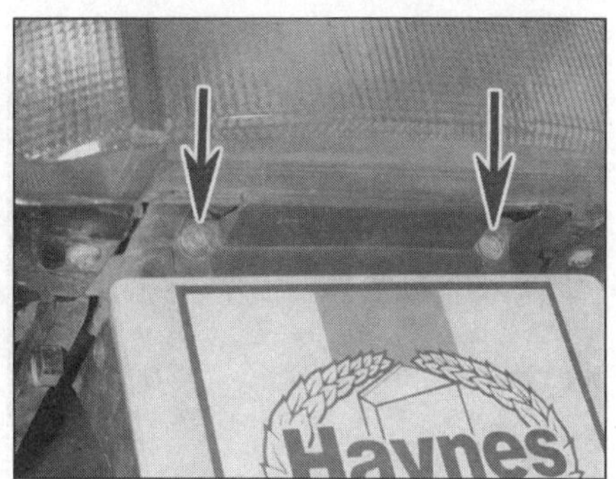

10.4b . . . and the two outer screws (arrowed) and remove the taillight

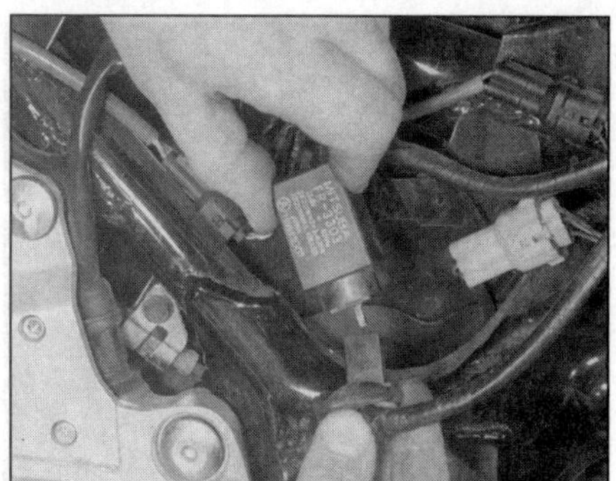

11.3 Disconnect the relay wiring connector and test as described

12.1 Release the mirror/turn signal housing from its clips . . .

12.2 . . . then remove the bulbholder . . .

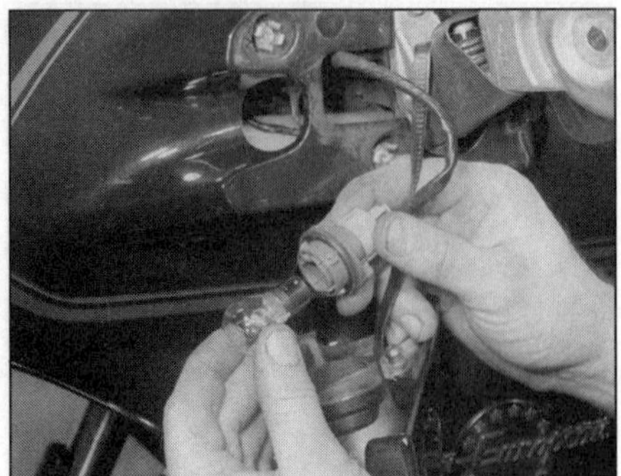
12.3 . . . and the bulb

access (see Chapter 8). Turn the ignition OFF when the check is complete.

4 If no power was present at the relay, check the wiring from the relay to the ignition (main) switch for continuity.

5 If power was present at the relay, using the appropriate wiring diagram at the end of this Chapter, check the wiring between the relay, turn signal switch and turn signal lights for continuity. If the wiring and switch are sound, replace the relay with a new one.

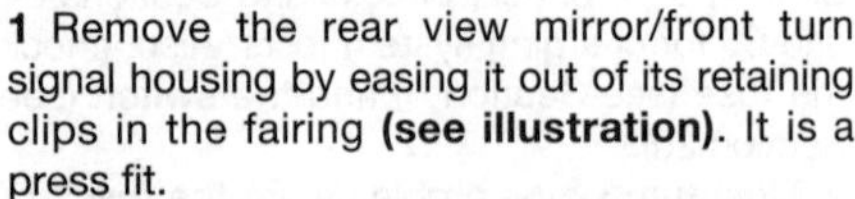

12 Turn signal bulbs - replacement

Front turn signals

1 Remove the rear view mirror/front turn signal housing by easing it out of its retaining clips in the fairing **(see illustration)**. It is a press fit.

2 Turn the bulbholder anti-clockwise and withdraw it from the housing **(see illustration)**.

3 Push the bulb into the holder and twist it anti-clockwise to remove it **(see illustration)**. Check the socket terminals for corrosion and clean them if necessary. Line up the pins of the new bulb with the slots in the socket, then push the bulb in and turn it clockwise until it locks into place. **Note:** *On US models, the front turn signals double as running lights - the pins on the bulb are offset so it can only be installed one way.*

4 Install the bulbholder back into the housing, then press the housing back into its retaining clips in the fairing, making sure it is securely held.

5 To replace the lens unit, remove the three screws securing the unit to the housing and withdraw the unit **(see illustration)**.

Rear turn signals

6 The rear turn signals are housed within the tail light assembly. Remove the seat (see Chapter 8).

7 Fold the tail light cover side pieces in to the middle, then fold the middle piece down to access the bulbholders **(see illustrations 9.1a and b)**. The turn signal bulbholders are the outer two of the four.

8 Turn the bulbholder anti-clockwise and withdraw it from the tail light **(see illustration)**.

9 Push the bulb into the holder and twist it anti-clockwise to remove it **(see illustration)**. Check the socket terminals for corrosion and clean them if necessary. Line up the pins of the new bulb with the slots in the socket, then push the bulb in and turn it clockwise until it locks into place.

10 Install the bulbholder into the tail light and turn it clockwise to secure it.

11 Close the tail light covers, then install the seat (see Chapter 8).

HAYNES HiNT *If the socket contacts are dirty or corroded, scrape them clean and spray with electrical contact cleaner before a new bulb is installed.*

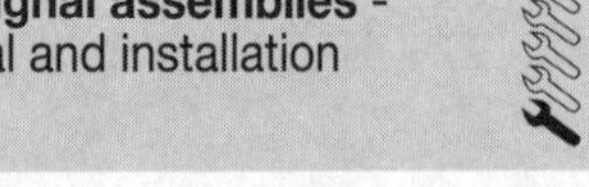

13 Turn signal assemblies - removal and installation

Front

Removal

1 Remove the rear view mirror/front turn signal housing by easing it out of its retaining clips in the fairing **(see illustration 12.1)**. It is a press fit.

2 Turn the bulbholder anti-clockwise and withdraw it from the housing **(see illustration 12.2)**. The housing is now retained by its safety strap. Release the strap and remove the housing.

Installation

3 Installation is the reverse of removal. Make sure the housing is securely held. Check the operation of the turn signals.

Rear

Removal

4 The rear turn signals are housed within the tail light assembly. Refer to Section 10 for tail light assembly removal.

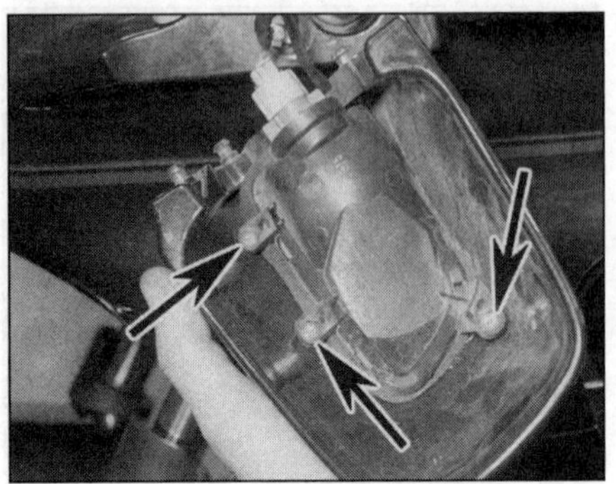
12.5 The lens unit is secured by three screws (arrowed)

12.8 Remove the bulbholder . . .

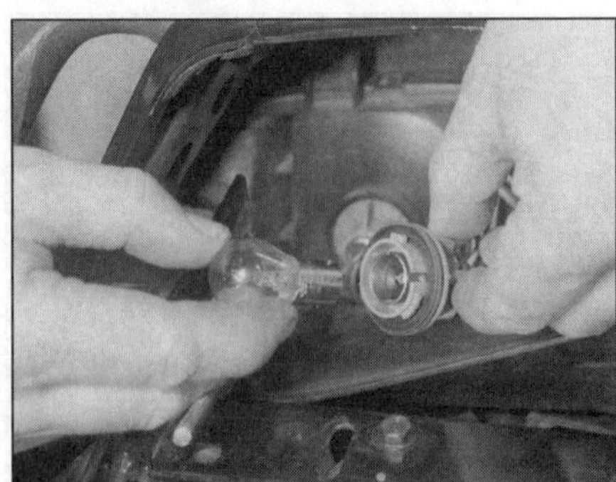
12.9 . . . and the bulb

14.5 Disconnect the switch wiring connectors . . .

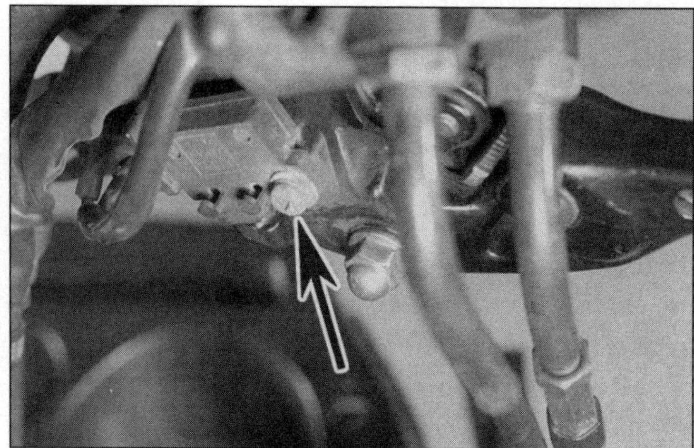

14.6 . . . and remove the single screw (arrowed) securing it to the master cylinder

Installation

5 Installation is the reverse of removal. Check the operation of the tail light, the brake light and the rear turn signals.

14 Brake light switches - check and replacement

Circuit check

1 Before checking any electrical circuit, check the bulb (see Section 9) and fuse (see Section 5).

2 Using a multimeter or test light connected to a good earth (ground), check for voltage at the brake light switch wiring connector **(see illustration 14.5 or 14.8)**. If there's no voltage present, check the wire between the switch and the ignition switch (see the *wiring diagrams* at the end of this Chapter).

3 If voltage is available, touch the probe of the test light to the other terminal of the switch, then pull the brake lever in or depress the brake pedal. If no reading is obtained or the test light doesn't light up, replace the switch.

4 If a reading is obtained or the test light does light up, check the wiring between the switch and the brake light bulb (see the *wiring diagrams* at the end of this Chapter).

Switch replacement

Front brake lever switch

5 The switch is mounted on the underside of the brake master cylinder. Disconnect the wiring connectors from the switch **(see illustration)**.

6 Remove the single screw securing the switch to the bottom of the master cylinder and remove the switch **(see illustration)**.

7 Installation is the reverse of removal. The switch isn't adjustable.

Rear brake pedal switch

8 The switch is mounted on the inside of the right-hand footrest bracket. Remove the right-hand side panel for access to the switch and its connector (see Chapter 8). Trace the wiring from the switch and disconnect it at the connector **(see illustrations)**.

9 Detach the lower end of the switch spring from the brake pedal, then unscrew the switch.

10 Installation is the reverse of removal. Make sure the brake light is activated just before the rear brake pedal takes effect. If adjustment is necessary, hold the switch and turn the adjusting nut on the switch body until the brake light is activated when required.

15 Instrument cluster and speedometer cable - removal and installation

Instrument cluster

Removal

1 Remove the windshield, trim and inner screen (see Chapter 8).

2 Remove the fairing pockets (see Chapter 8).

3 Disconnect the clock wiring connectors from under the instrument cluster.

4 Remove the instrument surround (see Chapter 8, Section 6, Step 5).

5 On ABS/TCS or CBS/LBS-ABS/TCS models, remove the two bolts securing the ignition control unit and displace it **(see illustration)**. There is no need to disconnect the wiring connectors.

6 Unscrew the knurled ring securing the speedometer cable and withdraw it from the speedometer.

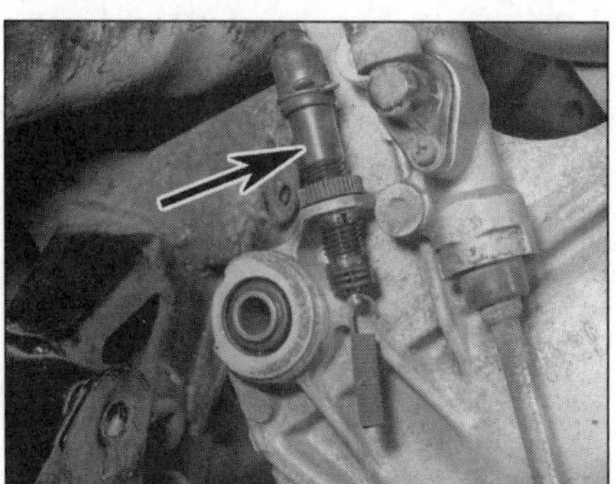

14.8a The rear brake light switch (arrowed) is on the inside of the right-hand footrest bracket (shown displaced for clarity)

14.8b Disconnect the switch wiring connector

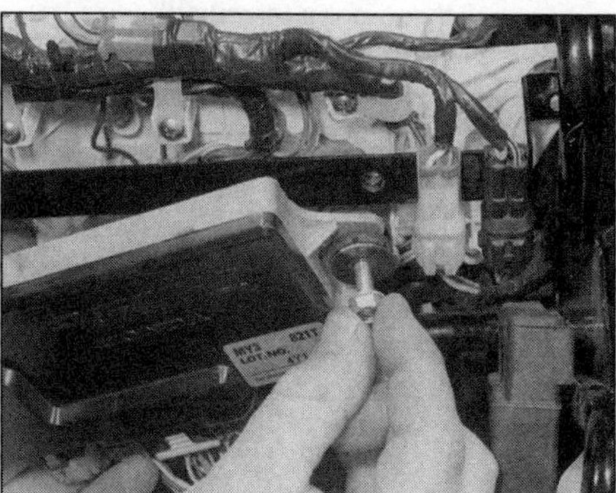

15.5 Remove the two bolts and displace the ignition control unit

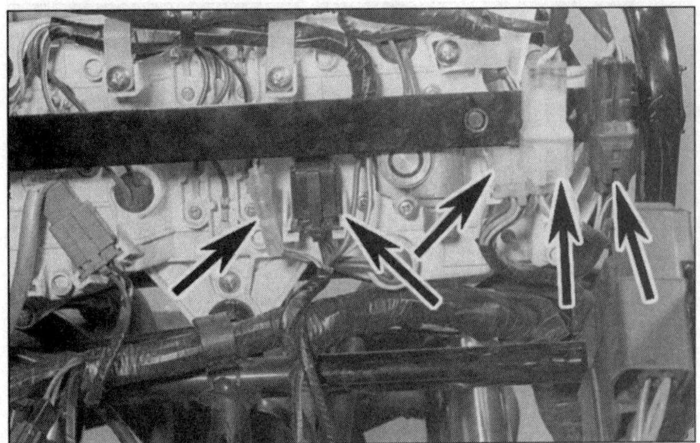
15.7a Instrument wiring connectors (arrowed) - ABS/TCS and CBS/LBS-ABS/TCS models

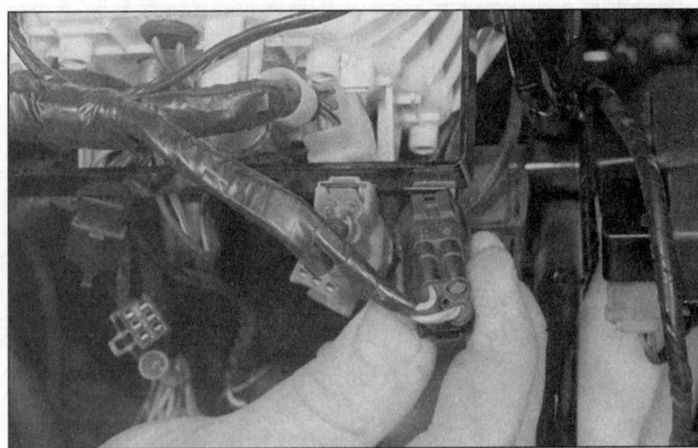
15.7b Some of the connectors are mounted on the bracket

7 Disconnect the instrument cluster wiring connectors - there are three on standard models and five on ABS/TCS models. Where appropriate, remove the connectors from their clips **(see illustrations)**.

8 Unscrew the three bolts securing the instrument cluster and remove them with their collars, where fitted **(see illustration)**.

9 Carefully remove the instrument cluster.

Installation

10 Installation is the reverse of removal. Tighten the bolts to the torque setting specified at the beginning of the Chapter. Make sure that the speedometer cable and wiring connectors are correctly routed and secured.

15.8 The instrument cluster is secured by three bolts (arrowed)

Speedometer cable

Removal

11 Remove the windshield, trim and inner screen (see Chapter 8).

12 On ABS/TCS or CBS/LBS-ABS/TCS models, remove the two bolts securing the ignition control unit and displace it **(see illustration 15.5)**. There is no need to disconnect the wiring connectors.

13 Unscrew the knurled ring securing the speedometer cable to the rear of the instrument cluster and detach the cable.

14 Remove the screw securing the lower end of the cable to the drive housing on the left-hand side of the front wheel **(see illustration)**.

15 Withdraw the cable through the hole in the middle fairing inner panel and remove it from the bike, noting its correct routing.

Installation

16 Route the cable up through the hole in the inner fairing panel to the back of the instrument cluster.

17 Connect the cable upper end to the speedometer and tighten the retaining ring securely.

18 Connect the cable lower end to the drive housing, aligning the slot in the cable end with the drive tab, and tighten the retaining screw securely **(see illustration)**.

19 Check that the cable doesn't restrict steering movement or interfere with any other components.

16 Instruments - check and replacement

Speedometer

Check

1 Special instruments are required to properly check the operation of this meter. If it is believed to be faulty, take the motorcycle to a Honda dealer for assessment.

Replacement

2 Remove the instrument cluster (see Section 15).

3 Unscrew the two nuts and the five screws and lift the front panel off the cluster **(see illustrations)**.

4 Remove the two screws securing the

15.14 Remove the screw (arrowed) and withdraw the cable

15.18 Align the slot with the tab and insert the cable, then secure it with the screw

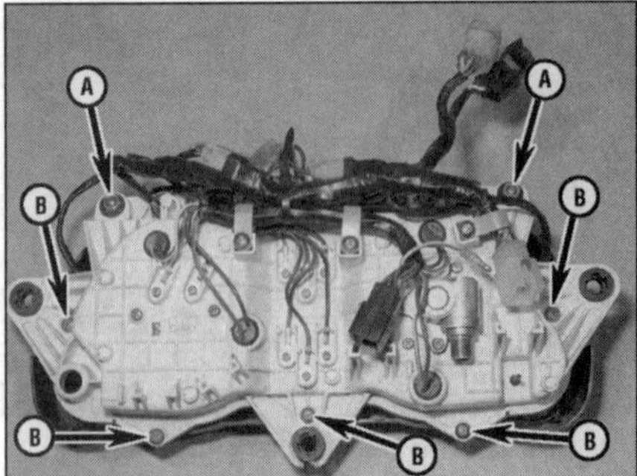

16.3a Remove the two nuts (A) and the five screws (B) . . .

16.3b ... then lift off the front cover

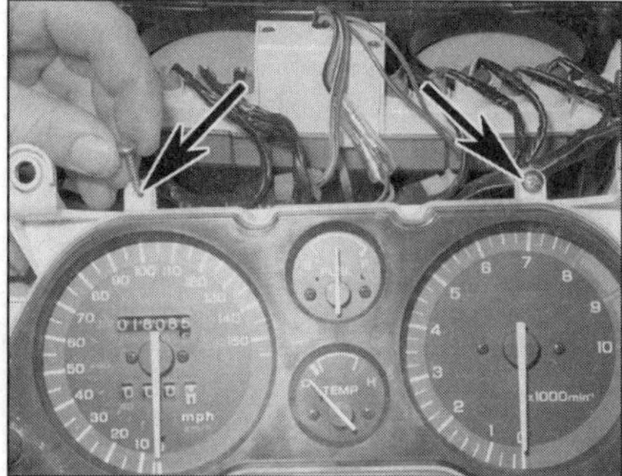
16.4a Remove the screws (arrowed) and lift off the screen ...

16.4b ... and the inner cover

instrument screen and lift off the screen and the inner cover **(see illustrations)**.

5 Remove the two screws securing the speedometer gearbox and lift off the box. Remove the O-ring from the speedometer for safekeeping. Remove the two screws securing the speedometer to the casing, then carefully withdraw the speedometer from the front **(see illustrations)**.

6 Installation is the reverse of removal.

Tachometer

Check

7 Special instruments are required to properly check the operation of this meter. If it is believed to be faulty, take the motorcycle to a Honda dealer for assessment.

Replacement

8 Remove the instrument cluster (see Section 15).

9 Unscrew the two nuts and the five screws and lift the front panel off the cluster **(see illustrations 16.3a and b)**.

10 Remove the two screws securing the instrument screen and lift off the screen and the inner cover **(see illustrations 16.4a and b)**.

11 Remove the screw securing each wiring connector, making a note of which fits where, then remove the two screws securing the tachometer to the casing and carefully withdraw the tachometer from the front **(see illustration)**.

12 Installation is the reverse of removal. Make sure the wires are correctly and securely connected.

Fuel gauge

Check

13 Remove the fuel tank cover (see Chapter 8). Trace the fuel level sender wiring from the left-hand side of the fuel tank and disconnect it at the connector **(see illustration overleaf)**.

14 Connect a jumper wire between the terminals on the wiring loom side of the connector. With the ignition switched ON, the fuel gauge should read FULL. If it doesn't,

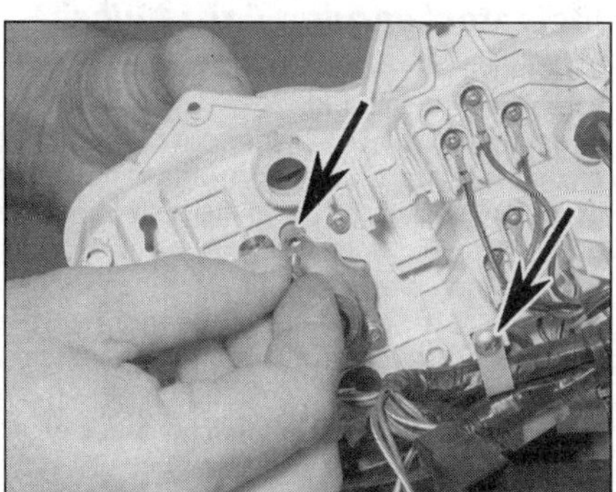
16.5a Remove the two screws (arrowed) ...

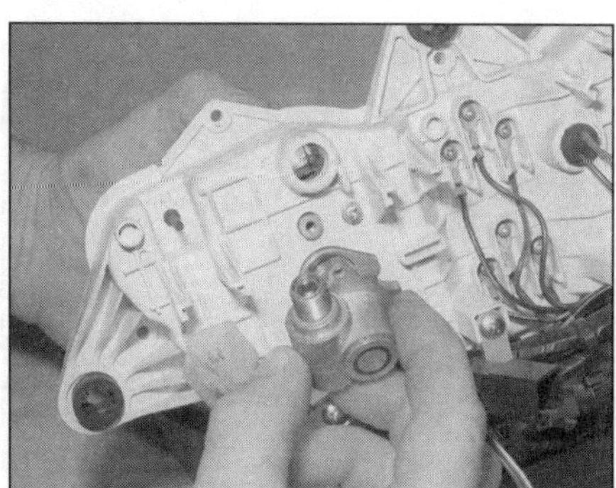
16.5b ... and lift off the gearbox

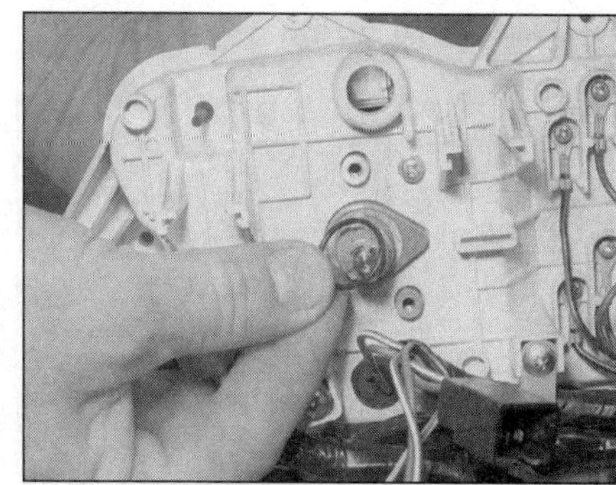
16.5c Remove the O-ring and keep it safe

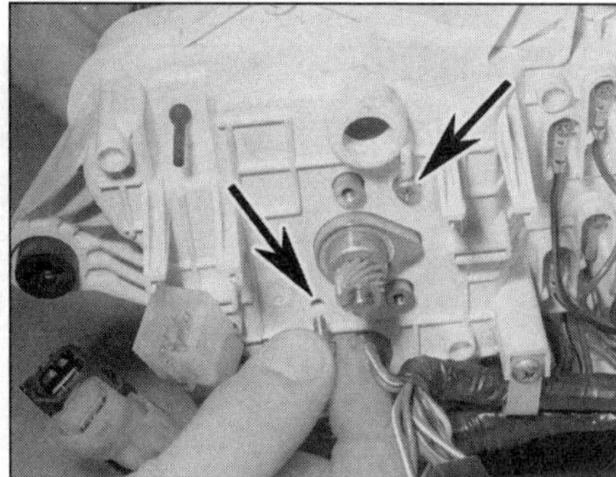
16.5d Remove the two screws (arrowed) ...

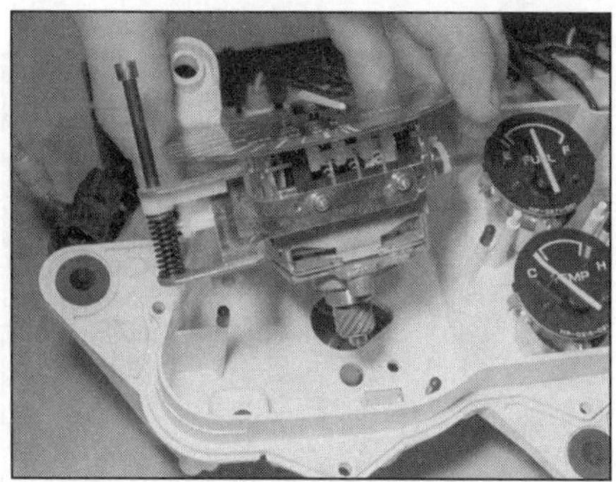
16.5e ... and remove the speedometer

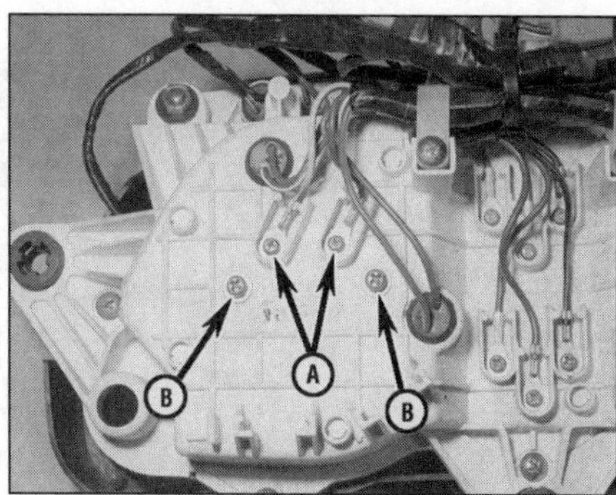

16.11 Remove the two wiring screws (A) and the two tachometer screws (B), then remove the tachometer

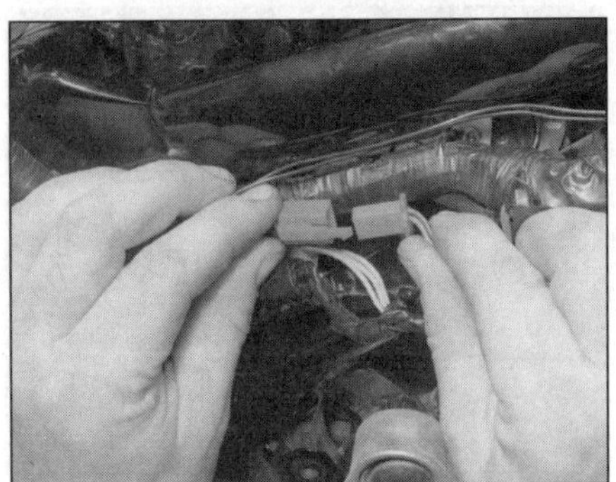

16.13 Disconnect the fuel level sender wiring connector

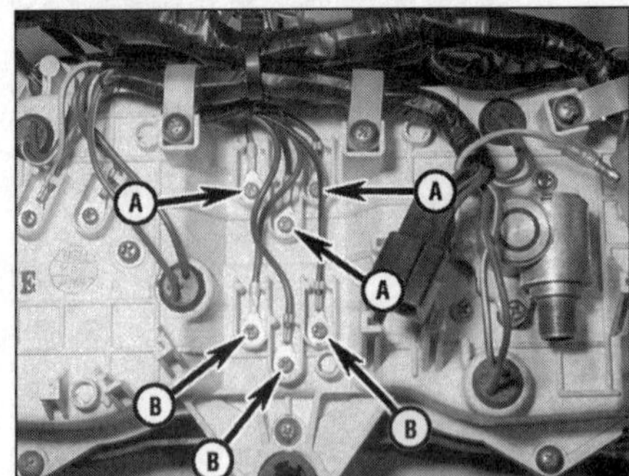

16.19 Fuel gauge wiring connectors (A), temperature gauge wiring connectors (B)

check the wiring between the connector and the gauge, and check for voltage at the black/brown wire on the back of the fuel gauge. If the wiring is good, then the gauge is faulty.

15 If the gauge reads FULL, check the fuel level sender inside the fuel tank (see Section 27).

Replacement

16 Remove the instrument cluster (see Section 15).

17 Unscrew the two nuts and the five screws and lift the front panel off the cluster **(see illustrations 16.3a and b)**.

18 Remove the two screws securing the instrument screen and lift off the screen and the inner cover **(see illustrations 16.4a and b)**.

19 Remove the screw securing each wiring connector, making a note of which fits where, then carefully withdraw the fuel gauge from the front **(see illustration)**.

20 Installation is the reverse of removal. Make sure the wires are correctly and securely connected.

Coolant temperature gauge

Check

21 See Chapter 3.

Replacement

22 Remove the instrument cluster (see Section 15).

23 Unscrew the two nuts and the five screws and lift the front panel off the cluster **(see illustrations 16.3a and b)**.

24 Remove the two screws securing the instrument screen and lift off the screen and the inner cover **(see illustrations 16.4a and b)**.

25 Remove the screw securing each wiring connector, making a note of which fits where, then carefully withdraw the temperature gauge from the front **(see illustration 16.19)**.

26 Installation is the reverse of removal. Make sure the wires are correctly and securely connected.

17 Instrument and warning light bulbs - replacement

Instrument light bulbs

1 Remove the windshield, trim and inner screen (see Chapter 8).

2 Gently pull the bulbholder out of the instrument casing, then pull the bulb out of the bulbholder **(see illustrations)**. If the socket contacts are dirty or corroded, scrape them clean and spray with electrical contact cleaner before a new bulb is installed. Carefully push the new bulb into the holder and install the windshield, trim and inner screen (see Chapter 8).

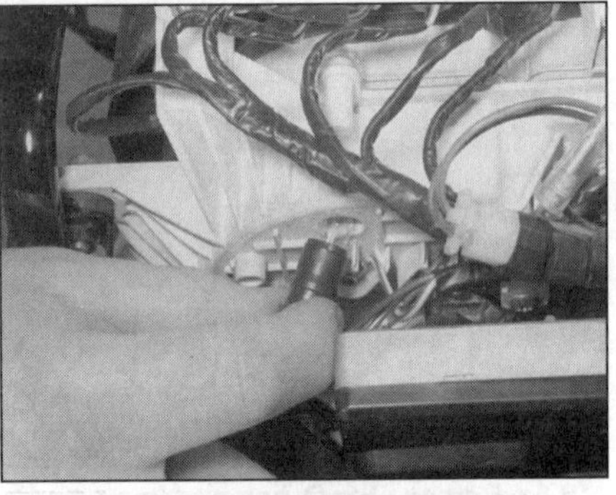

17.2a Pull the bulbholder out of the instrument casing . . .

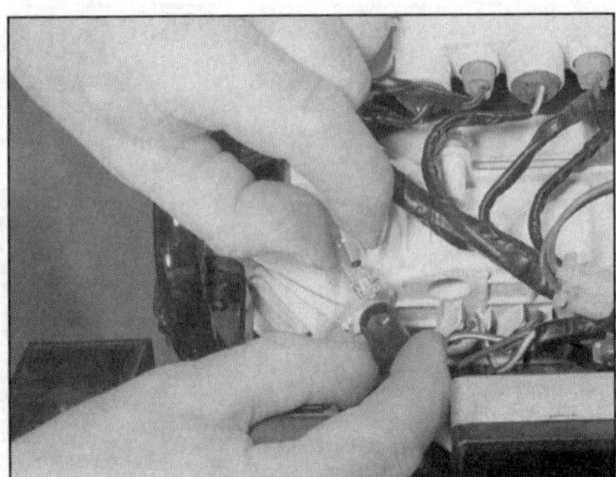

17.2b . . . and remove the bulb

Indicator/warning light bulbs

3 Remove the windshield, trim and inner screen (see Chapter 8).

4 Gently pull the bulbholder out of the panel, or in the case of the turn signal indicator bulbs, the casing, then pull the bulb out of the bulbholder. To access the ABS/TCS LEDs, remove the screws securing the cover, then remove the cover and withdraw the bulbholder **(see illustrations)**. If the socket contacts are dirty or corroded, scrape them clean and spray with electrical contact cleaner before a new bulb is installed. Carefully push the new bulb into the holder and install the windshield, trim and inner screen (see Chapter 8).

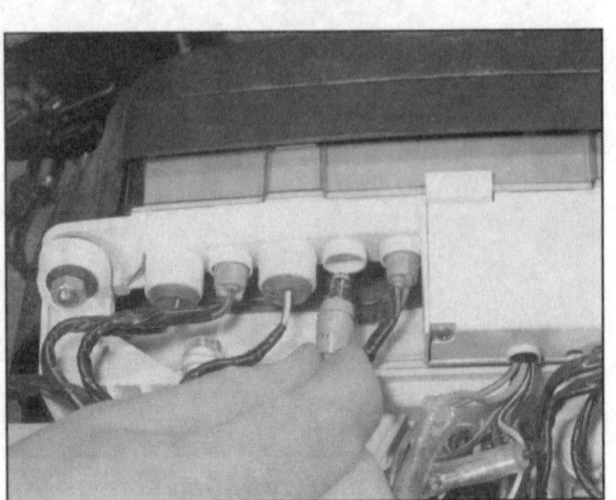

17.4a Pull the bulbholder out of the panel . . .

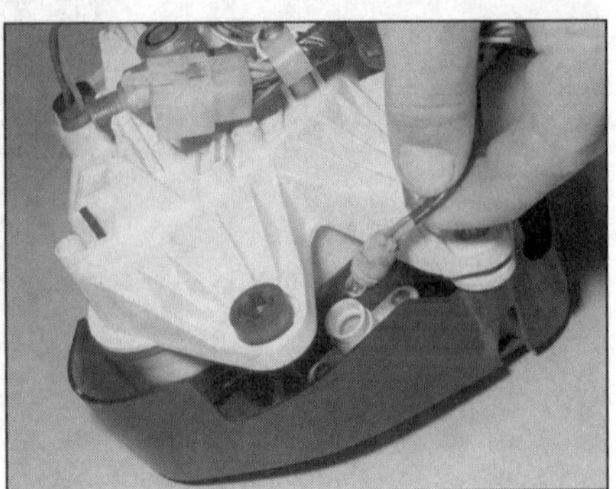

17.4b . . . or casing . . .

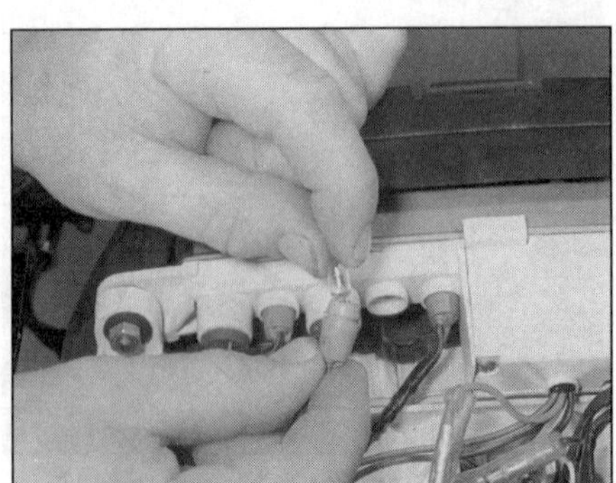

17.4c . . . and remove the bulb

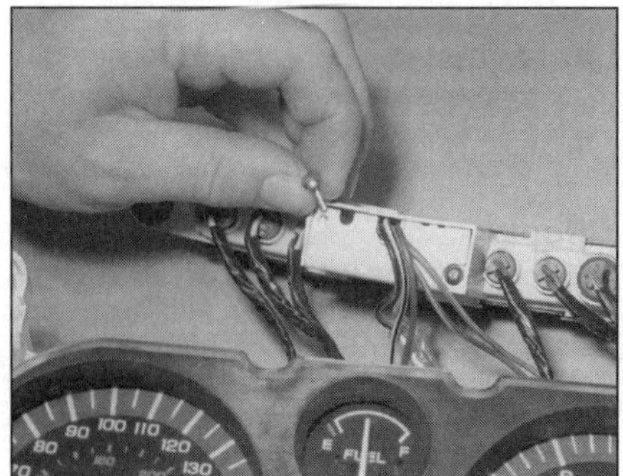

17.4d Remove the panel . . .

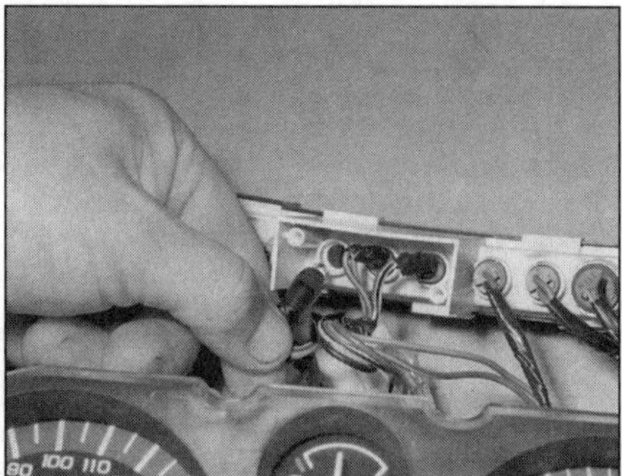

17.4e . . . to access the ABS/TCS LEDs

18 Oil pressure switch - check, removal and installation

Check

1 The oil pressure warning light should come on when the ignition (main) switch is turned ON and extinguish a few seconds after the engine is started. If the oil pressure warning light comes on whilst the engine is running, stop the engine immediately and carry out an oil level check, and if the level is correct, an oil pressure check (see Chapter 1).

2 If the oil pressure warning light does not come on when the ignition is turned on, check the bulb (see Section 17) and fuse (see Section 5).

3 The oil pressure switch is screwed into the crankcase between the cylinders and is accessed by removing the right-hand maintenance cover (see Chapter 8). Pull the rubber cover off the switch and detach the wiring connector **(see illustrations)**. With the ignition switched ON, earth (ground) the wire on the crankcase and check that the warning light comes on. If the light comes on, the switch is defective and must be replaced.

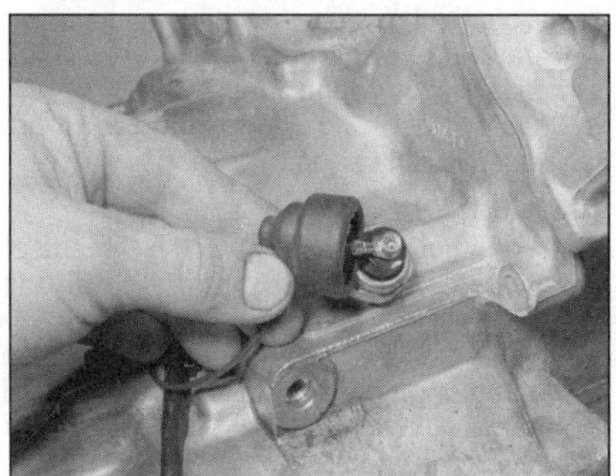

18.3a Pull back the rubber cover . . .

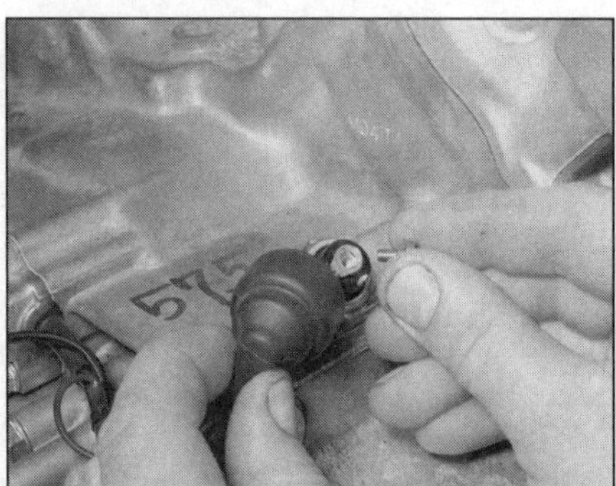

18.3b . . . then remove the terminal screw and detach the wiring

4 If the light still does not come on, check for voltage at the wire terminal. If there is no voltage present, check the wire between the switch, the instrument cluster and fusebox for continuity (see the *Wiring diagrams* at the end of this Chapter).

5 If the warning light comes on whilst the engine is running, yet the oil pressure is satisfactory, remove the wire from the oil pressure switch. With the wire detached and the ignition switched ON the light should be out. If it is illuminated, the wire between the switch and instrument cluster must be earthed (grounded) at some point. If the wiring is good, the switch must be assumed faulty and replaced.

Removal

6 Remove the right-hand middle fairing panel (see Chapter 8), and on ABS/TCS and CBS/LBS-ABS/TCS models, remove the coolant reservoir (see Chapter 3).

7 Pull the rubber cover off the switch and detach the wiring connector **(see illustrations 18.3a and b)**.

8 Unscrew the oil pressure switch and withdraw it from the crankcase.

Installation

9 Apply a suitable sealant to the upper portion of the switch threads near the switch body, leaving the bottom 3 to 4 mm of thread clean. Install the switch in the crankcase and tighten it to the torque setting specified at the beginning of the Chapter. Attach the wiring connector **(see illustration 18.3b)**.

10 Run the engine and check that the switch operates correctly.

11 Install the middle fairing panel (see Chapter 8).

19 Ignition (main) switch - check, removal and installation

Warning: To prevent the risk of short circuits, disconnect the battery negative (-ve) lead before making any ignition (main) switch checks.

Check

1 Remove the air filter housing (see Chapter 4). Trace the ignition (main) switch wiring back from the base of the switch and disconnect it at the white connector behind the steering head **(see illustration)**.

2 Using an ohmmeter or a continuity tester, check the continuity of the connector terminal pairs (see the *wiring diagrams* at the end of this Chapter). Continuity should exist between the terminals connected by a solid line on the diagram when the switch is in the indicated position.

3 If the switch fails any of the tests, replace it.

Removal

Note: *Support the bike on its centrestand or an auxiliary stand and tie the back end down so that all weight is off the front end of the bike.*

4 Displace the handlebars (see Chapter 6). Although not essential, it is wise to remove the upper fairing and the fuel tank cover (see Chapter 8) to avoid the possibility of damage should a tool slip. Unscrew the steering stem nut, then slacken the fork clamp bolts in the top yoke **(see illustration)**. Gently ease the top yoke up off the fork tubes.

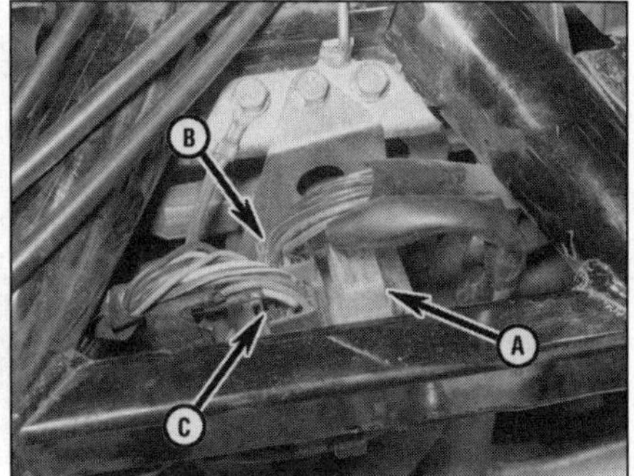

19.1 Ignition switch wiring connector (A), right-side handlebar switch connector (B), left-side handlebar connector (C)

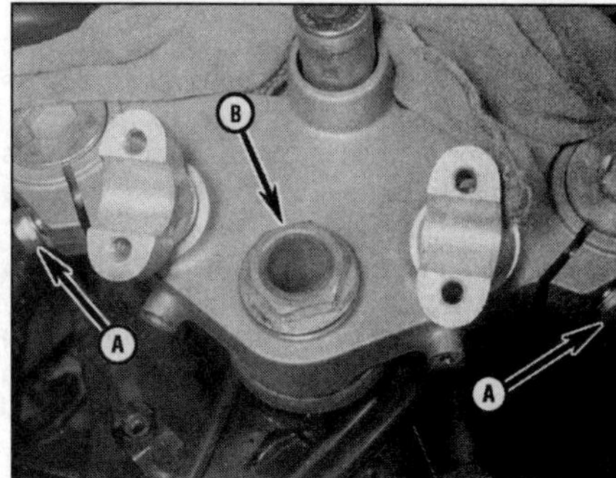

19.4 Slacken the clamp bolts (A), and remove the steering stem nut and washer (B)

19.6 The ignition switch is secured by two Torx bolts (arrowed)

5 Remove the air filter housing (see Chapter 4). Trace the ignition (main) switch wiring back from the base of the switch and disconnect it at the white connector behind the steering head **(see illustration 19.1)**. Draw the wiring through to the switch, noting its routing

6 Two Torx bolts mount the ignition switch to the underside of the top yoke **(see illustration)**. Remove the bolts and withdraw the switch from the top yoke.

Installation

7 Installation is the reverse of removal. Make sure wiring is securely connected and correctly routed.

20 Handlebar switches - check

1 Generally speaking, the switches are reliable and trouble-free. Most troubles, when they do occur, are caused by dirty or corroded contacts, but wear and breakage of internal parts is a possibility that should not be overlooked. If breakage does occur, the entire switch and related wiring harness will have to be replaced with a new one, since individual parts are not available.

2 The switches can be checked for continuity using an ohmmeter or a continuity test light. Always disconnect the battery negative (-ve) cable, which will prevent the possibility of a short circuit, before making the checks.

3 Trace the wiring harness of the switch in question back to its connector and disconnect it. The connectors are behind the steering stem - remove the air filter housing for access (see Chapter 4) **(see illustration 19.1)**.

4 Check for continuity between the terminals of the switch harness with the switch in the various positions (i.e. switch off - no continuity, switch on - continuity) - see the *wiring diagrams* at the end of this Chapter.

5 If the continuity check indicates a problem exists, refer to Section 21, remove the switch and spray the switch contacts with electrical contact cleaner. If they are accessible, the contacts can be scraped clean with a knife or polished with crocus cloth. If switch components are damaged or broken, it will be obvious when the switch is disassembled.

21 Handlebar switches - removal and installation

Right-hand handlebar switch

Removal

1 If the switch is to be removed from the bike, rather than just displaced from the handlebar, remove the air filter housing (see Chapter 4) and trace the wiring harness back from the switch to the red wiring connector behind the steering head and disconnect it **(see illustration 19.1)**. Work back along the harness, freeing it from all the relevant clips and ties, whilst noting its correct routing.

2 Disconnect the two wires from the brake light switch **(see illustration 14.5)**.

3 Remove the throttle cables from the switch (see Chapter 4 - this procedure incorporates switch removal).

Installation

4 Installation is the reverse of removal. Make sure the locating pin in the lower half of the switch locates in the hole in the underside of the handlebar. Refer to Chapter 4 for installation of the throttle cables.

Left-hand handlebar switch

Removal

5 If the switch is to be removed from the bike, rather than just displaced from the handlebar, remove the air filter housing (see Chapter 4) and trace the wiring harness back from the switch to the black wiring connector behind the steering head and disconnect it **(see illustration 19.1)**. Work back along the harness, freeing it from all the relevant clips and ties, whilst noting its correct routing.

6 Disconnect the two wires from the clutch switch **(see illustration 24.2)**.

7 Remove the choke cable from the switch (see Chapter 4 - this procedure incorporates switch removal).

Installation

8 Installation is the reverse of removal. Make sure the locating pin in the lower half of the switch locates in the hole in the underside of the handlebar. Refer to Chapter 4 for installation of the choke cable.

22.2a The neutral switch (arrowed) threads into the transmission casing

22 Neutral switch - check, removal and installation

Check

1 Before checking the electrical circuit, check the bulb (see Section 17) and fuse (see Section 5).

2 The switch is located in the left-hand side of the transmission casing on the back of the engine. Remove the left-hand middle fairing panel for access (see Chapter 8). Detach the wiring connector from the switch **(see illustrations)**. Make sure the transmission is in neutral.

3 With the connector disconnected and the ignition switched ON, the neutral light should be out. If not, the wire between the connector and instrument cluster must be earthed (grounded) at some point.

4 Check for continuity between the switch terminal and the crankcase. With the transmission in neutral, there should be continuity. With the transmission in gear, there should be no continuity. If the tests prove otherwise, then the switch is faulty.

5 If the continuity tests prove the switch is good, check for voltage at the wire terminal using a test light. If there's no voltage present, check the wire between the switch, the instrument cluster and fusebox (see the *wiring diagrams* at the end of this Chapter).

Removal

6 Remove the left-hand middle fairing panel (see Chapter 8).

7 Detach the wiring connector from the switch **(see illustration 22.2b)**.

8 Unscrew the switch and withdraw it from the transmission casing.

Installation

9 Apply a smear of sealant to the threads of the switch, taking care not to cover the contact point.

10 Install the switch and tighten it to the torque setting specified at the beginning of the Chapter.

11 Check the operation of the neutral light.

12 Install the left-hand middle fairing panel (see Chapter 8).

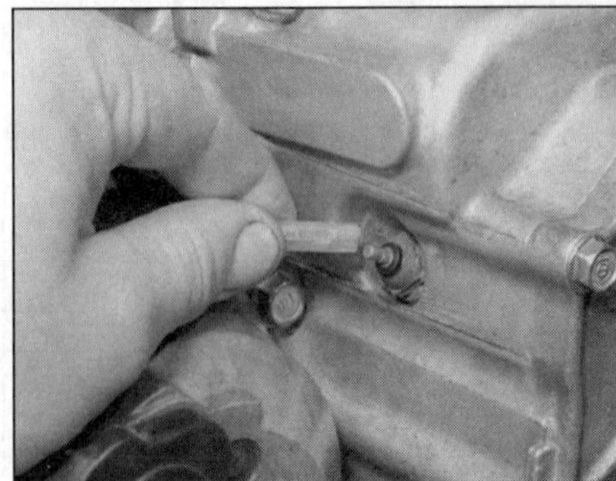
22.2b Disconnect the wiring connector

23.2 Disconnect the sidestand switch wiring connector

23.6 The switch is secured to the stand by a single bolt

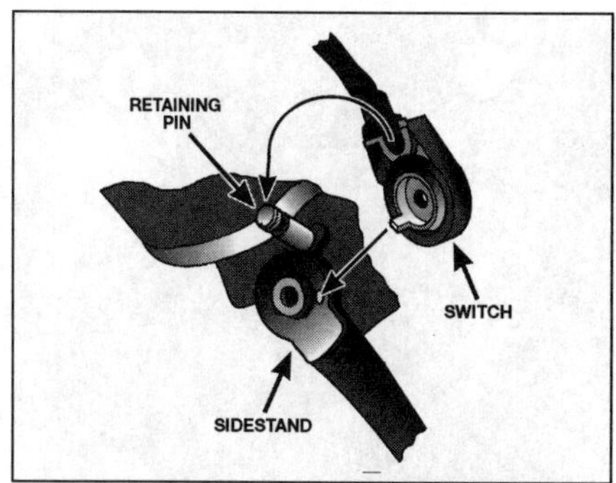

23.8 Make sure the lug on the switch locates in the hole in the stand, and the cutout in the switch locates around the retaining pin

23 Sidestand switch - check and replacement

Check

1 The sidestand switch is mounted on the top of the sidestand. The switch is part of the safety circuit which prevents or stops the engine running if the transmission is in gear whilst the sidestand is down, and prevents the engine from starting if the transmission is in gear unless the sidestand is up, and unless the clutch is pulled in. Before checking the electrical circuit, check the indicator bulb (see Section 17) and fuse (see Section 5).

2 Place the machine on the centrestand and remove the left-hand side panel (see Chapter 8). Trace the wiring back from the switch to its connector and disconnect it **(see illustration)**.

3 Check the operation of the switch using an ohmmeter or continuity test light. Connect the meter to the green/white and green wires on the switch side of the connector. With the sidestand up there should be continuity (zero resistance) between the terminals, and with the stand down there should be no continuity (infinite resistance). Now connect the meter to the yellow/black and green wires on the switch side of the connector. With the sidestand down there should be continuity (zero resistance) between the terminals, and with the stand up there should be no continuity (infinite resistance).

4 If the switch does not perform as expected, it is defective and must be replaced.

5 If the switch is good, check the wiring between the various components in the starter safety circuit (see the *Wiring diagrams* at the end of this book).

Replacement

6 The sidestand switch is mounted on the top of the sidestand **(see illustration)**. Place the machine on the centrestand and remove the left-hand side panel and swingarm pivot cover (see Chapter 8). Trace the wiring back from the switch to its connector and disconnect it **(see illustration 23.2)**. Work back along the switch wiring, freeing it from any relevant retaining clips and ties, noting its correct routing.

7 Unscrew the switch bolt and remove the switch from the stand, noting how it fits.

8 Fit the new switch onto the sidestand, making sure the pin locates in the hole in the sidestand, and the lug above the stand locates into the cutout in the switch body **(see illustration)**. Install the switch retaining bolt and tighten it to the specified torque setting.

9 Make sure the wiring is correctly routed up to the connector and retained by all the necessary clips and ties.

10 Reconnect the wiring connector and check the operation of the sidestand switch.

24 Clutch switch - check and replacement

Check

1 The clutch switch is situated on the front of the clutch master cylinder **(see illustration)**. The switch is part of the safety circuit which prevents or stops the engine running if the transmission is in gear whilst the sidestand is down, and prevents the engine from starting if the transmission is in gear unless the sidestand is up and the clutch lever is pulled in.

2 To check the switch, disconnect the wiring connectors from the switch **(see illustration 24.1)**. Connect the probes of an ohmmeter or a continuity test light to the two switch terminals. With the clutch lever pulled in, continuity should be indicated. With the clutch lever out, no continuity (infinite resistance) should be indicated.

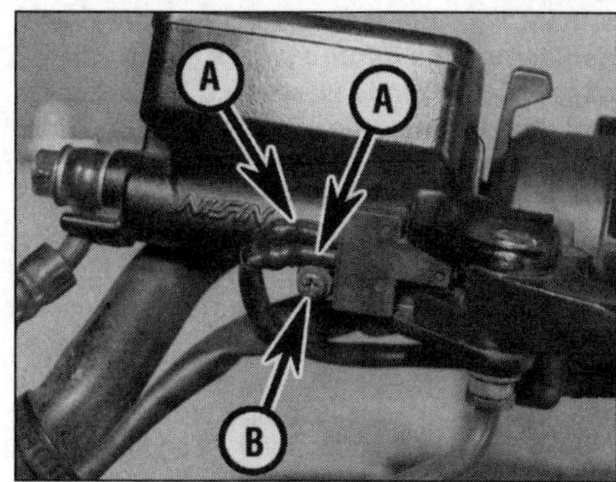

24.1 Clutch switch wiring connectors (A) and retaining screw (B)

3 If the switch is good, check the other components in the starter circuit as described in the relevant sections of this Chapter. If all components are good, check the wiring between the various components (see the *wiring diagrams* at the end of this book).

Replacement

4 Disconnect the wiring connectors from the clutch switch **(see illustration 24.1)**. Remove the retaining screw and remove the switch.

5 Installation is the reverse of removal. The switch isn't adjustable.

25 Diode - check and replacement

Check

1 The diode is a small block that plugs into a connector in the main wiring harness. The diode is part of the safety circuit which prevents or stops the engine running if the transmission is in gear whilst the sidestand is down, and prevents the engine from starting if the transmission is in gear unless the sidestand is up and the clutch lever is pulled in. Disconnect the diode from the harness.

2 Using an ohmmeter or continuity tester, connect the positive (+ve) probe to one of the outer terminals of the diode and the negative (-ve) probe to the middle (light green) terminal of the diode. The diode should show continuity. Now reverse the probes. The diode should show no continuity. Repeat the tests between the other outer terminal and the middle terminal. The same results should be achieved. If it doesn't behave as stated, replace the diode.

3 If the diode is good, check the other components in the starter circuit as described in the relevant sections of this Chapter. If all components are good, check the wiring between the various components (see the *wiring diagrams* at the end of this book).

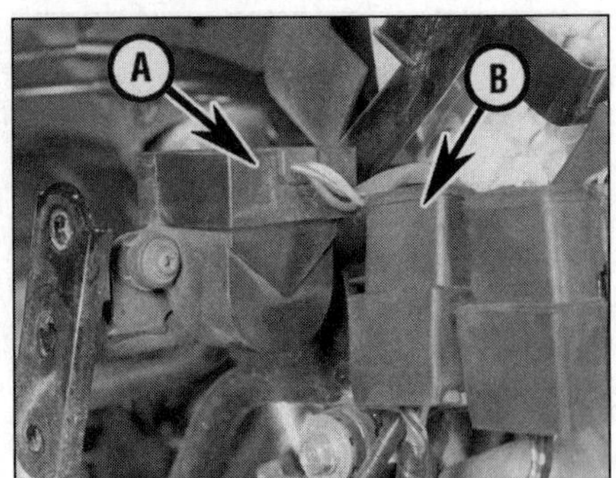

26.1 Lean angle sensor (A), lean angle sensor relay (B) - ABS/TCS model shown

27.5 The fuel level sender is mounted in the left-hand side of the tank

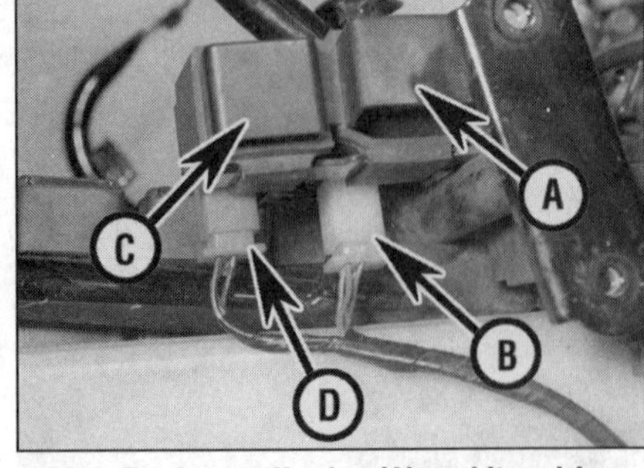

28.1 Fuel cut-off relay (A) and its wiring connector (B); indicator light check unit (C) and its wiring connector (D)

Replacement

4 The diode is a small block that plugs into a connector in the main wiring harness. Disconnect the diode and connect the new one.

26 Lean angle sensor and relay - check and replacement

Check

1 Remove the upper fairing (see Chapter 8). The lean angle sensor and its relay are mounted on the right-hand side of the fairing stay **(see illustration)**.

2 Trace the wiring from the sensor and disconnect it at the connector. Turn the ignition switch "ON", then using a multimeter set to the 0-20 V DC scale, connect the positive (+ve) probe to the red/white terminal of the sensor, and the negative (-ve) probe to the green terminal. There should be a reading of 0 to 3.0 V. Now connect the positive (+ve) probe to the white terminal of the sensor, and the keep the negative (-ve) probe on the green terminal. There should be a reading of 10.0 to 14.0 V. If the readings obtained are different, check the voltage supply to the sensor and the wiring. If the wiring is good, the sensor is faulty.

3 If the sensor is good, disconnect the meter and turn the ignition switch "OFF". Remove the screws securing the sensor, but keep the wiring connector connected.

4 Make sure the sensor is horizontal, then turn the ignition switch "ON". The sensor relay should click and there should be continuity between its main black/yellow and black terminals.

5 Now lean the sensor either way to an angle of approximately 50 degrees from the horizontal. The relay should click and there should now be no continuity between its main black/yellow and black terminals. If the sensor is good and the relay does not click as described, the relay is faulty.

6 If the relay is good, check the other components in the starter circuit as described in the relevant sections of this Chapter. If all components are good, check the wiring between the various components (see the *wiring diagrams* at the end of this book).

7 Note that a modified lean angle sensor was fitted to UK R and AR models onward, and US 1994 models onward; this unit may already have been subsequently installed on earlier machines. The modified unit can be identified by the moulded UP mark on its side, as opposed to the white painted UP mark on the earlier unit.

Replacement

8 Remove the upper fairing (see Chapter 8). The lean angle sensor and its relay are mounted on the right-hand side of the fairing stay **(see illustration 26.1)**.

9 Trace the wiring from the sensor and /or relay and disconnect it at the connector. The sensor is secured by two screws, while the relay sits in a rubber sleeve mounted on a bracket.

10 Install the new unit and connect the wiring connector. Make sure the UP mark on the back of the sensor faces up. Check the operation of the sensor and relay.

27 Fuel level sender - check and replacement

Warning: Petrol (gasoline) is extremely flammable, so take extra precautions when you work on any part of the fuel system. Don't smoke or allow open flames or bare light bulbs near the work area, and don't work in a garage where a natural gas-type appliance is present. If you spill any fuel on your skin, rinse it off immediately with soap and water. When you perform any kind of work on the fuel system, wear safety glasses and have a fire extinguisher suitable for a class B type fire (flammable liquids) on hand.

Check

1 If the fuel gauge fails to operate, remove the fuel tank cover (see Chapter 8) and trace the wiring back from the fuel level sender in the left-hand side of the fuel tank and disconnect it at the connector **(see illustration 16.13)**.

2 Using an ohmmeter set to ohms x 100 scale, connect its probes to the terminals on the sender side of the connector. Check the resistance reading with the tank empty and full. Compare the readings with those listed in the specifications at the beginning of this Chapter. Alternatively, remove the sender from the tank (see Steps 4 and 5 below) and, with the meter connected as above, manually move the float up and down to emulate the different positions.

3 If the readings taken differ to those listed in the specifications, replace the sender.

Replacement

4 Drain and remove the fuel tank (see Chapter 4).

5 Remove the retainer securing the sender to the tank and withdraw the sender, taking care not to bend the float arm **(see illustration)**. Discard the gasket as a new one must be used.

6 Install the sender by reversing the removal process, using a new gasket.

28 Fuel pump and cut-off relay - check, removal and installation

Warning: Gasoline (petrol) is extremely flammable, so take extra precautions when you work on any part of the fuel system. Don't smoke or allow open flames or bare light bulbs near the work area, and don't work in a garage where a natural gas-type appliance (such as a water heater or clothes dryer) is present. If you spill any fuel on your skin, rinse it off immediately with soap and water. When you perform any kind of work on the fuel system, wear safety glasses and have a fire extinguisher suitable for a class B type fire (flammable liquids) on hand.

Check

1 The fuel pump is located inside the fuel tank. The fuel cut-off relay is located behind the instrument cluster surround (see Chapter 8, Section 6, Steps 3 to 5 for removal of the surround) **(see illustration)**.

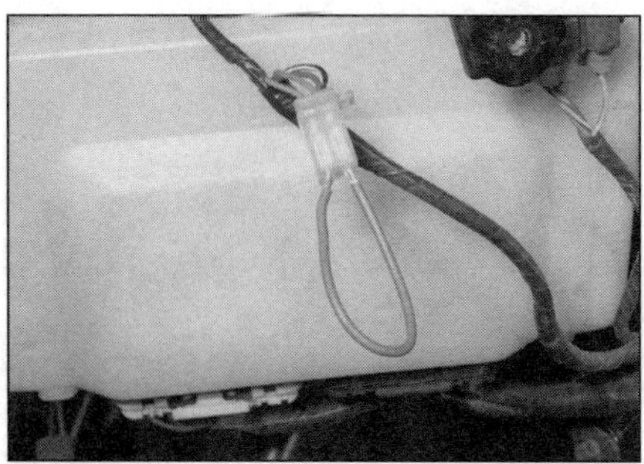
28.4 Connect a jumper wire between the specified terminals of the relay wiring connector

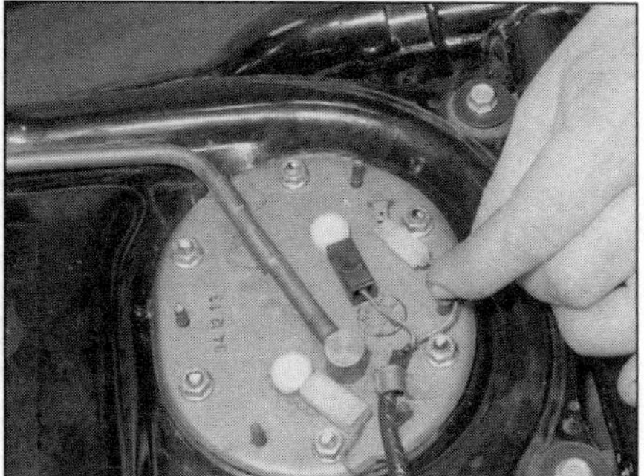
28.8 Disconnect the fuel pump wiring connectors

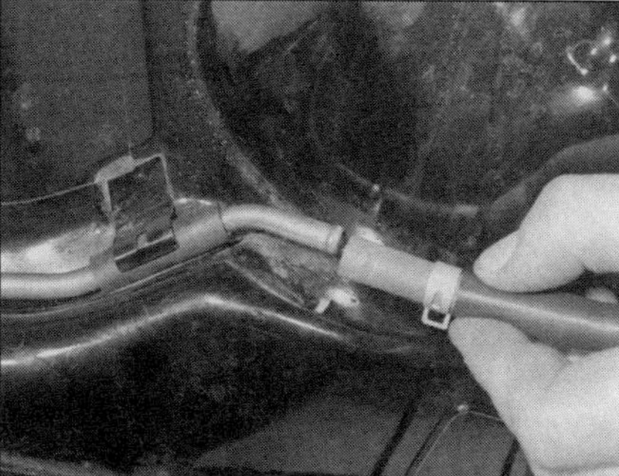
28.17a Detach the pipe from the hose . . .

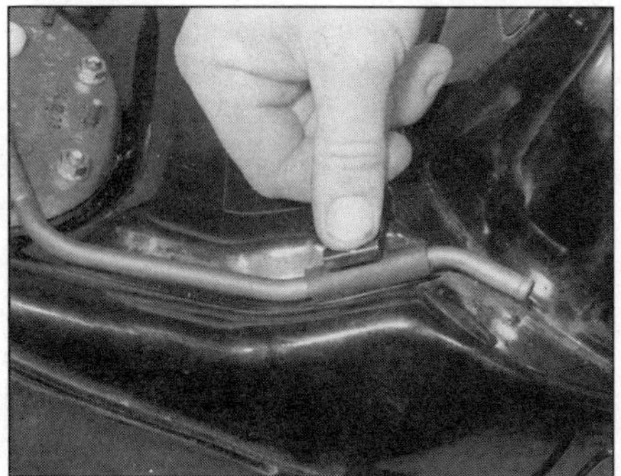
28.17b . . . and release it from the clamp

28.18a Remove the six nuts (arrowed) . . .

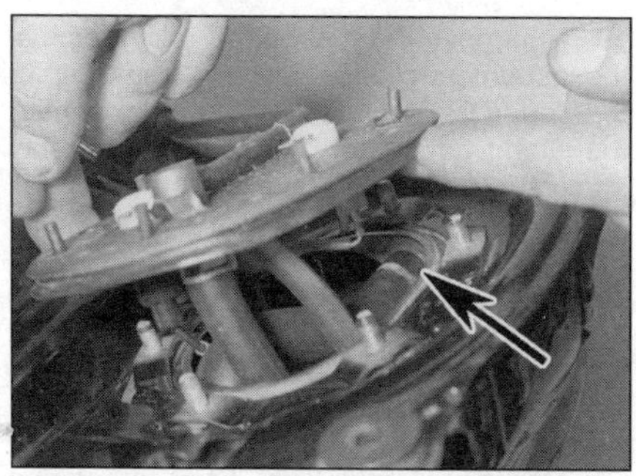
28.18b . . . and withdraw the pump far enough to detach the vent pipe from its union (arrowed)

2 The fuel pump is controlled through the fuel cut-off relay so that it runs whenever the ignition is switched ON and the ignition is operative (i.e., only when the engine is turning over). As soon as the ignition is killed, the relay will cut off the fuel pump's electrical supply (so that there is no risk of fuel being sprayed out under pressure in the event of an accident).

3 It should be possible to hear the fuel pump running whenever the engine is turning over - remove the seat (see Chapter 8) and place your ear close to the cover on the rear of the tank. If you can't hear anything, check the circuit fuse (see Section 5). If the fuse is good, check the pump and relay for loose or corroded connections or physical damage and rectify as necessary.

4 If the circuit is fine so far, switch the ignition OFF, unplug the relay's wiring connector **(see illustration 28.1)** and connect across the relay's black/white and brown/red terminals on the loom side of the connector with a short length of insulated jumper wire **(see illustration)**. Switch the ignition ON; the pump should operate.

5 If the pump now works, either the relay or its wiring is at fault. Test the wiring as follows.

6 Check for full battery voltage at the relay's black/white terminal with the ignition switch ON. If there is no battery voltage, there is a fault in the circuit between the relay and the fuse - turn off the ignition, then trace and rectify the fault as outlined in Section 2; refer to the wiring diagrams at the end of this Chapter.

7 Disconnect the wiring connectors from the relay, fuel pump and ignition control module. Using an ohmmeter, check for continuity between the blue/yellow wire on the relay's wire connector and the blue/yellow wire on the control module's wire connector. Check for continuity between the brown/red wire on the relay's wire connector and the brown/red wire on the fuel pump's wire connector. Also check for continuity between the green wire on the relay connector and earth. Continuity should be indicated in all tests; if not, trace and rectify the fault as described in Section 2. Reconnect all wire connectors.

8 If the pump still does not work, remove the seat (see Chapter 8) and disconnect the pump wiring connectors from the fuel tank, noting which fits where **(see illustration)**. Using a fully charged 12 volt battery and two insulated jumper wires, connect the positive (+) terminal of the battery to the pump's brown/red terminal, and the negative (-) terminal of the battery to the pump's green terminal. The pump should operate. If the pump does not operate it must be replaced.

9 If the pump works and all the relevant wiring and connectors are good, then the relay is at fault. The only definitive test of the relay is to substitute one that is known to be good. If substitution does not cure the problem, bear in mind that the ignition control module could be faulty.

10 If the pump operates but is thought to be delivering an insufficient amount of fuel, first check that the fuel tank breather hose is unobstructed (except California models), that all fuel hoses are in good condition and not pinched or trapped. Check that the fuel filter is not blocked.

11 The fuel pump's output can be checked as follows: make sure the ignition switch is OFF. Remove the seat and the fuel tank cover (see Chapter 8).

12 Disconnect the fuel outlet hose from the rear (fuel tank side) of the fuel filter and place the end into a graduated beaker.

13 Using a short length of insulated jumper wire, connect across the black/white and the brown/red wire terminals of the cut-off relay wiring connector as in Step 4 **(see illustration 28.4)**.

14 Turn the ignition switch ON and let fuel flow from the pump into the beaker for 5 seconds, then switch the ignition OFF.

15 Measure the amount of fuel that has flowed into the beaker, then multiply that amount by 12 to determine the fuel pump flow rate per minute. The minimum flow rate required is 640cc per minute. If the flow rate recorded is below the minimum required, then the fuel pump must be replaced.

Removal

16 Make sure the ignition is switched OFF. Remove the seat (see Chapter 8).

17 Disconnect the fuel pump wiring connectors **(see illustration 28.8)** and detach the fuel outlet pipe from the fuel hose. Release the pipe from its clamp **(see illustrations)**.

18 Unscrew the six nuts securing the fuel pump assembly to the tank, then withdraw the assembly part-way and detach the vent hose from its union. Withdraw the pump and discard the rubber base gasket as a new one should be used **(see illustrations)**.

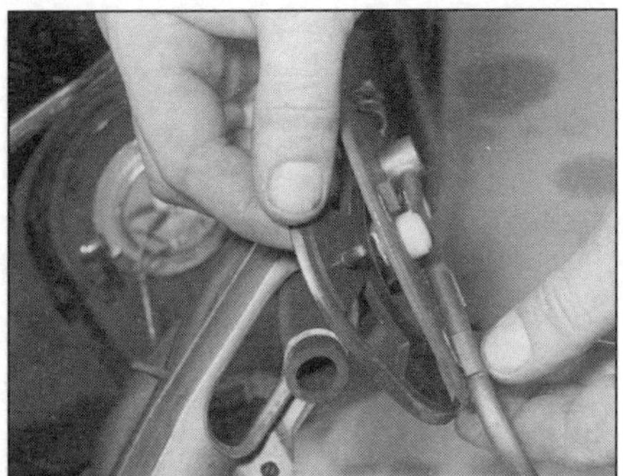
28.18c A new base gasket should be used

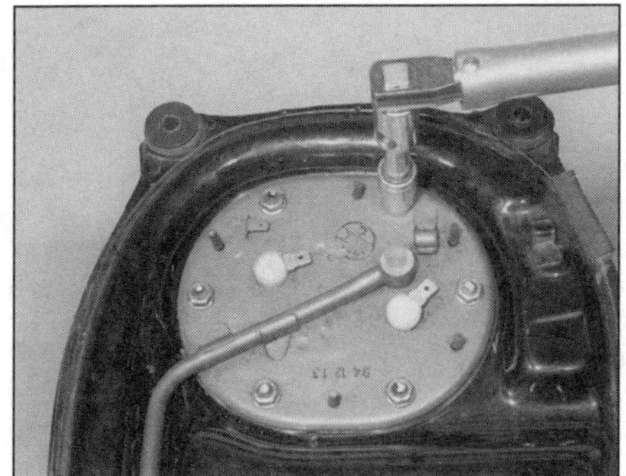
28.20 Tighten the fuel pump cover nuts to the specified torque setting

30.1 The horn is secured by a single bolt

19 To remove the fuel cut-off relay, remove the instrument cluster surround (see Chapter 8, Section 6, Steps 3 to 5), then disconnect the wiring connector and remove the relay from its mounting lugs **(see illustration 28.1)**.

Installation

20 Installation is a reverse of the removal procedure. Make sure the fuel hoses are correctly and securely fitted to the pump. Tighten the pump assembly nuts to the torque setting specified at the beginning of the Chapter **(see illustration)**. Start the engine and look carefully for any signs of leaks at the pipe connections. Make sure the wiring is correctly routed, making sure it cannot be trapped between the seat and the frame.

29 Fuel indicator light circuit - check

1 The fuel indicator light on the instrument cluster should come on when the ignition switch is turned ON, then go out after a few seconds. It should also come on whenever the fuel level is too low.

2 If the light does not come on as stated, first check the bulb (see Section 17) and the fuse (see Section 5).

3 The circuit check unit is located behind the instrument cluster surround in front of the fuel cut-off relay **(see illustration 28.1)**. See Chapter 8, Section 6, Steps 3 to 5 for removal of the surround.

4 Disconnect the unit wiring connector. Using a multimeter set to 0-20 V DC, connect the positive (+ve) probe to the black/brown terminal of the connector, and the negative (-ve) probe to the green/black terminal. Battery voltage should be present.

5 If battery voltage was recorded, the check unit is faulty and must be replaced. If there was no voltage present, check the wiring (see *wiring diagrams* at the end of the Chapter.

30 Horn(s) - check and replacement

Check

1 The horn is mounted just ahead of the radiator on the left-hand side **(see illustration)**. Remove the middle fairing inner panel for access (see Chapter 8).

2 Unplug the wiring connectors from the horn **(see illustration)**. Using two jumper wires, apply battery voltage directly to the terminals on the horn. If the horn sounds, check the switch (see Section 21) and the wiring between the switch and the horn (see the *wiring diagrams* at the end of this Chapter).

3 If the horn doesn't sound, replace it.

Replacement

4 The horn is mounted just ahead of the radiator on the left-hand side **(see illustration 30.1)**. Remove the middle fairing inner panel for access (see Chapter 8).

5 Unplug the wiring connectors from the horn, then unscrew the bolt securing the horn and remove it from the bike **(see illustration 30.2)**.

6 Install the horn and securely tighten the bolt. Connect the wiring connectors to the horn.

31 Starter relay - check and replacement

Check

1 If the starter circuit is faulty, first check the fuse (see Section 5).

2 The starter relay is located behind the left-hand side panel. Remove the side panel for access (see Chapter 8). Disconnect the relay wiring connector to provide access to the rear terminals, then lift the rubber terminal cover and unscrew the bolt securing the starter motor lead **(see illustrations)**; position the lead away from the relay terminal. Reconnect the wiring connector. With the ignition switch ON, the engine kill switch in the RUN position, the transmission in neutral and the clutch pulled in, press the starter switch. The relay should be heard to click.

3 If the relay doesn't click, switch off the ignition and remove the relay as described below; test it as follows.

4 Set a multimeter to the ohms x 1 scale and connect it across the relay's starter motor and battery lead terminals. Using a fully-charged

30.2 Disconnect the horn wiring connectors

31.2a Disconnect the relay wiring connectors . . .

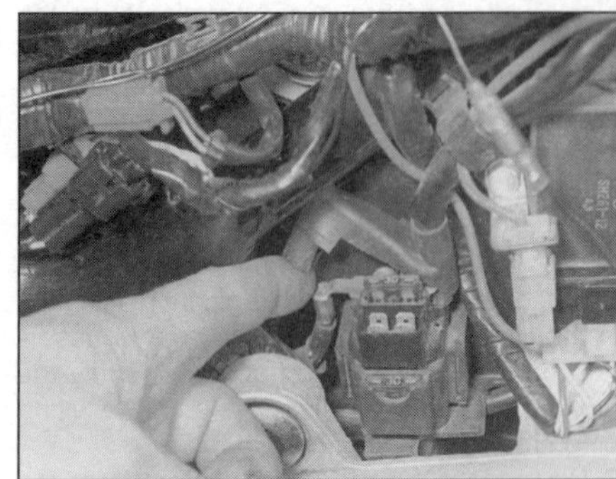
31.2b . . . then lift the rubber terminal cover

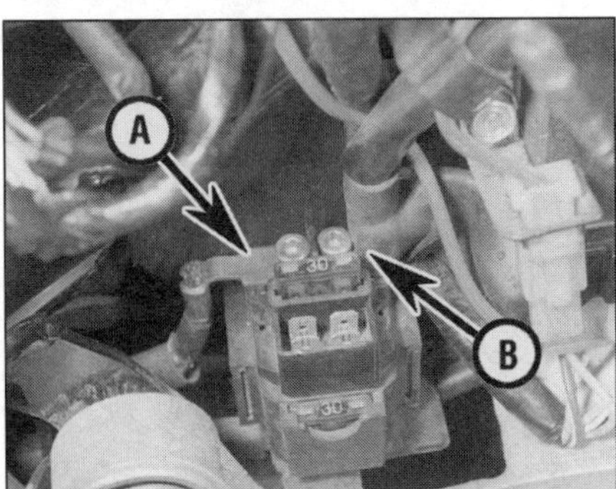

31.2c Starter motor lead (A), battery lead (B)

12 volt battery and two insulated jumper wires, connect the positive (+ve) terminal of the battery to the yellow/red wire terminal of the relay, and the negative (-ve) terminal to the green/red wire terminal of the relay. At this point the relay should be heard to click and the multimeter read 0 ohms (continuity). If this is the case the relay is proved good. If the relay does not click when battery voltage is applied and indicates no continuity (infinite resistance) across its terminals, it is faulty and must be replaced.

5 If the relay is good, check for battery voltage between the yellow/red wire and the green/red wire when the starter button is pressed. Check the other components in the starter circuit as described in the relevant sections of this Chapter. If all components are good, check the wiring between the various components (see the *Wiring diagrams* at the end of this book).

Replacement

6 Remove the left-hand side panel (see Chapter 8).

7 Disconnect the battery terminals, remembering to disconnect the negative (-ve) terminal first.

8 Disconnect the relay wiring connector, then unscrew the two bolts securing the starter motor and battery leads to the relay and detach the leads **(see illustrations 31.2a, b and c)**. Remove the relay with its rubber sleeve from its mounting lug on the frame.

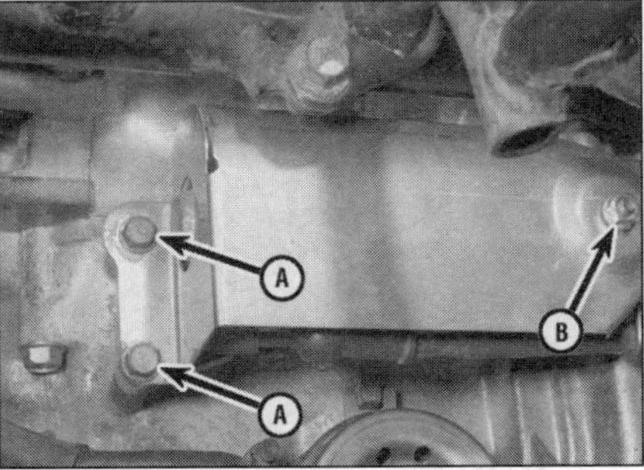

32.2 Remove the two bolts (A) and the nut (B) and remove the guard. The two bolts (A) also secure the starter motor

9 Installation is the reverse of removal. Make sure the terminal bolts are securely tightened. Connect the negative (-ve) lead last when reconnecting the battery.

32 Starter motor - removal and installation

Removal

1 Remove the left-hand side panel (see Chapter 8). Disconnect the battery negative (-ve) lead. The starter motor is mounted above the oil filter on the left-hand side of the engine. Remove the left-hand middle fairing panel for access (see Chapter 8).

2 Unscrew the two bolts and the nut securing the heat guard, noting that the bolts also secure the starter motor to the engine **(see illustration)**. Remove the heat guard.

3 Peel back the rubber terminal cover and remove the nut securing the starter lead to the motor **(see illustration)**. Detach the lead and withdraw it from its guide, if required.

4 Slide the starter motor out from the crankcase and remove it from the machine **(see illustration)**.

5 Remove the O-ring on the end of the starter motor and discard it as a new one must be used.

Installation

6 Install a new O-ring on the end of the starter motor and ensure it is seated in its groove

32.3 Pull off the rubber cover to access the terminal nut

32.4 Slide the starter motor out of the engine

(see illustration). Apply a smear of engine oil to the O-ring to aid installation.

7 Manoeuvre the motor into position and slide it into the crankcase **(see illustration 32.4)**. Ensure that the starter motor teeth mesh correctly with those of the starter idle/reduction gear.

8 Connect the starter lead to the motor, making sure it is fitted in its guide, and secure it with the screw or nut **(see illustration)**. Make sure the rubber cover is correctly seated over the terminal.

9 Fit the heat guard onto the starter motor and install the motor/guard mounting bolts and tighten them securely **(see illustration)**. Also fit the heat guard nut.

10 Connect the battery negative (-ve) lead and install the middle fairing panel and the side panel (see Chapter 8).

32.6 Fit a new O-ring onto the starter motor

32.8 Attach the lead to the terminal and secure it with its nut

32.9 Fit the heat guard and install the mounting bolts

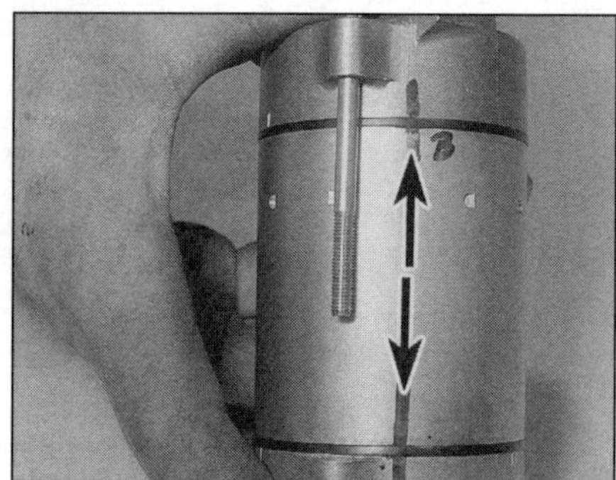
33.2 Make alignment marks between the main housing and the front and rear covers (arrowed)

33 Starter motor - disassembly, inspection and reassembly

Disassembly

1 Remove the starter motor as described in Section 32.

2 Make alignment marks between the main housing and the front and rear covers **(see illustration)**.

3 Unscrew the two long bolts then remove the rear cover from the motor along with its sealing ring **(see illustration)**. Discard the sealing ring as a new one must be used for reassembly. Remove the shim(s) from the rear end of the armature noting how many and their correct fitted positions.

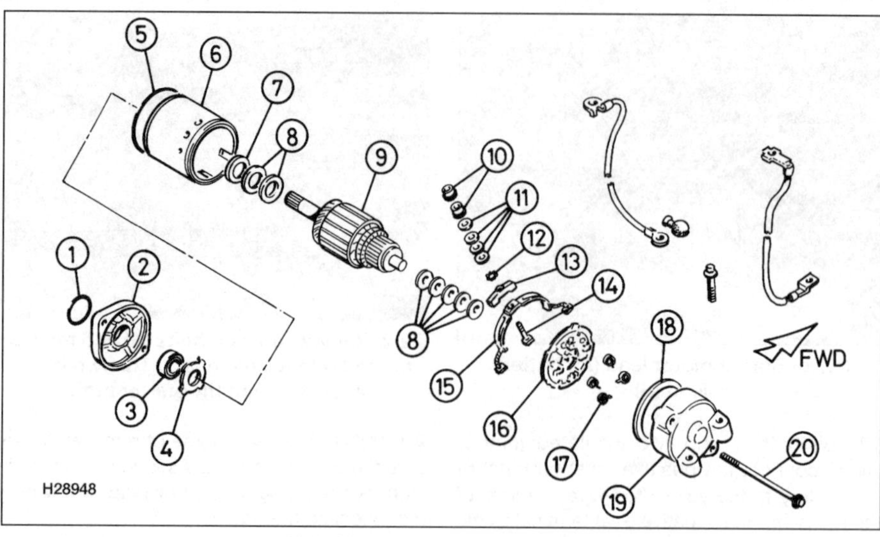

33.3 Starter motor components

1 O-ring
2 Front cover
3 Oil seal
4 Toothed washer
5 Sealing ring
6 Main housing
7 Insulating washer
8 Shims
9 Armature
10 Nuts
11 Insulating washers
12 O-ring
13 Insulator
14 Terminal bolt
15 Brush assembly
16 Brush plate
17 Brush springs
18 Sealing ring
19 Rear cover
20 Long bolt

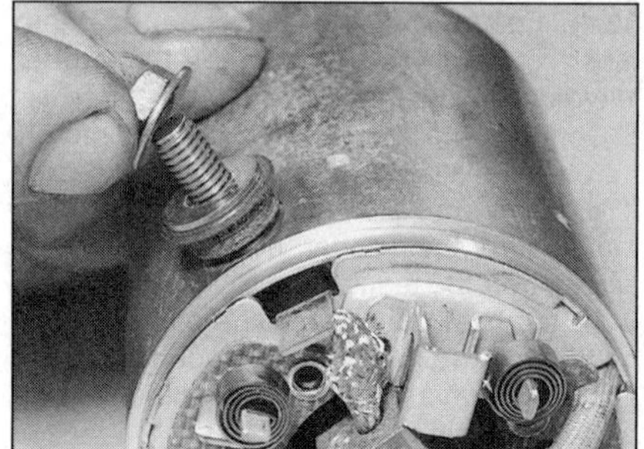
33.6 Unscrew the nut and remove the washers from the terminal bolt, noting their correct order

4 Remove the front cover from the motor along with its sealing ring. Discard the sealing ring as a new one must be used for reassembly. Recover the toothed washer from the cover and slide the insulating washer and shim(s) from the front end of the armature, noting the number of shims and their correct fitted order.

5 Withdraw the armature from the main housing.

6 Noting the correct fitted location of each washer, unscrew the nut from the terminal bolt and remove the plain washer, the various insulating washers and the rubber O-ring **(see illustration)**. Withdraw the terminal bolt, brush and brushplate assembly from the main housing and recover the insulator.

7 Lift each brush spring end onto the top of each brush holder and slide the brushes out from their holders **(see illustration)**.

Inspection

8 The parts of the starter motor that are most likely to require attention are the brushes. Measure the length of the brushes and compare the results to the brush length listed in this Chapter's Specifications **(see illustration)**. If any of the brushes are worn beyond the service limit, replace the brush assembly with a new one. If the brushes are not worn excessively, nor cracked, chipped, or otherwise damaged, they may be re-used.

9 Inspect the commutator bars on the armature for scoring, scratches and discoloration. The commutator can be cleaned and polished with crocus cloth, but do not use sandpaper or emery paper. After cleaning, wipe away any residue with a cloth soaked in electrical system cleaner or denatured alcohol.

10 Using an ohmmeter or a continuity test light, check for continuity between the commutator bars. Continuity should exist between each bar and all of the others. Also, check for continuity between the commutator bars and the armature shaft **(see illustrations)**.

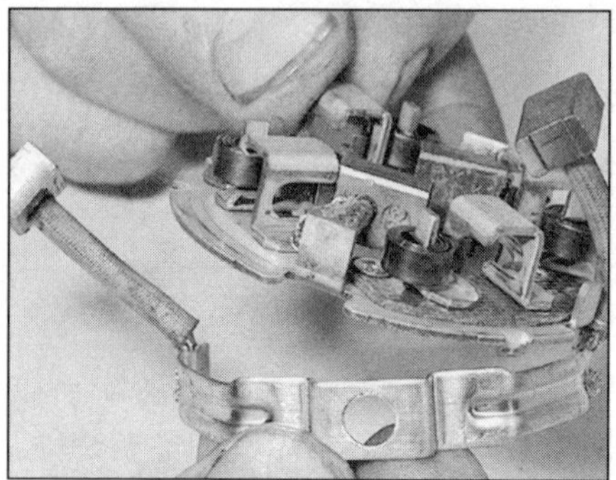
33.7 Lift each brush spring onto the top of its holder and slide the brushes out

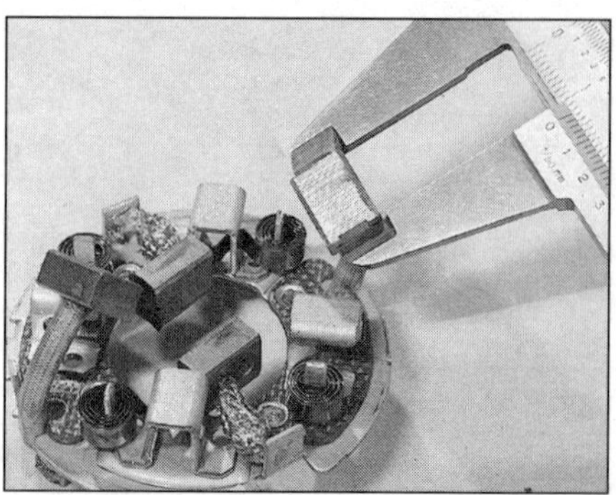
33.8 Measure the brush length

33.10a Continuity should exist between the commutator bars

33.10b There should be no continuity between the commutator bars and the armature shaft

There should be no continuity (infinite resistance) between the commutator and the shaft. If the checks indicate otherwise, the armature is defective.

11 Check for continuity between each brush and the terminal bolt. There should be continuity (zero resistance). Check for continuity between the terminal bolt and the housing (when assembled). There should be no continuity (infinite resistance).

12 Check the starter pinion gear for worn, cracked, chipped and broken teeth. If the gear is damaged or worn, replace the starter motor.

13 Inspect the end cover for signs of cracks or wear. Inspect the magnets in the main housing and the housing itself for cracks.

33.16b . . . and install the brushplate assembly and terminal bolt

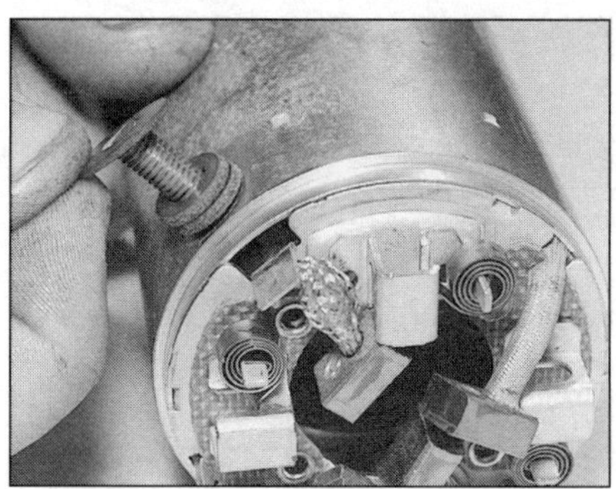

33.17b . . . followed by the insulating washers . . .

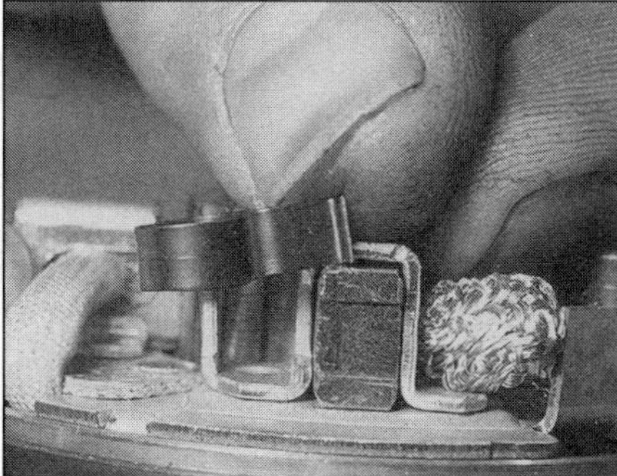

33.15 Retain the brush spring on the holder to allow easy entry of the shaft through the brushes

14 Inspect the insulating washers, O-ring and front cover oil seal for signs of damage and replace if necessary.

Reassembly

15 Slide all the brushes back into position in their holders. Make sure that each brush spring is retained against the top of its brush holder so that it will not exert any pressure on the brush **(see illustration)**.

Lifting the end of the brush spring so that it is against the top of the brush holder and not pressing the brush inwards makes it much easier to install the armature on reassembly.

33.16c Make sure the tab on the brushplate (arrowed) locates in the slot in the main housing

33.17c . . . and the plain washer, then fit the nut and tighten it

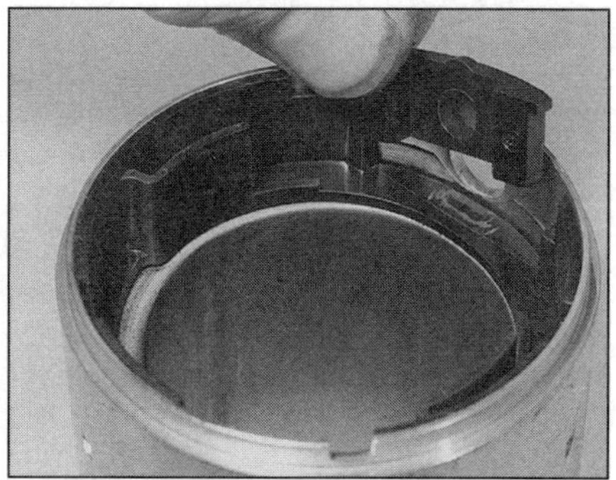

33.16a Locate the insulator in the housing . . .

16 Fit the insulator to the main housing, then insert the terminal bolt through the brushplate and housing and install the brushplate assembly, making sure its tab is correctly located in the housing slot **(see illustrations)**.

17 Slide the rubber O-ring and small insulating washer(s) onto the terminal bolt, followed by the large insulating washer(s) and the plain washer. Fit the nut to the terminal bolt and tighten it securely **(see illustrations)**.

18 Insert the armature in the front of the housing and locate the brushes on the commutator bars. Slip each brush spring end off the top of the brush housing and onto the brush end **(see illustrations)**. Check that each brush is securely pressed against the commutator by its spring and is free to move easily in its holder.

19 Fit the toothed washer to the front cover

33.17a Slide the rubber O-ring onto the terminal bolt . . .

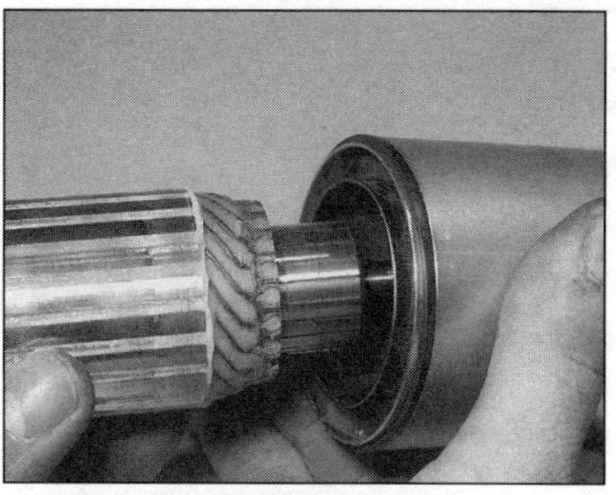

33.18a Install the armature into the housing

33.18b Fit the brush spring ends onto the brushes

so that its teeth are correctly located with the cover ribs **(see illustration)**. Apply a smear of grease to the cover oil seal lip.

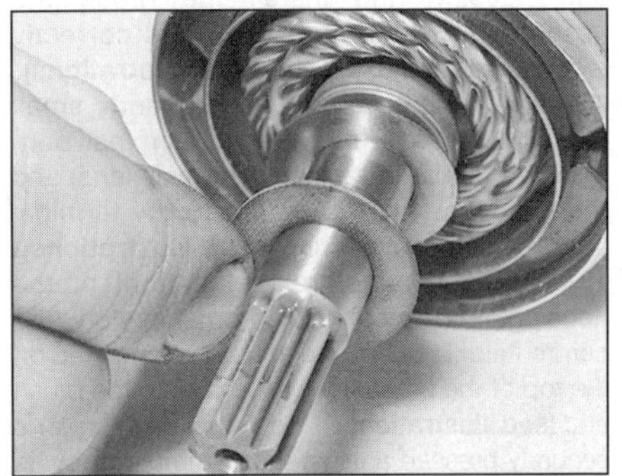

33.20a Slide the shim(s), followed by the insulating washer, onto the front of the shaft

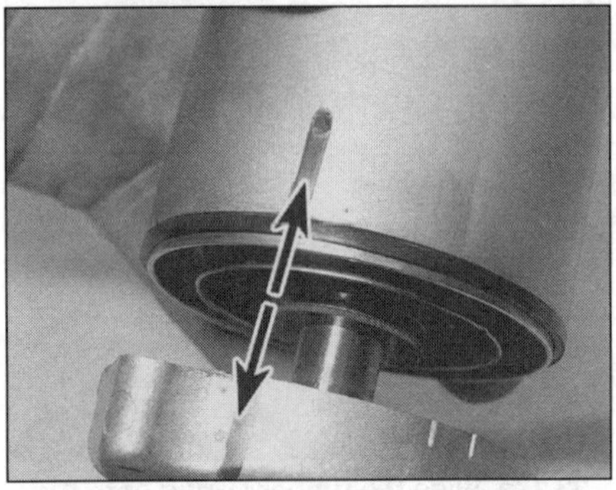

33.20c . . . then install the front cover, aligning the marks (arrowed)

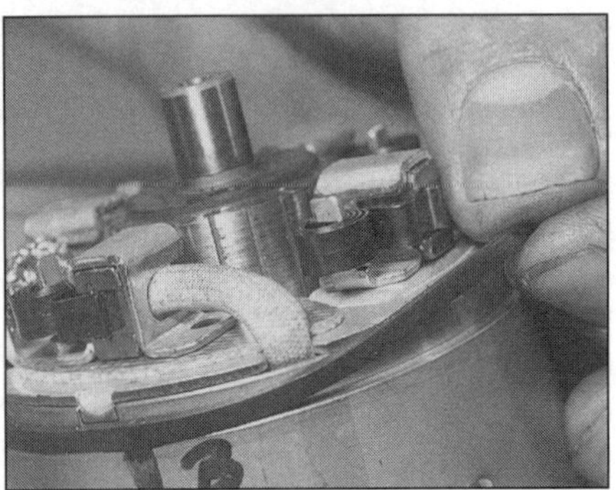

33.22a Fit a new sealing ring to the housing . . .

33.19 Fit the toothed washer to the front cover

20 Slide the shim(s) onto the front end of the armature shaft then fit the insulating washer. Fit a new sealing ring to the housing and carefully slide the front cover into position, aligning the marks made on removal **(see illustrations)**.

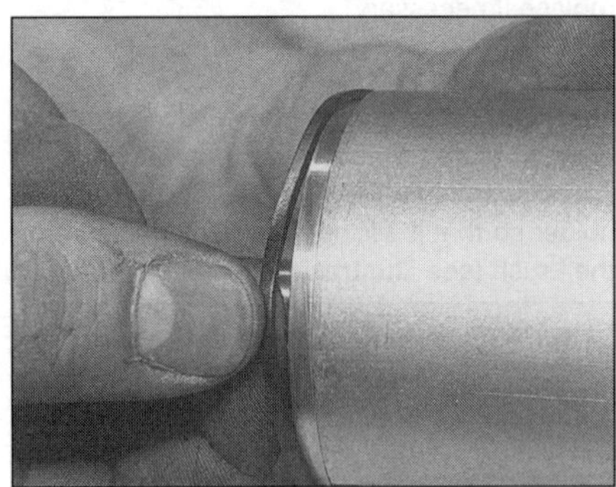

33.20b Fit a new sealing ring to the housing . . .

33.21 Fit the shims onto the end of the shaft

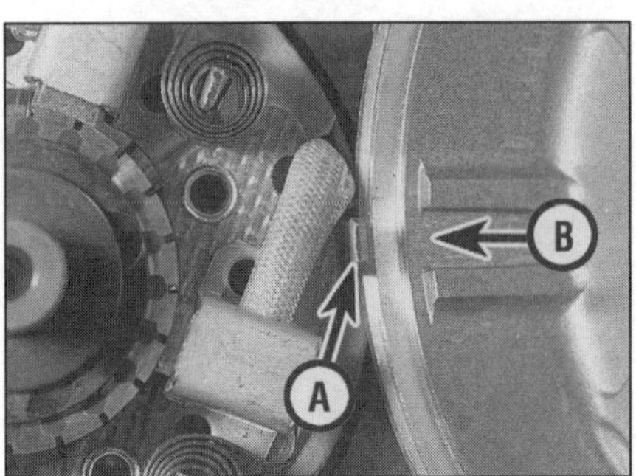

33.22b . . . then install the rear cover, aligning the tab on the brushplate (A) with the groove (B)

21 Fit the shims to the rear of the armature shaft **(see illustration)**.

22 Fit a new sealing ring to the housing. Align the rear cover groove with the brushplate outer tab and install the cover **(see illustrations)**.

23 Check the marks made on removal are correctly aligned then fit the long bolts and tighten them securely **(see illustration)**.

24 Install the starter motor (see Section 32).

34 Charging system testing - general information and precautions

1 If the performance of the charging system is suspect, the system as a whole should be checked first, followed by testing of the individual components. **Note:** *Before beginning the checks, make sure the battery is fully charged and that all system connections are clean and tight.*

2 Checking the output of the charging system and the performance of the various components within the charging system requires the use of a multimeter (with voltage, current and resistance checking facilities).

3 When making the checks, follow the procedures carefully to prevent incorrect connections or short circuits, as irreparable damage to electrical system components may result if short circuits occur.

4 If a multimeter is not available, the job of checking the charging system should be left to a Honda dealer.

35 Charging system - leakage and output test

1 If the charging system of the machine is thought to be faulty, remove the left-hand side panel (see Chapter 8) and perform the following checks.

Leakage test

Caution: Always connect an ammeter in series, never in parallel with the battery, otherwise it will be damaged. Do not turn

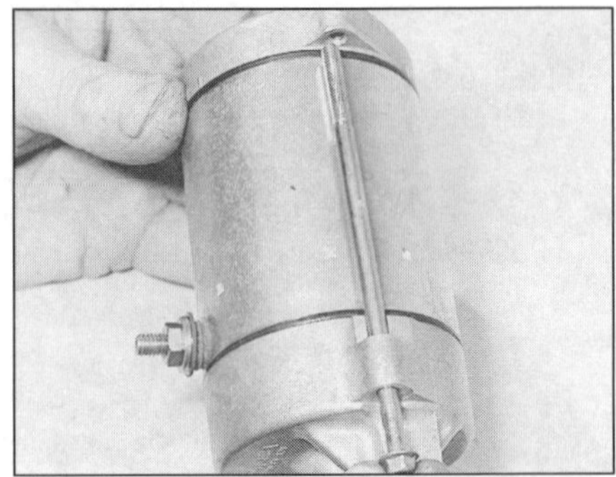

33.23 Align the marks made on removal and install the two long bolts

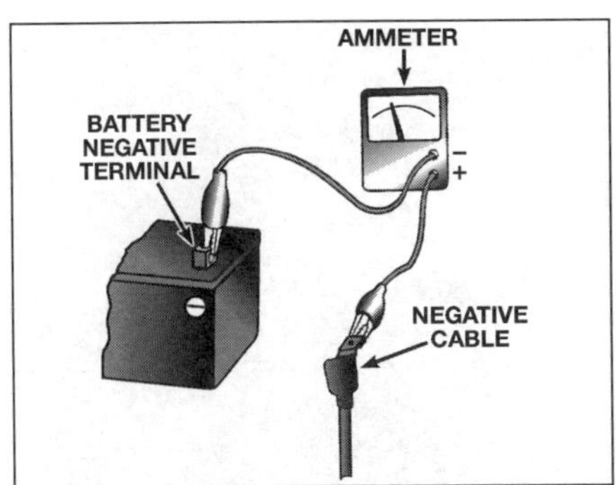

35.3 Checking the charging system leakage rate. Connect the meter as shown

the ignition ON or operate the starter motor when the ammeter is connected - a sudden surge in current will blow the meter's fuse.

2 Turn the ignition switch OFF and disconnect the lead from the battery negative (-ve) terminal.

3 Set the multimeter to the Amps function and connect its negative (-ve) probe to the battery negative (-ve) terminal, and positive (+ve) probe to the disconnected negative (-ve) lead **(see illustration)**. Always set the meter to a high amps range initially and then bring it down to the mA (milli Amps) range; if there is a high current flow in the circuit it may blow the meter's fuse.

4 If the current leakage indicated exceeds the amount specified at the beginning of the Chapter, there is probably a short circuit in the wiring. Disconnect the meter and connect the negative (-ve) lead to the battery, tightening it securely,

5 If leakage is indicated, use the wiring diagrams at the end of this book to systematically disconnect individual electrical components and repeat the test until the source is identified.

Output test

6 Start the engine and warm it up to normal operating temperature.

7 Allow the engine to idle and connect a multimeter set to the 0-20 volts DC scale (voltmeter) across the terminals of the battery (positive (+ve) lead to battery positive (+ve) terminal, negative (-ve) lead to battery negative (-ve) terminal). Slowly increase the engine speed to 5000 rpm and note the reading obtained. The regulated voltage should be as specified at the beginning of the Chapter. If the voltage is outside these limits, check the alternator and the regulator (see Section 36).

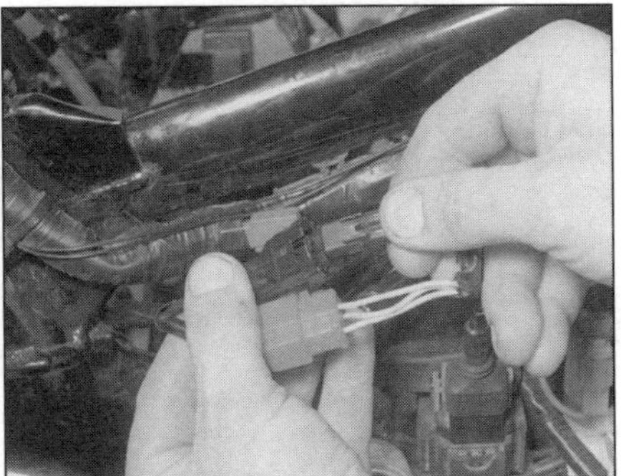

36.5a Disconnect the alternator wiring connectors

Clues to a faulty regulator are constantly blowing bulbs, with brightness varying considerably with engine speed, and battery overheating.

36 Alternator/regulator/rectifier - check, removal and installation

UK L, M, N, AN, P, AP, R, AR, S, AS models and US 1991 to 1995 models

Alternator check

1 Remove the left-hand side panel. Trace the wiring from the stator cover and disconnect it at the connectors.

2 Using a multimeter or continuity tester, connect the probes between each pair of the yellow wire terminals on the stator side of the connector, making three measurements in all. There should be continuity between each pair of yellow terminals. Now connect one probe to earth and check each terminal in turn. There should be no continuity between any terminal and earth.

36.5b Unscrew the three bolts (arrowed) . . .

3 To check the rotor coil resistance, measure the resistance between the black and white terminals on the alternator side of the 2-pin black wiring connector and compare the reading to that specified at the beginning of the Chapter. To check the stator coil resistance, measure the resistance between the yellow terminals on the alternator side of the 3-pin red wiring connector, taking three readings in all, and compare the readings to that specified at the beginning of the Chapter.

4 If any of the tests above do not produce the expected results, replace the component concerned.

Alternator removal

5 To remove the stator coil assembly, leaving the rotor in place, remove the swingarm and the gearchange pedal (see Chapter 6). Trace the wiring from the stator cover and disconnect it at the connectors. Unscrew the three Allen bolts securing the stator coil assembly to the alternator, then draw the stator off **(see illustrations)**. Remove the O-ring and discard it as a new one must be used.

6 To remove the complete alternator, remove the engine, the sump and the oil strainer (see Chapter 2). Reach into the sump and insert a 6 mm bolt into one of the holes in the front of the alternator driven gear. This prevents the teeth of the sprung gear becoming misaligned when the alternator is removed, making it much easier to mesh with the drive gear on installation. Unscrew the three alternator mounting bolts and remove the alternator **(see illustrations)**.

36.5c . . . and remove the stator

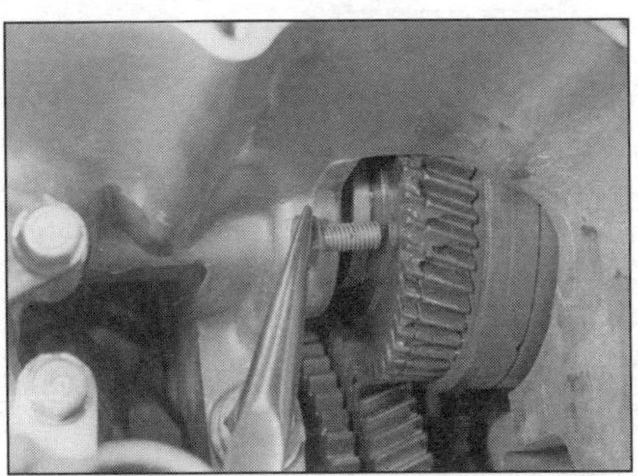

36.6a Insert a 6 mm bolt into one of the holes in the driven gear before removing the alternator

36.6b Unscrew the four bolts (arrowed) . . .

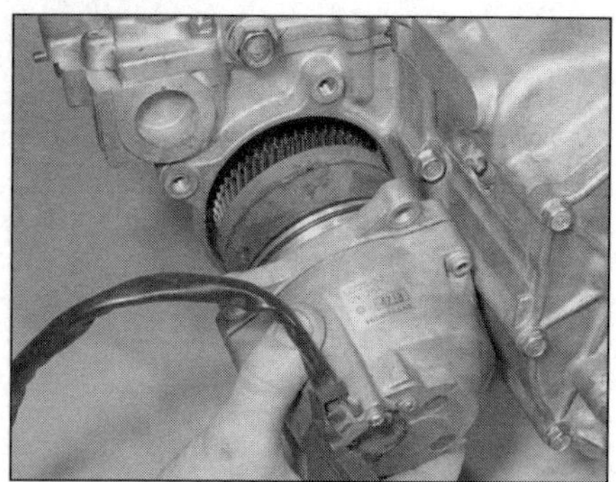
36.6c ... and remove the alternator

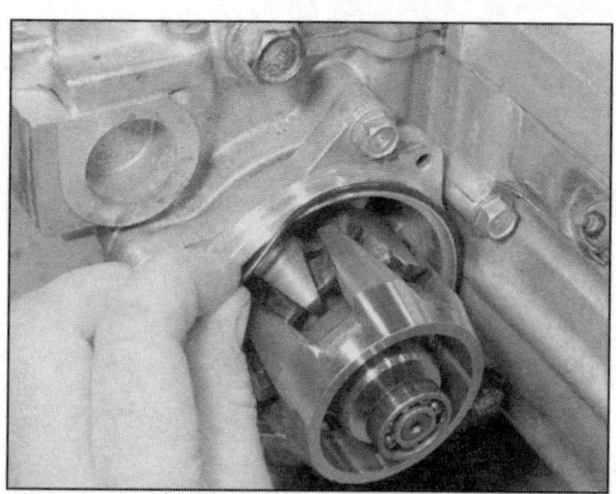
36.7a Fit a new O-ring and smear it with oil ...

36.7b ... and apply copper grease to the stator bolts

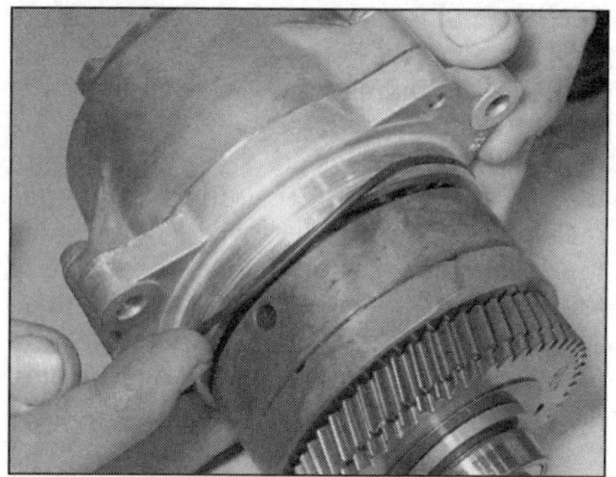
36.8a Fit a new O-ring and smear it with oil

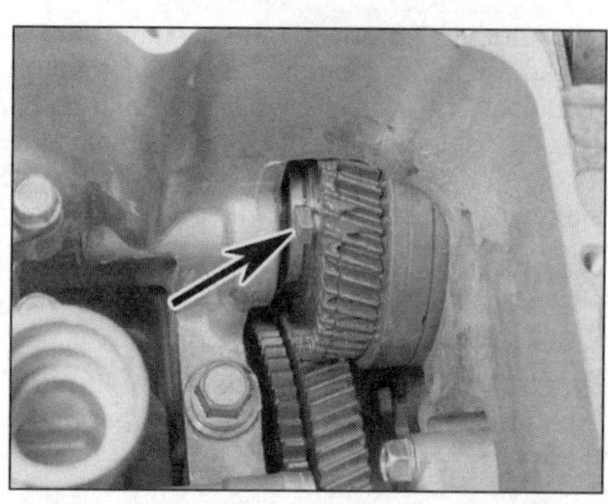
36.8b Do not forget to remove the 6 mm bolt (arrowed)

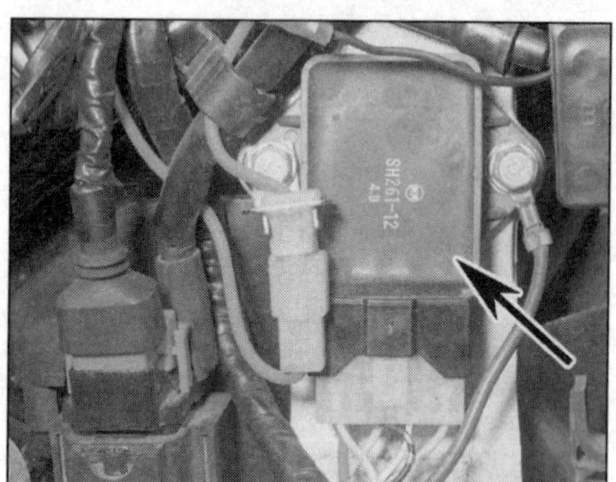
36.9 Regulator/rectifier

Remove the O-ring and discard it as a new one must be used.

Alternator installation

7 To install the stator assembly, fit a new O-ring onto the alternator and smear it with oil, then install the stator and tighten the bolts securely **(see illustrations)**. Install the swingarm and gearchange pedal (see Chapter 6).

> **HAYNES HiNT** *It is advisable to apply copper grease to the bolt threads as their ends are exposed and liable to corrode*

8 Check the condition of the alternator shaft bearing. If it is worn, place the alternator driven gear in a vice with two pieces of wood to protect the gear teeth - do not clamp the damper housing behind the gear otherwise it will distort. Remove the nut and washer from the shaft end, followed by the bearing. Fit the new bearing and tighten the shaft nut to the torque setting specified at the beginning of the Chapter. To install the rotor assembly, fit a new O-ring onto the alternator and smear it with oil **(see illustration)**. Apply molybdenum disulphide grease to the driven gear teeth, then install the rotor and tighten the bolts to the specified torque setting. Remove the 6 mm bolt previously inserted in the hole in the driven gear **(see illustration)**, then install the oil strainer, sump and engine (see Chapter 2).

Regulator/rectifier check

9 The regulator/rectifier is mounted behind the left-hand side panel **(see illustration)**. Remove the side panel for access (see Chapter 8).

10 Disconnect the wiring connector from the bottom of the regulator/rectifier. Using a multimeter set to the appropriate resistance scale check the resistance between the various terminals of the regulator/rectifier connectors as shown in the table **(see illustration)**. If the readings do not compare closely with those shown in the accompanying table the regulator/rectifier unit can be considered faulty. **Note:** *The use of certain multimeters could lead to false readings being obtained. Therefore, if the above check shows the regulator/rectifier unit to be faulty take the unit to a Honda dealer for*

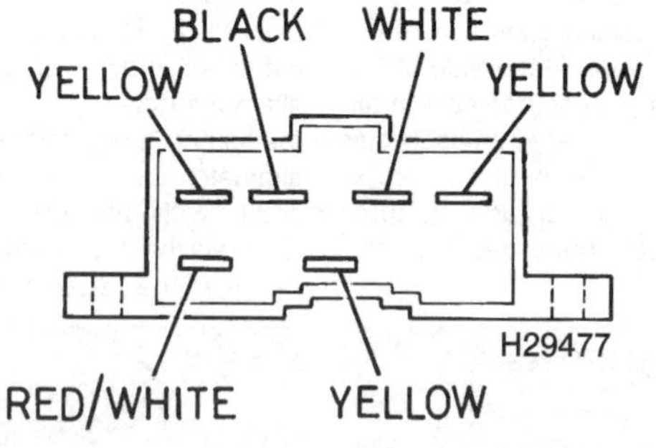

– +	Red/white	Yellow 1	Yellow 2	Yellow 3	White
Red/white		∞	∞	∞	∞
Yellow 1	7.5		∞	∞	∞
Yellow 2	7.5	∞		∞	∞
Yellow 3	7.5	∞	∞		∞
White	60	28	28	28	

36.10 Regulator/rectifier test connections

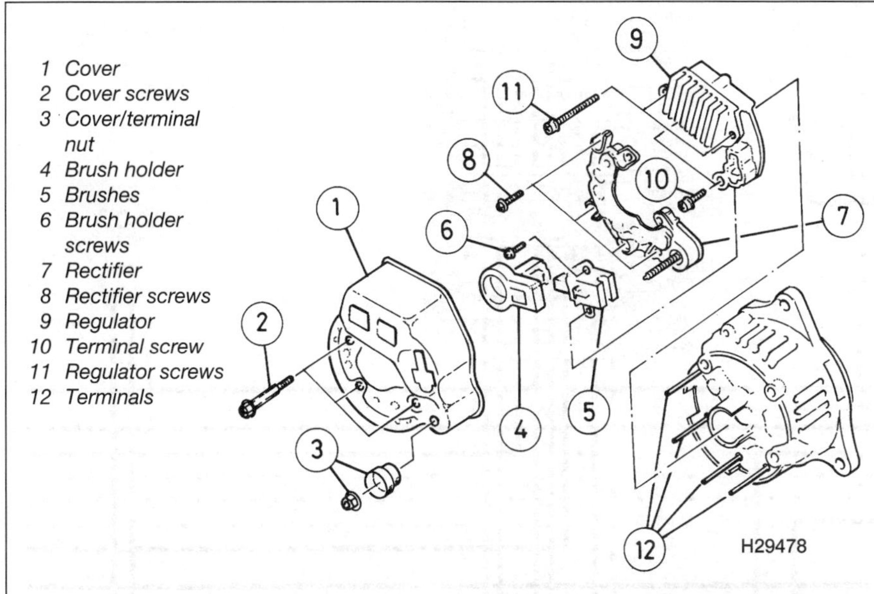

36.14 Alternator/regulator/rectifier components - UK T, AT, V and AV, and US 1996-on models

confirmation of its condition before replacing it.

Regulator/rectifier removal

11 The regulator/rectifier is mounted behind the left-hand side panel **(see illustration 36.9)**. Remove the side panel for access (see Chapter 8).

12 Disconnect the wiring connector from the bottom of the regulator/rectifier. Unscrew the two bolts and remove the regulator/rectifier, noting the earth lead secured by the right-hand bolt.

Regulator/rectifier installation

13 Install the regulator/rectifier, not forgetting to secure the earth lead with the right-hand bolt. Make sure the wiring connector is free from corrosion and securely connected.

UK T, AT, V and AV, and US 1996-on models

Check

14 Remove the alternator (see below) **(see illustration)**. Unscrew the three bolts and the nut securing the alternator end cover and remove the cover.

15 Remove the screws securing the brush holder and remove the holder, noting how it fits. Inspect the holder for any signs of damage. Measure the brush lengths and compare the measurements with the figures given in the Specifications at the beginning of the Chapter. Clean the slip rings with a rag moistened with some solvent. Slip ring diameter can be measured and compared with the figures given in the Specifications at the beginning of the Chapter, although access is difficult with the rotor installed in the alternator body.

16 Check for continuity between the slip rings. There should be continuity (zero resistance). If there is no continuity, replace the rotor. Check for continuity between the slip rings and the rotor or shaft. There should be no continuity (infinite resistance). If there is continuity, replace the rotor.

17 To check the rotor coil resistance, measure the resistance between the slip rings and compare the reading to the Specifications. If it is higher than specified, replace the rotor. To check the stator coil resistance, measure the resistance between each pair of terminals on the stator, taking six readings in all, and compare the readings to that specified at the beginning of the Chapter.

18 To test the rectifier it is necessary to remove it from the alternator. With the rectifier removed from the alternator, use a multimeter set to the ohms x 1 scale to check its six diodes **(see illustration)**. Each diode is checked in both directions by reversing the meter probes. Continuity should only exist in one direction only; if no continuity is shown in both directions, or continuity is shown if both directions, the diode is faulty.

B to P1	*P1 to B*
B to P2	*P2 to B*
B to P3	*P3 to B*
B to P4	*P4 to B*
E to P1	*P1 to E*
E to P2	*P2 to E*
E to P3	*P3 to E*
E to P4	*P4 to E*

19 Any further testing or dismantling of the alternator assembly must be carried out by an electrical specialist or Honda dealer.

Removal

20 Remove the fuel tank (see Chapter 4) and the swingarm (see Chapter 6).

21 Disconnect the 2-pin white wiring connector from the alternator. Pull back the rubber cover on the other terminal, then remove the terminal nut and detach the cable.

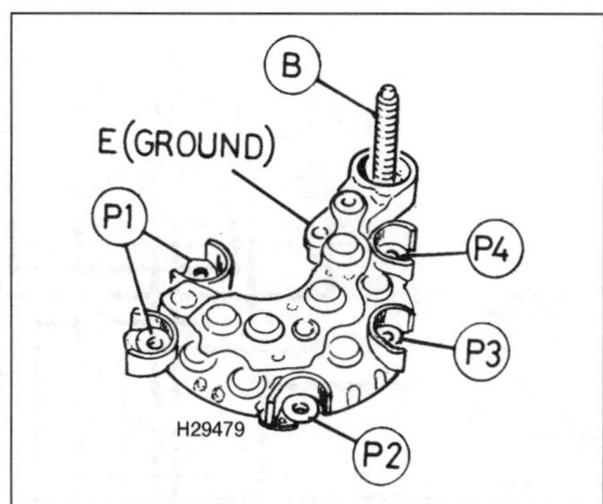

36.18 Rectifier test connections - UK T, AT, V and AV, and US 1996-on models

22 Unscrew the three bolts securing the alternator to the engine. Before removing the alternator, rotate it clockwise until the outer alternator base mounting bolt hole is uncovered, then insert one of the bolts into this hole and tighten it. This prevents the shaft and driven gear assembly coming out with the alternator. Remove the alternator and discard its O-ring as a new one must be used.

23 To remove the alternator shaft and driven gear assembly, remove the sump and the oil strainer (see Chapter 2). Reach into the sump and insert a 6 mm bolt into one of the holes in the front of the alternator driven gear **(see illustration 36.6a)**. This prevents the teeth of the sprung gear becoming misaligned when the base is removed, making it much easier to mesh with the drive gear on installation. Remove the single bolt that was previously inserted and remove the shaft and driven gear assembly.

Installation

24 Check the condition of the alternator shaft bearing. If it is worn, place the alternator driven gear in a vice with two pieces of wood to protect the gear teeth - do not clamp the damper housing behind the gear otherwise it will distort. Remove the nut and washer from the shaft end, followed by the bearing. Fit the new bearing and tighten the shaft nut to the torque setting specified at the beginning of the Chapter. To install the shaft and driven gear assembly, apply molybdenum disulphide grease to the driven gear teeth, then install the assembly and remove the 6 mm bolt previously inserted in the hole in the driven gear **(see illustration 36.8b)**, then install the oil strainer and sump (see Chapter 2).

25 Fit a new O-ring to the front of the alternator and smear it with oil. Install the alternator and tighten the bolts securely.

26 Connect the wiring connector and fit the lead on the terminal, making sure the nut is secure.

27 Install the swingarm (see Chapter 6) and the fuel tank (see Chapter 4).

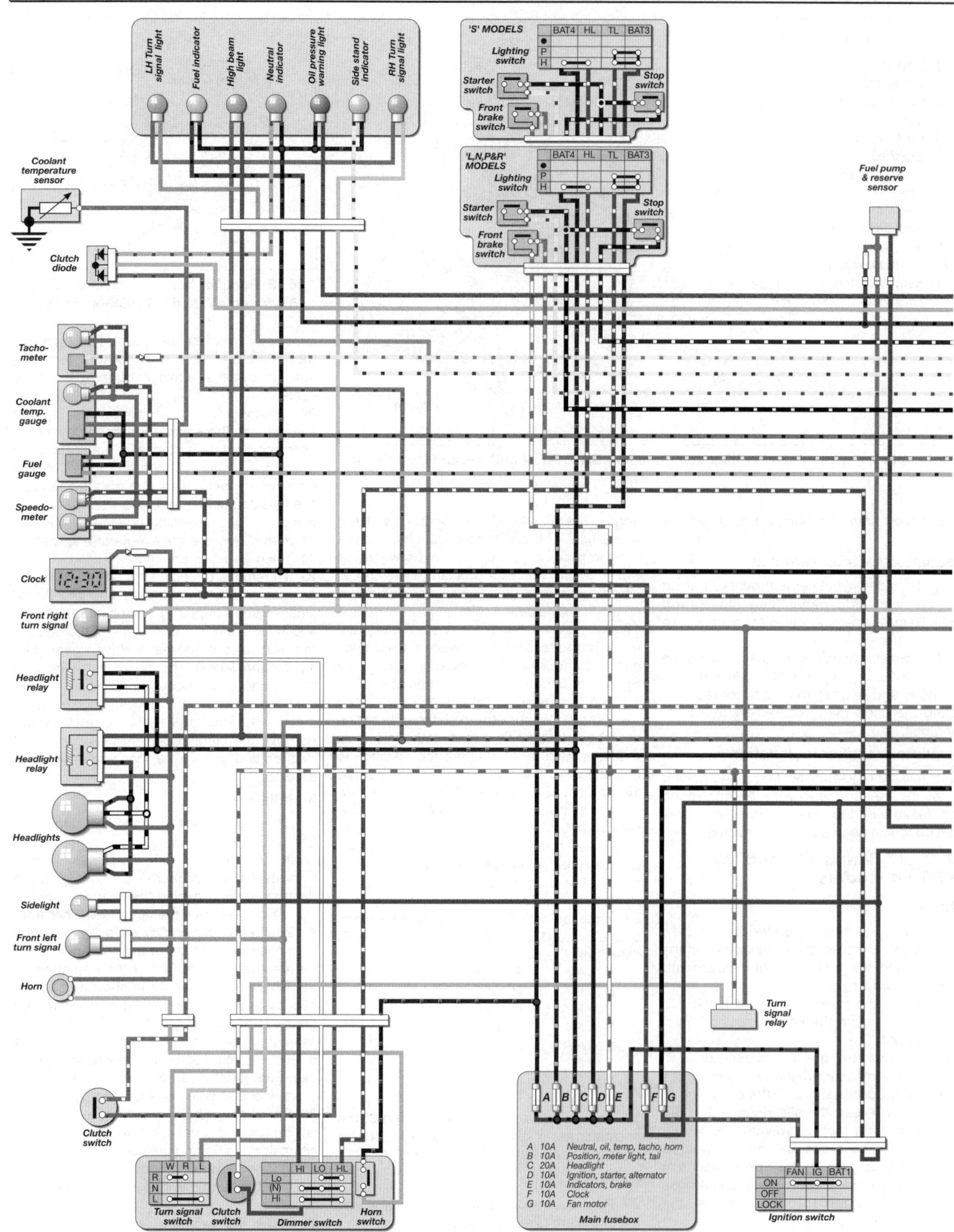

Honda ST1100 L, M, N, P, R and S standard UK models

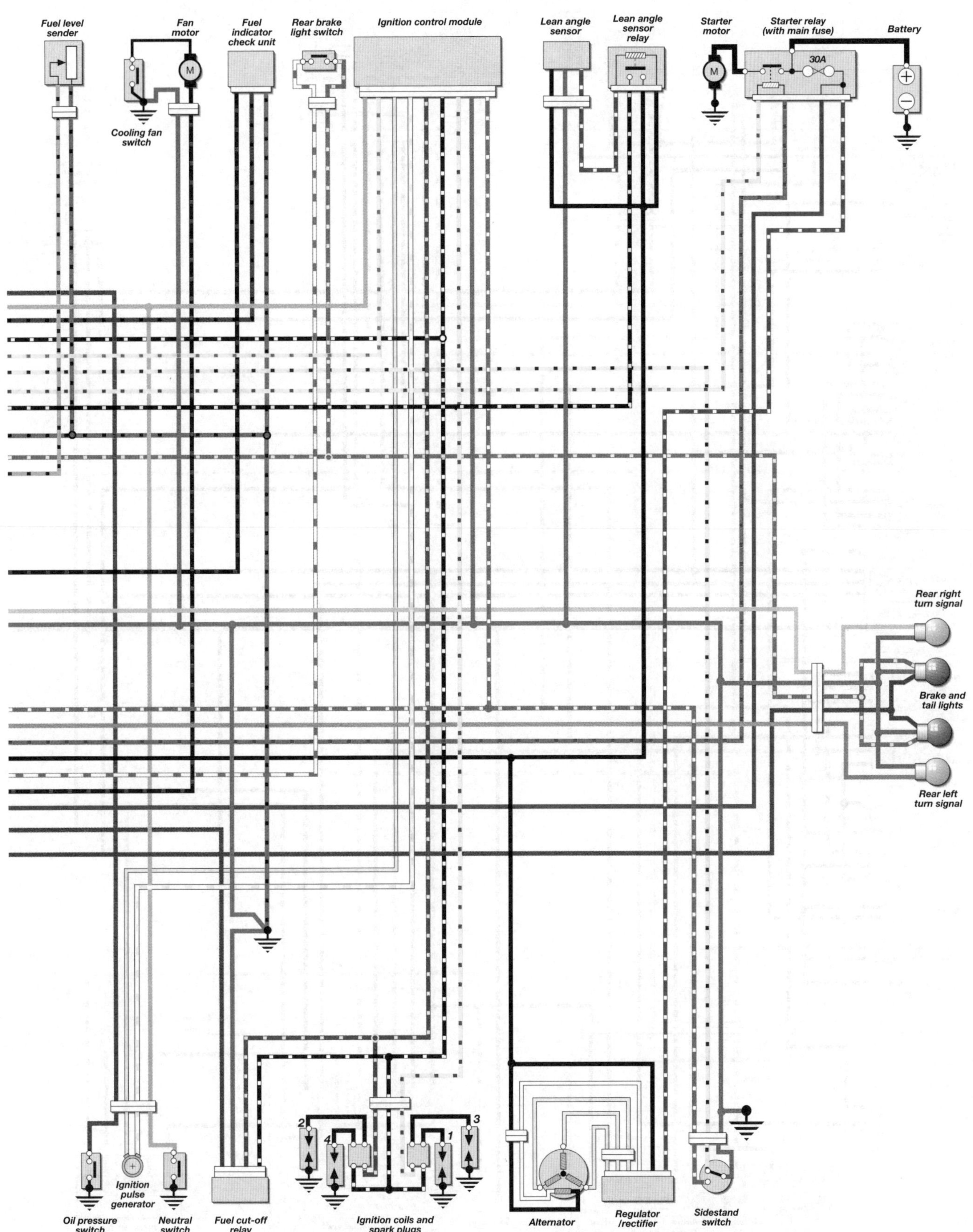

Honda ST1100 L, M, N, P, R and S standard UK models (continued)

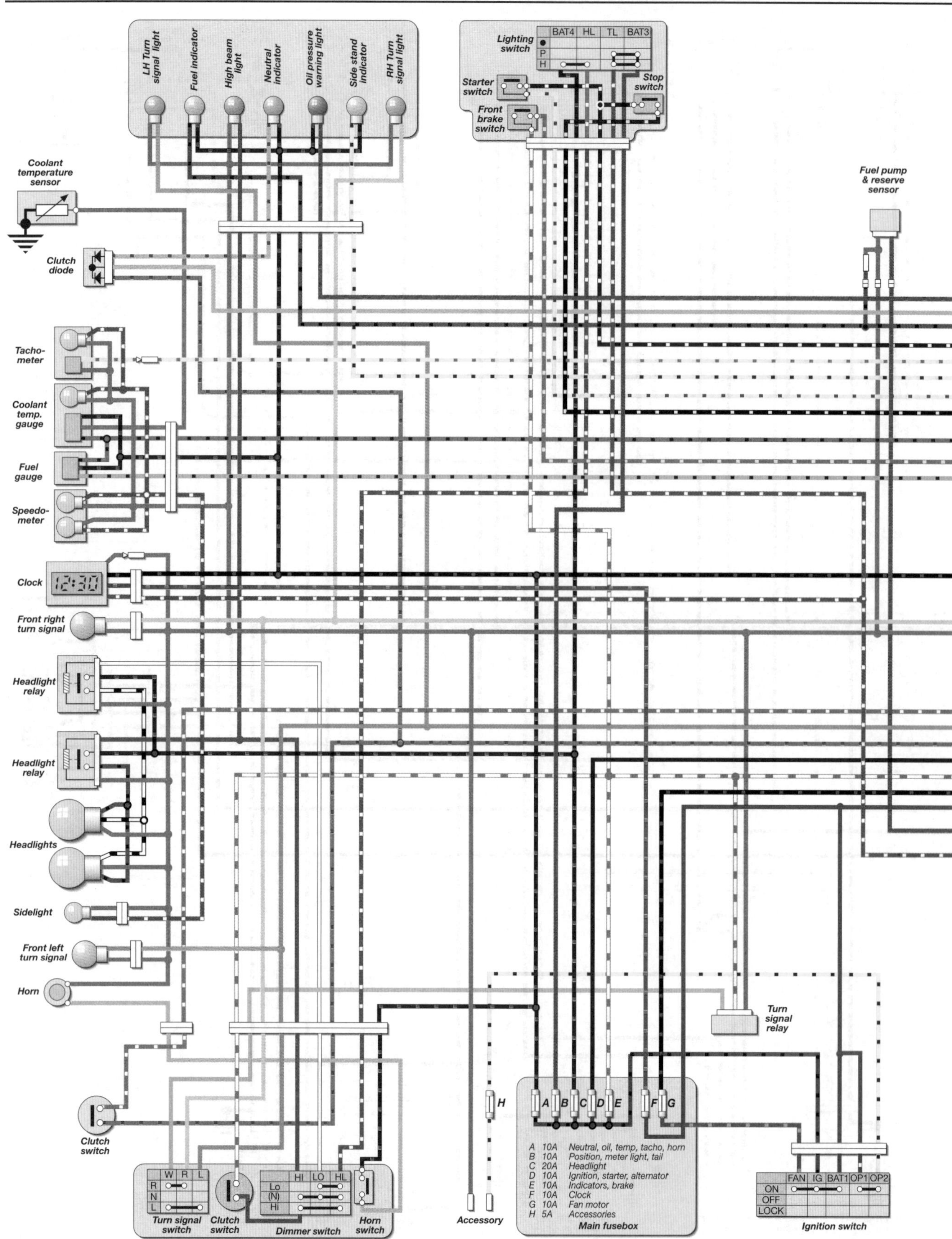

Honda ST1100 T and V standard UK models

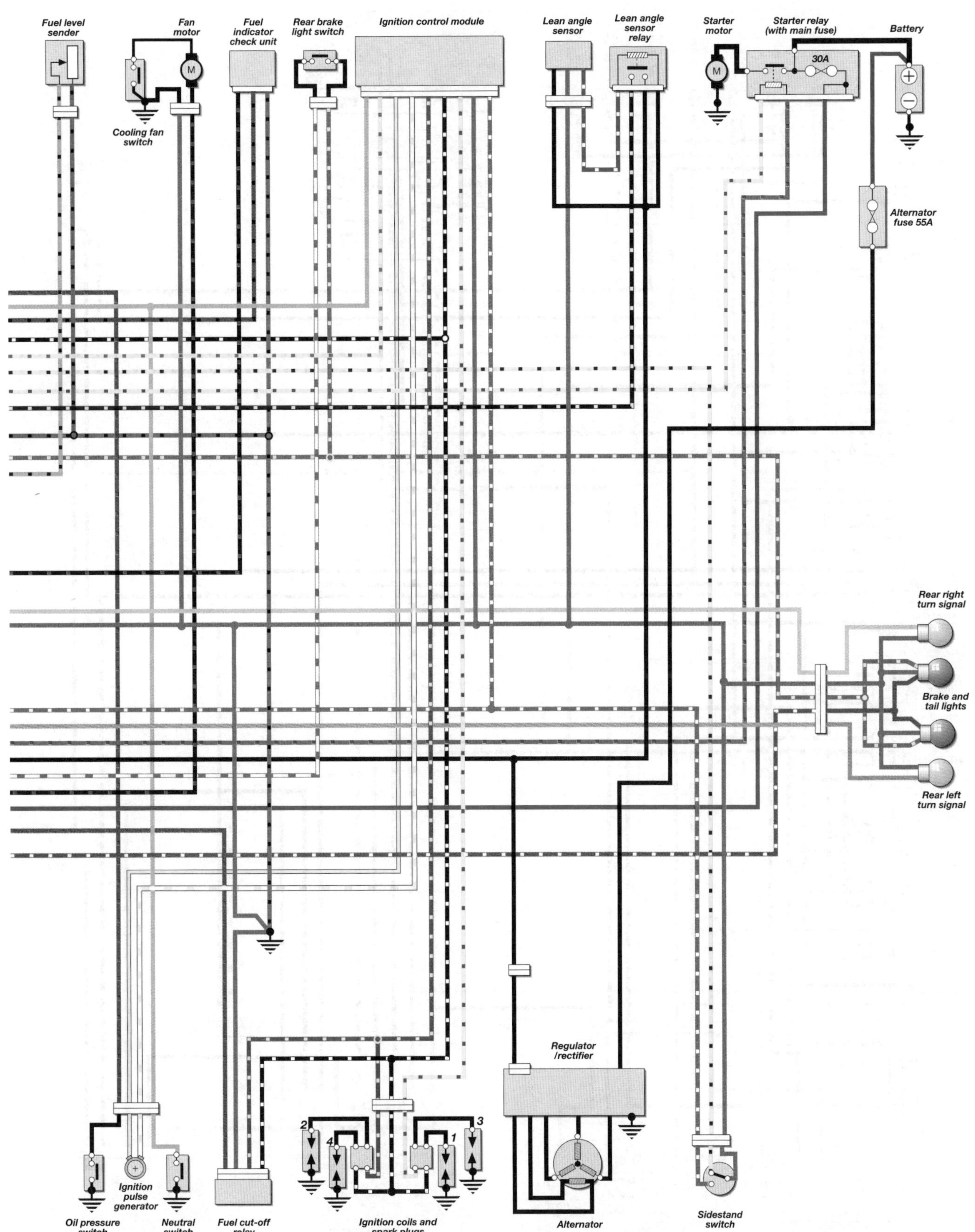

Honda ST1100 T and V standard UK models (continued)

C.J. Turk
H29568

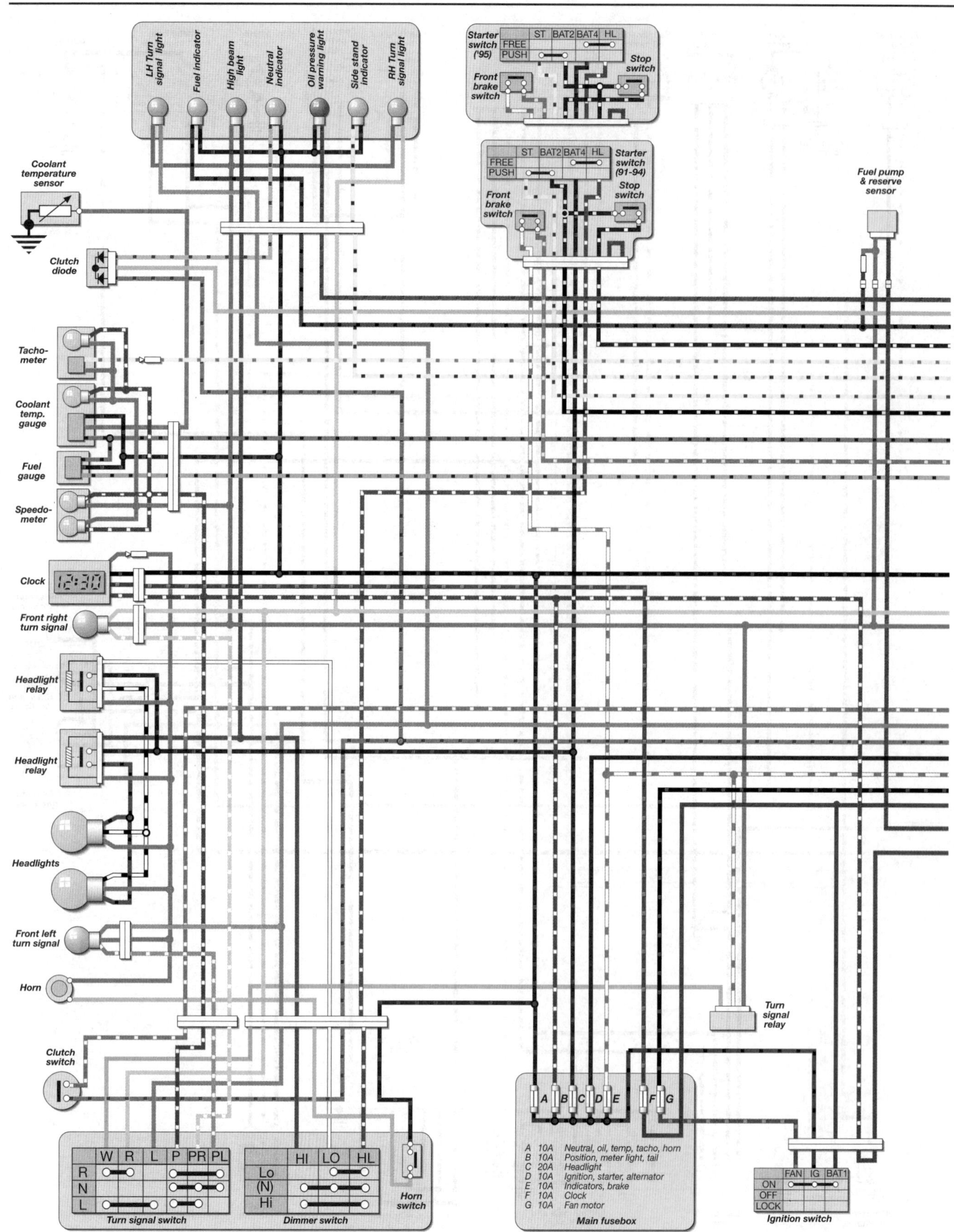

Honda ST1100 1991-95 standard US models

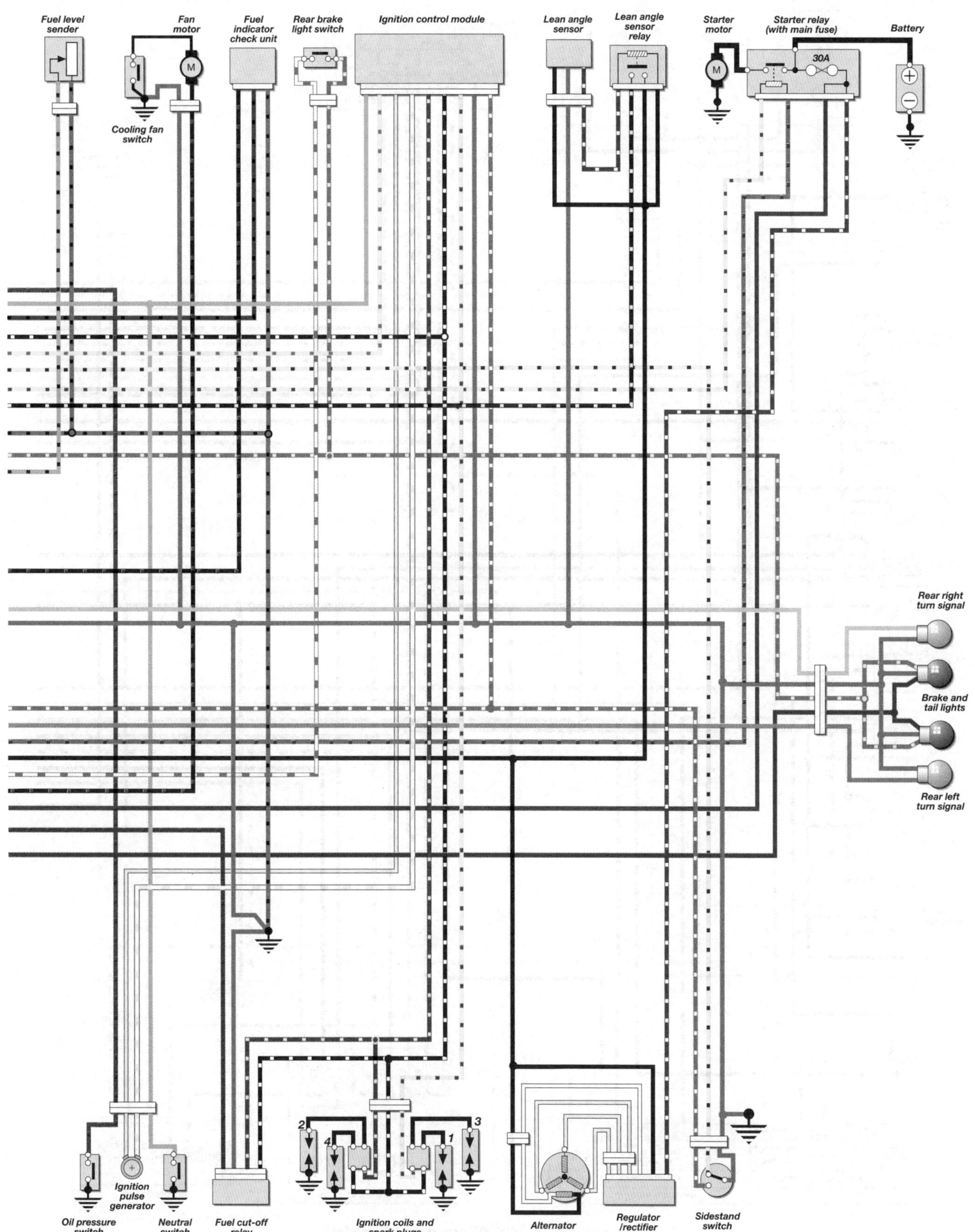

Honda ST1100 1991-95 standard US models (continued)

C.J. Turk
H29564

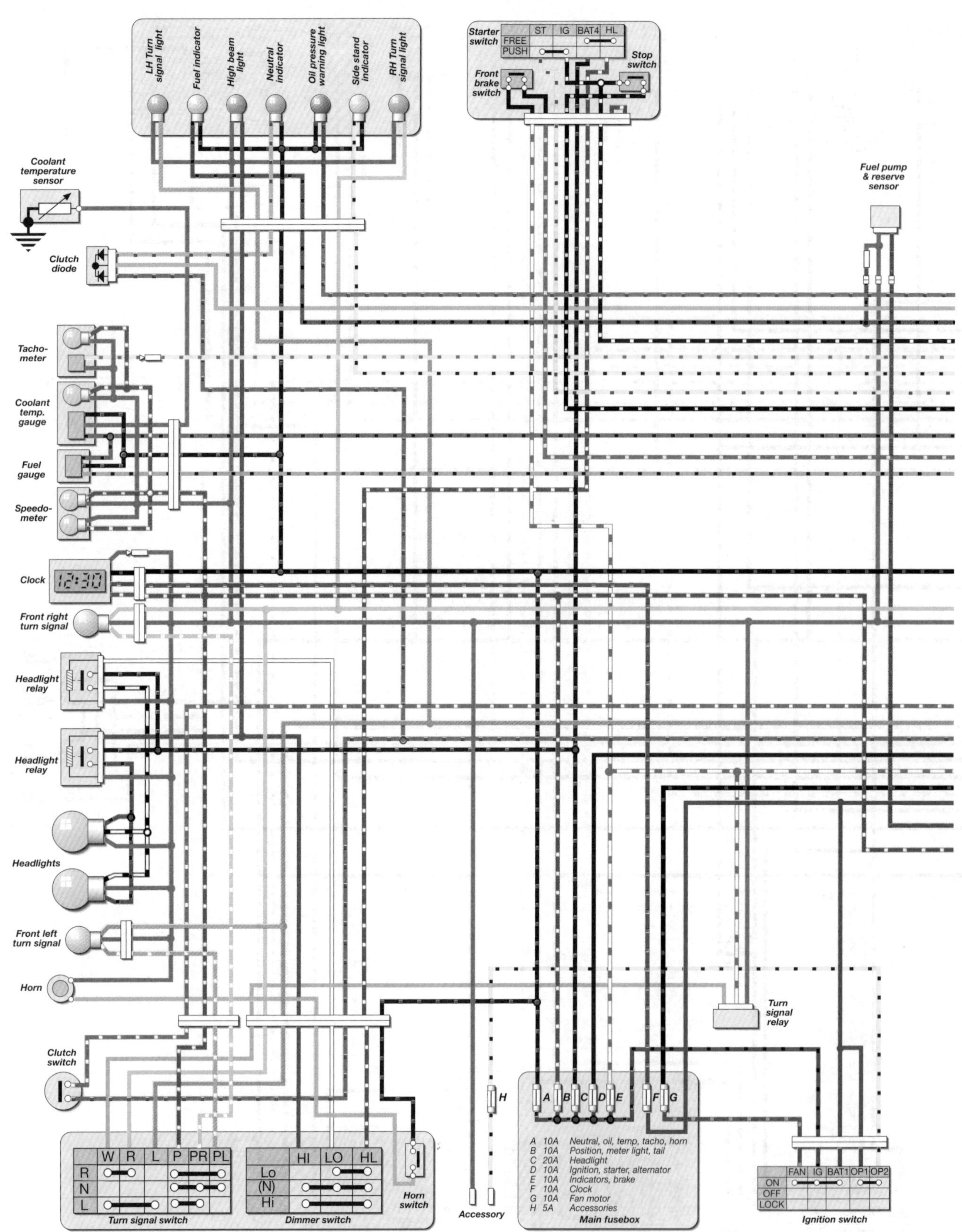

Honda ST1100 1996-97 standard US models

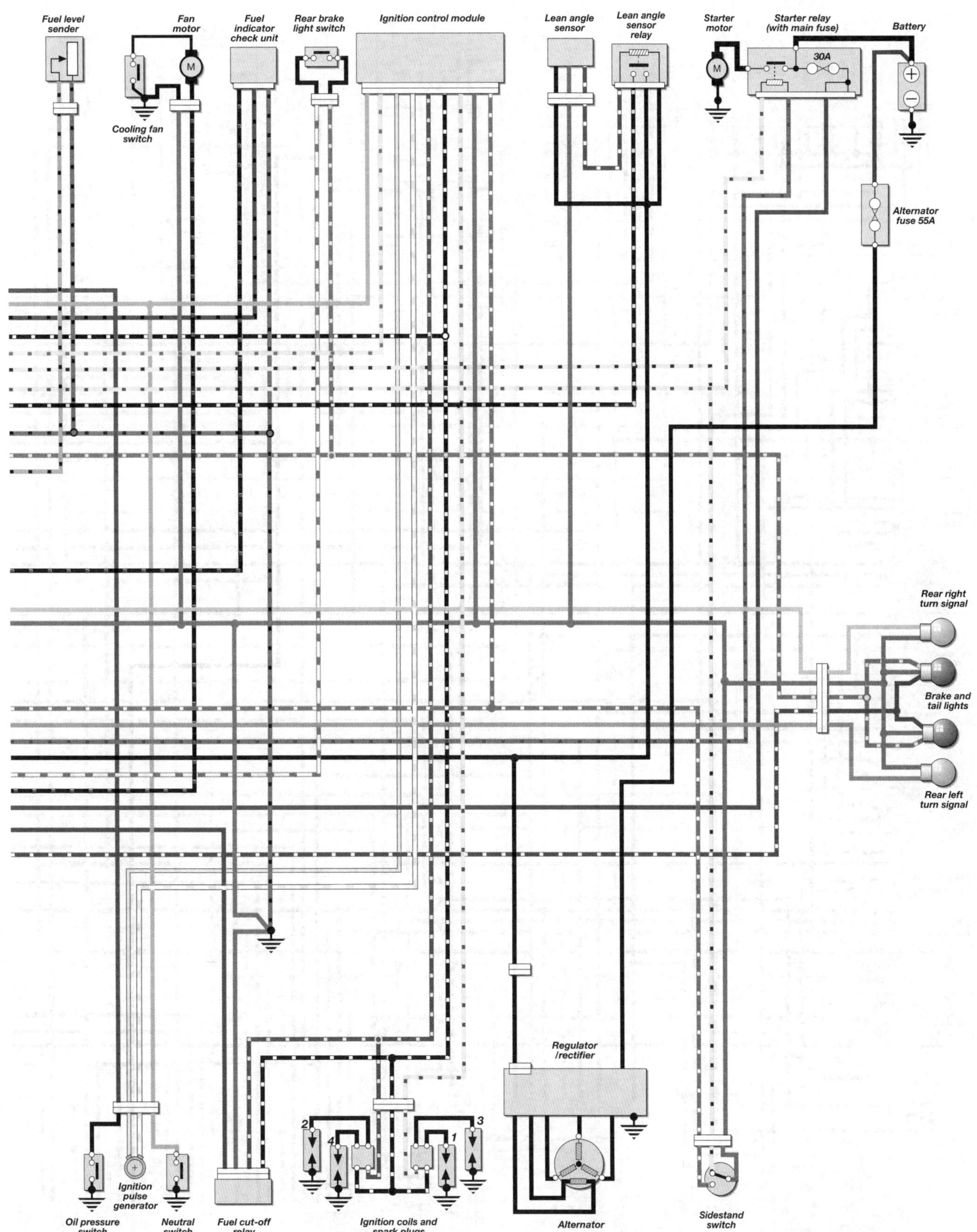

Honda ST1100 1996-97 standard US models (continued)

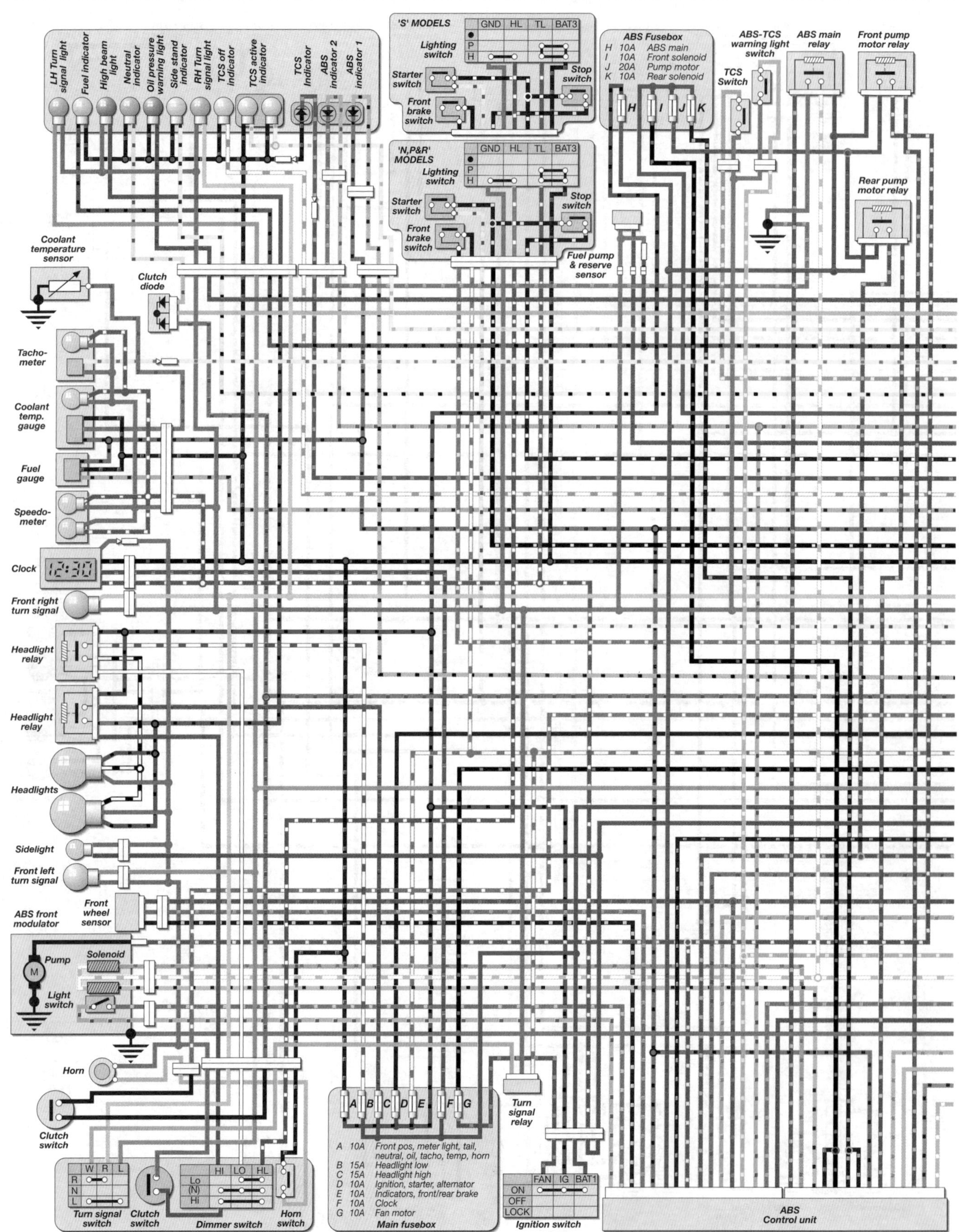

Honda ST1100 AN, AP, AR and AS ABS/TCS UK models

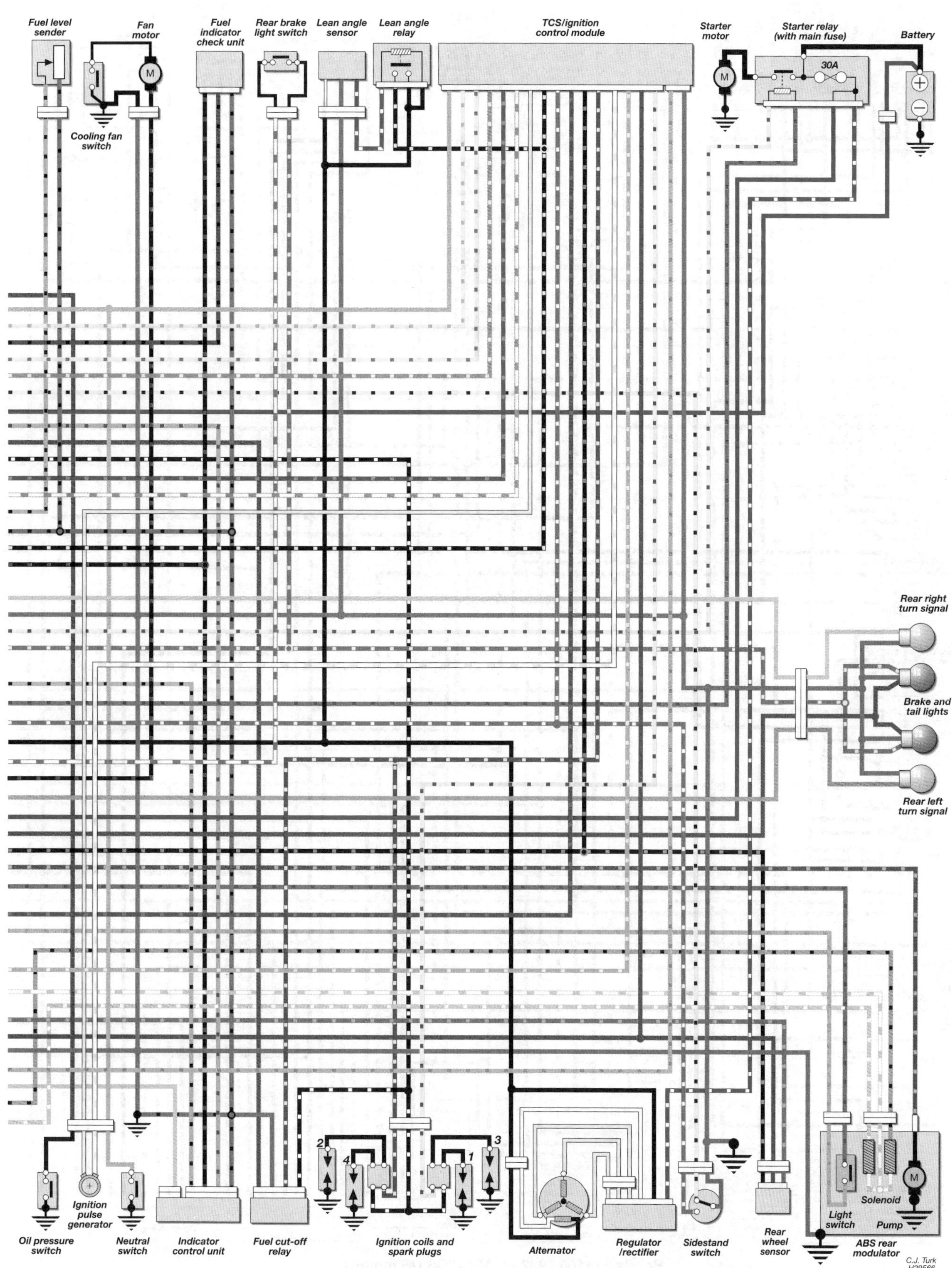

Honda ST1100 AN, AP, AR and AS ABS/TCS UK models (continued)

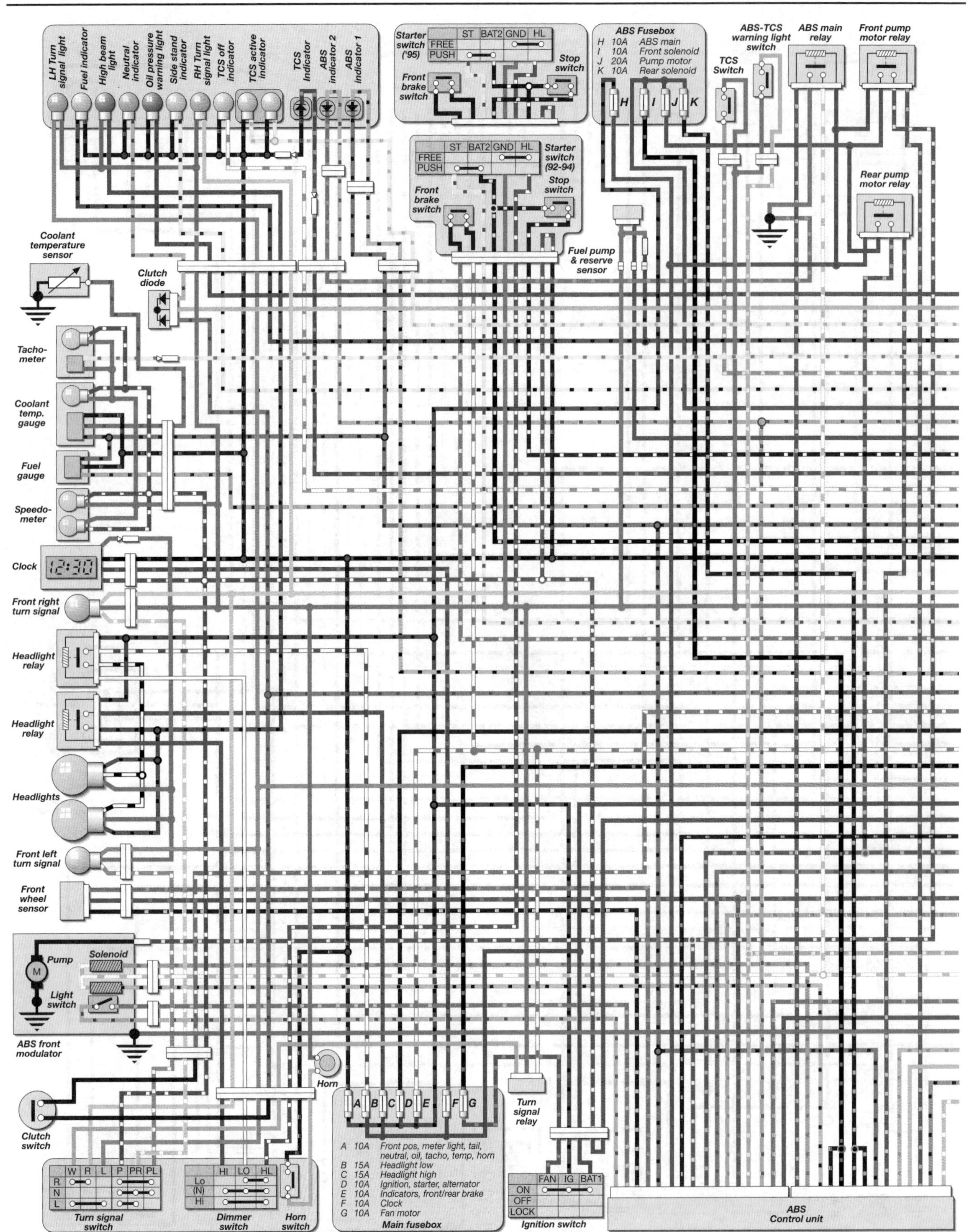

Honda ST1100 1992-95 ABS/TCS US models

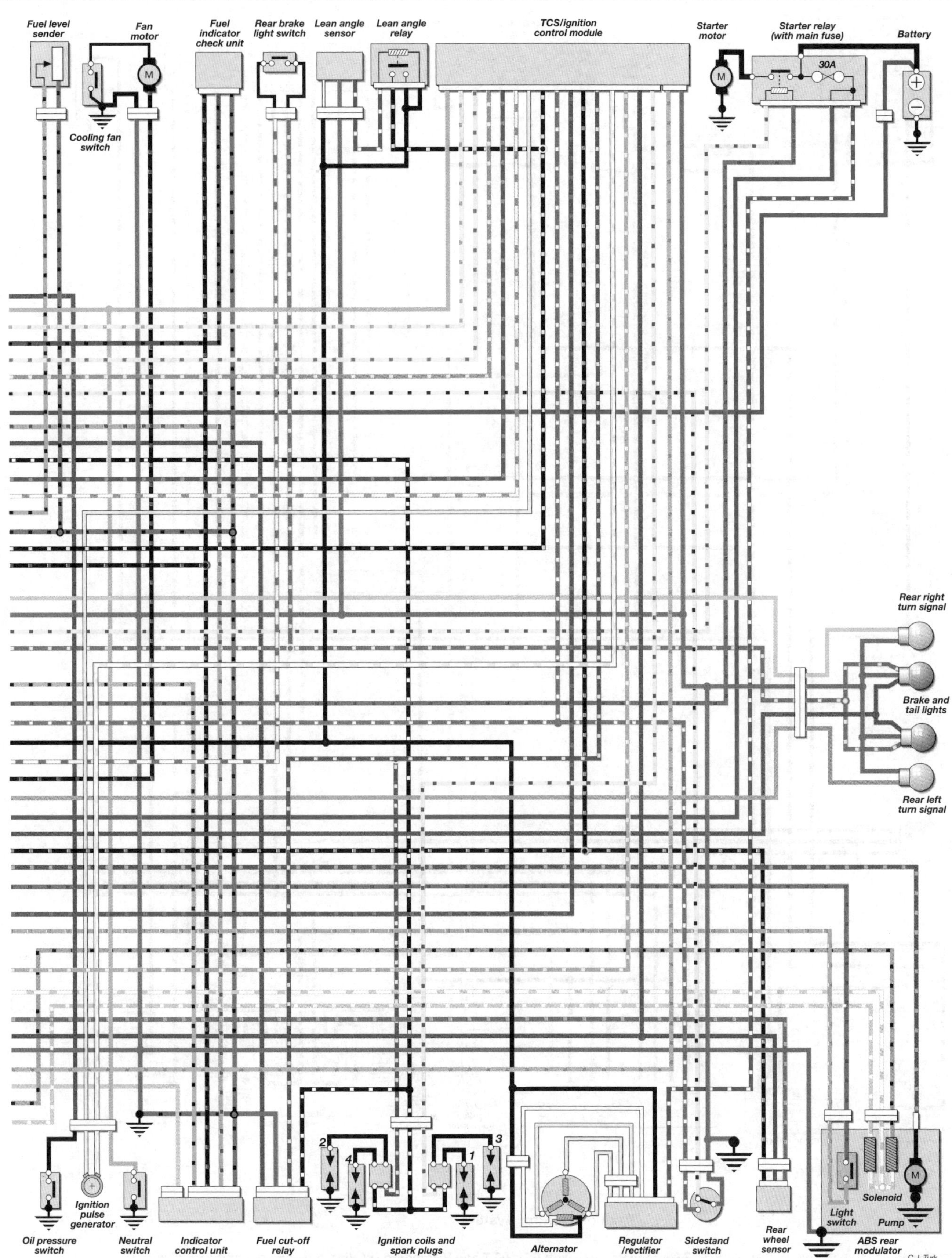

Honda ST1100 1992-95 ABS/TCS US models (continued)

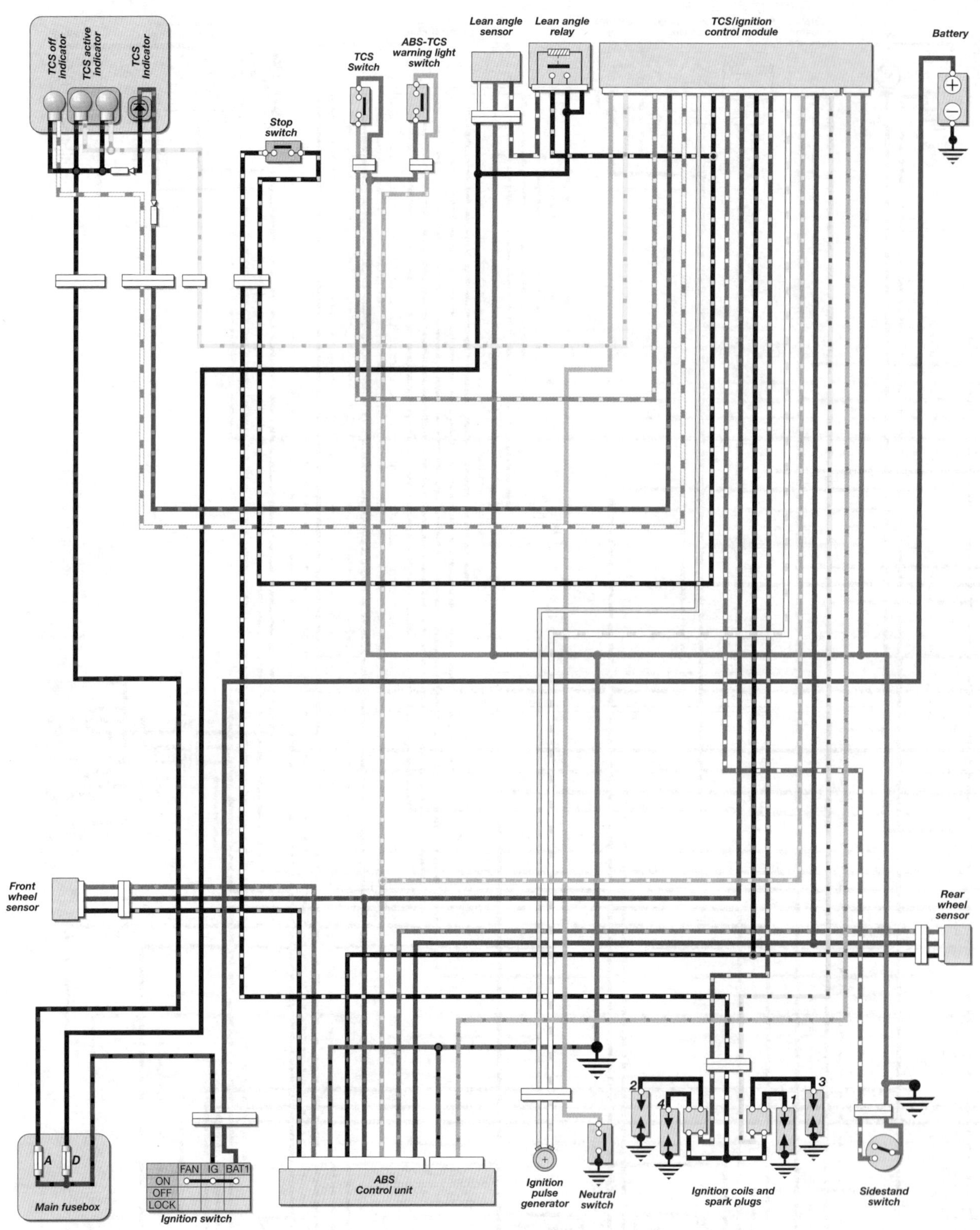

Traction Control System

UK: Honda ST1100 AT and AV CBS-ABS/TCS UK models - use with ST1100 T and V standard UK diagram and adjacent ABS diagram
US: Honda ST1100 1996-97 LBS-ABS/TCS US models - use with ST1100 1996-97 standard US diagram and adjacent ABS diagram

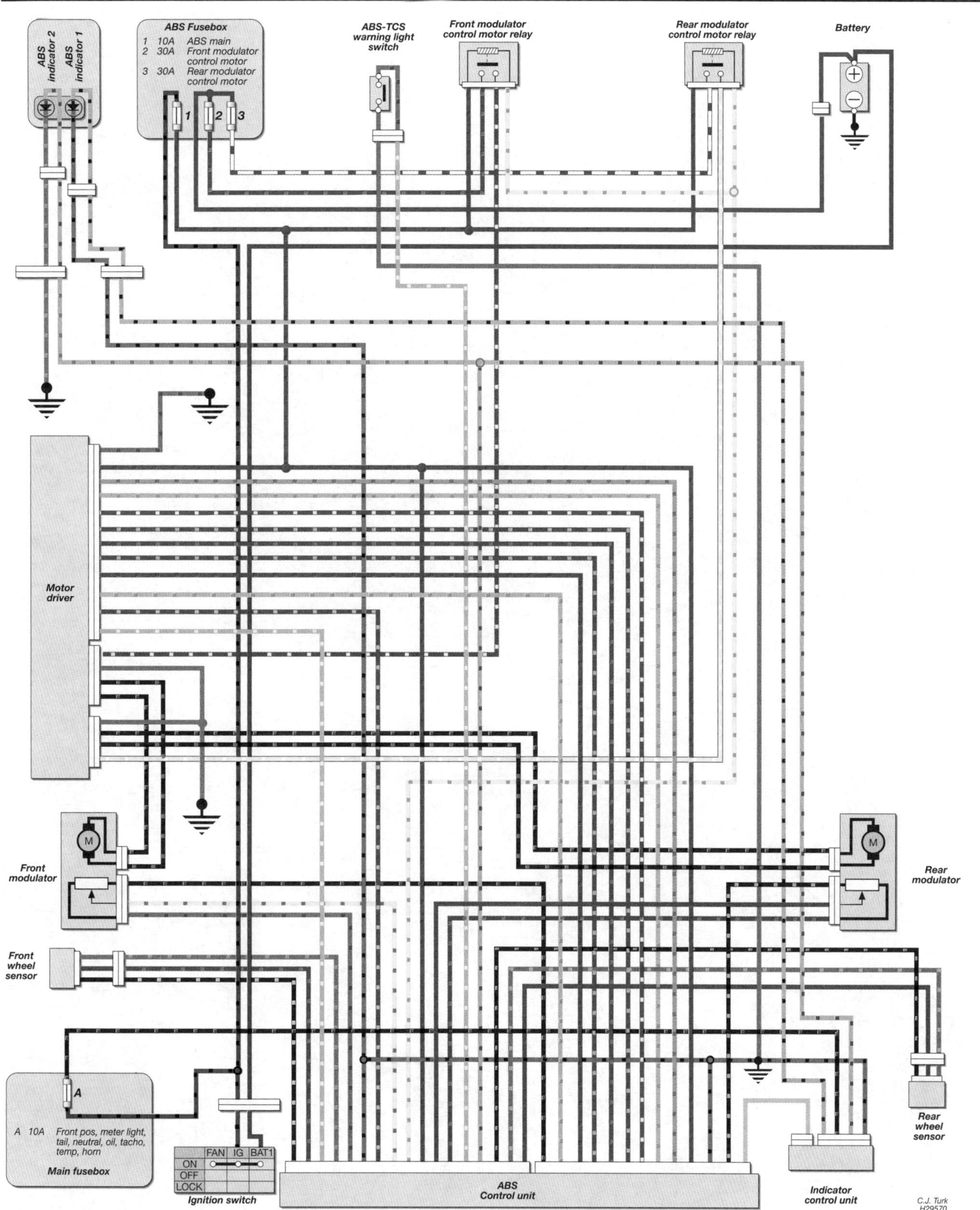

Anti-lock Braking System

UK: Honda ST1100 AT and AV CBS-ABS/TCS UK models - use with ST1100 T and V standard UK diagram and adjacent TCS diagram
US: Honda ST1100 1996-97 LBS-ABS/TCS US models - use with ST1100 1996-97 standard US diagram and adjacent TCS diagram

Notes

Dimensions and Weights .REF•1
Tools and Workshop Tips . . . . .REF•2
Conversion Factors . . . . .REF•20
Motorcycle Chemicals and Lubricants . . . . .REF•21
MOT Test Checks . . . . .REF•22
Storage . . . . .REF•26
Fault Finding . . . . .REF•28
Fault Finding Equipment . . . . .REF•36
Technical Terms Explained . . . . .REF•40
Index . . . . .REF•44

Dimensions and Weights

Wheelbase
All models . . . . .1555 mm

Length
All models . . . . .2285 mm

Width
UK L, M, N, P and R models, US 1991 to 1994 models . . . . . .835 mm
UK S, T and V models, US 1995 to 1997 models . . . . .835 mm

Overall height
UK L, M, N, P and R models, US 1991 to 1994 models . . . . .1395 mm
UK S, T and V models, US 1995 to 1997 models . . . . .1405 mm

Seat height
All models . . . . .800 mm

Minimum ground clearance
All models . . . . .145 mm

Weight (dry)
UK ST1100 L, M, N, P and R standard models . . . . .283 kg
UK ST1100 S, T and V standard models . . . . .287 kg
UK ST1100 AN, AP and AR ABS/TCS models . . . . .293 kg
UK AS, AT and AV CBS-ABS/TCS models . . . . .297 kg
US ST1100 1991 to 1994 standard models . . . . .284 kg*
US ST1100 1995 to 1997 standard models . . . . .288 kg*
US ST1100A 1992 to 1994 ABS/TCS models . . . . .297 kg*
US ST1100A 1995 to 1997 LBS-ABS/TCS models . . . . .298 kg*
**Add 1 kg for California models*

Buying tools

A toolkit is a fundamental requirement for servicing and repairing a motorcycle. Although there will be an initial expense in building up enough tools for servicing, this will soon be offset by the savings made by doing the job yourself. As experience and confidence grow, additional tools can be added to enable the repair and overhaul of the motorcycle. Many of the specialist tools are expensive and not often used so it may be preferable to hire them, or for a group of friends or motorcycle club to join in the purchase.

As a rule, it is better to buy more expensive, good quality tools. Cheaper tools are likely to wear out faster and need to be renewed more often, nullifying the original saving.

> ⚠ ***Warning: To avoid the risk of a poor quality tool breaking in use, causing injury or damage to the component being worked on, always aim to purchase tools which meet the relevant national safety standards.***

The following lists of tools do not represent the manufacturer's service tools, but serve as a guide to help the owner decide which tools are needed for this level of work. In addition, items such as an electric drill, hacksaw, files, hammers, soldering iron and a workbench equipped with a vice, may be needed. Although not classed as tools, a selection of bolts, screws, nuts, washers and pieces of tubing always come in useful.

For more information about tools, refer to the Haynes *Motorcycle Workshop Practice Manual* (Bk. No. 1454).

Manufacturer's service tools

Inevitably certain tasks require the use of a service tool. Where possible an alternative tool or method of approach is recommended, but sometimes there is no option if personal injury or damage to the component is to be avoided. Where required, service tools are referred to in the relevant procedure.

Service tools can usually only be purchased from a motorcycle dealer and are identified by a part number. Some of the commonly-used tools, such as rotor pullers, are available in aftermarket form from mail-order motorcycle tool and accessory suppliers.

Maintenance and minor repair tools

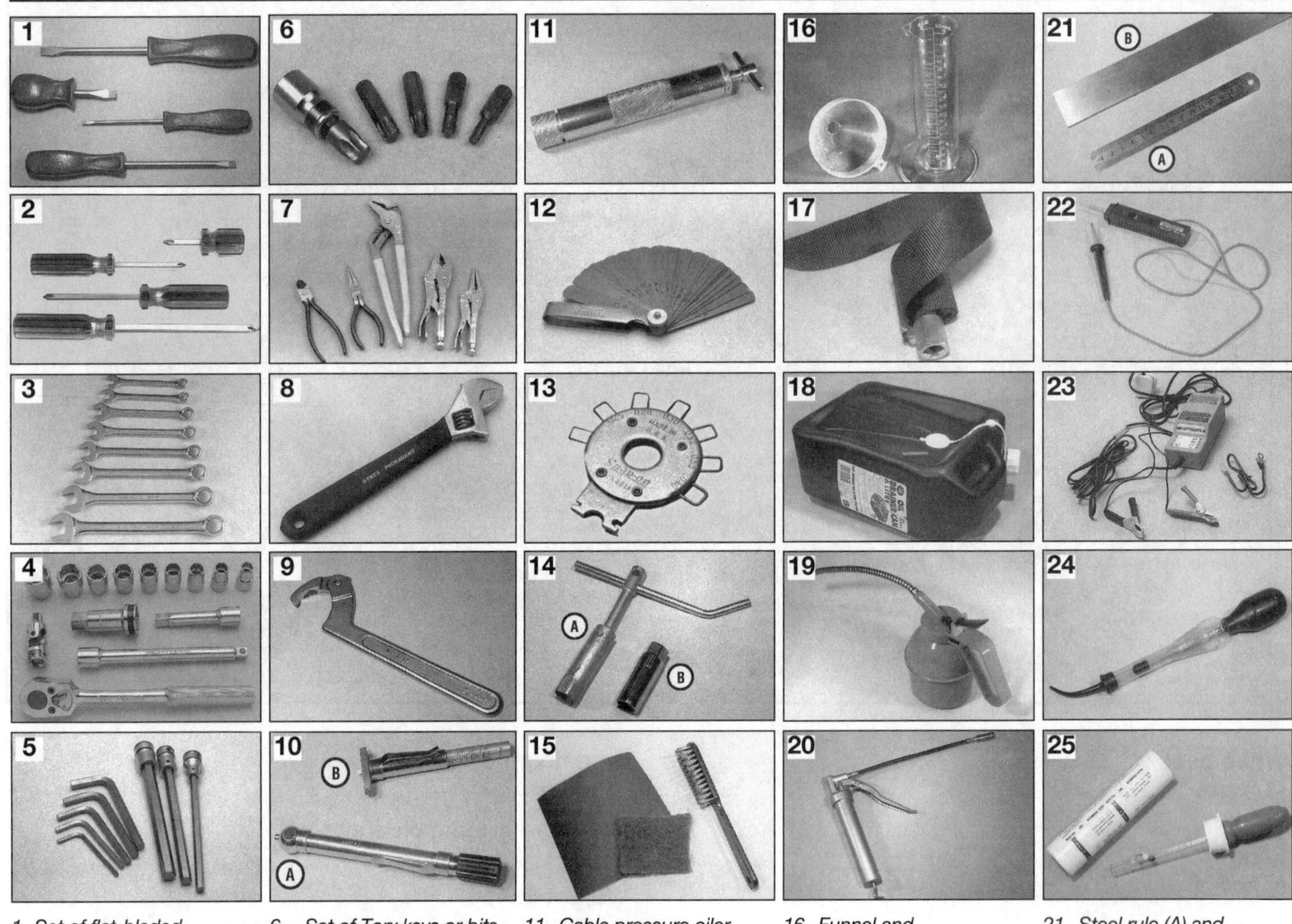

1 Set of flat-bladed screwdrivers
2 Set of Phillips head screwdrivers
3 Combination open-end & ring spanners
4 Socket set (3/8 inch or 1/2 inch drive)
5 Set of Allen keys or bits
6 Set of Torx keys or bits
7 Pliers and self-locking grips (Mole grips)
8 Adjustable spanner
9 C-spanner (ideally adjustable type)
10 Tyre pressure gauge (A) & tread depth gauge (B)
11 Cable pressure oiler
12 Feeler gauges
13 Spark plug gap measuring and adjusting tool
14 Spark plug spanner (A) or deep plug socket (B)
15 Wire brush and emery paper
16 Funnel and measuring vessel
17 Strap wrench, chain wrench or oil filter removal tool
18 Oil drainer can or tray
19 Pump type oil can
20 Grease gun
21 Steel rule (A) and straight-edge (B)
22 Continuity tester
23 Battery charger
24 Hydrometer (for battery specific gravity check)
25 Anti-freeze tester (for liquid-cooled engines)

Repair and overhaul tools

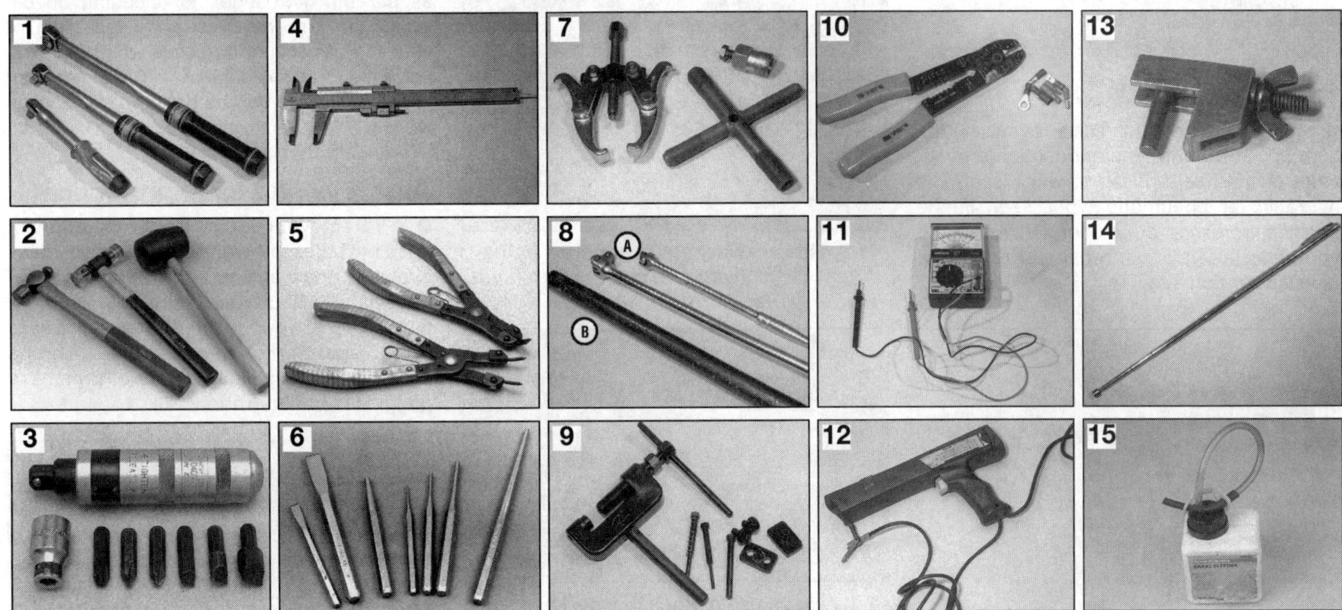

1 *Torque wrench (small and mid-ranges)*
2 *Conventional, plastic or soft-faced hammers*
3 *Impact driver set*
4 *Vernier gauge*
5 *Circlip pliers (internal and external, or combination)*
6 *Set of punches and cold chisels*
7 *Selection of pullers*
8 *Breaker bars (A) and length of tubing (B)*
9 *Chain breaking/ riveting tool*
10 *Wire crimper tool*
11 *Multimeter (measures amps, volts and ohms)*
12 *Stroboscope (for dynamic timing checks)*
13 *Hose clamp (wingnut type shown)*
14 *Magnetic arm (telescopic type shown)*
15 *One-man brake/clutch bleeder kit*

Specialist tools

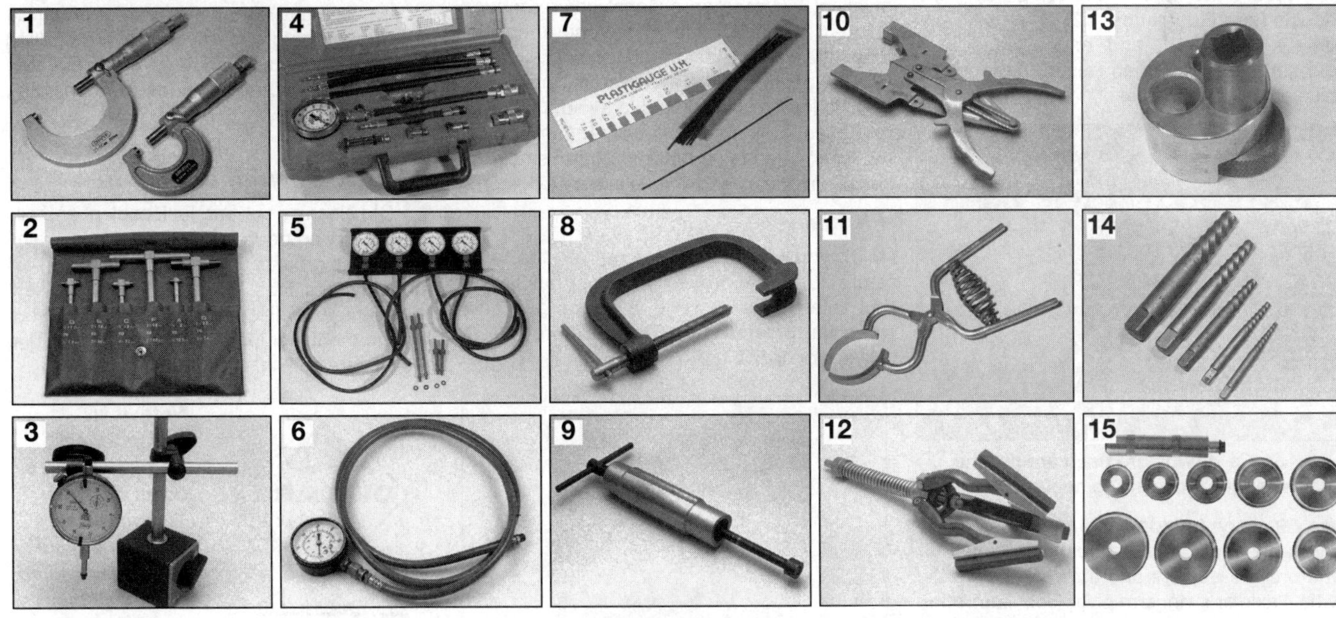

1 *Micrometer (external type)*
2 *Telescoping gauges or small-hole gauges*
3 *Dial gauge*
4 *Cylinder compression gauge*
5 *Vacuum gauges (shown) or manometer*
6 *Oil pressure gauge*
7 *Plastigauge kit*
8 *Valve spring compressor (4-stroke engines)*
9 *Piston pin drawbolt tool*
10 *Piston ring removal and installation tool*
11 *Piston ring clamp*
12 *Cylinder bore hone (stone type shown)*
13 *Stud extractor*
14 *Screw extractor set*
15 *Bearing driver set*

1 Workshop equipment and facilities

The workbench

- Work is made much easier by raising the bike up on a ramp - components are much more accessible if raised to waist level. The hydraulic or pneumatic types seen in the dealer's workshop are a sound investment if you undertake a lot of repairs or overhauls **(see illustration 1.1)**.

1.1 Hydraulic motorcycle ramp

- If raised off ground level, the bike must be supported on the ramp to avoid it falling. Most ramps incorporate a front wheel locating clamp which can be adjusted to suit different diameter wheels. When tightening the clamp, take care not to mark the wheel rim or damage the tyre - use wood blocks on each side to prevent this.
- Secure the bike to the ramp using tie-downs **(see illustration 1.2)**. If the bike has only a sidestand, and hence leans at a dangerous angle when raised, support the bike on an auxiliary stand.

1.2 Tie-downs are used around the passenger footrests to secure the bike

- Auxiliary (paddock) stands are widely available from mail order companies or motorcycle dealers and attach either to the wheel axle or swingarm pivot **(see illustration 1.3)**. If the motorcycle has a centrestand, you can support it under the crankcase to prevent it toppling whilst either wheel is removed **(see illustration 1.4)**.

1.3 This auxiliary stand attaches to the swingarm pivot

1.4 Always use a block of wood between the engine and jack head when supporting the engine in this way

Fumes and fire

- Refer to the Safety first! page at the beginning of the manual for full details. Make sure your workshop is equipped with a fire extinguisher suitable for fuel-related fires (Class B fire - flammable liquids) - it is not sufficient to have a water-filled extinguisher.
- Always ensure adequate ventilation is available. Unless an exhaust gas extraction system is available for use, ensure that the engine is run outside of the workshop.
- If working on the fuel system, make sure the workshop is ventilated to avoid a build-up of fumes. This applies equally to fume build-up when charging a battery. Do not smoke or allow anyone else to smoke in the workshop.

Fluids

- If you need to drain fuel from the tank, store it in an approved container marked as suitable for the storage of petrol (gasoline) **(see illustration 1.5)**. Do not store fuel in glass jars or bottles.

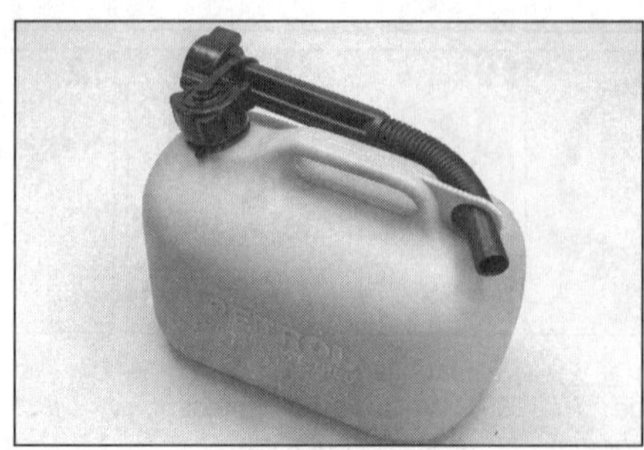

1.5 Use an approved can only for storing petrol (gasoline)

- Use proprietary engine degreasers or solvents which have a high flash-point, such as paraffin (kerosene), for cleaning off oil, grease and dirt - never use petrol (gasoline) for cleaning. Wear rubber gloves when handling solvent and engine degreaser. The fumes from certain solvents can be dangerous - always work in a well-ventilated area.

Dust, eye and hand protection

- Protect your lungs from inhalation of dust particles by wearing a filtering mask over the nose and mouth. Many frictional materials still contain asbestos which is dangerous to your health. Protect your eyes from spouts of liquid and sprung components by wearing a pair of protective goggles **(see illustration 1.6)**.

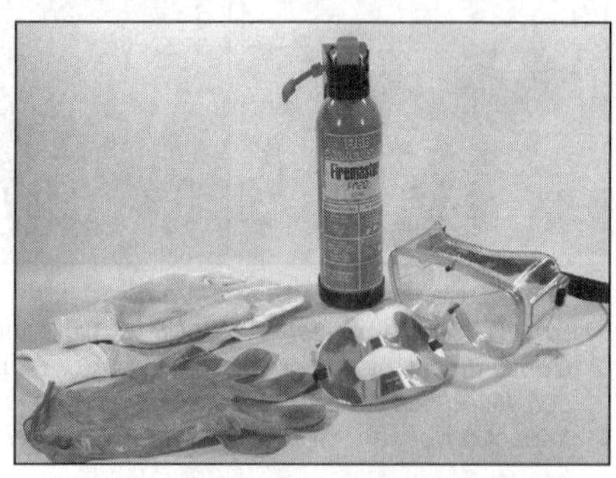

1.6 A fire extinguisher, goggles, mask and protective gloves should be at hand in the workshop

- Protect your hands from contact with solvents, fuel and oils by wearing rubber gloves. Alternatively apply a barrier cream to your hands before starting work. If handling hot components or fluids, wear suitable gloves to protect your hands from scalding and burns.

What to do with old fluids

- Old cleaning solvent, fuel, coolant and oils should not be poured down domestic drains or onto the ground. Package the fluid up in old oil containers, label it accordingly, and take it to a garage or disposal facility. Contact your local authority for location of such sites or ring the oil care hotline.

Note: It is antisocial and illegal to dump oil down the drain. To find the location of your local oil recycling bank, call this number free.

In the USA, note that any oil supplier must accept used oil for recycling.

2 Fasteners - screws, bolts and nuts

Fastener types and applications

Bolts and screws

● Fastener head types are either of hexagonal, Torx or splined design, with internal and external versions of each type **(see illustrations 2.1 and 2.2)**; splined head fasteners are not in common use on motorcycles. The conventional slotted or Phillips head design is used for certain screws. Bolt or screw length is always measured from the underside of the head to the end of the item **(see illustration 2.11)**.

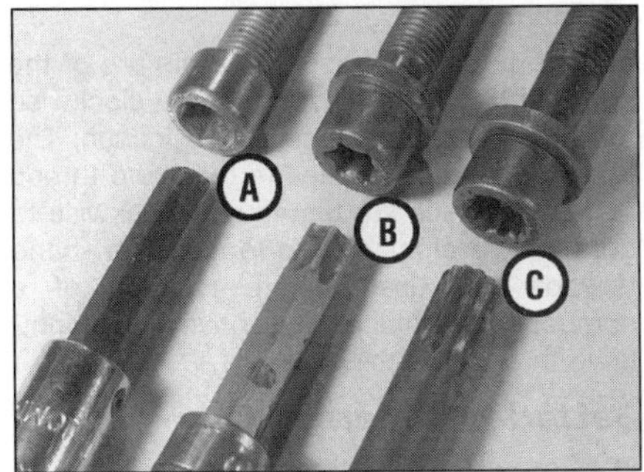

2.1 Internal hexagon/Allen (A), Torx (B) and splined (C) fasteners, with corresponding bits

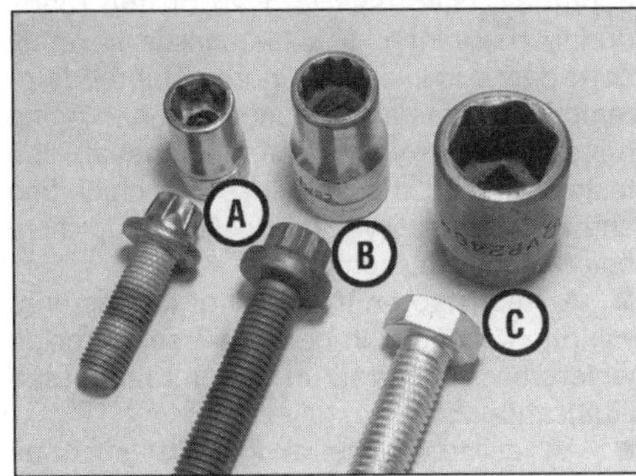

2.2 External Torx (A), splined (B) and hexagon (C) fasteners, with corresponding sockets

● Certain fasteners on the motorcycle have a tensile marking on their heads, the higher the marking the stronger the fastener. High tensile fasteners generally carry a 10 or higher marking. Never replace a high tensile fastener with one of a lower tensile strength.

Washers (see illustration 2.3)

● Plain washers are used between a fastener head and a component to prevent damage to the component or to spread the load when torque is applied. Plain washers can also be used as spacers or shims in certain assemblies. Copper or aluminium plain washers are often used as sealing washers on drain plugs.

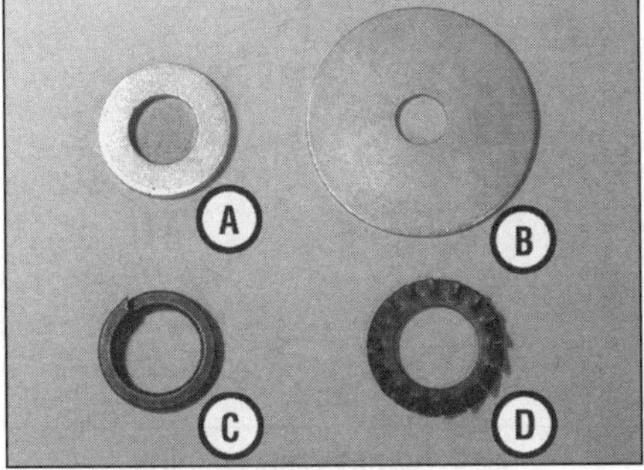

2.3 Plain washer (A), penny washer (B), spring washer (C) and serrated washer (D)

● The split-ring spring washer works by applying axial tension between the fastener head and component. If flattened, it is fatigued and must be renewed. If a plain (flat) washer is used on the fastener, position the spring washer between the fastener and the plain washer.

● Serrated star type washers dig into the fastener and component faces, preventing loosening. They are often used on electrical earth (ground) connections to the frame.

● Cone type washers (sometimes called Belleville) are conical and when tightened apply axial tension between the fastener head and component. They must be installed with the dished side against the component and often carry an OUTSIDE marking on their outer face. If flattened, they are fatigued and must be renewed.

● Tab washers are used to lock plain nuts or bolts on a shaft. A portion of the tab washer is bent up hard against one flat of the nut or bolt to prevent it loosening. Due to the tab washer being deformed in use, a new tab washer should be used every time it is disturbed.

● Wave washers are used to take up endfloat on a shaft. They provide light springing and prevent excessive side-to-side play of a component. Can be found on rocker arm shafts.

Nuts and split pins

● Conventional plain nuts are usually six-sided **(see illustration 2.4)**. They are sized by thread diameter and pitch. High tensile nuts carry a number on one end to denote their tensile strength.

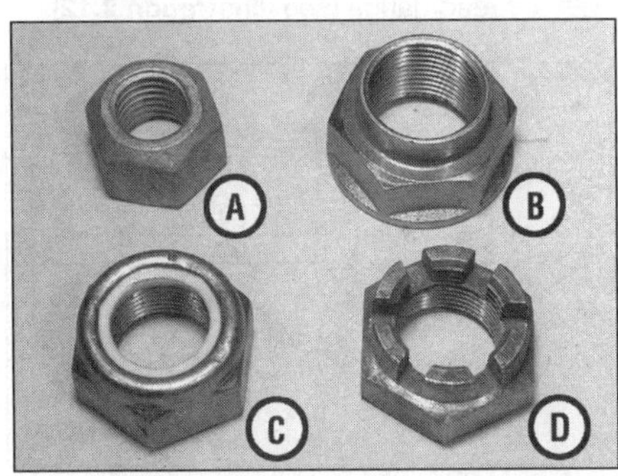

2.4 Plain nut (A), shouldered locknut (B), nylon insert nut (C) and castellated nut (D)

● Self-locking nuts either have a nylon insert, or two spring metal tabs, or a shoulder which is staked into a groove in the shaft - their advantage over conventional plain nuts is a resistance to loosening due to vibration. The nylon insert type can be used a number of times, but must be renewed when the friction of the nylon insert is reduced, ie when the nut spins freely on the shaft. The spring tab type can be reused unless the tabs are damaged. The shouldered type must be renewed every time it is disturbed.

● Split pins (cotter pins) are used to lock a castellated nut to a shaft or to prevent slackening of a plain nut. Common applications are wheel axles and brake torque arms. Because the split pin arms are deformed to lock around the nut a new split pin must always be used on installation - always fit the correct size split pin which will fit snugly in the shaft hole. Make sure the split pin arms are correctly located around the nut **(see illustrations 2.5 and 2.6)**.

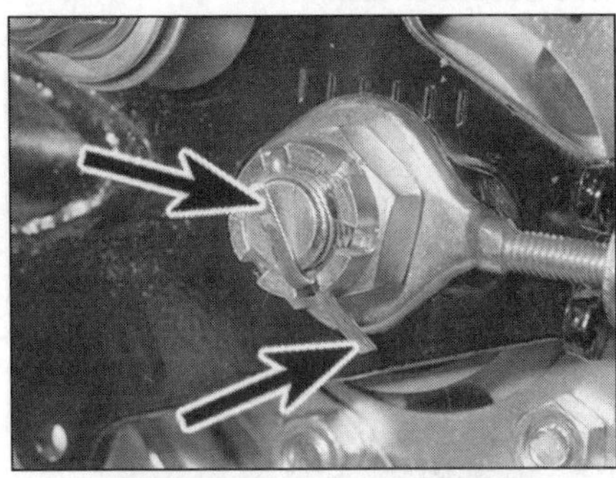

2.5 Bend split pin (cotter pin) arms as shown (arrows) to secure a castellated nut

2.6 Bend split pin (cotter pin) arms as shown to secure a plain nut

Caution: If the castellated nut slots do not align with the shaft hole after tightening to the torque setting, tighten the nut until the next slot aligns with the hole - never slacken the nut to align its slot.

● R-pins (shaped like the letter R), or slip pins as they are sometimes called, are sprung and can be reused if they are otherwise in good condition. Always install R-pins with their closed end facing forwards **(see illustration 2.7)**.

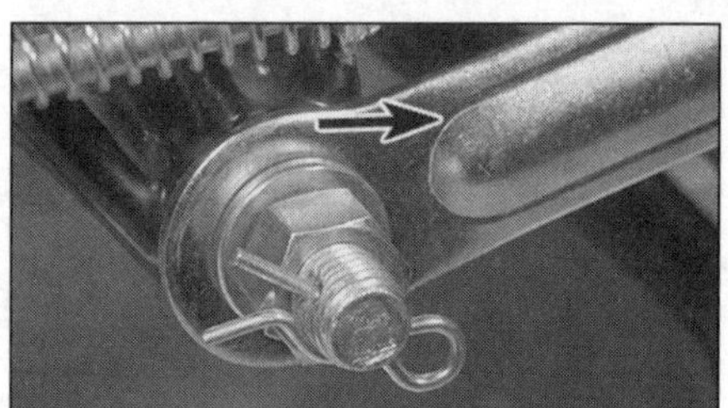

2.7 Correct fitting of R-pin. Arrow indicates forward direction

Circlips (see illustration 2.8)

● Circlips (sometimes called snap-rings) are used to retain components on a shaft or in a housing and have corresponding external or internal ears to permit removal. Parallel-sided (machined) circlips can be installed either way round in their groove, whereas stamped circlips (which have a chamfered edge on one face) must be installed with the chamfer facing away from the direction of thrust load **(see illustration 2.9)**.

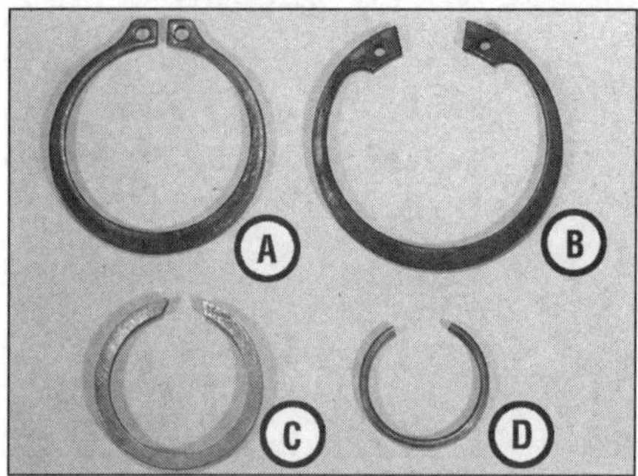

2.8 External stamped circlip (A), internal stamped circlip (B), machined circlip (C) and wire circlip (D)

● Always use circlip pliers to remove and install circlips; expand or compress them just enough to remove them. After installation, rotate the circlip in its groove to ensure it is securely seated. If installing a circlip on a splined shaft, always align its opening with a shaft channel to ensure the circlip ends are well supported and unlikely to catch **(see illustration 2.10)**.

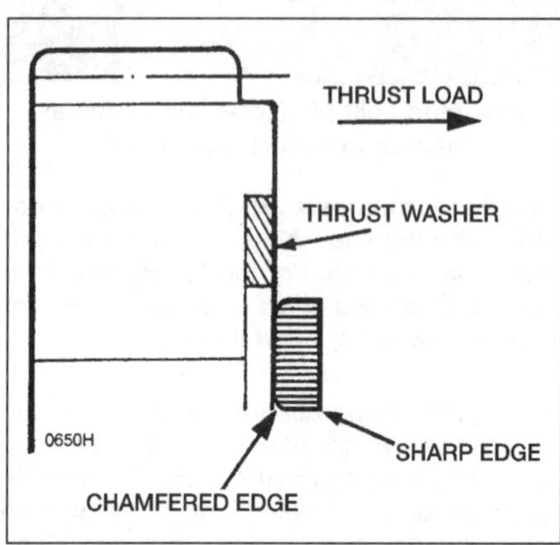

2.9 Correct fitting of a stamped circlip

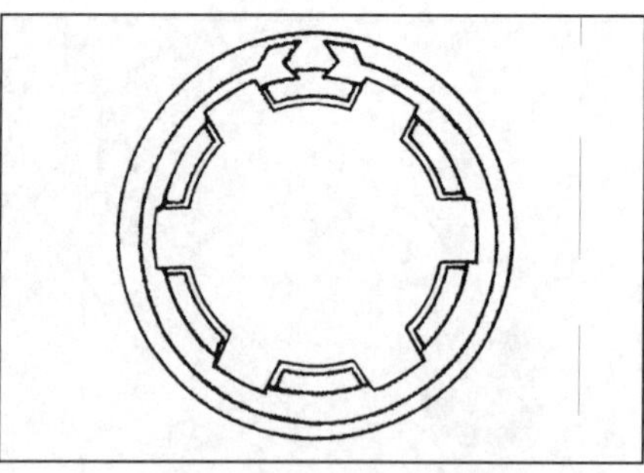

2.10 Align circlip opening with shaft channel

● Circlips can wear due to the thrust of components and become loose in their grooves, with the subsequent danger of becoming dislodged in operation. For this reason, renewal is advised every time a circlip is disturbed.

● Wire circlips are commonly used as piston pin retaining clips. If a removal tang is provided, long-nosed pliers can be used to dislodge them, otherwise careful use of a small flat-bladed screwdriver is necessary. Wire circlips should be renewed every time they are disturbed.

Thread diameter and pitch

● Diameter of a male thread (screw, bolt or stud) is the outside diameter of the threaded portion **(see illustration 2.11)**. Most motorcycle manufacturers use the ISO (International Standards Organisation) metric system expressed in millimetres, eg M6 refers to a 6 mm diameter thread. Sizing is the same for nuts, except that the thread diameter is measured across the valleys of the nut.

● Pitch is the distance between the peaks of the thread **(see illustration 2.11)**. It is expressed in millimetres, thus a common bolt size may be expressed as 6.0 x 1.0 mm (6 mm thread diameter and 1 mm pitch). Generally pitch increases in proportion to thread diameter, although there are always exceptions.

● Thread diameter and pitch are related for conventional fastener applications and the following table can be used as a guide. Additionally, the AF (Across Flats), spanner or socket size dimension of the bolt or nut **(see illustration 2.11)** is linked to thread and pitch specification. Thread pitch can be measured with a thread gauge **(see illustration 2.12)**.

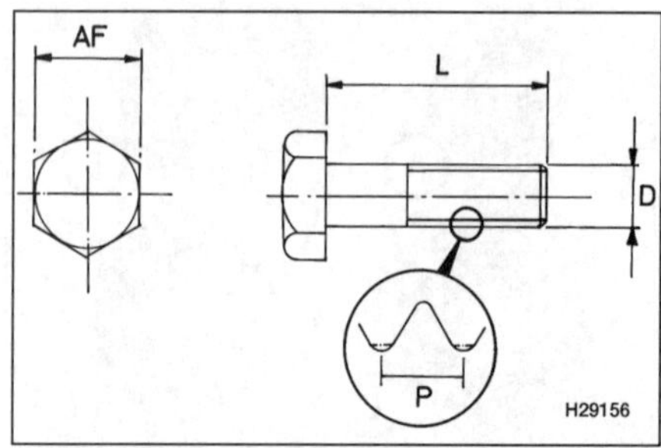

2.11 Fastener length (L), thread diameter (D), thread pitch (P) and head size (AF)

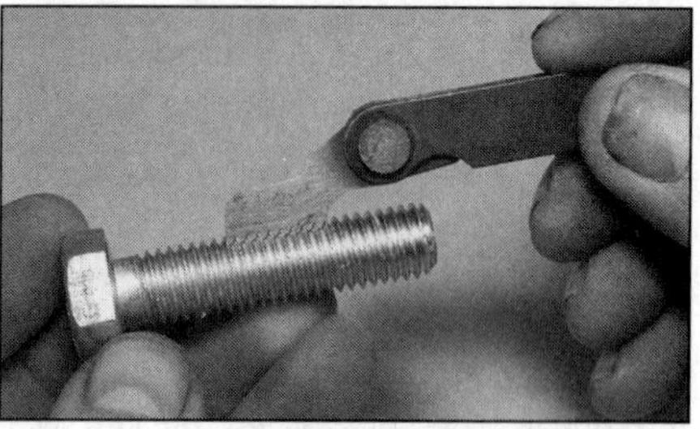

2.12 Using a thread gauge to measure pitch

AF size	Thread diameter x pitch (mm)
8 mm	M5 x 0.8
8 mm	M6 x 1.0
10 mm	M6 x 1.0
12 mm	M8 x 1.25
14 mm	M10 x 1.25
17 mm	M12 x 1.25

● The threads of most fasteners are of the right-hand type, ie they are turned clockwise to tighten and anti-clockwise to loosen. The reverse situation applies to left-hand thread fasteners, which are turned anti-clockwise to tighten and clockwise to loosen. Left-hand threads are used where rotation of a component might loosen a conventional right-hand thread fastener.

Seized fasteners

● Corrosion of external fasteners due to water or reaction between two dissimilar metals can occur over a period of time. It will build up sooner in wet conditions or in countries where salt is used on the roads during the winter. If a fastener is severely corroded it is likely that normal methods of removal will fail and result in its head being ruined. When you attempt removal, the fastener thread should be heard to crack free and unscrew easily - if it doesn't, stop there before damaging something.

● A smart tap on the head of the fastener will often succeed in breaking free corrosion which has occurred in the threads **(see illustration 2.13)**.

● An aerosol penetrating fluid (such as WD-40) applied the night beforehand may work its way down into the thread and ease removal. Depending on the location, you may be able to make up a Plasticine well around the fastener head and fill it with penetrating fluid.

2.13 A sharp tap on the head of a fastener will often break free a corroded thread

● If you are working on an engine internal component, corrosion will most likely not be a problem due to the well lubricated environment. However, components can be very tight and an impact driver is a useful tool in freeing them **(see illustration 2.14)**.

2.14 Using an impact driver to free a fastener

● Where corrosion has occurred between dissimilar metals (eg steel and aluminium alloy), the application of heat to the fastener head will create a disproportionate expansion rate between the two metals and break the seizure caused by the corrosion. Whether heat can be applied depends on the location of the fastener - any surrounding components likely to be damaged must first be removed **(see illustration 2.15)**. Heat can be applied using a paint stripper heat gun or clothes iron, or by immersing the component in boiling water - wear protective gloves to prevent scalding or burns to the hands.

2.15 Using heat to free a seized fastener

● As a last resort, it is possible to use a hammer and cold chisel to work the fastener head unscrewed **(see illustration 2.16)**. This will damage the fastener, but more importantly extreme care must be taken not to damage the surrounding component.

Caution: Remember that the component being secured is generally of more value than the bolt, nut or screw - when the fastener is freed, do not unscrew it with force, instead work the fastener back and forth when resistance is felt to prevent thread damage.

2.16 Using a hammer and chisel to free a seized fastener

Broken fasteners and damaged heads

● If the shank of a broken bolt or screw is accessible you can grip it with self-locking grips. The knurled wheel type stud extractor tool or self-gripping stud puller tool is particularly useful for removing the long studs which screw into the cylinder mouth surface of the crankcase or bolts and screws from which the head has broken off **(see illustration 2.17)**. Studs can also be removed by locking two nuts together on the threaded end of the stud and using a spanner on the lower nut **(see illustration 2.18)**.

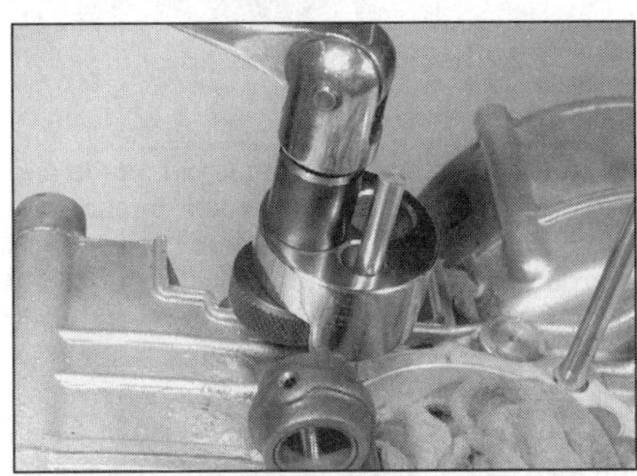

2.17 Using a stud extractor tool to remove a broken crankcase stud

2.18 Two nuts can be locked together to unscrew a stud from a component

● A bolt or screw which has broken off below or level with the casing must be extracted using a screw extractor set. Centre punch the fastener to centralise the drill bit, then drill a hole in the fastener **(see illustration 2.19)**. Select a drill bit which is

2.19 When using a screw extractor, first drill a hole in the fastener . . .

approximately half to three-quarters the diameter of the fastener and drill to a depth which will accommodate the extractor. Use the largest size extractor possible, but avoid leaving too small a wall thickness otherwise the extractor will merely force the fastener walls outwards wedging it in the casing thread.

● If a spiral type extractor is used, thread it anti-clockwise into the fastener. As it is screwed in, it will grip the fastener and unscrew it from the casing **(see illustration 2.20)**.

2.20 . . . then thread the extractor anti-clockwise into the fastener

● If a taper type extractor is used, tap it into the fastener so that it is firmly wedged in place. Unscrew the extractor (anti-clockwise) to draw the fastener out.

Warning: Stud extractors are very hard and may break off in the fastener if care is not taken - ask an engineer about spark erosion if this happens.

● Alternatively, the broken bolt/screw can be drilled out and the hole retapped for an oversize bolt/screw or a diamond-section thread insert. It is essential that the drilling is carried out squarely and to the correct depth, otherwise the casing may be ruined - if in doubt, entrust the work to an engineer.

● Bolts and nuts with rounded corners cause the correct size spanner or socket to slip when force is applied. Of the types of spanner/socket available always use a six-point type rather than an eight or twelve-point type - better grip

2.21 Comparison of surface drive ring spanner (left) with 12-point type (right)

is obtained. Surface drive spanners grip the middle of the hex flats, rather than the corners, and are thus good in cases of damaged heads **(see illustration 2.21)**.

● Slotted-head or Phillips-head screws are often damaged by the use of the wrong size screwdriver. Allen-head and Torx-head screws are much less likely to sustain damage. If enough of the screw head is exposed you can use a hacksaw to cut a slot in its head and then use a conventional flat-bladed screwdriver to remove it. Alternatively use a hammer and cold chisel to tap the head of the fastener round to slacken it. Always replace damaged fasteners with new ones, preferably Torx or Allen-head type.

A dab of valve grinding compound between the screw head and screw-driver tip will often give a good grip.

Thread repair

● Threads (particularly those in aluminium alloy components) can be damaged by overtightening, being assembled with dirt in the threads, or from a component working loose and vibrating. Eventually the thread will fail completely, and it will be impossible to tighten the fastener.

● If a thread is damaged or clogged with old locking compound it can be renovated with a thread repair tool (thread chaser) **(see illustrations 2.22 and 2.23)**; special thread chasers are available for spark plug hole threads. The tool will not cut a new thread, but clean and true the original thread. Make sure that you use the correct diameter and pitch tool. Similarly, external threads can be cleaned up with a die or a thread restorer file **(see illustration 2.24)**.

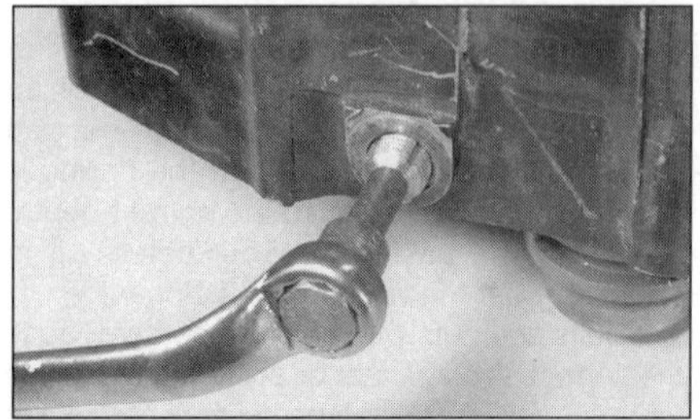
2.22 A thread repair tool being used to correct an internal thread

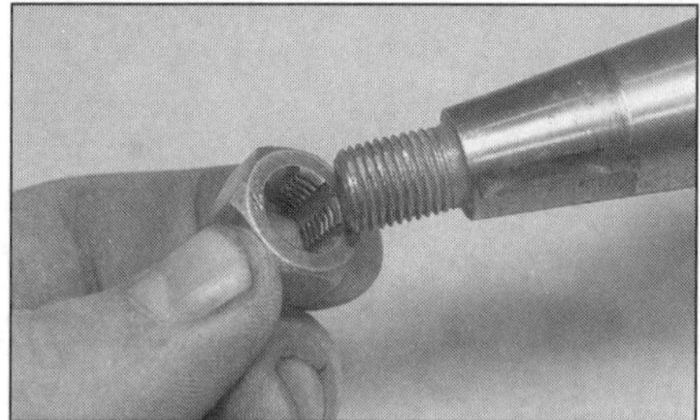
2.23 A thread repair tool being used to correct an external thread

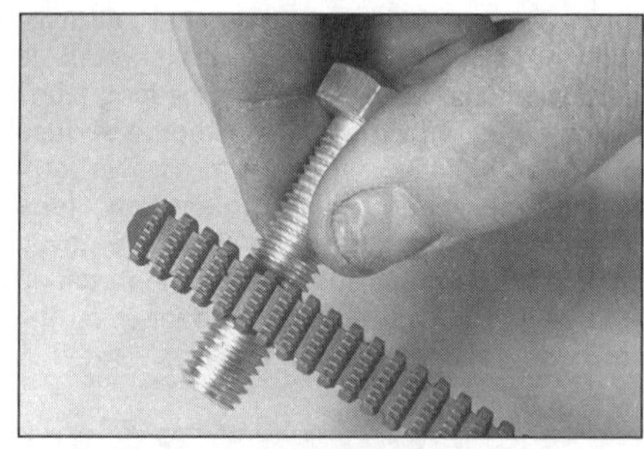
2.24 Using a thread restorer file

● It is possible to drill out the old thread and retap the component to the next thread size. This will work where there is enough surrounding material and a new bolt or screw can be obtained. Sometimes, however, this is not possible - such as where the bolt/screw passes through another component which must also be suitably modified, also in cases where a spark plug or oil drain plug cannot be obtained in a larger diameter thread size.

● The diamond-section thread insert (often known by its popular trade name of Heli-Coil) is a simple and effective method of renewing the thread and retaining the original size. A kit can be purchased which contains the tap, insert and installing tool **(see illustration 2.25)**. Drill out the damaged thread with the size drill specified **(see illustration 2.26)**. Carefully retap the thread **(see illustration 2.27)**. Install the insert on the installing tool and thread it slowly into place using a light downward pressure **(see illustrations 2.28 and 2.29)**. When positioned between a 1/4 and 1/2 turn below the surface withdraw the installing tool and use the break-off tool to press down on the tang, breaking it off **(see illustration 2.30)**.

● There are epoxy thread repair kits on the market which can rebuild stripped internal threads, although this repair should not be used on high load-bearing components.

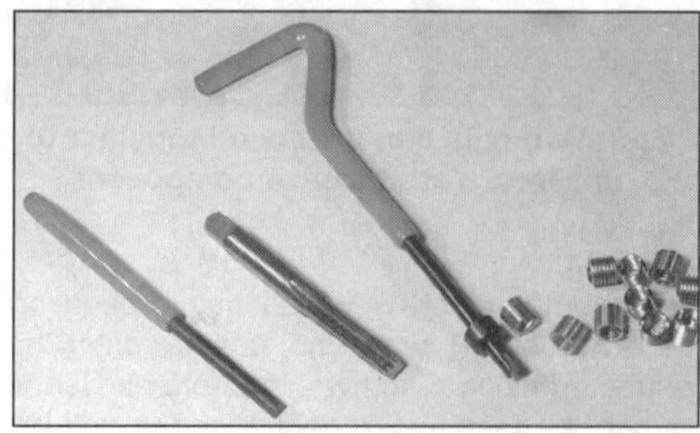
2.25 Obtain a thread insert kit to suit the thread diameter and pitch required

2.26 To install a thread insert, first drill out the original thread . . .

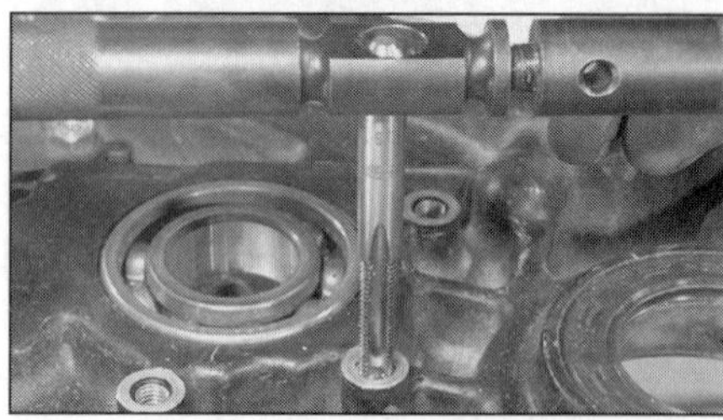
2.27 . . . tap a new thread . . .

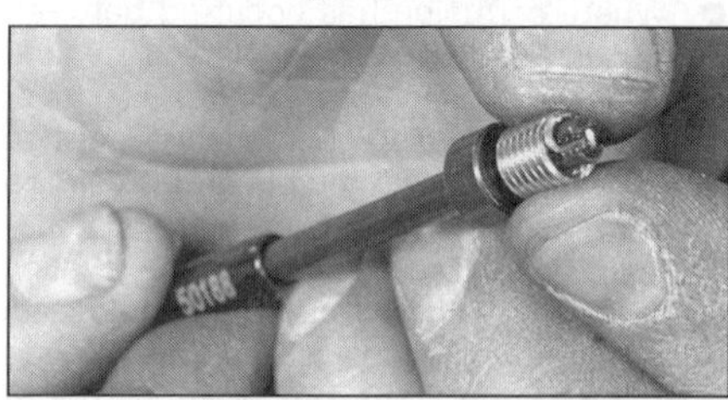
2.28 . . . fit insert on the installing tool . . .

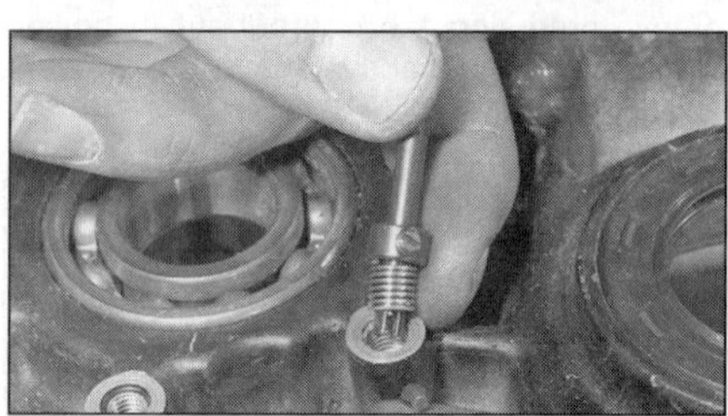
2.29 . . . and thread into the component . . .

2.30 . . . break off the tang when complete

Thread locking and sealing compounds

● Locking compounds are used in locations where the fastener is prone to loosening due to vibration or on important safety-related items which might cause loss of control of the motorcycle if they fail. It is also used where important fasteners cannot be secured by other means such as lockwashers or split pins.

● Before applying locking compound, make sure that the threads (internal and external) are clean and dry with all old compound removed. Select a compound to suit the component being secured - a non-permanent general locking and sealing type is suitable for most applications, but a high strength type is needed for permanent fixing of studs in castings. Apply a drop or two of the compound to the first few threads of the fastener, then thread it into place and tighten to the specified torque. Do not apply excessive thread locking compound otherwise the thread may be damaged on subsequent removal.

● Certain fasteners are impregnated with a dry film type coating of locking compound on their threads. Always renew this type of fastener if disturbed.

● Anti-seize compounds, such as copper-based greases, can be applied to protect threads from seizure due to extreme heat and corrosion. A common instance is spark plug threads and exhaust system fasteners.

3 Measuring tools and gauges

Feeler gauges

● Feeler gauges (or blades) are used for measuring small gaps and clearances **(see illustration 3.1)**. They can also be used to measure endfloat (sideplay) of a component on a shaft where access is not possible with a dial gauge.

● Feeler gauge sets should be treated with care and not bent or damaged. They are etched with their size on one face. Keep them clean and very lightly oiled to prevent corrosion build-up.

3.1 Feeler gauges are used for measuring small gaps and clearances - thickness is marked on one face of gauge

● When measuring a clearance, select a gauge which is a light sliding fit between the two components. You may need to use two gauges together to measure the clearance accurately.

Micrometers

● A micrometer is a precision tool capable of measuring to 0.01 or 0.001 of a millimetre. It should always be stored in its case and not in the general toolbox. It must be kept clean and never dropped, otherwise its frame or measuring anvils could be distorted resulting in inaccurate readings.

● External micrometers are used for measuring outside diameters of components and have many more applications than internal micrometers. Micrometers are available in different size ranges, eg 0 to 25 mm, 25 to 50 mm, and upwards in 25 mm steps; some large micrometers have interchangeable anvils to allow a range of measurements to be taken. Generally the largest precision measurement you are likely to take on a motorcycle is the piston diameter.

● Internal micrometers (or bore micrometers) are used for measuring inside diameters, such as valve guides and cylinder bores. Telescoping gauges and small hole gauges are used in conjunction with an external micrometer, whereas the more expensive internal micrometers have their own measuring device.

External micrometer

Note: *The conventional analogue type instrument is described. Although much easier to read, digital micrometers are considerably more expensive.*

● Always check the calibration of the micrometer before use. With the anvils closed (0 to 25 mm type) or set over a test gauge (for

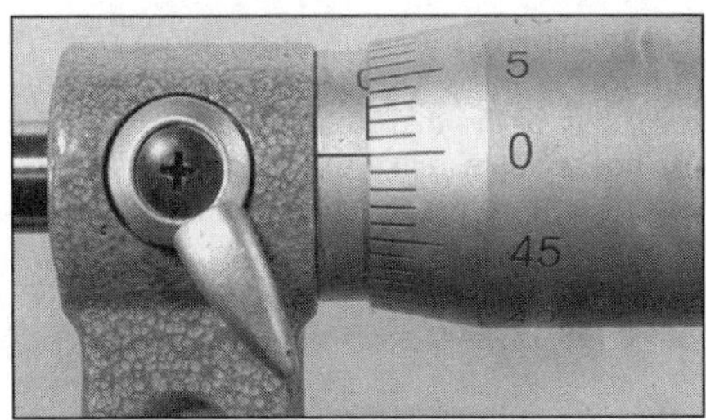

3.2 Check micrometer calibration before use

the larger types) the scale should read zero **(see illustration 3.2)**; make sure that the anvils (and test piece) are clean first. Any discrepancy can be adjusted by referring to the instructions supplied with the tool. Remember that the micrometer is a precision measuring tool - don't force the anvils closed, use the ratchet (4) on the end of the micrometer to close it. In this way, a measured force is always applied.

● To use, first make sure that the item being measured is clean. Place the anvil of the micrometer (1) against the item and use the thimble (2) to bring the spindle (3) lightly into contact with the other side of the item **(see illustration 3.3)**. Don't tighten the thimble down because this will damage the micrometer - instead use the ratchet (4) on the end of the micrometer. The ratchet mechanism applies a measured force preventing damage to the instrument.

● The micrometer is read by referring to the linear scale on the sleeve and the annular scale on the thimble. Read off the sleeve first to obtain the base measurement, then add the fine measurement from the thimble to obtain the overall reading. The linear scale on the sleeve represents the measuring range of the micrometer (eg 0 to 25 mm). The annular scale

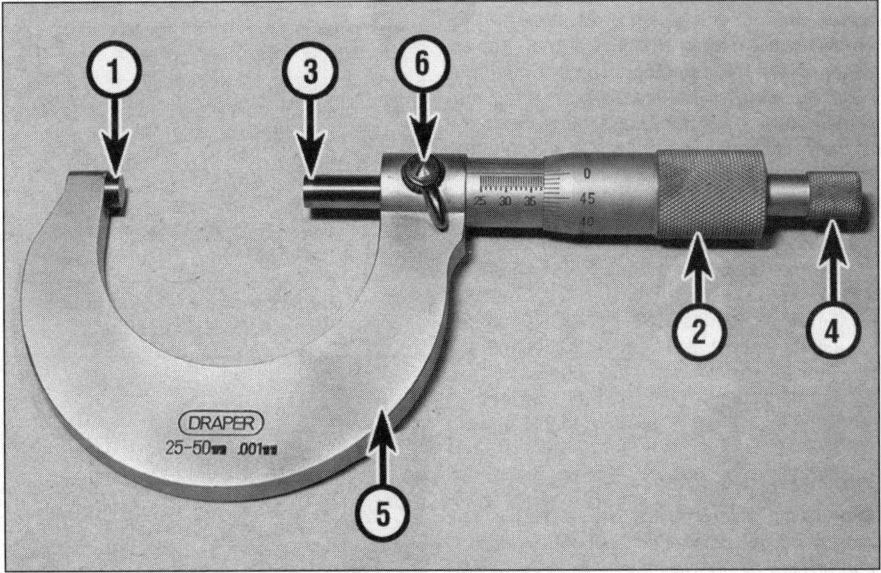

3.3 Micrometer component parts

1 Anvil
2 Thimble
3 Spindle
4 Ratchet
5 Frame
6 Locking lever

on the thimble will be in graduations of 0.01 mm (or as marked on the frame) - one full revolution of the thimble will move 0.5 mm on the linear scale. Take the reading where the datum line on the sleeve intersects the thimble's scale. Always position the eye directly above the scale otherwise an inaccurate reading will result.

In the example shown the item measures 2.95 mm **(see illustration 3.4)**:

Linear scale	2.00 mm
Linear scale	0.50 mm
Annular scale	0.45 mm
Total figure	**2.95 mm**

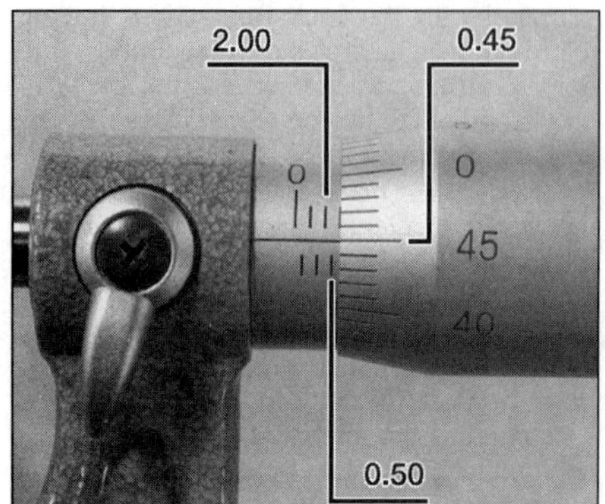

3.4 Micrometer reading of 2.95 mm

Most micrometers have a locking lever (6) on the frame to hold the setting in place, allowing the item to be removed from the micrometer.

● Some micrometers have a vernier scale on their sleeve, providing an even finer measurement to be taken, in 0.001 increments of a millimetre. Take the sleeve and thimble measurement as described above, then check which graduation on the vernier scale aligns with that of the annular scale on the thimble **Note:** *The eye must be perpendicular to the scale when taking the vernier reading - if necessary rotate the body of the micrometer to ensure this.* Multiply the vernier scale figure by 0.001 and add it to the base and fine measurement figures.

In the example shown the item measures 46.994 mm **(see illustrations 3.5 and 3.6)**:

Linear scale (base)	46.000 mm
Linear scale (base)	00.500 mm
Annular scale (fine)	00.490 mm
Vernier scale	00.004 mm
Total figure	**46.994 mm**

Internal micrometer

● Internal micrometers are available for measuring bore diameters, but are expensive and unlikely to be available for home use. It is suggested that a set of telescoping gauges and small hole gauges, both of which must be used with an external micrometer, will suffice for taking internal measurements on a motorcycle.

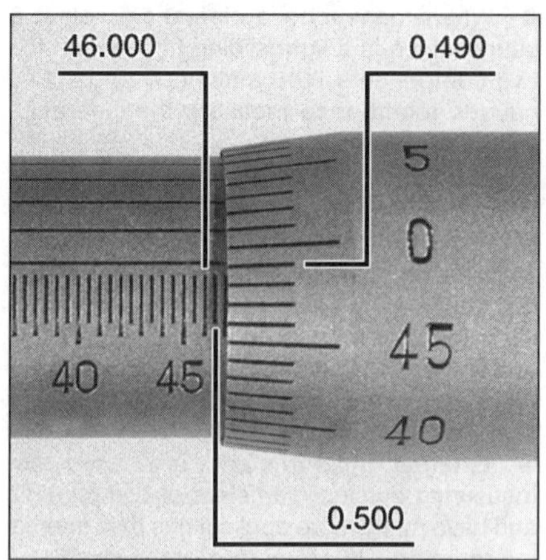

3.5 Micrometer reading of 46.99 mm on linear and annular scales . . .

3.6 . . . and 0.004 mm on vernier scale

● Telescoping gauges can be used to measure internal diameters of components. Select a gauge with the correct size range, make sure its ends are clean and insert it into the bore. Expand the gauge, then lock its position and withdraw it from the bore **(see illustration 3.7)**. Measure across the gauge ends with a micrometer **(see illustration 3.8)**.

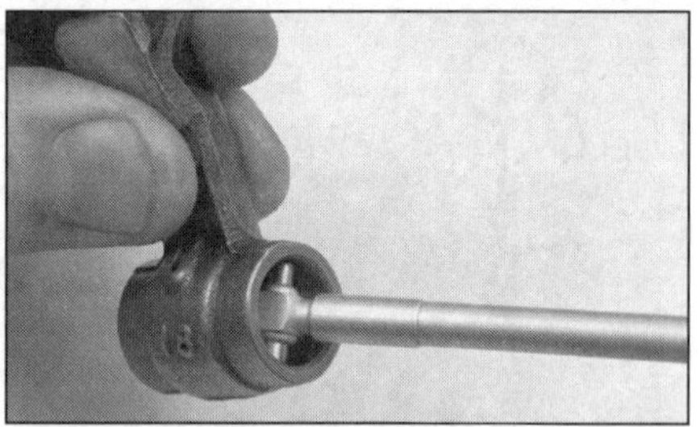

3.7 Expand the telescoping gauge in the bore, lock its position . . .

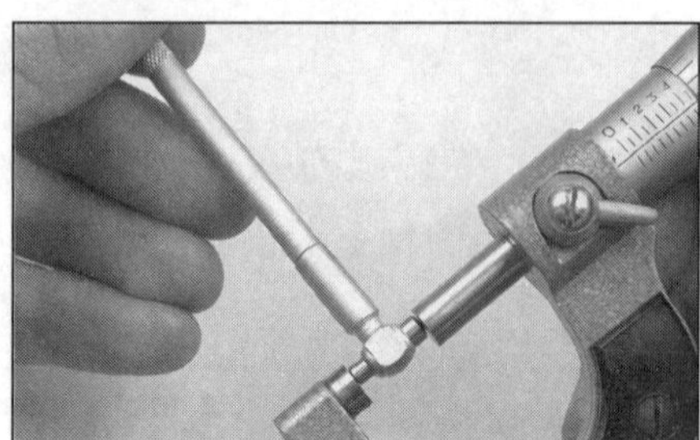

3.8 . . . then measure the gauge with a micrometer

3.9 Expand the small hole gauge in the bore, lock its position . . .

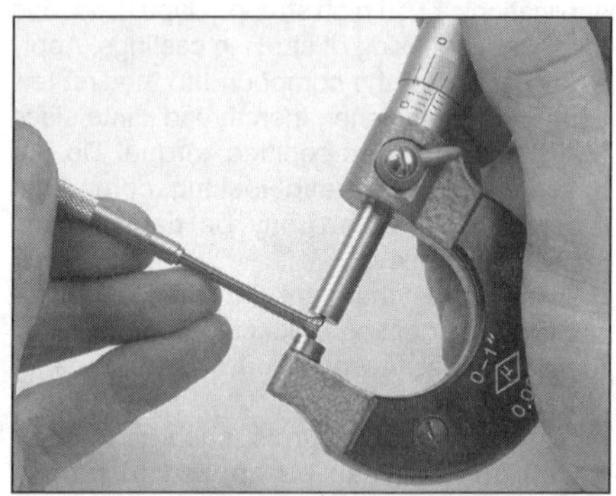

3.10 . . . then measure the gauge with a micrometer

● Very small diameter bores (such as valve guides) are measured with a small hole gauge. Once adjusted to a slip-fit inside the component, its position is locked and the gauge withdrawn for measurement with a micrometer **(see illustrations 3.9 and 3.10)**.

Vernier caliper

Note: *The conventional linear and dial gauge type instruments are described. Digital types are easier to read, but are far more expensive.*

● The vernier caliper does not provide the precision of a micrometer, but is versatile in being able to measure internal and external diameters. Some types also incorporate a depth gauge. It is ideal for measuring clutch plate friction material and spring free lengths.

● To use the conventional linear scale vernier, slacken off the vernier clamp screws (1) and set its jaws over (2), or inside (3), the item to be measured **(see illustration 3.11)**. Slide the jaw into contact, using the thumb-wheel (4) for fine movement of the sliding scale (5) then tighten the clamp screws (1). Read off the main scale (6) where the zero on the sliding scale (5) intersects it, taking the whole number to the left of the zero; this provides the base measurement. View along the sliding scale and select the division which lines up exactly with any of the divisions on the main scale, noting that the divisions usually represents 0.02 of a millimetre. Add this fine measurement to the base measurement to obtain the total reading.

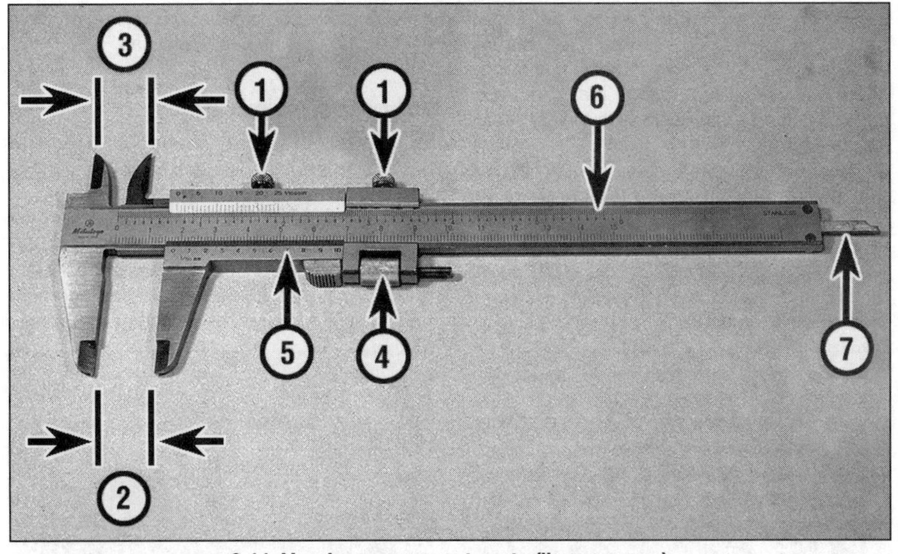

3.11 Vernier component parts (linear gauge)

1 Clamp screws *3 Internal jaws* *5 Sliding scale* *7 Depth gauge*
2 External jaws *4 Thumbwheel* *6 Main scale*

In the example shown the item measures 55.92 mm **(see illustration 3.12)**:

Base measurement	55.00 mm
Fine measurement	00.92 mm
Total figure	**55.92 mm**

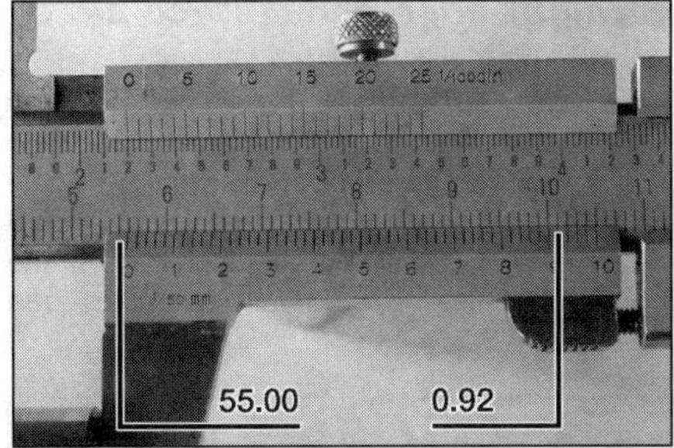

3.12 Vernier gauge reading of 55.92 mm

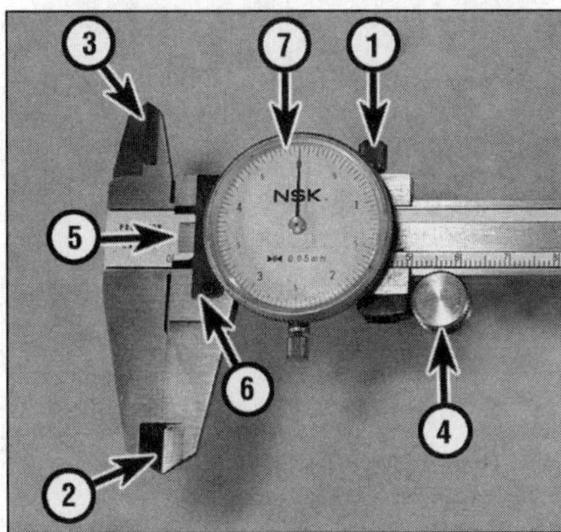

3.13 Vernier component parts (dial gauge)

1 Clamp screw *5 Main scale*
2 External jaws *6 Sliding scale*
3 Internal jaws *7 Dial gauge*
4 Thumbwheel

● Some vernier calipers are equipped with a dial gauge for fine measurement. Before use, check that the jaws are clean, then close them fully and check that the dial gauge reads zero. If necessary adjust the gauge ring accordingly. Slacken the vernier clamp screw (1) and set its jaws over (2), or inside (3), the item to be measured **(see illustration 3.13)**. Slide the jaws into contact, using the thumbwheel (4) for fine movement. Read off the main scale (5) where the edge of the sliding scale (6) intersects it, taking the whole number to the left of the zero; this provides the base measurement. Read off the needle position on the dial gauge (7) scale to provide the fine measurement; each division represents 0.05 of a millimetre. Add this fine measurement to the base measurement to obtain the total reading.

In the example shown the item measures 55.95 mm **(see illustration 3.14)**:

Base measurement	55.00 mm
Fine measurement	00.95 mm
Total figure	**55.95 mm**

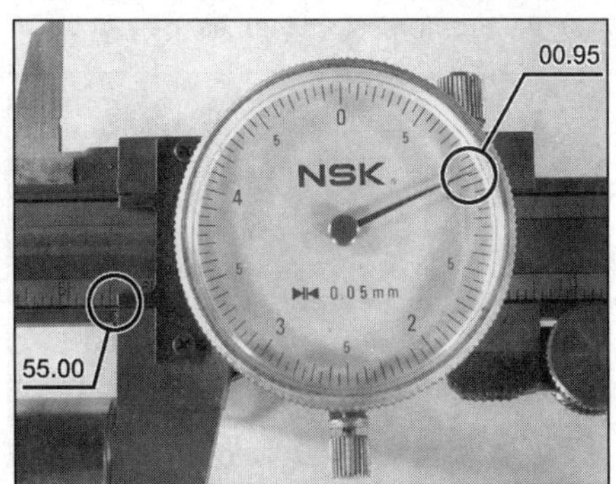

3.14 Vernier gauge reading of 55.95 mm

Plastigauge

● Plastigauge is a plastic material which can be compressed between two surfaces to measure the oil clearance between them. The width of the compressed Plastigauge is measured against a calibrated scale to determine the clearance.

● Common uses of Plastigauge are for measuring the clearance between crankshaft journal and main bearing inserts, between crankshaft journal and big-end bearing inserts, and between camshaft and bearing surfaces. The following example describes big-end oil clearance measurement.

● Handle the Plastigauge material carefully to prevent distortion. Using a sharp knife, cut a length which corresponds with the width of the bearing being measured and place it carefully across the journal so that it is parallel with the shaft **(see illustration 3.15)**. Carefully install both bearing shells and the connecting rod. Without rotating the rod on the journal tighten its bolts or nuts (as applicable) to the specified torque. The connecting rod and bearings are then disassembled and the crushed Plastigauge examined.

3.15 Plastigauge placed across shaft journal

● Using the scale provided in the Plastigauge kit, measure the width of the material to determine the oil clearance **(see illustration 3.16)**. Always remove all traces of Plastigauge after use using your fingernails.

Caution: Arriving at the correct clearance demands that the assembly is torqued correctly, according to the settings and sequence (where applicable) provided by the motorcycle manufacturer.

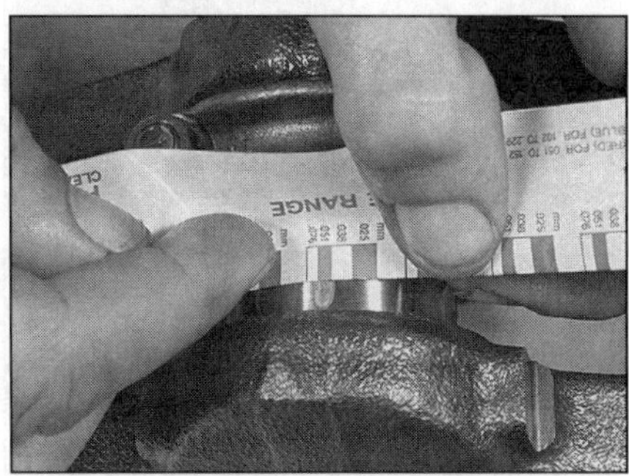

3.16 Measuring the width of the crushed Plastigauge

Dial gauge or DTI (Dial Test Indicator)

● A dial gauge can be used to accurately measure small amounts of movement. Typical uses are measuring shaft runout or shaft endfloat (sideplay) and setting piston position for ignition timing on two-strokes. A dial gauge set usually comes with a range of different probes and adapters and mounting equipment.
● The gauge needle must point to zero when at rest. Rotate the ring around its periphery to zero the gauge.
● Check that the gauge is capable of reading the extent of movement in the work. Most gauges have a small dial set in the face which records whole millimetres of movement as well as the fine scale around the face periphery which is calibrated in 0.01 mm divisions. Read off the small dial first to obtain the base measurement, then add the measurement from the fine scale to obtain the total reading.

In the example shown the gauge reads 1.48 mm **(see illustration 3.17)**:

Base measurement	1.00 mm
Fine measurement	0.48 mm
Total figure	**1.48 mm**

3.17 Dial gauge reading of 1.48 mm

● If measuring shaft runout, the shaft must be supported in vee-blocks and the gauge mounted on a stand perpendicular to the shaft. Rest the tip of the gauge against the centre of the shaft and rotate the shaft slowly whilst watching the gauge reading **(see illustration 3.18)**. Take several measurements along the length of the shaft and record the maximum gauge reading as the amount of runout in the shaft. **Note:** *The reading obtained will be total runout at that point - some manufacturers specify that the runout figure is halved to compare with their specified runout limit.*

3.18 Using a dial gauge to measure shaft runout

● Endfloat (sideplay) measurement requires that the gauge is mounted securely to the surrounding component with its probe touching the end of the shaft. Using hand pressure, push and pull on the shaft noting the maximum endfloat recorded on the gauge **(see illustration 3.19)**.

3.19 Using a dial gauge to measure shaft endfloat

● A dial gauge with suitable adapters can be used to determine piston position BTDC on two-stroke engines for the purposes of ignition timing. The gauge, adapter and suitable length probe are installed in the place of the spark plug and the gauge zeroed at TDC. If the piston position is specified as 1.14 mm BTDC, rotate the engine back to 2.00 mm BTDC, then slowly forwards to 1.14 mm BTDC.

Cylinder compression gauges

● A compression gauge is used for measuring cylinder compression. Either the rubber-cone type or the threaded adapter type can be used. The latter is preferred to ensure a perfect seal against the cylinder head. A 0 to 300 psi (0 to 20 Bar) type gauge (for petrol/gasoline engines) will be suitable for motorcycles.
● The spark plug is removed and the gauge either held hard against the cylinder head (cone type) or the gauge adapter screwed into the cylinder head (threaded type) **(see illustration 3.20)**. Cylinder compression is measured with the engine turning over, but not running - carry out the compression test as described in *Fault Finding Equipment*. The gauge will hold the reading until manually released.

3.20 Using a rubber-cone type cylinder compression gauge

Oil pressure gauge

● An oil pressure gauge is used for measuring engine oil pressure. Most gauges come with a set of adapters to fit the thread of the take-off point **(see illustration 3.21)**. If the take-off point specified by the motorcycle manufacturer is an external oil pipe union, make sure that the specified replacement union is used to prevent oil starvation.

3.21 Oil pressure gauge and take-off point adapter (arrow)

● Oil pressure is measured with the engine running (at a specific rpm) and often the manufacturer will specify pressure limits for a cold and hot engine.

Straight-edge and surface plate

● If checking the gasket face of a component for warpage, place a steel rule or precision straight-edge across the gasket face and measure any gap between the straight-edge and component with feeler gauges **(see illustration 3.22)**. Check diagonally across the component and between mounting holes **(see illustration 3.23)**.

3.22 Use a straight-edge and feeler gauges to check for warpage

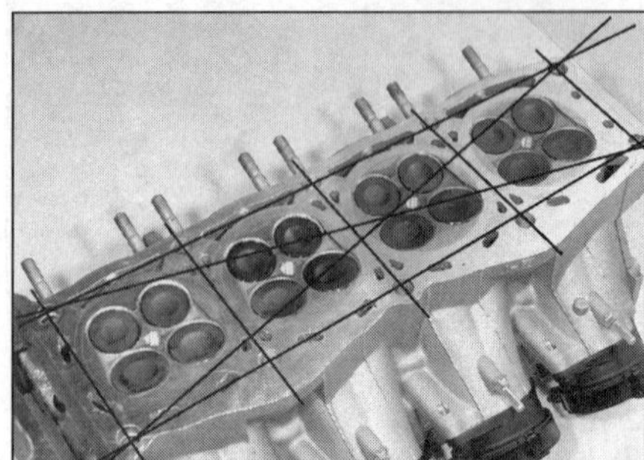
3.23 Check for warpage in these directions

● Checking individual components for warpage, such as clutch plain (metal) plates, requires a perfectly flat plate or piece or plate glass and feeler gauges.

4 Torque and leverage

What is torque?

● Torque describes the twisting force about a shaft. The amount of torque applied is determined by the distance from the centre of the shaft to the end of the lever and the amount of force being applied to the end of the lever; distance multiplied by force equals torque.

● The manufacturer applies a measured torque to a bolt or nut to ensure that it will not slacken in use and to hold two components securely together without movement in the joint. The actual torque setting depends on the thread size, bolt or nut material and the composition of the components being held.

● Too little torque may cause the fastener to loosen due to vibration, whereas too much torque will distort the joint faces of the component or cause the fastener to shear off. Always stick to the specified torque setting.

Using a torque wrench

● Check the calibration of the torque wrench and make sure it has a suitable range for the job. Torque wrenches are available in Nm (Newton-metres), kgf m (kilograms-force metre), lbf ft (pounds-feet), lbf in (inch-pounds). Do not confuse lbf ft with lbf in.

● Adjust the tool to the desired torque on the scale **(see illustration 4.1)**. If your torque wrench is not calibrated in the units specified, carefully convert the figure (see *Conversion Factors*). A manufacturer sometimes gives a torque setting as a range (8 to 10 Nm) rather than a single figure - in this case set the tool midway between the two settings. The same torque may be expressed as 9 Nm ± 1 Nm. Some torque wrenches have a method of locking the setting so that it isn't inadvertently altered during use.

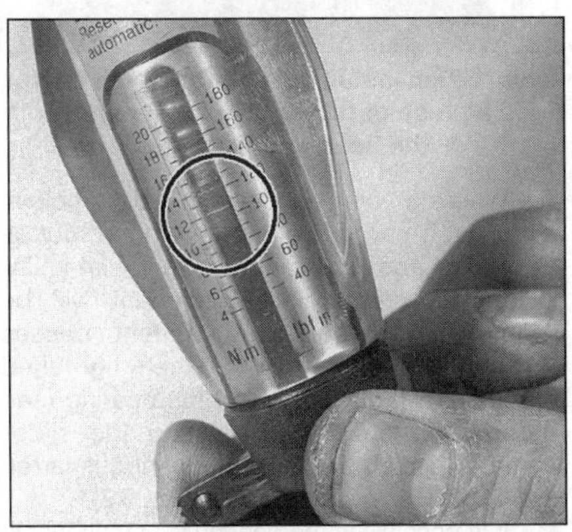

4.1 Set the torque wrench index mark to the setting required, in this case 12 Nm

● Install the bolts/nuts in their correct location and secure them lightly. Their threads must be clean and free of any old locking compound. Unless specified the threads and flange should be dry - oiled threads are necessary in certain circumstances and the manufacturer will take this into account in the specified torque figure. Similarly, the manufacturer may also specify the application of thread-locking compound.

● Tighten the fasteners in the specified sequence until the torque wrench clicks, indicating that the torque setting has been reached. Apply the torque again to double-check the setting. Where different thread diameter fasteners secure the component, as a rule tighten the larger diameter ones first.

● When the torque wrench has been finished with, release the lock (where applicable) and fully back off its setting to zero - do not leave the torque wrench tensioned. Also, do not use a torque wrench for slackening a fastener.

Angle-tightening

● Manufacturers often specify a figure in degrees for final tightening of a fastener. This usually follows tightening to a specific torque setting.

● A degree disc can be set and attached to the socket **(see illustration 4.2)** or a protractor can be used to mark the angle of movement on the bolt/nut head and the surrounding casting **(see illustration 4.3)**.

4.2 Angle tightening can be accomplished with a torque-angle gauge . . .

4.3 . . . or by marking the angle on the surrounding component

Loosening sequences

● Where more than one bolt/nut secures a component, loosen each fastener evenly a little at a time. In this way, not all the stress of the joint is held by one fastener and the components are not likely to distort.

● If a tightening sequence is provided, work in the REVERSE of this, but if not, work from the outside in, in a criss-cross sequence **(see illustration 4.4)**.

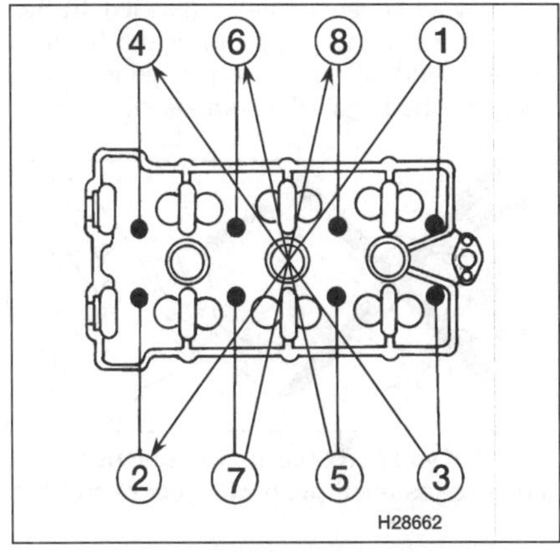

4.4 When slackening, work from the outside inwards

Tightening sequences

● If a component is held by more than one fastener it is important that the retaining bolts/nuts are tightened evenly to prevent uneven stress build-up and distortion of sealing faces. This is especially important on high-compression joints such as the cylinder head.

● A sequence is usually provided by the manufacturer, either in a diagram or actually marked in the casting. If not, always start in the centre and work outwards in a criss-cross pattern **(see illustration 4.5)**. Start off by securing all bolts/nuts finger-tight, then set the torque wrench and tighten each fastener by a small amount in sequence until the final torque is reached. By following this practice,

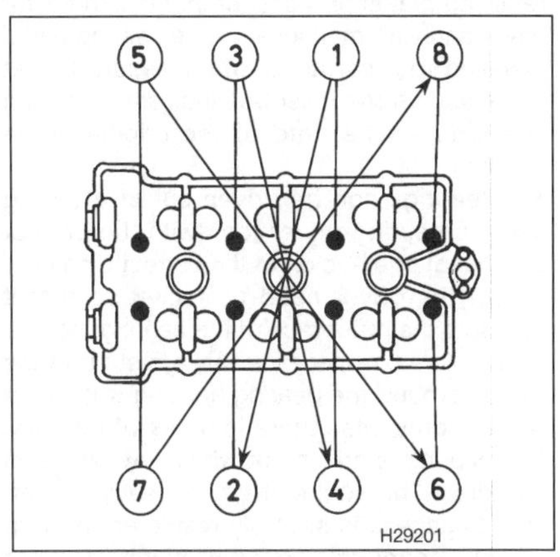

4.5 When tightening, work from the inside outwards

the joint will be held evenly and will not be distorted. Important joints, such as the cylinder head and big-end fasteners often have two- or three-stage torque settings.

Applying leverage

● Use tools at the correct angle. Position a socket wrench or spanner on the bolt/nut so that you pull it towards you when loosening. If this can't be done, push the spanner without curling your fingers around it **(see illustration 4.6)** - the spanner may slip or the fastener loosen suddenly, resulting in your fingers being crushed against a component.

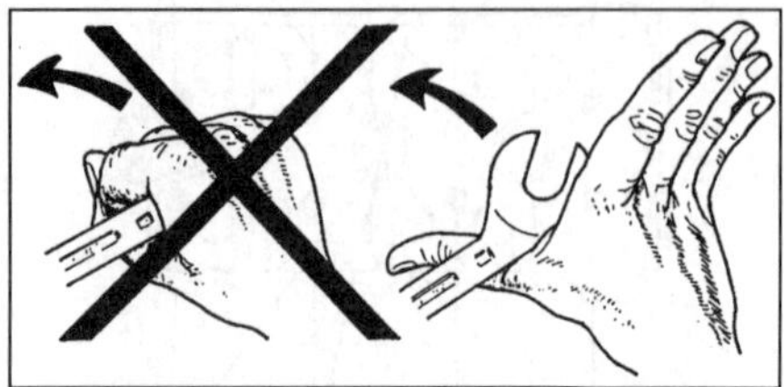

4.6 If you can't pull on the spanner to loosen a fastener, push with your hand open

● Additional leverage is gained by extending the length of the lever. The best way to do this is to use a breaker bar instead of the regular length tool, or to slip a length of tubing over the end of the spanner or socket wrench.

● If additional leverage will not work, the fastener head is either damaged or firmly corroded in place (see *Fasteners*).

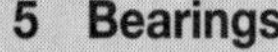

5 Bearings

Bearing removal and installation

Drivers and sockets

● Before removing a bearing, always inspect the casing to see which way it must be driven out - some casings will have retaining plates or a cast step. Also check for any identifying markings on the bearing and if installed to a certain depth, measure this at this stage. Some roller bearings are sealed on one side - take note of the original fitted position.

● Bearings can be driven out of a casing using a bearing driver tool (with the correct size head) or a socket of the correct diameter. Select the driver head or socket so that it contacts the outer race of the bearing, not the balls/rollers or inner race. Always support the casing around the bearing housing with wood blocks, otherwise there is a risk of fracture. The bearing is driven out with a few blows on the driver or socket from a heavy mallet. Unless access is severely restricted (as with wheel bearings), a pin-punch is not recommended unless it is moved around the bearing to keep it square in its housing.

● The same equipment can be used to install bearings. Make sure the bearing housing is supported on wood blocks and line up the bearing in its housing. Fit the bearing as noted on removal - generally they are installed with their marked side facing outwards. Tap the bearing squarely into its housing using a driver or socket which bears only on the bearing's outer race - contact with the bearing balls/rollers or inner race will destroy it **(see illustrations 5.1 and 5.2)**.

● Check that the bearing inner race and balls/rollers rotate freely.

5.1 Using a bearing driver against the bearing's outer race

5.2 Using a large socket against the bearing's outer race

Pullers and slide-hammers

● Where a bearing is pressed on a shaft a puller will be required to extract it **(see illustration 5.3)**. Make sure that the puller clamp or legs fit securely behind the bearing and are unlikely to slip out. If pulling a bearing off a gear shaft for example, you may have to locate the puller behind a gear pinion if there is no access to the race and draw the gear pinion off the shaft as well **(see illustration 5.4)**.

Caution: Ensure that the puller's centre bolt locates securely against the end of the shaft and will not slip when pressure is applied. Also ensure that puller does not damage the shaft end.

5.3 This bearing puller clamps behind the bearing and pressure is applied to the shaft end to draw the bearing off

5.4 Where no access is available to the rear of the bearing, it is sometimes possible to draw off the adjacent component

● Operate the puller so that its centre bolt exerts pressure on the shaft end and draws the bearing off the shaft.

● When installing the bearing on the shaft, tap only on the bearing's inner race - contact with the balls/rollers or outer race with destroy the bearing. Use a socket or length of tubing as a drift which fits over the shaft end **(see illustration 5.5)**.

5.5 When installing a bearing on a shaft use a piece of tubing which bears only on the bearing's inner race

● Where a bearing locates in a blind hole in a casing, it cannot be driven or pulled out as described above. A slide-hammer with knife-edged bearing puller attachment will be required. The puller attachment passes through the bearing and when tightened expands to fit firmly behind the bearing **(see illustration 5.6)**. By operating the slide-hammer part of the tool the bearing is jarred out of its housing **(see illustration 5.7)**.

● It is possible, if the bearing is of reasonable weight, for it to drop out of its housing if the casing is heated as described below. If this

5.6 Expand the bearing puller so that it locks behind the bearing . . .

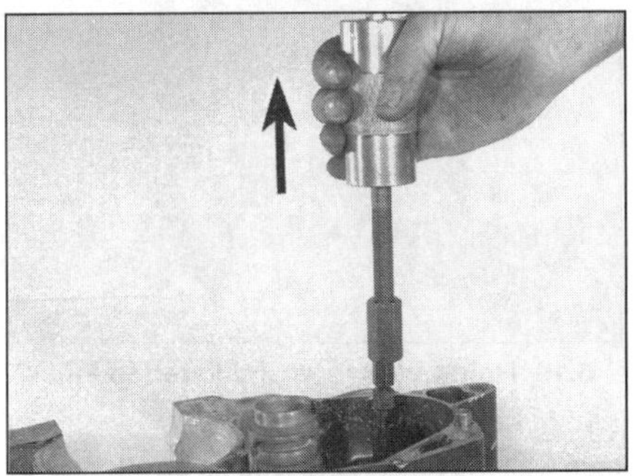
5.7 . . . attach the slide hammer to the bearing puller

method is attempted, first prepare a work surface which will enable the casing to be tapped face down to help dislodge the bearing - a wood surface is ideal since it will not damage the casing's gasket surface. Wearing protective gloves, tap the heated casing several times against the work surface to dislodge the bearing under its own weight **(see illustration 5.8)**.

5.8 Tapping a casing face down on wood blocks can often dislodge a bearing

- Bearings can be installed in blind holes using the driver or socket method described above.

Drawbolts

- Where a bearing or bush is set in the eye of a component, such as a suspension linkage arm or connecting rod small-end, removal by drift may damage the component. Furthermore, a rubber bushing in a shock absorber eye cannot successfully be driven out of position. If access is available to a engineering press, the task is straightforward. If not, a drawbolt can be fabricated to extract the bearing or bush.

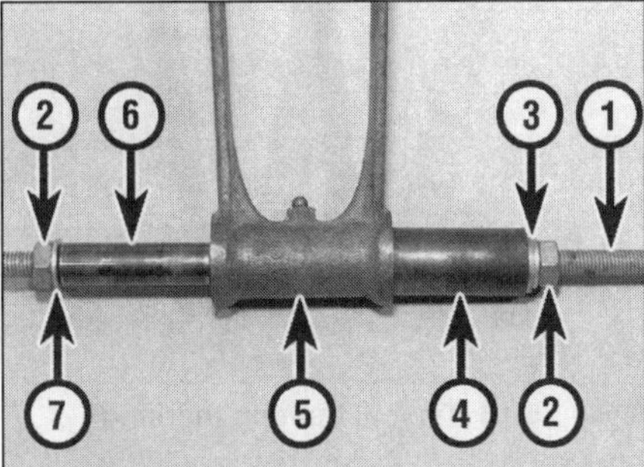

5.9 Drawbolt component parts assembled on a suspension arm

1 *Bolt or length of threaded bar*
2 *Nuts*
3 *Washer (external diameter greater than tubing internal diameter)*
4 *Tubing (internal diameter sufficient to accommodate bearing)*
5 *Suspension arm with bearing*
6 *Tubing (external diameter slightly smaller than bearing)*
7 *Washer (external diameter slightly smaller than bearing)*

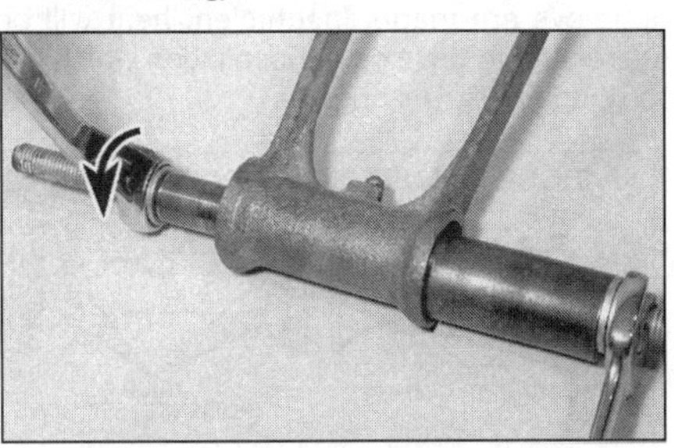
5.10 Drawing the bearing out of the suspension arm

- To extract the bearing/bush you will need a long bolt with nut (or piece of threaded bar with two nuts), a piece of tubing which has an internal diameter larger than the bearing/bush, another piece of tubing which has an external diameter slightly smaller than the bearing/ bush, and a selection of washers **(see illustrations 5.9 and 5.10)**. Note that the pieces of tubing must be of the same length, or longer, than the bearing/bush.
- The same kit (without the pieces of tubing) can be used to draw the new bearing/bush back into place **(see illustration 5.11)**.

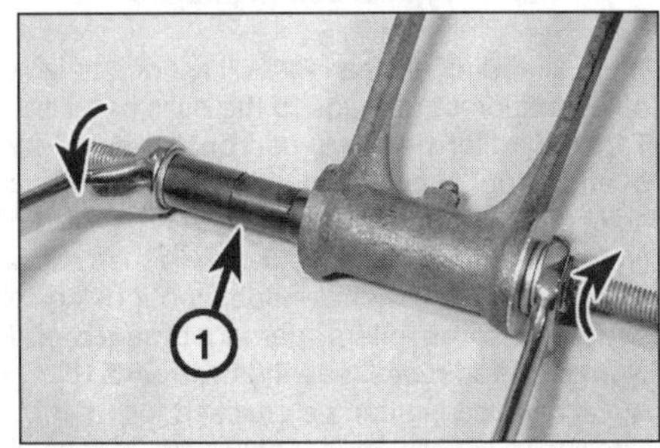

5.11 Installing a new bearing (1) in the suspension arm

Temperature change

- If the bearing's outer race is a tight fit in the casing, the aluminium casing can be heated to release its grip on the bearing. Aluminium will expand at a greater rate than the steel bearing outer race. There are several ways to do this, but avoid any localised extreme heat (such as a blow torch) - aluminium alloy has a low melting point.
- Approved methods of heating a casing are using a domestic oven (heated to 100°C) or immersing the casing in boiling water **(see illustration 5.12)**. Low temperature range localised heat sources such as a paint stripper heat gun or clothes iron can also be used **(see illustration 5.13)**. Alternatively, soak a rag in boiling water, wring it out and wrap it around the bearing housing.

Warning: All of these methods require care in use to prevent scalding and burns to the hands. Wear protective gloves when handling hot components.

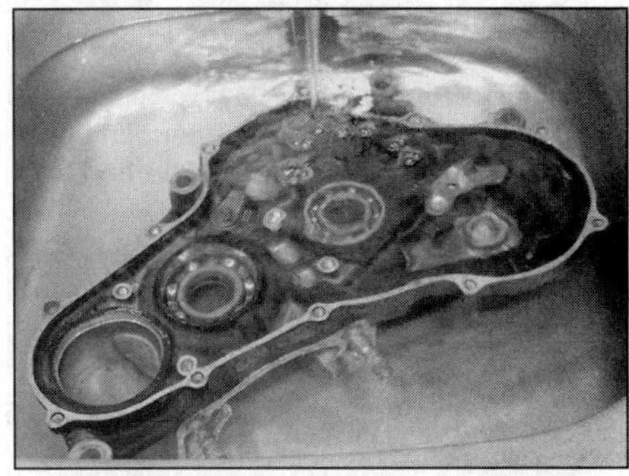
5.12 A casing can be immersed in a sink of boiling water to aid bearing removal

5.13 Using a localised heat source to aid bearing removal

- If heating the whole casing note that plastic components, such as the neutral switch, may suffer - remove them beforehand.
- After heating, remove the bearing as described above. You may find that the expansion is sufficient for the bearing to fall out of the casing under its own weight or with a light tap on the driver or socket.
- If necessary, the casing can be heated to aid bearing installation, and this is sometimes the recommended procedure if the motorcycle manufacturer has designed the housing and bearing fit with this intention.

● Installation of bearings can be eased by placing them in a freezer the night before installation. The steel bearing will contract slightly, allowing easy insertion in its housing. This is often useful when installing steering head outer races in the frame.

Bearing types and markings

● Plain shell bearings, ball bearings, needle roller bearings and tapered roller bearings will all be found on motorcycles **(see illustrations 5.14 and 5.15)**. The ball and roller types are usually caged between an inner and outer race, but uncaged variations may be found.

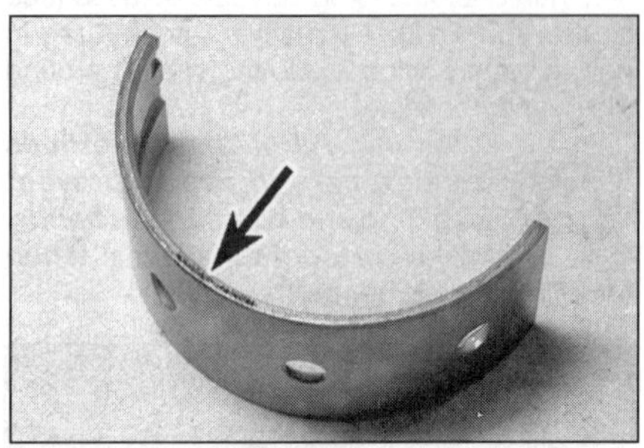

5.14 Shell bearings are either plain or grooved. They are usually identified by colour code (arrow)

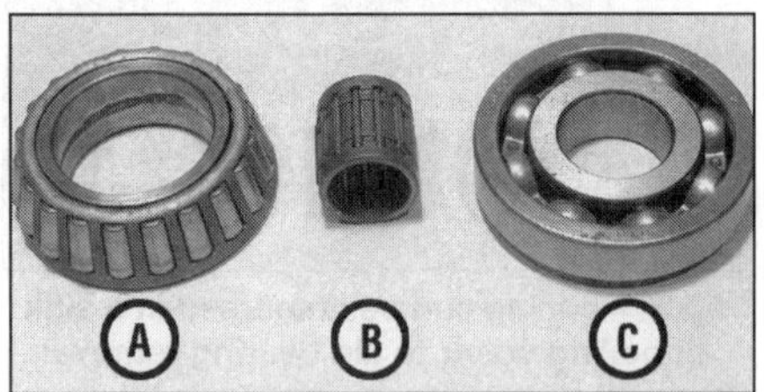

5.15 Tapered roller bearing (A), needle roller bearing (B) and ball journal bearing (C)

● Shell bearings (often called inserts) are usually found at the crankshaft main and connecting rod big-end where they are good at coping with high loads. They are made of a phosphor-bronze material and are impregnated with self-lubricating properties.

● Ball bearings and needle roller bearings consist of a steel inner and outer race with the balls or rollers between the races. They require constant lubrication by oil or grease and are good at coping with axial loads. Taper roller bearings consist of rollers set in a tapered cage set on the inner race; the outer race is separate. They are good at coping with axial loads and prevent movement along the shaft - a typical application is in the steering head.

● Bearing manufacturers produce bearings to ISO size standards and stamp one face of the bearing to indicate its internal and external diameter, load capacity and type **(see illustration 5.16)**.

● Metal bushes are usually of phosphor-bronze material. Rubber bushes are used in suspension mounting eyes. Fibre bushes have also been used in suspension pivots.

5.16 Typical bearing marking

Bearing fault finding

● If a bearing outer race has spun in its housing, the housing material will be damaged. You can use a bearing locking compound to bond the outer race in place if damage is not too severe.

● Shell bearings will fail due to damage of their working surface, as a result of lack of lubrication, corrosion or abrasive particles in the oil **(see illustration 5.17)**. Small particles of dirt in the oil may embed in the bearing material whereas larger particles will score the bearing and shaft journal. If a number of short journeys are made, insufficient heat will be generated to drive off condensation which has built up on the bearings.

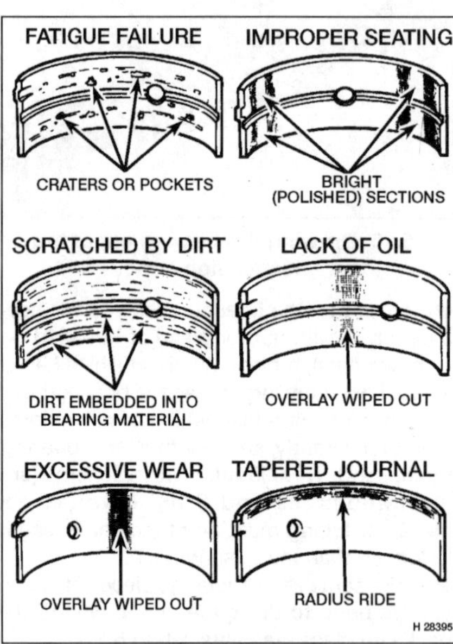

5.17 Typical bearing failures

● Ball and roller bearings will fail due to lack of lubrication or damage to the balls or rollers. Tapered-roller bearings can be damaged by overloading them. Unless the bearing is sealed on both sides, wash it in paraffin (kerosene) to remove all old grease then allow it to dry. Make a visual inspection looking to dented balls or rollers, damaged cages and worn or pitted races **(see illustration 5.18)**.

● A ball bearing can be checked for wear by listening to it when spun. Apply a film of light oil to the bearing and hold it close to the ear - hold the outer race with one hand and spin the inner race with the other hand **(see illustration 5.19)**. The bearing should be almost silent when spun; if it grates or rattles it is worn.

5.18 Example of ball journal bearing with damaged balls and cages

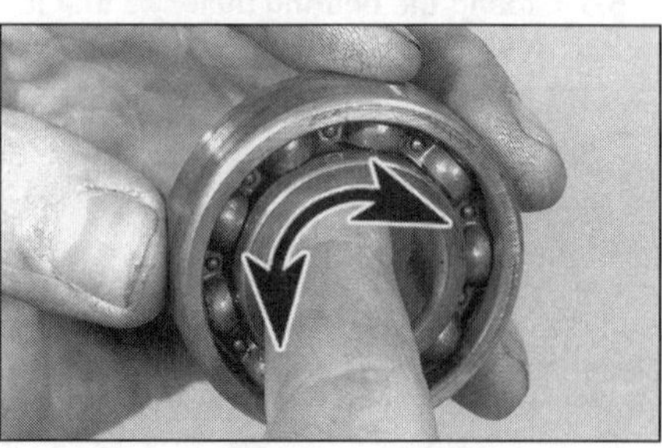

5.19 Hold outer race and listen to inner race when spun

6 Oil seals

Oil seal removal and installation

● Oil seals should be renewed every time a component is dismantled. This is because the seal lips will become set to the sealing surface and will not necessarily reseal.

● Oil seals can be prised out of position using a large flat-bladed screwdriver **(see illustration 6.1)**. In the case of crankcase seals, check first that the seal is not lipped on the inside, preventing its removal with the crankcases joined.

6.1 Prise out oil seals with a large flat-bladed screwdriver

● New seals are usually installed with their marked face (containing the seal reference code) outwards and the spring side towards the fluid being retained. In certain cases, such as a two-stroke engine crankshaft seal, a double lipped seal may be used due to there being fluid or gas on each side of the joint.

● Use a bearing driver or socket which bears only on the outer hard edge of the seal to install it in the casing - tapping on the inner edge will damage the sealing lip.

Oil seal types and markings

● Oil seals are usually of the single-lipped type. Double-lipped seals are found where a liquid or gas is on both sides of the joint.

● Oil seals can harden and lose their sealing ability if the motorcycle has been in storage for a long period - renewal is the only solution.

● Oil seal manufacturers also conform to the ISO markings for seal size - these are moulded into the outer face of the seal **(see illustration 6.2)**.

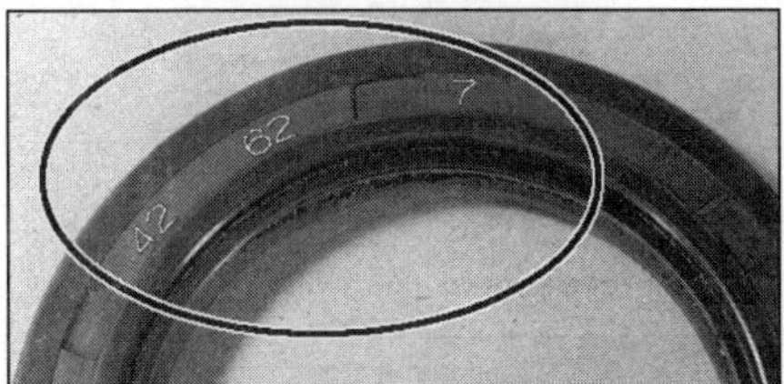

6.2 These oil seal markings indicate inside diameter, outside diameter and seal thickness

7 Gaskets and sealants

Types of gasket and sealant

● Gaskets are used to seal the mating surfaces between components and keep lubricants, fluids, vacuum or pressure contained within the assembly. Aluminium gaskets are sometimes found at the cylinder joints, but most gaskets are paper-based. If the mating surfaces of the components being joined are undamaged the gasket can be installed dry, although a dab of sealant or grease will be useful to hold it in place during assembly.

● RTV (Room Temperature Vulcanising) silicone rubber sealants cure when exposed to moisture in the atmosphere. These sealants are good at filling pits or irregular gasket faces, but will tend to be forced out of the joint under very high torque. They can be used to replace a paper gasket, but first make sure that the width of the paper gasket is not essential to the shimming of internal components. RTV sealants should not be used on components containing petrol (gasoline).

● Non-hardening, semi-hardening and hard setting liquid gasket compounds can be used with a gasket or between a metal-to-metal joint. Select the sealant to suit the application: universal non-hardening sealant can be used on virtually all joints; semi-hardening on joint faces which are rough or damaged; hard setting sealant on joints which require a permanent bond and are subjected to high temperature and pressure. **Note:** *Check first if the paper gasket has a bead of sealant impregnated in its surface before applying additional sealant.*

● When choosing a sealant, make sure it is suitable for the application, particularly if being applied in a high-temperature area or in the vicinity of fuel. Certain manufacturers produce sealants in either clear, silver or black colours to match the finish of the engine. This has a particular application on motorcycles where much of the engine is exposed.

● Do not over-apply sealant. That which is squeezed out on the outside of the joint can be wiped off, whereas an excess of sealant on the inside can break off and clog oilways.

Breaking a sealed joint

● Age, heat, pressure and the use of hard setting sealant can cause two components to stick together so tightly that they are difficult to separate using finger pressure alone. Do not resort to using levers unless there is a pry point provided for this purpose **(see illustration 7.1)** or else the gasket surfaces will be damaged.

● Use a soft-faced hammer **(see illustration 7.2)** or a wood block and conventional hammer to strike the component near the mating surface. Avoid hammering against cast extremities since they may break off. If this method fails, try using a wood wedge between the two components.

Caution: If the joint will not separate, double-check that you have removed all the fasteners.

7.1 If a pry point is provided, apply gently pressure with a flat-bladed screwdriver

7.2 Tap around the joint with a soft-faced mallet if necessary - don't strike cooling fins

Removal of old gasket and sealant

● Paper gaskets will most likely come away complete, leaving only a few traces stuck on the sealing faces of the components. It is imperative that all traces are removed to ensure correct sealing of the new gasket.

● Very carefully scrape all traces of gasket away making sure that the sealing surfaces are not gouged or scored by the scraper **(see illustrations 7.3, 7.4 and 7.5)**. Stubborn deposits can be removed by spraying with an aerosol gasket remover. Final preparation of

Most components have one or two hollow locating dowels between the two gasket faces. If a dowel cannot be removed, do not resort to gripping it with pliers - it will almost certainly be distorted. Install a close-fitting socket or Phillips screwdriver into the dowel and then grip the outer edge of the dowel to free it.

7.3 Paper gaskets can be scraped off with a gasket scraper tool . . .

7.4 . . . a knife blade . . .

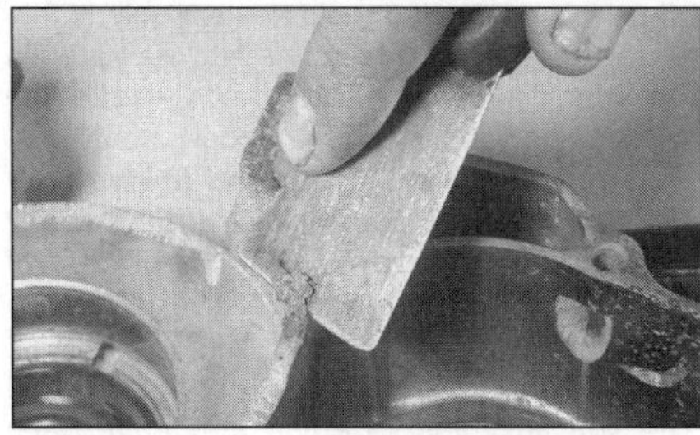

7.5 . . . or a household scraper

7.6 Fine abrasive paper is wrapped around a flat file to clean up the gasket face

7.7 A kitchen scourer can be used on stubborn deposits

the gasket surface can be made with very fine abrasive paper or a plastic kitchen scourer **(see illustrations 7.6 and 7.7)**.

- Old sealant can be scraped or peeled off components, depending on the type originally used. Note that gasket removal compounds are available to avoid scraping the components clean; make sure the gasket remover suits the type of sealant used.

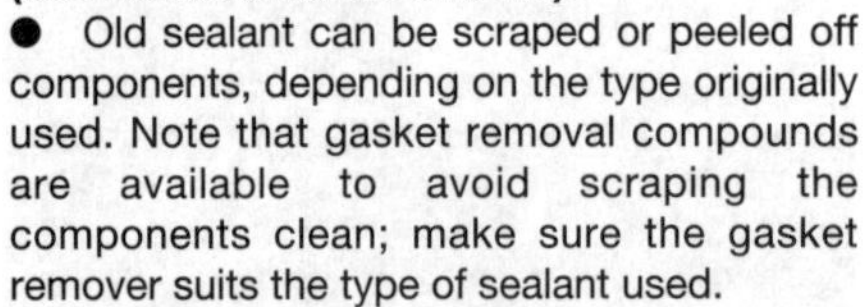

8 Chains

Breaking and joining final drive chains

- Drive chains for all but small bikes are continuous and do not have a clip-type connecting link. The chain must be broken using a chain breaker tool and the new chain securely riveted together using a new soft rivet-type link. Never use a clip-type connecting link instead of a rivet-type link, except in an emergency. Various chain breaking and riveting tools are available, either as separate tools or combined as illustrated in the accompanying photographs - read the instructions supplied with the tool carefully.

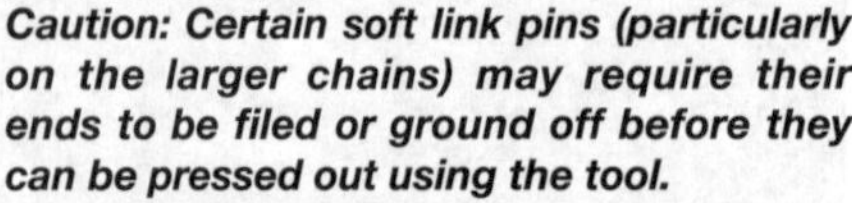

Warning: The need to rivet the new link pins correctly cannot be overstressed - loss of control of the motorcycle is very likely to result if the chain breaks in use.

- Rotate the chain and look for the soft link. The soft link pins look like they have been deeply centre-punched instead of peened over like all the other pins **(see illustration 8.9)** and its sideplate may be a different colour. Position the soft link midway between the sprockets and assemble the chain breaker tool over one of the soft link pins **(see illustration 8.1)**. Operate the tool to push the pin out through the chain **(see illustration 8.2)**. On an O-ring chain, remove the O-rings **(see illustration 8.3)**. Carry out the same procedure on the other soft link pin.

Caution: Certain soft link pins (particularly on the larger chains) may require their ends to be filed or ground off before they can be pressed out using the tool.

- Check that you have the correct size and strength (standard or heavy duty) new soft link - do not reuse the old link. Look for the size marking on the chain sideplates **(see illustration 8.10)**.
- Position the chain ends so that they are engaged over the rear sprocket. On an O-ring chain, install a new O-ring over each pin of the link and insert the link through the two chain ends **(see illustration 8.4)**. Install a new O-ring over the end of each pin, followed by the sideplate (with the chain manufacturer's marking facing outwards) **(see illustrations 8.5 and 8.6)**. On an unsealed chain, insert the link through the two chain ends, then install the sideplate with the chain manufacturer's marking facing outwards.
- Note that it may not be possible to install the sideplate using finger pressure alone. If using a joining tool, assemble it so that the plates of the tool clamp the link and press the sideplate over the pins **(see illustration 8.7)**. Otherwise, use two small sockets placed over

8.1 Tighten the chain breaker to push the pin out of the link . . .

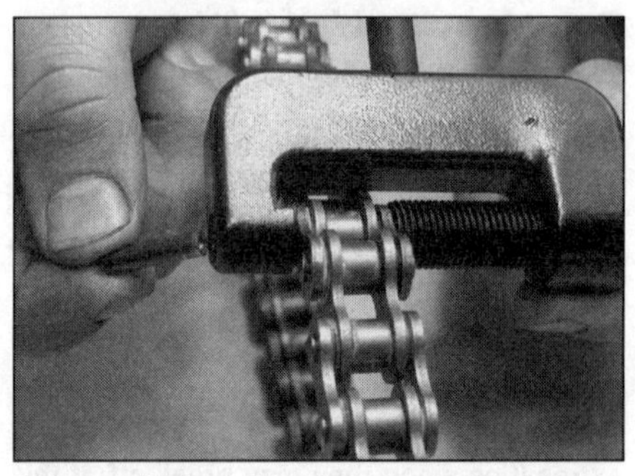

8.2 . . . withdraw the pin, remove the tool . . .

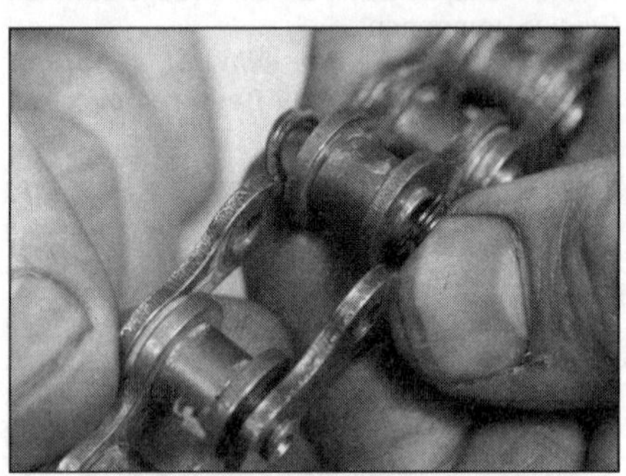

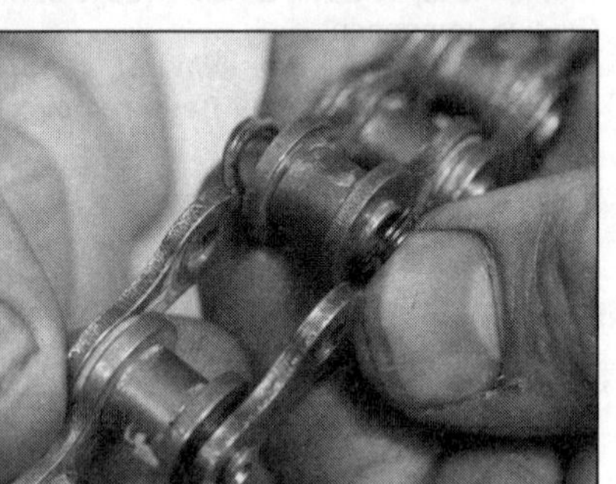

8.3 . . . and separate the chain link

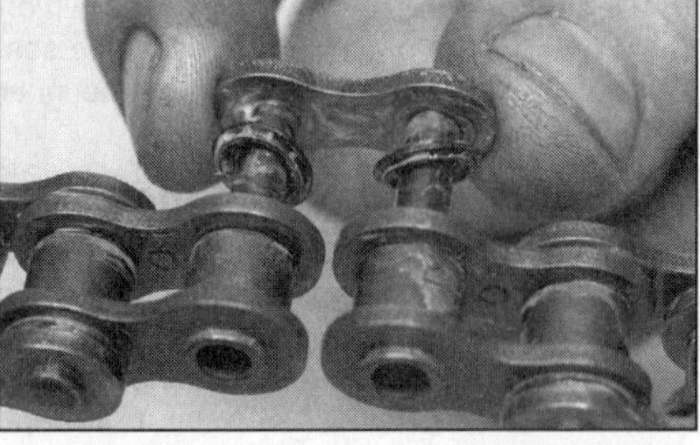

8.4 Insert the new soft link, with O-rings, through the chain ends . . .

8.5 . . . install the O-rings over the pin ends . . .

8.6 . . . followed by the sideplate

8.7 Push the sideplate into position using a clamp

8.8 Assemble the chain riveting tool over one pin at a time and tighten it fully

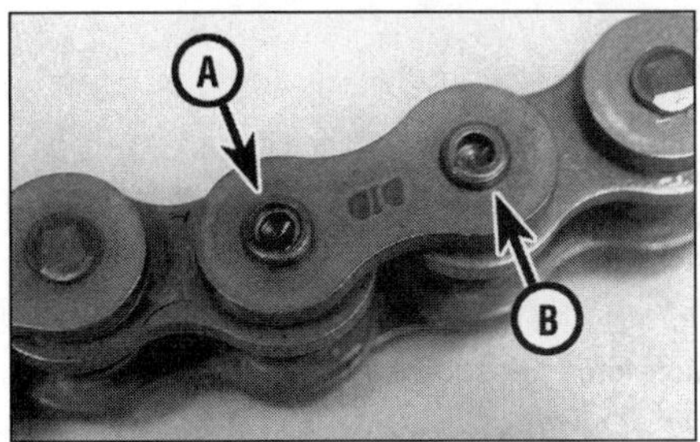

8.9 Pin end correctly riveted (A), pin end unriveted (B)

the rivet ends and two pieces of the wood between a G-clamp. Operate the clamp to press the sideplate over the pins.

● Assemble the joining tool over one pin (following the maker's instructions) and tighten the tool down to spread the pin end securely **(see illustrations 8.8 and 8.9)**. Do the same on the other pin.

Warning: Check that the pin ends are secure and that there is no danger of the sideplate coming loose. If the pin ends are cracked the soft link must be renewed.

Final drive chain sizing

● Chains are sized using a three digit number, followed by a suffix to denote the chain type **(see illustration 8.10)**. Chain type is either standard or heavy duty (thicker sideplates), and also unsealed or O-ring/X-ring type.

● The first digit of the number relates to the pitch of the chain, ie the distance from the centre of one pin to the centre of the next pin **(see illustration 8.11)**. Pitch is expressed in eighths of an inch, as follows:

8.10 Typical chain size and type marking

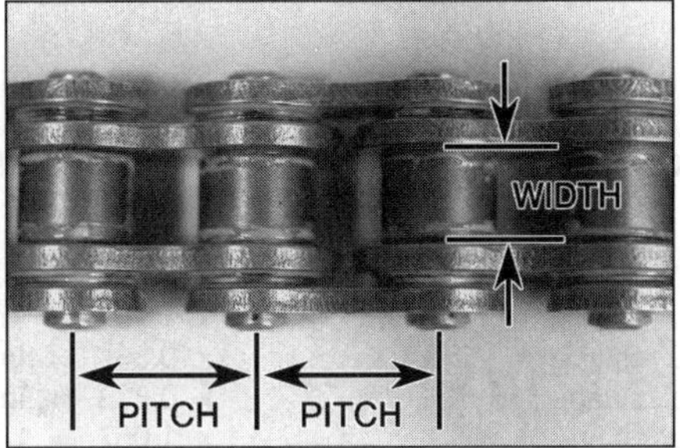

8.11 Chain dimensions

Sizes commencing with a 4 (eg 428) have a pitch of 1/2 inch (12.7 mm)

Sizes commencing with a 5 (eg 520) have a pitch of 5/8 inch (15.9 mm)

Sizes commencing with a 6 (eg 630) have a pitch of 3/4 inch (19.1 mm)

● The second and third digits of the chain size relate to the width of the rollers, again in imperial units, eg the 525 shown has 5/16 inch (7.94 mm) rollers **(see illustration 8.11)**.

9 Hoses

Clamping to prevent flow

● Small-bore flexible hoses can be clamped to prevent fluid flow whilst a component is worked on. Whichever method is used, ensure that the hose material is not permanently distorted or damaged by the clamp.

*a) A brake hose clamp available from auto accessory shops **(see illustration 9.1)**.*

*b) A wingnut type hose clamp **(see illustration 9.2)**.*

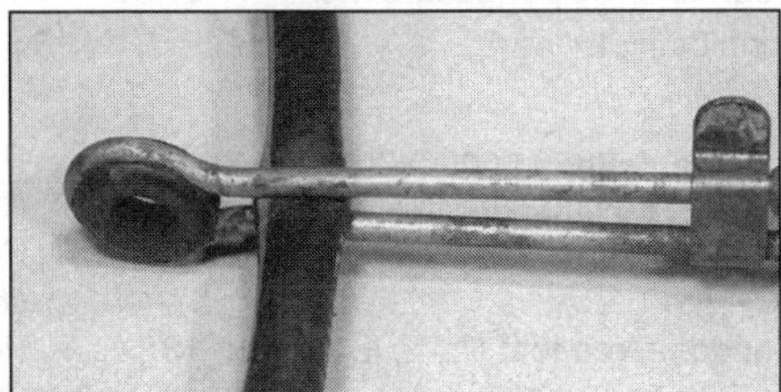

9.1 Hoses can be clamped with an automotive brake hose clamp . . .

9.2 . . . a wingnut type hose clamp . . .

*c) Two sockets placed each side of the hose and held with straight-jawed self-locking grips **(see illustration 9.3)**.*

*d) Thick card each side of the hose held between straight-jawed self-locking grips **(see illustration 9.4)**.*

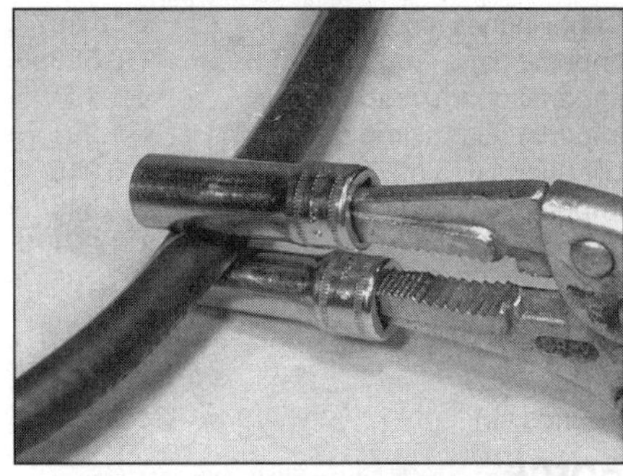

9.3 . . . two sockets and a pair of self-locking grips . . .

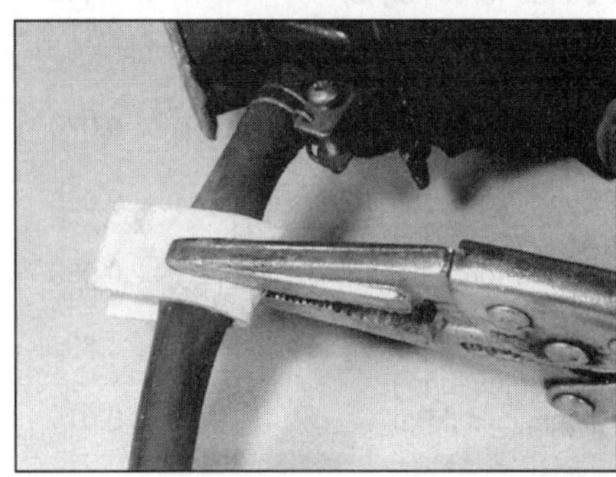

9.4 . . . or thick card and self-locking grips

Freeing and fitting hoses

● Always make sure the hose clamp is moved well clear of the hose end. Grip the hose with your hand and rotate it whilst pulling it off the union. If the hose has hardened due to age and will not move, slit it with a sharp knife and peel its ends off the union **(see illustration 9.5)**.

● Resist the temptation to use grease or soap on the unions to aid installation; although it helps the hose slip over the union it will equally aid the escape of fluid from the joint. It is preferable to soften the hose ends in hot water and wet the inside surface of the hose with water or a fluid which will evaporate.

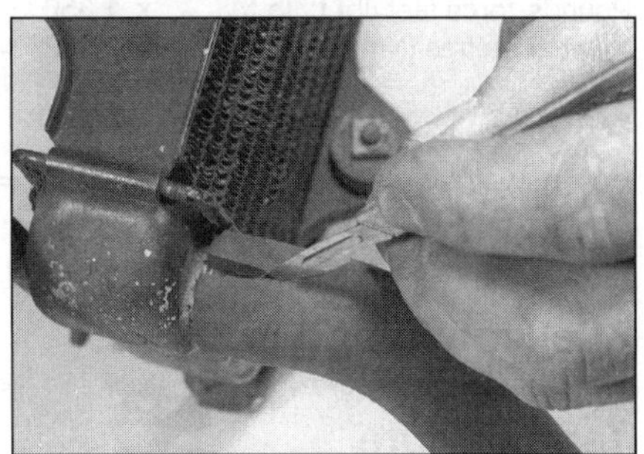

9.5 Cutting a coolant hose free with a sharp knife

Conversion Factors

Length (distance)

Inches (in)	x 25.4	=	Millimetres (mm)	x 0.0394	=	Inches (in)
Feet (ft)	x 0.305	=	Metres (m)	x 3.281	=	Feet (ft)
Miles	x 1.609	=	Kilometres (km)	x 0.621	=	Miles

Volume (capacity)

Cubic inches (cu in; in³)	x 16.387	=	Cubic centimetres (cc; cm³)	x 0.061	=	Cubic inches (cu in; in³)
Imperial pints (Imp pt)	x 0.568	=	Litres (l)	x 1.76	=	Imperial pints (Imp pt)
Imperial quarts (Imp qt)	x 1.137	=	Litres (l)	x 0.88	=	Imperial quarts (Imp qt)
Imperial quarts (Imp qt)	x 1.201	=	US quarts (US qt)	x 0.833	=	Imperial quarts (Imp qt)
US quarts (US qt)	x 0.946	=	Litres (l)	x 1.057	=	US quarts (US qt)
Imperial gallons (Imp gal)	x 4.546	=	Litres (l)	x 0.22	=	Imperial gallons (Imp gal)
Imperial gallons (Imp gal)	x 1.201	=	US gallons (US gal)	x 0.833	=	Imperial gallons (Imp gal)
US gallons (US gal)	x 3.785	=	Litres (l)	x 0.264	=	US gallons (US gal)

Mass (weight)

Ounces (oz)	x 28.35	=	Grams (g)	x 0.035	=	Ounces (oz)
Pounds (lb)	x 0.454	=	Kilograms (kg)	x 2.205	=	Pounds (lb)

Force

Ounces-force (ozf; oz)	x 0.278	=	Newtons (N)	x 3.6	=	Ounces-force (ozf; oz)
Pounds-force (lbf; lb)	x 4.448	=	Newtons (N)	x 0.225	=	Pounds-force (lbf; lb)
Newtons (N)	x 0.1	=	Kilograms-force (kgf; kg)	x 9.81	=	Newtons (N)

Pressure

Pounds-force per square inch (psi; lbf/in²; lb/in²)	x 0.070	=	Kilograms-force per square centimetre (kgf/cm²; kg/cm²)	x 14.223	=	Pounds-force per square inch (psi; lbf/in²; lb/in²)
Pounds-force per square inch (psi; lbf/in²; lb/in²)	x 0.068	=	Atmospheres (atm)	x 14.696	=	Pounds-force per square inch (psi; lbf/in²; lb/in²)
Pounds-force per square inch (psi; lbf/in²; lb/in²)	x 0.069	=	Bars	x 14.5	=	Pounds-force per square inch (psi; lbf/in²; lb/in²)
Pounds-force per square inch (psi; lbf/in²; lb/in²)	x 6.895	=	Kilopascals (kPa)	x 0.145	=	Pounds-force per square inch (psi; lbf/in²; lb/in²)
Kilopascals (kPa)	x 0.01	=	Kilograms-force per square centimetre (kgf/cm²; kg/cm²)	x 98.1	=	Kilopascals (kPa)
Millibar (mbar)	x 100	=	Pascals (Pa)	x 0.01	=	Millibar (mbar)
Millibar (mbar)	x 0.0145	=	Pounds-force per square inch (psi; lbf/in²; lb/in²)	x 68.947	=	Millibar (mbar)
Millibar (mbar)	x 0.75	=	Millimetres of mercury (mmHg)	x 1.333	=	Millibar (mbar)
Millibar (mbar)	x 0.401	=	Inches of water (inH_2O)	x 2.491	=	Millibar (mbar)
Millimetres of mercury (mmHg)	x 0.535	=	Inches of water (inH_2O)	x 1.868	=	Millimetres of mercury (mmHg)
Inches of water (inH_2O)	x 0.036	=	Pounds-force per square inch (psi; lbf/in²; lb/in²)	x 27.68	=	Inches of water (inH_2O)

Torque (moment of force)

Pounds-force inches (lbf in; lb in)	x 1.152	=	Kilograms-force centimetre (kgf cm; kg cm)	x 0.868	=	Pounds-force inches (lbf in; lb in)
Pounds-force inches (lbf in; lb in)	x 0.113	=	Newton metres (Nm)	x 8.85	=	Pounds-force inches (lbf in; lb in)
Pounds-force inches (lbf in; lb in)	x 0.083	=	Pounds-force feet (lbf ft; lb ft)	x 12	=	Pounds-force inches (lbf in; lb in)
Pounds-force feet (lbf ft; lb ft)	x 0.138	=	Kilograms-force metres (kgf m; kg m)	x 7.233	=	Pounds-force feet (lbf ft; lb ft)
Pounds-force feet (lbf ft; lb ft)	x 1.356	=	Newton metres (Nm)	x 0.738	=	Pounds-force feet (lbf ft; lb ft)
Newton metres (Nm)	x 0.102	=	Kilograms-force metres (kgf m; kg m)	x 9.804	=	Newton metres (Nm)

Power

Horsepower (hp)	x 745.7	=	Watts (W)	x 0.0013	=	Horsepower (hp)

Velocity (speed)

Miles per hour (miles/hr; mph)	x 1.609	=	Kilometres per hour (km/hr; kph)	x 0.621	=	Miles per hour (miles/hr; mph)

Fuel consumption*

Miles per gallon (mpg)	x 0.354	=	Kilometres per litre (km/l)	x 2.825	=	Miles per gallon (mpg)

Temperature

Degrees Fahrenheit = (°C x 1.8) + 32

Degrees Celsius (Degrees Centigrade; °C) = (°F - 32) x 0.56

** It is common practice to convert from miles per gallon (mpg) to litres/100 kilometres (l/100km), where mpg x l/100 km = 282*

A number of chemicals and lubricants are available for use in motorcycle maintenance and repair. They include a wide variety of products ranging from cleaning solvents and degreasers to lubricants and protective sprays for rubber, plastic and vinyl.

- **Contact point/spark plug cleaner** is a solvent used to clean oily film and dirt from points, grime from electrical connectors and oil deposits from spark plugs. It is oil free and leaves no residue. It can also be used to remove gum and varnish from carburettor jets and other orifices.
- **Carburettor cleaner** is similar to contact point/spark plug cleaner but it usually has a stronger solvent and may leave a slight oily reside. It is not recommended for cleaning electrical components or connections.
- **Brake system cleaner** is used to remove grease or brake fluid from brake system components (where clean surfaces are absolutely necessary and petroleum-based solvents cannot be used); it also leaves no residue.
- **Silicone-based lubricants** are used to protect rubber parts such as hoses and grommets, and are used as lubricants for hinges and locks.
- **Multi-purpose grease** is an all purpose lubricant used wherever grease is more practical than a liquid lubricant such as oil. Some multi-purpose grease is coloured white and specially formulated to be more resistant to water than ordinary grease.
- **Gear oil** (sometimes called gear lube) is a specially designed oil used in transmissions and final drive units, as well as other areas where high friction, high temperature lubrication is required. It is available in a number of viscosities (weights) for various applications.
- **Motor oil**, of course, is the lubricant specially formulated for use in the engine. It normally contains a wide variety of additives to prevent corrosion and reduce foaming and wear. Motor oil comes in various weights (viscosity ratings) of from 5 to 80. The recommended weight of the oil depends on the seasonal temperature and the demands on the engine. Light oil is used in cold climates and under light load conditions; heavy oil is used in hot climates and where high loads are encountered. Multi-viscosity oils are designed to have characteristics of both light and heavy oils and are available in a number of weights from 5W-20 to 20W-50.
- **Petrol additives** perform several functions, depending on their chemical makeup. They usually contain solvents that help dissolve gum and varnish that build up on carburettor and inlet parts. They also serve to break down carbon deposits that form on the inside surfaces of the combustion chambers. Some additives contain upper cylinder lubricants for valves and piston rings.
- **Brake and clutch fluid** is a specially formulated hydraulic fluid that can withstand the heat and pressure encountered in brake/clutch systems. Care must be taken that this fluid does not come in contact with painted surfaces or plastics. An opened container should always be resealed to prevent contamination by water or dirt.
- **Chain lubricants** are formulated especially for use on motorcycle final drive chains. A good chain lube should adhere well and have good penetrating qualities to be effective as a lubricant inside the chain and on the side plates, pins and rollers. Most chain lubes are either the foaming type or quick drying type and are usually marketed as sprays. Take care to use a lubricant marked as being suitable for O-ring chains.
- **Degreasers** are heavy duty solvents used to remove grease and grime that may accumulate on engine and frame components. They can be sprayed or brushed on and, depending on the type, are rinsed with either water or solvent.
- **Solvents** are used alone or in combination with degreasers to clean parts and assemblies during repair and overhaul. The home mechanic should use only solvents that are non-flammable and that do not produce irritating fumes.
- **Gasket sealing compounds** may be used in conjunction with gaskets, to improve their sealing capabilities, or alone, to seal metal-to-metal joints. Many gasket sealers can withstand extreme heat, some are impervious to petrol and lubricants, while others are capable of filling and sealing large cavities. Depending on the intended use, gasket sealers either dry hard or stay relatively soft and pliable. They are usually applied by hand, with a brush, or are sprayed on the gasket sealing surfaces.
- **Thread locking compound** is an adhesive locking compound that prevents threaded fasteners from loosening because of vibration. It is available in a variety of types for different applications.
- **Moisture dispersants** are usually sprays that can be used to dry out electrical components such as the fuse block and wiring connectors. Some types can also be used as treatment for rubber and as a lubricant for hinges, cables and locks.
- **Waxes and polishes** are used to help protect painted and plated surfaces from the weather. Different types of paint may require the use of different types of wax polish. Some polishes utilise a chemical or abrasive cleaner to help remove the top layer of oxidised (dull) paint on older vehicles. In recent years, many non-wax polishes (that contain a wide variety of chemicals such as polymers and silicones) have been introduced. These non-wax polishes are usually easier to apply and last longer than conventional waxes and polishes.

About the MOT Test

In the UK, all vehicles more than three years old are subject to an annual test to ensure that they meet minimum safety requirements. A current test certificate must be issued before a machine can be used on public roads, and is required before a road fund licence can be issued. Riding without a current test certificate will also invalidate your insurance.

For most owners, the MOT test is an annual cause for anxiety, and this is largely due to owners not being sure what needs to be checked prior to submitting the motorcycle for testing. The simple answer is that a fully roadworthy motorcycle will have no difficulty in passing the test.

This is a guide to getting your motorcycle through the MOT test. Obviously it will not be possible to examine the motorcycle to the same standard as the professional MOT tester, particularly in view of the equipment required for some of the checks. However, working through the following procedures will enable you to identify any problem areas before submitting the motorcycle for the test.

It has only been possible to summarise the test requirements here, based on the regulations in force at the time of printing. Test standards are becoming increasingly stringent, although there are some exemptions for older vehicles. More information about the MOT test can be obtained from the HMSO publications, *How Safe is your Motorcycle* and *The MOT Inspection Manual for Motorcycle Testing.*

Many of the checks require that one of the wheels is raised off the ground. If the motorcycle doesn't have a centre stand, note that an auxiliary stand will be required. Additionally, the help of an assistant may prove useful.

Certain exceptions apply to machines under 50 cc, machines without a lighting system, and Classic bikes - if in doubt about any of the requirements listed below seek confirmation from an MOT tester prior to submitting the motorcycle for the test.

Check that the frame number is clearly visible.

> **HAYNES HiNT** *If a component is in borderline condition, the tester has discretion in deciding whether to pass or fail it. If the motorcycle presented is clean and evidently well cared for, the tester may be more inclined to pass a borderline component than if the motorcycle is scruffy and apparently neglected.*

Electrical System

Lights, turn signals, horn and reflector

✔ With the ignition on, check the operation of the following electrical components. **Note:** *The electrical components on certain small-capacity machines are powered by the generator, requiring that the engine is run for this check.*

a) *Headlight and tail light. Check that both illuminate in the low and high beam switch positions.*
b) *Position lights. Check that the front position (or sidelight) and tail light illuminate in this switch position.*
c) *Turn signals. Check that all flash at the correct rate, and that the warning light(s) function correctly. Check that the turn signal switch works correctly.*
c) *Hazard warning system (where fitted). Check that all four turn signals flash in this switch position.*
d) *Brake stop light. Check that the light comes on when the front and rear brakes are independently applied. Models first used on or after 1st April 1986 must have a brake light switch on each brake.*
e) *Horn. Check that the sound is continuous and of reasonable volume.*

✔ Check that there is a red reflector on the rear of the machine, either mounted separately or as part of the tail light lens.

✔ Check the condition of the headlight, tail light and turn signal lenses.

Headlight beam height

✔ The MOT tester will perform a headlight beam height check using specialised beam setting equipment **(see illustration 1)**. This equipment will not be available to the home mechanic, but if you suspect that the headlight is incorrectly set or may have been maladjusted in the past, you can perform a rough test as follows.

✔ Position the bike in a straight line facing a brick wall. The bike must be off its stand, upright and with a rider seated. Measure the height from the ground to the centre of the headlight and mark a horizontal line on the wall at this height. Position the motorcycle 3.8 metres from the wall and draw a vertical line up the wall central to the centreline of the motorcycle. Switch to dipped beam and check that the beam pattern falls slightly lower than the horizontal line and to the left of the vertical line **(see illustration 2)**.

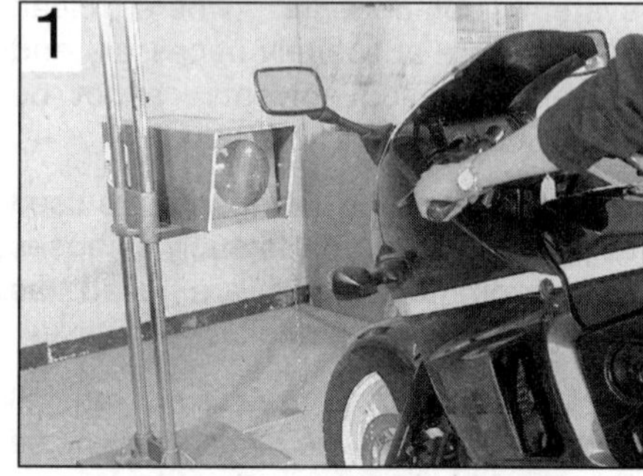
1 Headlight beam height checking equipment

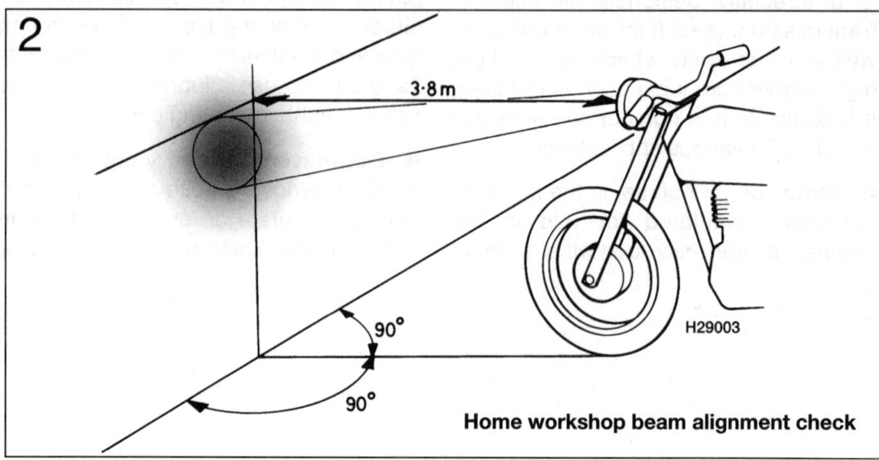

2 Home workshop beam alignment check

Exhaust System and Final Drive

Exhaust

✔ Check that the exhaust mountings are secure and that the system does not foul any of the rear suspension components.

✔ Start the motorcycle. When the revs are increased, check that the exhaust is neither holed nor leaking from any of its joints. On a linked system, check that the collector box is not leaking due to corrosion.

✔ Note that the exhaust decibel level ("loudness" of the exhaust) is assessed at the discretion of the tester. If the motorcycle was first used on or after 1st January 1985 the silencer must carry the BSAU 193 stamp, or a marking relating to its make and model, or be of OE (original equipment) manufacture. If the silencer is marked NOT FOR ROAD USE, RACING USE ONLY or similar, it will fail the MOT.

Final drive

✔ On chain or belt drive machines, check that the chain/belt is in good condition and does not have excessive slack. Also check that the sprocket is securely mounted on the rear wheel hub. Check that the chain/belt guard is in place.

✔ On shaft drive bikes, check for oil leaking from the drive unit and fouling the rear tyre.

Steering and Suspension

Steering

✔ With the front wheel raised off the ground, rotate the steering from lock to lock. The handlebar or switches must not contact the fuel tank or be close enough to trap the rider's hand. Problems can be caused by damaged lock stops on the lower yoke and frame, or by the fitting of non-standard handlebars.

✔ When performing the lock to lock check, also ensure that the steering moves freely without drag or notchiness. Steering movement can be impaired by poorly routed cables, or by overtight head bearings or worn bearings. The tester will perform a check of the steering head bearing lower race by mounting the front wheel on a surface plate, then performing a lock to lock check with the weight of the machine on the lower bearing **(see illustration 3)**.

✔ Grasp the fork sliders (lower legs) and attempt to push and pull on the forks **(see illustration 4)**. Any play in the steering head bearings will be felt. Note that in extreme cases, wear of the front fork bushes can be misinterpreted for head bearing play.

✔ Check that the handlebars are securely mounted.

✔ Check that the handlebar grip rubbers are secure. They should by bonded to the bar left end and to the throttle cable pulley on the right end.

3 Front wheel mounted on a surface plate for steering head bearing lower race check

4 Checking the steering head bearings for freeplay

Front suspension

✔ With the motorcycle off the stand, hold the front brake on and pump the front forks up and down **(see illustration 5)**. Check that they are adequately damped.

✔ Inspect the area above and around the front fork oil seals **(see illustration 6)**. There should be no sign of oil on the fork tube (stanchion) nor leaking down the slider (lower leg). On models so equipped, check that there is no oil leaking from the anti-dive units.

✔ On models with swingarm front suspension, check that there is no freeplay in the linkage when moved from side to side.

Rear suspension

✔ With the motorcycle off the stand and an assistant supporting the motorcycle by its handlebars, bounce the rear suspension **(see illustration 7)**. Check that the suspension components do not foul on any of the cycle parts and check that the shock absorber(s) provide adequate damping.

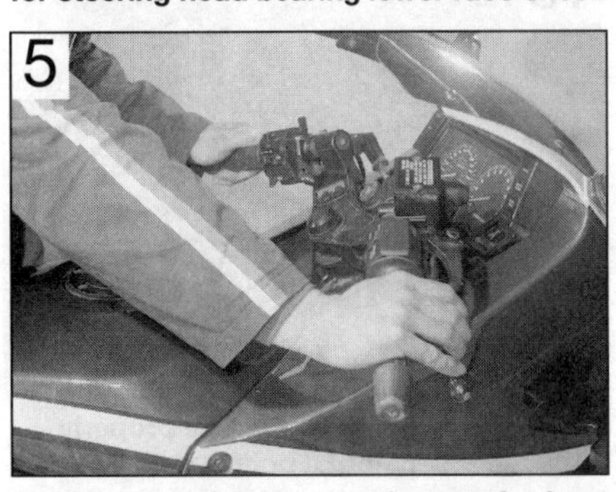

5 Hold the front brake on and pump the front forks up and down to check operation

6 Inspect the area around the fork dust seal for oil leakage (arrow)

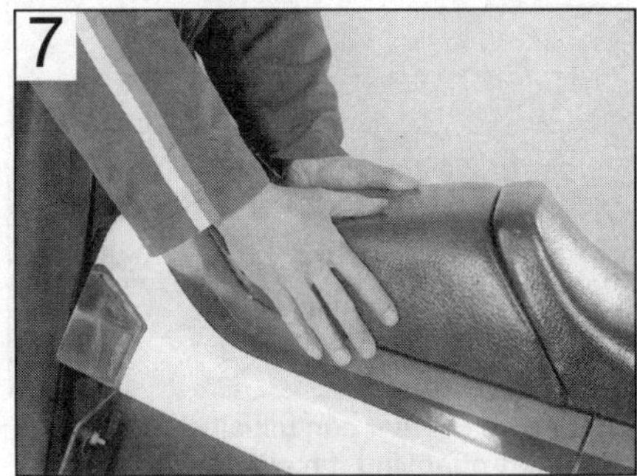

7 Bounce the rear of the motorcycle to check rear suspension operation

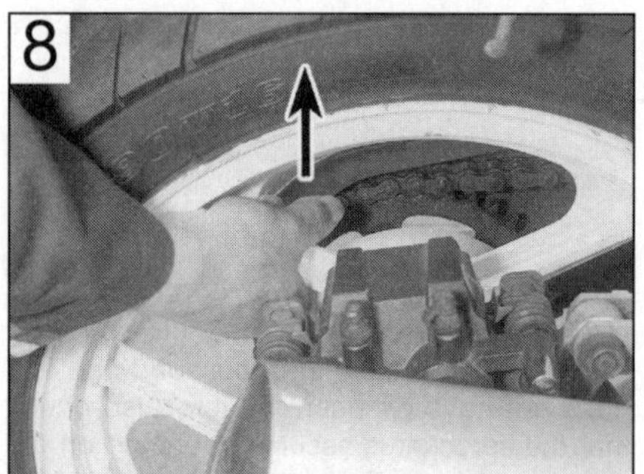

Checking for rear suspension linkage play

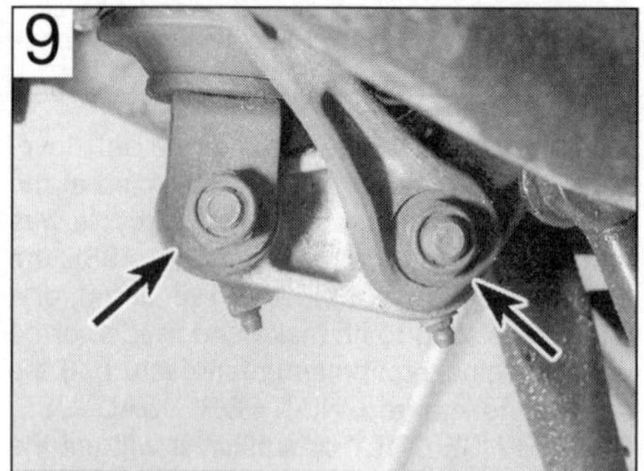

Worn suspension linkage pivots (arrows) are usually the cause of play in the rear suspension

Grasp the swingarm at the ends to check for play in its pivot bearings

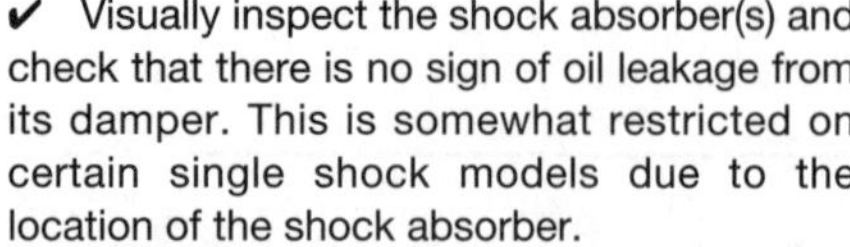

✔ Visually inspect the shock absorber(s) and check that there is no sign of oil leakage from its damper. This is somewhat restricted on certain single shock models due to the location of the shock absorber.

✔ With the rear wheel raised off the ground, grasp the wheel at the highest point and attempt to pull it up **(see illustration 8)**. Any play in the swingarm pivot or suspension linkage bearings will be felt as movement. **Note:** *Do not confuse play with actual suspension movement.* Failure to lubricate suspension linkage bearings can lead to bearing failure **(see illustration 9)**.

✔ With the rear wheel raised off the ground, grasp the swingarm ends and attempt to move the swingarm from side to side and forwards and backwards - any play indicates wear of the swingarm pivot bearings **(see illustration 10)**.

Brakes, Wheels and Tyres

Brakes

✔ With the wheel raised off the ground, apply the brake then free it off, and check that the wheel is about to revolve freely without brake drag.

✔ On disc brakes, examine the disc itself. Check that it is securely mounted and not cracked.

✔ On disc brakes, view the pad material through the caliper mouth and check that the pads are not worn down beyond the limit **(see illustration 11)**.

✔ On drum brakes, check that when the brake is applied the angle between the operating lever and cable or rod is not too great **(see illustration 12)**. Check also that the operating lever doesn't foul any other components.

✔ On disc brakes, examine the flexible hoses from top to bottom. Have an assistant hold the brake on so that the fluid in the hose is under pressure, and check that there is no sign of fluid leakage, bulges or cracking. If there are any metal brake pipes or unions, check that these are free from corrosion and damage. Where a brake-linked anti-dive system is fitted, check the hoses to the anti-dive in a similar manner.

✔ Check that the rear brake torque arm is secure and that its fasteners are secured by self-locking nuts or castellated nuts with split-pins or R-pins **(see illustration 13)**.

✔ On models with ABS, check that the self-check warning light in the instrument panel works.

✔ The MOT tester will perform a test of the motorcycle's braking efficiency based on a calculation of rider and motorcycle weight. Although this cannot be carried out at home, you can at least ensure that the braking systems are properly maintained. For hydraulic disc brakes, check the fluid level, lever/pedal feel (bleed of air if its spongy) and pad material. For drum brakes, check adjustment, cable or rod operation and shoe lining thickness.

Wheels and tyres

✔ Check the wheel condition. Cast wheels should be free from cracks and if of the built-up design, all fasteners should be secure. Spoked wheels should be checked for broken, corroded, loose or bent spokes.

✔ With the wheel raised off the ground, spin the wheel and visually check that the tyre and wheel run true. Check that the tyre does not foul the suspension or mudguards.

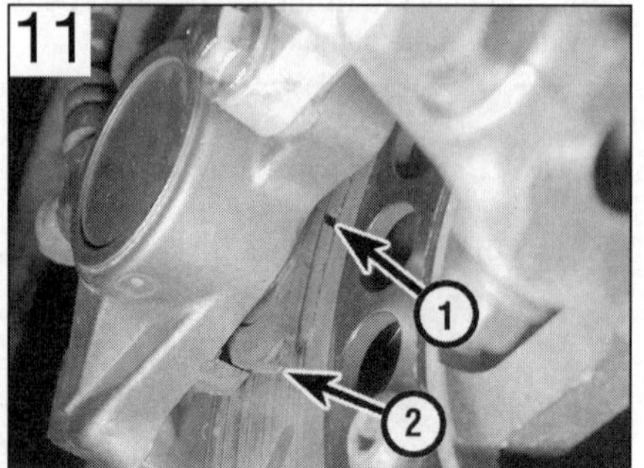

Brake pad wear can usually be viewed without removing the caliper. Most pads have wear indicator grooves (1) and some also have indicator tangs (2)

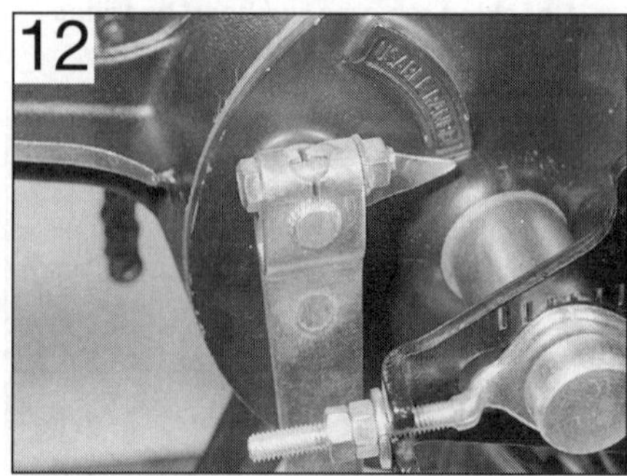

On drum brakes, check the angle of the operating lever with the brake fully applied. Most drum brakes have a wear indicator pointer and scale.

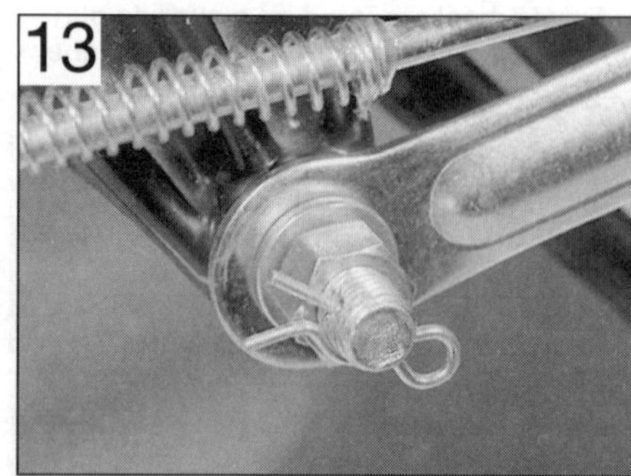

Brake torque arm must be properly secured at both ends

Check for wheel bearing play by trying to move the wheel about the axle (spindle)

Castellated type wheel axle (spindle) nut must be secured by a split pin or R-pin

✔ With the wheel raised off the ground, grasp the wheel and attempt to move it about the axle (spindle) **(see illustration 14)**. Any play felt here indicates wheel bearing failure.

✔ Check the tyre tread depth, tread condition and sidewall condition **(see illustration 15)**.

Checking the tyre tread depth

Two straightedges are used to check wheel alignment

✔ Check the tyre type. Front and rear tyre types must be compatible and be suitable for road use. Tyres marked NOT FOR ROAD USE, COMPETITION USE ONLY or similar, will fail the MOT.

Tyre direction of rotation arrow can be found on tyre sidewall

✔ If the tyre sidewall carries a direction of rotation arrow, this must be pointing in the direction of normal wheel rotation **(see illustration 16)**.

✔ Check that the wheel axle (spindle) nuts (where applicable) are properly secured. A self-locking nut or castellated nut with a split-pin or R-pin can be used **(see illustration 17)**.

✔ Wheel alignment is checked with the motorcycle off the stand and a rider seated. With the front wheel pointing straight ahead, two perfectly straight lengths of metal or wood and placed against the sidewalls of both tyres **(see illustration 18)**. The gap each side of the front tyre must be equidistant on both sides. Incorrect wheel alignment may be due to a cocked rear wheel (often as the result of poor chain adjustment) or in extreme cases, a bent frame.

General checks and condition

✔ Check the security of all major fasteners, bodypanels, seat, fairings (where fitted) and mudguards.

✔ Check that the rider and pillion footrests, handlebar levers and brake pedal are securely mounted.

✔ Check for corrosion on the frame or any load-bearing components. If severe, this may affect the structure, particularly under stress.

Sidecars

A motorcycle fitted with a sidecar requires additional checks relating to the stability of the machine and security of attachment and swivel joints, plus specific wheel alignment (toe-in) requirements. Additionally, tyre and lighting requirements differ from conventional motorcycle use. Owners are advised to check MOT test requirements with an official test centre.

Preparing for storage

Before you start

If repairs or an overhaul is needed, see that this is carried out now rather than left until you want to ride the bike again.

Give the bike a good wash and scrub all dirt from its underside. Make sure the bike dries completely before preparing for storage.

Engine

● Remove the spark plug(s) and lubricate the cylinder bores with approximately a teaspoon of motor oil using a spout-type oil can **(see illustration 1)**. Reinstall the spark plug(s). Crank the engine over a couple of times to coat the piston rings and bores with oil. If the bike has a kickstart, use this to turn the engine over. If not, flick the kill switch to the OFF position and crank the engine over on the starter **(see illustration 2)**. If the nature on the ignition system prevents the starter operating with the kill switch in the OFF position, remove the spark plugs and fit them back in their caps; ensure that the plugs are earthed (grounded) against the cylinder head when the starter is operated **(see illustration 3)**.

Warning: It is important that the plugs are earthed (grounded) away from the spark plug holes otherwise there is a risk of atomised fuel from the cylinders igniting.

On a single cylinder four-stroke engine, you can seal the combustion chamber completely by positioning the piston at TDC on the compression stroke.

Squirt a drop of motor oil into each cylinder

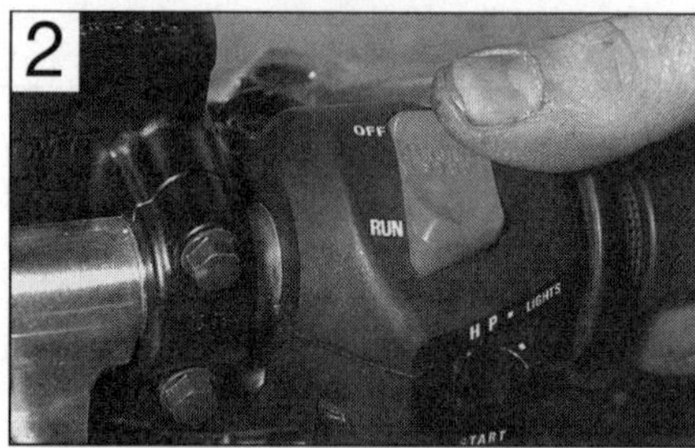

Flick the kill switch to OFF . . .

. . . and ensure that the metal bodies of the plugs (arrows) are earthed against the cylinder head

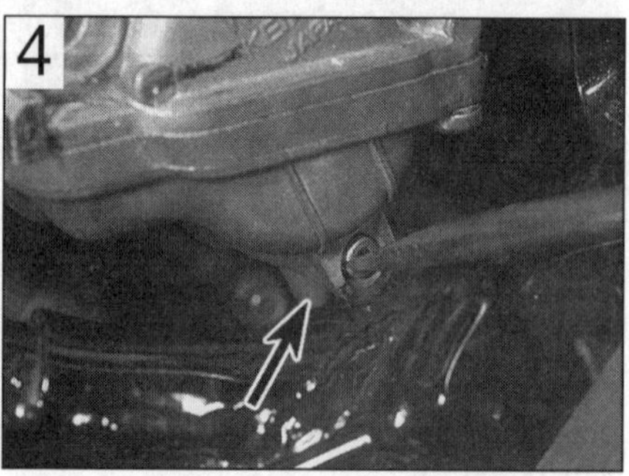

Connect a hose to the carburettor float chamber drain stub (arrow) and unscrew the drain screw

● Drain the carburettor(s) otherwise there is a risk of jets becoming blocked by gum deposits from the fuel **(see illustration 4)**.

● If the bike is going into long-term storage, consider adding a fuel stabiliser to the fuel in the tank. If the tank is drained completely, corrosion of its internal surfaces may occur if left unprotected for a long period. The tank can be treated with a rust preventative especially for this purpose. Alternatively, remove the tank and pour half a litre of motor oil into it, install the filler cap and shake the tank to coat its internals with oil before draining off the excess. The same effect can also be achieved by spraying WD40 or a similar water-dispersant around the inside of the tank via its flexible nozzle.

● Make sure the cooling system contains the correct mix of antifreeze. Antifreeze also contains important corrosion inhibitors.

● The air intakes and exhaust can be sealed off by covering or plugging the openings. Ensure that you do not seal in any condensation; run the engine until it is hot, then switch off and allow to cool. Tape a piece of thick plastic over the silencer end(s) **(see illustration 5)**. Note that some advocate pouring a tablespoon of motor oil into the silencer(s) before sealing them off.

Exhausts can be sealed off with a plastic bag

Battery

● Remove it from the bike - in extreme cases of cold the battery may freeze and crack its case **(see illustration 6)**.

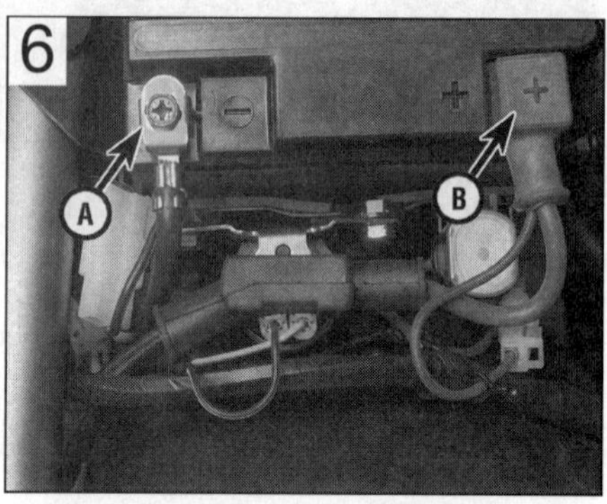

Disconnect the negative lead (A) first, followed by the positive lead (B)

● Check the electrolyte level and top up if necessary (conventional refillable batteries). Clean the terminals.

● Store the battery off the motorcycle and away from any sources of fire. Position a wooden block under the battery if it is to sit on the ground.

● Give the battery a trickle charge for a few hours every month **(see illustration 7)**.

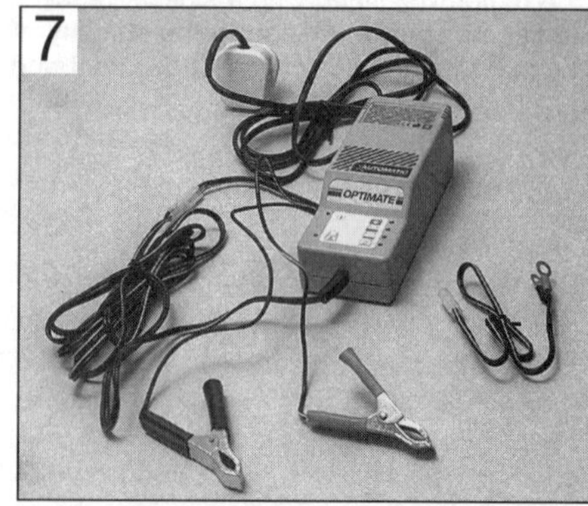

Use a suitable battery charger - this kit also assess battery condition

Tyres

● Place the bike on its centrestand or an auxiliary stand which will support the motorcycle in an upright position. Position wood blocks under the tyres to keep them off the ground and to provide insulation from damp. If the bike is being put into long-term storage, ideally both tyres should be off the ground; not only will this protect the tyres, but will also ensure that no load is placed on the steering head or wheel bearings.
● Deflate each tyre by 5 to 10 psi, no more or the beads may unseat from the rim, making subsequent inflation difficult on tubeless tyres.

Pivots and controls

● Lubricate all lever, pedal, stand and footrest pivot points. If grease nipples are fitted to the rear suspension components, apply lubricant to the pivots.
● Lubricate all control cables.

Cycle components

● Apply a wax protectant to all painted and plastic components. Wipe off any excess, but don't polish to a shine. Where fitted, clean the screen with soap and water.
● Coat metal parts with Vaseline (petroleum jelly). When applying this to the fork tubes, do not compress the forks otherwise the seals will rot from contact with the Vaseline.
● Apply a vinyl cleaner to the seat.

Storage conditions

● Aim to store the bike in a shed or garage which does not leak and is free from damp.
● Drape an old blanket or bedspread over the bike to protect it from dust and direct contact with sunlight (which will fade paint). This also hides the bike from prying eyes. Beware of tight-fitting plastic covers which may allow condensation to form and settle on the bike.

Getting back on the road

Engine and transmission

● Change the oil and replace the oil filter. If this was done prior to storage, check that the oil hasn't emulsified - a thick whitish substance which occurs through condensation.
● Remove the spark plugs. Using a spout-type oil can, squirt a few drops of oil into the cylinder(s). This will provide initial lubrication as the piston rings and bores comes back into contact. Service the spark plugs, or fit new ones, and install them in the engine.
● Check that the clutch isn't stuck on. The plates can stick together if left standing for some time, preventing clutch operation. Engage a gear and try rocking the bike back and forth with the clutch lever held against the handlebar. If this doesn't work on cable-operated clutches, hold the clutch lever back against the handlebar with a strong elastic band or cable tie for a couple of hours **(see illustration 8)**.

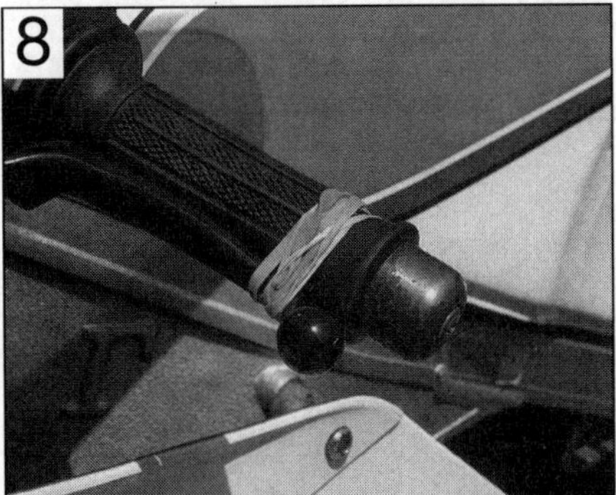

Hold clutch lever back against the handlebar with elastic bands or a cable tie

● If the air intakes or silencer end(s) were blocked off, remove the bung or cover used.
● If the fuel tank was coated with a rust preventative, oil or a stabiliser added to the fuel, drain and flush the tank and dispose of the fuel sensibly. If no action was taken with the fuel tank prior to storage, it is advised that the old fuel is disposed of since it will go off over a period of time. Refill the fuel tank with fresh fuel.

Frame and running gear

● Oil all pivot points and cables.
● Check the tyre pressures. They will definitely need inflating if pressures were reduced for storage.
● Lubricate the final drive chain (where applicable).
● Remove any protective coating applied to the fork tubes (stanchions) since this may well destroy the fork seals. If the fork tubes weren't protected and have picked up rust spots, remove them with very fine abrasive paper and refinish with metal polish.
● Check that both brakes operate correctly. Apply each brake hard and check that it's not possible to move the motorcycle forwards, then check that the brake frees off again once released. Brake caliper pistons can stick due to corrosion around the piston head, or on the sliding caliper types, due to corrosion of the slider pins. If the brake doesn't free after repeated operation, take the caliper off for examination. Similarly drum brakes can stick due to a seized operating cam, cable or rod linkage.
● If the motorcycle has been in long-term storage, renew the brake fluid and clutch fluid (where applicable).
● Depending on where the bike has been stored, the wiring, cables and hoses may have been nibbled by rodents. Make a visual check and investigate disturbed wiring loom tape.

Battery

● If the battery has been previously removal and given top up charges it can simply be reconnected. Remember to connect the positive cable first and the negative cable last.
● On conventional refillable batteries, if the battery has not received any attention, remove it from the motorcycle and check its electrolyte level. Top up if necessary then charge the battery. If the battery fails to hold a charge and a visual checks show heavy white sulphation of the plates, the battery is probably defective and must be renewed. This is particularly likely if the battery is old. Confirm battery condition with a specific gravity check.
● On sealed (MF) batteries, if the battery has not received any attention, remove it from the motorcycle and charge it according to the information on the battery case - if the battery fails to hold a charge it must be renewed.

Starting procedure

● If a kickstart is fitted, turn the engine over a couple of times with the ignition OFF to distribute oil around the engine. If no kickstart is fitted, flick the engine kill switch OFF and the ignition ON and crank the engine over a couple of times to work oil around the upper cylinder components. If the nature of the ignition system is such that the starter won't work with the kill switch OFF, remove the spark plugs, fit them back into their caps and earth (ground) their bodies on the cylinder head. Reinstall the spark plugs afterwards.
● Switch the kill switch to RUN, operate the choke and start the engine. If the engine won't start don't continue cranking the engine - not only will this flatten the battery, but the starter motor will overheat. Switch the ignition off and try again later. If the engine refuses to start, go through the fault finding procedures in this manual. **Note:** *If the bike has been in storage for a long time, old fuel or a carburettor blockage may be the problem. Gum deposits in carburettors can block jets - if a carburettor cleaner doesn't prove successful the carburettors must be dismantled for cleaning.*
● Once the engine has started, check that the lights, turn signals and horn work properly.
● Treat the bike gently for the first ride and check all fluid levels on completion. Settle the bike back into the maintenance schedule.

This Section provides an easy reference-guide to the more common faults that are likely to afflict your machine. Obviously, the opportunities are almost limitless for faults to occur as a result of obscure failures, and to try and cover all eventualities would require a book. Indeed, a number have been written on the subject.

Successful troubleshooting is not a mysterious 'black art' but the application of a bit of knowledge combined with a systematic and logical approach to the problem. Approach any troubleshooting by first accurately identifying the symptom and then checking through the list of possible causes, starting with the simplest or most obvious and progressing in stages to the most complex.

Take nothing for granted, but above all apply liberal quantities of common sense.

The main symptom of a fault is given in the text as a major heading below which are listed the various systems or areas which may contain the fault. Details of each possible cause for a fault and the remedial action to be taken are given, in brief, in the paragraphs below each heading. Further information should be sought in the relevant Chapter.

1 Engine doesn't start or is difficult to start

- ☐ Starter motor doesn't rotate
- ☐ Starter motor rotates but engine does not turn over
- ☐ Starter works but engine won't turn over (seized)
- ☐ No fuel flow
- ☐ Engine flooded
- ☐ No spark or weak spark
- ☐ Compression low
- ☐ Stalls after starting
- ☐ Rough idle

2 Poor running at low speed

- ☐ Spark weak
- ☐ Fuel/air mixture incorrect
- ☐ Compression low
- ☐ Poor acceleration

3 Poor running or no power at high speed

- ☐ Firing incorrect
- ☐ Fuel/air mixture incorrect
- ☐ Compression low
- ☐ Knocking or pinging
- ☐ Miscellaneous causes

4 Overheating

- ☐ Engine overheats
- ☐ Firing incorrect
- ☐ Fuel/air mixture incorrect
- ☐ Compression too high
- ☐ Engine load excessive
- ☐ Lubrication inadequate
- ☐ Miscellaneous causes

5 Clutch problems

- ☐ Clutch slipping
- ☐ Clutch not disengaging completely

6 Gearchanging problems

- ☐ Doesn't go into gear, or lever doesn't return
- ☐ Jumps out of gear
- ☐ Overshifts

7 Abnormal engine noise

- ☐ Knocking or pinging
- ☐ Piston slap or rattling
- ☐ Valve noise
- ☐ Other noise

8 Abnormal driveline noise

- ☐ Clutch noise
- ☐ Transmission noise
- ☐ Final drive noise

9 Abnormal frame and suspension noise

- ☐ Front end noise
- ☐ Shock absorber noise
- ☐ Brake noise

10 Oil pressure warning light comes on

- ☐ Engine lubrication system
- ☐ Electrical system

11 Excessive exhaust smoke

- ☐ White smoke
- ☐ Black smoke
- ☐ Brown smoke

12 Poor handling or stability

- ☐ Handlebar hard to turn
- ☐ Handlebar shakes or vibrates excessively
- ☐ Handlebar pulls to one side
- ☐ Poor shock absorbing qualities

13 Braking problems

- ☐ Brakes are spongy, don't hold
- ☐ Brake lever or pedal pulsates
- ☐ Brakes drag

14 Electrical problems

- ☐ Battery dead or weak
- ☐ Battery overcharged

1 Engine doesn't start or is difficult to start

Starter motor doesn't rotate

- ☐ Engine kill switch OFF.
- ☐ Fuse blown. Check main fuse and starter circuit fuse (Chapter 9).
- ☐ Battery voltage low. Check and recharge battery (Chapter 9).
- ☐ Starter motor defective. Make sure the wiring to the starter is secure. Make sure the starter relay clicks when the start button is pushed. If the relay clicks, then the fault is in the wiring or motor.
- ☐ Starter relay faulty. Check it according to the procedure in Chapter 9.
- ☐ Starter switch not contacting. The contacts could be wet, corroded or dirty. Disassemble and clean the switch (Chapter 9).
- ☐ Wiring open or shorted. Check all wiring connections and harnesses to make sure that they are dry, tight and not corroded. Also check for broken or frayed wires that can cause a short to ground (earth) (see wiring diagram, Chapter 9).
- ☐ Ignition (main) switch defective. Check the switch according to the procedure in Chapter 9. Replace the switch with a new one if it is defective.
- ☐ Engine kill switch defective. Check for wet, dirty or corroded contacts. Clean or replace the switch as necessary (Chapter 9).
- ☐ Faulty neutral, side stand or clutch switch. Check the wiring to each switch and the switch itself according to the procedures in Chapter 9.

Starter motor rotates but engine does not turn over

- ☐ Starter motor clutch defective. Inspect and repair or replace (Chapter 2).
- ☐ Damaged idler or starter gears. Inspect and replace the damaged parts (Chapter 2).

Starter works but engine won't turn over (seized)

- ☐ Seized engine caused by one or more internally damaged components. Failure due to wear, abuse or lack of lubrication. Damage can include seized valves, followers, camshafts, pistons, crankshaft, connecting rod bearings, or transmission gears or bearings. Refer to Chapter 2 for engine disassembly.

No fuel flow

- ☐ No fuel in tank.
- ☐ Fuel pump failure or in-line filter blockage (see Chapters 1 and 9 respectively).
- ☐ Fuel tank breather hose obstructed (not California models).
- ☐ Fuel tap filter clogged. Remove the tap and clean it and the filter (Chapter 1).
- ☐ Fuel line clogged. Pull the fuel line loose and carefully blow through it.
- ☐ Float needle valve clogged. For all of the valves to be clogged, either a very bad batch of fuel with an unusual additive has been used, or some other foreign material has entered the tank. Many times after a machine has been stored for many months without running, the fuel turns to a varnish-like liquid and forms deposits on the inlet needle valves and jets. The carburettors should be removed and overhauled if draining the float chambers doesn't solve the problem.

Engine flooded

- ☐ Float height too high. Check as described in Chapter 4.
- ☐ Float needle valve worn or stuck open. A piece of dirt, rust or other debris can cause the valve to seat improperly, causing excess fuel to be admitted to the float chamber. In this case, the float chamber should be cleaned and the needle valve and seat inspected. If the needle and seat are worn, then the leaking will persist and the parts should be replaced with new ones (Chapter 4).
- ☐ Starting technique incorrect. Under normal circumstances (i.e., if all the carburettor functions are sound) the machine should start with little or no throttle. When the engine is cold, the choke should be operated and the engine started without opening the throttle. When the engine is at operating temperature, only a very slight amount of throttle should be necessary. If the engine is flooded, turn the fuel tap OFF and hold the throttle open while cranking the engine. This will allow additional air to reach the cylinders. Remember to turn the fuel tap back ON after the engine starts.

No spark or weak spark

- ☐ Ignition switch OFF.
- ☐ Engine kill switch turned to the OFF position.
- ☐ Battery voltage low. Check and recharge the battery as necessary (Chapter 9).
- ☐ Spark plugs dirty, defective or worn out. Locate reason for fouled plugs using spark plug condition chart and follow the plug maintenance procedures (Chapter 1).
- ☐ Spark plug caps or secondary (HT) wiring faulty. Check condition. Replace either or both components if cracks or deterioration are evident (Chapter 5).
- ☐ Spark plug caps not making good contact. Make sure that the plug caps fit snugly over the plug ends.
- ☐ Ignition control unit defective. Check the unit, referring to Chapter 5 for details.
- ☐ Pulse generator defective. Check the unit, referring to Chapter 5 for details.
- ☐ Ignition HT coils defective. Check the coils, referring to Chapter 5.
- ☐ Ignition or kill switch shorted. This is usually caused by water, corrosion, damage or excessive wear. The switches can be disassembled and cleaned with electrical contact cleaner. If cleaning does not help, replace the switches (Chapter 9).
- ☐ Wiring shorted or broken between:
  - *a) Ignition (main) switch and engine kill switch (or blown fuse)*
  - *b) Ignition control unit and engine kill switch*
  - *c) Ignition control unit and ignition HT coils*
  - *d) Ignition HT coils and spark plugs*
  - *e) Ignition control unit and pulse generator*
- ☐ Make sure that all wiring connections are clean, dry and tight. Look for chafed and broken wires (Chapters 5 and 9).

Compression low

- ☐ Spark plugs loose. Remove the plugs and inspect their threads. Reinstall and tighten to the specified torque (Chapter 1).
- ☐ Cylinder head not sufficiently tightened down. If the cylinder head is suspected of being loose, then there's a chance that the gasket or head is damaged if the problem has persisted for any length of time. The head bolts should be tightened to the proper torque in the correct sequence (Chapter 2).
- ☐ Improper valve clearance. This means that the valve is not closing completely and compression pressure is leaking past the valve. Check and adjust the valve clearances (Chapter 1).
- ☐ Cylinder and/or piston worn. Excessive wear will cause compression pressure to leak past the rings. This is usually accompanied by worn rings as well. A top-end overhaul is necessary (Chapter 2).
- ☐ Piston rings worn, weak, broken, or sticking. Broken or sticking piston rings usually indicate a lubrication or carburation problem that causes excess carbon deposits or seizures to form on the pistons and rings. Top-end overhaul is necessary (Chapter 2).
- ☐ Piston ring-to-groove clearance excessive. This is caused by excessive wear of the piston ring lands. Piston replacement is necessary (Chapter 2).
- ☐ Cylinder head gasket damaged. If the head is allowed to become loose, or if excessive carbon build-up on the piston crown and combustion chamber causes extremely high compression, the head gasket may leak. Retorquing the head is not always sufficient to restore the seal, so gasket replacement is necessary (Chapter 2).

1 Engine doesn't start or is difficult to start (continued)

- ☐ Cylinder head warped. This is caused by overheating or improperly tightened head bolts. Machine shop resurfacing or head replacement is necessary (Chapter 2).
- ☐ Valve spring broken or weak. Caused by component failure or wear; the springs must be replaced (Chapter 2).
- ☐ Valve not seating properly. This is caused by a bent valve (from over-revving or improper valve adjustment), burned valve or seat (improper carburation) or an accumulation of carbon deposits on the seat (from carburation or lubrication problems). The valves must be cleaned and/or replaced and the seats serviced if possible (Chapter 2).

Stalls after starting

- ☐ Improper choke action. Make sure the choke linkage shaft is getting a full stroke and staying in the out position (Chapter 4).
- ☐ Ignition malfunction. See Chapter 5.
- ☐ Carburettor malfunction. See Chapter 4.
- ☐ Fuel contaminated. The fuel can be contaminated with either dirt or water, or can change chemically if the machine is allowed to sit for several months or more. Drain the tank and float chambers (Chapter 4).
- ☐ Intake air leak. Check for loose carburettor-to-intake manifold connections, loose or missing vacuum gauge adapter screws or hoses, or loose carburettor tops (Chapter 4).
- ☐ Engine idle speed incorrect. Turn idle adjusting screw until the engine idles at the specified rpm (Chapter 1).

Rough idle

- ☐ Ignition malfunction. See Chapter 5.
- ☐ Idle speed incorrect. See Chapter 1.
- ☐ Carburettors not synchronised. Adjust carburettors with vacuum gauge or manometer set as described in Chapter 1.
- ☐ Carburettor malfunction. See Chapter 4.
- ☐ Fuel contaminated. The fuel can be contaminated with either dirt or water, or can change chemically if the machine is allowed to sit for several months or more. Drain the tank and float chambers (Chapter 4).
- ☐ Intake air leak. Check for loose carburettor-to-intake manifold connections, loose or missing vacuum gauge adapter screws or hoses, or loose carburettor tops (Chapter 4).
- ☐ Air filter clogged. Replace the air filter element (Chapter 1).

2 Poor running at low speeds

Spark weak

- ☐ Battery voltage low. Check and recharge battery (Chapter 9).
- ☐ Spark plugs fouled, defective or worn out. Refer to Chapter 1 for spark plug maintenance.
- ☐ Spark plug cap or HT wiring defective. Refer to Chapters 1 and 5 for details on the ignition system.
- ☐ Spark plug caps not making contact.
- ☐ Incorrect spark plugs. Wrong type, heat range or cap configuration. Check and install correct plugs listed in Chapter 1.
- ☐ Ignition control unit defective. See Chapter 5.
- ☐ Pulse generator defective. See Chapter 5.
- ☐ Ignition HT coils defective. See Chapter 5.

Fuel/air mixture incorrect

- ☐ Pilot screws out of adjustment (Chapter 4).
- ☐ Pilot jet or air passage clogged. Remove and overhaul the carburettors (Chapter 4).
- ☐ Air bleed holes clogged. Remove carburettor and blow out all passages (Chapter 4).
- ☐ Air filter clogged, poorly sealed or missing (Chapter 1).
- ☐ Air filter housing poorly sealed. Look for cracks, holes or loose clamps and replace or repair defective parts.
- ☐ Fuel level too high or too low. Check the float height (Chapter 4).
- ☐ Fuel tank breather hose obstructed (not California models).
- ☐ Carburettor intake manifolds loose. Check for cracks, breaks, tears or loose clamps. Replace the rubber intake manifold joints if split or perished.

Compression low

- ☐ Spark plugs loose. Remove the plugs and inspect their threads. Reinstall and tighten to the specified torque (Chapter 1).
- ☐ Cylinder head not sufficiently tightened down. If the cylinder head is suspected of being loose, then there's a chance that the gasket and head are damaged if the problem has persisted for any length of time. The head bolts should be tightened to the proper torque in the correct sequence (Chapter 2).
- ☐ Improper valve clearance. This means that the valve is not closing completely and compression pressure is leaking past the valve. Check and adjust the valve clearances (Chapter 1).
- ☐ Cylinder and/or piston worn. Excessive wear will cause compression pressure to leak past the rings. This is usually accompanied by worn rings as well. A top end overhaul is necessary (Chapter 2).
- ☐ Piston rings worn, weak, broken, or sticking. Broken or sticking piston rings usually indicate a lubrication or carburation problem that causes excess carbon deposits or seizures to form on the pistons and rings. Top-end overhaul is necessary (Chapter 2).
- ☐ Piston ring-to-groove clearance excessive. This is caused by excessive wear of the piston ring lands. Piston replacement is necessary (Chapter 2).
- ☐ Cylinder head gasket damaged. If the head is allowed to become loose, or if excessive carbon build-up on the piston crown and combustion chamber causes extremely high compression, the head gasket may leak. Retorquing the head is not always sufficient to restore the seal, so gasket replacement is necessary (Chapter 2).
- ☐ Cylinder head warped. This is caused by overheating or improperly tightened head bolts. Machine shop resurfacing or head replacement is necessary (Chapter 2).
- ☐ Valve spring broken or weak. Caused by component failure or wear; the springs must be replaced (Chapter 2).
- ☐ Valve not seating properly. This is caused by a bent valve (from over-revving or improper valve adjustment), burned valve or seat (improper carburation) or an accumulation of carbon deposits on the seat (from carburation, lubrication problems). The valves must be cleaned and/or replaced and the seats serviced if possible (Chapter 2).

Poor acceleration

- ☐ Carburettors leaking or dirty. Overhaul the carburettors (Chapter 4).
- ☐ Timing not advancing. The pulse generator or the ignition control module may be defective. If so, they must be replaced with new ones, as they can't be repaired.
- ☐ Carburettors not synchronised. Adjust them with a vacuum gauge set or manometer (Chapter 1).
- ☐ Engine oil viscosity too high. Using a heavier oil than that recommended in Chapter 1 can damage the oil pump or lubrication system and cause drag on the engine.
- ☐ Brakes dragging. Usually caused by debris which has entered the brake piston seals, or from a warped disc or bent axle. Repair as necessary (Chapter 7).

3 Poor running or no power at high speed

Firing incorrect

- ☐ Air filter restricted. Clean or replace filter (Chapter 1).
- ☐ Spark plugs fouled, defective or worn out. See Chapter 1 for spark plug maintenance.
- ☐ Spark plug caps or HT wiring defective. See Chapters 1 and 5 for details of the ignition system.
- ☐ Spark plug caps not in good contact. See Chapter 5.
- ☐ Incorrect spark plugs. Wrong type, heat range or cap configuration. Check and install correct plugs listed in Chapter 1.
- ☐ Ignition control unit defective. See Chapter 5.
- ☐ Ignition coils defective. See Chapter 5.

Fuel/air mixture incorrect

- ☐ Main jet clogged. Dirt, water or other contaminants can clog the main jets. Clean the fuel tap filter, the in-line filter, the float chamber area, and the jets and carburettor orifices (Chapter 4).
- ☐ Main jet wrong size. The standard jetting is for sea level atmospheric pressure and oxygen content.
- ☐ Throttle shaft-to-carburettor body clearance excessive. Refer to Chapter 4 for inspection and part replacement procedures.
- ☐ Air bleed holes clogged. Remove and overhaul carburettors (Chapter 4).
- ☐ Air filter clogged, poorly sealed, or missing (Chapter 1).
- ☐ Air filter housing poorly sealed. Look for cracks, holes or loose clamps, and replace or repair defective parts.
- ☐ Fuel level too high or too low. Check the float height (Chapter 4).
- ☐ Fuel tank breather hose obstructed (not California models).
- ☐ Carburettor intake manifolds loose. Check for cracks, breaks, tears or loose clamps. Replace the rubber intake manifolds if they are split or perished (Chapter 4).

Compression low

- ☐ Spark plugs loose. Remove the plugs and inspect their threads. Reinstall and tighten to the specified torque (Chapter 1).
- ☐ Cylinder head not sufficiently tightened down. If the cylinder head is suspected of being loose, then there's a chance that the gasket and head are damaged if the problem has persisted for any length of time. The head bolts should be tightened to the proper torque in the correct sequence (Chapter 2).
- ☐ Improper valve clearance. This means that the valve is not closing completely and compression pressure is leaking past the valve. Check and adjust the valve clearances (Chapter 1).
- ☐ Cylinder and/or piston worn. Excessive wear will cause compression pressure to leak past the rings. This is usually accompanied by worn rings as well. A top-end overhaul is necessary (Chapter 2).
- ☐ Piston rings worn, weak, broken, or sticking. Broken or sticking piston rings usually indicate a lubrication or carburation problem that causes excess carbon deposits or seizures to form on the pistons and rings. Top-end overhaul is necessary (Chapter 2).
- ☐ Piston ring-to-groove clearance excessive. This is caused by excessive wear of the piston ring lands. Piston replacement is necessary (Chapter 2).
- ☐ Cylinder head gasket damaged. If the head is allowed to become loose, or if excessive carbon build-up on the piston crown and combustion chamber causes extremely high compression, the head gasket may leak. Retorquing the head is not always sufficient to restore the seal, so gasket replacement is necessary (Chapter 2).
- ☐ Cylinder head warped. This is caused by overheating or improperly tightened head bolts. Machine shop resurfacing or head replacement is necessary (Chapter 2).
- ☐ Valve spring broken or weak. Caused by component failure or wear; the springs must be replaced (Chapter 2).
- ☐ Valve not seating properly. This is caused by a bent valve (from over-revving or improper valve adjustment), burned valve or seat (improper carburation) or an accumulation of carbon deposits on the seat (from carburation or lubrication problems). The valves must be cleaned and/or replaced and the seats serviced if possible (Chapter 2).

Knocking or pinging

- ☐ Carbon build-up in combustion chamber. Use of a fuel additive that will dissolve the adhesive bonding the carbon particles to the crown and chamber is the easiest way to remove the build-up. Otherwise, the cylinder head will have to be removed and decarbonized (Chapter 2).
- ☐ Incorrect or poor quality fuel. Old or improper grades of fuel can cause detonation. This causes the piston to rattle, thus the knocking or pinging sound. Drain old fuel and always use the recommended fuel grade.
- ☐ Spark plug heat range incorrect. Uncontrolled detonation indicates the plug heat range is too hot. The plug in effect becomes a glow plug, raising cylinder temperatures. Install the proper heat range plug (Chapter 1).
- ☐ Improper air/fuel mixture. This will cause the cylinder to run hot, which leads to detonation. Clogged jets or an air leak can cause this imbalance. See Chapter 4.

Miscellaneous causes

- ☐ Throttle valve doesn't open fully. Adjust the throttle grip freeplay (Chapter 1).
- ☐ Clutch slipping. May be caused by loose or worn clutch components. Refer to Chapter 2 for clutch overhaul procedures.
- ☐ Timing not advancing.
- ☐ Engine oil viscosity too high. Using a heavier oil than the one recommended in Chapter 1 can damage the oil pump or lubrication system and cause drag on the engine.
- ☐ Brakes dragging. Usually caused by debris which has entered the brake piston seals, or from a warped disc or bent axle. Repair as necessary.

4 Overheating

Engine overheats

- ☐ Coolant level low. Check and add coolant (Chapter 1).
- ☐ Leak in cooling system. Check cooling system hoses and radiator for leaks and other damage. Repair or replace parts as necessary (Chapter 3).
- ☐ Thermostat sticking open or closed. Check and replace as described in Chapter 3.
- ☐ Faulty radiator cap. Remove the cap and have it pressure tested.
- ☐ Coolant passages clogged. Have the entire system drained and flushed, then refill with fresh coolant.
- ☐ Water pump defective. Remove the pump and check the components (Chapter 3).
- ☐ Clogged radiator fins. Clean them by blowing compressed air through the fins from the backside.
- ☐ Cooling fan or fan switch fault (Chapter 3).

Firing incorrect

- ☐ Spark plugs fouled, defective or worn out. See Chapter 1 for spark plug maintenance.
- ☐ Incorrect spark plugs.
- ☐ Ignition control unit defective. See Chapter 5.
- ☐ Faulty ignition HT coils (Chapter 5).

Fuel/air mixture incorrect

- ☐ Main jet clogged. Dirt, water and other contaminants can clog the main jets. Clean the fuel tap filter, the fuel pump in-line filter, the float chamber area and the jets and carburettor orifices (Chapter 4).
- ☐ Main jet wrong size. The standard jetting is for sea level atmospheric pressure and oxygen content.
- ☐ Air filter clogged, poorly sealed or missing (Chapter 1).
- ☐ Air filter housing poorly sealed. Look for cracks, holes or loose clamps and replace or repair.
- ☐ Fuel level too low. Check float height (Chapter 4).
- ☐ Fuel tank breather hose obstructed (not California models).
- ☐ Carburettor intake manifolds loose. Check for cracks, breaks, tears or loose clamps. Replace the rubber intake manifold joints if split or perished.

Compression too high

- ☐ Carbon build-up in combustion chamber. Use of a fuel additive that will dissolve the adhesive bonding the carbon particles to the piston crown and chamber is the easiest way to remove the build-up. Otherwise, the cylinder head will have to be removed and decarbonized (Chapter 2).
- ☐ Improperly machined head surface or installation of incorrect gasket during engine assembly.

Engine load excessive

- ☐ Clutch slipping. Can be caused by damaged, loose or worn clutch components. Refer to Chapter 2 for overhaul procedures.
- ☐ Engine oil level too high. The addition of too much oil will cause pressurisation of the crankcase and inefficient engine operation. Check Specifications and drain to proper level (Chapter 1).
- ☐ Engine oil viscosity too high. Using a heavier oil than the one recommended in Chapter 1 can damage the oil pump or lubrication system as well as cause drag on the engine.
- ☐ Brakes dragging. Usually caused by debris which has entered the brake piston seals, or from a warped disc or bent axle. Repair as necessary.

Lubrication inadequate

- ☐ Engine oil level too low. Friction caused by intermittent lack of lubrication or from oil that is overworked can cause overheating. The oil provides a definite cooling function in the engine. Check the oil level (Chapter 1).
- ☐ Poor quality engine oil or incorrect viscosity or type. Oil is rated not only according to viscosity but also according to type. Some oils are not rated high enough for use in this engine. Check the Specifications section and change to the correct oil (Chapter 1).

Miscellaneous causes

- ☐ Modification to exhaust system. Most aftermarket exhaust systems cause the engine to run leaner, which make them run hotter. When installing an accessory exhaust system, always rejet the carburettors.

5 Clutch problems

Clutch slipping

- ☐ Clutch master cylinder reservoir fluid level too high (see *Daily (pre-ride) checks*).
- ☐ Friction plates worn or warped. Overhaul the clutch assembly (Chapter 2).
- ☐ Plain plates warped (Chapter 2).
- ☐ Clutch springs broken or weak. Old or heat-damaged (from slipping clutch) springs should be replaced with new ones (Chapter 2).
- ☐ Clutch release mechanism defective. Replace any defective parts (Chapter 2).
- ☐ Clutch centre or outer drum unevenly worn. This causes improper engagement of the plates. Replace the damaged or worn parts (Chapter 2).

Clutch not disengaging completely

- ☐ Clutch master cylinder reservoir fluid level too low (see *Daily (pre-ride) checks*).
- ☐ Clutch plates warped or damaged. This will cause clutch drag, which in turn will cause the machine to creep. Overhaul the clutch assembly (Chapter 2).
- ☐ Clutch spring tension uneven. Usually caused by a sagged or broken spring. Check and replace the springs as a set (Chapter 2).
- ☐ Engine oil deteriorated. Old, thin, worn out oil will not provide proper lubrication for the plates, causing the clutch to drag. Replace the oil and filter (Chapter 1).
- ☐ Engine oil viscosity too high. Using a heavier oil than recommended in Chapter 1 can cause the plates to stick together, putting a drag on the engine. Change to the correct weight oil (Chapter 1).
- ☐ Clutch outer drum guide seized on mainshaft. Lack of lubrication, severe wear or damage can cause the guide to seize on the shaft. Overhaul of the clutch, and perhaps transmission, may be necessary to repair the damage (Chapter 2).
- ☐ Clutch release mechanism defective. Overhaul the clutch cover components (Chapter 2).
- ☐ Loose clutch centre nut. Causes drum and centre misalignment putting a drag on the engine. Engagement adjustment continually varies. Overhaul the clutch assembly (Chapter 2).

6 Gearchanging problems

Doesn't go into gear or lever doesn't return

- ☐ Clutch not disengaging. See Section 27.
- ☐ Shift fork(s) bent or seized. Often caused by dropping the machine or from lack of lubrication. Overhaul the transmission (Chapter 2).
- ☐ Gear(s) stuck on shaft. Most often caused by a lack of lubrication or excessive wear in transmission bearings and bushings. Overhaul the transmission (Chapter 2).
- ☐ Gearshift drum binding. Caused by lubrication failure or excessive wear. Replace the drum and bearing (Chapter 2).
- ☐ Gearshift lever return spring weak or broken (Chapter 2).
- ☐ Gearshift lever broken. Splines stripped out of lever or shaft, caused by allowing the lever to get loose or from dropping the machine. Replace necessary parts (Chapter 2).
- ☐ Gearshift mechanism stopper arm broken or worn. Full engagement and rotary movement of shift drum results. Replace the arm (Chapter 2).
- ☐ Stopper arm spring broken. Allows arm to float, causing sporadic shift operation. Replace spring (Chapter 2).

Jumps out of gear

- ☐ Shift fork(s) worn. Overhaul the transmission (Chapter 2).
- ☐ Gear groove(s) worn. Overhaul the transmission (Chapter 2).
- ☐ Gear dogs or dog slots worn or damaged. The gears should be inspected and replaced. No attempt should be made to service the worn parts.

Overshifts

- ☐ Stopper arm spring weak or broken (Chapter 2).
- ☐ Gearshift shaft return spring post broken or distorted (Chapter 2).

7 Abnormal engine noise

Knocking or pinging

- ☐ Carbon build-up in combustion chamber. Use of a fuel additive that will dissolve the adhesive bonding the carbon particles to the piston crown and chamber is the easiest way to remove the build-up. Otherwise, the cylinder head will have to be removed and decarbonized (Chapter 2).
- ☐ Incorrect or poor quality fuel. Old or improper fuel can cause detonation. This causes the pistons to rattle, thus the knocking or pinging sound. Drain the old fuel and always use the recommended grade fuel (Chapter 4).
- ☐ Spark plug heat range incorrect. Uncontrolled detonation indicates that the plug heat range is too hot. The plug in effect becomes a glow plug, raising cylinder temperatures. Install the proper heat range plug (Chapter 1).
- ☐ Improper air/fuel mixture. This will cause the cylinders to run hot and lead to detonation. Clogged jets or an air leak can cause this imbalance. See Chapter 4.

Piston slap or rattling

- ☐ Cylinder-to-piston clearance excessive. Caused by improper assembly. Inspect and overhaul top-end parts (Chapter 2).
- ☐ Connecting rod bent. Caused by over-revving, trying to start a badly flooded engine or from ingesting a foreign object into the combustion chamber. Replace the damaged parts (Chapter 2).
- ☐ Piston pin or piston pin bore worn or seized from wear or lack of lubrication. Replace damaged parts (Chapter 2).
- ☐ Piston ring(s) worn, broken or sticking. Overhaul the top-end (Chapter 2).
- ☐ Piston seizure damage. Usually from lack of lubrication or overheating. Replace the pistons and bore the cylinders, as necessary (Chapter 2).
- ☐ Connecting rod upper or lower end clearance excessive. Caused by excessive wear or lack of lubrication. Replace worn parts.

Valve noise

- ☐ Incorrect valve clearances. Adjust the clearances by referring to Chapter 1.
- ☐ Valve spring broken or weak. Check and replace weak valve springs (Chapter 2).
- ☐ Camshaft or cylinder head worn or damaged. Lack of lubrication at high rpm is usually the cause of damage. Insufficient oil or failure to change the oil at the recommended intervals are the chief causes. Since there are no replaceable bearings in the head, the head itself will have to be replaced if there is excessive wear or damage (Chapter 2).

Other noise

- ☐ Cylinder head gasket leaking.
- ☐ Exhaust pipe leaking at cylinder head connection. Caused by improper fit of pipe(s) or loose exhaust flange. All exhaust fasteners should be tightened evenly and carefully. Failure to do this will lead to a leak.
- ☐ Crankshaft runout excessive. Caused by a bent crankshaft (from over-revving) or damage from an upper cylinder component failure. Can also be attributed to dropping the machine on either of the crankshaft ends.
- ☐ Engine mounting bolts loose. Tighten all engine mount bolts (Chapter 2).
- ☐ Crankshaft bearings worn (Chapter 2).
- ☐ Cam chain tensioner defective. Replace according to the procedure in Chapter 2.
- ☐ Cam chain, sprockets or guides worn (Chapter 2).

8 Abnormal driveline noise

Clutch noise

- ☐ Clutch outer drum/friction plate clearance excessive (Chapter 2).
- ☐ Loose or damaged clutch pressure plate and/or bolts (Chapter 2).

Transmission noise

- ☐ Bearings worn. Also includes the possibility that the shafts are worn. Overhaul the transmission (Chapter 2).
- ☐ Gears worn or chipped (Chapter 2).
- ☐ Metal chips jammed in gear teeth. Probably pieces from a broken clutch, gear or shift mechanism that were picked up by the gears. This will cause early bearing failure (Chapter 2).
- ☐ Engine oil level too low. Causes a howl from transmission. Also affects engine power and clutch operation (Chapter 1).

Final drive noise

- ☐ Final drive oil level low (Chapter 1).
- ☐ Final drive gear lash incorrect (Chapter 5).
- ☐ Final drive gears worn or damaged (Chapter 5).
- ☐ Final drive bearings worn (Chapter 5).
- ☐ Driveshaft splines worn and slipping (Chapter 5).
- ☐ Wheel coupling damper worn. Replace damper (Chapter 5).

9 Abnormal frame and suspension noise

Front end noise

- ☐ Low fluid level or improper viscosity oil in forks. This can sound like spurting and is usually accompanied by irregular fork action (Chapter 6).
- ☐ Spring weak or broken. Makes a clicking or scraping sound. Fork oil, when drained, will have a lot of metal particles in it (Chapter 6).
- ☐ Steering head bearings loose or damaged. Clicks when braking. Check and adjust or replace as necessary (Chapters 1 and 6).
- ☐ Fork triple clamps loose. Make sure all clamp pinch bolts are tight (Chapter 6).
- ☐ Fork tube bent. Good possibility if machine has been dropped. Replace tube with a new one (Chapter 6).
- ☐ Front axle or axle clamp bolt loose. Tighten them to the specified torque (Chapter 6).

Shock absorber noise

- ☐ Fluid level incorrect. Indicates a leak caused by defective seal. Shock will be covered with oil. Replace shock or seek advice on repair from a Honda dealer (Chapter 6).
- ☐ Defective shock absorber with internal damage. This is in the body of the shock and can't be remedied. The shock must be replaced with a new one (Chapter 6).
- ☐ Bent or damaged shock body. Replace the shock with a new one (Chapter 6).

Brake noise

- ☐ Squeal caused by pad shim not installed or positioned correctly - rear caliper (Chapter 7).
- ☐ Squeal caused by dust on brake pads. Usually found in combination with glazed pads. Clean using brake cleaning solvent (Chapter 7).
- ☐ Contamination of brake pads. Oil, brake fluid or dirt causing brake to chatter or squeal. Clean or replace pads (Chapter 7).
- ☐ Pads glazed. Caused by excessive heat from prolonged use or from contamination. Do not use sandpaper, emery cloth, carborundum cloth or any other abrasive to roughen the pad surfaces as abrasives will stay in the pad material and damage the disc. A very fine flat file can be used, but pad replacement is suggested as a cure (Chapter 7).
- ☐ Disc warped. Can cause a chattering, clicking or intermittent squeal. Usually accompanied by a pulsating lever and uneven braking. Replace the disc (Chapter 7).
- ☐ Loose or worn wheel bearings. Check and replace as needed (Chapter 7).

10 Oil pressure warning light comes on

Engine lubrication system

- ☐ Engine oil pump defective, blocked oil strainer gauze or failed relief valve. Carry out oil pressure check (Chapter 2).
- ☐ Engine oil level low. Inspect for leak or other problem causing low oil level and add recommended oil (Chapter 1).
- ☐ Engine oil viscosity too low. Very old, thin oil or an improper weight of oil used in the engine. Change to correct oil (Chapter 1).
- ☐ Camshaft or journals worn. Excessive wear causing drop in oil pressure. Replace cam and/or/cylinder head. Abnormal wear could be caused by oil starvation at high rpm from low oil level or improper weight or type of oil (Chapter 1).
- ☐ Crankshaft and/or bearings worn. Same problems as paragraph 4. Check and replace crankshaft and/or bearings (Chapter 2).

Electrical system

- ☐ Oil pressure switch defective. Check the switch according to the procedure in Chapter 9. Replace it if it is defective.
- ☐ Oil pressure indicator light circuit defective. Check for pinched, shorted, disconnected or damaged wiring (Chapter 9).

11 Excessive exhaust smoke

White smoke

- ☐ Piston oil ring worn. The ring may be broken or damaged, causing oil from the crankcase to be pulled past the piston into the combustion chamber. Replace the rings with new ones (Chapter 2).
- ☐ Cylinders worn, cracked, or scored. Caused by overheating or oil starvation. The cylinders will have to be rebored and new pistons installed.
- ☐ Valve oil seal damaged or worn. Replace oil seals with new ones (Chapter 2).
- ☐ Valve guide worn. Perform a complete valve job (Chapter 2).
- ☐ Engine oil level too high, which causes the oil to be forced past the rings. Drain oil to the proper level (Chapter 1).
- ☐ Head gasket broken between oil return and cylinder. Causes oil to be pulled into the combustion chamber. Replace the head gasket and check the head for warpage (Chapter 2).
- ☐ Abnormal crankcase pressurisation, which forces oil past the rings. Clogged breather hose is usually the cause.

Black smoke

- ☐ Air filter clogged. Clean or replace the element (Chapter 1).
- ☐ Main jet too large or loose. Compare the jet size to the Specifications (Chapter 4).
- ☐ Choke cable or linkage shaft stuck, causing fuel to be pulled through choke circuit (Chapter 4).
- ☐ Fuel level too high. Check and adjust the float height(s) as necessary (Chapter 4).
- ☐ Float needle valve held off needle seat. Clean the float chambers and fuel line and replace the needles and seats if necessary (Chapter 4).

Brown smoke

- ☐ Main jet too small or clogged. Lean condition caused by wrong size main jet or by a restricted orifice. Clean float chambers and jets and compare jet size to Specifications (Chapter 4).
- ☐ Fuel flow insufficient. Float needle valve stuck closed due to chemical reaction with old fuel. Float height incorrect. Restricted fuel line. Clean line and float chamber and adjust floats if necessary.
- ☐ Carburettor intake manifold clamps loose (Chapter 4).
- ☐ Air filter poorly sealed or not installed (Chapter 1).

12 Poor handling or stability

Handlebar hard to turn

- ☐ Steering head bearing adjuster nut too tight. Check adjustment as described in Chapter 1.
- ☐ Bearings damaged. Roughness can be felt as the bars are turned from side-to-side. Replace bearings and races (Chapter 6).
- ☐ Races dented or worn. Denting results from wear in only one position (e.g., straight ahead), from a collision or hitting a pothole or from dropping the machine. Replace races and bearings (Chapter 6
- ☐ Steering stem lubrication inadequate. Causes are grease getting hard from age or being washed out by high pressure car washes. Disassemble steering head and repack bearings (Chapter 6).
- ☐ Steering stem bent. Caused by a collision, hitting a pothole or by dropping the machine. Replace damaged part. Don't try to straighten the steering stem (Chapter 6).
- ☐ Front tire air pressure too low (Chapter 1).

Handlebar shakes or vibrates excessively

- ☐ Tires worn or out of balance (Chapter 7).
- ☐ Swingarm bearings worn. Replace worn bearings by referring to Chapter 6.
- ☐ Rim(s) warped or damaged. Inspect wheels for runout (Chapter 7).
- ☐ Wheel bearings worn. Worn front or rear wheel bearings can cause poor tracking. Worn front bearings will cause wobble (Chapter 7).
- ☐ Handlebar clamp bolts loose (Chapter 6).
- ☐ Fork triple clamp bolts loose. Tighten them to the specified torque (Chapter 6).
- ☐ Engine mounting bolts loose. Will cause excessive vibration with increased engine rpm (Chapter 2).

Handlebar pulls to one side

- ☐ Frame bent. Definitely suspect this if the machine has been dropped. May or may not be accompanied by cracking near the bend. Replace the frame (Chapter 6).
- ☐ Wheels out of alignment. Caused by improper location of axle spacers or from bent steering stem or frame (Chapter 6).
- ☐ Swingarm bent or twisted. Caused by age (metal fatigue) or impact damage. Replace the arm (Chapter 6).
- ☐ Steering stem bent. Caused by impact damage or by dropping the motorcycle. Replace the steering stem (Chapter 6).
- ☐ Fork tube bent. Disassemble the forks and replace the damaged parts (Chapter 6).
- ☐ Fork oil level uneven. Check and add or drain as necessary (Chapter 6).

Poor shock absorbing qualities

- ☐ Too hard:
  - *a) Fork oil level excessive (Chapter 6).*
  - *b) Fork oil viscosity too high. Use a lighter oil (see the Specifications in Chapter 6).*
  - *c) Fork tube bent. Causes a harsh, sticking feeling (Chapter 6).*
  - *d) Shock shaft or body bent or damaged (Chapter 6).*
  - *e) Fork internal damage (Chapter 6).*
  - *f) Shock internal damage.*
  - *g) Tire pressure too high (Chapter 1).*
- ☐ Too soft:
  - *a) Fork or shock oil insufficient and/or leaking (Chapter 6).*
  - *b) Fork oil level too low (Chapter 6).*
  - *c) Fork oil viscosity too light (Chapter 6).*
  - *d) Fork springs weak or broken (Chapter 6).*
  - *e) Shock internal damage or leakage (Chapter 6).*

13 Braking problems

Brakes are spongy, don't hold

- ☐ Air in brake line. Caused by inattention to master cylinder fluid level or by leakage. Locate problem and bleed brakes (Chapter 7).
- ☐ Pad or disc worn (Chapters 1 and 7).
- ☐ Brake fluid leak. See paragraph 1.
- ☐ Contaminated pads. Caused by contamination with oil, grease, brake fluid, etc. Clean or replace pads. Clean disc thoroughly with brake cleaner (Chapter 7).
- ☐ Brake fluid deteriorated. Fluid is old or contaminated. Drain system, replenish with new fluid and bleed the system (Chapter 7).
- ☐ Master cylinder internal parts worn or damaged causing fluid to bypass (Chapter 7).
- ☐ Master cylinder bore scratched by foreign material or broken spring. Repair or replace master cylinder (Chapter 7).
- ☐ Disc warped. Replace disc (Chapter 7).

Brake lever or pedal pulsates

- ☐ Disc warped. Replace disc (Chapter 7).
- ☐ Axle bent. Replace axle (Chapter 7).
- ☐ Brake caliper bolts loose (Chapter 7).
- ☐ Brake caliper sliders damaged or sticking (rear caliper), causing caliper to bind. Lubricate the sliders or replace them if they are corroded or bent (Chapter 7).
- ☐ Wheel warped or otherwise damaged (Chapter 7).
- ☐ Wheel bearings damaged or worn (Chapter 7).

Brakes drag

- ☐ Master cylinder piston seized. Caused by wear or damage to piston or cylinder bore (Chapter 7).
- ☐ Lever balky or stuck. Check pivot and lubricate (Chapter 7).
- ☐ Brake caliper binds. Caused by inadequate lubrication or damage to caliper sliders (Chapter 7).
- ☐ Brake caliper piston seized in bore. Caused by wear or ingestion of dirt past deteriorated seal (Chapter 7).
- ☐ Brake pad damaged. Pad material separated from backing plate. Usually caused by faulty manufacturing process or from contact with chemicals. Replace pads (Chapter 7).
- ☐ Pads improperly installed (Chapter 7).

ABS/TCS problems

- ☐ ABS warning light in instrument panel stays on after initial self-checking process and blinks. Have system checked by a Honda dealer.
- ☐ TCS warning light in instrument panel stays on after initial self-checking process and blinks. Have system checked by a Honda dealer.

14 Electrical problems

Battery dead or weak

- ☐ Battery faulty. Caused by sulphated plates which are shorted through sedimentation. Also, broken battery terminal making only occasional contact (Chapter 9).
- ☐ Battery cables making poor contact (Chapter 9).
- ☐ Load excessive. Caused by addition of high wattage lights or other electrical accessories.
- ☐ Ignition (main) switch defective. Switch either grounds (earths) internally or fails to shut off system. Replace the switch (Chapter 9).
- ☐ Regulator/rectifier defective (Chapter 9).
- ☐ Alternator stator coil open or shorted (Chapter 9).
- ☐ Wiring faulty. Wiring grounded (earthed) or connections loose in ignition, charging or lighting circuits (Chapter 9).

Battery overcharged

- ☐ Regulator/rectifier defective. Overcharging is noticed when battery gets excessively warm (Chapter 9).
- ☐ Battery defective. Replace battery with a new one (Chapter 9).
- ☐ Battery amperage too low, wrong type or size. Install manufacturer's specified amp-hour battery to handle charging load (Chapter 9).

Fault Finding Equipment

Checking engine compression

● Low compression will result in exhaust smoke, heavy oil consumption, poor starting and poor performance. A compression test will provide useful information about an engine's condition and if performed regularly, can give warning of trouble before any other symptoms become apparent.

● A compression gauge will be required, along with an adapter to suit the spark plug hole thread size. Note that the screw-in type gauge/adapter set up is preferable to the rubber cone type.

● Before carrying out the test, first check the valve clearances as described in Chapter 1.

1 Run the engine until it reaches normal operating temperature, then stop it and remove the spark plug(s), taking care not to scald your hands on the hot components.

2 Install the gauge adapter and compression gauge in No. 1 cylinder spark plug hole **(see illustration 1)**.

3 On kickstart-equipped motorcycles, make sure the ignition switch is OFF, then open the throttle fully and kick the engine over a couple of times until the gauge reading stabilises.

4 On motorcycles with electric start only, the procedure will differ depending on the nature of the ignition system. Flick the engine kill switch (engine stop switch) to OFF and turn

Screw the compression gauge adapter into the spark plug hole, then screw the gauge into the adapter

the ignition switch ON; open the throttle fully and crank the engine over on the starter motor for a couple of revolutions until the gauge reading stabilises. If the starter will not operate with the kill switch OFF, turn the ignition switch OFF and refer to the next paragraph.

5 Install the spark plugs back into their suppressor caps and arrange the plug electrodes so that their metal bodies are earthed (grounded) against the cylinder head; this is essential to prevent damage to the ignition system as the engine is spun over **(see illustration 2)**. Position the plugs well away from the plug holes otherwise there is a risk of atomised fuel escaping from the combustion chambers and igniting. As a safety precaution, cover the top of the valve cover with rag. Now turn the ignition switch ON and kill switch ON, open the throttle fully and crank the engine over on the starter motor for a couple of revolutions until the gauge reading stabilises.

All spark plugs must be earthed (grounded) against the cylinder head

6 After one or two revolutions the pressure should build up to a maximum figure and then stabilise. Take a note of this reading and on multi-cylinder engines repeat the test on the remaining cylinders.

7 The correct pressures are given in Chapter 2 Specifications. If the results fall within the specified range and on multi-cylinder engines all are relatively equal, the engine is in good condition. If there is a marked difference between the readings, or if the readings are lower than specified, inspection of the top-end components will be required.

8 Low compression pressure may be due to worn cylinder bores, pistons or rings, failure of the cylinder head gasket, worn valve seals, or poor valve seating.

9 To distinguish between cylinder/piston wear and valve leakage, pour a small quantity of oil into the bore to temporarily seal the piston rings, then repeat the compression tests **(see illustration 3)**. If the readings show a noticeable increase in pressure this confirms that the cylinder bore, piston, or rings are worn. If, however, no change is indicated, the cylinder head gasket or valves should be examined.

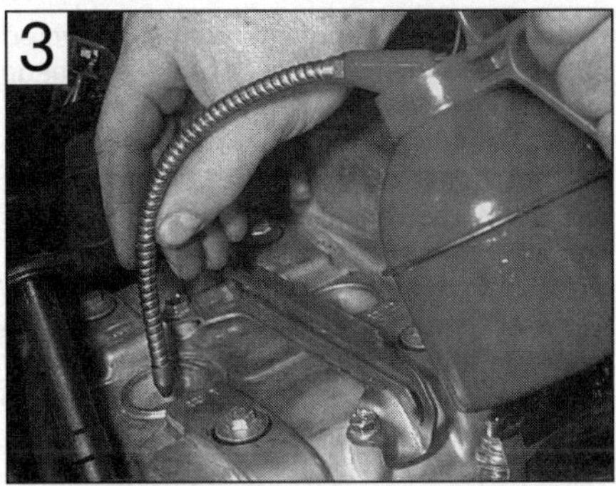

Bores can be temporarily sealed with a squirt of motor oil

10 High compression pressure indicates excessive carbon build-up in the combustion chamber and on the piston crown. If this is the case the cylinder head should be removed and the deposits removed. Note that excessive carbon build-up is less likely with the used on modern fuels.

Checking battery open-circuit voltage

Warning: The gases produced by the battery are explosive - never smoke or create any sparks in the vicinity of the battery. Never allow the electrolyte to contact your skin or clothing - if it does, wash it off and seek immediate medical attention.

- Before any electrical fault is investigated the battery should be checked.
- You'll need a dc voltmeter or multimeter to check battery voltage. Check that the leads are inserted in the correct terminals on the meter, red lead to positive (+ve), black lead to negative (-ve). Incorrect connections can damage the meter.
- A sound fully-charged 12 volt battery should produce between 12.3 and 12.6 volts across its terminals (12.8 volts for a maintenance-free battery). On machines with a 6 volt battery, voltage should be between 6.1 and 6.3 volts.

1 Set a multimeter to the 0 to 20 volts dc range and connect its probes across the battery terminals. Connect the meter's positive (+ve) probe, usually red, to the battery positive (+ve) terminal, followed by the meter's negative (-ve) probe, usually black, to the battery negative terminal (-ve) **(see illustration 4)**.

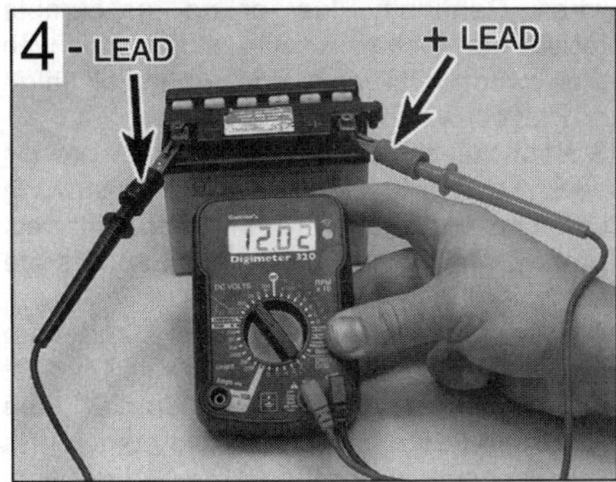

Measuring open-circuit battery voltage

2 If battery voltage is low (below 10 volts on a 12 volt battery or below 4 volts on a six volt battery), charge the battery and test the voltage again. If the battery repeatedly goes flat, investigate the motorcycle's charging system.

Checking battery specific gravity (SG)

Warning: The gases produced by the battery are explosive - never smoke or create any sparks in the vicinity of the battery. Never allow the electrolyte to contact your skin or clothing - if it does, wash it off and seek immediate medical attention.

- The specific gravity check gives an indication of a battery's state of charge.
- A hydrometer is used for measuring specific gravity. Make sure you purchase one which has a small enough hose to insert in the aperture of a motorcycle battery.
- Specific gravity is simply a measure of the electrolyte's density compared with that of water. Water has an SG of 1.000 and fully-charged battery electrolyte is about 26% heavier, at 1.260.
- Specific gravity checks are not possible on maintenance-free batteries. Testing the open-circuit voltage is the only means of determining their state of charge.

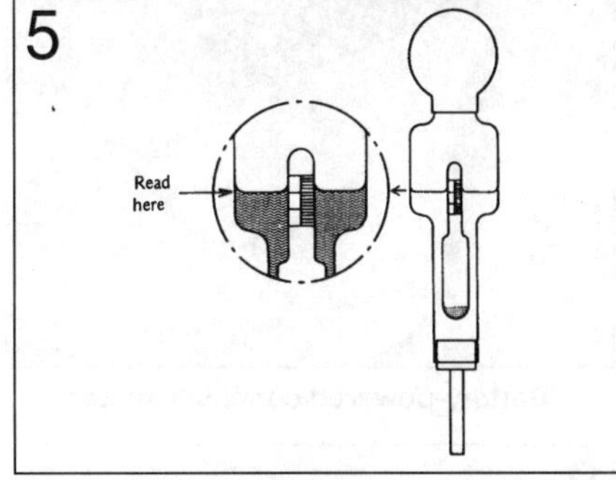

Float-type hydrometer for measuring battery specific gravity

1 To measure SG, remove the battery from the motorcycle and remove the first cell cap. Draw some electrolyte into the hydrometer and note the reading **(see illustration 5)**. Return the electrolyte to the cell and install the cap.

2 The reading should be in the region of 1.260 to 1.280. If SG is below 1.200 the battery needs charging. Note that SG will vary with temperature; it should be measured at 20°C (68°F). Add 0.007 to the reading for every 10°C above 20°C, and subtract 0.007 from the reading for every 10°C below 20°C. Add 0.004 to the reading for every 10°F above 68°F, and subtract 0.004 from the reading for every 10°F below 68°F.

3 When the check is complete, rinse the hydrometer thoroughly with clean water.

Checking for continuity

- The term continuity describes the uninterrupted flow of electricity through an electrical circuit. A continuity check will determine whether an **open-circuit** situation exists.
- Continuity can be checked with an ohmmeter, multimeter, continuity tester or battery and bulb test circuit **(see illustrations 6, 7 and 8)**.

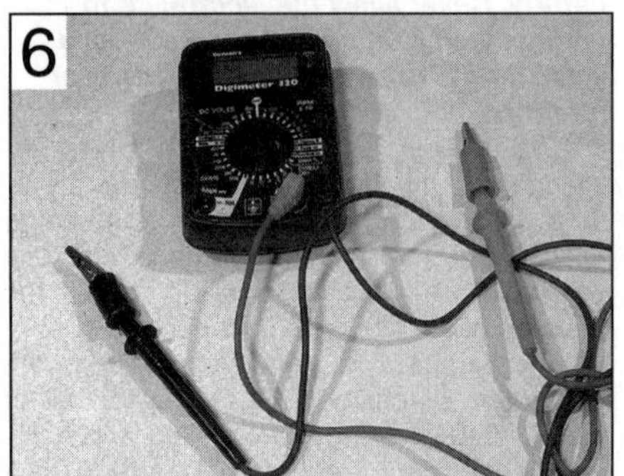

6 Digital multimeter can be used for all electrical tests

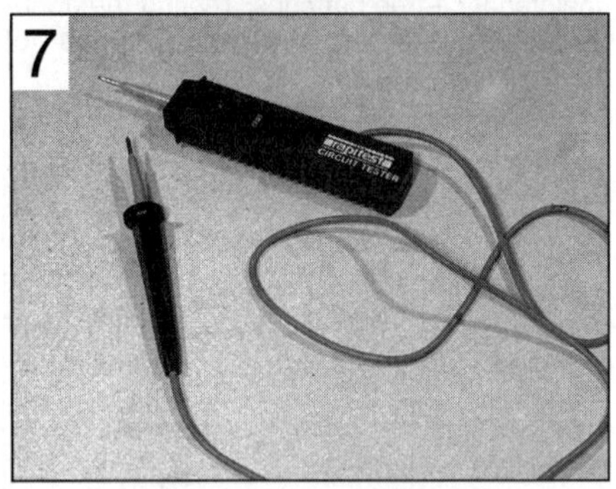

7 Battery-powered continuity tester

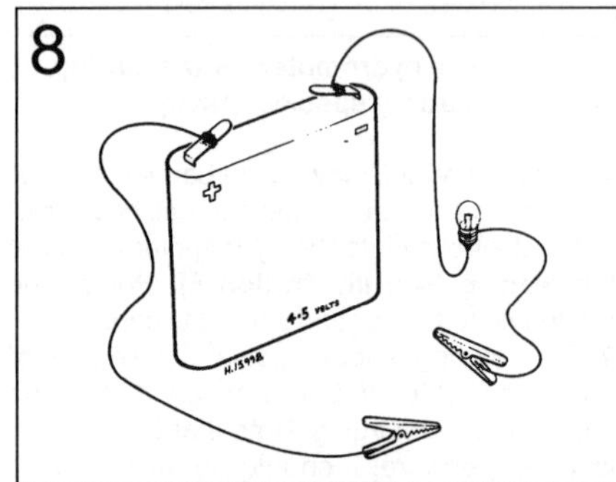

8 Battery and bulb test circuit

- All of these instruments are self-powered by a battery, therefore the checks are made with the ignition OFF.
- As a safety precaution, always disconnect the battery negative (-ve) lead before making checks, particularly if ignition switch checks are being made.
- If using a meter, select the appropriate ohms scale and check that the meter reads infinity (∞). Touch the meter probes together and check that meter reads zero; where necessary adjust the meter so that it reads zero.
- After using a meter, always switch it OFF to conserve its battery.

Switch checks

1 If a switch is at fault, trace its wiring up to the wiring connectors. Separate the wire connectors and inspect them for security and condition. A build-up of dirt or corrosion here will most likely be the cause of the problem - clean up and apply a water dispersant such as WD40.

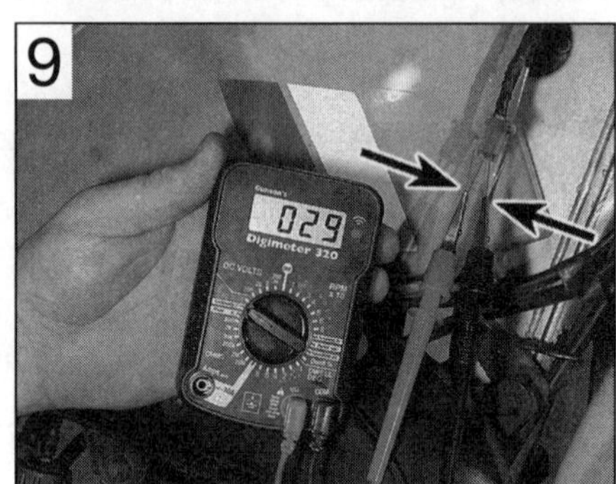

9 Continuity check of front brake light switch using a meter - note split pins used to access connector terminals

2 If using a test meter, set the meter to the ohms x 10 scale and connect its probes across the wires from the switch **(see illustration 9)**. Simple ON/OFF type switches, such as brake light switches, only have two wires whereas combination switches, like the ignition switch, have many internal links. Study the wiring diagram to ensure that you are connecting across the correct pair of wires. Continuity (low or no measurable resistance - 0 ohms) should be indicated with the switch ON and no continuity (high resistance) with it OFF.

3 Note that the polarity of the test probes doesn't matter for continuity checks, although care should be taken to follow specific test procedures if a diode or solid-state component is being checked.

4 A continuity tester or battery and bulb circuit can be used in the same way. Connect its probes as described above **(see illustration 10)**. The light should come on to indicate continuity in the ON switch position, but should extinguish in the OFF position.

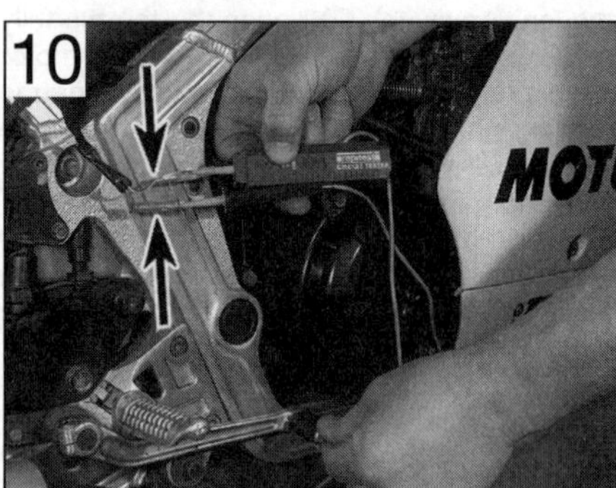

10 Continuity check of rear brake light switch using a continuity tester

Wiring checks

- Many electrical faults are caused by damaged wiring, often due to incorrect routing or chaffing on frame components.
- Loose, wet or corroded wire connectors can also be the cause of electrical problems, especially in exposed locations.

1 A continuity check can be made on a single length of wire by disconnecting it at each end and connecting a meter or continuity tester across both ends of the wire **(see illustration 11)**.

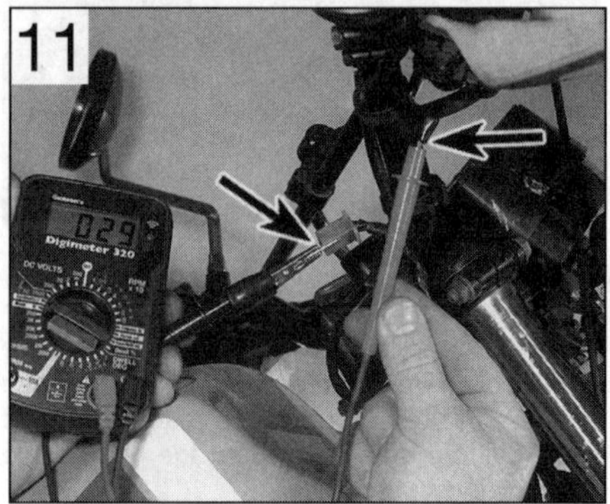

11 Continuity check of front brake light switch sub-harness

2 Continuity (low or no resistance - 0 ohms) should be indicated if the wire is good. If no continuity (high resistance) is shown, suspect a broken wire.

Checking for voltage

- A voltage check can determine whether current is reaching a component.
- Voltage can be checked with a dc voltmeter, multimeter set on the dc volts scale, test light or buzzer **(see illustrations 12 and 13)**. A meter has the advantage of being able to measure actual voltage.

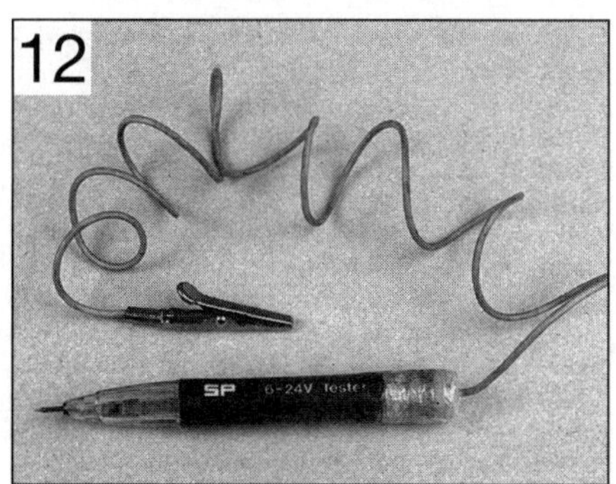

A simple test light can be used for voltage checks

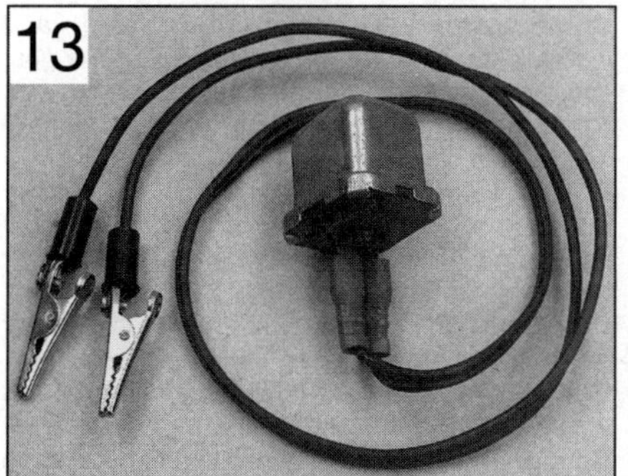

A buzzer is useful for voltage checks

● When using a meter, check that its leads are inserted in the correct terminals on the meter, red to positive (+ve), black to negative (-ve). Incorrect connections can damage the meter.

● A voltmeter (or multimeter set to the dc volts scale) should always be connected in parallel (across the load). Connecting it in series will destroy the meter.

● Voltage checks are made with the ignition ON.

1 First identify the relevant wiring circuit by referring to the wiring diagram at the end of this manual. If other electrical components share the same power supply (ie are fed from the same fuse), take note whether they are working correctly - this is useful information in deciding where to start checking the circuit.

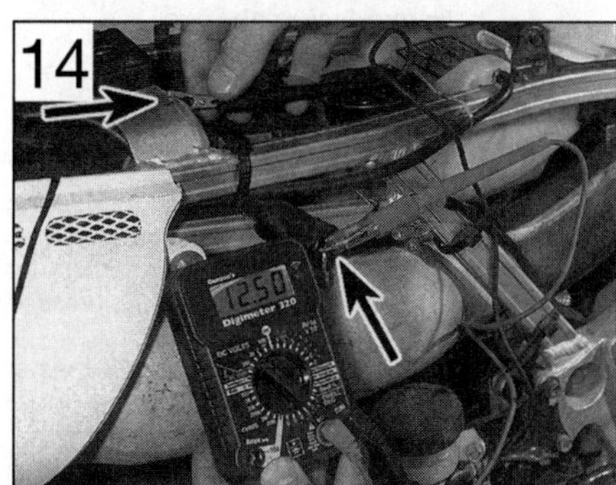

Checking for voltage at the rear brake light power supply wire using a meter . . .

2 If using a meter, check first that the meter leads are plugged into the correct terminals on the meter (see above). Set the meter to the dc volts function, at a range suitable for the battery voltage. Connect the meter red probe (+ve) to the power supply wire and the black probe to a good metal earth (ground) on the motorcycle's frame or directly to the battery negative (-ve) terminal **(see illustration 14)**. Battery voltage should be shown on the meter with the ignition switched ON.

3 If using a test light or buzzer, connect its positive (+ve) probe to the power supply terminal and its negative (-ve) probe to a good earth (ground) on the motorcycle's frame or directly to the battery negative (-ve) terminal **(see illustration 15)**. With the ignition ON, the test light should illuminate or the buzzer sound.

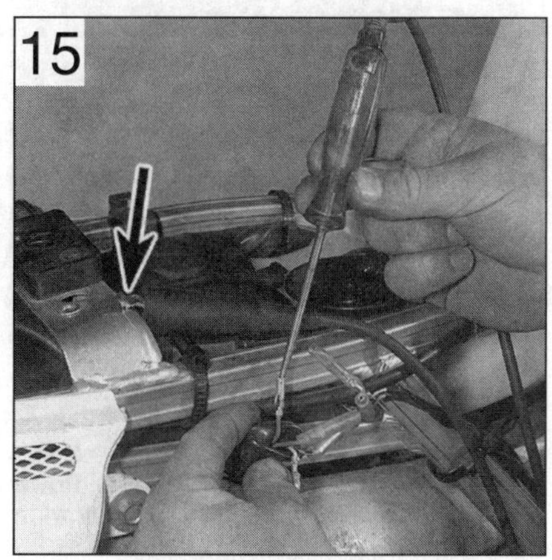

. . . or a test light - note the earth connection to the frame (arrow)

4 If no voltage is indicated, work back towards the fuse continuing to check for voltage. When you reach a point where there is voltage, you know the problem lies between that point and your last check point.

Checking the earth (ground)

● Earth connections are made either directly to the engine or frame (such as sensors, neutral switch etc. which only have a positive feed) or by a separate wire into the earth circuit of the wiring harness. Alternatively a short earth wire is sometimes run directly from the component to the motorcycle's frame.

● Corrosion is often the cause of a poor earth connection.

● If total failure is experienced, check the security of the main earth lead from the negative (-ve) terminal of the battery and also the main earth (ground) point on the wiring harness. If corroded, dismantle the connection and clean all surfaces back to bare metal.

1 To check the earth on a component, use an insulated jumper wire to temporarily bypass its earth connection **(see illustration 16)**. Connect one end of the jumper wire between the earth terminal or metal body of the component and the other end to the motorcycle's frame.

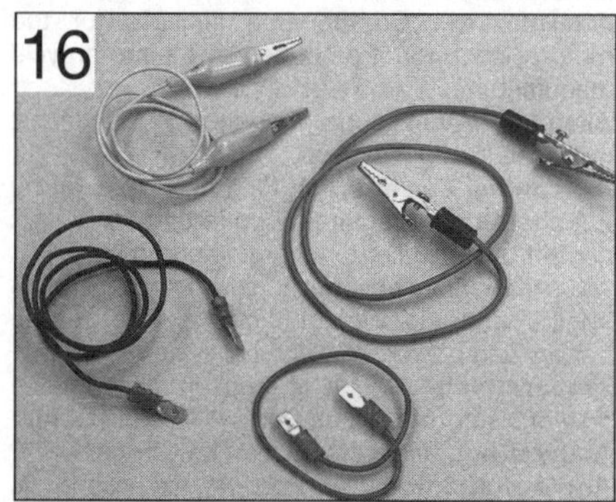

A selection of jumper wires for making earth (ground) checks

2 If the circuit works with the jumper wire installed, the original earth circuit is faulty. Check the wiring for open-circuits or poor connections. Clean up direct earth connections, removing all traces of corrosion and remake the joint. Apply petroleum jelly to the joint to prevent future corrosion.

Tracing a short-circuit

● A short-circuit occurs where current shorts to earth (ground) bypassing the circuit components. This usually results in a blown fuse.

● A short-circuit is most likely to occur where the insulation has worn through due to wiring chafing on a component, allowing a direct path to earth (ground) on the frame.

1 Remove any bodypanels necessary to access the circuit wiring.

2 Check that all electrical switches in the circuit are OFF, then remove the circuit fuse and connect a test light, buzzer or voltmeter (set to the dc scale) across the fuse terminals. No voltage should be shown.

3 Move the wiring from side to side whilst observing the test light or meter. When the test light comes on, buzzer sounds or meter shows voltage, you have found the cause of the short. It will usually shown up as damaged or burned insulation.

4 Note that the same test can be performed on each component in the circuit, even the switch.

A

ABS (Anti-lock braking system) A system, usually electronically controlled, that senses incipient wheel lockup during braking and relieves hydraulic pressure at wheel which is about to skid.
Aftermarket Components suitable for the motorcycle, but not produced by the motorcycle manufacturer.
Allen key A hexagonal wrench which fits into a recessed hexagonal hole.
Alternating current (ac) Current produced by an alternator. Requires converting to direct current by a rectifier for charging purposes.
Alternator Converts mechanical energy from the engine into electrical energy to charge the battery and power the electrical system.
Ampere (amp) A unit of measurement for the flow of electrical current. Current = Volts ˆ Ohms.
Ampere-hour (Ah) Measure of battery capacity.
Angle-tightening A torque expressed in degrees. Often follows a conventional tightening torque for cylinder head or main bearing fasteners **(see illustration)**.

Angle-tightening cylinder head bolts

Antifreeze A substance (usually ethylene glycol) mixed with water, and added to the cooling system, to prevent freezing of the coolant in winter. Antifreeze also contains chemicals to inhibit corrosion and the formation of rust and other deposits that would tend to clog the radiator and coolant passages and reduce cooling efficiency.
Anti-dive System attached to the fork lower leg (slider) to prevent fork dive when braking hard.
Anti-seize compound A coating that reduces the risk of seizing on fasteners that are subjected to high temperatures, such as exhaust clamp bolts and nuts.
API American Petroleum Institute. A quality standard for 4-stroke motor oils.
Asbestos A natural fibrous mineral with great heat resistance, commonly used in the composition of brake friction materials. Asbestos is a health hazard and the dust created by brake systems should never be inhaled or ingested.
ATF Automatic Transmission Fluid. Often used in front forks.
ATU Automatic Timing Unit. Mechanical device for advancing the ignition timing on early engines.
ATV All Terrain Vehicle. Often called a Quad.
Axial play Side-to-side movement.
Axle A shaft on which a wheel revolves. Also known as a spindle.

B

Backlash The amount of movement between meshed components when one component is held still. Usually applies to gear teeth.
Ball bearing A bearing consisting of a hardened inner and outer race with hardened steel balls between the two races.
Bearings Used between two working surfaces to prevent wear of the components and a build-up of heat. Four types of bearing are commonly used on motorcycles: plain shell bearings, ball bearings, tapered roller bearings and needle roller bearings.
Bevel gears Used to turn the drive through 90°. Typical applications are shaft final drive and camshaft drive **(see illustration)**.

Bevel gears are used to turn the drive through 90°

BHP Brake Horsepower. The British measurement for engine power output. Power output is now usually expressed in kilowatts (kW).
Bias-belted tyre Similar construction to radial tyre, but with outer belt running at an angle to the wheel rim.
Big-end bearing The bearing in the end of the connecting rod that's attached to the crankshaft.
Bleeding The process of removing air from an hydraulic system via a bleed nipple or bleed screw.
Bottom-end A description of an engine's crankcase components and all components contained there-in.
BTDC Before Top Dead Centre in terms of piston position. Ignition timing is often expressed in terms of degrees or millimetres BTDC.
Bush A cylindrical metal or rubber component used between two moving parts.
Burr Rough edge left on a component after machining or as a result of excessive wear.

C

Cam chain The chain which takes drive from the crankshaft to the camshaft(s).
Canister The main component in an evaporative emission control system (California market only); contains activated charcoal granules to trap vapours from the fuel system rather than allowing them to vent to the atmosphere.
Castellated Resembling the parapets along the top of a castle wall. For example, a castellated wheel axle or spindle nut.
Catalytic converter A device in the exhaust system of some machines which converts certain pollutants in the exhaust gases into less harmful substances.
Charging system Description of the components which charge the battery, ie the alternator, rectifer and regulator.
Circlip A ring-shaped clip used to prevent endwise movement of cylindrical parts and shafts. An internal circlip is installed in a groove in a housing; an external circlip fits into a groove on the outside of a cylindrical piece such as a shaft. Also known as a snap-ring.
Clearance The amount of space between two parts. For example, between a piston and a cylinder, between a bearing and a journal, etc.
Coil spring A spiral of elastic steel found in various sizes throughout a vehicle, for example as a springing medium in the suspension and in the valve train.
Compression Reduction in volume, and increase in pressure and temperature, of a gas, caused by squeezing it into a smaller space.
Compression damping Controls the speed the suspension compresses when hitting a bump.
Compression ratio The relationship between cylinder volume when the piston is at top dead centre and cylinder volume when the piston is at bottom dead centre.
Continuity The uninterrupted path in the flow of electricity. Little or no measurable resistance.
Continuity tester Self-powered bleeper or test light which indicates continuity.
Cp Candlepower. Bulb rating common found on US motorcycles.
Crossply tyre Tyre plies arranged in a criss-cross pattern. Usually four or six plies used, hence 4PR or 6PR in tyre size codes.
Cush drive Rubber damper segments fitted between the rear wheel and final drive sprocket to absorb transmission shocks **(see illustration)**.

Cush drive rubbers dampen out transmission shocks

D

Degree disc Calibrated disc for measuring piston position. Expressed in degrees.
Dial gauge Clock-type gauge with adapters for measuring runout and piston position. Expressed in mm or inches.
Diaphragm The rubber membrane in a master cylinder or carburettor which seals the upper chamber.
Diaphragm spring A single sprung plate often used in clutches.
Direct current (dc) Current produced by a dc generator.

Decarbonisation The process of removing carbon deposits - typically from the combustion chamber, valves and exhaust port/system.
Detonation Destructive and damaging explosion of fuel/air mixture in combustion chamber instead of controlled burning.
Diode An electrical valve which only allows current to flow in one direction. Commonly used in rectifiers and starter interlock systems.
Disc valve (or rotary valve) A induction system used on some two-stroke engines.
Double-overhead camshaft (DOHC) An engine that uses two overhead camshafts, one for the intake valves and one for the exhaust valves.
Drivebelt A toothed belt used to transmit drive to the rear wheel on some motorcycles. A drivebelt has also been used to drive the camshafts. Drivebelts are usually made of Kevlar.
Driveshaft Any shaft used to transmit motion. Commonly used when referring to the final driveshaft on shaft drive motorcycles.

E

Earth return The return path of an electrical circuit, utilising the motorcycle's frame.
ECU (Electronic Control Unit) A computer which controls (for instance) an ignition system, or an anti-lock braking system.
EGO Exhaust Gas Oxygen sensor. Sometimes called a Lambda sensor.
Electrolyte The fluid in a lead-acid battery.
EMS (Engine Management System) A computer controlled system which manages the fuel injection and the ignition systems in an integrated fashion.
Endfloat The amount of lengthways movement between two parts. As applied to a crankshaft, the distance that the crankshaft can move side-to-side in the crankcase.
Endless chain A chain having no joining link. Common use for cam chains and final drive chains.
EP (Extreme Pressure) Oil type used in locations where high loads are applied, such as between gear teeth.
Evaporative emission control system Describes a charcoal filled canister which stores fuel vapours from the tank rather than allowing them to vent to the atmosphere. Usually only fitted to California models and referred to as an EVAP system.
Expansion chamber Section of two-stroke engine exhaust system so designed to improve engine efficiency and boost power.

F

Feeler blade or gauge A thin strip or blade of hardened steel, ground to an exact thickness, used to check or measure clearances between parts.
Final drive Description of the drive from the transmission to the rear wheel. Usually by chain or shaft, but sometimes by belt.
Firing order The order in which the engine cylinders fire, or deliver their power strokes, beginning with the number one cylinder.
Flooding Term used to describe a high fuel level in the carburettor float chambers, leading to fuel overflow. Also refers to excess fuel in the combustion chamber due to incorrect starting technique.
Free length The no-load state of a component when measured. Clutch, valve and fork spring lengths are measured at rest, without any preload.
Freeplay The amount of travel before any action takes place. The looseness in a linkage, or an assembly of parts, between the initial application of force and actual movement. For example, the distance the rear brake pedal moves before the rear brake is actuated.
Fuel injection The fuel/air mixture is metered electronically and directed into the engine intake ports (indirect injection) or into the cylinders (direct injection). Sensors supply information on engine speed and conditions.
Fuel/air mixture The charge of fuel and air going into the engine. See **Stoichiometric ratio.**
Fuse An electrical device which protects a circuit against accidental overload. The typical fuse contains a soft piece of metal which is calibrated to melt at a predetermined current flow (expressed as amps) and break the circuit.

G

Gap The distance the spark must travel in jumping from the centre electrode to the side electrode in a spark plug. Also refers to the distance between the ignition rotor and the pickup coil in an electronic ignition system.
Gasket Any thin, soft material - usually cork, cardboard, asbestos or soft metal - installed between two metal surfaces to ensure a good seal. For instance, the cylinder head gasket seals the joint between the block and the cylinder head.
Gauge An instrument panel display used to monitor engine conditions. A gauge with a movable pointer on a dial or a fixed scale is an analogue gauge. A gauge with a numerical readout is called a digital gauge.
Gear ratios The drive ratio of a pair of gears in a gearbox, calculated on their number of teeth.
Glaze-busting see **Honing**
Grinding Process for renovating the valve face and valve seat contact area in the cylinder head.
Gudgeon pin The shaft which connects the connecting rod small-end with the piston. Often called a piston pin or wrist pin.

H

Helical gears Gear teeth are slightly curved and produce less gear noise that straight-cut gears. Often used for primary drives.

Installing a Helicoil thread insert in a cylinder head

Helicoil A thread insert repair system. Commonly used as a repair for stripped spark plug threads **(see illustration)**.
Honing A process used to break down the glaze on a cylinder bore (also called glaze-busting). Can also be carried out to roughen a rebored cylinder to aid ring bedding-in.
HT High Tension Description of the electrical circuit from the secondary winding of the ignition coil to the spark plug.
Hydraulic A liquid filled system used to transmit pressure from one component to another. Common uses on motorcycles are brakes and clutches.
Hydrometer An instrument for measuring the specific gravity of a lead-acid battery.
Hygroscopic Water absorbing. In motorcycle applications, braking efficiency will be reduced if DOT 3 or 4 hydraulic fluid absorbs water from the air - care must be taken to keep new brake fluid in tightly sealed containers.

I

lbf ft Pounds-force feet. An imperial unit of torque. Sometimes written as ft-lbs.
lbf in Pound-force inch. An imperial unit of torque, applied to components where a very low torque is required. Sometimes written as in-lbs.
IC Abbreviation for Integrated Circuit.
Ignition advance Means of increasing the timing of the spark at higher engine speeds. Done by mechanical means (ATU) on early engines or electronically by the ignition control unit on later engines.
Ignition timing The moment at which the spark plug fires, expressed in the number of crankshaft degrees before the piston reaches the top of its stroke, or in the number of millimetres before the piston reaches the top of its stroke.
Infinity (∞) Description of an open-circuit electrical state, where no continuity exists.
Inverted forks (upside down forks) The sliders or lower legs are held in the yokes and the fork tubes or stanchions are connected to the wheel axle (spindle). Less unsprung weight and stiffer construction than conventional forks.

J

JASO Quality standard for 2-stroke oils.
Joule The unit of electrical energy.
Journal The bearing surface of a shaft.

K

Kickstart Mechanical means of turning the engine over for starting purposes. Only usually fitted to mopeds, small capacity motorcycles and off-road motorcycles.
Kill switch Handebar-mounted switch for emergency ignition cut-out. Cuts the ignition circuit on all models, and additionally prevent starter motor operation on others.
km Symbol for kilometre.
kph Abbreviation for kilometres per hour.

L

Lambda (λ) sensor A sensor fitted in the exhaust system to measure the exhaust gas oxygen content (excess air factor).

Lapping see **Grinding.**
LCD Abbreviation for Liquid Crystal Display.
LED Abbreviation for Light Emitting Diode.
Liner A steel cylinder liner inserted in a aluminium alloy cylinder block.
Locknut A nut used to lock an adjustment nut, or other threaded component, in place.
Lockstops The lugs on the lower triple clamp (yoke) which abut those on the frame, preventing handlebar-to-fuel tank contact.
Lockwasher A form of washer designed to prevent an attaching nut from working loose.
LT Low Tension Description of the electrical circuit from the power supply to the primary winding of the ignition coil.

M

Main bearings The bearings between the crankshaft and crankcase.
Maintenance-free (MF) battery A sealed battery which cannot be topped up.
Manometer Mercury-filled calibrated tubes used to measure intake tract vacuum. Used to synchronise carburettors on multi-cylinder engines.
Micrometer A precision measuring instrument that measures component outside diameters **(see illustration).**

Tappet shims are measured with a micrometer

MON (Motor Octane Number) A measure of a fuel's resistance to knock.
Monograde oil An oil with a single viscosity, eg SAE80W.
Monoshock A single suspension unit linking the swingarm or suspension linkage to the frame.
mph Abbreviation for miles per hour.
Multigrade oil Having a wide viscosity range (eg 10W40). The W stands for Winter, thus the viscosity ranges from SAE10 when cold to SAE40 when hot.
Multimeter An electrical test instrument with the capability to measure voltage, current and resistance. Some meters also incorporate a continuity tester and buzzer.

N

Needle roller bearing Inner race of caged needle rollers and hardened outer race. Examples of uncaged needle rollers can be found on some engines. Commonly used in rear suspension applications and in two-stroke engines.
Nm Newton metres.
NOx Oxides of Nitrogen. A common toxic pollutant emitted by petrol engines at higher temperatures.

O

Octane The measure of a fuel's resistance to knock.
OE (Original Equipment) Relates to components fitted to a motorcycle as standard or replacement parts supplied by the motorcycle manufacturer.
Ohm The unit of electrical resistance. Ohms = Volts ÷ Current.
Ohmmeter An instrument for measuring electrical resistance.
Oil cooler System for diverting engine oil outside of the engine to a radiator for cooling purposes.
Oil injection A system of two-stroke engine lubrication where oil is pump-fed to the engine in accordance with throttle position.
Open-circuit An electrical condition where there is a break in the flow of electricity - no continuity (high resistance).
O-ring A type of sealing ring made of a special rubber-like material; in use, the O-ring is compressed into a groove to provide the seal.
Oversize (OS) Term used for piston and ring size options fitted to a rebored cylinder.
Overhead cam (sohc) engine An engine with single camshaft located on top of the cylinder head.
Overhead valve (ohv) engine An engine with the valves located in the cylinder head, but with the camshaft located in the engine block or crankcase.
Oxygen sensor A device installed in the exhaust system which senses the oxygen content in the exhaust and converts this information into an electric current. Also called a Lambda sensor.

P

Plastigauge A thin strip of plastic thread, available in different sizes, used for measuring clearances. For example, a strip of Plastigauge is laid across a bearing journal. The parts are assembled and dismantled; the width of the crushed strip indicates the clearance between journal and bearing.
Polarity Either negative or positive earth (ground), determined by which battery lead is connected to the frame (earth return). Modern motorcycles are usually negative earth.
Pre-ignition A situation where the fuel/air mixture ignites before the spark plug fires. Often due to a hot spot in the combustion chamber caused by carbon build-up. Engine has a tendency to 'run-on'.
Pre-load (suspension) The amount a spring is compressed when in the unloaded state. Preload can be applied by gas, spacer or mechanical adjuster.
Premix The method of engine lubrication on older two-stroke engines. Engine oil is mixed with the petrol in the fuel tank in a specific ratio. The fuel/oil mix is sometimes referred to as "petroil".
Primary drive Description of the drive from the crankshaft to the clutch. Usually by gear or chain.
PS Pfedestärke - a German interpretation of BHP.
PSI Pounds-force per square inch. Imperial measurement of tyre pressure and cylinder pressure measurement.
PTFE Polytetrafluroethylene. A low friction substance.
Pulse secondary air injection system A process of promoting the burning of excess fuel present in the exhaust gases by routing fresh air into the exhaust ports.

Quartz halogen bulb Tungsten filament surrounded by a halogen gas. Typically used for the headlight **(see illustration).**

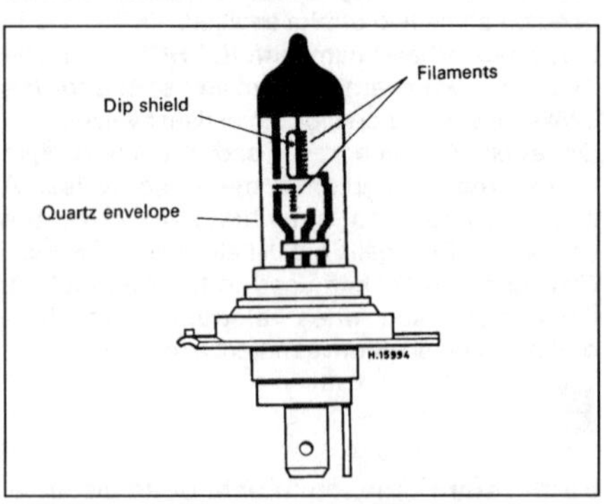

Quartz halogen headlight bulb construction

R

Rack-and-pinion A pinion gear on the end of a shaft that mates with a rack (think of a geared wheel opened up and laid flat). Sometimes used in clutch operating systems.
Radial play Up and down movement about a shaft.
Radial ply tyres Tyre plies run across the tyre (from bead to bead) and around the circumference of the tyre. Less resistant to tread distortion than other tyre types.
Radiator A liquid-to-air heat transfer device designed to reduce the temperature of the coolant in a liquid cooled engine.
Rake A feature of steering geometry - the angle of the steering head in relation to the vertical **(see illustration).**

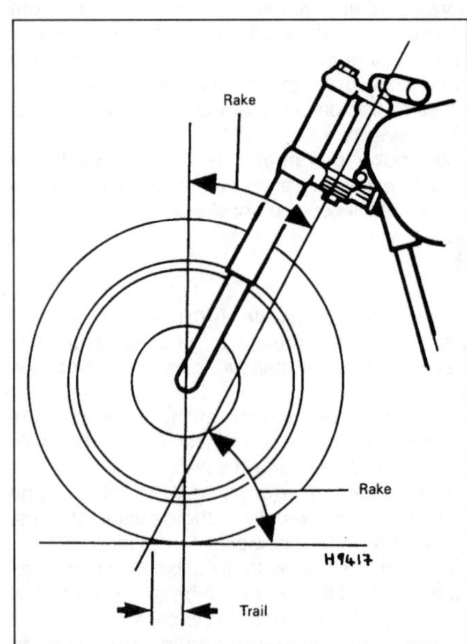

Steering geometry

Rebore Providing a new working surface to the cylinder bore by boring out the old surface. Necessitates the use of oversize piston and rings.
Rebound damping A means of controlling the oscillation of a suspension unit spring after it has been compressed. Resists the spring's natural tendency to bounce back after being compressed.
Rectifier Device for converting the ac output of an alternator into dc for battery charging.
Reed valve An induction system commonly used on two-stroke engines.
Regulator Device for maintaining the charging voltage from the generator or alternator within a specified range.
Relay A electrical device used to switch heavy current on and off by using a low current auxiliary circuit.
Resistance Measured in ohms. An electrical component's ability to pass electrical current.
RON (Research Octane Number) A measure of a fuel's resistance to knock.
rpm revolutions per minute.
Runout The amount of wobble (in-and-out movement) of a wheel or shaft as it's rotated. The amount a shaft rotates 'out-of-true'. The out-of-round condition of a rotating part.

S

SAE (Society of Automotive Engineers) A standard for the viscosity of a fluid.
Sealant A liquid or paste used to prevent leakage at a joint. Sometimes used in conjunction with a gasket.
Service limit Term for the point where a component is no longer useable and must be renewed.
Shaft drive A method of transmitting drive from the transmission to the rear wheel.
Shell bearings Plain bearings consisting of two shell halves. Most often used as big-end and main bearings in a four-stroke engine. Often called bearing inserts.
Shim Thin spacer, commonly used to adjust the clearance or relative positions between two parts. For example, shims inserted into or under tappets or followers to control valve clearances. Clearance is adjusted by changing the thickness of the shim.
Short-circuit An electrical condition where current shorts to earth (ground) bypassing the circuit components.
Skimming Process to correct warpage or repair a damaged surface, eg on brake discs or drums.
Slide-hammer A special puller that screws into or hooks onto a component such as a shaft or bearing; a heavy sliding handle on the shaft bottoms against the end of the shaft to knock the component free.
Small-end bearing The bearing in the upper end of the connecting rod at its joint with the gudgeon pin.
Spalling Damage to camshaft lobes or bearing journals shown as pitting of the working surface.
Specific gravity (SG) The state of charge of the electrolyte in a lead-acid battery. A measure of the electrolyte's density compared with water.
Straight-cut gears Common type gear used on gearbox shafts and for oil pump and water pump drives.
Stanchion The inner sliding part of the front forks, held by the yokes. Often called a fork tube.
Stoichiometric ratio The optimum chemical air/fuel ratio for a petrol engine, said to be 14.7 parts of air to 1 part of fuel.
Sulphuric acid The liquid (electrolyte) used in a lead-acid battery. Poisonous and extremely corrosive.
Surface grinding (lapping) Process to correct a warped gasket face, commonly used on cylinder heads.

T

Tapered-roller bearing Tapered inner race of caged needle rollers and separate tapered outer race. Examples of taper roller bearings can be found on steering heads.
Tappet A cylindrical component which transmits motion from the cam to the valve stem, either directly or via a pushrod and rocker arm. Also called a cam follower.
TCS Traction Control System. An electronically-controlled system which senses wheel spin and reduces engine speed accordingly.
TDC Top Dead Centre denotes that the piston is at its highest point in the cylinder.
Thread-locking compound Solution applied to fastener threads to prevent slackening. Select type to suit application.
Thrust washer A washer positioned between two moving components on a shaft. For example, between gear pinions on gearshaft.
Timing chain See **Cam Chain.**
Timing light Stroboscopic lamp for carrying out ignition timing checks with the engine running.
Top-end A description of an engine's cylinder block, head and valve gear components.
Torque Turning or twisting force about a shaft.
Torque setting A prescribed tightness specified by the motorcycle manufacturer to ensure that the bolt or nut is secured correctly. Undertightening can result in the bolt or nut coming loose or a surface not being sealed. Overtightening can result in stripped threads, distortion or damage to the component being retained.
Torx key A six-point wrench.
Tracer A stripe of a second colour applied to a wire insulator to distinguish that wire from another one with the same colour insulator. For example, Br/W is often used to denote a brown insulator with a white tracer.
Trail A feature of steering geometry. Distance from the steering head axis to the tyre's central contact point.
Triple clamps The cast components which extend from the steering head and support the fork stanchions or tubes. Often called fork yokes.
Turbocharger A centrifugal device, driven by exhaust gases, that pressurises the intake air. Normally used to increase the power output from a given engine displacement.
TWI Abbreviation for Tyre Wear Indicator. Indicates the location of the tread depth indicator bars on tyres.

U

Universal joint or U-joint (UJ) A double-pivoted connection for transmitting power from a driving to a driven shaft through an angle. Typically found in shaft drive assemblies.
Unsprung weight Anything not supported by the bike's suspension (ie the wheel, tyres, brakes, final drive and bottom (moving) part of the suspension).

V

Vacuum gauges Clock-type gauges for measuring intake tract vacuum. Used for carburettor synchronisation on multi-cylinder engines.
Valve A device through which the flow of liquid, gas or vacuum may be stopped, started or regulated by a moveable part that opens, shuts or partially obstructs one or more ports or passageways. The intake and exhaust valves in the cylinder head are of the poppet type.
Valve clearance The clearance between the valve tip (the end of the valve stem) and the rocker arm or tappet/follower. The valve clearance is measured when the valve is closed. The correct clearance is important - if too small the valve won't close fully and will burn out, whereas if too large noisy operation will result.
Valve lift The amount a valve is lifted off its seat by the camshaft lobe.
Valve timing The exact setting for the opening and closing of the valves in relation to piston position.
Vernier caliper A precision measuring instrument that measures inside and outside dimensions. Not quite as accurate as a micrometer, but more convenient.
VIN Vehicle Identification Number. Term for the bike's engine and frame numbers.
Viscosity The thickness of a liquid or its resistance to flow.
Volt A unit for expressing electrical "pressure" in a circuit. Volts = current x ohms.

W

Water pump A mechanically-driven device for moving coolant around the engine.
Watt A unit for expressing electrical power. Watts = volts x current.
Wear limit see **Service limit**
Wet liner A liquid-cooled engine design where the pistons run in liners which are directly surrounded by coolant **(see illustration).**

Wet liner arrangement

Wheelbase Distance from the centre of the front wheel to the centre of the rear wheel.
Wiring harness or loom Describes the electrical wires running the length of the motorcycle and enclosed in tape or plastic sheathing. Wiring coming off the main harness is usually referred to as a sub harness.
Woodruff key A key of semi-circular or square section used to locate a gear to a shaft. Often used to locate the alternator rotor on the crankshaft.
Wrist pin Another name for gudgeon or piston pin.

Note: *References throughout this index relate to Chapter•page number*

A

ABS system - 7•24
Acknowledgements - 0•7
Air filter
housing - 4•15
replacement - 1•15
Air mixture adjustment - 4•4
Alternator - 9•23
Antifreeze - 0•13, 1•2
Asbestos - 0•10

B

Battery - 0•10
charging - 9•4
removal, installation, inspection and maintenance - 9•3
Bleeding
brake system - 7•17
clutch - 2•30
Bodywork - 8•1 *et seq*
fairing panels - 8•2
fairing pockets - 8•4
fuel tank cover - 8•2
mirrors - 8•5
mudguard - 8•6
panniers - 8•2
rear panel - 8•6
seat - 8•2
side panels - 8•2
swingarm pivot covers - 8•5
windshield - 8•6
Brake fluid - 0•12, 1•2
change - 1•16
Brakes, wheels and tyres - 7•1 *et seq*
ABS system - 7•24
bleeding - 7•17
calipers - 7•5, 7•12
check - 1•12
delay valve - 7•11, 7•12
discs - 7•7
hoses, pipes and unions - 1•20, 7•16
light bulb - 9•6
master cylinder - 7•8, 7•11, 7•14
pads - 1•7, 7•4
pedal - 6•3
proportional control valve - 7•11, 7•12
secondary master cylinder - 7•11
switches - 9•9
TCS system - 7•24
tyres - 7•24
wheels - 7•17, 7•18, 7•20, 7•21
Burning - 0•10

C

Cables - 1•8, 1•13, 4•13, 4•14
Calipers
removal, overhaul and installation - 7•12
seals replacement - 1•20
removal, overhaul and installation - 7•5
Camshafts and followers
removal, inspection and installation - 2•14
Carburettors
disassembly, cleaning and inspection - 4•6
overhaul - 4•5
reassembly - 4•10
removal and installation - 4•5
separation and joining - 4•9
synchronisation - 1•10
Centrestand removal and installation - 6•3
Charging system
leakage and output test - 9•22
testing - 9•22
Choke cable - 4•14
check - 1•8
Clutch
bleeding - 2•30
check - 1•12
fluid - 0•11, 1•2, 1•16
hoses - 1•20
master cylinder - 2•27
release cylinder - 2•29
removal, inspection and installation - 2•22
switch - 9•15
Coils
check, removal and installation - 5•2, 5•3
Connecting rods
removal, inspection and installation - 2•48
Contents - 0•2
Conversion factors - REF•20
Coolant - 0•13, 1•2
Cooling system - 3•1 *et seq*
check - 1•11
fan - 3•2
draining, flushing and refilling - 1•18
hoses - 3•7
radiator - 3•5
radiator pressure cap - 3•2
reservoir - 3•2
temperature gauge and sensor - 3•3, 9•12
thermostat - 3•4
water pump - 3•6
Crankcase halves and cylinder bores
inspection and servicing - 2•46
Crankcase halves
separation and reassembly - 2•44
Crankshaft bearings
removal, inspection and installation - 2•52
Cylinder compression check - 1•20
Cylinder heads
disassembly, inspection and reassembly - 2•19
removal and installation - 2•18

D

Daily (pre-ride) checks - 0•11 *et seq*
Dimensions - REF•1
Direction indicators - 0•14
light bulbs replacement - 9•12
removal and installation - 9•8
bulbs - 9•8
circuit check - 9•8
Discs
inspection, removal and installation - 7•7
Driveshaft
bearing replacement - 6•19
inspection - 6•19
joints - 6•19
removal and installation - 6•17

E

Electrical system - 9•1 *et seq*
alternator - 9•23
battery - 9•3, 9•4
brake light - 9•6, 9•9
cables - 9•9
charging system - 9•22
clutch switch - 9•15
coolant temperature gauge - 9•12
direction indicators - 9•8, 9•12
fault finding - 9•3
fuel gauge - 9•11
fuel indicator light - 9•18
fuel level sender - 9•16
fuel pump and cut-off relay - 9•16
fuses - 9•4
handlebar switches - 9•14
headlight - 9•5, 9•6
horn(s) - 9•18
ignition (main) switch - 9•13
indicators - 9•8, 9•12
instrument bulbs - 9•12
instrument cluster - 9•9
instrument light bulbs - 9•12
instruments - 9•10
lean angle sensor - 9•16
lighting system - 9•5
neutral switch - 9•14

oil pressure switch - 9•13
regulator/rectifier - 9•23
sidelights - 9•5, 9•6
sidestand switch - 9•15
speedometer - 9•9, 9•10
starter motor - 9•19, 9•20
starter relay - 9•18
switches - 9•9, 9•13, 9•14, 9•15
tachometer - 9•11
taillight - 9•5, 9•6, 9•7
temperature gauge - 9•12
turn signal - 9•8
warning light bulbs - 9•12
Electricity - 0•10
Emission control systems check - 1•11
Engine numbers - 0•8
Engine oil - 0•11, 1•2, 1•9
pressure check - 1•20
Engine, clutch and transmission - 2•1 *et seq*
camshafts and followers - 2•14
clutch - 2•22, 2•27, 2•29, 2•30
connecting rods - 2•47, 2•48
crankcase bores - 2•46
crankcase cylinder bores - 2•46
crankcase halves - 2•44, 2•46
crankshaft - 2•52
cylinder heads - 2•18, 2•19
disassembly and reassembly - 2•9
gearchange - 2•34
main bearings - 2•52
oil cooler - 2•9
oil pressure relief valve - 2•32
oil pump - 2•32
oil strainer - 2•31
oil sump - 2•31
piston rings - 2•52
pistons - 2•50
removal and installation - 2•6
running-in procedure - 2•55
selector drum and forks - 2•42
starter clutch - 2•54
sump - 2•31
timing belt - 2•11, 2•13
transmission - 2•36, 2•37, 2•38
valve covers - 2•10
valves - 2•19
Evaporative Emission Control System (EVAP) - 4•18
Exhaust system - 4•16

F

Fairing panels removal and installation - 8•2
Fairing pockets removal and installation - 8•4
Fault Finding - 9•3, REF•28 *et seq*
Fault Finding Equipment - REF•36 *et seq*
Filter
air - 1•15, 4•15
fuel - 1•8
oil - 1•9
Final drive - 0•13
removal, inspection and installation - 6•19
oil - 1•2, 1•11, 1•19
Fire - 0•10
Float height check - 4•10
Footrests removal and installation - 6•2
Forks - 6•17
disassembly, inspection and reassembly - 6•7
oil - 1•20, 6•1
removal and installation - 6•6
Frame numbers - 0•8
Frame, suspension and final drive - 6•1 *et seq*
brake pedal - 6•3
centrestand - 6•3
driveshaft - 6•17, 6•19
final drive - 6•19
footrests - 6•2
forks - 6•1, 6•6, 6•7, 6•17
gearchange lever - 6•3
handlebars - 6•4
levers - 6•5
shock absorber - 6•16, 6•17
sidestand - 6•4
steering head bearings - 6•15
steering stem - 6•14
suspension adjustments - 6•17
swingarm - 6•17, 6•19
Fuel and exhaust systems - 4•1 *et seq*
air filter housing - 4•15
carburettors - 4•5, 4•6, 4•9, 4•10
check - 1•8
choke cable - 4•14
Evaporative Emission Control System (EVAP) - 4•18
exhaust system - 4•16
filter - 1•8
float height - 4•10
fuel tank - 4•3, 4•4, 8•2
fuel tap - 4•3
gauge check and replacement - 9•11
hoses replacement - 1•20
idle fuel/air mixture adjustment - 4•4
level sender and light - 9•16, 9•18
Pulse Secondary Air Injection System (PAIR) - 4•18
pump and cut-off relay - 9•16
throttle cables - 4•13
Fumes - 0•10
Fuses check and replacement - 9•4

G

Gearchange
lever - 6•3
mechanism - 2•34

H

Handlebars
removal and installation - 6•4
switches - 9•14
Headlight
aim - 1•12
bulb replacement - 9•5
removal and installation - 9•6
system check - 9•5
Horn(s) check and replacement - 9•18
HT coils check, removal and installation - 5•2

I

Identification numbers - 0•8
Idle fuel adjustment - 4•4
Idle speed check and adjustment - 1•7
Ignition (main) switch
check, removal and installation - 9•13
Ignition system - 5•1 *et seq*
check - 5•2
control unit - 5•4
HT coils - 5•2
pulse generator coil - 5•3
timing - 5•5
Indicators - 0•14
light bulbs replacement - 9•12
removal and installation - 9•8
bulbs - 9•8
circuit check - 9•8
Instruments
check and replacement - 9•10
cluster - 9•9
light bulbs - 9•12
Introduction - 0•4

L

Lean angle sensor and relay
check and replacement - 9•16
Levers
removal and installation - 6•5
pivots lubrication - 1•13
Lighting - 0•14
check - 9•5
Lubricants - REF•21

M

Main bearings
removal, inspection and installation - 2•52
Maintenance schedule - 1•3
Master cylinder
removal, overhaul and installation - 2•27, 7•8, 7•11, 7•14
seals - 1•20
Mirrors removal and installation - 8•5
Mixture adjustment - 4•4
MOT test checks - REF•22 *et seq*
Mudguard removal and installation - 8•6

N

Neutral switch
check, removal and installation - 9•14
Nuts and bolts tightness check - 1•14

O

Oil
engine/transmission - 0•11, 1•2, 1•9, 1•20
final drive - 1•2, 1•11, 1•19
forks - 1•20, 6•1

Oil cooler removal and installation - 2•9
Oil filter - 1•9
Oil pressure switch
check, removal and installation - 9•13
Oil pump and pressure relief valve
removal, inspection and installation - 2•32
Oil strainer
removal, inspection and installation - 2•31
Oil sump and oil strainer
removal, inspection and installation - 2•31

P

Pads
replacement - 7•4
wear check - 1•7
Panniers removal and installation - 8•2
Pedals - 6•3
Piston rings
inspection and installation - 2•52
Pistons
removal, inspection and installation - 2•50
Proportional control valve
removal, overhaul and installation - 7•11
Pulse generator coil - 5•3
Pulse Secondary Air Injection System (PAIR) - 4•18

R

Radiator - 3•5
pressure cap - 3•2
Reference - REF•1 *et seq*
Regulator/rectifier - 9•23
Release cylinder
removal, overhaul and installation - 2•29
Routine maintenance and servicing - 1•1 *et seq*
air filter - 1•15
antifreeze - 1•2
brake caliper - 1•20
brake fluid - 1•2, 1•16
brake hoses - 1•20
brake pads - 1•7
brake system - 1•12
cables - 1•8, 1•13
calipers - 1•20
carburettor synchronisation - 1•10
choke cable - 1•8
clutch - 1•12
clutch fluid - 1•2, 1•16
clutch hose - 1•20
coolant - 1•2
cooling system - 1•11, 1•18
cylinder compression - 1•20
emission control systems - 1•11
engine oil - 1•2, 1•9
engine oil pressure - 1•20
filter
air - 1•15
fuel - 1•8
oil - 1•9
final drive oil - 1•2, 1•11, 1•19
forks oil - 1•20
fuel filter - 1•8
fuel hoses - 1•20
fuel system - 1•8
headlight aim - 1•12
idle speed - 1•7
lever pivots - 1•13
maintenance schedule - 1•3
master cylinder - 1•20
nuts and bolts tightness - 1•14
oil filter - 1•9
oil pressure - 1•20
spark plugs - 1•6, 1•9
stands - 1•13
steering head bearings - 1•14, 1•20
suspension - 1•13
swingarm bearings - 1•20
throttle cable - 1•8
transmission oil - 1•2
tyres - 1•14
valve clearances - 1•16
wheel bearings - 1•20
wheels - 1•14
Running-in procedure - 2•55

S

Safety first! - 0•10, 0•14
Seat removal and installation - 8•2
Servicing - 1•1 *et seq*
Shock absorber - 6•17
removal, inspection and installation - 6•16
Side panels removal and installation - 8•2
Sidelight bulb replacement - 9•5
Sidestand removal and installation - 6•4
Sidestand switch check and replacement - 9•15
Signalling - 0•14
Spare parts - 0•7
Spark plugs
gaps - 1•6
replacement - 1•9
Speedometer
cable - 9•10
check and replacement - 9•10
Stands
lubrication - 1•13
removal and installation - 6•3
Starter motor
clutch assembly - 2•54
disassembly, inspection and reassembly - 9•20
removal and installation - 9•19
Starter relay check and replacement - 9•18
Steering - 0•13
Steering head bearings
freeplay - 1•14
inspection and replacement - 6•15
lubrication - 1•20
Steering stem removal and installation - 6•14
Storage - REF•26 *et seq*
Sump removal, inspection and installation - 2•31
Suspension - 0•13
adjustments - 6•17
check - 1•13
Swingarm
bearings - 1•20, 6•19
inspection - 6•19
pivot covers - 8•5
removal and installation - 6•17
Switches - 3•2, 9•13, 9•14, 9•15

T

Tachometer check and replacement - 9•11
Taillight
removal and installation - 9•7
bulbs - 9•6
system check - 9•5
TCS system - 7•24
Technical Terms Explained - REF•40 *et seq*
Temperature gauge and sensor check - 3•3
Thermostat - 3•4
Throttle cable - 4•13
check - 1•8
Timing - 5•5
Timing belt
removal, inspection and installation - 2•11
cover - 2•11
pulleys - 2•13
Tools and Workshop Tips - REF•2 *et seq*
Transmission oil - 0•11, 1•2
Transmission shafts - 2•37, 2•38
Turn signals - 0•14
assemblies - 9•8
bulbs - 9•8
circuit check - 9•8
Tyre pressures - 0•14
Tyres - 1•14, 7•24

V

Valve clearances
check and adjustment - 1•16
Valve covers
removal and installation - 2•10
Valves
disassembly, inspection and reassembly - 2•19
servicing - 2•19

W

Warning light bulbs replacement - 9•12
Water pump - 3•6
Weights - REF•1
Wheel bearings
check - 1•20
removal, inspection and installation - 7•21
Wheels - 1•14
alignment - 7•18
inspection and repair - 7•17
removal and installation - 7•18, 7•20
Windshield removal and installation - 8•6
Wiring diagrams - 9•26 *et seq*

Haynes Motorcycle Manuals - The Complete List

Title	Book No.
BMW	
BMW 2-valve Twins (70 - 96)	0249
BMW K100 & 75 2-valve Models (83 - 96)	1373
BMW R850 & R1100 4-valve Twins (93 - 97)	3466
BSA	
BSA Bantam (48 - 71)	0117
BSA Unit Singles (58 - 72)	0127
BSA Pre-unit Singles (54 - 61)	0326
BSA A7 & A10 Twins (47 - 62)	0121
BSA A50 & A65 Twins (62 - 73)	0155
BULTACO	
Bultaco Competition Bikes (72 - 75)	0219
CZ	
CZ 125 & 175 Singles (69 - 90)	◇ 0185
DUCATI	
Ducati 600, 750 & 900 2-valve V-Twins (91 - 96)	3290
HARLEY-DAVIDSON	
Harley-Davidson Sportsters (70 - 97)	0702
Harley-Davidson Big Twins (70 - 97)	0703
HONDA	
Honda SH50 City Express (84 - 89)	◇ 1597
Honda NB, ND, NP & NS50 Melody (81 - 85)	◇ 0622
Honda NE/NB50 Vision & SA50 Vision Met-in (85 - 95)	◇ 1278
Honda MB, MBX, MT & MTX50 (80 - 93)	0731
Honda C50, C70 & C90 (67 - 95)	0324
Honda ATC70, 90, 110, 185 & 200 (71 - 85)	0565
Honda CR80R & CR125R (86 - 97)	2220
Honda XR80R & XR100R (85 - 96)	2218
Honda XL/XR 80, 100, 125, 185 & 200 2-valve Models (78 - 87)	0566
Honda CB100N & CB125N (78 - 86)	◇ 0569
Honda H100 & H100S Singles (80 - 92)	◇ 0734
Honda CB/CD125T & CM125C Twins (77 - 88)	◇ 0571
Honda CG125 (76 - 94)	◇ 0433
Honda NS125 (86 - 93)	◇ 3056
Honda MBX/MTX125 & MTX200 (83 - 93)	◇ 1132
Honda CD/CM185 200T & CM250C 2-valve Twins (77 - 85)	0572
Honda XL/XR 250 & 500 (78 - 84)	0567
Honda XR250L, XR250R & XR400R (86 - 97)	2219
Honda CB250RS Singles (80 - 84)	◇ 0732
Honda CB250 & CB400N Super Dreams (78 - 84)	◇ 0540
Honda CR250R & CR500R (86 - 97)	2222
Honda Elsinore 250 (73 - 75)	0217
Honda TRX300 Shaft Drive ATVs (88 - 95)	2125
Honda VFR400 & RVF400 V-Fours (89 - 98)	3496
Honda CB400 & CB550 Fours (73 - 77)	0262
Honda CX/GL500 & 650 V-Twins (78 - 86)	0442
Honda CBX550 Four (82 - 86)	◇ 0940
Honda XL600R & XR600R (83 - 96)	2183
Honda CBR600F1 & 1000F Fours (87 - 96)	1730
Honda CBR600F2 & F3 Fours (91 - 98)	2070
Honda CB650 sohc Fours (78 - 84)	0665
Honda NTV600 & 650 V-Twins (88 - 96)	3243
Honda CB750 sohc Four (69 - 79)	0131
Honda V45/65 Sabre & Magna (82 - 88)	0820
Honda VFR750 & 700 V-Fours (86 - 97)	2101
Honda CB750 & CB900 dohc Fours (78 - 84)	0535
Honda CBR900RR FireBlade (92 - 97)	2161
Honda ST1100 Pan European V-Fours (90 - 97)	3384
Honda GL1000 Gold Wing (75 - 79)	0309
Honda GL1100 Gold Wing (79 - 81)	0669

Title	Book No.
Honda Gold Wing 1200 (USA) (84 - 87)	2199
Honda Gold Wing 1500 (USA) (88 - 98)	2225
KAWASAKI	
Kawasaki AE/AR 50 & 80 (81 - 95)	1007
Kawasaki KC, KE & KH100 (75 - 93)	1371
Kawasaki AR125 (82 - 94)	◇ 1006
Kawasaki KMX125 & 200 (86 - 96)	◇ 3046
Kawasaki 250, 350 & 400 Triples (72 - 79)	0134
Kawasaki 400 & 440 Twins (74 - 81)	0281
Kawasaki 400, 500 & 550 Fours (79 - 91)	0910
Kawasaki EN450 & 500 Twins (Ltd/Vulcan) (85 - 93)	2053
Kawasaki EX500 (GPZ500S) Twins (87 - 93)	2052
Kawasaki ZX600 (Ninja ZX-6, ZZ-R600) Fours (90 - 97)	2146
Kawasaki ZX600 (GPZ600R, GPX600R, Ninja 600R & RX) & ZX750 (GPX750R, Ninja 750R) Fours (85 - 97)	1780
Kawasaki 650 Four (76 - 78)	0373
Kawasaki 750 Air-cooled Fours (80 - 91)	0574
Kawasaki ZR550 & 750 Zephyr Fours (90 - 97)	3382
Kawasaki ZX750 (Ninja ZX-7 & ZXR750) Fours (89 - 96)	2054
Kawasaki 900 & 1000 Fours (73 - 77)	0222
Kawasaki ZX900, 1000 & 1100 Liquid-cooled Fours (83 - 97)	1681
MOTO GUZZI	
Moto Guzzi 750, 850 & 1000 V-Twins (74 - 78)	0339

Title	Book No.
MZ	
MZ TS125 (76 - 86)	◇ 1270
MZ ETZ Models (81 - 95)	◇ 1680
NORTON	
Norton 500, 600, 650 & 750 Twins (57 - 70)	0187
Norton Commando (68 - 77)	0125
PIAGGIO	
Piaggio (Vespa) Scooters (91 - 98)	3492
SUZUKI	
Suzuki FR50, 70 & 80 (74 - 87)	◇ 0801
Suzuki GT, ZR & TS50 (77 - 90)	◇ 0799
Suzuki TS50X (84 - 95)	◇ 1599
Suzuki 100, 125, 185 & 250 Air-cooled Trail bikes (79 - 89)	0797
Suzuki GP100 & 125 Singles (78 - 93)	◇ 0576
Suzuki GS & DR125 Singles (82 - 94)	◇ 0888
Suzuki 250 & 350 Twins (68 - 78)	0120
Suzuki GT250X7, GT200X5 & SB200 Twins (78 - 83)	◇ 0469
Suzuki GS/GSX250, 400 & 450 Twins (79 - 85)	0736
Suzuki GS500E Twin (89 - 97)	3238
Suzuki GS550 (77 - 82) & GS750 Fours (76 - 79)	0363
Suzuki GS/GSX550 4-valve Fours (83 - 88)	1133
Suzuki GSF600 & 1200 Bandit Fours (95 - 97)	3367
Suzuki GS850 Fours (78 - 88)	0536

Title	Book No.
Suzuki GS1000 Four (77 - 79)	0484
Suzuki GSX-R750, GSX-R1100, GSX600F, GSX750F, GSX1100F (Katana) Fours (85 - 96)	2055
Suzuki GS/GSX1000, 1100 & 1150 4-valve Fours (79 - 88)	0737
TOMOS	
Tomos A3K, A3M, A3MS & A3ML Mopeds (82 - 91)	◇ 1062
TRIUMPH	
Triumph Tiger Cub & Terrier (52 - 68)	0414
Triumph 350 & 500 Unit Twins (58 - 73)	0137
Triumph Pre-Unit Twins (47 - 62)	0251
Triumph 650 & 750 2-valve Unit Twins (63 - 83)	0122
Triumph Trident & BSA Rocket 3 (69 - 75)	0136
Triumph Triples & Fours (91 - 95)	2162
VESPA	
Vespa P/PX125, 150 & 200 Scooters (78 - 95)	0707
Vespa Scooters (59 - 78)	0126
YAMAHA	
Yamaha RD50 & 80 (78 - 89)	◇ 1255
Yamaha DT50 & 80 Trail Bikes (78 - 95)	◇ 0800
Yamaha T50 & 80 Townmate (83 - 95)	◇ 1247
Yamaha YT, YFM, YTM & YTZ ATVs (80 - 85)	1154
Yamaha YB100 Singles (73 - 91)	◇ 0474
Yamaha 100, 125 & 175 Trail bikes (71 - 85)	0210
Yamaha RS/RXS100 & 125 Singles (74 - 95)	0331
Yamaha RD & DT125LC (82 - 87)	◇ 0887
Yamaha TZR125 (87 - 93) & DT125R (88 - 95)	◇ 1655
Yamaha TY50, 80, 125 & 175 (74 - 84)	◇ 0464
Yamaha XT & SR125 (82 - 96)	1021
Yamaha 250 & 350 Twins (70 - 79)	0040
Yamaha XS250, 360 & 400 sohc Twins (75 - 84)	0378
Yamaha YBF250 Timberwolf ATV (92 - 96)	2217
Yamaha YFM350 Big Bear and ER ATVs (87 - 95)	2126
Yamaha RD250 & 350LC Twins (80 - 82)	0803
Yamaha RD350 YPVS Twins (83 - 95)	1158
Yamaha RD400 Twin (75 - 79)	0333
Yamaha XT, TT & SR500 Singles (75 - 83)	0342
Yamaha XZ550 Vision V-Twins (82 - 85)	0821
Yamaha FJ, FZ, XJ & YX600 Radian (84 - 92)	2100
Yamaha XJ600S (Seca II, Diversion) & XJ600N Fours (92 - 95 UK) (92 - 96 USA)	2145
Yamaha 650 Twins (70 - 83)	0341
Yamaha XJ650 & 750 Fours (80 - 84)	0738
Yamaha XS750 & 850 Triples (76 - 85)	0340
Yamaha FZR600, 750 & 1000 Fours (87 - 96)	2056
Yamaha XV V-Twins (81 - 96)	0802
Yamaha XJ900F Fours (83 - 94)	3239
Yamaha FJ1100 & 1200 Fours (84 - 96)	2057
PRACTICAL MANUALS	
Motorcycle Basics Manual	1083
Motorcycle Carburettor Manual	0603
TECHBOOKS	
ATV Basics	10450
Motorcycle Electrical Manual (3rd Edition)	3471
Motorcycle Workshop Practice Manual (2nd Edition)	3470

◇ *= not available in the USA* **Bold type** *= Superbike*

Preserving Our Motoring Heritage

The Model J Duesenberg Derham Tourster. Only eight of these magnificent cars were ever built – this is the only example to be found outside the United States of America

Almost every car you've ever loved, loathed or desired is gathered under one roof at the Haynes Motor Museum. Over 300 immaculately presented cars and motorbikes represent every aspect of our motoring heritage, from elegant reminders of bygone days, such as the superb Model J Duesenberg to curiosities like the bug-eyed BMW Isetta. There are also many old friends and flames. Perhaps you remember the 1959 Ford Popular that you did your courting in? The magnificent 'Red Collection' is a spectacle of classic sports cars including AC, Alfa Romeo, Austin Healey, Ferrari, Lamborghini, Maserati, MG, Riley, Porsche and Triumph.

A Perfect Day Out

Each and every vehicle at the Haynes Motor Museum has played its part in the history and culture of Motoring. Today, they make a wonderful spectacle and a great day out for all the family. Bring the kids, bring Mum and Dad, but above all bring your camera to capture those golden memories for ever. You will also find an impressive array of motoring memorabilia, a comfortable 70 seat video cinema and one of the most extensive transport book shops in Britain. The Pit Stop Cafe serves everything from a cup of tea to wholesome, home-made meals or, if you prefer, you can enjoy the large picnic area nestled in the beautiful rural surroundings of Somerset.

John Haynes O.B.E., Founder and Chairman of the museum at the wheel of a Haynes Light 12.

The 1936 490cc sohc-engined International Norton – well known for its racing success

MOTOR MUSEUM
A359 CASTLE CARY
A303 ANDOVER
A303 EXETER TO M5 J 25 TAUNTON
SPARKFORD
A359 YEOVIL
HAYNES PUBLISHING
OLD A303
NOT TO SCALE

The Museum is situated on the A359 Yeovil to Frome road at Sparkford, just off the A303 in Somerset. It is about 40 miles south of Bristol, and 25 minutes drive from the M5 intersection at Taunton.

Open 9.30am - 5.30pm (10.00am - 4.00pm Winter) 7 days a week, *except Christmas Day, Boxing Day and New Years Day*

Special rates available for schools, coach parties and outings Charitable Trust No. 292048